Fourth Edition

American Heritage

An Interdisciplinary Approach

Fourth Edition

American Heritage
An Interdisciplinary Approach

Frank W. Fox
Clayne L. Pope

Brigham Young University

Kendall/Hunt
Publishing Company
Dubuque, Iowa

Cover photo: Copyright Yale University Art Gallery

Contents

Part 2 ECONOMICS

Part 3 HISTORY

Preface

The authors wish to acknowledge the efforts of a number of people in making this book possible. Brian Dunsmore, Annette Bay Pimentel, Christopher Dahlin, Kimberly James, Gary Novak, Rebecca L. Reynolds, Karl N. Snow, Curtis W. Southworth, Todd and Susan Maynes, Frank Sesto, and Philip J. Perry all made valuable contributions as research assistants. Photographs and other illustrations were ferreted out by Joan H. Shrum, Daniel B. Shrum, Lou J. Royer, and John A. Scruggs. Graphics were done by Mary Ann Reynolds and Chris Sorensen of BYU Instructional Graphics. Expert assistance in preparing the fourth edition was rendered by Craig Hunsaker, Craig Merrill, and Brett Hugh Latimer (a descendent of Bishop Hugh Latimer who was burned at the stake by Mary I in her attempt to return England to Catholicism), all three of whom performed yeoman service. Todd Galbraith checked the manuscript for errors.

Special mention needs to be made of the contributions of Joan H. Shrum and Linda L. Jensen, both of the American Heritage staff, who have served in a dozen capacities, from business managers, to research assistants, to editors, to proofreaders.

The interpretations of American government, American history, and the American economic system set forth in this book were developed over a period of years by the American Heritage Committee at Brigham Young University. Members of the committee include Noel B. Reynolds, Martin B. Hickman, and David B. Magleby (political science); Larry T. Wimmer and Clayne L. Pope (economics); James B. Allen, Thomas G. Alexander, and Frank W. Fox (history). Although not an official member of the committee, Louis C. Midgley made a number of extremely helpful contributions, and we owe a special debt of gratitude to the work of R. Richard Vetterli, whose research in the area of American public virtue has shown how important that subject is. Ralph C. Hancock's knowledge and insight in political philosophy were instrumental in the revisions which appear in the present edition.

We would like to thank Mrs. Mildred Mikita for the use of her family history in chapter twenty-one. Her father, Stevan Lazich, and her daughter, Carole Mikita York, were good enough to help us with innumerable specific details.

We owe a final thanks to the College of Family, Home, and Social Sciences, to the General Education Program, and to the departments of economics, history, and political science, all of BYU, for support, encouragement, released time and material assistance in completing this project.

Introduction: The America Question

This book is not a conventional history of the United States. Neither is it a conventional study of the American government or economic system. All three of these subjects—history, government, and economics—will be found within its pages, but the book's real focus lies beyond the traditional disciplines. It is an attempt to answer a very broad and elusive, yet extremely important, question. We might call it the America Question.

The America Question grows out of the fact that the United States is a nation quite unlike any other. Stop and think of the things for which it has become known. It was the first of the modern-day republics. It adopted the first written constitution. It originated the theory and practice of federalism. It pioneered modern democracy. It found a way to bring not only a decent living but veritable abundance to the great mass of its people. Its backyard inventors produced marvels of innovation while its industry burgeoned into history's mightiest colossus. Its successes at arms excited global admiration while, paradoxically, it became a pioneer of world peace. And, most astonishing, its array of achievements remained consistent with human liberty.

Why, then, an America Question? The answer is that the United States, being so very unique, has seemed to operate on a different set of principles from other nations, and it has never been entirely clear what those principles are. We have often spoken of the "American genius" or the "American spirit" without knowing what such terms really mean. Of course, no one worried about that during flush times, when national self-confidence abounded. But what about when times are not flush? Ever since the war in Vietnam (coupled with the fiasco of Watergate), Americans have seemed to falter. The issues that worry

George Boughton's *Pilgrims Going to Church:* People
who knew what they were about. (Library of Congress)

us in the 1980s— crime, inflation, productivity, credibility, morality in government,
loss of world prestige, collapsing values—
are not the concerns of a confident people.
In this situation self- knowledge becomes
more than important; it becomes critical.
For if we do not adequately comprehend
our successes, we are even less likely to
comprehend our failures. The America
Question is simply this: *What was it that
made for those successes?*

*   *   *   *   *

The America Question is one we have
posed before, of course, most often in times
of uncertainty. It came up during the Great
Depression of the 1930s and before that,
during the Civil War. But it was asked with
greatest poignancy, though perhaps in a
different way, by the first colonists to set
foot on these shores. Having committed

their lives to an American future, it be-
hooved them to know, for better or worse,
just what that future held in store.

Consider, for example, the group we
call the Pilgrims. Standing at the rail of the
Mayflower and watching the coast of Cape
Cod looming out of the mist, they undoubtedly reflected on how little they
knew of what lay ahead. They had read a
pamphlet or two about "Virginia," as the
whole of the seaboard was called, and had
interviewed a couple of Jamestown survivors. Beyond that, America was shrouded
in mystery.

In the years that followed, the Pilgrims answered the America Question for
themselves. The New World, they learned,
was full of surprises. They had come to it
with one objective in view: to preserve
their way of life at all costs. And in the
space of a single generation, America
turned that way of life upside down and
inside out.

Take the matter of government, for example. Where the Pilgrims came from, government was exclusively in the hands of kings. God had planned it that way, the kings explained, so that the Christian world would remain orderly and obedient. The Pilgrims accepted that. In London, prior to their departure, they took pains to insure that the king's seal was affixed to all the right documents. But in Plymouth, somehow, the Pilgrims wound up governing themselves. This was not intentional. There were several accidents and miscues involved, not the least of which was that they made landfall too far to the north, in a place where "none had power to command them."

So, willy-nilly, the Pilgrims had to devise their own government. They drafted a kind of charter, laid out an organization, elected a group of magistrates, and began making rules. London eyebrows went up at the news of this, but, travel being what it was in those days, nothing was done to curtail it. And the jury-rigged government was not half bad. In the beginning, at least, it was essentially democratic—all adult males could vote—and the laws tempered Old Testament justice with New Testament mercy. People who bridled at the stern regimes of the Puritans in Massachusetts sometimes sought freedom down in Plymouth.

Or take economics. Where the Pilgrims came from, economic life was highly regulated. The same kings who ran government ran business as well by granting licenses, privileges, and outright monopolies to various court favorites. And there was little more freedom on the community level, where, often as not, a rigid collectivism prevailed. The people of a given village typically tilled communal lands, herded communal cows, and sheared communal sheep, and as for the prices of things bought and sold, they looked to the church to see what was just. With all of this the Pilgrims agreed. In fact, their intention to replicate just such a system in the New World was strengthened by their pastor, John Robinson, who often lectured them on the evils of self-love. Why should one seek profit, Robinson asked, indeed why should one seek private ownership, "if not because thou thinkest to live better than thy neighbor?" Self-love, said the pastor, was "a deadly plague."

But in America, once again, expectations were defeated. For one thing, no one but the settlers themselves was in a position to direct Plymouth's economic activities. Plans that looked fine in London often fell to tatters in Plymouth, and, conversely, what worked out in Plymouth was often the unexpected. Farming, for example, hardly broke even in Plymouth's stony soil, but fishing, furring, and seafaring—none of which the Pilgrims had thought about—turned out to be New England's hidden treasures.

And for another thing, self-love turned out to be a much stronger force than John Robinson had reckoned. When it came to laboring in the common fields, the Pilgrims, like other mortals, were often either ill, indisposed, or just plain AWOL. The colony had to pass through some extremely harrowing times—including wholesale starvation—before seeing the folly of it all. The only sure way to boost production, they learned, was to give individuals their own private land and let the profit motive drive them to make the most of it.

Or, again, take society. Where the Pilgrims came from, the compelling social ideal was purity. English Anglicans wanted to live among their own kind, and so did French Catholics, German Lutherans, and

Swiss Calvinists. The idea of mixing different cultures, nationalities, and religious points of view struck most Europeans as sheer madness. And again the Pilgrims agreed. They had tried living among the Anglicans of Nottinghamshire, and they had tried living among the Dutch in Leyden, and neither attempt had gone well. The English Anglicans, who were culturally much like the Pilgrims, were nonetheless brutally intolerant of their religion; while the Dutch, who were tolerant to a fault, seemed culturally rather bizarre. America alone, with its vast lands and empty horizons, offered the promise of total purity.

But would such a promise be kept? The Pilgrims seriously hoped so. They made strenuous efforts to keep foreign influences away from Plymouth. Worldly Anglicans who came too near—such as Thomas Morton, the owner of a furring station down the coast—were arrested and shipped back to England. And those in their own midst who would not conform—such as Samuel Gorton, a freethinking dissident—were summarily expelled. But it was no use. America threw them together with "strangers" (members of their own company who were not of the Pilgrim faith), with Puritans, with Anglicans, with Quaker evangelists, with radical dissenters like Roger Williams, and even with a host of nonwhite, non-English, nonbelieving savages.

In the end, America reshaped every part of the Pilgrims' lives. It changed the structure of their houses, changed their clothing, changed their personal habits, changed the organization of their towns, changed the way they made a living, changed their diet, changed their pleasures, changed everything about them. It even, alas, changed the religion that they crossed the ocean to preserve. If America was nothing else, it was a place for innovation.

But America, for the Pilgrims, meant more than change: it meant *successful* change—change in the right direction. It might have been otherwise. Consider, for comparison, the case of another colonization effort, undertaken by the French somewhat earlier. Landing on the coast of what is now South Carolina, Jean Ribaut established what he hoped would be a permanent French outpost in the New World. Like Plymouth, the planting of Port Royal was filled with hope and expectation.

No sooner had Ribaut returned to France for supplies, however, than trouble set in. The colonists, unmindful of the need to feed themselves, went off hunting gold, and soon they were facing starvation. They acquired food from the local Indians, who originally thought them to be gods, but now came to regard them with pity. One of their number, a rude soldier named Albert, set himself up as the colony's dictator, putting to terror all who got in his way. At length, Albert overextended himself by banishing one of his subjects to a small island to starve, and in the ensuing revolt he was killed. Anarchy now prevailed. In desperation, the survivors constructed a jerry-built raft and started home for France. Before they arrived, famished, crazed, and delirious from drinking salt water, they had to resort to cannibalism. It was not a happy story.

For the English Pilgrims, by contrast, self-government did not lead to tyranny or anarchy. It led to freedom. And private ownership did not lead to monopoly, exploitation, or economic chaos. It led to general prosperity. Nor did social tension lead to a military free-for-all. It led the Pilgrims to seek better harmony with their neighbors, peace with the Indians, and accommodation with religious dissenters.

Here, then, is where the America Question comes into sharp focus. What was it, exactly, that the English Pilgrims had going for them that the French colonists of Port Royal did not? *What made for those successes?* Whatever it was, it made the difference between building a free and prosperous society, on the one hand, and sinking into degradation, on the other.

And, whatever it was, we still think about it today. It is the thing we have in the back of our minds when we sentimentalize the Pilgrims, write poetry about them, reenact their Thanksgiving in the wilderness. Clearly we have come to see in the Pilgrims some sort of reflection of ourselves.

So, before beginning our study of the American experience in earnest, let us take one more glance at the Pilgrims and fix the America Question firmly in mind. An agreeable image of them is presented in George H. Boughton's noted painting, *Pilgrims Going to Church*. A group of black-clad figures are trudging through the snowy woods to their Sabbath meeting. Some of them carry guns over their shoulders, ready for trouble. Some carry Bibles in their hands. Guns and books become the painting's key symbols.

Clearly enough, the people in the painting know precisely what they are about. They have come a long way and have braved a great deal of hardship to attend this church meeting, and nothing so trivial as a wild bear or an Indian ambush is going to stop them. They are, symbolically, people of the gun. And yet, equally symbolically, they are also people of the book. Mirrored in their faces is a quality of more than conventional sectarian piety. They possess a broad moral vision of the world and their own place in it. They have not only mastered the wilderness, they have mastered themselves. And, in a curiously American way, they seem to have mastered their destiny in the process.

*   *   *   *   *

It ought to be clear, then, why the America Question is not likely to get a simple or quick answer. It is a question that not only runs into the cracks between academic disciplines, it runs into the cosmos beyond. In attempting to grapple with it, Americans of the 1980s are not just seeking out their national roots or recapitulating their accomplishments. They are, in a very real way, attempting to recover that wondrous sense of themselves as children of the ages, the hope of mankind.

Part 1

Government

We begin our exploration of the America Question with the study of government. Possibly excepting religion, government is the oldest human institution, and we can trace evidence of it back to the dawn of history. Beginning with the government of families, clans, and tribes, political forms were elaborated and adapted to the use of cities, kingdoms, and empires. People lived with good or bad government, it seemed, but never without government of some kind.

This was because government seemed to address a fundamental human need. Without some way to control the selfish, or hostile, or exploitative actions of individuals, society itself would not be possible. Indeed, so obvious was the need for government that some supposed it to be of divine origin. The ruler, be he king, emperor, sachem, pharaoh, czar, rajah, sultan, mogul (or any of the feminine equivalents), was frequently understood to be God's vicar on earth.

Accordingly, government became bathed in an ineffable mystique. To many, the king was not just a powerful politician or ruler of the realm, he was a demigod, and as such he evoked awe in his subjects. In the France of Louis XIV there was a magnificent ritual attending the king's daily act of rising from bed. And if you think the mystique of monarchy is entirely dead, consider the fuss always made over a royal visit to the United States—where there have been no kings since the Revolution. The clothing and coiffure of Princess Di are the only things that can top Hollywood for popular interest.

The founding and development of the American colonies happened to coincide with significant changes in European political thought. On the one hand, national states, whose growth dated from the Renaissance and whose grasp for power lengthened with the discovery of the New World, grew ever more energetic and expansive. England's King James I, who hounded thousands of Puritans out of his kingdom and across the Atlantic, resurrected the notion that kings ruled by "divine right" and used it to enhance his own authority. On the other hand, many Europeans began questioning the old assumptions. Was government really divine, they asked, or was it merely a human institution? And if the latter, could it not be altered to suit changing needs? While the American colonies were coming into maturity, there was a hot debate about every aspect of political society.

The American colonies played a crucial role in that debate. Unlike the nations of Europe, colonial governments were not the result of established, centuries-old tradition, but rather were recent and practical inventions. In the Old World the discussion of what government was and what it should do was largely academic since the existing governments had little inclination to change. In the New World, by contrast, the discussion of how government, not yet fully formed, should ultimately be shaped, had both relevance and immediacy. The very notion of *creating* government (as opposed to receiving it from God) was full of revolutionary implications.

What came out of the interaction between European ideas and American practice was both a new theory of government and a startling application of it. Americans learned for themselves that while bad government made for human misery, good government made for "life, liberty, and the pursuit of happiness," and they began altering their own governments accordingly. This development was the first of America's striking departures from the Old World and its ways.

1
The Will to Be Free

Concepts

The Human Predicament
Tyranny
Anarchy
Freedom

Hitler's speech in Vienna (UPI/Bettmann Newsphotos)

The Face of Tyranny

Before its work was done, the Nuremberg Court, set up to try Nazi war criminals at the end of World War II, was to review some ghastly evidence. But even this group fell into a hush of horror the day the chief British prosecutor, Sir Hartley Shawcross, read aloud the sworn affidavit of one Hermann Graebe, a German living in the town of Dubno in the Ukraine, who on October 5, 1942, had witnessed the SS's liquidation of Dubno's five thousand Jews.

My foreman and I went directly to the pits. I heard rifle shots in quick succession from behind one of the earth mounds. The people who had got off the trucks—men, women and children of all ages—had to undress upon the order of an S.S. man, who carried a riding or dog whip. They had to put down their clothes in fixed places, sorted according to shoes, top clothing and under-clothing. I saw a heap of shoes of about 800 to 1,000 pairs, great piles of under-linen and clothing.

Without screaming or weeping these people undressed, stood around in family groups, kissed each other, said farewells and waited for a sign from another S.S. man, who stood near the pit, also with a whip in his hand. During the fifteen minutes that I stood near the pit I heard no complaint or plea for mercy. . . .

An old woman with snow-white hair was holding a one-year-old child in her arms and singing to it and tickling it. The child was cooing with delight. The parents were looking on with tears in their eyes. The father was holding the hand of a boy about 10 years old and speaking to him softly; the boy was fighting his tears. The father pointed to the sky, stroked his head and seemed to explain something to him.

At that moment the S.S. man at the pit shouted something to his comrade. The latter counted off about twenty persons and instructed them to go behind the earth mound. . . . I well remember a girl, slim and with black hair, who, as she passed close to me, pointed to herself and said: "twenty-three years old."

I walked around the mound and found myself confronted by a tremendous grave. People were closely wedged together and lying on top of each other so that only their heads were visible. Nearly all had blood running over their shoulders from their heads. Some of the people were still moving. Some were lifting their arms and turning their heads to show that they were still alive. The pit was already two-thirds full. I estimated that it contained about a thousand people. I looked for the man who did the shooting. He was an S.S. man, who sat at the edge of the narrow end of the pit, his feet dangling into the pit. He had a tommy gun on his knees and was smoking a cigarette.

The people, completely naked, went down some steps and clambered over the heads of the people lying there to the place to which the S.S. man directed them. They lay down in front of the dead or wounded people; some caressed those who were still alive and spoke to them in a low voice. Then I heard a series of shots. I looked into the pit and saw that the bodies were twitching or the heads lying already motionless on top of the bodies that lay beneath them. Blood was running from their necks.

The next batch was approaching already. They went down into the pit, lined themselves up against the previous victims and were shot.

It is not pleasant reading, is it? But free people must summon themselves from time to time to think about the unthinkable. For what Mr. Graebe beheld in the execution pits of Dubno was nothing less than the face of tyranny. When we speak of being free, this is what we are really, by indirection, speaking about. We mean free from tyranny—free from this. Tyranny knows no bounds, no limits. Once it is unleashed, there is nothing to stop it from going straight to Hitler's genocide.

Yet, almost as detestable is tyranny's partner, anarchy. Stories could be told of it, too. There was the anarchy of the French Revolution, where serial violence claimed the lives of thousands. There was the anarchy in Mexico a century later—great armies of peasants criss-crossing the landscape with swaths of destruction. There was the mad, senseless anarchy of the Russian Revolution, and the Chinese, and the Iranian. And, yes, there was the anarchy of the German Revolution as well. Germans still recall it with a shudder. Throughout the 1920s, the Weimar Republic groaned under the Allied war debt, its economy plummeted, its currency sank into oblivion, while gangs roamed the streets of Berlin, fighting pitched battles with one another, and politicians hawked simple cures.

Adolf Hitler had been one of those. His cure for what ailed Germany was to get the Jews, and in the end he got them. At the same time, he put Germans back to work, brought order to the cities, built the *autobahns*, brought forth the Volkswagen. And, when he stood in the Nuremberg *Sportpalast* and spewed forth his venom, Germans by the millions cheered him wildly. Perhaps tyranny was not ideal, they conceded to one another, but it certainly beat anarchy. Such, apparently, were the only choices they thought life offered.

Nazi executioners: The things free people must think about. (Library of Congress)

The constant flight from tyranny (UPI/Bettmann Newsphotos)

Twentieth-century peoples have not been the only ones to live on the razor's edge between tyranny and anarchy. Having to face that grim choice runs as far back as recorded history. The biblical Israelites—just to name one example—found themselves in the most abject sort of bondage in Egypt. Yet as soon as Moses led them to freedom, they immediately lapsed into anarchy. So incapable were they of living as free men, that, according to the scriptural account, they were left wandering in the desert until a new generation came forth. There are many such examples throughout history. Taken as a whole, they seem to point up a basic feature of life, one we might call the human predicament.

The Human Predicament

One pole of the human predicament is tyranny. The other is anarchy. And between them a dynamic (if destructive) relationship appears to exist. Alexander Hamilton described it well:

The same state of passions which fits the multitude for opposition to tyranny and oppression very naturally leads them to a contempt and disregard for all authority. When minds are loosened from their attachment to ancient establishments and courses, they seem to grow giddy and are apt to run into anarchy.

Both in life and literature, the human predicament has been illustrated many times. In William Golding's celebrated novel, *Lord of the Flies,* a group of well-born English schoolchildren, finding themselves marooned on a remote island, shed their civilized values and revert to barbarism. First, anarchy appears and they dissolve into hostile factions. Then, as one faction gradually becomes dominant, tyranny takes over and the tyrants embark on a binge of murder. The book's behaviors are familiar enough in other contexts—but among the well spoken offspring of England's upper crust, they seem uniquely horrifying. The message appears to be that *anyone* is capable of inhumanity.

Tyranny

Tyranny is defined most simply as the rule of will. If you are living under a tyranny and find that you must do something (or refrain from doing something), it is always for the same reason: because the tyrant so wills it. The tyrant may be a single individual or a junta. His methods may be brutal or subtle. The action he demands (or forbids) may be for your own good, for the good of society, or for no good whatsoever. Some tyrants, such as Pisistratus of ancient Athens, have acted out of the best of motives, and their subjects have been uncommonly lucky. But luck is the best one can hope for under tyranny because there are literally no other safeguards.

Most of us have daydreamed about being tyrants ourselves. For, we have often found ourselves in situations where our own will counts for precious little. This probably explains the deathless appeal of Superman. Like the great mass of his fans, Superman's alter ego, Clark Kent, is always getting kicked around. However, when he steps into that phone booth and peels off his coat and tie, he is magically transformed into a will that can defy anything.

Consequences of anarchy in Lebannon (UPI/ Bettmann Newsphotos)

As he majestically swoops down on some hapless crew of wrongdoers, we can easily imagine the thrill of tyrannical power. The lesson is clear. Tyranny is a reflection of the human heart.

Fortunately for society, the tyrant in each of us rarely gets a chance to come forth. In those situations when he does come forth, the result is almost never a happy one. Battered children constitute a particularly grim reminder of this fact. For, once people are given real power over others, the worst features of the human nature seem to possess them. "Power tends to corrupt," observed Lord Acton, "and absolute power corrupts absolutely."

Power and Evil in the *Lord of the Rings*

Does absolute power indeed corrupt absolutely? In J.R.R. Tolkien's *The Lord of the Rings*, familiar throughout the Western world, it does seem to have that effect. The Ring of Power, the possession of which is something like holding the blueprints to an H-bomb, sorely tempts anyone who comes into contact with it. Staunch and faithful Boromir turns into a madman when he thinks the ring might be his, the once-fair Gollum degenerates into a loathsome reptilian, and even Frodo himself experiences moments of real doubt. But the Ring's most unexpected transformation is wrought upon Samwise Gamgee, Frodo's honest, humble, self- effacing manservant, who unexpectedly finds the ring in his own custody:

> As Sam stood there, even though the Ring was not on him but hanging by its chain about his neck, he felt himself enlarged, as if he were robed in a huge distorted shadow of himself. . . . Already the Ring tempted him, gnawing at his will and reason. Wild fantasies arose in his mind; and he saw Samwise the Strong, Hero of the Age, striding with a flaming sword across the darkened land, and armies flocking to his call as he marched to the overthrow of Barad-dor. And then all the clouds rolled away, and the white sun shone, and at his command the vale of Gorgoroth became a garden of flowers and trees and brought forth fruit. He had only to put on the Ring and claim it for his own, and all this could be.

> At this rate, it is remarkable that anyone has guts enough to cast the ring to its destruction. And, indeed, no one does. Frodo, in the end, can't bring himself to pull the thing off his finger, and only the greed of Gollum, making a last desperate grab for it, plummets it into the fiery Crack of Doom.

History, unsurprisingly, has been full of tyranny. The tyrants have not always been as coldly methodical as Adolph Hitler but they have been, on the whole, a pretty vicious lot. Scan through the illustrations of a history book for ready evidence. Here are the Christian martyrs being fed to the lions. Here are the torture devices of the Inquisition: the rack, the wheel, the thumbscrew, the spit. Here is Peter Brueghel's horrifying *Massacre of the Innocents*—soldiers butchering Flemish children as their mothers plead piteously. And here are bodies dangling from gibbets outside the walls of the Kremlin—reminders left by Peter the Great that he tolerated no opposition. The human record has not been a happy one.

Anarchy

Anarchy may be defined as no rule whatever. In a situation of pure anarchy, each person's will operates independently of every other's, and the result is chaos. Anarchy is rarely pure, however. In real life, when there is an absence of overriding authority, people with similar interests and outlooks get together and form factions, and it is these factions contending with one another that generates the mayhem.

The same history book that furnished examples of tyranny will provide an equal abundance of anarchy. Here are the Visigoths sacking Rome. Here is the desolate German countryside after the Thirty Years War. Here are mobs in the streets of Paris crying for the blood of some partisan. And here, in Detroit, is a scene of pandemonium from the 1930s—policemen clubbing striking auto workers.

Once in a while, anarchical situations can go on indefinitely, propelled by the inability of any single faction to gain control. In the recent past, Lebanon seemed to present just such a case. But far more often, one faction, or a cooperating group of factions, does gain control and imposes its will on the others. It is at this point that anarchy is transformed into tyranny.

Anarchy, too, is undoubtedly rooted in the human heart. Just as each of us would secretly like to be Superman, each of us instinctively reaches out toward like-minded individuals for the advancement of common interests. Take the case of sports fans. One usually becomes a fan of this or that team for the most accidental of reasons, and the allegiance can change abruptly when one moves to a new town or enrolls in a different school. But, when the fans of a given team get together, frightening things can happen. The otherwise rational fans of the Liverpool soccer team turned, Jekyll-and-Hyde-like, into a howling mob at the 1985 playoffs in Belgium and wound up committing wholesale murder.

The Economic Dimension

Although we usually think of the human predicament in political terms, similar situations exist in the realm of economics. Political tyranny, for example, has a close economic cousin. Whenever the will of a ruler can reign freely, it usually follows that he, or the group he represents, will use his power to exploit and deprive others economically. Circumstances in which there are a few rich and great many poor are made-to-order for tyranny. For the rich, fearing to lose their advantage, will use their political power to the fullest—and the poor will find themselves also the powerless.

Similarly, political anarchy has almost always led to, or otherwise accompanied, economic anarchy. When mobs and factions contend with one another politically, they often wreak economic havoc as well. In the course of insurrections, for example, various rebel groups typically seize the custom house, the mint, or the local bank and make whatever use they can of its assets. Prosperous nations have been laid to waste by such upheaval.

Freedom

If tyranny and anarchy were all we could find in the human heart, the world would be a sad place indeed. Fortunately, there are some better qualities too: a desire for truth, a respect for justice, a sense of mercy, and, most importantly, the will to be free. Our instinctive love of freedom runs as far back in history as anarchy and tyranny do. Let us return to the example of the Hebrews. In addition to the tyranny of the Pharaoh, they suffered under that of the Philistines, the Assyrians, and the Chaldeans, who not only enslaved them but carried them off to Babylon. Then came the Greeks, the Romans, the Arabians, and the Turks, not to mention the various princes of Europe among whom they were scattered in the Diaspora. Not all their foreign rulers compared with Hitler, perhaps, but unspeakable atrocities were inflicted upon them over the centuries. Still, no amount of horror could extinguish their desire to be free: it burns as incandescently today as it did in Old Testament times.

Although most of us have never known that sort of oppression, we have experienced the fuming outrage that oppression can kindle. There is that memory of the parent who said no, who rejected all reason, who answered the profoundest arguments with a resounding: "Because I say so, that's why." Or there was the boss who got the story wrong, who jumped to conclusions, who dismissed all explanations with a preemptory wave of the hand. And so on. Life has brought us enough of those situations to give us an inkling of what freedom must have meant to millions far less fortunate than ourselves. There is an old story of a man living in the Punjab, many of whose family had been killed by tigers. "Why do you not move somewhere else?" asked a traveler who had paused for conversation. "Because," the man replied, "here there is freedom."

One reason that freedom (tigers and all) is so attractive is that it has a dimension which transcends the mere absence of tyranny and anarchy. Freedom is an aspect—possibly the highest aspect—of the human personality. It is a unique condition that both challenges and ennobles man's nature. Animals might live in a world untroubled by the tyrant or the demagogue, yet they can never be free in the human sense. When human beings actually govern their own affairs, their lives take on a bold and exhilarating new significance. Human freedom at once expresses realization of the self, aspirations of the community, and fulfillment of the soul.

Exemplars of Freedom

Some few peoples have known moments of true freedom. The conspicuous example is that of the classical republics. Throughout the world of ancient Greece one city-state after another succeeded in throwing off the yoke of monarchy, oligarchy, or dictatorship and devising governments of democratic self-rule. To be sure, it was a precarious sort of freedom. One false move and the dictators and oligarchs were back—or else the democratic government simply dissolved into factional chaos.

But while it lasted, the democratic freedom of the ancient world was remarkable indeed. In Athens, largest of the democracies, citizens of the city-state quite literally governed their own lives. They took their seats in the popular Assembly and cast their votes for the laws. They served on the massive juries and in them resolved the ultimate questions of the commonwealth. They even served in the upper chamber, the Council, on the basis of random lots and directed day-to-day policy. Much of their daily life was taken up with politics, but they rarely seemed to complain. Surviving records suggest that they enjoyed themselves enormously.

A second starburst of freedom was recorded in both the Swiss and Dutch republics of the late Renaissance. Both were special cases. The Swiss, safely ensconced in the Alps, worked out various formulas of self-rule in their separate cantons and organized a determined military force to defend it. The Netherlands had been under the thumb of Spain for several centuries but had found ways to play off their Spanish overlords against the other powers. As with the classical republics, the freedom of the Dutch was hard won and difficult to preserve. Each province had its own political arrangements, and as a group they worked together only with difficulty. Yet their fragile liberty survived.

England presented an especially significant case. It was neither a republic nor a constitutional monarchy. It fell victim to many of the abuses of European tyrannies and, occasionally, to firestorms of anarchy. Yet everyone could see that English institutions worked differently from those of other monarchies. It was clear, for example, that the English king was not all powerful. When fighting a foreign war, he was obliged to go to Parliament, more or less hat in hand, and request the funds to pay for it. Nor could he successfully control the law courts. Cases of great moment came before the common-law judges and were decided quite independently of the crown.

While there was no English constitution as such, kings and queens of the realm kept hearing about the ancient rights and liberties of their subjects. In the 1640s a civil war resulted in King Charles I being tried by Parliament, removed from the throne, and ignominiously executed, after which Parliament itself ruled for a decade. Then, in 1688, another monarch, James II, finding himself in equally hot water, fled England for the continent. This time Parliament, while installing a Dutch nobleman as James' successor, made it clear that the English monarch ruled only "in Parliament"—that is, with the cooperation of a parliamentary majority. Political thinkers energetically debated just what this meant. To ordinary Englishmen, it meant an unprecedented degree of freedom.

The Blessings of Freedom

In all three cases, the corollary benefits of freedom were no less remarkable than the freedom itself. Athens, for example, witnessed a veritable explosion of creativity. While power was lodged in the city's democratic Assembly, Pathagoras worked out his geometric theorem, Sophocles wrote *Oedipus Rex*, Herodotus became the "father of history," Socrates taught Plato his philosophical idealism, and Phidias constructed the Parthenon.

The Netherlands enjoyed a similar flowering of the human spirit. When the Dutch first won their independence, they were bedraggled from the long years of struggle: their economy was ravaged, entire towns had been devastated, and society was wracked with dissension. Fifty years later the Dutch had built a trading empire extending from the Cape of Good Hope to the Hudson River. Their navy had come to dwarf those of England and France combined. Amsterdam had become the center of world commerce. And Rembrandt was at work on his masterpieces.

The lesson that political freedom, economic prosperity, and social well-being were somehow interconnected was plain to see. It was especially so in England. There, too, the tyranny and anarchy of earlier times had left ugly scars. But England's increasingly liberal political system unlocked hidden sources of energy. By the early 1600s English trade was expanding rapidly, and a rising middle class was enjoying bounding prosperity. Francis Drake and company were ravaging Spanish shipping on the high seas. Shakespeare was writing his plays. And there were projects afoot to colonize the coast of North America.

The Human Predicament in Pop Culture

All too frequently, our common understanding of tyranny and anarchy comes not from the history books, where it stands forth in stark horror, but from popular culture, where it is presented as entertainment.

Anarchy, for instance, is the ordinary world of many movies and television shows. Murder occurs in the streets, the parks, the playgrounds. Grisly corpses are found in bedrooms, hallways, garages, or come tumbling out of closets. Psychopaths run amok with axes, cleavers, chain-saws, sniper rifles. Hit men burst through doors with uzis, shotguns, AK-47s and spray the air with death. If things begin to lull, the inevitable chase scene picks them up: vehicles roar down the wrong side of the freeway; trucks careen out of control; twenty cars collide in an intersection; something or other blows up. The police, of course, are part of the fun. Their cars spin around corners, ski-jump down hills, leap across raising drawbridges, skid off the end of docks. The cops don't have to worry a lot about trials and such because the bad guys usually end up in a ball of fire before the commercial.

Pop culture has concocted some equally memorable tyrants. There were those never-say-die Nazis who kept trying to swipe the Arc of the Covenant from Indiana Jones. Darth Vader, with his perennial breathing problems, gave nightmares to many a ten-year- old. Even those nasty eye-gougers in TV wrestling are the very embodiment of pop tyranny. But what could compare with the tyrants that James Bond has encountered over the years? Each had a scheme for world conquest more grandiose than the last. One wanted to smash Russian and American satellites and start World War III. Another sought to detonate a nuclear device in some innocent German town. A third tried to touch off the great California Earthquake and send Silicon Valley into the sea.

It is, of course, all in good fun. The tyrants get beaten every time by a miscellany of good guys, and the anarchists are simply enjoying themselves. For example, the A Team, over the years, has fired off some twenty million rounds of ammunition without so much as causing a scratch. But the very fun of it all may be precisely the problem. The implicit message, absorbed unawares by millions of American children, might well be that tyranny and anarchy aren't really such serious matters.

And freedom? That, alas, does not seem to be terribly interesting to pop culture.

Does Liberty Have a Short Lifespan?

If the fruits of liberty were impressive, so were its costs and attendant difficulties. Nowhere, it seemed, did the course of liberalization run smoothly. In England, for example, there were the Stuart kings, beginning with James I in 1603, who dug in their heels at the notion of sharing power with some Parliament. Kings ruled by "divine right," James sniffed, and if they ruled wrongly or unjustly that was just too bad. More than once, James illustrated his own point by committing some outrage.

There was no king to commit outrages in the Netherlands, but old-fashioned anarchy was never far away. Some of the provinces were Catholic, others Lutheran, still others Calvinist. Some of them favored moderate kingship while others preferred out-and-out democracy. When the enemy was close at hand, they closed ranks and forged real unity, but when the foreign threat became remote, they fell back to wrangling. Their iron self-discipline failed them too. While fighting the Spanish they could be heroic to a fault, but peace and prosperity seemed to sap their will. By 1700 corruption had depleted the tax revenues, rivalries were besetting the government, and strong leadership had vanished. A century after its birth the Dutch Republic had fallen on bad times.

Was freedom, then, doomed to an ephemerally short life? The case could certainly be made. One needed only to look back at the republics of ancient Greece for confirmation. In their common evolution they had managed to get rid of their tyrants and oligarchs and to work out formulas of freedom. But how long had the freedom lasted? In the Athenian Republic, true democracy did not begin until the reforms of Cleisthenes in 508 BC. Though it briefly reemerged in the fourth century, by the end of the Peloponnesian War in 404 BC it had been reduced to a shambles. It had not flourished much longer than a single human lifespan.

The Enlightenment

How to achieve and secure freedom—really secure it—thus became one of the great philosophical problems of all time. Thinkers from the ancient world to the present have devoted their energies to solving it. In their quest they have combed the records of history, written masterful treatises, conducted political experiments, and engaged one another in endless debate.

Mostly they have studied and analyzed human nature. The reason for this is that the various behaviors involved in the human predicament—grasping for power, misusing power, supporting tyrants, following demagogues—seemed to be patterned behaviors. Specific situations, be they in classical Rome, Renaissance France, or present-day Central America, appeared to have likely, if not wholly predictable, outcomes. Tyranny and anarchy seemed as deeply rooted in the human heart as freedom was.

A period which has come to be known as the Enlightenment was marked by a special excitement in the quest for freedom. Though there was no precise beginning date for the Enlightenment, it came into flower toward the end of the seventeenth century—the 1600s—at about the time of England's Glorious Revolution. During the first half of that century, the human predicament had been especially grim. War and revolution had torn Europe asunder, and thousands of English Puritans had sailed for the American colonies. In the latter decades of the century, however, a new spirit seemed to dawn. The slaughter in Europe was finally brought to an end, along with the English Civil War. Political society appeared to be making progress at last.

It was just at this point that the discoveries of Sir Isaac Newton revolutionized the world of ideas. Astronomers had been observing the motion of the planets for some time and attempting to make sense of it. Newton demonstrated conclusively that such motion made overwhelming sense—it was governed by the single, elegant law of universal gravitation. "Every particle of matter in the universe attracts every other particle with a force varying inversely as the square of the distance between them and directly proportional to the product of their masses."

Laws of nature! It was an astounding concept. Philosophers had debated the existence of such laws, and suddenly here was a stupendous and unchallengeable example. The falling of an apple to the earth was not a random, accidental event, and neither was the orbit of Jupiter about the sun. What happened in the universe happened according to rules which could be given precise mathematical definition.

With this discovery came a whole new understanding of how and why things were as they were. For ancient and medieval thinkers, God provided the ultimate purpose in nature: things were as they were because that was how God made them. And since God's ways were inscrutable, man could never know what the final purpose really was. Newton's laws, by contrast, were anything but inscrutable. Through observation and reason man was able to discern precisely what they were and how they affected his life.

Take the case of lightning, for example. At the beginning of the Enlightenment, no one understood what lightning was or what caused it; it was a random hazard of nature. Ben Franklin's experiments demonstrated that lightning was nothing more than static electricity—the same thing one could produce in the parlor with raw wool and a piece of rosin. Like any natural occurrence, static electricity was known to obey certain laws, one of which Franklin described as the "law of points." If a static charge were to jump across a gap of space, it would always, if it could, hit something pointed. (Mathematical reasons for this would eventually be worked out.) Here was the key to protecting oneself from lightning. Put a

pointed metal object on the rooftop, said Franklin, and run a wire from it down to the earth. If lightning should strike your house, it would obey the law of points, zap the lightning rod, and travel harmlessly to ground. Understanding the laws of nature gave man mastery over a phenomenon once mysterious and terrifying.

There was an important next question. If there were laws of *physical* nature, undoubtedly there were laws of *human* nature as well. Just as the apple *must* fall to the earth, so too, perhaps, the ruler *must* be corrupted by power, the demagogue *must* arise from a spirit of licentiousness, the free republic *must* topple into anarchy. Like physical events, political events had also been viewed as God's mysterious handiwork. Now, suddenly, they too seemed open to man's understanding.

Such became the basis of the Enlightenment's spirit of optimism. Here for the first time was a hopeful sense that people could figure out the rules. And, just as a knowledge of physical nature made for the control of lightning, a knowledge of human nature—a *scientific* knowledge of human nature—might well make for the control of tyranny, anarchy, and the human predicament.

The philosophers of the Enlightenment were an amorphous group, international in character. Yet many of them knew each other well, exchanged correspondence, bombarded one another with prolix disquisitions. Those on the continent included Grotius, Bynkershoek, Pufendorf, Burlamaqui, Barbeyrac, Rousseau, Montesquieu, and Voltaire. In England were Milton, Hobbes, Harrington, Locke, Sidney, Cumberland, Selden, Neville, and Ludlow. And in Scotland were Robertson, Smollett, Hume, Hutcheson, Kames, Furgeson, Rutherford, and Smith. Some focused their interest on law, others on politics, and still others on economics, but all were broadly concerned with human nature and the human predicament. We might think of them as the first political scientists.

It would be difficult to overstate the enthusiasm sparked by the Enlightenment. Mankind seemed to be on the brink of something important—something virtually transcending human history. Enlightenment ideas were known to have taken root in the British colonies of North America, where, beginning in the spring of 1775 a liberal revolution was in progress, but, more broadly, they appeared to be taking root everywhere. In France, long known for political backwardness, the new spirit seemed especially effervescent. There the Enlightenment *philosophes* were stirring the popular imagination with ideas of "liberty, equality, and fraternity." In 1789, events reached a historic climax with the outbreak of the French Revolution.

The Irony of History

It would be nice to report that 1789 changed the world—that with the French Revolution the Enlightenment finally solved the human predicament once and for all. Many believed precisely that to be the case, at the time.

Actually, it was the human predicament that proved to be the winner. The French Revolution, so filled with idealism at the outset, itself began to sour into anarchy. Various groups, claiming to speak exclusively for the people, set themselves on the aristocrats of the old regime, imprisoning some, butchering others, sacking the graceful estates of still others, wreaking an increasingly violent havoc. Soon the murder became coldly systematic, and the

Adolph Hitler: Absolute power corrupts absolutely. (Library of Congress)

shadow of the guillotine loomed ever larger. Lords and ladies of the once-proud monarchy fell like wheat in the notorious Reign of Terror.

And terror begat more terror. Each faction of revolutionaries seemed more radical and virulent than its predecessor, and each seemed to hate rivals worse than enemies. By 1793 the revolutionaries were executing *each other*. One at a time Marat, Danton, then finally Robespierre himself joined the twenty thousand Frenchmen to die in the name of liberty, equality, and fraternity.

It all began to seem familiar. As power passed from the king to the National Assembly, to the National Convention, to the Committee of Public Safety, to the Directory, the revolution seemed to become a ghostly rehearsal of the ancient republics and their downfall. Was dictatorship ahead? thoughtful Frenchmen asked.

Indeed it was. In 1804, in the cathedral of Notre Dame in Paris, Napoleon Bonaparte, who had been the country's de facto dictator for the past five years, had himself crowned Napoleon I, Emperor of the French.

So the pattern of the ages still held. Tyranny had passed into anarchy and anarchy back into tyranny. Where the Enlightenment had promised a rational understanding of the human predicament and ultimately a way out of it, events actually delivered a new sort of nightmare, a secular religion which vowed to pull down all gods, transcend all faiths, remake human nature, and start history over again at the Year One. Needless to say, Frenchmen who had read the *philosophes* and dreamed of true liberty were severely disappointed.

Modern Versions of the Human Predicament

Horrors and all, the human predicament is something a free people must keep squarely in view. Americans of the present century have become so used to a world of comparative freedom that it is difficult for them to comprehend the true condition of mankind.

Pause and consider just a few of the historical benchmarks since the failed French Revolution. In 1914 a war broke out in Europe which eventually engulfed the entire West. In the wake of its thirteen million or so casualties, World War I brought revolution and upheaval to the Russian Empire, the German Empire, and the Turkish Empire, and despair to every democracy left standing. From these events it is fair to conclude that anarchy, far from being banished in the modern world, is in fact still close at hand.

Taking the place of the demolished Russian Empire was the Soviet Union, pledged to the violent overthrow of all existing governments, and led by the ruthless dictator Joseph Stalin. Taking the place of the German Empire, after a shaky try at democracy, was Adolph Hitler, pledged to the violent overthrow of communism, the forced unification of all Germans, and the systematic extermination of all Jews. At the same time Italy fell under the sway of Mussolini, Spain under Franco, and Japan under an oligarchy of Samuri bent upon the conquest of China. Right behind anarchy, so it seemed, was tyranny such as the world had never seen.

We should note, too, that science—the hope of the Enlightenment—far from making these tyrannical situations better, was directly complicit in making them worse. Hitler's technicians set to work perfecting heavier *panzers*, faster bombers, and deadlier submarines, while his scientists developed advanced rocketry and even nuclear weapons. Before the end of the World War II, German "scientists" were using Jewish guinea pigs in their ghastly medical research.

These events were not mere aberrations of modern history. Indeed, from the standpoint of millions, they *were* modern history. During Stalin's collectivization of Soviet agriculture in the 1920s, more than ten million Ukrainians were cynically starved to death. Who knows how many Chinese were killed in the Japanese invasion of their homeland, or who died in the war and revolution that followed. And within the past generation there have been horrendous famines in Biafra, Bangladesh, and Ethiopia, either caused or complicated by the human predicament.

Scientific Tyranny

For many philosophers of the Enlightenment, science was the answer to the human predicament. When man learned the scientific rules that governed his behavior, he would be able to wipe tyranny and anarchy from the earth.

But there was another direction that science might lead. With science, after all, man could perfect his mastery over things. He could master the elements—witness the lightning rod—master Nature itself. Perhaps he could even master *human* nature. If he really discovered what made human beings tick, he might be able to change the very tickings themselves.

The idea certainly occurred to Jean Jacques Rousseau. For this Enlightenment philosopher, pondering the significance of what science was teaching, human nature seemed to become supremely malleable. Humans, he wrote, were products of the institutions of society. Alter those institutions and you alter the human animal. It proved to be an intoxicating idea.

A few of the more extreme French revolutionaries actually tried it out. They would, they vowed, wipe out all existing institutions and start mankind over from scratch. They would destroy the church, remake the government, and radically alter the school. The months of the year would be renamed. The week would have ten days. The calendar would begin anew. This would be the Year One.

And what to do about anyone who stood in their way? Put them to the guillotine, of course. The new world could not come forth while tatters of the old world still lingered.

Was such thinking possible only in the bad old days? Unfortunately not. Ghastly as the Terror was in France, Pol Pot and his Cambodian revolutionaries went it one better. Hear the words of Dith Pran narrating his all-but-indescribable experience under the Khmer Rouge:

> They tell us that God is dead, and now the party they call the Angka will provide everything for us. He says Angka has identified and proclaims the existence of a bad new disease, diagnosed as 'thinking too much.' He says we are surrounded by enemies. The enemy is inside us. No one can be trusted. We must be like the ox, and have no thought except for the party; no love but for the Angka. We must honor the comrade children, whose minds are not corrupted by the past. Now is the year zero, and everything is to start anew."

If this sounds a lot like the style of brain-washing experienced by Winston Smith in *Nineteen Eighty-Four*, indeed it is. Its object was not simply to control particular people—but to control the human mind itself.

The killing fields of Cambodia (UPI/Bettmann Newsphotos)

In an odd mirror of this history, science fiction writers have projected tyranny and anarchy into a stark and forbidding future. From Aldous Huxley's *Brave New World* to George Orwell's *Nineteen Eighty-Four*, the imagined tomorrow has been filled with horror. Yet little in that reading surpasses what actually took place in Cambodia after the victory of the Khmer Rouge in 1975. The tales of it have become familiar, as has the nightmare imagery created by the film, *The Killing Fields.* Here, in real life, human beings were put to death by the millions to satisfy the whims of the rulers. The skulls really did pile up in vast boneyards, and the rivers really did run with blood. One Cambodian in every five failed to survive it.

To the extent that freedom survives today it does so in a tense and threatening world. Genocidal conflict has been raging in the Persian Gulf for almost a decade. The Middle East exists in a state of armed truce. Car bombs explode periodically in Spain (the work of Basque separatists) and Northern Ireland (the work of religious zealots). The Soviet Union has laid waste to much of Afghanistan. Central Americans are perennially at war with themselves. Drug lords topple sovereign governments. Travelers are terrorized on airliners. As we survey the human condition, we can see why the man in the Punjab took his chances with the tigers.

All of which is to reaffirm a certain fundamental truth. There is as yet no simple, clear, sure-fire solution to the human predicament and there probably never will be. If there is still cause for hope—and certainly there is—there is little justification for complacency. Neither man as a whole nor the individual nations have come up with a full answer to the riddle of the ages.

Freedom—the highest of human aspirations—still remains essentially a puzzle.

2

The Freedom Puzzle

Concepts
Human Nature
Public Virtue
Christian Virture
Self-Interest
Structure
Natural Law
Natural Rights

Socrates addressing the Athenians: Freedom
imposed a heavy burden. (Library of Congress)

High Noon

On the very day that Marshall Will Kane turned in his badge, word arrived in Hadleyville that the notorious Frank Miller, whom the marshall had sent to prison five years ago, had inexplicably been pardoned and was on his way back. "I'll kill you, Will Kane," he had vowed. "I swear I'll come back and kill you!" He was due to arrive in an hour and twenty minutes, on the high noon train. Three members of his old gang were already waiting at the station.

For a western movie, the plot of Stanley Kramer's 1952 classic, *High Noon,* started out ordinarily enough. Viewers expected to see plenty of action, a fisticuff or two, some fancy gunplay, and in the end, the unambiguous triumph of right. What they saw instead was a psychological drama that left many of them shaken. *High Noon* did not seem like a western at all. Rather, in a vague and indefinable way, it seemed to be about the viewers' own lives.

Hadleyville owed a lot to Marshall Kane. Before he came it had been a two-fisted frontier hell, ruled by the Miller bunch. Now, thanks to the law and order Kane had established, Hadleyville was peaceful and prosperous. "You cleaned up the town," says an admirer, "Made it fit for women and children to live in."

But had peace and prosperity been good for Hadleyville? The viewer began to wonder. As Marshall Kane pinned his star back on and attempted to recruit his old posse, it became clear that all was not well. Those who had helped to break the Miller gang five years earlier were not willing to break it again. Their reasons were a study in political psychology.

The deputy, Howard Pell, for instance, merely wants to play politics. He will strap on his gun and help the marshall out if the latter will make him his successor. Otherwise, Kane can go to hell.

The marshall's friend, Sam Fuller, cravenly hides in his bedroom and orders his wife to lie. "You want me to get killed?" he shrieks to her. "You want to be a widow?"

The boys at the saloon are more subtle in their cowardice. "Things were different then, Kane," one of them explains of the earlier time. "You had six steady deputies to start off with, every one a top gun. You ain't got but two now."

Gradually it becomes clear that certain elements in the town are not upset about the return of Frank Miller. Business has been off at the local saloon; gambling is in a slump; prostitution has declined. Explains a resentful hotel clerk: "There's plenty of people around who think he's got a comeuppance coming."

The broader significance of this remark is established by the town judge, while packing his bags to clear out. "No time for a lesson in civics, my boy," he says but delivers one anyway. "In the fifth century B.C. the citizens of Athens, having suffered grievously under a tyrant, managed to depose and banish him. However, when he returned some years later with an army of mercenaries, those same citizens not only opened the gates for him but stood by while he executed members of the legal government."

So much for the corrupt elements of Hadleyville. What about the law-and-order people—those whose way of life Kane is defending? Their reasons for bailing out— appropriately given at a church meeting—are even more convoluted. Why should we get involved in a personal feud between Kane and Miller? Whose problem is this, anyway, but the politicians' up north who turned Miller loose? Why should we fight Miller when we pay taxes for law-enforcement?

Kane's staunchest supporter then delivers this speech: "People up north are thinking about this town. Thinking about sending money down here to build stores and factories. It'll mean a lot to this town, an awful lot. But if they're going to read about shooting and killing in the streets, what're they going to think then? If Will isn't here when Miller gets into town, my hunch is there won't be any trouble. Not one bit."

The last, and most devastating, defection is Will's best friend and fellow lawman, Mart. "Yeah," he says, "been a lawman all my life. It's a great life. You risk your skin catching killers, and the juries turn 'em loose so they can come back and shoot at you again. If you're honest, you're poor your whole life. And in the end you wind up dyin' all alone on some dirty street. For what? For nothin'. For a tin star."

Kane, however, refuses to buy any of this. He will stay and fight at whatever cost. "I've never run from anybody before," is the sum and substance of his explanation. As the townspeople, in their corruption and cowardice, make ever more rational sense, Will Kane makes ever less. All he seems to know is that he stands for the right—come what may. If need be he will face the Miller gang alone.

Which is, of course, precisely what he has to do. As the last deputy quits— "There's a limit how much you can ask of a man. I got a wife and kids"—the marshall loads his guns, makes out his will, and heads through the deserted streets to meet the high noon train.

When the American Founders issued the Declaration of Independence and cut their ties to England, they spoke as children of the ages. They drew not only upon their own wisdom and experience but that of all mankind. They were, of course, closely in touch with the Enlightenment. Their personal libraries were stocked with the works of Hume, Rousseau, Montesquieu, Puffendorf, Sidney, and Locke, to name only a few, and several of them were personally in contact with European philosophers and scientists. Yet their sources of inspiration ran far beyond the Enlightenment. They were acquainted with the classics— Herodotus, Plutarch, Polybius, Cato, Livy— and could quote passages of them by heart.

They more or less accepted the unity of human experience. An event that had transpired in fifth- century Athens might be as relevant to their world as the Boston Tea Party.

The Founders began their quest for freedom with some fundamental assumptions. They assumed, first of all, that freedom really was possible; it was not just an empty dream. Their own colonial experience—though not without its difficulties—seemed to confirm that optimism. Secondly, they assumed that freedom was difficult both to achieve and to preserve. This insight also reflected their own experience, as well as their understanding of classical antiquity, where freedom had been tragically short-lived.

The Founders' third, and most important, assumption was that a vital connection existed between freedom and human nature. In order to achieve a lasting liberty, they believed, it was necessary to put aside all preconceived notions and peer into the heart of man.

Freedom and Human Nature

The idea of a link between qualities of the social order and qualities of the individual soul is well established in western thought. Put simply, it was believed that good people made for a good society, and vice versa. Most of us have had the experience of meeting some stranger who, quite beyond his foreign accent, impresses us as, say, a German, a Russian, or a Brazilian. His nationality is somehow reflected in the way he thinks and acts. The ancient Spartans, we are told, were a rugged, mirthless, unpitying people, and they quite naturally lived under a rugged, mirthless and unpitying form of government.

Thus, many of the principal thinkers of the Enlightenment were psychologists as well as philosophers. Hobbes, Locke, Hume, Rousseau, and Smith all wrote learned disquisitions on human nature. How did human beings learn things? How did they decide what was, or wasn't, true? How did they acquire their sense of right and wrong, their personal conscience, their ideas of justice and honor? Was the final reality of life only material reality, atoms in motion creating endless change, or was there a spiritual reality as well?

There was no easy way to get answers to such questions. One technique was to scan the human record and see what kind of overall sense could be made of it. A second was to study abstract philosophy and apply the power of reason. A third approach—especially favored by the Enlightenment—was to make use of science. In the spirit of Isaac Newton, one could perhaps devise experiments in which human actions could be observed and analyzed. Would an infant, for example, thrust its hand into a fire—or would it somehow know in advance that fire equals hot?

Probably the most favored technique was to shrewdly and dispassionately observe life around them. As men of affairs, which they often were, the enlightenment philosophers were in a position to experience firsthand many of the shocks and abrasions of political life. They knew what privilege was, for some of them traveled in the highest circles, but they also knew tyranny. Thomas Hobbes' work was banned in England. William Rutherford's was publicly burned. And Jean Jacques Rousseau was forced to flee France for Switzerland. One group of English thinkers lived through the Civil War and another through the Glorious Revolution. Both were the wiser for it.

The investigation into human nature rewarded the philosophers with a wealth of information. Yet its precise meaning was not always clear. In some situations human beings had acted to secure and protect their freedom while in other situations they had fostered tyranny and anarchy. Within the larger puzzle of liberty, there were innumerable smaller puzzles to sort out. Here are a few of the patterns that had to be explained:

There were rulers who had seemed worthy of the most sacred public trust but who, once in power, had grossly abused their authority. During the reign of Megacles in Athens, Draco was given the weighty office of lawgiver because of his reputed integrity and compassion. But his only "reform" was to introduce capital punishment for all offenses, prompting Athenians to say that the laws of Draco were written in blood.

There were instances when the people themselves, presumably enjoying their liberty, had somehow thrown in with the tyrants and helped to destroy it. In ancient Corinth, for example, the comparatively harmless Bacchiadae aristocracy was overthrown by Cypselus the tyrant with full support of the people—who later sorely regretted their action.

There were cases—plenty of these—in which the people struggled mightily for their freedom only to become licentious and turbulent after winning it, dissolving into warring factions. So dreadful was the havoc in Athens at the time of the "Thirty Tyrants" that it resulted in more casualties—including the gentle Socrates—than the entire Peloponnesian War.

How such behavior could be explained was the first and most important dimension of the freedom puzzle.

Public Virtue

The ancients' understanding of human nature was based on the concept of virtue. Where we think of virtue as the will to do right, they thought of it more in terms of human excellence. The virtuous man was the one who achieved highest self-realization in the arts, in learning, in warfare, in athletics, and, most importantly, in government. The virtuous man—stern, forthright, rigidly self-disciplined, politically independent—was the key to the virtuous society.

Virtue not only led the individual to excel, it also led him, at critical points, to subordinate his own private interests to the good of the whole. In the free society, those who held high office had to exhibit enormous virtue. They had to withstand the human tendency to be tempted by power and fall into the abuse of it. For example, Cleisthenes, a tyrant of sixth- century Athens, held absolute power, but instead of using it destructively, he used it to reform the constitution and establish democracy.

Still, for every "good" tyrant like Cleisthenes, there were a hundred of the other kind. Since the Greeks agreed with Lord Acton that power corrupts and absolute power corrupts absolutely, it followed that the virtue of the rulers was unlikely to be sufficient by itself. Freedom must have far stronger protections.

Thus, the more important virtue was that of the ordinary citizen. This *public virtue*, as it was called, was held to consist of basically four elements. First, there must be a willingness to obey the law, to obey it at all costs, whether or not there was a likelihood of punishment. If citizens lacked this virtue, no power on earth could spare them from anarchy.

Second, there must be a willingness to contribute one's own time and energy to the public well-being. The citizen had to keep himself well informed. He had to participate energetically in the political process. He had to be ready to make whatever sacrifices in order to keep the democracy sound and operating. For, when threats to the democracy occurred, there were none but the citizens to save it.

Third, there must be a strong sense of justice. Justice in civic affairs had to grow out of justice in the individual. And no system could long afford to be *unjust*, for out of injustice grew hatred, and out of hatred grew anarchy and tyranny.

The Strange Death of the Peanut Shower

The peanut shower was an ancient and honored custom at Wardwell Elementary School in Emmett, Idaho. Students would get together and arrange a prior signal—say, someone blowing his nose or asking a certain question. And when the signal was given, everyone would pull handfuls of peanuts from pocket or purse and shower them at the teacher. It is not recorded whether Wardwell teachers liked the peanut shower. (Perhaps they did if they liked peanuts.) In any event, they rarely, if ever, punished its perpetrators, for the entire class was complicitous.

One day, however, a certain predictable joke was played. While arranging a peanut shower, the group secretly determined that one of the students—we'll call him Goat—would be allowed to make a fool of himself. At the prearranged signal, he alone would stand up and throw the peanuts; his classmates would sit demurely in their seats. It worked like a charm. The signal was given. Goat stood up and bravely showered the peanuts, looking about in puzzlement. This time the teacher was definitely not amused. (She had a single, identifiable culprit to punish.) She made Goat stay after school and clean up the mess.

And, after that, there was never another peanut shower at Wardwell Elementary. Why not? Because no one ever again could be sure that the same joke was not being planned against *him*. As long as each had confidence in the "virtue" of every other, all were willing to stand up and throw the peanuts. The moment it became thinkable for the virtue of the group to fail, it did fail, catastrophically.

If I can be sure of your virtue, I may be virtuous too. If I can't be sure of your virtue, I will very likely lapse into strategic behavior and, depending on my estimate of the probable outcome, I may not be virtuous at all.

Finally, there must be an intense and unremitting vigilance toward those who held the public trust. One could not count on *their* virtue. One had to watch them carefully—audit their accounts, monitor their speeches, closely observe their actions. If the virtue of the leaders should falter, only the alertness and courage of the citizens could avert disaster.

The Difficulty with Public Virtue

In theory, public virtue was not necessarily altruistic. That is, the virtuous citizen did not have to be unhumanly or unrealistically good. For, in serving the cause of freedom he was in reality only serving his own best interest. In practice, however, public virtue might require substantial sacrifice—and the sacrifice might well have to be made up front. If I discover a conspiracy to subvert the democracy, do I, if need be, oppose the conspirators single-handedly? More than one citizen of the ancient republics had to answer that question the hard way.

And of course the answer was not always yes. Sometimes, given the difficulty of the demand, the citizens simply proved weak. They slipped back, opted for cowardice or inaction, chose immediate gratifications over iron self-discipline.

Sometimes they engaged in a kind of strategic behavior in which the virtue of one person would depend on the virtue of another. *I* will oppose the conspiracy if *you* oppose the conspiracy—you go first.

So it was, according to John Adams' reading of history, that the reforms of Solon ended in anarchy. In 594, Solon gave the lower orders of Athenian society the right to participate in government in the belief that their virtue would act as a check on the rulers. But the temptations of their new power proved too great for them. They lost their virtue, redrew Solon's constitution to suit their own selfish desires, and wound up bringing ruin to the democracy.

For the ancient democracies, then, the chief problem was how to keep virtue—especially public virtue—brightly shining. The answer they came up with was to approach virtue as a kind of crusade. Virtue was preached constantly throughout society. It was sermonized at the pulpit. It was taught in the school. It was celebrated in ritual and pageant. It was extolled in athletic contests. At no time could the pressure be relaxed, it was believed, or the people might let down their guard.

The relentless pursuit of virtue helps account for the poverty of material comforts found in Greek society. "Their beds had no springs," as a noted text puts it, "their houses had no drains, and their food consisted chiefly of barley cakes, onions, and fish, washed down with diluted wine." At the standard wage of one drachma a day, few luxuries were afforded or desired. What the average citizen wanted was a tolerable living, few material distractions, and plenty of time for public affairs.

Public virtue, conceived in this way, became the mainstay of the classical republics. The design of government and the precise way it operated were qualities of less importance. What counted for the ancients was not whether the ambition of one could be set against, or made to nullify, the ambition of another, but whether the virtue of all could be maintained at a sufficiently high level to preserve free government.

Virtue and Human Nature

How well did the classical solution to the freedom puzzle succeed? In a few instances, it succeeded well enough. The Athenian democracy survived more or less intact for a century. In many other cases, however, the results were more mixed. Some of the city-states could scarcely maintain their freedom for a single generation before corruption, war, or foreign intrigue put an end to it.

What seemed to be the undoing of classical virtue was the difficulty of maintaining such a demanding intensity. Even without material comforts to distract the attention, people were constantly slipping back into private concerns, contented lives, and attitudes of repose. Ironically, the happy and fulfilled private life—an important product of a free society—was ever the bane of the classical republic.

Christian Virtue

The sort of virtue taught by Jesus and practiced in varying degrees by the Christian world may not seem directly relevant to the freedom puzzle. After all, Christianity was directed not toward politics but salvation. Nevertheless, Christian virtue had important implications for liberty. A community that actually practiced the charity and humility set forth in the Sermon on the Mount could hardly be imagined to support tyranny or anarchy.

Moreover, Christian virtue proved on the whole to be stronger and more durable than the virtue of the classical republics. For the ancient Greeks, virtue was in large measure its own reward. For Christians, by contrast, there was a heavenly prize awaiting those who were virtuous on earth. Thus, where classical virtue was always pulling against self-interest, Christian virtue in a sense encompassed and included it.

For Christians, moreover, virtue was ordained by God, a second important point. The Christian truth was Truth with a capital T. It stood above and transcended lesser human truth. Philosophers did not need to debate—as Plato had had to do—fine points regarding the virtuous life and its relation to the public good. No abstract subtleties needed to be worked through. God commanded and mortals obeyed, and that was that. The Christian could turn whole attention to actually living the virtuous life.

Accordingly, while the Christian community was not noted for its liberty in the classical sense, its was well noted for its social harmony and unity of purpose. Christians were expected to go the extra mile and turn the other cheek. They were expected to love neighbor as self. In economic life, the Christian merchant was expected to charge "just" prices for his goods and share his profits with the poor. When it was truly practiced, Christian virtue could exercise an important moderating influence on both tyranny and anarchy.

The Difficulty With Christian Virtue

Nevertheless, we should note that the spread of Christianity did anything but ease the human predicament. To the contrary, it often appeared to intensify it.

David Hume: Man is what he is. (Library of Congress)

Those were, after all, Christian monarchs who claimed to rule by "divine right" and for that reason must rule unopposed. And those were Christian armies that marched off to the Crusades sowing mayhem. The Inquisition that tortured and murdered Spanish heretics was a professedly Christian institution, and the horrific Thirty Years War a Christian conflict. We are well justified in asking what went wrong with Christian political virtue.

There are hints of explanation in the scriptures themselves. Part of the problem, certainly, was that Jesus had said "My Kingdom is not of this world," and "Render unto Caesar that which is Caesar's." Many Christians were willing to put up with a great deal of worldly evil in the interest of their heavenly reward. Where the virtue of the Greeks had been *public* in nature—pulling people into the center of

Self-Interest and Social Engineering

We live in a world in which self-interest is often ignored. People learn to give high-minded reasons for their actions, when the real reason is material self-interest. This truth offers some possibilities for social engineering. To wit:

Why do trucks speed on the highways? Truck drivers are usually paid by the mile. The faster they go, the more they make. If we paid truck drivers by the hour, trucks would be the slowest-moving vehicles on the road.

Why are those do-it-yourself salad bars so messy? Because people get to eat everything they can manage to pile on their plate. Some get very good at it, using slices of cucumber to extend the edges of the plate a little further. But it's an untidy process. Things are always tumbling off the top of the heap and cascading onto the floor. If we started weighing the salads and charging by the ounce, there would be more weight- watchers in the world.

Why is there a rush to spend the last nickel in the budget by year's end? Because if you don't completely exhaust your budget, some higher-up might get the idea that you didn't really need it all. (Which of course is true.) If we told all department heads they could keep what was left over and spend it on Christmas bonuses, we would see a startling new frugality in the workplace.

civic affairs— Christian virtue was inherently *private*. It wasn't considered part of a Christian's duty to debate policy or keep an eye on the government. And if the rulers saw fit to smite him, he was supposed to turn the other cheek.

A second—and perhaps more important—part of the problem was that Christian virtue operated entirely without brakes. When the authors of the Inquisition quite reasonably deduced that heretics were in league with the devil and therefore must be destroyed, nothing that Jesus had said, and no feature of Christian political life, acted to stop them. Virtue by itself, without safeguards of some kind, could turn men into fanatics.

Of course, Christian virtue did not always lead to bad outcomes. For many followers of Jesus it led to very good outcomes. The point is that there was no easy way to determine which doctrines, which practices, or which groups might suddenly turn destructive.

Self-Interest

There was no wholesale abandonment of the idea of virtue in the Enlightenment. Philosophers continued to stress public virtue especially, and to insist on its relevance to the freedom puzzle. Harrington, Sidney, Montesquieu, and even Hume, who was skeptical about the very notion of virtue, found a place for it somewhere in their writings. Nevertheless, taking Enlightenment thought as a whole, the shift away from relying on virtue was remarkable. Human virtue was fine as far as it went, said the Enlightenment majority, but there were better ways to secure freedom.

The Problem of Sally's Two Dates

Sally Johnson would not see herself as a study in human nature. But Sally's dilemma presents some key issues of human nature in particularly convenient terms. Her difficulty is that she has two different dates for Saturday night.

It should be explained at the outset that Sally is a very nice person. She is radiant, wholesome, and attractive. Along with a career in marketing, she wants to marry, raise a family, live in the suburbs, and seek the Good Life. She is a good student at Wellesley College, is popular and well liked, is active in her church and an officer in her sorority. Toward other people she has been taught to behave with compassion and respect. She is the all-American girl.

But she has a problem. On Tuesday last, Fred Schultz called and asked her for a date on Saturday. Good old Fred. A date with him would unvaryingly include two lines of bowling at the student union, a frozen yogurt, twenty minutes in the video arcade, and a walk back to the dorm. Fred was, alas, something of a nerd, bless his heart. However, Sally wasn't doing anything on Saturday night, and so she accepted.

Then, on Wednesday, who should telephone but Lance—*the* Lance. Lance W. Rockefeller IV. He had seen her at the Black and White Formal, he said, and would like to get to know her. On Friday he and some friends were going to take the lear jet down to the Bahamas for the weekend. There would be swimming and tennis, a short cruise on the family yacht, dinner at the Royal Poinciana, and perhaps a stroll along the beach at sunset. Mom and Dad were staying at the villa themselves, so everything would be chaperoned and aboveboard. Would she like to come along?

Would she ever! But there is that problem of the other date—with Fred. Breaking it would be a simple enough matter. She could call Fred and make up an excuse. Of course, that would mean telling a lie. It would also mean breaching a commitment and violating a trust. Sally has been taught that trusts and commitments are matters of no small moment, and that lies are unthinkable.

What should she do? Here are the thoughts that flit through her mind while the decision is being made:

In fact, their starting point was an entirely different, even opposite, conception of human nature. *Self-interest*, they said, was a much better guide than virtue to political behavior. Human beings may often invoke and proclaim high ideals in their political discourse; they may speak glowingly of compassion, honor, and justice—but in practice they are more likely to act out of plain self-interest.

The Scottish philosopher David Hume put the case pointedly. Some people may be virtuous, he allowed. ("You and I certainly are," he would say with a wink. "It's just all those *other* people we can't be sure of.") But most people, most of the time act out of self-interest. For Hume, unlike traditional Christian thinkers, the mind had no innate ideas or values, so there was no

In the real world there is such a thing as a permissible lie. Indeed, the real world is quite patently founded on permissible lies. And lies aimed at averting hurt feelings are obviously permissible.

Lance Rockefeller, with all his millions, is probably not the marrying kind. Courtship with him—allowing the imagination to soar—might well prove tantalizing, frustrating, and in the end, disastrous. Fred, bless his heart, *is* the marrying kind and would probably make someone a good husband.

Suppose word got around that Sally Johnson broke dates, jettisoned commitments, jumped at the best opportunity. This might not be good for her reputation, not in the long run.

Actually, it might be wrong *not* to break the date. She could never marry Fred. She was just leading him on. To go with Fred and be hating him every minute *would not be fair to Fred*. For Fred's own good she should be up-front with him and let him find someone his own speed.

Who was this Lance, anyway, that she should compromise her integrity for him? What could a single date, no matter how glorious, have to compare with her idea of herself? "This, above all, to thine own self be true. . . ."

On the other hand, why not do it to Fred? Fred would probably do it to her. Others had. Bad things happened in the world. It was a bad world.

Suppose she turned Lance down. Maybe he would call again. Indeed, maybe he would respect her the more for her honesty. Maybe forthrightness would give her the winning edge over competitors.

Then, again, suppose he never called again. Suppose this was her only chance. Suppose he took some other—less upright— girl to the Bahamas and wound up marrying her. "The saddest words of tongue and pen. . . ."

Mrs. Lance W. Rockefeller IV. . . .

There they are, the sentiments of mankind. Enlightened self-interest. Corrupt self-interest. Virtue for its own sake. Virtue by calculation. All of them occur to Sally as indeed they would occur to most of us in her situation.

The question is, which of them will determine the outcome?

Truth—with a capital T—to command virtuous conduct. People learned what they knew solely on the basis of sense impressions of pleasure and pain. As a result, they sought their own pleasure, tried to avoid pain, and directed their political behavior accordingly.

Hume's argument was not without its difficulties, but it did explain some of the ancient puzzles. Why did the supposedly virtuous politician behave so differently after achieving power? Because he was never really virtuous in the first place— only self-interested. Why would the supposedly virtuous citizen cooperate with a tyrant to destroy his own freedom? Because the tyrant made it immediately and handsomely worth his while to do so. Why would a free people relax their vigilance in the face of material prosperity? Because material prosperity was more important to them than some remote political ideal.

And all that talk about virtue? Mostly just talk, Hume would say. People wanted to feel good about themselves. They wanted to believe they were acting out of the right motives. So they would deceive themselves and others with high-sounding patter about honor and justice. At bottom, their ideals were usually quite empty.

Self-interest, said Hume and his fellows, was nothing less than a law of human behavior analogous to the physical laws of the universe. And, like them, it held out much promise for mankind.

Self-Interest and Politics

What sort of political society did self-interest imply? To some Enlightenment thinkers, the answer was rather grim. To Machiavelli, conduct based on self-interest would naturally lead to systematic lying, manipulating, and other cynical behavior. The task of the ruler, said Machiavelli, was to speak glibly of high motives while shrewdly playing the interests of everyone against everyone else. And for Thomas Hobbes, self-interest led toward universal anarchy—what he termed "the war of each against all"—which could be controlled only by the all-powerful king.

But most of the Enlightenment thinkers were more optimistic. If self-interest had its downside, it had its up-side too. In fact, men of the Scottish Enlightenment—Smith, Hume, Ferguson—saw in self-interest precisely the missing key to solving the freedom puzzle. They basically advanced three arguments.

First, although some people would act only in the narrowest, blindest, and most cynical kind of self-interest—such as co-operating with a tyrant to destroy one's own freedom—many, and probably most, would act in a broader and more *enlightened* self-interest. They would resist the temptations of instant gratification in favor of their longer-term good.

Second, material self-interest, frankly avowed, was an effective antidote to excessive zeal. A commercial society, with its general prosperity and multiplicity of interests, was apt to be quite mellow in political matters. Put bluntly, people with comfortable homes and fine carriages might not care much about burning witches at the stake.

Finally, as Adam Smith noted, self-interest possessed an almost magical property. When each member of society was free to pursue his own gain, the result was often more to the public good than if all had acted solely out of virtue. This was especially true in economic matters, where, in the market system advocated by Smith, the pursuit of each person's private good added up to a general prosperity for all.

The Control of Self-Interest

To be sure, Smith and the others recognized that self-interest would not be harmless or beneficial on all occasions. Some individuals would not temper their selfishness with enlightenment. Some would not behave themselves in regard to power and privilege. The outcome of self-interested behavior was by no means automatically assured to be good.

But Enlightenment thinkers developed a general solution to this problem. It was possible, they came to believe, to control excessive self-interest by means of certain structural devices. Suppose, for example, that two children discover a small cake. They agree to divide it between them but neither wants to divide it quite fairly. So they bicker and squabble over the question of who will do the dividing and how it will be done. The children may be virtuous enough in other matters but in this matter they are exclusively—and destructively—self-interested.

Suddenly an adult comes onto the scene and alters its basic structure. Handing the knife to one of the children, the adult says, "Johnny, you may cut the cake—but Billy gets first choice of the pieces." Johnny and Billy now find themselves in a new situation. Their self-interest has been turned toward dividing the cake *evenly*. Johnny cuts the cake *exactly* down the middle, for he knows that if one piece is the slightest bit larger, he will have done himself a grave disservice.

Broadly conceived, the idea of structure was to set ambition against ambition—to make self-interest in effect control *itself*. The operation of a good structure depended on what the philosophers called *counterpoise*—the careful balancing of interests on both sides—it did *not* depend on virtue. Of course virtue might be present, and so much the better if it was. But it didn't *have* to be present in order to achieve a favorable outcome.

Political Structure

As the Enlightenment philosophers thought about it, they could see a number of ways in which structure could be applied to politics. This had not been the case in the ancient republics, where the reliance had been chiefly on virtue. The classical governments had had their various divisions—assemblies, councils, law courts and the like—but these had not been organized on the principle of counterpoise.

For the Enlightenment philosophers, thinking about self- interest, the precise structure of government could mean everything. Structure could operate to control self-interest. It could also operate to mobilize virtue and bring it to bear more effectively. Here were the main elements of structure as the Enlightenment philosophers conceived them:

Written constitutions with enumerated powers. The structure of a government and the description of its powers could be set down in black and white like a formal contract. All parties to the contract would have an interest in seeing to it that the *other* parties didn't violate its terms.

Separation of powers. Broadly speaking, there were two powers of government, the rule-making and the rule-enforcing power. If those two powers were held in different hands, and if a wall of separation stood between them, the result might be much like the cake example given above. The rule-maker would make the rules fairly because he would not be able to enforce them (and thus would have no reason to make them unfairly), and the rule- enforcer would administer them fairly because they could not reflect his particular purposes. And each would jealously check the other.

Checks and balances. Some of the powers of government could be divided in other ways for quite a different purpose. If two separate branches of government held parts of the same power, they would necessarily have to cooperate in order to exercise that power. At the same time, each would pull against the other out of sheer jealousy. They might wind up wrangling a good deal, but neither would be likely to dominate the other.

Fame and the Football

During the 1984 college football season, in which BYU was destined to win the national championship, Brigham Young fans were feeling their oats. Those seated behind the end zones took to catching the footballs kicked for the point-after-touchdown and hurling them around the stands, a sort of game of "keep-away" from the ushers. This was a bit dangerous: unattentive spectators could be bonked from the blind side as the ball was pitched from section to section. So the university hit upon a plan. Anyone catching the football and obediently turning it in would be given a real trophy: a football autographed by the members of the team.

It was a study in human nature. Everyone, of course, wanted an autographed football for his very own. In order to get it, however, he had to play the fink, and what was worse, he had to play it *in public*. There were his classmates, there were his friends, there was the coed he so wanted to impress. Should he hand the ball over meekly—and be richly rewarded—or should he do the macho thing?

Could the answer be in doubt? It was a perfect application of the principle of "fame" in governing human nature. BYU students, otherwise known for their submissiveness, continued to hurl the football until a desperate university put up nets behind the goal posts. There were worse things, it seemed, than losing out on a coveted prize. Like being known as a fink.

Representation. In the process of electing representatives to act in their behalf, the people would presumably choose men of exceptional virtue. If these representatives then chose representatives of their own, men of even greater virtue might come forth. And so on. Representation had another benefit. The more indirectly a given representative was chosen, the farther removed he was from popular passions and the more his virtue could act independently.

Fame. By structuring the government carefully, it could be insured that those who held greatest power were also the best known and most trusted throughout the land. Such individuals would recognize a vested interest in preserving their fame—and making sure it didn't become infamy.

Bills of Rights. These could limit the power and scope of government by declaring that certain rights were beyond government authority. Moreover, by protecting the right of free expression, a bill of rights also protected those (such as newspaper reporters) who kept watch on the government.

Government By Consent

The philosophers pursuing freedom had to think about more than human nature. They also had to think about the nature of government. Indeed, a bold new conception of government came out of the Enlightenment and addressed itself to the materialistic, self-interested view of human nature.

Natural Law and Natural Rights

That man needed government seemed to go without saying. From this fact alone it was possible to conclude that government had been created by God and was divine by nature. In a religious world, "divine" government could more easily command the loyalty of the people. It was also more difficult to correct or oppose.

Thus, while the notion of divine government had suited the medieval world well, Enlightenment thinkers had serious difficulty with it. How, they asked, could man make progress toward freedom if tyranny and anarchy could masquerade as God's will? On the other hand, if government were depicted as a mere human contrivance to suit the need for order, how could it hope to command loyalty and respect?

The way out of this impasse proved to be the concept of natural law. With Newton's discoveries in mind, one could accept the idea of a higher Truth in the universe without having to accept the divine claims of this or that monarch. Instead of thinking about God in the Christian sense, one could think about Nature—with a capital N. Nature had obviously ordained certain truths in the form of natural law; look at the law of gravity. And one didn't need a priest to illuminate the laws of Nature— they could be discovered through the use of man's own *reason*.

In fact, from the laws of Nature could be reasoned the precise freedom for which men had been searching. For reason suggested, did it not, that all men had a natural right to be free. How else could one explain the universal yearning for liberty?

The philosophy of natural law imparted a radically new meaning to government. Government was no longer a gift that

John Locke: There was a time when all men were free. (Library of Congress)

God had capriciously bestowed on some prince. It was a product of Nature—with a capital N—and its only conceivable function was to defend and protect man's natural rights.

John Locke

Here is how it all worked out in the philosophy of John Locke, one of the most influential Enlightenment thinkers. Locke reasoned that human society had existed long before government, and that in this premordial state—which he described as a "state of nature"—man had enjoyed the natural rights of life, liberty, and property. Life may have been reasonably orderly in the state of nature, but it *was* characterized by self-interest, and self- interest led to ill-disposed behavior on the part of a few.

For that reason *and that reason alone*, government came into the world. It was created by the people themselves for their own protection, much as one might hire a watchman to guard his home. Accordingly, in the compact between people and king which originally set government on course, the people did not surrender their natural rights. They merely agreed to give the king their obedience and loyalty so that he might protect those rights effectively.

By this view of things, government was appreciably less than divine and human beings appreciably less than angels. The king could not run roughshod over the rights of his subjects—indeed his only job was to protect those rights—nor were the subjects called upon to behave with saintly virtue. The entire arrangement was based on self-interest. And if the king failed at his job of protecting natural rights, self-interest just might lead the people to discharge him—as you might discharge a watchman who slept on the job—and find a replacement.

Here was a whole new approach to the freedom puzzle. Think of government not as something mystical and sublime but as a simple contract between king and people. As with any contract, there were duties and obligations on both sides. If both parties to the contract lived up to their own side of the bargain, government would *have* to be free.

What made Locke's approach so powerful was not simply its abstract reasoning; it was the fact that it suited the needs of self-interest so well *and* that it was timed to coincide with the Glorious Revolution. In that event, remember, the people of England, acting through Parliament, did precisely what Locke said they had a right to do: got rid of their king. They sent James II packing and then, with calm deliberation, looked about Europe to find a suitable replacement. History seemed to be proving that Locke was right.

Theory and Practice in England

Enlightenment thinkers often pointed reverently to England. Its constitution, evolving over the centuries, had come to embody important aspects of the Enlightenment approach. There was a rough and ready separation of powers between the rule-maker, Parliament, and the rule-enforcer, the court system. There were a few checks and balances, too. Parliament was divided into two houses, Commons and Lords, and both had to approve a bill before it became law. As for the king, he was not, as James II discovered, all powerful, for he was constantly pulling and hauling against Parliament and the courts. England even had a Bill of Rights, and James' successors* had to acknowledge its authority before taking the throne.

There was something else about England that fit into the Enlightenment conception of things. Since the days of Henry VII England had become ever more a commercial society, sending its ships all around Europe and to the New World, arranging and financing a variety of commercial transactions, steadily building the power and wealth of the middle class. Commerce created a multiplicity of private interests—the wool merchants, the cloth merchants, the wine merchants—and each group pursued its own political aims. With self-interest tugging the government this way and that, it was difficult for a single group to gain tyrannical control. Private interest drove public policy toward moderation—just as Adam Smith said it would.

England might have been a little less receptive to Locke's ideas if it had seen where they could lead. For, if government

*James' successor, William of Orange, was Stadtholder—something like president—of the Dutch Republic and a distant kin of the deposed monarch. He ruled conjointly with his wife, Mary, who also had some claim to the throne.

was founded on the consent of the governed, then the people, by right, might do more than substitute one king for another. They might take the entire government apart, alter it, transform it, or create a new government to take its place.

And if the people could actually make government themselves, it stood to reason that they could make it from scratch. They could scan through history and philosophical theory, pick out the ingredients that wisdom and experience found worthwhile, and stir them into their own recipe. That is exactly what the Americans would do—cook up their own government.

A Tentative Solution to the Freedom Puzzle

With rare exceptions, Enlightenment thinkers did not hold political power, reform European governments, or do much to alter existing conditions. They were theorists only. They had produced some exciting ideas, but the ideas were not without their difficulties.

The foremost problem was that neither virtue nor self- interest, by itself, gave a completely satisfactory account of human nature nor a completely promising solution to the freedom puzzle. Thinking about human beings solely in terms of virtue had not worked well in the past and didn't seem likely to work in the future. Virtue might be real enough in human nature, but it was unpredictable, unreliable, and occasionally tinged with fanaticism. Think about Hitler's Germans putting aside all private interest for the sake of European conquest and you will see where the notion of pure virtue could lead.

Thinking about human beings solely in terms of self-interest seemed scarcely more satisfying. If self-interest was really all there was in life, could freedom truly be possible? For example, would Hitler have ever been stopped if all Russians, all Englishmen, and all Americans had acted in their own narrow self-interest? It is doubtful.

As a practical matter, then, the freedom puzzle resolved itself into two interlocking propositions. First, human nature appeared to be multidimensional. Both virtue *and* self-interest seemed to play a role in it. The double challenge of free government was to find ways of encouraging and mobilizing virtue, on the one hand, and, on the other hand, bending self-interest to serve the public good.

Second, the idea of structure, broadly conceived, represented a general approach to both problems. Structure might be used to harness virtue and direct it toward the right outcome. Structure might also be used to control self-interest and keep it "enlightened."

The only task remaining was to do it.

3

A Republican Revolution

Concepts

Converging Experience
Moral Founding
General Religion
Threat of Tyranny
Patronage

Battle of Bunker's Hill—June 17, 1775 (Library of Congress)

John Dickinson Addresses the Continental Congress

Here it was, the speech the Patriots had dreaded. All morning the delegates to the Continental Congress had sat through the suffocating heat while President Hancock had droned his way through letter after letter, fourteen in all, waiting for the final showdown on The Question. Three weeks earlier, on June 7, 1776, Richard Henry Lee had submitted a motion for the colonies formally to declare independence from Great Britain. The motion had been tabled in order to give both sides, those in favor and those against, an opportunity to marshall their forces. The problem for the Patriots (those in favor) was that many of their best orators had gone off to their respective colonies to do just that, marshall their forces. Gadsden was in South Carolina, Chase was in Maryland, Caesar Rodney was in Delaware, and, most distressingly, Lee himself had returned to Virginia. Now John Dickinson was going to have his say, for better or worse, and John Adams was going to have to answer him.

Adams was well suited to the task, however. He had been keeping tabs on the Continental Congress for months. He knew every person in it, every like and dislike, every strength and weakness, indeed, every item of apparel that each customarily wore. He knew that Pennsylvania's John Dickinson, who today was wearing his plum-colored coat and breeches, was far and away the most persuasive of the "cool considerate men" who sought to block independence. And he even knew more or less what Dickinson was about to say. Independence, in the name of republicanism, would antagonize every monarch in Europe. It would cause serious division among the colonies themselves. It would bring on democracy and mob rule. It would pull the rug from under the peace commissioners soon expected from England. It would overwhelm the colonies with debt. Adams had heard it all before, from Carter Braxton, from John Jay, from Robert Morris, from James Wilson, from both Rutledges, but most effectively of all, from John Dickinson. This speech would be Dickinson's final try.

Finishing the last letter, Hancock picked up his mace and ceremoniously handed it to the clerk, signaling that the floor was open. At once, Dickinson was on his feet. The heat was now blazing. Several flies buzzed in the room. Cousin Sam sat motionless at his table, but every so often he shot a knowing glance at John. Yes, it was the same speech all right.

The Pennsylvanian, as usual, spoke slowly, deliberately, at times almost haltingly, but with a sincerity of conviction that seemed to well up from within. "If we declare a separation without waiting to hear from France, we may be overwhelmed with debt. We shall ruin ourselves and Britain will be ruined with us. France will rise on those ruins. Britain will push the war with a severity hitherto unimagined. Indians will be set loose on our frontiers."

In spite of himself, John Adams was impressed. Dickinson was truly speaking from the heart, he thought. But was he changing any minds? John looked around the room. How he wished that Lee were there, or Caesar Rodney.

Just then the door at the back of the hall opened and a messenger walked up the aisle. He handed Hancock a large envelope and then came around to John Adams with a smaller one. Adams looked at the postmark—Annapolis—then quickly tore it open. "I am this Moment from the House," he read, "with an Unan: Vote of our Convention for Independence. Now for a government. Your Friend, S. Chase." Adams looked across the room at Hancock, who had also finished his letter. Raising document, Hancock formed with his lips the word "Maryland." Whispers rustled in the room: *"Maryland for Independence!"*

Dickinson was coming to his favorite simile. "To escape from the protection of Britain by declaring independence, all unprepared as we are," he was saying, "would be like destroying our house in winter and exposing a growing family before we have got another shelter." John Adams smiled at his cousin but not mirthfully. That business of the house and the weather was a hard one to answer. Dickinson was always appealing to *experience*, blast him, and experience carried weight. Every man in the room knew what it was to be without a shelter in the winter.

The speech ended on a particularly ominous note. If independence were declared, Dickinson said, the nation born of it would, in time, certainly become unwieldy and break into pieces. As if the elements somehow concurred, the light suddenly faded in the room, and there was a distant roll of thunder.

Dickinson mopped his forehead and sat down. The storm was moving nearer. Save for the rumbles of thunder, there was no sound in the room, as the delegates waited for Adams to make his reply. The latter was angry that all of this had to be hashed over yet again. But Dickinson had spoken from the heart and spoken well; he could not go unanswered. Adams drew in his breath slowly and rose to his feet. Just then the storm broke, ratting heavily against the windows. John Adams looked at the delegates of the united colonies of America and began speaking, once again, for the cause of independence.

John Dickenson: Presented the case against independence. (Library of Congress)

Why was the anxiety so great on that warm July afternoon? In part because the American colonists were putting much at risk in a war with mighty Britain. But even heavier on their souls weighed the fear of political failure. After all, monarchy was alive and well in the modern world. Oligarchies could be found everywhere. Every cruel and tyrannical form of government known to man was operating somewhere on the earth in 1776. But republicanism had been dead for two thousand years.

So the delegates to the Continental Congress faced a sobering prospect: if they were to succeed where all others had failed, they must literally depart from the course of history.

What was it that made this tiny band of provincials think that they, of all people, should attempt such a feat? Two things. First, they had their own special faith in the Enlightenment. American statesmen had not only watched its development with great attention, they had also actively contributed to it. Young Thomas Jefferson had corresponded with the best minds of Europe. John Adams, in his well-stocked Braintree library, had collected hundreds of volumes of political theory—four copies of Rousseau's *Social Contract* alone. And Benjamin Franklin, world famous for his electrical discoveries, had become synonymous with the Enlightenment itself.

Even more importantly, however, Americans were convinced that their own history somehow embodied the republican quest. Dickinson's appeal to experience hit home with the delegates at Philadelphia precisely because experience was important to them. Pure reason could mislead. It often did. But to Englishmen steeped in long tradition, experience was like the immovable boulder in the stream.

In America, quite in contrast to Europe, republican theory and practical experience tended to merge together. Quite apart from working out republican *ideas* on paper, the colonists saw themselves as having worked out republican *practice* in their lives. In this chapter we shall examine the colonial experience and determine why Americans deemed it so useful.

A Natural Birth in Freedom

To begin with, we must understand that Americans were, in a very real sense, born free. In sharp contrast to that dreary catalogue of peoples who had had to make their

Benjamin Franklin: A man of the Enlightment in a coonskin cap. (Library of Congress)

choice between tyranny and anarchy, most American colonists had faced neither alternative. Travelers to the colonies observed that nowhere in Europe, nowhere in the civilized world, did men enjoy a greater degree of liberty nor a more widespread material prosperity than the citizens of Boston, New York, or Philadelphia. For this there were some important reasons:

The Idea of Freedom. Even before Columbus, it seemed, restless Europeans had looked westward beyond the sunset and imagined the existence of marvelous lands—Elysium, Arcadia, Utopia,—where gold abounded, innocence flourished, and freedom was wondrously real. They wrote about this dream in wistful novels of the day, and even committed it to the painted canvas. When Columbus' expedition returned with the electrifying news that there was indeed a world out there, the European imagination soared. Reporting on the islanders of Hispaniola, Peter Martyr concluded that they were "living in a golden age, without laws, without lying judges, without books, satisfied with their life, and in no wise solicitous for the future." America was seen as not just a new place—but a new beginning.

In Search of Freedom. Those who were most interested in beginning anew were also most heavily represented in the ensuing migration. They signed aboard American settlement expeditions for any number of reasons, from escaping creditors, to avoiding civil punishment, to forsaking wife and family. Still, it was the quest for religious freedom that attracted the majority. In 1630, a fleet of some thirty ships set sail from Bristol and made landfall slightly north of Cape Cod. Aboard the flagship was John Winthrop, Esq., lately of Groton Manor and soon to be governor of Massachusetts Bay, and accompanying him were literally thousands of fellow Puritans. They wanted to show the world what the Lord's people could accomplish if given elbow room and freedom of conscience. Eventually, they populated most of New England.

Later on, there arrived comparable contingents of Quakers, spreading themselves from Pennsylvania to New Jersey. They had been exceedingly unpopular in the Old World, and it was not until they strolled in wonder along Philadelphia's Market Street that they knew what freedom really was. The Appalachian frontier attracted still other heretics, its snug valleys

sheltering a wide assortment of Lutherans, Mennonites, and Moravians, not to mention those Anabaptist sects with the strange-sounding names: Dunkards, River Brethren, Schwenkfelders, Amish. Even genteel Maryland was founded as a religious refuge—for England's downtrodden Catholics.

Few Institutions of Tyranny. In the Old World there were any number of institutions more or less expressly designed to maintain tyrannical control. These were the institutions that Rousseau had in mind when he wrote: "Man is born free, and everywhere he is in chains." One reason Americans were not in chains was that the institutions of tyranny were not easily transported across the Atlantic.

Consider monarchy, for example. True, the English king was more or less sovereign in most of the American colonies, but making his power truly effective proved to be difficult. Because the machinery of executive bureaucracy was not easily stretched across the Atlantic, the king had to rely on an appointed governor and council, most of whose members were colonists themselves. In political battles, the king's men were far from home and socially isolated. In some colonies their very salaries could be pulled from under them.

For similar reasons, it was difficult to transplant standing armies. Defense was critically necessary in the colonies, of course, but because of the stretched supply lines, tangled authority, and exorbitant cost of any London-based army, defense needs were met by local militias. These as a whole were most unmilitary. They elected their own officers, framed their own bylaws, and maintained such discipline as they could

The Most Vivid People of the Century

What sort of people emigrated to the colonies? Were they the most courageous, the most imaginative, and the most daring of their time? For Alfred North Whitehead, at least, they were indeed. He called them the "most vivid people of the century."

What little we know about them as individuals seems to confirm Whitehead's belief. Take Capt. John Smith, for example. During the voyage to Jamestown, he quarreled with other passengers on the *Susan Constant* and wound up below decks in irons. Once ashore, he took himself off in a small boat and mapped the entire Chesapeake, little minding the not-always- friendly Indians he encountered. Later on, when the colony was starving, Smith knew exactly where to go for food. Having thus saved Jamestown, he was forthwith elected its president, and he ruled it with an iron hand.

But for John Smith such feats were ordinary. While still a young boy, he had run away to Holland. There he had known court life and squalor, adventure and misadventure. More exciting still was the odyssey of his return home. On one voyage he was shipwrecked and became a hermit. On another he wound up in a sea battle. On a third he was blamed for causing a storm his impiety) and was summarily tossed into the sea. Luckily there was an island nearby.

Smith found even more excitement in the East, where he went to fight the Turks. He told of taking on three gigantic gladiators in a single combat and emerging with all three of their heads. He told of being captured and sold as a slave to the wife of the Turkish Pasha (who straightaway fell in love with him), and of his eventual escape by murdering her cruel brother. The saga went on and on.

For Capt. John Smith, then, being saved from death by the lovely Pocahontas was relatively mild stuff. He was used to *real* adventure.

Here was a genuinely vivid early American, even if, as historians suspect, he was not always a truthful one.

John Smith: Always vivid, if not always truthful. (Library of Congress)

among the "good old boys" of the town. When George Washington asked a Connecticut militiaman to procure him a shovel, the reply was: "Go fetch it yerself." Needless to say, such forces were not good weapons for tyranny.

Aristocracy, a third instrument of Old World tyranny, made valiant efforts to cross the Atlantic. With American fiefs swimming before their eyes, Lord Say and Seal, Lord Culpepper, Lord Albemarle, Lord Carteret, and a number of other English noblemen were awarded gigantic tracts of land in the colonies. Lord Baltimore was granted the whole of Maryland, complete with kingly powers, while the Duke of York was given the entire valley of the Hudson. Yet, despite all expectation, aristocracy in America fell flat. Colonists who had fled from privilege in Europe had little interest in submitting to it here, and with so much land available, they didn't have to. They simply settled elsewhere.

Most fortunate of all for the cause of American liberty was the eventual demise of established churches. Such churches (like the Church of England) were as difficult to supervise from across the Atlantic as standing armies were, and their authority was next to impossible to enforce. When dissenting sects began to sprout like mushrooms, no official could imagine how to stop them. Soon, no matter what their theology or worship, the dissenters were commonly demanding complete religious freedom. Under the circumstances, it was the only thing that made sense.

Cheap Land. In Europe the ownership of land determined both an individual's station in life and his sense of self-worth. In the colonies, however, most of the Old-World definitions lost their meaning. Anyone who could pay his own passage across the Atlantic was given more land in Virginia than belonged to the wealthiest family he may have known in Europe. And even a lowly servant, once free of his indenture, could gain title to a good hundred acres. America made property owners out of people formerly considered refuse.

And property owning, in turn, did wonders for them. People who would not lift a finger in a London poorhouse, when given their own land in the colonies, were suddenly willing to push a plow day and night. Moreover, such settlers acquired a stake in their community, a political interest in its well-being. Because suffrage was customarily based on land ownership, most American farmers could meet the minimal requirement as a matter of course. Studies have shown that in Virginia more than ninety percent of all adult white males were qualified to vote, while in Massachusetts, the figure was even higher. Thus, at town meetings or county courts, the Yankee freeholder could take his place among other men of property and forcefully speak his mind.

Frontier Life. Life on the frontier, far from most social controls, had an equally bracing effect. There were people in the Carolina backcountry who lived out their entire lives without ever seeing an official of the colony, a minister of the church, or a gentleman in a powdered wig. Travelers who visited them, such as the Reverend Charles Woodmason, were forcibly struck by the effects. "Nakedness is not censurable or indecent here," he noted, "and

"DANCE-HOUSE."

Frontier life: Far from social controls (Library of Congress)

frontier girls expose themselves often quite Naked, with Ceremony, Rubbing themselves and their Hair with Bears oil, and tying it up behind in a Bunch like the Indians, being hardly one degree removed from them." These frontier Americans were the forerunners of Daniel Boone, Davey Crockett, and the Wild Bunch. Freedom was a way of life for them.

Americans' experience with freedom gave them insight into the human condition. They learned firsthand that, contrary to what some philosophers had imagined, freedom did not banish injustice, assure prosperity, or bring about personal fulfillment. If people were free to succeed in America, they were also free to fail. What

freedom did, rather, was to create possibilities. Thus, almost incredibly, indentured servants who had survived starvation in early Jamestown began building mansions along the Chesapeake estuaries; settlers on the Pennsylvania frontier started sending their children to college; and the sons of tinkers and cobblers found themselves sitting in colonial assemblies. People whose limits were once fixed now had something to strive for.

Freedom also created dignity. In the Old World, some people were valued much higher than others, and most of the distinctions were permanent. In the colonies, by contrast, what counted most was not birth or inheritance but brains, talent, and fortitude—qualities that anyone might possess. By degrees, the colonists came to understand that even though freedom could not guarantee a full stomach or a happy marriage, it was nevertheless the essence of humanity.

The Threat of Tyranny

If freedom was one powerful force in shaping the American experience, the threat of tyranny was another. Here and there in the colonies, there had turned up an especially corrupt or despotic governor whose very presence had reminded Americans what tyranny was like. The notorious William Berkeley, an early governor of Virginia, had given his colony such a bad time that he was eventually overthrown in a violent revolt.

What happened in the 1760s and 1770s, however, was not just another chance misfortune. It was the result of a calculated attempt on the part of English politicians to alter the nature of their colonial empire. That empire had begun as a ramshackle affair. Various colonies, without plan or forethought, had grown up in a tangle of legal relations and supervisory authorities, and the whole thing had come to border on chaos. Then, too, some Americans took their responsibilities in the empire rather lightly. When bargains were offered them by Dutch merchants, for example, several colonies forgot about their English affiliation and channeled their commerce through Amsterdam. As a result, the so-called Navigation Acts were passed for the purpose of making the colonies behave.

Even with the Navigation Acts, though, the British Empire was no model of efficiency. American merchants could often evade the trade laws and smugglers could blatantly violate them. The Spanish,

whose own empire was tightly organized and smoothly run, looked on the English colonies with pity and disgust. And there were English admirers of the Spanish example. "All these Colloneys," declared Lord Cornbury with a loud harrumph, "ought to be kept entirely dependent upon and subservient to England."

At the close of the French and Indian War in 1763, the time seemed right to follow Lord Cornbury's advice and overhaul colonial administration. But this was difficult to accomplish "legally." The American colonists thought of themselves as Englishmen, and believed that their rights were the same as Englishmen's anywhere. Moreover, among those rights they numbered many of the existing loose arrangements. They truly believed, for example, that no one but their own colonial assemblies had the right to tax them—just because that had come to be the practical reality.

It was a situation made for disaster. Everything the English tried to do seemed wrongheaded. When new customs officers were sent into the colonies to improve the enforcement of the Navigation Acts, they turned out to be corrupt and incompetent. One of them, Thomas Scottowe, found his income so plentiful and his work so dull that he left the customhouse to subordinates and went off on a permanent vacation. On top of the invasion of the customs men, a new legal jurisdiction was announced. Owing to the difficulty of convicting American smugglers in American courts, violations of the Navigation Acts would henceforth be tried before Vice-Admiralty courts—which did not use juries. To a people who took seriously the Magna Carta's promise of trial by jury, this was a sinister innovation indeed.

Self-Interest in the Empire

If the American colonists needed to be reminded that self-interest governed the British Empire, there was always the Louisbourg incident to think about. Fort Louisbourg was the eighteenth century's version of the Maginot Line. Built by France on Cape Breton Island, it was the largest, best armed, and most formidable military installation in the New World, and its thirty-six-pound batteries, glowering at the gray Atlantic, were regarded as literally unapproachable. For that reason, the place was a haven for French privateers, who harassed American shipping and kept Yankee seiners out of the northern fisheries.

When war broke out with France in 1744, Massachusetts Gov. William Shirley somehow got it into his head to assemble a colonial strike force and have a go at Louisbourg. Though initially protested as sheer madness, Shirley's plan eventually won support. New York contributed cannon; Pennsylvania and New Jersey chipped in provisions; and feisty New England put up the men, some 4,200 of them. On March 24, 1745, they set sail in ninety vessels, many of them mere fishing smacks, on what one chronicler termed a "mad frolic."

Little of the expedition bespoke discipline. The New England farm boys got drunk on captured brandy and paid their respects to "2 pritty gurls" left behind by the French. When it came to fighting, though, they were all business. They hauled their siege guns through miles of trackless bog and began battering the fortress from the rear. "We gave them," reported the commander, merchant William Pepperell, "about nine thousand cannon-balls and six hundred bombs," many of the former chased down by the Americans, loaded into their own cannons, and fired back. "Never was a place more mauled."

After some two months of this, the French garrison called it quits. A thrill of pride rang through the English-speaking colonies—Yankee militiamen had achieved the

It was in the matter of taxes, however, that the British truly put their foot in it. Of all powers of government, the power of taxation was the one most closely associated with tyranny, and Americans were known to fear it almost morbidly. But the Whitehall politicians bowled ahead. They rammed through Parliament a series of taxes which, had the Americans acceded to them, would have required revenue stamps—much like those on liquor bottles today—for the purchase of a variety of articles. The Americans, however, did not accede. They gathered in the streets and all but mobbed the would-be stamp vendors.

They would pay only those taxes levied by their own assemblies, they vowed, adding: "Taxation without representation is tyranny."

And so it went. Parliament repealed the Stamp Act yet wrathfully reasserted its right to tax the colonies. Two years later it tried again, this time with new import duties. There was another firestorm in the streets and another grudging withdrawal—except for the tax on tea. The British lawmakers scratched their heads. Somehow, they said, a way had to be found to make the Americans pay that tea tax.

William Pepperell at the Siege of Louisbourg: "Never was a place more mauled." (Library of Congress)

impossible—but the lords of the empire were not so pleased. They were at a delicate point in their negotiations to end the war, and news of the French surrender upset everything. In the end, in fact, it was politically necessary to give Louisbourg back to the French, who immediately reinforced it and put it back into operation. At this, American resentment was almost palpable. "Perhaps this goodly land itself," reasoned one colonial statesman, "may be the purchase of a future peace."

They simply must be brought into the new order.

Few things are harder to bear than the threatened loss of a valued treasure. By 1770, Americans up and down the colonies were convinced that a conspiracy existed to deprive them of their liberty, and they were ready to resist violently. On a cold evening in March, a group of them, nettled by the presence of British soldiers in their midst, took to the streets in Boston, just as a contingent of redcoats was changing the guard. Insults were hurled back and forth, followed by snowballs packed around oyster shells. The situation soon got out of hand. When the soldiers found themselves cornered by the now-howling mob, they panicked and fired into it, killing five and wounding several others.

The Boston Massacre gave Americans much to think about. For 150 years they had escaped the dilemma of tyranny versus anarchy, but now, within the space of a decade, tyranny was glowering at them from across the sea and anarchy was lurking in their own streets. The American people, uniquely born free, had come at last to confront the human predicament.

Mastering the Art of Republican Government

While the American colonists were enjoying their freedom—and fretting about losing it—they were also learning the art of republican government. That art, as noted earlier, was largely one of coming to understand political self-interest and then finding ways of controlling it. As provincials in a foreign empire, they learned a lot about self-interest, much of it the hard way. They learned, for example, that laws supposedly benefiting the entire empire mostly benefited British merchants. They learned that while their own goods sold cheaply in the restricted English market, the foreign goods *they* purchased, after being funneled through Fleet Street, wound up costing a fortune. And as for the military protection that theoretically came free of charge, they learned that whenever trouble broke out they had better be able to provide their own.

Where Americans really witnessed self-interest was in the daily grind of colonial politics. While some of their British governors were capable men, a rather large number consisted of broken-down aristocrats who were sent to the colonies to recover lost fortunes, escape political embarrassment, or simply get out of town. (New York's Lord Bellomont, for example, enjoyed parading about in women's clothing.) With such types holding the reins of royal authority, the Americans soon learned to defend their own interests. Over the years, a great many of them gained hands-on experience in the art of controlling human nature.

Colonial Experience and Enlightenment Ideas

Colonial experience bore an interesting relationship to the European Enlightenment. The philosophers of the Enlightenment were largely confined to questions of theory, since they had little opportunity to exercise power on their own. The American Founders, by contrast, were schooled in real politics. And yet, there came to be striking parallels between European theory and American practice, for at one time or another the American provincials, wittingly or otherwise, utilized many of the ideas of the Enlightenment. They were especially successful with the following:

Natural Law and Government by Consent. Where John Locke had theorized about a state of nature before the invention of government, Americans actually seemed to be living in such a condition, especially on the western frontier. So who better than they understood natural law and natural rights, or the idea of government by consent? Locke had only imagined people coming together and forming their own government; the Americans had actually done it. In a number of backcountry communities, they had literally gathered themselves together, worked out a constitutional structure, and then submitted themselves to its authority. The effect of this on the imagination of European intellectuals should not be hard to guess. It explains why Benjamin Franklin, a master manipulator of symbols, often wore his beaver hat to the Paris salons or affairs of the French court. He was playing the Man of Nature to the hilt.

Written Constitutions. Americans had lived by written constitutions, too, for the design and operation of their colonial governments had come to depend upon written charters granted by the king. The charters themselves were merely words on paper, of course, but in a society of law, words on paper could have a momentous effect.

In Massachusetts Bay, for example, a delegation of citizens appeared at the governor's office one day and demanded to see the colony's charter. It was duly produced. Here was a provision, they pointed out, that in practice was not being kept. The governor more or less gulped and called a hasty meeting with his council to correct the indicated deficiency. The slightest departure from the written compact, so it seemed, could bring sobering consequences.

Divided Power. When the philosophers of the Enlightenment were only discussing divided power, colonial governments divided their powers naturally. In such governments there were always two separate powers at work: that of Great Britain (or a British proprietor) and that of the colonists themselves. The former was expressed by some sort of executive authority and the latter by some sort of elected assembly.

Neither the English king nor the proprietary lords had much liking for colonial assemblies. They often deleted the assembly provision from working drafts of a charter, and in one or two instances, put existing assemblies out of business. And yet, because the colonists themselves unwaveringly demanded it, every single colony came to have its assembly. The various assemblies, moreover, all behaved more or less alike. All of them came to exercise the sole power of taxation, and all of them demanded legislative independence. They seemed to see themselves as little parliaments.

Representation and the Electoral Process. In the English government of the day, there was a kind of representation already at work, but we would hardly recognize it today. Members of Parliament did not represent geographical districts or specific groups of voters; they represented generalized points of view. If you were a Whig, a Tory, or whatever, the idea was that somewhere in Parliament there would be someone to speak up for you, whether you actually elected him or not. It was called virtual representation.

The problem with virtual representation was that the representatives rarely had to live with the results of their own decisions. For example, somewhere in Parliament there were supposed to be those who, although not elected by Americans, nevertheless espoused an American point of view. But many of these virtual representatives went along with the Stamp Tax (which they did not have to pay), the Townshend Duties (which did not apply to them), and a raft of other legislation that Americans themselves found outrageous. Virtual representation proved to be no bar against tyranny.

American colonists came to regard representation differently. They found it better to define constituencies precisely, so that voters knew in advance exactly who was electing whom. With that innovation, representatives truly *represented*. Thus, your delegate to, say, the Virginia House of Burgesses was quite literally your neighbor down the road. Your problems were his problems, and, more importantly, your taxes were also his. This, of course, was the Enlightenment's view of representation, and it had an obvious application to liberty.

Free Inquiry and Expression. No eighteenth-century man of affairs liked to have reporters spading about in his garden. All too often, there was dirt to dig up on anybody, and what usually got dirtiest was the government. Although newspapers in England were among the freest in Europe, even they were muzzled by the laws of libel. But newspapers in the colonies were harder to control. There were a great number of them, and their editors were aggressive, determined, and slippery.

In New York, for example, there was something of a scandal sheet published by a young German immigrant named John Peter Zenger, and it made life difficult for Gov. William Cosby. In 1735 Cosby had Zenger arrested and charged with seditious libel. Zenger, however, had a good lawyer, one James Hamilton, who rather novelly argued that the truth of Zenger's allegations ought to constitute a sufficient defense. It was of considerable significance to the idea of free speech that Hamilton's argument won the day.

Becoming a Republican People

So much for the Humean side of the colonial experience. In their growth to maturity, the American Founders had come to know self- interest well and to understand how it might be controlled mechanically. Such was the art of republican government. Yet the Founders had also come to realize that government comprised only half of the republican equation. It was equally important—indeed critically necessary—to perfect a republican *citizenry*.

That brought the Founders to consider the Rousseauean side of the problem, the side of public virtue. And consider it they did. Beginning before the Revolution and continuing well beyond the Constitution, they conducted a searching and spirited debate on the nature of republican citizenship. Was there or was there not, they asked themselves, sufficient virtue in human nature to make republican government possible?

For answers, they combed through philosophy and history once again, and reexamined their own experience. They discovered something very much like public virtue in the annals of their own past. In order to comprehend the essence of American nationhood, we need to understand what the colonial idea of public virtue was—and why it was uniquely American.

The First Founding

For the ancients, we recall, virtue was understood as being essentially opposed to self-interest. Thus, the active promotion of virtue as the mainstay of freedom meant that they effectively had to rid themselves of self-interest. Using every means at the state's disposal, they applied unremitting pressure on individuals to suppress their natural selfishness in favor of republican ideals. Such all-engrossing public-spiritedness was not without its rewards, perhaps, but it proved impossible to maintain the high standards indefinitely. Eventually one after another of the classical republics succumbed to corruption and disorder.

Life in the American colonies was significantly different. No one in Boston or Philadelphia sacrificed for the common good because he lacked self-interest or because the government was hounding him about patriotism. American colonials were notoriously self-interested, and patriotism was something they rarely mentioned. Yet, in their own way, they possessed every bit as much public virtue as the citizens of ancient Athens. The question is, why?

Religion and Social Ethics. It is difficult for people in the twentieth century to understand the once awesome power of religion. In the sixteenth and seventeenth centuries, wars were fought over it; nations stood or fell by it; politics and diplomacy were shaped in its image. In the England of James I, dissenters from the Anglican establishment (the Church of England) took religion especially seriously—they had to be willing to die for it. But the Anglicans themselves were sober about religious matters. It was in Anglican Virginia, not Puritan Massachusetts, that a man had his tongue nailed to a tree for the offense of blasphemy.

That underscored another point. Those who were serious about religion were equally serious about virtue, as we have seen. No one could read the Ten Commandments, the Sermon on the Mount, or the twelfth chapter of Romans without concluding that Judeo- Christianity imposed high standards of conduct. They were standards, moreover, that had to be supported primarily from within. A God-fearing man was expected to rise early in the morning, work hard, treat neighbors kindly, conduct all business honestly, respect his wife, and teach his children to "walk uprightly," not just because of legal obligation, but because of the strength of his faith. True Christian behavior could never be enforced—it had to be self-generated.

The phenomenon of self-generated virtue was a difficult one to explain. Most theologians agreed, however, that it could only be accomplished through some sort of divine intervention. Some of them called it "grace," others "salvation," still others "the inner light." But the principle was basically the same. God, through His own power, would see fit to lift a person from his sinful nature toward the virtuous life. Thus religion—especially dissenting religion—implied moral regeneration.

For many of the dissenters, then, the problem of dealing with self-interest in society was distinctly different than it had been for the ancient Greeks. Rather than seeking to banish self-interest through an externally monitored and regulated behavior, as was done in ancient Athens, they came to rely on the *self*-regulated, but otherwise free, individual. As long as the individual walked uprightly before the Lord, they said, it was immaterial whether he also possessed wealth, sought power, or relished the honors of men. If the tree itself was good, it could not bring forth evil fruit.

The Puritan Example. Here, for example, was the way it worked for the Puritans of New England. When a person received divine grace, he would make a covenant with the Lord to act in ways that would further the latter's glory. This meant more than prayer and psalm-singing; it included old-fashioned worldly success. For when God's own were successful in the world—when they laid out farms, built cities, founded commercial empires—it established the worth of the gospel. Men would look and say "Behold!"

Wealth per se, then, was not considered evil. What really counted was how the wealth was used. If used only for frippery and finery, it would stand as a condemnation to its possessor, but if used for the building of God's Kingdom, it would redound to the saint's credit forever. A prosperous business, for example, was a fine thing to possess—*if* it charged fair prices, paid fair wages, and enhanced the life of the community. In the Puritan scheme of things, there was no purely private concept of self-interest. Every action that enhanced the saint before God also enhanced the godly community.

Although not every religious group taught this precise doctrine, most of them worked to harmonize individual and community. Isaac Norris might glide through the streets of Philadelphia in a monogrammed carriage, yet he used his fortune for constructive social purposes. Charles Carroll may, in his words, "have been blessed with great wealth, prosperity and most of the good things which the world can bestow," but his greatest blessing was "that I have practised the duties of my religion." So strong and pervasive was the ethic of community service that we are justified in regarding it as the moral founding of American nationhood.

From the First Founding to the Second

The concept of fusing virtue and self-interest together—rather than pulling them apart—was something decidedly new. While it wasn't an exclusively American phenomenon, it acquired a peculiar force in the context of American circumstances. For in America there was a constant fear that religious faith was somehow slipping away, and that repeated efforts must be put forth to renew it. In the great religious revivals of the eighteenth century, hell-fire and damnation preachers assailed their audiences with the notion that sinfulness was engulfing society, and that only the most heroic actions could save the sinners. Audiences were swept into such a state that women swooned, men barked like dogs, and stolid rationalists like Ben Franklin emptied their pockets into the collection plate. Many, it seemed, felt the common sense of loss—and resolved to change their ways.

The General Religion. Changing their ways, however, did not for Americans necessarily mean going back to church. Rather, it tended to mean rededicating oneself to the moral life. Thus, long after many Americans had grown bored with sectarian wrangling and ceased to attend worship, there was still a reawakening of the moral conscience and a rededication to social responsibility. Where the colonies had often been founded in sectarian strife, their mature religion became a kind of generalized Christianity—the "general religion," as Jefferson called it—consisting of those aspects of the gospel which were common to all of the churches. Central to the General Religion were Christian ethics—going the extra mile, turning the other cheek—and the old Puritan notion that society as a whole, not just the individual, must be pleasing to the Lord.

There was no better illustration of the General Religion's influence than in the lives of the Founders. As a group, they were men of pronounced self-interest. George Washington was an energetic businessman and land speculator. Thomas Jefferson arranged for himself an extremely lucrative marriage. James Madison lived a princely life on his tidewater estate while

George Washington at Valley Forge: Self-interest did not preclude public virtue. (Library of Congress)

John Adams believed so profoundly in such values that he defended the British soldiers accused in the Boston Massacre. And if, above all, public virtue meant placing public ahead of private interests, Franklin abandoned his beloved inventions to go abroad as a diplomat; Jefferson took on the thankless task of governing Virginia during the war; and Washington gave up his pleasant life at Mount Vernon for the horrors of Valley Forge.

How did the Founders explain such conduct? Most often in terms of the General Religion. "Here is my creed," wrote Ben Franklin, supposedly the group's leading skeptic: "I believe in one God, Creator of the universe. That he governs it by his providence. That the most acceptable service we render to him is in doing good to his other children." Sam Adams called Franklin's points "the religion of America." To Jefferson, they were principles in which "God has united us all." George Washington referred to religion and morality as the "indispensible supports [of] political prosperity." "Our Constitution," affirmed John Adams, "was made only for a moral and religious people. It is wholly inadequate to the government of any other." James Madison hoped for a career in the ministry and abandoned it only with reluctance. Even Thomas Paine professed a strong belief. "I consider myself in the hands of my Creator," he wrote in *The Age of Reason*, adding, "To do good is my religion."

slaves did all the work. Benjamin Franklin was a cunning entrepreneur. John Adams was a two-fisted trial lawyer. And Alexander Hamilton's ambitions were so strong that they eventually led to his downfall.

And yet, see their lives again in terms of public virtue. If public virtue began with the willingness of the citizen to take part, the Founders spent most of their time in civic affairs. If it meant being watchful of the government in power, the Founders watched that of His Majesty like so many professional auditors. If it included respect for the law and for the rights of others,

The American strain of political virtue was different from that of classical antiquity. It depended on inner conviction and self-restraint rather than compulsion from outside. It respected the identity and integrity of the individual—leaving intact his pursuit of self-interest. And it existed

Life Under Patronage

What life could be like in a patronage society was aptly illustrated by New Hampshire under Gov. Benning Wentworth. Assuming the governorship in 1741, Wentworth began assiduously packing the Council with friends and relatives. Packing the elected Assembly was not much more difficult; the governor merely made the enfranchisement of new communities conditional upon electing pro-Wentworth representatives. He also made free with civil commissions, appointing so many of his followers justice of the peace that the office became a colony-wide joke. As for military commissions, the governor's faithful supporters instantly became full colonels in the militia, while his two adolescent sons and a ten-year-old nephew had to be satisfied as captains. One advantage, though, was that government business could be conducted at Wentworth family reunions.

Having passed around the favors, Wentworth now exacted his pound of flesh. Every new township in the province had to reserve five hundred to eight hundred acres as the governor's personal property. The New Hampshire mast industry—the mainstay of its economy—was regulated for the benefit of His Majesty's surveyor

---

beyond the control of the state. In the classical republics, it was the government that maintained the virtue of the people. What created American patriotism was the people themselves.

From Virtue to Revolution

It was their sense of public virtue that ultimately pushed the American colonies toward revolution. In order to understand why, we must first understand what Americans perceived as the opposite of virtue: *corruption*.

Public Virtue and Patronage

The alternative to a social ethic based on virtue was a social ethic based on patronage. Under a patronage system every person in society was dependent on some higher person—his patron—for many of the important opportunities of life. In order to gain an education, or to secure the right spouse, or to find worthwhile employment, a person counted not on his own resourcefulness, but on his patron, someone more elevated, someone with even higher patrons of his own. It was the classic case of not *what* you knew but *whom* you knew that counted.

Although patronage has always played a role in human affairs, in certain times and places it has assumed overwhelming importance. Georgian England was one of them. There, jobs were passed out, marriages arranged, property bought and sold, and careers made and ruined, solely on the basis of favors. When Samuel Johnson wanted to finish his great dictionary, he went to Lord Chesterfield, hat in hand, to request the necessary funds, proposing to dedicate the work to Chesterfield as a favor-in-return.

general, who also happened to be Benning Wentworth. Smuggling operations were similarly widespread, similarly lucrative, and similarly controlled by the governor. The list went on. New Hampshire was likened to a "field of battle" and the governor's minions to "the vultures and ravens glutting on the carnage."

In vain did the Assembly try to fight back. It withheld Wentworth's salary—but he seemed to need none. It hauled his friends into court—but Wentworth was paying the judges' salaries also, out of his own pocket. It refused to seat his private representatives—but Wentworth knew how to deal with that too: he simply disallowed the Assembly's choice for speaker and thus tied its proceedings into knots. Finally, in desperation, the colonists appealed over Wentworth's head to the British Lords of Trade. That plan backfired disastrously. John Tomlinson, the man who received their petition, just happened to be Wentworth's patron, and he was in no mood to discuss corruption in the provinces. "[If the] address was calculated to turn out the Governor," Tomlinson replied tartly, "it would not have been in your power, or in the power of the most sanguine of his enemies to remove him."

So on and on the saga went. In his old age, Benning Wentworth could sit back on the veranda of his fifty-two-room mansion and look out happily on the bustling panorama of Portsmouth Harbor below him—master of all he surveyed.

Laws were passed the same way. If the king desired a certain piece of legislation, he had his ministers ply members of Parliament with an assortment of favors in the hope that they would vote right. This, of course, effectively neutralized Parliament as a check against royal power. "The king in Great Britain is absolute," observed one critic, "for though he doth not act without the Parliament, by places, honors, and promises he obtained the sanction of the Parliament for doing as he pleases." Patronage, in other words, could spell tyranny.

Patronage was especially handy in running an empire, for out-of-the-way colonies were perfect places to perform quiet favors. Ne'er-do-wells with good connections were often sent there to recoup lost fortunes, and with a little graft here and there, they could usually succeed. Once in the colonies, these "place-men," as they were called, continued to spin out their patronage webs. Some of the provincials themselves fell in with the system, but many others did not. Far from the center of favor-making and possessing their own sense of the world, they came to find patronage distasteful in the extreme.

In the American colonies patronage collided headlong with public virtue. Where public virtue required a person to stand proud and self-reliant, patronage required him to grovel before others. Where public virtue made a person confront the morality of his actions, patronage enabled him to blame someone else. And where public virtue drew people into the life of the community, patronage pulled them back into the self, whispering, "Better get yours while you can."

Virtue and Enlightenment at Princeton

In the autumn of 1770, Princeton College still bore the luster of newness. Its cluster of Georgian buildings stood squarely symmetrical on their campus and looked out placidly at the world. Not all was placid within, however, for the college was astir with ferment. The new mood seemed to emanate from the president, John Witherspoon, a small, bespectacled man known affectionately to his students as "W.S." An Edinburgh-trained Presbyterian, Witherspoon was more than a little tinged with old-fashioned Puritanism but equally steeped in the Enlightenment. Somewhere along the way he had read the works of fellow Scot Francis Hutchinson and become convinced of the importance of virtue.

Over and over, in the gleaming new lecture hall, W.S. hammered away at the message that in politics, as in religion, virtue counted for everything. By "virtue" Witherspoon did not mean meek submission to injustice. Quite the reverse. The man himself had known injustice at the hands of self-important churchmen and had resisted with fiery resolve. There was an obligation to resist other kinds of tyranny, he said—such as the tyranny of kings and princes.

One of Witherspoon's students was young James Madison. The boy was to have attended the College of William and Mary in his home province of Virginia, but at the last minute his parents, hearing favorably of Princeton, changed their minds. For the next four years, he sat at the feet of John Witherspoon—and in a class of revolutionary firebrands.

What their education was like was hinted at by the graduation ceremonies in September of 1770. James Witherspoon, the president's son, explained why the law of nature obliged subjects to resist tyrannical kings. John Ogden defended the boycott against British goods as "a noble Exertion of Self-denial." And valedictorian Robert Stewart declaimed grandly on a theme of "Public Spirit."

So it was that revolutionary feeling grew and intensified in the colonies. Proper young men from the finest homes explored religion and politics and found that the two came together. Young Madison joined the college's radically tinged American Whig Society, energetically debated British tyranny, and graduated an ardent patriot. His mentor, W.S., became a signer of the Declaration of Independence and served with distinction in the Continental Congress.

The Impending Crisis

It was the close of the French and Indian War in 1763 that brought the patronage issue to the fore. It was not hard to see why. England's decision to impose order on its ramshackle empire made necessary a vastly expanded bureaucracy, and the resulting swarms of new place-men represented patronage at its worst. The question was what, exactly, would Americans make of it.

And what they made of it was unparalleled sinfulness—in terms that echoed the old revivals. Americans were becoming corrupt, cried preachers in their jeremiad sermons: they were caught up with pride and arrogance, with the wearing of costly apparel, with outright vice and depravity. Moreover, corruption would beget more corruption. Soon the webs of patronage would lie in every dark corner. No man would be able to stand proud and self-reliant. No virtue would be able to survive. And liberty would be the final casualty.

Sin, corruption, loss of virtue—loss of liberty. Here in new guise were elements of the age-old pattern. Pamphlets appeared on the street corners pointing out what every student of the Enlightenment already knew, that "foreign corruption" went back as far as ancient Greece, that around every king, including their own, "evil counselors" were constantly inventing new corruption, that corruption sapped away at the virtue of the people and in the end stifled liberty.

It was not only in lighted drawing rooms that such ideas were being discussed—it was also in the taverns, on the street corners, and down at the docks. Soon, gangs of youths were wandering the streets, loudly voicing their alarm. "Isn't it awful, Mr. Crockett, how we're losing our

Tar and feathering a Tory: Not only in lighted drawing rooms. (Library of Congress)

virtue these days?" they would ask an occasionally waylaid official. Yes, Mr. Crockett would agree, it was awful. "Well, what's to be done about it, sir?" Mr. Crockett wouldn't know. But to escape from the interview he would likely be obliged to throw his hat in the air and cry "Huzzah for liberty!" It was a pointless exercise, perhaps, and yet one that was increasingly full of meaning. For many Americans talk was not enough—they must act.

The Logic of Liberty

The Declaration of Independence represented the outcome of two different logical processes. First, Americans believed they had to free themselves from a political conspiracy to enslave them, a conspiracy

Congress voting independence—July 4th, 1776
(James L. Shaffer)

symbolized by the various imposts and taxations, and brought to the flashpoint by the trickery over tea. Second, they believed they had to free themselves from a moral conspiracy to corrupt them, one symbolized by the workings of patronage. The intertwined conclusions were all too clear: Americans had to be free in order to preserve their virtue, and virtuous in order to preserve their freedom.

The colonists' unique historical experience had thus addressed both halves of the republican equation. Membership in the British Empire taught them that self-interested behavior could be controlled by human means. And within their own midst welled up a fountain of virtue capable of sustaining the republican spirit. It was the dawning of this awareness that gave Americans the confidence to push ahead, to convert a colonial rebellion into a republican revolution.

So it was that in Philadelphia, in the hot summer of 1776, while British forces were driving Washington's army from its bases on Long Island, the resistance of the colonists was almost magically transformed. To the wild cheering of the people and the tumultuous ringing of the bells, the American Republic suddenly became a reality.

4
The Rule of Law

Concepts

Legalism
Administrative Law
Substantive Law
Rule of Law
Generality
Prospectivity
Publicity
Consent
Due Process
Respect for Law

The Boston Massacre: March 5, 1770: Anarchy was lurking in their own streets. (Library of Congress)

The Trial of the Accused Soldiers

All Boston was scandalized. The soldiers accused of murder in the Boston Massacre were to be defended in court, not by the king's attorneys—there was not a one of them who would touch the case— but by native Yankees: Robert Auchmuty, Josiah Quincy, and, worst of all, John Adams himself. None of the three had volunteered. Adams, for one, took the job only because of a dramatic personal appeal by one of the soldiers' friends.

But that decision was not without its price. John's cousin Sam, leader of the Liberty party, turned precipitantly cool toward him. Rocks were thrown through his windows and a mudball spattered his cheek. There were whistles and catcalls wherever he went, and a voice behind a fence asked him why he left his red coat at home. He found solace from a passage in Beccaria: "If, by supporting the rights of mankind and of invincible truth, I shall contribute to save from the agonies of death one unfortunate victim of tyranny . . . his blessing and tears of transport will be sufficient consolation to me for the contempt of all mankind."

The defense attorneys prepared their case well. Of the three, Adams was best versed in the English Common Law, and he grilled his colleagues for days on the distinctions between homicide justifiable, homicide excusable, and homicide felonious. To many Bostonians such distinctions seemed irrelevant. They sided with the *Boston Gazette* when it piously thundered: "Whoso sheddeth Man's blood, by Man shall his blood be shed!"

That was tommyrot, and John Adams knew it. The soldiers had been cornered by a wild mob spoiling for their blood. One of the casualties himself, lingering before death, forgave the soldiers and confessed that the fault had been on his side. But to go too far into that, as John Adams also knew, would be to put the town of Boston on trial, and to harm the cause of liberty. So the defense strategy would be to stick to the law, and to the law's venerable distinctions. They would argue that this was a case of homicide justifiable.

The trial itself was the event of the decade. People drove in from the countryside and picnicked on the common while awaiting it. The courtroom was packed to overflowing, and the spillover thronged the steps outside. The defense began with lengthy interviews of prospective jurors, throwing out one after another, and including in the final roster not a single Bostonian. Then the charge was read, the pleas entered, and the trial formally commenced.

Auchmuty and Quincy acquitted themselves well. The latter's impassioned rhetoric on the soldiers' behalf made the jurors stop and think. But John Adams was the trial's real hero. Standing before the court in his barrister's wig and gown, he seemed to personify the law itself and its ancient traditions.

He stepped near to the jury and addressed it earnestly as he spoke. "Place yourselves in the situation of Killroy or the sentry, with the bells ringing—and you know well there is no fire—the people shouting, huzzahing and making the mob whistle as they call it. The people are crying, Kill them! kill them! knock them down!—and heaving snow balls, oyster shells, clubs, white birch sticks three and a half inches in diameter. . . . Consider yourselves in this situation and then judge if a reasonable man would not consider they were going to kill him." The law, said Adams, did not require a man to stand still for that. The law allowed him the right of self-defense—even if the result was homicide.

In the closing arguments, the defense appealed to good, hard, common sense. That and the law. Adams quoted Algernon Sidney that "The law no passion can disturb. 'Tis void of desire and fear, lust and anger. 'Tis written reason, retaining some measure of the divine perfection. 'Tis deaf, inexorable, inflexible." Then he added his own wisdom. "The law," he said, "on the one hand is inexorable to the cries and lamentations of the prisoners. On the other it is deaf, deaf as an adder to the clamors of the populace."

The jury considered the matter for two and a half hours and returned a verdict of not guilty for six of the soldiers, guilty of manslaughter (a lesser charge) for the remaining two. The punishment was a mere branding on the thumb. Then and there, with jurors and spectators alike craning their necks to see, an iron was heated, the two soldiers stretched out their hands, and the requirements of justice were met.

As Adams walked over to the prisoners, they seized his hand in gratitude. "God bless you, Mr. Adams!" they said. "We owe our lives to you and Mr. Quincy." Matthew Killroy, reputedly the toughest of the eight, sat weeping in his chair. Montgomery, the other brandee, held up his thumb as one might exhibit a trophy. "A small price to pay for our lives, Sir," he said with a smile.

John Adams: Much more at stake than mere propaganda. (Library of Congress)

Adams' performance was one that Americans still typically admire. Along with crime shows, westerns, and the ever-popular soap operas, we have a special place in our hearts for a good courtroom thriller. True, we never quite trust the lawyer at the center of it, and we often scorn his sly tricks. But we venerate the law itself, which has a unique power and meaning for us. Just why this should be so, and just what it has to do with the republican quest for liberty are the subjects of this chapter.

Inventing America

The American republic was an invention. People literally sat down and made it up. Most European countries, by contrast, were the products of a historical process tracing back beyond memory. It took thousands of years to evolve the language, culture, religion, and institutions of a France or a Germany. The United States was made in a day.

It should come as no surprise, therefore, to learn that on the eve of the Revolution the colonists did not think of themselves as "Americans" at all, but rather as Rhode Islanders, New Jerseyans, or people of the Carolinas. After all, each colony had its own geography, its own institutions, sometimes its own religion, and often its own ethnic mix. True, there was a shared English heritage in most of the colonies, but two of them, New York and Pennsylvania, lacked even that.

Accordingly, when Americans thought of creating republican government, they did so in terms of the individual states, or, as they would have said, the individual countries. After all, a *country* to them was a sovereign political unit roughly the size of England. Anything larger would be a *continent*, too large for a single government and *much* too large for a republic. (The classical republics had been about the size of Rhode Island.) The assumption was that the thirteen republics of America would join into some loose confederation for the purpose of defense, but otherwise would remain separate.

So the process of invention was carried on differently in the different states. Each state drew upon its own past and the lessons it had learned. Each adapted its existing institutions to a new republican identity. And each drew upon the thinking of its own statesmen and scholars. These various inventors, working in their separate laboratories, would be the forerunners of the American Founders a decade later.

Idea of the Rule of Law

Most of the inventors worked from a common store of ideas. They generally accepted the importance of public virtue in creating a republican society, and the necessity of limiting self-interest by means of structure. Public virtue and auxiliary precautions, as they termed the latter, were recognized as the main components of a republic—just as bricks and mortar were recognized as the main components of an edifice.

Republicanism's Achilles Heel

But that left open the question of architecture. Bricks and mortar *by themselves* did not make a building, and it was possible that public virtue and auxiliary precautions *by themselves* did not make a republic either. Not all of the Enlightenment ideas were destined to work out in practice, and a few of them were destined to boomerang disastrously. In the course of the French Revolution, for example, partisans would develop an array of structural controls and a tidal wave of patriotic fervor—yet France would fail to establish a working republic.

The trouble was, republicanism had an Achilles heel. It was possible to have all of the structural controls in place and operating, and to have the spirit of virtue strong in the people, and yet *still* not to find freedom. Here was the way it could happen:

Let us suppose that John Locke's sovereign people get together and decide to found a republic. They send their king packing, write themselves a constitution, and hold free elections to a representative assembly. Well and good. But now to the

first item of business. It is moved and sec-
onded that all of the king's supporters, a
small but vocal minority, be forthwith put
to the guillotine. The loyalists themselves
object to this, of course, but they are outvoted. The entire process is republican and
orderly, and the outcome—getting rid of
these undesirables— might even be considered a desirable outcome. The question
is, is it freedom?

Of course not. It is virtually the antithesis of freedom. The rule of a despot's will
has merely been replaced by the rule of a
mob's, and one kind of tyranny exchanged
for another. This, in sum, was what happened in the French Revolution: each faction that managed to gain control felt it had
to wipe out its political rivals, and the result
was rule by guillotine. And even in the
American Revolution, thousands of Tories
were reviled and persecuted for being loyal
to the king. They lost their homes, their
property, and sometimes even their lives
simply for opposing a popular majority.

We could devise other grim scenarios
for our hypothetical republic. What if there
came along a powerful leader, able to mes-
merize the people with his rhetoric? What
if a gang of corruptionists subverted our
carefully designed structure? What if
someone in the government gained a kind
of power that could be wielded unchecked? In all three cases we would still
be left with the rule of will.

Here, then, was republicanism's
Achilles heel. It was possible to establish
an apparently successful republic—and
still wind up with the rule of will. It was
a problem that the Enlightenment had
never really considered. The American republican inventors now had to meet it head
on.

Sam Adams: Wanted a political trial and a public
execution. (Library of Congress)

John Adams and the Rule of Law

John Adams was one of those inventors.
The trial of the soldiers accused in the
Boston Massacre presented him a situation
very much like the above. The republicans
of Boston, led by Cousin Sam, had rounded
up some "evil" monarchists and wanted to
make an example of them. Undoubtedly,
they had a political trial in mind and probably even a public execution. John himself
was not unmindful of the propaganda
value of the "massacre." He was as eager
as Sam to embarrass the British government, and here was a heaven-sent opportunity to do so.

But John, unlike Sam, knew the peril
of such a course. His training in the law
helped him to see that there was much
more at stake than mere propaganda. For,

Tyranny of the Majority

Were there actual situations in which people were simply voted to death? Indeed. In the French Revolution, in fact, it occurred several times. The incident the world remembered best was the execution of the king.

In truth, Louis XVI posed a difficult problem for the Revolution. Now he would accept the new order of affairs and now he wouldn't. He was docile one moment and hostile the next. It began to occur to the Jacobins that as long as Louis Capet was alive and dithering, he would be a rallying point for royalism within the country and a focal point for intrigue without.

But how, exactly, to get rid of the king? Most of the deputies favored some sort of trial. After all, if law was really to govern the new republic, then bring Louis before a high court, charge him with treason, present evidence, and carry out the sentence.

At that point, however, the constitutional scholars began scratching their heads. The new constitution specified "inviolability" for most of the king's actions. And even if the king could be said to have abdicated at the time of his flight to Varennes, there were still other technicalities to deal with. Finally, what, precisely, were the crimes that Louis could be charged with, and where was the evidence for his guilt? Figuring it all out seemed hopeless.

But Robespierre, the leader of the Jacobins, cut through the tangles cleanly. Addressing the Assembly on December 3, 1792, he recast the issues in the most practical terms. "This is no question of a trial," he said, "Louis is not a defendant; you are not judges, but statesmen, and the representatives of the people. You have not to give a verdict for or against an individual, but to adopt a measure of public safety. . . . We talk of a republic, and Louis still lives!" The logic seemed convincing. Call it a trial if you will, and call the deputies judges, but don't worry about specific laws or details of evidence. Just vote.

On January 14, the voting began. The first question was whether Louis was guilty. (No crime was alleged, just guilt.) By a vote of 683 to 65, it was decided that indeed he was. The second question was what the punishment should be. There, the vote was closer: 361 for immediate death, 72 for temporary reprieve, and 288 for imprisonment or exile. If the votes for reprieve and imprisonment were added together, they came to 360. One could argue, then, that Louis lost by a single vote.

---

to railroad the soldiers, as Sam and the radicals wanted to do, would be to show the world that republican Boston, no less than monarchical London, acted by the rule of will. On the other hand, to turn the soldiers loose, as local Tories advocated, would be just as willful, for in many minds the accused were guilty of murder. Adams realized that neither alternative would do.

He knew what must happen instead was that the soldiers be given a fair trial. If found to have violated the laws of the land, they must assuredly be punished, and if found not to have violated those laws, they must equally assuredly be set free. The

Violence during the French Revolution: The
majority could be a tyrant too. (Library of Congress)

The sentence was carried out in the Place de la Revolution on the morning of
January 21, 1793. Like all affairs of the guillotine, it was short and simple. And at the
end of it the people shouted: *"Le Roi est mort: Vive la nation!"*
One vote!

politics of the situation, its propaganda
value, the sense of outrage on the part of
this or that group—all had no part to play
in determining the soldiers' punishment.
For John Adams realized that the only alternative to the rule of will—be it the will
of a tyrant or the will of a mob—was the
rule of law.

Legalism

Before explaining what the rule of law is,
we must explain what it is not. It is not
merely using the law to rule. That is what
tyrants do. Instead of saying "Let us kill all
the Druids among us," they say "Druidism
is hereby declared unlawful; let us enforce

the law." The same trick is used by tyrannical majorities, which can actually "pass" their laws through some legislature. But none of this is the rule of law. If the law is used only as a cosmetic to cover up the exercise of someone's will, then it clearly does not rule. It is only empty legalism.

And such legalism does exist. Under totalitarian regimes, people are rounded up every day for having supposedly violated the law, but in reality they are only the victims of some tyrant. Even in the Western democracies there are laws that forbid citizens to "interfere with the police"—meaning that if two policemen want to do away with someone, they can simply beat him to death for "resisting arrest" and no one can legally stop them. In Idi Amin's Uganda, that was a daily occurrence.

The rule of law, then, is not law itself. It is not something that could be put into words and passed by a legislature. It is, rather, a philosophical ideal, like truth and justice. It is a kind of shared agreement among the people that government has to be conducted in a certain way. We can state the ideal generally in terms of the examples set forth above. The law must not be used for tyrannical purposes. It must not be used to get somebody. It must not be the expression of anyone's will, even the majority's, without certain important limitations.

In John Adams' day there were laws on the books against murder. Those laws were made blind, as it were, without any particular murderers in mind, only abstract definitions of action. An innocent person could not be railroaded as long as he was judged according to that sort of law—which is why the king's soldiers were acquitted. Generally speaking, the rule of law is simply an agreement to use *that* sort of law all the time.

Two Kinds of Law

We now have a general idea of what the rule of law is. Before making the definition more precise, we must learn to distinguish between two different types of lawmaking.

Administrative Law. In some ways government is like a large private corporation in that it has certain resources at its disposal, certain personnel on its payroll, and certain tasks to perform. Many of its official actions have only to do with these responsibilities: treating sewage, funding schools, operating airports, supplying the military, and so on. The measures that are passed to accomplish these purposes are not really laws so much as in-house administrative instructions.

In running its own affairs, the government, like any corporation, must have a relatively free hand. It must be able to address particular points of concern, correct past mistakes, and single out individuals for reward or punishment. Consider road building, for example. If the government builds a road, it might, like any private contractor, determine that a certain favored supplier is to be generously rewarded. It might determine that no Democrats—let's say it is a Republican administration—get to work on the road. It might determine that certain subcontractors have done inferior work in the past and are therefore not to be used again. And it might determine that "inferior work" is whatever a state inspector says it is. Most of these decisions have the force of law and some might actually be passed by the legislature, but they are *laws* only in a narrow, administrative sense.

Substantive Law. A second type of law-making applies to the private sector. It addresses relations among private individuals, private corporations, and—a possible point of confusion—government itself. But here the government is not *administering* anything; it is *governing*. It is laying down the rules that everyone must live by. These laws, unlike their administrative cousins, must be enforced by coercion, and if they are violated someone must be punished.

We speak of both kinds of action as *law*, and there is a good deal of confusion between them. It should be clear, however, that the two are markedly dissimilar and demand drastically different approaches. For if the government addressed its task of governing the way it must address administration, the result would be . . . well, let's imagine:

Suppose that the road in our example above is complete and ready for use. The government's job now becomes that of enforcing the traffic rules—of *governing*, not *administering*. But suppose the government is not sensitive to the shift in roles (as indeed some governments are not) and continues to behave as it did earlier. What might happen? The government may determine that a certain client's vehicles may speed. It may determine that Democrats may not drive on the road at all. It may determine that a few of its critics have driven recklessly in the past and will accordingly have their licenses revoked. And it may determine that "reckless driving" is what any highway patrolman says it is.

All of these actions, of course, are analogous to the administrative ones which were perfectly acceptable. And yet these, clearly, are *not* acceptable. Like John Adams, we instinctively feel that they violate some fundamental principle, and indeed they do. We are ready now to define the rule of law more precisely.

The Definition

The rule of law means that in the private sphere of human activities, government may not act except in the enforcement of a known general rule. It may not administer the lives of private citizens the way it administers its own affairs. If the king's soldiers have killed citizens in the streets of Boston, we may not deal with that fact the way we might deal with, say, incompetence in the Boston fire department. We may only deal with it by applying a known general rule against murder.

And what does this accomplish? To the extent that we approach the ideal rule of law, it makes the actions of government predictable. In place of the rule of will, which is arbitrary, capricious, and unpredictable, we wind up with something very much like the laws of nature. Knowing the laws of nature we can make use of them. We can decide whether to leave the space shuttle in orbit or bring it back to earth, because we understand the law of gravity. Similarly, we can make use of laws of society. If we know that by stealing a car we will go to jail and, more importantly, that by not stealing the car we will *not* go to jail, we can decide whether or not to go to jail by deciding whether or not to steal the car.

Those living under the rule of will cannot make such choices. They may decide not to steal the car and *still* wind up in jail, and, conversely, they may decide to steal the car and get away with it completely—depending on whom they know down at city hall. Life under the rule of will is similar to our bizarre highway above. Some are allowed to speed and some are not. And some cannot travel on the highway at all.

The practical outcome of the rule of law is that people can govern their own lives. For, when the laws of society become certain, like the laws of nature, people can make plans with fullest confidence. Understanding gravity, I choose not to step into an open manhole; and, understanding murder, I choose not to settle quarrels with a gun. I cannot be ordered about or "administered" by anyone, for I alone am responsible for what happens to me. The rule of law *has made me free.*

Principles of the Rule of Law

How do we know if the rule of law exists? There is no simple answer. Despite the fact that most countries have governments, laws, and enforcement agencies of an apparently republican character, not all of them enjoy the rule of law. Most face a situation where tyrants (or tyrannical majorities) manipulate the laws for their own ends, leaving only the rule of will. This causes great uncertainty as individuals try to figure out which levers to pull in order to secure and advance themselves. Generally speaking, we know the rule of law does not exist when the people themselves do not feel free.

But there are more precise tests. If the following conditions are met, there is a very great likelihood that the rule of law exists.

Generality

The laws must be general. They must be stated in abstract terms, without reference to particular persons, places, or things.

Thomas Wentworth, Earl of Strafford: The victim of a special law. (Library of Congress)

Only thus can they be truly blind. All laws single out certain categories, of course, but in most of them it is impossible to ascertain who does and does not fall within the category. A law aimed at "drivers" is essentially blind, for it is impossible to know in advance who may or may not be a driver. By contrast, a law aimed at "drivers of red Volkswagens" is not blind, for it describes a specific and ascertainable group.

England departed from generality on several occasions when its Parliament passed *bills of attainder.* These were legislative acts, much like those of the present, except that their function was to charge a particular individual with some crime and then specify his guilt. The classic case was that of the Earl of Strafford, just before the English Civil War. For political reasons, Strafford was accused of treason. In his trial before the House of Lords, he grilled the witnesses against him and all but demolished their evidence. As English law then stood, it was impossible to find him guilty, so, in desperation, the Lords passed a bill of attainder against him instead. Strafford's punishment was to be butchered alive.

False Generality. On their very face, of course, bills of attainder seem tyrannical. But legislatures since Strafford's time have grown more sophisticated in undermining generality. Instead of singling out a person or thing by name, they have learned to describe their targets in terms that *appear* general. In 1970, for example, the California state legislature voted special giveaways for all cities of between 188,000 and 189,000 population. Scarcely more adroit was the German tariff that sought to levy special duties on Swiss and Austrian cows; the rate applied to all "brown and dappled cows reared at a level of at least 300 meters above the sea and passing at least one month every summer at a height of at least 800 meters."

If these examples are easy to pick out, others are not. What about a law that lays a special tax on all cities of, say, a million or more people? We have to know how many cities meet the requirement before knowing if the law violates generality. (If only one city does, the law should be in trouble.) Or what about a law exempting voters from paying a poll tax if their grandfathers were qualified to vote? It sounds general enough— until we learn that it was used in the South after the Civil War, and that the grandfathers of blacks had all been slaves.

So, how do we know which classifications are on the level and which are not? For borderline cases there is no easy answer, but for most others there is a workable rule of thumb. If the legitimacy of the classification is recognized by those who are being classified, then it is probably all right. Thus Hitler's laws against the Jews or Jim Crow laws against southern blacks would both fail the test, for Jews in the one case and blacks in the other did not accept the legitimacy of being singled out. On the other hand, users of, say, pesticides generally understand why special rules must be applied to them.

Equality Before the Law. If specific groups do have to be singled out in the law, we try to make sure that they are not groups defined by politics, religion, race, or gender—all touchy subjects for Americans. But what about the touchiest subject of all, money? Should there be one law for the rich and another for the poor? In Georgian England, precisely that was the case. Commoners could not race their horses, for horse racing was considered a gentleman's sport, nor could they drive carriages, wear powdered wigs, or dress in a manner above their station. The law may have been general in the formal sense but it was not socially equal.

But the American Founders—themselves men of wealth—bridled at such distinctions. They realized that in a republic, unlike any other form of government, no one, no matter how rich and powerful, could be above the law. Legal equality would be difficult to maintain amid the many inequalities of mankind—but for freedom to flourish it was critically necessary.

Prospectivity

The laws must be prospective. They must be addressed to future, not past, action. That principle, too, was violated by the

The Noble Experiment

What happens to respect for the law when masses of citizens cannot bring themselves to obey it? Before the days of Prohibition, no one thought to ask. After all, among a law-abiding people, laws were supposed to be respected automatically. As Prohibition Commissioner John F. Kramer said of the Volstead Act: "This law will be obeyed, and where it is not obeyed it will be enforced." But it turned out that Prohibition was neither obeyed nor enforced, for American drinkers simply continued their drinking.

At home in their basements, "wets" (as they were called) brewed hard cider, cheap wine, and makeshift brandy, and in their bathrooms they literally concocted bathtub gin. Where simple fermentation would not do, as in the making of higher octane beverages, they rigged up stills, some of them fairly sophisticated. One still, steaming away in a New York cemetery, had produced fifty-one barrels of moonshine by the time Prohibition agents got onto it.

Most people, however, simply bought their bootleg ready-made. This could be done at the local *speakeasy*, a club or cafe with a secret back room, or at a variety of other establishments. Near Cornell University it was a soda fountain. In lower Manhattan it was a store that sold "sacramental wine." In Baltimore it was a sidewalk fish market, with tiny bottles of booze in the cash register drawer. In Atlanta it was a confectionery, and in New Orleans it was a taxi—*any* taxi. One woman bought a milk shake in New York's Van Cortlandt Park and wrote indignantly that by mistake it was filled with gin. (Bad gin, too, she reported.) Another complained that in a grocery store in Harlem, a clerk "charged me two dollars for a can of tomatoes, and when I got home I found there was nothing in it but a lot of nasty-smelling water." And nosing around in Brooklyn pawn shops, agents uncovered ten thousand dollars worth of liquor wrapped in the clothing left as pledges.

Nor was the illicit trade in alcohol confined to lowbrow establishments. In New York's posh Half Past Nine Club, a large stock of contraband was found in a stuffed grizzly bear. In a fashionable Madison Avenue delicatessen, the beribboned baskets of fruit concealed small bottles of rye. Before the "noble experiment" was over, Manhattan lost some of its most exclusive nightspots: Jack's, Shanley's, the Beaux Arts, Reisenweber's.

English bills of attainder, for those acts not only singled out individuals for punishment, they also defined their crimes retroactively. Think of the effect of retroactive legislation on the ideal of predictability. You wake up one morning to learn that what you did last Wednesday (when it was legal) has now been declared illegal and you are to be punished for it. Not very predictable.

Tyrants, on the other hand, relish ex post facto laws. They know that their enemies can dodge prospective laws simply by not violating them, so they create retroactive ones instead. In Argentina's "Dirty War," the junta declared many activities illegal and applied the penalties retroactively. As a consequence, students criticizing the government, editors writing

Raiding a moonshine still: The country was
becoming downright lawless. (National Archives)

People regarded the mass evasion as good, clean fun. At the football game, they
pulled flasks out of hip pockets, garter belts, and racoon coats, and had a wonderful
time. Only dimly were they aware of names like Johnny Torrio, Frankie Yale, and Al
Capone; and the connection between big-time gangsters and the good, clean fun
seemed tenuous at best. Then, on St. Valentine's Day of 1929, two carloads of Al
Capone's hitmen battered their way into a Chicago warehouse and gunned down
seven employees of "Bugs" Moran. Americans were puzzled to learn that the massacre
took place in a bootleg distillery. Somehow, it seemed, the country was becoming
downright lawless.

in their newspapers, and labor leaders complaining about working conditions, simply disappeared.

Publicity

The laws must be known *and* certain. Tyranny always works best in secret. Whether behind the high walls of the Kremlin or at a remote hideaway like Hitler's Wolf's Lair, the farther from news reporters and question askers the better. This explains why tyrannical edicts often seem to pop out of nowhere, and the victim learns of them only too late. After the victory of Pol Pot in 1975, Cambodians received a number of such shocks. A woman wiping her mouth with a handkerchief was told that handkerchiefs were bourgeois and was taken out and shot. A man wearing eyeglasses was informed that these were a mark of intellectualism and was similarly put to death. So it was that Cambodia lost some two million of its citizens.

But it is not enough that the laws be known; they must also be certain. Certainty means that people know in advance what the law will or will not sanction and can act accordingly. We sometimes doubt the certainty of the law and suppose that smart lawyers can sniff out its loopholes. This does happen. Far more often, though, the law is applied predictably and methodically, and more often still, there is no need to apply the law at all, for the would-be lawbreaker, assessing his chances, has had second thoughts.

At times, however, the reverse has been true. Some governments, unwilling or unable to apply the laws evenhandedly, apply them capriciously instead and hope that by making an example of a few offenders, they will somehow deter the rest. They don't. In the United States during the Prohibition era, moonshiners flourished in the hills, rumrunners landed nightly along the coasts, and bootleggers of every description amassed fortunes. The federal government settled for enforcing the prohibition laws capriciously, raiding a speakeasy every now and then but winking at everything else. As a result, the reputation of the law suffered disastrously. Prohibition agents became the butt of jokes, while gangland dons like Al Capone became popular heroes.

Consent

The laws must be made by consent. This idea traced back to John Locke, who reasoned that if government was truly to be just, the people themselves must consent to be governed by it. The American colonists consented to be governed by their colonial assemblies. They expressed that consent by organizing the assemblies themselves and by electing the people who sat in them. They did not consent to be governed by the British Parliament, whose thinking they found bewildering and whose members they did not elect. To them it was nothing but a foreign government.

English politicians had trouble grasping this point of view. After all, Parliament was larger, older, and far more prestigious than any colonial assembly, and its members included the most distinguished men of the realm. But that was not the point. The Americans had learned (from hard experience) that human beings did not look out for the interests of others quite in the way they looked out for their own. If I must vote on laws that will apply to me—taxes that I will have to pay, restrictions that I will have to face—you may be sure that I will take a very hard look at them. Psychologically, consent is almost foolproof.

Original Consent. Consent is bestowed in two different ways. The first might be called *original consent*, where the people as a whole agree to adopt a given form of government. Although such an event occurs only rarely, original consent is renewed each time fundamental changes are made. In the United States, if we amend our Constitution, we give original consent to an altered form of government. And if, after thinking about it, we decide not to amend the Constitution, we renew our consent to the original. Simply because the amendment process exists, the government enjoys a continuous assurance of original consent.

A public trial in the ancient English tradition: A part of the heritage of liberty. (Library of Congress)

Periodic Consent. With original consent we agree to what the government is; with *periodic consent* we agree to what the government does. By periodically electing our own representatives, we have a direct impact on the laws they make. In 1932, in the midst of the Great Depression, American voters were presented with a clear choice between lawmakers who would continue the policies of the past and those who would make radical changes. Overwhelmingly they chose the latter. Thereafter, whether they liked Franklin Roosevelt's New Deal or whether they didn't, the voters had only themselves to hold responsible. Compare this with the situation of the colonists in 1775. They, too, would like to have changed the government in power, for it had steadily angered them for more than a decade. But in that case no machinery for consent was available: there were no elections, no amending process, no way for the people to say, "We do not accept the rules you are making." The only way to be heard, alas, was to start shooting.

Due Process

The laws must be applied impartially. It is possible to have laws that are general, prospective, public, and consented to—and yet

Smokey and the Rule of Law

Americans have difficulty imagining what life would be like without the rule of law. If there were laws in society that didn't have to meet the test of generality, prospectivity, publicity, consent, and due process, what would it be like, say, to be arrested? Well, it would be like running up against "Smokey," that legendary redneck cop of American popular culture. Suppose, for instance, that you are in the Deep South back in the early days of the Civil Rights Revolution. You and your friends have come to help register black voters in the little town of Cotton Blossom. On the bumpers of your car are stickers that say saucy things about segregation and racism. That is why Smokey decides to pull you over. The conversation goes something like this:

"Lemme see your driver's license."

"Sure. Anything wrong? I wasn't speeding, was I?"

"No, you wasn't speedin'. But you done violated our law agin' bumper stickers. They ain't legal around here."

"Bumper stickers? Are you sure? We've seen other cars with bumper stickers. Lots of them."

"Yeah. But you got *Yankee* bumper stickers. They's agin' the law."

"Excuse me, sir. I'm not from around here. What is a Yankee' bumper sticker?"

"It's any kind I don't like. I'm gonna have to run you in."

"Excuse me, again, but do you mean that there is a law in the municipal code of this town against *bumper stickers*?"

The cop gives you a hard look. "Well," he says, a glint of mischief in his eye, "maybe it ain't in the municipal code. But we got laws around here that we don't write down. Come on."

still misused. Such is the case when the laws are enforced in an irresponsible way. Englishmen learned that lesson centuries ago. That is why they became so concerned over what we have come to call *due process of law*. Due process simply means that there is a right way and a wrong way to enforce any law—and the wrong way isn't legal.

Trial by Jury. The oldest—and still central—element of due process is trial by jury. There were, of course, other ways to determine guilt or innocence. Among them were burning the accused with a hot iron to see if the burns would heal (if they did not, he was guilty), throwing him into a pond of water to see if he would float or sink (if he sank, he was guilty), and subjecting him to various tortures to see how well he withstood pain (if he confessed, he was guilty). All of them seemed to have defects. By contrast, the use of juries worked out well.

The idea was simple. A jury composed of ordinary people, like the accused, would presumably identify with the person on trial. In order to be satisfied that the law was dealing fairly with him, they had to be satisfied that the law would also deal fairly with them. Juries can be fooled, of course, and they are often put through an emotional wringer, but by and large they do a

"Just a minute, please." You are beginning to feel a little desperate. "When was this law passed?"

Another glint of mischief. "Few minutes ago. Ain't that right, Turley?" He turns to his sidekick, still seated in the patrol car. Turley nods.

"Well, who passed it, then?"

"Me and Turley. Ain't that right, Turley?" Turley nods again.

You are now thinking about the possibility of a week in the Cotton Blossom jail. You try a new tack. "Excuse me, I don't mean to seem rude. But if this law was passed a few minutes ago, it can't possibly apply to us. We've been here for several days—while bumper stickers were legal. We've only just learned of the law."

Another hard look. "Ignorance of the law ain't no excuse. Besides, this here law took effect *last year*. You broke it clean when you come drivin' down here lookin' for trouble. Come on, let's go."

"Just a moment." Your desperation is visibly mounting. "I'd like to call a lawyer."

"You ain't callin' no lawyer, Yankee." Here comes Smokey's final triumph. "We got laws in this town 'bout makin' phone calls on Saturday."

Pure fantasy? Three northern civil rights workers were murdered in Mississippi in 1964. The culprits were all police officers. In 1985 a U.S. drug-enforcement agent, Enrique Camarena, was beaten to death in Guadalajara, Mexico. The culprits were once again police officers. In the course of Argentina's "Dirty War" in the 1970s, thousands of citizens turned up missing. Put on trial for abduction and murder were policemen, military officers, and officials of the government.

remarkably good job. In our age of scientific marvels, we have not yet found a replacement for them.

Habeas Corpus. This is another ancient device, a guard against summary arrest. In medieval England, a man could be jailed on nothing more than the say-so of the powerful. *Writs of habeas corpus* were developed to counter such practices. More recently the temptation of the autocratic ruler has been to arrest his enemies "on suspicion of" some charge and then just leave them in jail. In this situation the writ of habeas corpus demands that evidence be produced and a trial date set. If no good evidence is available, the prisoner goes free.

Just why the English were devoted to such devices as jury trial and habeas corpus comes nicely into focus in the 1670 trial of William Penn for "inciting riot" in the streets of London. What Penn was actually doing was holding Quaker services, and the Church of England wanted them stopped. When the jury returned a verdict of not guilty, the judge in the case, somewhat less than impartial, had the jurors locked up until they changed their minds. The strange proceeding ended with the release of the jurors on a writ of habeas corpus.

Other Safeguards. To these oldest elements of due process, we have added a number of others. The right to counsel, freedom from unreasonable searches and seizures, protection against self-incrimination, freedom from torture and intimidation, and freedom from cruel and unusual punishment, have all become necessary to the evenhanded enforcement of the law. Each of them reflects painful experience with the ways of power. For example, anciently there was no right to remain silent when accused. A person could be tortured until he talked, even if all he said was "I am not guilty." One of the people accused of witchcraft in Salem was put to death in this way. Giles Cory would not speak in his own defense, and so he was stretched out on the ground and rocks were piled on him, one at a time, until he suffocated. The only words he choked out were a defiant: "More weight!"

We must keep the Giles Corys of history in mind when we encounter what seems to be an excess of due process. Forgetting the tyrant and his tricks, we are impatient with safeguards like the Miranda Rule (named for the 1966 Supreme Court case of *Miranda v. Arizona*), where the arresting officer is made to recite a long list of rights to the still panting criminal. Yet experience has shown us that these are necessary costs of freedom.

Establishing the Rule of Law

Generality, prospectivity, publicity, consent, and due process—when they are present they make the law predictable and the people free. How, then, do we secure their presence? There is no easy answer. We have already seen that in many republican revolutions they were indeed not present and could not be produced. That fact gave the Founders much to ponder.

Historical Experience

History has taught us, however, that where the rule of law does exist, it exists most importantly in the hearts of the people. Conversely, where the rule of law does not exist, it is usually not greatly missed. Aleksandr Solzhenitsyn makes this point tellingly in the pages of his *Gulag Archipelago*. Why, he asks, did the Russian people allow themselves to be hoodwinked by a tiny minority, to have their constitution overthrown, their freedom curtailed, and their lives put in terror? His answer is that they never possessed a tradition of liberty. When the communist rulers began ordering them around, it seemed quite natural to obey.

Americans were more fortunate. Their historical experience was that of Old England, not the England of George III and his muscle-flexing Parliament but the earlier England of John Locke and the Glorious Revolution. Then there had been, as the Americans recalled, a profound respect for the law, not only the official, written law but the unofficial, unwritten law, the law which held that all power must be limited, all court judgments reasonable, and all government fair.

It was this inarticulate memory that first led the Americans to resist Parliament. In the beginning they didn't know why they resisted and gave muddled explanations for their action. Gradually, however, they began to think matters through. Parliament limited the power of the king, they reasoned, but what limited the power of Parliament? In theory nothing

Law Versus Will in A MAN FOR ALL SEASONS

Nowhere was the power of the law to thwart tyranny depicted more clearly than in the struggle between Henry VIII and Sir Thomas More. King Henry, having married his late brother's wife, Catherine of Aragon, found himself with no son and, more importantly, no heir. He thus determined to divorce Catherine and try again with someone else—someone more comely. But there was a hitch: the king was Catholic, and the pope would not sanction his divorce. Henry plunged ahead anyway. He went through with the divorce, married Anne Boleyn, and repudiated the authority of Rome.

Sir Thomas More was the king's chancellor, a high officer in his government. He was a wise, saintly man, devoutly religious, and respected all over the realm. Had he ratified the king's bold actions, it would have gone far toward making them acceptable. But this his conscience would not permit. Of course, he would not renounce the divorce either, nor condemn the king's break with Rome, for that would amount to treason. He simply said nothing. A master of English jurisprudence, More knew exactly what the law would and would not condone. He also knew that English respect for the law was such that the king himself feared to break it.

Just where that left him was aptly illustrated by his trial in 1535, imaginatively recreated in *A Man For All Seasons:*

Thomas Cromwell (the prosecutor): "Let us consider now the circumstances of the prisoner's silence. The oath was put to loyal subjects up and down the country and they all declared his grace's title to be just and good. But when it came to the prisoner, he refused. He calls this 'silence.' Yet is there a man in this court, is there a man in this country who does not know Sir Thomas More's opinion of this title? Yet how can this be? Because this silence betokened, nay, this silence was not silence at all but most eloquent denial."

More: "Not so. Not so, Master Secretary. The maxim is 'qui tacet consentire videtur.' The maxim of the law is 'Silence gives consent.' If therefore you wish to construe what my silence betokens, you must construe that I consented, not that I denied."

Cromwell: "Is that in fact what the world construes from it? Do you pretend that is what you wish the world to construe from it?"

More: "The world must construe according to its wits. This court must construe according to the law."

In the end, tragically, More was condemned and executed anyway, but only because his enemies found a witness willing to testify against him falsely. Short of such outright skulduggery, the law of England steadfastly shielded him, even from the wrath of a tyrannical king. It was an example that was not lost on the authors of the American Constitution.

did. But Americans, graced with their sense of playing by the rules, strongly believed otherwise. They could not accept the proposition advanced by constitutional scholars that Parliament could do absolutely anything it wished. When it enacted bills of attainder and ex post facto laws, when it showered favors on the politically fortunate, when it singled out American colonists for special taxes and regulations, something was terribly wrong.

Constitutional Prohibitions

A second method of institutionalizing the rule of law is more practical. In certain limited ways, the rule of law could actually be written into a constitutional document. In the American Constitution, for instance, the Founders did what they could to insure that procedures in the new republic would at least meet the tests outlined above. To protect generality, they stipulated that Congress could pass no bills of attainder (Article I, Section 9), nor establish a hereditary nobility (Article I, Section 9), nor provide for more than a single category of citizenship (Article IV, Section 2). To insure that the laws remained prospective, Congress was forbidden to pass any ex post facto law (Article I, Section 9).

Publicity was a bit more difficult to achieve, but here as well the Founders did what they could. In Article I, Section 5, they required publication of the proceedings of Congress. Later on, in the First Amendment, they took special pains to guarantee freedom of the press, knowing that ambitious reporters would be even more effective at keeping the public informed.

Much of the rest of the Constitution was addressed to providing consent. In addition to the machinery for both constitutional ratification and constitutional amendment—aimed at securing original consent—there was the machinery for providing regularly scheduled elections—periodic consent. Where the latter seemed most critical, in the House of Representatives, the Founders set the term of office at a bare two years, so that consent would operate directly and continuously.

And as for due process, the Founders wrote a number of special protections for it into the Bill of Rights. Although these features will be discussed in detail later on, we might point out here that the Founders included every procedural guarantee they could think of, from old standards like jury trial, to such new innovations as freedom from unreasonable search.

Insofar as specific prohibitions could entrench the rule of law in the U.S. Constitution, the Founders made sure they did so. But there was a problem with prohibitions. We have described the rule of law as a metalegal principle, meaning that, like justice or mercy, it cannot really be expressed in so many words. Besides, any prohibition that could be written *into* the Constitution could be amended right back *out* of it. That brings us to the third, and most important, way that the rule of law could be institutionalized.

The Architecture of Government

The government itself could be designed with the rule of law in mind. How? By using certain kinds of structure specifically designed to promote rule-of-law outcomes. Consider generality and prospectivity, for example. It is one thing to stipulate that Congress shall pass, say, no bill of attainder, but how does one actually *keep* Congress from doing so? In 1943 Congress passed a bill pronouncing three named individuals guilty of espionage. Was this a bill of attainder? A majority of both houses thought not, for they cheerfully voted the measure into law. But the Supreme Court disagreed. When called upon to enforce the new legislation, the Court held that it indeed violated the bill-of-attainder clause.

What does this episode tell us about the architecture of government? Simply that if there is a separation of powers between the lawmaker (Congress) and the law enforcer (the court system), the principles of generality and prospectivity are far more likely to be respected. For if Congress cannot enforce its own laws, it has little incentive to aim those laws at specific, identifiable targets, such as the three spies mentioned above. By employing separation of powers in the Constitution's basic design, the Framers did a great deal to preserve the rule of law.

Indeed, anything that reduces the scope of will in government automatically enhances the rule of law. If the chief executive is a potential tyrant, then any device capable of curbing his will must be useful. If Congress is the one to watch out for, then the same goes for Congress. And so on. Willful officers in the government, willful agencies of the government, even willful majorities behind the government, must all be restrained if the law is truly to rule. In deciding which controls to use in the Constitution and precisely how to deploy them, the concept of the rule of law was to prove extremely valuable.

Toward the Constitution

The inventors of the first American republics (as the states considered themselves) did not clearly perceive all of this. Because the process of invention typically goes by trial and error, they had to learn many things the hard way. Not all of the new republican governments would succeed in establishing the rule of law, and even the first national government would have its difficulties. To the Founders of 1787 it would gradually become clear that successful republics could not be thrown together piecemeal; they must be carefully crafted to minimize the role of will and maximize the rule of law. It was only when citizens could organize their own lives, calculate their own chances, and seek out their own happiness, that they would truly be free.

5
Republican Experiments

Concepts

The Confederation
Unpredictability of Public Virtue
Factional Behavior
Experimental Republicanism
Dissonant Experience
Legislative Tyranny

First meeting of the Virginia Colonial Assembly:
The beginning of American republican experiment.
(Library of Congress)

Shays' Rebellion

While rebellion was nothing new in a monarchy, it was not supposed to occur in a republic—and here it was in republican Massachusetts. Americans were dumbfounded. They knew only that farmers back in the Massachusetts hinterland claimed to be having difficulties with taxes, debts, and currency deflation, and that when no relief was provided by the government in Boston, they oiled up their Revolutionary War flintlocks and started shutting down local courts. Though there was little overt violence in their actions, there was a great deal of intimidation. By January of 1787, the rebels had put the county courts of Worcester, Middlesex, Bristol, and Berkshire completely out of business. Then, needing muskets and cannon for who knew what further purpose, they proceeded to march on the federal arsenal at Springfield.

It was there that Shays' Rebellion, as it was coming to be known, drew blood. On January 26, Daniel Shays, a former Revolutionary War captain and the movement's nominal leader, marched a force of twelve hundred men in open column platoons toward the town. Drawn up in the low hills ahead of them was a state militia unit of roughly one thousand, under the command of Col. William Shepard. Of Shepard's several howitzers, one was loaded with grapeshot, and all were primed and ready.

Shays himself rode up, a drawn sword in one hand and a pistol in the other, his horse breaking holes through the hard crusted snow. Samuel Buffington, Shepard's aide, stepped in front of him and commenced a sermonette.

"I'm here in defense of that country you are endeavoring to destroy," he said.

"If you are in defense of that country, we are both defending the same cause," Shays shot back. He was a young man, powerfully built, and he had served the Revolution well. But he had never commanded a large force, and the attack he had planned on the arsenal was already badly askew.

"I expect we'll take different parts before night."

"The part I'll take," replied Shays, attempting humor, "is on the hill on which the arsenal and the public buildings stand. Will they fight?"

"You can count on it."

As the invaders advanced on the double, confident that their Massachusetts neighbors would not really fire, Shepard's artillerymen sent two rounds over their heads, and then trained the grapeshot howitzer on their center. "The fourth or fifth shot put the whole column into the utmost confusion," Shepard reported, adding, "I . . . could have killed the greater part of [Shays'] whole army within twenty five minutes." As it was, he killed four, and left a score of others wounded.

But, if the insurrectos cleared the field hurriedly, they still refused to disband. They beat a retreat to Amherst, then to Pelham, and finally to Petersham. There they were cooking breakfast on a cold, crisp morning when the state troops surrounded them in an ambush. Shays, along with 150 of his men, was taken prisoner and marched back to Boston to stand trial. Although the leaders were condemned to be hanged, all of them, including Shays, were pardoned by Gov. Hancock. After all, they had never fired a shot!

The affair raised some nettlesome questions. Was it true, as the Tories had charged, that liberty inevitably led to license? And what about republican government: was it incapable of defending itself? Massachusetts responded effectively enough to the insurrection but the national Congress simply dithered. After days of debate it timidly voted for a military expedition— to be disguised as a raid against the Indians! George Washington, for one, was heartsick. "Let us have a government by which our lives, liberties, and properties maybe secured," he said, "or let us know the worst."

Finally, what sort of society was this where men were always reaching for their muskets? All too clearly, westerners did not understand easterners, country people did not understand city people, and debtors did not understand creditors. The question was, did anyone understand anyone? Josiah Tucker, dean of Gloucester, declared that the "antipathies and clashing interests of Americans" insured that they would remain "a disunited people to the end of time." So much, it seemed, for public virtue.

And, indeed, the bitterness of Shays' Rebellion was a long time passing. When Colonel Shepard retired to his home in Westfield, many of his neighbors made it clear they could never forgive him for the part he had taken. One of them, Roland Parks, who had once served with the British Army, made a habit of donning his British uniform on Sunday afternoons and trotting disdainfully past Shepard's house.

Long afterward, when people reflected on the Confederation period in American history, Shays' Rebellion was what often came to mind. It seemed symbolic of a certain deep sense of malaise. For, in those early years after the Revolution, American republicanism didn't seem to be panning out after all, and no one knew why. "I feel infinitely more than I can express for the disorders which have arisen," wrote Washington. "Who besides a Tory could have foreseen, or a Briton have predicted them?"

Experiments, of course, often have their setbacks—which is why laboratories come equipped with fire extinguishers. But the occasional workbench explosion should not obscure the quieter, less visible progress which is often being made. At the very moment of Shays' Rebellion, the American republican inventors were pushing rapidly ahead on a number of fronts and were learning some extremely valuable lessons. They had, for example, already created the world's first republican supergovernment, the Confederation.

The Confederation

In contrast to the Constitution a decade later, whose wording would be haggled over bitterly, the writing of the Articles of Confederation in 1777 was simplicity itself. John Dickinson of Pennsylvania was asked by the Continental Congress to draft a plan for the union of the American republics, and he set to work on it immediately. Political confederation had been attempted before in America, so Dickinson more or less knew where the pitfalls lay. He knew, for example, that the American states would not surrender a particle of their sovereignty to any continent-wide government. Several had already proclaimed themselves to be "free, sovereign, and independent," and that was exactly what they had meant. So Dickinson simply banded them into a loose association of sovereign states and let it go at that.

The government of the Confederation essentially consisted of a unicameral (one-house) legislature. There was no executive to speak of and no national court system.

Voting in the legislature was by states, not by populations, meaning that small states like Rhode Island marshaled just as much power as large states like New York. The large states did not seem to mind, however, for, in truth, there was little power to marshal. The Confederation had neither the authority to tax, nor coin money, nor regulate commerce. Beyond coordinating a common defense (which of course *had* to be done), it was left with such matters as foreign affairs and trade with the Indians, and even here the states proved their independence by sending their own diplomats abroad and commissioning their own navies.

So the Confederation was not so much a government as an alliance among friendly nations. (Think of it as an old-time version of NATO.) What it critically lacked was *sovereignty*—the ultimate power of decision-making which every true government must possess. Without sovereignty it could not impose its will on a recalcitrant state, nor could it deal directly with individual citizens. In a difficult situation, it could only beg and cajole, as NATO would have to do if one of its partners decided to give it a bad time. Still, the Confederation experience was valuable experimentally and was not without its lessons for the republican inventors.

The Confederation and the Rule of Law

Despite its limitations, the Confederation still needed to achieve the rule of law, if only among the states. There had to be generality, prospectivity, publicity, and consent in whatever the government did if the union was to succeed politically. In some tasks the Confederation performed admirably. It brought the war with England to a successful conclusion. It surveyed western lands in an orderly fashion and began parceling them out to settlers. It provided for the political organization of the West on terms that assured equality of the new states with the old. And it provided a large measure of the peace and order necessary for further constitutional development. But it failed disastrously in other ways.

*   *   *   *   *

Summary of the Articles of Confederation

1. States are sovereign.
2. No independent executive.
3. No federal courts—national laws are enforced by state courts.
4. No taxing power in Congress.
5. Congress has no power over interstate or foreign commerce.
6. Congress is an assembly of delegates chosen by state legislatures—delegates may be recalled at any time.
7. Articles may be amended only by the consent of all of the states.
8. Congress has only specific delegated powers.
9. The central government cannot act directly upon the people.

Revenue. In the matter of fund raising, for example, the Confederation was hobbled from the outset by its inability to tax. Having inherited the debts of the old Continental Congress, it lacked all means of effectively retiring them. Superintendent of Finance Robert Morris requisitioned the states for $10 million. He received a scant $1.5 million, which did not even cover the interest. And so it went. There were mutinous rumblings in the unpaid army, disaffection among domestic lenders, and a scandalous loss of credit abroad, but the government could only continue holding out its hat. Rufus King wrote to a friend about the "humiliating condition of the Union. You may depend on it," he added, "that the Treasury now is literally without a penny."

Commerce. Unable as well to impose commercial peace, the Confederation wound up presiding over economic mayhem. New York slapped a fee on ships arriving from Connecticut and New Jersey. New Jersey retaliated by taxing a New York-owned lighthouse, and Connecticut retaliated by embargoing New York goods completely. States with large seaports took advantage of those with small ones, and the latter sought ways to get even. Easterners made deals that cost westerners dearly, and westerners countered by flirting with secession. No one escaped the confusion.

Disputes. The Confederation was crippled even worse by its lack of a national judiciary. For, when the highest tribunal in the land was a state court, there was no way to settle interstate disputes. For example, the Wyoming Valley in Pennsylvania was also claimed by Connecticut (under the terms of its old colonial charter), and settlers from Connecticut were the ones who got there first. Sporadic evictions, burnings, and bushwhackings punctuated life in the valley until the winter of 1784, when flooding left the New Englanders stricken and defenseless. The Pennsylvania militia, supposedly sent to help out, went on a rampage instead, and turned the "accursed Yankees" out of their homes. Scores died of exhaustion and exposure.

The government of the Confederation repeatedly tried to resolve the dispute, but, without legal jurisdiction, it had little chance of success. James Madison was among those who deplored the situation. Without national courts, he said, there would never be an abiding peace. The wills of the states would clash in a perpetual free-for-all, and the sense of American nationhood would gradually fray into tatters.

Diplomacy. In foreign affairs the Confederation *had* to be effective. Sometimes it was. What it could not do, however, was oblige the states to live up to the agreements it made with foreign governments. With the Treaty of Paris ending the Revolutionary War, for example, the states had little interest in honoring the American side of the bargain. Where the United States promised to pay outstanding debts to British merchants, Virginians replied: "If we are now to pay the debts . . . what have we been fighting for this while?" Where the United States promised to protect Loyalists, South Carolinians continued to expropriate their property and threaten their lives, going so far as to lynch one Isaac Love when he returned to his home. The British struck back, of course, violating *their* side of the treaty. They kept their troops stationed along the Great Lakes and continued to trade with the Indians for Yankee scalps. It was not a high moment for American diplomacy.

While it is possible to exaggerate the failings of the Confederation, the fact remains that it did not achieve the rule of law. The actions of the national government were general, prospective, public, and consensual—but they woefully lacked

The Pennamite Wars: State Fighting State

Amos Ogden readied his men for the attack. He, with his lieutenants, was ensconced on a hill known as Bullock's Mountain, watching the Connecticut settlers in the valley below. They were leaving their blockhouse on the bank of the Susquehanna and making ready for a day's work in the fields nearby. Ogden noted with satisfaction that they carried no weapons.

In order to take these Yankee intruders by surprise, Ogden and his 140 Pennsylvanians had reached Bullock's Mountain by a circuit of briar infested Indian paths leading all the way back to Fort Allen on the Lehigh. But now he had them. He lowered his glasses and gave the final orders. All detachments would commence hostilities in unison, relying on the sound of gunfire for coordination. The unarmed New Englanders would scatter like sheep.

And so they did. As the Pennsylvania strike force swept into the Wyoming Valley on that lovely September day, the Connecticut farmers, who believed their title to the valley was as good as any Pennsylvanian's, were caught completely by surprise. Groups of them fled in this direction and that, to be rounded up, clapped in irons, and marched off to the Easton jail.

A number of them, however, made it safely back to the blockhouse. Mud-spattered and terrified, they huddled in the log redoubt and tried to regroup. There was some hope, they supposed, if they could dispatch messengers to Coshuntunk on the Delaware and bring back help. The messengers waited until nightfall and crept out. Assuming that Ogden's men would be stationed on the main road, they headed toward Solomon's Gap instead. But the Pennsylvanians were waiting there too, camped in the pre-dawn chill without fires. Upon seizing this new contingent of prisoners, Ogden learned of the near hysteria inside the blockhouse and decided to attack at once.

Fort Durkee, as it was officially known, fell quickly. A detachment of Ogden's forces under Captain Craig stormed out of the rushes along the river, bowled over the solitary sentinel, and opened fire at the silhouettes within the gate. Minutes later the Pennsylvanians were trampling men, women, and children in the darkness, and thrusting bayonets at whatever moved. In the quarters of Captain Butler, the Connecticut officer in charge, they burst through the door, knocked the old man to the floor, and prepared to run him through, when Craig himself caught up with them and brought the bloodshed to a halt.

Morning saw the tethered Yankees led off toward Philadelphia, looking around them at the homes and fields they would see no more. Their possessions were being loaded up by the victors as bounty of war. It was a bitter parting.

The Pennamite Wars would go on and on like this, a continuous cycle of sieging, assaulting, bushwhacking, surrendering, defeating. It was a difficult thing to live in a land without law, where there was no civil way to settle disputes. It was not much better than life in the Old World.

certainty. Without real authority, the officers of the Confederation could only implore the states to comply with national policy, often to no avail. As a result, the policy itself remained unpredictable. Creditors couldn't count on seeing their money again, litigants couldn't count on enforceable judgments, and foreign diplomats couldn't count on the country's word. The wills of the states reigned supreme.

Even worse, a government that could not maintain the rule of law could not maintain the respect of its citizens either. Observing that the wrong sort of people benefited by the climate of uncertainty, Americans concluded that patriotism didn't pay. Smith would see that Jones could get away with murder and would decide to try it himself.

There was, then, a clear connection between the rule of law and the preservation of public virtue—another lesson for the republican inventors.

Virtue and Self-Interest: The Balance Tilts

Let us briefly review some points about human nature. Philosophers of the European Enlightenment, while they admitted the possibility of both self-interested and virtuous behavior in human beings, tended on the whole to expect the former. Most people, most of the time, they said, were likely to pursue their own self-interest. Accordingly, political theorists developed certain structural controls able to check self-interest internally. Were we to ask a Hume or a Montesquieu what the essential problem of government was, he might reply that it was getting the right controls in the right place to curtail the right people.

Americans, on the other hand, had come to espouse a somewhat different idea of human nature. Going back to that older concept of an inner-directed and self-motivated Christian virtue, they had come to believe strongly in their own capacity—possibly a unique capacity—for self-government. After all, public service had become part of their lives. Commitment to the law was second nature to them. And public-spirited self-sacrifice had been everywhere manifest in their struggle for independence. They had taken to writing homilies to one another of the temper of their patriotism; of the plain and simple clothing that befit a republican people; of renouncing false decoration in their parlors, ornamentation in their architecture, and luxuries in their cupboards. Put simply, virtue had come into high fashion.

Wartime Disillusionment

It was not long, however, before the passions of 1776 began to cool. War has always brought out the worst in human beings— hatred, greed, cynicism—and Americans were no different. They learned to hate their British enemy ferociously, and to treat him with savage cruelty. They learned to look out for themselves, too, even at the risk of their patriotism. And numbers of them forsook all loyalties and commitments in order to cash in on the great wartime bonanza.

There were farmers in Pennsylvania, for example, who, finding themselves between the British Army in Philadelphia and the Continental Army at Valley Forge, sold their produce to the highest bidder, which of course was the British. There were supply agents who bought cheaply and sold dearly, doubling, tripling, or quadrupling their investment in the process.

King of the Alley

William Duer came near to being one of the American Founders. He knew most of them personally, had political ties to several, and moved about easily in their world. He arrived in New York in 1768, the scion of a distinguished family and owner of prosperous plantations in the West Indies. If he was a cultivated English gentleman, he was also a high-velocity entrepreneur—and one who had difficulty keeping a straight trajectory. Duer typified the new morality of the Confederation period.

Despite his English background, Duer took up the Patriot cause and in 1777 was elected to the Continental Congress. There he became acquainted with such figures as Robert Morris, James Wilson, and Silas Deane, all of whom proved helpful to him. Deane, for example, introduced Duer to important foreign emissaries. Duer was soon doing business with a good half of them: supplying masts and spars to the Spanish navy, supplying food and clothing to the French army, and supplying bribes left and right in order to land the contracts.

Duer was willing to service American troops, too, if the business could be managed without risk. Once again friends helped out. Superintendent of Finance Robert Morris saw to it that Duer was always paid promptly, and in full, while other suppliers were left out in the cold. More than once, in fact, the government paid Duer in preference to the army itself. He made a good thing out of the Revolution.

After the war, Duer moved to New York City, the first national capital, and plunged into an array of enterprises. He also plunged into politics, serving as secretary to the Confederation's Board of Treasury. Private business and public office fit together perfectly for him: with inside knowledge of the government's fiscal operations, he encountered grand opportunities for speculation. Take the American debt to France, for example. After reading the confidential correspondence of the U.S. minister in Paris, Duer and his friends decided to buy up the entire debt and then bribe Congress to fund it at par. Fortunately for the United States, the scheme failed.

At the same time, however, Duer was at work on another one. Noting that soldiers of the Revolution had largely been paid in IOU's, and that these (owing to the treasury's inability to redeem them) were circulating at grossly depreciated value, Duer hit upon the idea of buying them up in quantity and then trading them for lands set aside for the veterans. If all went well, Duer and his associates would be able to secure rich farm land for ten cents an acre. The scheme was densely convoluted, and in the end it collapsed. A few hundred immigrants were ruined as a result of it, but Duer managed to escape unharmed.

The Duer story careened on and on, a veritable financial soap opera. It crashed to a halt only in 1792, after an attempt to corner stocks on the New York exchange left Duer $236,000 short. He asked Alexander Hamilton, who had made him second-in-command at the Treasury Department, to bail him out of the difficulty, but Hamilton's hands were tied. On March 23, 1792, he entered debtor's prison in New York City and spent the rest of his days there. Gone, said Jefferson, without too much regret, was the "King of the alley."

There were merchants who charged outrageous prices for whatever the American forces needed, calculating their profit in thousands of percent. There were speculators who bet on the fortunes of the war as one might bet on a horse race, buying this, selling that, in the hope that a nearby battle would drastically alter its value. There were militiamen who fought fiercely to defend *their own* communities but wouldn't lift a finger to defend someone else's. And there were politicians in Congress who wouldn't vote a nickel for army pay.

The problem was that the individualism which characterized American public virtue was a double-edged sword. If self-control was one of its possibilities, self-indulgence was the other, and the two were never far apart. So whether a man was acquisitive in a healthy way or avaricious in a sick one might depend on nothing more than the condition of his spirit. With the staunchest of patriots, it seemed, something could go wrong deep inside, and self-interest could sour into plain selfishness.

Factionalism

Then, too, war could galvanize other sentiments besides patriotism. The spirit of faction was one of them. There had always been groups of tradesmen, farmers, merchants, and the like who had recognized their common interest and acted on it politically. Traditionally, however, there had been much to restrain them. The very notion of patriotism precluded factional behavior. A politician who spoke *only* for the farmers or *only* for the merchants had scant hope of being thought a statesman.

But the Revolution unleashed new passions and changed the old rules. Factional behavior came to characterize both Patriot and Tory. As the tension between them mounted, the idea of gathering in the streets and raising havoc steadily gained acceptance. A few of the Revolution's leaders, such as Sam Adams in Boston, were closely tied to those crowds in the streets, but most of the Founders viewed them askance. They remembered the role of factionalism in the fall of ancient Athens, and told one another that factions were to anarchy what dictators were to tyranny. Factional behavior at its best, they said, could be irrational and hysterical, and at its worst it could sound the death knell of the republic. It is important for us to understand the reason for their fear.

Factional Behavior. A faction, according to the dictionary, is a group of persons forming a cohesive, usually contentious minority within a larger group. What holds it together is a common interest or passion. What makes it dangerous is that its actions frequently disregard the public good. Put simply, factionalism is self-interest run amok.

Our own world is filled with factions. They make headlines every day. When there is a kidnapping in the streets of Beirut, a car-bomb explosion in Belfast, an airline hijacking in the Persian Gulf, it is in every case almost certainly the work of a faction. By its very definition, then, factional behavior is extreme behavior.

It is also, alas, behavior of conflict. This is because factions, by their very nature, tend to produce counterfactions. I see that your group has mobilized itself for extreme measures, and my first thought is that my group, in self-defense, must follow suit. Thus, where there are Sandinistas in Nicaragua there must soon be Contras. Where a pro-Soviet faction takes power in Kabul, an anti-Soviet faction soon takes to

Kill the Umpire!

People don't really kill umpires, do they? In point of fact, they have. Violence in sports is alarmingly on the rise, not only in places like Belgium, where thirty-eight fans were killed in a soccer free-for-all in 1985, but right here at home. After the Pittsburgh Pirates defeated the Baltimore Orioles in the 1971 World Series, a crowd of one hundred thousand adrenaline-charged fans roamed through downtown Pittsburgh sowing mayhem. A similar riot followed the 1977 World Series after New York's victory over Los Angeles. Yankee second baseman Willie Randolph said it was "the scariest thing I've experienced in my life." In 1984, minutes after Detroit's final victory over San Diego, fans stormed the field in Tiger Stadium, tearing out turf, seats, and signs. They then surged into the parking lots, where they pelted police with bottles and rocks, smashed and overturned patrol cars, and embarked on a binge of violence. Before the bedlam was over, Raymond Dobrzynski, a visitor from Ypsilanti who was meeting a friend after the game, was shot to death while sitting quietly in his car.

Psychologists have attempted all sorts of explanations, from economic frustration to old-fashioned warlust. David Hume didn't know much about Freud, but he did observe that factional behavior, wherever found, often brings out the worst in human nature. "Where a considerable body of men act together," he wrote, "a man is sure to be approved of by his own party for what promotes the common interest, and he soon learns to despise the clamors of adversaries."

That, in a nutshell, was the secret of Maurice "The Rocket" Richard of the Montreal Canadiens. Instinctively recognizing the fascination of the fans with wild and disorderly behavior, Richard committed every sort of outrage on the ice, leaving it for his admirers to pay the fines. And when officials put him in the penalty box for good, his fans visited Montreal with its worst rampage in modern times. David Hume would have understood. For at bottom it was not really so different from politics.

the hills. Where white South Africans terrorize the blacks, black South Africans will soon turn the tables. Factions account for many of the world's worst headaches.

Factional behavior tends to follow an established set of rules, as valid now as they were in ancient Athens. Elements of the faction first of all separate themselves from the wider community, whose diverse interests and points of view seem increasingly unpalatable. The isolated group then turns inward and becomes self-reinforcing. If it is united by interest, the interest in question becomes steadily more well defined. If it is united by passion, the passion in question becomes ever more intense. Eventually, in the minds of the partisans, interest and passion and group merge all into one.

Factional psychology can oddly transform virtue. *Public* virtue, as the Founders understood it, cuts against the grain of factionalism, for one who believes in justice, honor, and the rule of law is ill at ease with the passions of the mob. Yet, once those passions take hold, virtue itself can be mobilized to serve the mob's ends. In the extreme case, we are left with the behavior

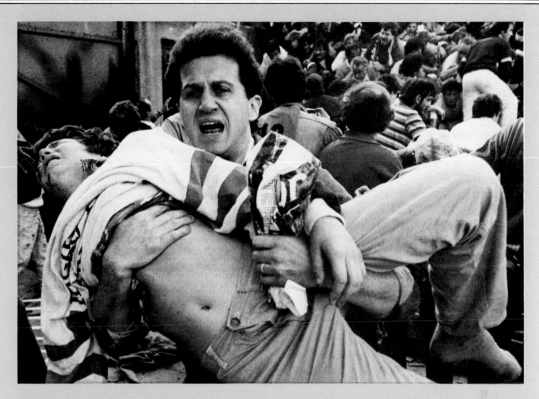

Soccer riot: consequence of factional behavior (UPI/
Bettmann Newsphotos)

of the kamikaze, who dutifully aims his own airplane at the enemy warship. The ordinary patriot becomes the fanatic.

Most of us have felt at least a tinge of factional compulsion. Take hometown athletics, for example. At the annual Big Game with our in-state rivals, many of us display factionalism at its worst. We arrive at the game as individuals, interested in sportsmanship, fair play, and other high values. As the game gets under way, however, we are transformed into a faction, interested only in winning. Our view of fair play suddenly becomes twisted, so that if the opposing team is caught in a foul, we believe that justice has been served—but, if *our* team is whistled down, it is because of poor officiating. As for sportsmanship, we greet a so-so play by the home team with an explosion of cheering—and greet a truly masterful play by the visiting team with icy silence. Occasionally, our fanhood becomes pathological. We begin throwing things onto the playing field or randomly picking fights. We want to kill the umpire, we say, and every so often someone has actually done it. Soccer riots alone have claimed more than a thousand lives!

Factions, then, bring out the worst in human nature. As individuals, we generally pay our taxes, abide by the laws, and behave civilly toward minorities. It is only as members of some faction that we would stuff ballot boxes or burn crosses on the neighbor's lawn.

A Second Look at Human Nature

Just such behavior was what the Founders witnessed as the war came to an end. On the one hand, there were promoters and speculators on every side, each of them vigorously pursuing his own advantage. And on the other hand, there was a seeming melee of factionalism as group after group joined in the general discord. For a fledgling republic which had been proclaiming its own virtue, both phenomena were unsettling.

It was the factions, however, that presented the greatest danger. Whether composed of farmers, artisans, or soldiers, factions of the Confederation period had each seen the Revolution as its own liberation: getting rid of the British was supposed to mean finding one's own place in the sun. Typically the factions consisted of working-class people, often deeply in debt, uprooted by the war, and politically outside of things. In the depression that followed the war their bitterness and frustration only deepened. Soon it fermented into anger.

Now, however, there were no British agents to tar and feather, only fellow Americans. That was what made Shays' Rebellion so startling. It was not a case of virtuous America against decadent England; it was a case of borrower against lender, tidewater against piedmont, have-not against have—the people against themselves. To conservatives, including most of the Founders, it seemed a chilling reminder of ancient Athens. "What, gracious God, is man that there should be such inconsistency and perfidiousness in his conduct?" exclaimed an exasperated George Washington. Like many others, he was back to wondering about human nature.

The republican inventors wondered too. Perhaps they had been wrong to place so much emphasis on patriotism. Just when they thought the Revolution of Virtue had been won, here were the people seething with contention. With a new humility, the Founders went back to the European Enlightenment for a second look at the nature of man.

The New Republics and the Rule of Law

It is against this background that we must examine constitution making in the states. A few of the states chose to write conservative constitutions. Three of them, in fact, simply revised their colonial charters and continued with the governments they had known. However, most of the states drafted bold new constitutions for the republican era before them. Reflecting the spirit of hope that marked the Revolution's outset, these documents sought to establish the power of the people. But that was when the people still seemed impeccably virtuous.

Thoughts on Government

While state constitution writing was in progress, John Adams sat down and penned out some advice on it. Adams was one of the best read of the American Founders and one with the fewest illusions about human nature. He believed in the American people and in the possibility of

The Contagion of Self-Interest

Public virtue seems to be inherently a product of individual behavior. You resolve within yourself, for reasons known only to you, to pay your taxes fairly, to take part in the political process, or to fight against some form of injustice. Self-interest, on the other hand, is patently contagious. Where there is one selfish person, we may be certain that quite soon there will be two.

We have all had the experience of sitting in a large stadium when someone down in front, in a climactic moment, impulsively leaps to his feet. (He cannot see any better standing than sitting, of course, but no matter.) At that point, the person seated behind him must also stand up or else miss the action entirely, and soon the entire crowd is on its feet. Each can see only as well as when all were seated comfortably, so nothing has really changed. Meanwhile, though, each has violated the rights of every other.

It works the same way in political society. I want to pay my fair share of the taxes—until I see that you are dodging yours. When it becomes a question of my paying more so that you can pay less, I suddenly want to dodge them too. We are all standing up, as it were, one right behind the other, and when we are all on our feet, each will have defrauded everyone else. Public virtue may, and hopefully will, restrain us, but public virtue, as Americans in the Confederation period were beginning to learn, can be anything but predictable. Just when needed most, it can vanish.

---

their genuine virtue, but his larger view of mankind was pessimistic. So, if he drew on Rousseau for the preparation of his *Thoughts on Government*, he also drew on Hume and de Mabley. Jotting down what he considered to be the essential checks necessary for republican order, Adams sent copies of the work around to the various states.

The document emphasized several points. One of them was the electoral process, which in Adams' view should be open, active and ongoing. "Where annual elections end," he declared, "there slavery begins." A second point was the judiciary, which Adams wished to keep completely independent of any other authority. Because judges were charged with enforcing the law impartially, Adams believed they

should be totally above the fray of politics. A third point was the executive veto (allowing the governor to kill undesirable legislative measures), which Adams characterized as a vitally necessary brake on the actions of a runaway legislature.

Indeed, curbing rambunctious legislatures turned out to be Adams' central theme. He pressed strongly for a legislature of two houses, each of them to operate as a check on the other. "A single assembly," he explained, "is liable to all the vices, follies, and frailties of an individual." Beyond that, he argued that the legislature should be given only lawmaking authority, not executive or judicial, and should be held accountable (by means of the veto) to a strong and independent governor.

In virtually all of these matters, Adams' advice ran counter to the prevailing republican spirit. More clearly than his contemporaries, the New Englander sensed the dangers of an all- powerful assembly directly controlled by the people. Such a body was likely to become a hotbed for corruption, he reasoned, and even more likely to become a factional battleground. Worst of all, a legislative assembly controlled by a *single* faction was nothing less than a tyranny.

Early State Constitutions

Adams' advice went mostly unheeded. State constitution writers generally adopted annual elections from his *Thoughts on Government*, but not much else. They made judges dependent on the legislature in matters of appointment, tenure, and salary. At the same time, they almost obliterated the executive branch of government, the office of governor. Every state deprived the governor of his traditional right to prorogue (dismiss) the legislature, and most of them trimmed back his appointive powers. Ten states made the governor an appointee himself, answerable to the legislature, while three others barred him from successive terms of office. (Four states eliminated the governorship entirely.) And where Adams had argued for the executive veto to keep legislatures under control, not a single state paid heed.

What they did instead, precisely as Adams had feared, was exalt the power of the legislature. The new look was exemplified by Pennsylvania. Here the office of governor was abolished completely and a plural executive put in its place. The legislature was made unicameral—with only one house—so as to exercise its authority to the fullest. It was then allowed to poke

fingers into every other branch of government. No executive felt safe in his seat, for the lawmakers could oust him without warning, and no judge could hand down a final decision, for the legislature functioned as a state-wide court of appeals. To some, the Pennsylvania government seemed the very embodiment of republicanism, for in it the people reigned supreme.

The Accounting

The way the new governments actually worked was less encouraging. Like the Confederation they did some things well, but their imperfections were both glaring and dangerous. By the war's end, when the states found themselves grappling with depression and discontent, it was apparent that many of them had serious constitutional difficulties on their hands.

For one thing, they were vulnerable to corruption. Where power was concentrated in a single legislative assembly, the task of the corruptionist was made easy: he simply calculated the votes necessary to pass a given measure and then started buying them up. State judges could do little to impede the shenanigans because the legislature controlled their salaries; and the governor, stripped of his veto, could do nothing at all. The only thing standing in the way of total corruption was the virtue of the lawmakers.

For another thing, the role of factions in such governments was all but decisive. Any group that would arm itself with pitchforks and shut down a county court would think nothing of taking over a state assembly if it had the necessary votes. And, once it did take over, there was little left to save the rule of law. We have already seen what tyrannical majorities did to the rule of law in France. What happened in the American state governments during the Confederation period, while more moderate in tone, had precisely the same effect.

There was, for example, a brisk demand for ex post facto legislation (violating the principle of prospectivity). For, if ordinary measures would not relieve the distress of the postwar depression, voters wanted measures beyond the ordinary. And they got them. Laws requiring creditors to accept depreciated paper currency in payment for loans, laws preventing the foreclosure of mortgages, and laws declaring certain commodities (such as land) legal tender were passed by several state legislatures. The effect of such measures was to allow debtors to escape their obligations and leave creditors holding the bag. In Rhode Island, 92 percent of the existing debt was simply wiped out. But the politicians didn't seem to mind: most of their constituents were debtors.

Even more ominously, some state governments began rewriting their own constitutions. It was not hard to do. Powers in most of the constitutions had been assigned by vaguely worded phrases, so there was nothing to stop one branch from invading the authority of the others. If, for example, the legislature had control over the salaries of the judges, what was to prevent it from using that control to dictate its own legal verdicts? And, if it had similar control over the governor's paycheck, what was to keep it from grabbing his power as well? Indeed, what was to stop the lawmakers from doing away with the other branches entirely?

In fact, Pennsylvania, the great experiment in republican liberalism, presented just such a scenario. Its all-powerful assembly, virtually unchecked by structural controls, violated first one provision of the state constitution and then another. It steadily eroded the authority of the executive branch and all but ravaged that of the judiciary. Judges' salaries were coldly manipulated to produce desirable court opinions, and in some cases, the assembly even handed down the opinions itself. Said Jefferson of this trend: "An *elective despotism* was not the government we fought for."

How to Recover the Rule of Law?

It became increasingly clear that such governments, no matter how liberal, how popular, or how self-consciously republican, had failed to institutionalize the rule of law. For what made them operate was will. In some cases it was the will of the corruptionists that shaped their policies, while in others it was the will of powerful factions. Either alternative produced the same result: uncertainty. People could not use the law to secure their personal freedom because the law was too easily and too often up simply manipulated.

According to republican theory, public virtue should have saved the day. Men of conscience should have sprung to their feet and denounced the abuses as they had earlier denounced those of Great Britain. An important reason why they didn't was that the systems themselves were not designed for virtuous expression. For when the power of government is exercised by a single authority, there is really nothing for the citizens, however well- intentioned, to mobilize against it. It is one thing to say that the people must act as a brake on government; it is quite another to provide them with a usable braking mechanism. In Pennsylvania, finally, they had to go beyond the constitution and set up a Council of Censors in order to bring the runaway government under control.

Alternatively (and also according to republican theory) the day should have been saved by structural controls placed in the constitutions for just such emergencies. But these controls proved disappointing as well. In the first place, there weren't enough of them in most state constitutions, and in the second place, they weren't used effectively. Take the separation of powers, for example. If the powers of government were truly separated from one another, as Montesquieu advocated, it would be very difficult for one branch to reach over and grab powers from another.

But how to make the powers truly separate? A constitution could proclaim that they *ought* to be separate, and most state constitution makers did just that. Thus, the Maryland constitution stipulated that "The legislative, executive, and judicial powers of government ought to be forever separate and distinct from each another." However, as we have learned, all such declarations have to be enforced by someone, and in most of the states there was simply no one authorized to enforce them. The lesson was clear. If separation of powers was to work, it could not just be declared—it had to be built into the system.

In fact, as experience was beginning to show, virtually everything had to be built into the system. The inventors could not sit back and hope for public virtue to materialize; they had to design the structure of government so that it *did* materialize. And now it was clear that separation of the powers must be achieved the same way. That was what John Adams had been trying to say in his *Thoughts on Government*. A successful constitution must be crafted with the greatest possible care.

Second Thoughts and Second Tries

By happy circumstance, the American states had a chance to learn from their mistakes and try again. It was Adams' own Massachusetts that led the way. The first Massachusetts constitution, written in 1775, had been far from exemplary. The all-powerful legislature had elected executive officers, appointed and removed judges, supervised government administration, and served as a court of impeachment. Massachusetts' drift from republican moorings had not been as alarming as Pennsylvania's, but it had nonetheless given the citizens pause. By 1780 they were ready to listen more carefully to John Adams' advice.

The New Massachusetts Constitution

Reflecting a growing awareness of the importance of structure, the framers of the new Massachusetts constitution made significant alterations. They dispensed entirely with declarations that the powers should remain separate or that justice should be prized. This time the powers were *made* separate and justice was built into the constitutional design.

Bicameral Legislature. To begin with, the new legislature was made strongly bicameral, as Adams had recommended. And not only did it include two separate houses, but each of them was made different from the other—and made responsible to different constituencies—so that neither would act as a mere rubber stamp. Moreover, each had its own powers. The assembly alone could initiate money bills (although the upper house could amend them) and the upper house alone could determine impeachments. Each half of the legislature needed the cooperation of the other, and each held the other in check. Neither, by itself, could go off hunting for power elsewhere.

Independent Judiciary. The judiciary was also made strong and independent, not by declaration, but by design. Judges were given life tenure and fixed salaries, so there was no way to intimidate them. Appeals were routed from the lower courts to the appellate ones higher up, and were pointedly kept away from the legislature. There was now a total separation between the lawmaking and law-enforcing powers in Massachusetts.

Strong Executive. Another design change applied to the executive branch, which was beefed up substantially. The people of Massachusetts, like their Yankee cousins elsewhere, had originally been distrustful of executive power. They had had to put up with some heavy-handed British governors in their day, and in memory of them the framers of the first constitution had hedged the governor's powers with multiple restrictions.

But further experience eased their suspicions. They learned that a legislature could be every bit as despotic as a governor. They also learned that in a world of factions, the executive could serve as an important safeguard. Factions represented specific constituencies in the electorate, and reflected only the narrowest of self-interest. Executives, on the other hand, were elected by everyone. A governor might enjoy the support of some groups more

CHECKS AND BALANCES

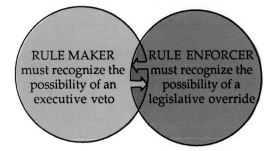

With checks and balances, both sides share certain powers. Each is compelled to deal co-operatively with the other.

SEPARATION OF POWERS AND CHECKS AND BALANCES

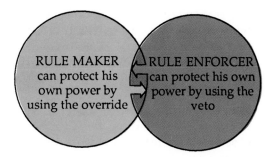

Combining both devices together, each side is able to protect its own power from invasions by the other.

than others, of course, but once in office he could not speak only for his supporters. In a very real sense, the governor had to represent all the people, and his outlook had to be correspondingly broad.

Accordingly, the framers of the 1780 constitution put aside their fears and gave the executive broad new authority. He could appoint many of the officers formerly chosen by the legislature. He was elected by the people, not by the legislature, and for a seven-year term (as opposed to annual terms in the assembly). Most importantly, he was handed back the veto power.

Use of the Veto to Maintain Separation of Powers. Veto power—the power of the executive to nullify laws passed by the legislature—was a delicate issue in John Adams' day. Its abuse by the British governors had branded it a tool of tyranny. There was a theoretical problem, too. Any executive who could block the action of two-thirds of a legislature was in effect wielding legislative power himself and was thus violating the separation of powers. The veto seemed inherently dangerous.

Yet actual experience again belied such fears. As the republican inventors looked back over their early work, they could see that their greatest difficulties had derived not from the excessive *strength* of the executive but from his excessive *weakness*. The long and short of their inability to maintain the separation of powers was that the executive had not been powerful enough to stop legislators from robbing his authority. With no legislative power of his own, he stood to have his orders countermanded, his salary reduced, and even himself eliminated by impeachment. If a hostile legislature chose to gang up on him, he simply could not fight back.

Except by the veto. Armed with that, the executive could protect himself. If the legislature tried to cut his pay, he could stop it cold. If it tried to harass or bully him, he could harass and bully back. He could not really tyrannize the lawmakers, for the veto power was only a negative one and was qualified at that. (Two-thirds of the legislature could override it.) But the point was, he could hold his own.

In truth, it was the strangest of paradoxes. In order to keep the powers of government effectively separate and distinct, there had to be a *sharing* of legislative power in the form of the executive veto. Theory alone could never have made such a discovery—only experience could.

The new constitution of Massachusetts marked a bold stride forward in republican statecraft, for it set forth a government in which the rule of will was truly minimized. It placed a heavy reliance on the virtue of its citizens, as freedom must always do, but it placed an equal reliance on structural devices that fragmented power, diffused responsibility, and curbed self- interest. It was the first republican experiment to really succeed.

Toward Philadelphia

South Carolina had already rewritten its original constitution in 1778. For many of the other states, the Massachusetts document served as a model. New Hampshire in 1784, Vermont in 1787, Georgia in 1789, Pennsylvania in 1790, and Delaware in 1792—all revised their original work. The six remaining states waited until the nineteenth century to rewrite their constitutions, but by the Civil War all of them had done so. All of the revisions moved toward a stronger executive and a more effective separation of powers. All of them strengthened the rule of law. Experimental republicanism was applying its lessons diligently, and was designing ever more effective structures of government.

The experience of doing this, of designing republican governments, trying them out, evaluating their performance, and then designing them anew, gave the American inventors a new sense of confidence. Government really *was* an instrument of the people and not the other way around. It was something that could be unplugged and hoisted onto the workbench for repairs, then reassembled and plugged back in. The Americans truly seemed masters of their own destiny.

It also boosted their confidence in republicanism to see that strong, capable governments could achieve the rule of law. The second Massachusetts constitution was far more self- controlled than its predecessor, yet it was also far stronger and more responsive. The rule of law, in other words, did not derive from governmental impotence, as some people had thought. Republican government could be both vigorous and effective. It could be boldly and imaginatively led. It could be energetic enough to deal with the many-sided challenges of modern life. And still it could hold itself in check.

If state governments could be overhauled, so could the national. The difficulty of the Confederation was not a drift toward tyranny, as in the states, but a drift toward anarchy and impotence. Self-interest had shown itself to be a powerful force in republican America, so powerful that public virtue alone could not control it. To an increasing number of Americans it was evident that a *real* government with *real* sovereignty was needed for the Union. Such a government would have to have its structure designed in just the right way, for it too would have to balance strength against freedom. But the inventors now knew it could be done.

In 1785, an informal conference was called at Mount Vernon, George Washington's estate on the Potomac, to work out interstate difficulties in the navigation of Chesapeake Bay. The conclave made enough progress for one of its participants, James Madison, to persuade the Virginia legislature to invite all thirteen states to attend a larger commercial convention at Annapolis the following year. That one was a disappointment—only five states showed up—but out of the deliberations came an intriguing proposal. The states should get together in 1787 at Philadelphia and discuss the inadequacies of the national government. American republicanism was ten years old that year. Perfecting it seemed like a good idea.

6
Federalism

Independence Hall (Library of Congress)

Serious Business

In its first item of business, the Constitutional Convention wisely elected George Washington to be its presiding officer. Solemnly escorted to the dais, the general made a little speech of acceptance, confessing his want of qualification and calling upon God for help. After that, though a lively interest never left his face, he took no further part in the proceedings. But his presence on the dais, day after day, through the heat, the flies, the sometimes bitter debates, meant everything. It was a presence that in earlier times had held together an easily divided army, and for the Philadelphia Convention it worked the same magic.

Washington was deeply concerned—sometimes painfully distressed—about the condition of the American Republic. It faced a host of difficulties, and there was no promise that it would ever surmount them. Had the threats been military, the old general would have known precisely how to deal with them, but they were political, intellectual, even spiritual in nature; and Washington, as he said, felt ill equipped in those areas. Accordingly, he did what he believed he could do best: made the delegates understand how serious a business this was.

Take the incident with Gouverneur Morris, for example. Himself affable and charming, Morris could not abide Washington's legendary reserve. He boasted one evening that he could be as familiar with the general as with any of his Philadelphia companions. At that, Alexander Hamilton came alight. "If you will, at the next reception evening, gently slap [Washington] on the shoulder and say, 'My dear General, how happy I am to see you look so well!' a supper and wine shall be provided for you and a dozen of your friends." Morris took the bait. A few evenings later, he shook the general's hand, placed an arm on his shoulder, and warmly recited Hamilton's words. Washington withdrew his hand, stepped back, and riveted a daunting frown upon the young Philadelphian. Constitution writing did not mix with idle intimacy.

Or take the matter of secrecy. The delegates resolved early that their procedings must be kept closely under wraps. For, if the public were looking over their shoulders, they could neither speak their minds freely nor work out delicate compromises. Thus, by agreement, the windows of Independence Hall were kept tightly shut. Sentries were posted at the doors. Members were forbidden to copy from the daily journal. Some, of course, took the secrecy rule more seriously than others. Ben Franklin, for one, was almost impossible to keep quiet. Someone had to be posted at every gathering he attended in order to steer conversations clear of danger.

How did Washington regard the secrecy rule? Early in the Convention, he was handed a paper dropped accidentally and left on the floor. That afternoon, just before adjournment, he rose from his seat. "Gentlemen!" he said, in a voice he might have used at the Battle of Germantown, "I am sorry to find that some one member of this body has been so neglectful of the secrets of the Convention as to drop in the State House a copy of their proceedings. . . . I know not whose paper it is, but there it is [throwing the paper down on the table], let him who owns it take it." Pierce, alarmed, instantly shot his hand into his own breast pocket to make sure that he was not the culprit. "It is something remarkable," he penned in his memoirs, "that no person ever owned the paper."

One for whom seriousness came naturally was James Madison. He was the first to arrive in Philadelphia, almost two weeks before the Convention got under way, and he used the time to full advantage. Having written to Jefferson, in France, for books on the subject of confederation, he spent days and nights poring through the hundreds of volumes he received in reply, writing out lengthy notes and even penning an essay on comparative government. Small—"no bigger than half a piece of soap," someone said—slight of figure, and so quietly spoken that he was repeatedly asked to speak up, Madison nevertheless dominated the proceedings. He sat on the front row of green baize-covered tables and took notes far more complete than those of the Convention's paid scribe. For him, too, constitution writing was a serious business.

There were, of course, moments of pleasure, even for the sober minded Virginians. Dr. Franklin had laid in a cask of porter for the Convention, and he doled it out lavishly to his many guests. Everywhere, it seemed, there were teas, formal receptions, and dazzling balls. If it was the hottest summer in Philadelphia's memory, it was also the most brilliant.

By day, however, the Convention was invariably back on task. And in its own perverse way, the heat may have actually helped out. Slatted blinds kept the sun from the Assembly chamber, but with the windows closed, the air inside grew lifeless and oppressive before midday. The New Englanders, who had come ill provided with woolen suits, stole envious glances at Washington, who, seated on the dais in his light camlet coat and breeches, seemed as imperturbable as a Gilbert Stuart portrait. But sitting through the suffocation, day after day, served as a reminder, if one were needed, that the American republic was in peril—and that the business of saving it was serious business indeed.

There was indeed a sense of intrigue in the launching of the Philadelphia Convention, and only part of it grew out of the air of secrecy. For, the Convention itself was more than a little subversive. Supposedly, it was meeting only for the purpose of reforming an existing government, not creating a new one, and most Americans did not wish the case to be otherwise. Difficulties and all, the 1780s marked a buoyant time in the new republic: settlers were moving into the West, merchants were exploring new markets, and entrepreneurs were tinkering with novel forms of enterprise. Hardly anyone was anticipating a second revolution.

Accordingly, most of the Convention delegates had only modest plans in mind, plans for a little strengthening here and shoring up there. They generally agreed that the Confederation needed the power of taxation, a national court system, and some kind of authority to regulate commerce. Those three powers, plus a workable means of amending the Articles, would have gratified the hopes of most. Still, there were a few who thought of going further. Alexander Hamilton of New York was one of them. His sympathy with monarchy was well known, and his disgust with the Confederation's weaknesses had become legendary. But Hamilton was so extreme—and so controversial— that his chances for real influence appeared slim. Such was not the case, however, with a small, slightly built, and softly spoken Virginian with whom Hamilton would soon be keeping close company. In the valise of James Madison was nothing less than a new plan of government.

Virginia Plan

What Madison had in mind was an expression of the man himself and his experience with republican revolution. A Virginian of the old school and by instinct rather moderate, Madison nevertheless had his revolutionary side. The ideals of the Enlightenment shimmered in his imagination, and he longed to translate them into reality. The world of practical politics, however, had repeatedly frustrated his attempts. For example, in the Virginia state legislature Madison and his friend Thomas Jefferson had labored for years to implement a range of republican reforms, everything from abolishing slavery to altering the laws of inheritance; yet, by 1787, the only real success they could report was on disestablishing the Church of England.

Why had all else come to naught? For the very reasons we examined in the previous chapter. The legislature of revolutionary Virginia was unprecedented in size and power, and new elements were making their first appearance in it. Radical firebrands like Patrick Henry rubbed shoulders with crusty conservatives like Edmund Pendleton. The play of factions, raucous enough back in the days of the Stamp Act, had increased in energy and tempo to the point where things had occasionally spun out of control. So concerned were all parties with the pursuit of private advantage

that virtually no one, so it seemed to Madison, cared a fig about the public good. Fumed his friend Jefferson: "One hundred and seventy three despots [are] surely as oppressive as one."

We might see this merely as politics. Madison saw it as something much worse. Indeed, to him it seemed as though republicanism was going awry. "The mutability of the laws of the States is found to be a serious evil," he wrote to Jefferson. "The injustice of them has been so frequent and so flagrant as to alarm the most steadfast friends of Republicanism." Madison and his colleagues returned to these themes time and again in their correspondence: the mutability and injustice of state legislatures might well wreck the great experiment. Some way had to be found for holding them permanently in check.

The Madison Plan

Of all the delegates to Philadelphia, Madison made the most careful and comprehensive preparations. He reread his bibles of political thought and spent weeks conversing and corresponding with friends. The more he thought about the problem of the American states, the more certain it seemed to him that the states had to go. Public virtue could never survive in the sharkpool of intrastate rivalries—and without public virtue the republic was doomed.

The plan that began to take shape in his mind was a radical departure from the ideas of classical republicanism. For Madison no longer envisioned America as a confederation of individual republics but rather as a *single* republic of continental size. The states might continue to exist in this new supersovereignty, but only as subordinate administrative units (like counties today). With only one republic and only one republican people, public virtue would be able to distance itself from the welter of private and local interests that clustered in state capitals.

Madison's means for accomplishing this end would be a powerful national executive and a powerful national legislature. The latter would be made national, as well as powerful, by basing its representation on the size of the respective populations of the states. Thus, Virginia, the largest state, would have the largest number of seats in congress, while Rhode Island, the smallest, would have only a few. What would really be represented in such a body was *the people of the United States* rather than the individual states of the union. (In the Confederation, we recall, the reverse was true.) In the exercise of their authority, the people of the United States, speaking through this legislature, would reign supreme.

Realist that he was, Madison toned his ideas down a little as he worked them from draft to draft. But he did not yield on his notion of the government's unitary nature. If all of France could be governed from Paris and all of England from Westminster, it was not ludicrous to suppose that all of America could be governed from New York or Philadelphia.

Madison's proposals, combined with assorted compatible elements, were presented to the Convention by his friend Edmund Randolph and thereafter became known as the Virginia Plan. Even watered down, the plan was a bombshell. Upon hearing it, some delegates jumped to their feet and reminded the Convention that its mandate was only to revise the Articles of Confederation, not to contrive a new government. On that note, the debate was joined in earnest.

The Sovereignty Question

Regardless of its nature, all true government has one thing in common: it can make final decisions. Sometimes a decision may have to ascend a long way through the channels of authority before it is finally made, and sometimes it will be reversed and rereversed on the way up, but if the government in question is real, it has the means at its disposal for laying any sort of issue to rest. The power of making final decisions is called *sovereignty*.

A glance at world history will show how important sovereignty is. For example, Herod Antipas, the infamous king of Judea, while he had the power to create much mischief, did not have sovereignty. If something really final had to be decided in his kingdom, it had to be decided in Rome, for Herod was merely Rome's puppet. Similarly, France after the Nazi takeover, Cuba in the days of Batista, and Poland under the Jaruzelski regime, though all supposedly free and independent, lacked the same essential element. Like Herod, they had to refer the big questions elsewhere.

Sovereignty was traditionally regarded as being indivisible: it could be exercised only by a single authority. The proposition, in fact, seemed self-evident. Suppose there were a kingdom somewhere that wished to divide its sovereignty between two kings. One would reign in, say, the north half of the kingdom and the other would reign in the south. But what would happen if an extremely difficult or divisive question came up? In all probability, one of the two kings would prove that he alone was the *real* sovereign. Alternatively, the kingdom might simply break in two.

Where the Buck Stops

Sovereignty is the power to make final decisions—to determine exactly when and where the buck stops. The concept may be a fuzzy one when presented in the abstract, but the reality of it is usually crystal clear. Consider, for example, the made-for-a-textbook case of Little Rock, Arkansas, in 1957.

In the fall of that year, a number of the community's citizens, angered by the prospect of school desegregation, decided to defy a federal court order and simply refuse to integrate. They knew, of course, about the supremacy clause of the Constitution, but they supposed that states had their rights too, and that somehow, such rights could be enforced independently of the federal judiciary. It was a classical question of where the buck stopped.

On the first day of school, nine black children appeared at Central High ready for class. There was trouble. A venomous crowd was milling about on the front steps and growling angrily about a lynching. Hesitantly, school authorities appealed to the Little Rock police department, and from there to the mayor's office, where it was decided to close the school. But the mayor of Little Rock was not sovereign, and so the decision was appealed still higher. The governor of the state, Orval Faubus, also decided against integration, and called out the state militia to support the local police. However, since a federal court order was also at stake, the issue had to go higher still. Ultimately, it wound up on the desk of Dwight Eisenhower, president of the United States, who decided that the court order should be upheld.

This decision turned out to be the final one. To emphasize that fact, Eisenhower nationalized the Arkansas state militia—meaning that Faubus lost command of his own troops—and sent in the 101st Airborne for good measure. The division's crack 327th Battle Group lined up outside Central High with fixed bayonets. Then the soldiers slowly advanced on the shouting throng of obstructionists. One stout soul had to approach within six inches of a gleaming bayonet before fully comprehending what sovereignty meant. Eventually, though, it came to him.

Could the president's decision have been appealed still higher? What about appealing to the Organization of American States or to the United Nations? These bodies were all larger than the United States and, organizationally speaking, all higher up. But, of course, they too lacked the power to make final decisions. Although they could have put in their two-bits worth about the Little Rock situation, they lacked the power to do what in the ultimate extremity had to be done: mobilize deadly force. That, unfortunately, is what sovereignty comes down to in the end.

In our world today, cities and counties, though they have the power to govern much of what we do, are not sovereign. For that matter, neither is the United Nations. So, if Americans had to make some life-or-death decision tomorrow, they would not bother to consult the mayor of Poughkeepsie, New York, or the U.N. secretary general, for neither one could lay the matter to rest. All this we accept without thinking.

But where did sovereignty lie in James Madison's America? That question is more difficult. If sovereignty truly was indivisible, then it could not exist in two different places at the same time: either the Confederation was sovereign or else the states were. And the answer, of course, is *the states*. They had been founded independently by various different colonizers, and each had come to possess its own distinctive identity. When the tie with England was cut, the states individually claimed for themselves all of the sovereignty of nationhood. True, they agreed to join together in the American Confederation—but they never agreed to give up their sovereign independence. Any of them, if they chose, could break their ties to the Confederation, with or without notice, and go their separate ways.

Understandably, then, the spokesmen of the states, now convened in Philadelphia, were not terribly interested in giving that sovereignty up. It was too precious a commodity, and too hard won, to cast aside at a whim. This was especially true of the smaller states, which had the most to lose. Their small populations would count for little in a continent-sized nation: a Rhode Island or New Hampshire might not have a single seat in the upper house of Madison's legislature, and the hope of their producing a president was nil.

Independence Hall: Birthplace of the American republic. (Courtesy of Bert R. Holfeltz)

Beyond the sovereignty issue, there were plenty of state politicians who liked things just the way they were. They didn't *want* a central government that was strong and energetic—and they especially didn't want one that would urge them to be virtuous.

The New Jersey Plan

Within a week or so of Madison's proposal the small states offered a proposal of their own, presented by New Jersey's William

Patterson. Patterson admitted that the Confederation had been a failure, and he was willing to support more than a cursory overhaul. He would accept taxing power, commercial regulation, and a national system of courts as necessary reforms. But, he said solemnly, the present states of America could not be destroyed. If there was to be a more perfect union, well and good, but it had to respect existing sovereignty.

Accordingly, the Patterson—or New Jersey—Plan differed markedly from the Virginia Plan in the composition of the legislature. Here, said Patterson, each state must have an equal voice. Things must not come to the point where two or three large states, by the very size of their populations, could simply order the smaller states around. Patterson feared that his own New Jersey, sandwiched between New York and Pennsylvania, might lose its very soul if its neighbors could outvote it.

Patterson asserted that the national legislature could be organized by "confederal" principles and still allow for a government of adequate authority. What counted, he believed, was not how the seats were filled in congress but how powers were assigned in the constitution. If the national government had constitutional authority to tax, regulate trade, and resolve interstate disputes, it would not be hobbled by the fact that all states had an equal say in its decisions.

But was that true? The history of the American colonies seemed to suggest otherwise.

The Confederation of New England

Back in 1643, when the New England colonies were still in their infancy, Massachusetts, which was by far the largest of them,

raised the question of whether and how they ought to be politically related. The five of them—Massachusetts, Plymouth, Connecticut, New Haven, and Rhode Island—had much in common: their ardent Puritanism, their maritime economies, and their often volatile relations with the Indians. Wouldn't it be a good idea for them all to form a confederation?

The resulting Confederation of the United Colonies of New England had an instructive, if somewhat short-lived, history. Each of its members pledged to act in concert with the others in all matters of common interest; they would make peace or war, conduct foreign policy, and carry on their Indian diplomacy with a single voice. But this was another case of confederal organization, where every member had exactly the same say as every other. And Massachusetts had a greater population than the rest of them combined.

What naturally happened, then, when the first tough issue came along? The Confederation fell apart. When Connecticut sought to tax the outlying village of Springfield, which Massachusetts also claimed, its commissioners persuaded the Confederation to support them. Massachusetts was outvoted but it still refused to go along—and it didn't have to. And again, when the Confederation voted to make war on the Dutch in 1652, Massachusetts, which would have borne the brunt of the fighting, simply balked. And that was that.

Quite clearly, then, confederal organization, no matter how it was dressed up, could not redistribute sovereignty. When final decisions have to be made by a confederation, they are made not by the group as a whole but by the group's individual members. It is hard to see how William Patterson's confederation would have been much different. For if political power in an organization is not apportioned according to population, there will always be a perception of unfairness. Someone will always be thinking that his vote does not equal someone else's, and as a consequence he will refuse to go along. Could the United States exist today if Rhode Island had exactly the same say in Congress as California? Could Nevada or Wyoming really compel Texas to act against its will? Or would the whole thing simply collapse of its own weight—like the Confederation of New England did?

Nevertheless, the small states were dead earnest about the Patterson Plan. Their delegates could not go home and announce that they had surrendered their sovereignty at Philadelphia—any more than, say, the U.S. ambassador to NATO could come home with a similar announcement today. And since it was universally agreed that sovereignty was indivisible, no political compromise seemed possible. Either Madison and the nationalists would have to win completely or else Patterson and the confederalists would. The sovereignty issue threatened to become the rock on which the Constitutional Convention would founder.

Large States, Small States, and Freedom

Matters were further complicated by another, parallel concern. The classical republics had all been geographically small themselves, and not by accident. Virtually all of the republican philosophers had assumed that size was an important consideration. For, only when the body politic was appropriately small could the citizens really exercise their responsibilities. They had to be close—physically close—to the

government in order to keep an eye on it and take an active part in its affairs. When Rome was small, it remained a republic; when it grew large, it became an empire.

For many Americans the classical models were still compelling. How indeed could a citizen watch the government, they asked, if the government was in New York City and he was in far-flung Tennessee? Might not the government become a power unto itself? Might it not lose contact with the people? Might it not begin to imagine that reality existed only there in the capital? And then there was the matter of corruption to think about. With so much power collected in a single place, wasn't there a constant temptation to misuse it? If the power remained scattered throughout the states, some of them might succumb to corruption and others might not. If it resided only in Philadelphia, the eggs were all in one basket.

We must remember, too, that their recent experience with the British was still much on the Americans' minds. When they thought of England, the small island nation of a few million inhabitants, they thought of King John and the Magna Carta, of John Locke and the Glorious Revolution, of Lord Coke and the common law—their own heritage of liberty. It was only when England had become the sprawling British Empire that corruption had begun to set in. "From the moment we become one great Republic," cried an opponent of the proposed new constitution, "we shall sink first into monarchy and then into despotism."

The Long, Hot Summer

For weeks the issue dragged on. Throughout the month of June and on into July the delegates unsuccessfully tried to

Benjamin Franklin and the Rising Sun

Ben Franklin seemed to view the world in similes. The comment in his *Autobiography* that "Keimer stared like a pig poisoned" was just the sort of thing he would come out with, and similes filled *Poor Richard's Almanac* from beginning to end. So it was only natural that the old diplomat was thinking in similes during the long, hot summer of 1787.

Franklin knew that settling the sovereignty issue would be difficult. As it happened, he had tried to settle it himself some thirty years earlier, at the time of the French and Indian War. Then, the much younger and less-experienced diplomat had conceived a plan for uniting the colonies in a common defense. The need for such unity had been real enough—almost critical—but the plan had been scuttled by the colonies' legendary jealousies and rivalries.

Only after the Constitution was signed did the old man reveal his doubts. "Whilst the last members were signing it," Madison recorded:

> Doctr. Franklin looking towards the President's Chair, at the back of which a rising sun happened to be painted, observed to a few members near him, that Painters had found it difficult to distinguish in their art a rising from a setting sun. I have, said he, often and often in the course of the Session, and the vicissitudes of my hopes and fears as to its issue, looked at that behind the President without being able to tell whether it was rising or setting: But now at length I have the happiness to know that it is a rising and not a setting Sun.

For the fledgling American Republic with its new Constituion, that simile seemed all but perfect.

resolve it. As the days slipped by, Philadelphia's bengal heat began to take its toll on them, and so did the flies. These were a "veritable torture," as one visitor recalled, constantly lighting on the face and hands, "stinging everywhere and turning everything black [with their] filth." Without window screens—not to mention air conditioning—the delegates warded off the oppression as best they could. Still it began to have its effect, and the speeches took on an angry tone.

William Patterson's was typical. "Can we consolidate [state] sovereignty and form one nation," he asked, "and annihilate the sovereignties of our states who have sent us here for other purposes?" He resoundingly replied in the negative. "I will never consent to the present system, and I shall make all the interest against it in the state which I represent that I can," he vowed. "Myself or my state will never submit to tyranny or despotism."

There was comparable vehemence on the other side. Pennsylvania's James Wilson, who answered Patterson point by point, also spoke in anger. "Shall New Jersey have the same right or council in the nation with Pennsylvania?" he asked. "I say no! It is unjust—I never will confederate on this plan. If no state will part with any of its sovereignty it is in vain to talk of a national government."

It was remarkable, in fact, that the Convention did not simply dissolve. A few delegates did leave. Lansing and Yates, New York men of the confederal persuasion, headed for home on July 10, resolving to fight any national system to the end. Even Hamilton—the only New Yorker remaining—took leave of the Convention, although he later returned. Getting away for a brief respite was not a bad idea, and several of the delegates gladly did so.

Still the wrangling continued. Various suggestions for compromise were made, some of them a little bizarre. Ben Franklin volunteered that if the issue of large states versus small could not otherwise be settled, he would see about ceding chunks of Pennsylvania to its diminutive neighbors. Mostly, however, business remained serious. Delaware's Gunning Bedford now pressed the attack for the confederalists. "The large states dare not dissolve the confederation," he taunted. "If they do, the small ones will find some foreign ally . . . who will take them by the hand and do them justice. You will annihilate your [confederal] government, and ruin must stare you in the face!"

It is in light of such vituperation that we must mention Benjamin Franklin's sudden plea for prayer. From a political man of the world it was a startling proposal, yet Franklin seemed entirely sincere in making it. He reminded the delegates that during the war the Continental Congress had often prayed for divine guidance in the very room where he now spoke. "I firmly believe," he went on, "that without [God's] concurring aid we shall succeed in

this political building no better than the builders of Babel. We shall be divided by our little partial local interests; our projects will be confounded and we ourselves shall become a reproach and bye word down to future ages." Franklin's motion was not adopted, most likely because the convention lacked funds to pay for a chaplain, yet it was not without its effect. For the words of this oldest and most highly respected of the delegates could not have fallen on deaf ears. They did stand at the judgment bar of history. The destiny of the United States did sit among them in this hall. Posterity would indeed not forgive them if they failed. "And what is worse," he added, "mankind may hereafter from this unfortunate instance despair of establishing government by human wisdom and leave it to chance, war, and conquest."

The Great Compromise

It became increasingly obvious that no political compromise would be forthcoming until some intellectual breakthroughs were made. Accordingly, every mind was fully engaged. The delegates dug out their copies of Pufendorf and Montesquieu and thumbed through them anew. Somewhere there had to be a path through the thicket.

Or, better yet, two paths. For there were two separate conceptual problems. First, sovereignty had to be made divisible in some way, so that sovereign state governments and a sovereign national government could exist side by side. Second, the delegates needed to be convinced that a large republic—as opposed to the small republics of antiquity—was practically feasible. Without progress in both areas the convention seemed doomed to fail.

Intellectual Breakthroughs

Curiously, it was two renowned thinkers of the European Enlightenment who came to the Founders' aid. John Locke, although long in his grave, helped them solve the sovereignty puzzle, and David Hume inspired a solution to the problem of the large republic.

Sovereignty in a Republic. Reflections on the philosophy of John Locke made the Founders begin to see sovereignty in a different light. The traditional view held that sovereignty was indivisible in nature, and hence that it had to be exercised by a single authority. Since most sovereigns of the world were in fact kings—solitary human individuals—there was a self-evidence about the proposition that was hard to deny.

Locke, however, viewed the whole matter differently, as we learned in chapter two. He saw the king merely as the agent of the people. It was the people, not the king, who gained their rights from nature, and it was they, not he, who chose a particular form of government. The conclusion was inescapable—sovereignty resided not with the king but with *the people.*

And the sovereignty of the people just might be divisible. True, if the people happened to vest their sovereignty in a single crowned head, the result would be unitary government. But what if they chose to vest it in two places, or three, or four? What if they placed the power to make some kinds of final decisions in a *state* government and the power to make other kinds of final decisions in a *national* one? The sovereignty itself would still be unitary—it would still rest ultimately with the people; but the exercise of it would be divided in two.

HUME'S FILTER

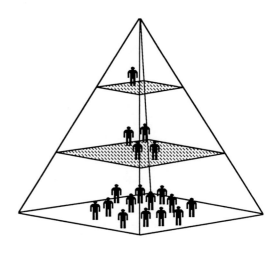

David Hume's idea of filtering the consent of the people through successive elections with representatives choosing representatives of their own, as if in an ascending pyramid. Those few at the top of the pyramid would be far removed from popular passions and hopefully patriotic individuals of national reputation.

Gradually, the delegates became convinced. It *was* possible to have two different governments and to regard both of them as sovereign. As long as they were not expected to exercise the same power, each could operate independently of the other and remain perfectly sovereign. That was the first important breakthrough.

Stability in Large Republics. It was David Hume who inspired a solution to the second problem, the problem of the large republic. Among Hume's ideas, we recall, was that of filtering the consent of the people through a process of successive elections. He believed that the various counties of a kingdom like Scotland could

Factional Takeover: The Case of Grenada

We know that it is difficult for single factions to take over large republics. Witness the United States. In small republics, by contrast, single factions can take charge much more easily. Witness Grenada.

In the spring of 1979, Grenada seemed anything but ripe for revolution. Life in the sleepy island had coursed along happily for more than twenty years under the uncontroversial Eric Matthew Gairy. True, there was some discontent. Youngsters unable to find work in the island's on-again, off-again economy often idled about, filling their afternoons with fishing off the rust-colored reefs. When agents from Castro's Cuba came preaching an angry new gospel in the mid–1970s, some of these kids were ready to listen. So began the New Jewel Movement.

The movement's tactics were peaceful at first. Its presidential candidate, Maurice Bishop, preached a mellifluous socialism and wrote blistering editorials in the *Torchlight*. Bishop was not content with constitutional politics, however, and his two lieutenants, Kendrick Radix and Bernard Coard, were even less so. With tactical and logistic support from Havana, they set about planning a coup.

The takeover proved to be absurdly easy. The NJM commandos merely waited until Gairy left the country, gathered up units of the People's Revolutionary Army, and began battering their way into the country's clapboard police stations. By the end of the day, March 13, 1979, Grenada was their very own.

Of course, consolidating the NJM's rule, especially among a nonideological and often unwilling populace, proved to be another matter. Gairy's entire government was jailed. His small defense force was rounded up and neutralized. Radio Free Grenada was set up to portray the former president as a fascist dictator, while the *Free West Indian* began inundating the island with Castroite propaganda. As for the *Torchlight*, which had earlier befriended the NJM, it was shut down completely. And when twenty-six leading citizens tried to launch a publication of their own, they were arrested and locked away in the Richmond Hill prison.

Meanwhile, Soviet "cruise liners" began putting in at St. George's, and one of them unloaded three thousand AK47 automatic rifles for the People's Revolutionary Army. Popular uprisings were well and good, as Grenada's new masters understood—but they had to be kept under control.

each elect representatives to a body of some sort, and that the members of that body could elect representatives of their own to a body still higher, and so on. The idea was to keep consent intact and operating while distancing the government from popular passions.

James Madison chanced to be thumbing through Hume's writings one day while pondering his own difficulty. At each step in Hume's filtering process, he reflected, the influence of a given faction grew less and less acute on the government. Suddenly it occurred to Madison precisely what was wrong with state governments. Lacking such filters, they were easy prey to the power of large factions. A political faction in Delaware, let us say, did not have to be very large at all in order to dominate state politics because the state itself was so very small.

But how easily could such a faction dominate the politics of a *large* republic? Let us think of a hypothetical situation and answer the question for ourselves. Suppose that the political life of Delaware is under the thumb of a large corporation. The company, let us say, employs thousands of people, spends billions of dollars, and altogether dwarfs the tiny state government in Dover. If it should choose to abuse its power, constitution or no constitution, there might not be a way of stopping it.

What if, though, Delaware were only a tiny county in the much larger republic of America? What voice would the local company have in *its* affairs? The answer is obvious. Just as the voice of any faction was increasingly muted in each of Hume's ascending elections, so too would the voice of any local interest tend to be lost in the larger clamor. In Delaware the firm might have few political competitors. In the United States as a whole it would have thousands of competitors—farmers, laborers, other kinds of industry, rival corporations—all of them jostling for place. Like the child's game of "king of the mountain," the more players scrambling for a position at the top of the hill, the more unlikely that any one of them could long remain there.

The implications of this insight were startling. Madison suddenly realized that the ancients had had it all backwards: not only were large republics not necessarily unstable, they were probably far *more* stable than small ones. Tiny Athens fell prey to a combination of local oligarchs; how many such courthouse politicians would it take to subvert the whole United States?

There was something else. Not only was the large republic advantageous, the large *commercial* republic was even more so. For with commerce and its attendant prosperity must come an even greater diversity of interests. In a primitive economy—such as those of the ancient republics—there were really only two interests: that of the rich and that of the poor. Each faced a temptation to dominate the other. When the tyrants and oligarchs ruled, they usually did so at the behest of the landowning haves. When the factions and demogogues held sway, it was usually in the name of the landless have-nots. In the commercial republic, by contrast, the more interests, the more *kinds* of interest, the better. Material self-interest could be a bad thing in the context of a chaotic state assembly—but it could be a very good thing in the context of a large republic.

Quiet Lobbying

Most of the real work toward a compromise was performed outside of the Convention proper. Madison and his allies talked to small groups of colleagues in secluded rooms of the City Queen, City Tavern, and London Coffee House, where the delegates gathered for relaxation. Over and over, they pressed home the points that sovereignty could be vested in more than a single authority, and that there was nothing to fear in a large republic.

MADISON'S THEORY OF LARGE REPUBLIC

Republic of America

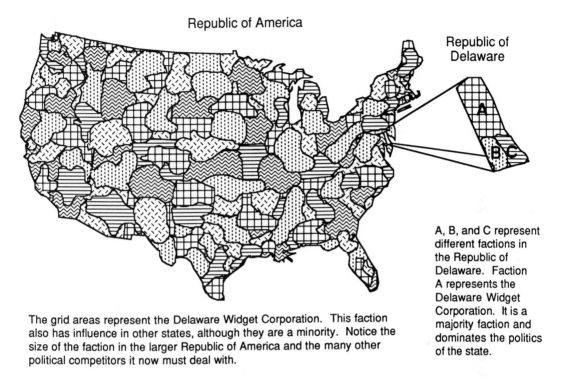

Republic of
Delaware

A, B, and C represent
different factions in
the Republic of
Delaware. Faction
A represents the
Delaware Widget
Corporation. It is a
majority faction and
dominates the politics
of the state.

The grid areas represent the Delaware Widget Corporation. This faction
also has influence in other states, although they are a minority. Notice the
size of the faction in the larger Republic of America and the many other
political competitors it now must deal with.

What is a majority faction in a small republic is a small minority faction in a
large republic. A minority faction has a small chance of taking over the
large republic.

Gradually, the doubters became convinced. Since the constitution would literally be written in black and white, it would be possible to carefully enumerate which powers were to be assigned to the national government and which were to be reserved for the states. Each kind of government would be completely sovereign in the exercise of its own authority. The states would handle all matters of local concern. Questions of health and safety, questions of education, questions of property and its disposal, questions of domestic order, questions affecting local commerce, and questions of applying criminal sanctions would all be settled there. National matters would be broader. Questions of war and peace, questions of diplomacy, questions affecting interstate or foreign commerce, and questions dealing with the national domain would be handled by the central government. There would remain

THE GREAT COMPROMISE

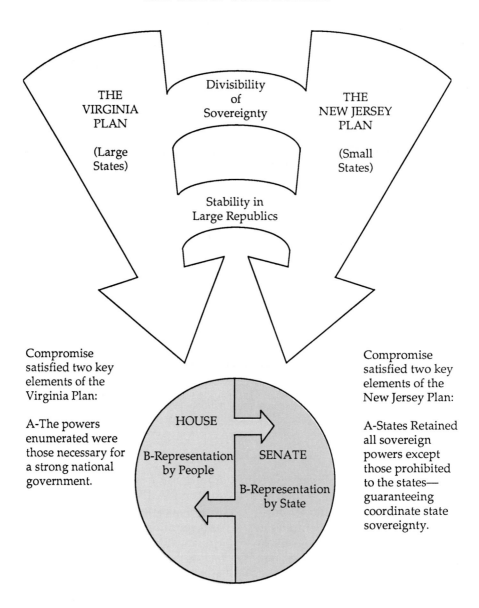

THE VIRGINIA PLAN

(Large States)

Divisibility of Sovereignty

THE NEW JERSEY PLAN

(Small States)

Stability in Large Republics

Compromise satisfied two key elements of the Virginia Plan:

A-The powers enumerated were those necessary for a strong national government.

HOUSE

B-Representation by People

SENATE

B-Representation by State

Compromise satisfied two key elements of the New Jersey Plan:

A-States Retained all sovereign powers except those prohibited to the states— guaranteeing coordinate state sovereignty.

No political compromise would have been possible unless some intellectual bridges were made between the Virginia Plan and the New Jersey Plan. Since it was already accepted that legislatures shold be Bi (two) Cameral (chamber), everything fit together perfectly.

a few problem areas where state and national authority might logically overlap, but these could be worked out. What counted was that there could be a national government for the United States of America *without dissolving the existing states*.

The Federal Structure

What became known as the Great Compromise was reached on July 16. Two kinds of government, both of them sovereign, would exist side by side in the American Republic. One would be national in character, much as Madison had originally envisioned, with power focused in a strong national legislature according to population. The other would be subnational in character—though still fully sovereign—consisting of thirteen individual states. The sovereignty of the states would be preserved by their legal equality in another legislature, one in which all of them, large and small, would be given exactly the same voice. The first legislative body would be the U.S. House of Representatives and the second would be the U.S. Senate. Since it was already accepted that legislatures should be divided into upper and lower houses, everything fit together perfectly.

By the principle of enumeration, the powers of the national government were then carefully described. Congress would have the power to tax and spend, to borrow and coin money, to regulate commerce, to

THE FEDERAL STRUCTURE

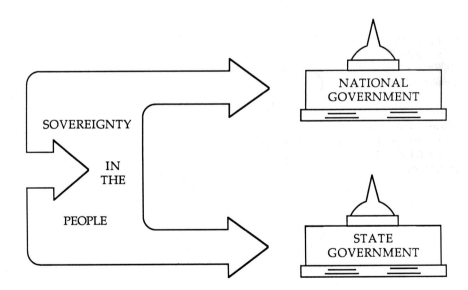

The exercise of popular sovereignty was divided in two. Powers delegated and prohibited to the National government were carefully enumerated. All other powers not designated National, nor prohibited to the States, were reserved to the States respectively, or to the people.

Father of the Constitution

Delegates to the Constitutional Convention who did not know James Madison could not understand how such a small, quiet, unimposing man could wield so much influence. The secret, if there was one, was preparation; he always did his homework. Preparation, in fact, remained the key to Madison throughout his long and highly accomplished life. He was the epitome of the scholar in politics.

Both his mother and father came from established Virginia families, and the Madison estate, Montpelier, might be mistaken today for a well-endowed college. James himself was uneasy about his wealth—always playing it down—and doubly uneasy about the nearly two hundred slaves who produced it. (When his trusted valet ran away and was recaptured, Madison, instead of selling him off into the West Indies, set him free and then hired him.) It was, in fact, "to depend as little as possible on the labor of slaves" that the young man took up the study of law.

And when James Madison took up anything, he did so with single-minded devotion. Under Donald Robertson, his first tutor; under Reverend Martin, with whom he later studied the classics; and finally under John Witherspoon at Princeton, Madison worked so diligently that he seriously endangered his health. More than once he confided that he did not expect to live long.

Once settled in such habits, Madison was loath to alter them. Whether it was working on a problem in the Virginia House of Burgesses, guiding the Revolution in the Continental Congress, or hammering out the new Federal Constitution, he addressed his tasks with a fearsome intensity. Much of his subsequent career was foreshadowed by his first term in Congress, where he did not utter a single speech for six months. When he did finally take the floor, however, he was so well prepared that he immediately rose to leadership.

Curiously, though, everything about him belied his volcanic drive. His delicate stature, his reserved manner, his thin, tinsel-toned voice combined to put adversaries off their guard. It was only upon looking closely that one noticed the exquisite tailoring, the finely powdered wig, the bright, scintillating eyes, the confident, bouncy

naturalize citizens, to set up a postal service, to issue patents, to declare war, to raise and support armies and navies, and to provide for the general welfare. All powers not designated as national were understood to be reserved for the states. This fact, too, enhanced state sovereignty, for the states (or the people) would retain the broad, undefined, residual powers of government.

As for the no man's land between state and national authority (where both might have a claim), the Founders opted for vagueness rather than precision, realizing that they could not anticipate all possible conflicts. They did, however, include a clause stating that "This Constitution, and the Laws of the United States which shall be made in Pursuance thereof . . . shall be

step. "In the affairs of the United States," wrote one of the delegates, "he perhaps has the most correct knowledge of any Man in the Union." It was true. He was prepared on everything and for everything. Every argument, every objection, every wrinkle in the tapestry of ideas he knew with loving intimacy and could address the same with cogency and conviction.

Madison reached the great watershed in his life with his work in Revolutionary Virginia. A passionate believer in public virtue, he lost his bid for reelection because he refused to canvass actively or ply the voters with rum. But virtue, as he found, didn't count for much in state politics. Indeed, after battling the factions and their special interests through the long years of the war, he gradually concluded that republicanism could never survive without a strong—and virtuous—central government. "The advice nearest to my heart and deepest in my convictions," he wrote, "is that the Union of the states be cherished and perpetuated."

There were ideas besides Madison's in Philadelphia, of course, and many of them found their way into the Constitution. But the heart of the document was his: it represented the strong and virtuous national republic that had shimmered before his eyes. When all else was said and done in the constitutional debates, there was just no gainsaying the boyish little Virginian with the amazing store of knowledge.

James Madison: Volcanic drive and amazing knowledge. (Library of Congress)

the supreme law of the land; and the Judges in every State shall be bound thereby, any Thing in the Constitution or Laws of any State to the Contrary notwithstanding."

This *federal* structure—as opposed to the earlier *confederal*—was something entirely new. Yet it was completely harmonious with the spirit of Enlightenment thinking. For one thing, it presented yet another way to divide the powers of government, not between executive and legislative authorities, but between state and national. And for another thing, it made possible the large republic, which, as Madison predicted, became a veritable rock of political stability.

Federalism's Ambiguities

One aspect of federalism's freshly minted newness was a certain degree of ambiguity. There were at least three questions about it that skeptics might well have raised, and that no one, at the time, would have been able to answer. The three need to be addressed here because of the effect they were to have on subsequent U.S. history.

Did Large Republics have Dangers of Their Own? If the only danger to republics were that of tyrannical factions, the advantage of a large geographical size would be complete and incontestable. At no time in American history has a single faction come close to dominating the federal government, while on several occasions such factions have overwhelmed individual states. But might the large republic not have other dangers, less well-understood?

As far as the Anti-Federalists—opponents of the new Constitution—were concerned, large republics still faced the danger of *distance*. Quite apart from the problem of factions, the seat of government in a large republic was bound to be far, far away from many of the citizens (Hawaii, for example, is closer to Peking than to Washington) and it remained unclear how those citizens could fulfill their responsibilities to it. Six months of arduous travel was required to reach gold-rush California. Had there been a conspiracy against the government in Washington, the forty-niners at least would have been hard put to stop it.

Add to this the fact that in a large republic there must be a great deal of power concentrated somewhere, and it becomes possible to see why the Anti-Federalists had their misgivings. History would show that an all-powerful national government could indeed lose its bearings, divorce itself from reality, and turn into an "Establishment."

In their own way, then, large republics placed a greater strain on human nature than small ones did. As a consequence, they had to have more and better designed structure in order to preserve freedom.

What Maintains Balance in a Federal Structure? When philosophers of the Enlightenment thought about governmental controls, they focused on devices that worked *automatically*. Thus, in the cake-dividing example, both of the children could behave wholly selfishly and still produce a favorable outcome. In the case of federalism, by contrast, there was no self-regulating device: the line between state and national authority was merely drawn on paper. What if, in time, the states found means to trim back national authority, a little here and a little there, as colonial assemblies had once done with British governors? Or, conversely, what if a powerful central government found means to chip away at the authority of the states?

In either case, only public virtue could save the day. If there were not a vigilant, wise, politically astute citizenry, such erosions in the federal balance could well be expected, and federalism itself might simply disappear.

How Would a Full-Scale Confrontation Be Settled? Suppose some issue were to arise which would pit state authority against national. Suppose the issue were so highly charged that people on neither side of it felt they could compromise. Suppose the issue plainly had to be resolved. The question is, which kind of government, state or national, would exercise the supreme sovereignty?

An academic question? The Founders might have thought so. After all, what issue imaginable to them could have such wrenching divisiveness? In point of fact, there was such an issue; it lay barely over the future horizon. And when it burst upon the American republic in the middle of the nineteenth century, it suddenly thrust this last, and most dangerous, ambiguity of federalism to the fore. When push came to shove on the question of human slavery, some Americans—mainly Northerners—concluded that the final decision had to be made by the nation as a whole, while other Americans—mainly Southerners—concluded that the final decision had to be made by the states. Needless to say, the argument was not easily resolved.

For the time being, however, all of this lay off in the future. What was immediately important was the fact that the Great Compromise enabled the work of constitution making to go forward. James Madison had not succeeded in obliterating the states, but he had succeeded in counterbalancing them. Obliged now to share their authority with a vigorous and responsible national government, the states were now far more likely to achieve the rule of law.

Of course, the national government had to achieve the rule of law, too, and the task might present its own difficulty. The large republic of the United States might have built-in safeguards against tyrannical majorities, but it needed plenty of protection from other dangers. What the Founders had to decide now was which structural controls to use and how to build them into an effective republican government.

7

Public Virtue
and Auxiliary
Precautions

Concepts

Public Virtue
Separation of Powers
Checks and Balances
Original Consent
Periodic Consent
Filtered Consent
Merging of virtue and Self-Interest

Signing of the Constitution: All brakes and no
engine. (Library of Congress)

President Adams Makes Peace with France

"How shall I describe to you my sensations and reflections at the moment?" The question was written in 1809, when John Adams could look back with some detachment. Ten years earlier, however, no detachment was possible. In 1798, Adams, second president of the United States, sitting in his Philadelphia office, had just finished reading a letter from George Washington. He had learned that the general was rejecting his, Adams', recommendations for appointments to high military command, and instead was insisting on his own. At the head of the list, as inspector general of the army, was the name of Alexander Hamilton. Hamilton was in effect being put in charge of the U.S. military.

Only recently, within the past few weeks, had the pieces of the puzzle come together for Adams. Though in theory he was chief executive of the United States and head of the Federalist party, in fact, so it now seemed, he was neither. The powerful members of his own cabinet had all turned out to be agents of Alexander Hamilton. Oliver Wolcott, secretary of the treasury, William McHenry, secretary of war, Timothy Pickering, secretary of state, were getting their ideas—nay, were taking their orders— from Hamilton. They were showing him secret correspondence. They were huddling with him to determine the policies of the government. They were conspiring with him to do who-knew-what with respect to the French War.

And Congress? Congress was dominated by the so-called High Federalists—Fisher Ames, Uriah Tracey, Theodore Sedgwick, Harrison Gray Otis—and they, in turn, were dominated by Alexander Hamilton. Hamilton! A private citizen. A simple lawyer. And now, apparently, he controlled Washington too. By arrangement, the old general would place him at the head of an American army, and the army would proceed to make war on France, on the allies of France, on the American friends of France, and quite certainly on the possessions of France in the Western Hemisphere.

Nor were these suppositions farfetched. Adams didn't yet know the worst. Hamilton was also in contact with Gen. James Wilkinson, commander of American forces in the West, and with a Venezuelan adventurer named Francisco de Miranda. Once the army of fifty thousand was whipped into shape, Wilkinson would board the flatboats waiting for him at Cincinnati and launch an expedition against New Orleans, while Miranda would go filibustering in South America. Hamilton would become the American Napoleon.

And if Hamilton's political rival, Jefferson, resisted this grand scheme, what then? Well, Jefferson and his followers would have to be broken. "Let a force," Hamilton wrote to Sedgwick, "be drawn towards Virginia for which there is an obvious pretext—and then let measures be taken to act upon the laws, and put Virginia to the Test of resistance." If Virginia bowed to Hamilton's army, the Jeffersonians would give no further trouble.

Of course, the success of these plans depended absolutely on going to war with France. No war, no Napoleon. But the prospect of war was coming along nicely. France had been outraged by the signing of Jay's Treaty with England (engineered by Hamilton), and from that point Franco-American relations had gone downhill. President Adams had sent commissioners to Paris to work through the difficulties, and the commissioners had been ignored and insulted. Soon French warships had begun

USS Constellation Dueling with *L'Insurgent* on high
seas: Peace came at a politically high price. (Library
of Congress)

potshooting at American merchantmen, and finally all hell had broken loose at sea.
Now, U.S. frigates were battling French cruisers almost daily, while channels of
diplomacy remained icebound. Fisher Ames explained the policy all too candidly.
"Wage war," he said, "and call it self-defense; forbear to call it war, on the contrary, let
it be said that we deprecate war . . . tell the citizens of danger and bring them to war
gradually."

But now, suddenly, the president's eyes were open. With the receipt of
Washington's letter, the last piece of the puzzle had fallen into place. "Honest John
Adams," they called him, "Atlas of the Revolution." Indeed he was honest and indeed
he was brave, but Adams, alas, was no politician. He had gotten himself into this mess
by failing to choose his own cabinet, by refusing to cultivate his own congressional
following, and by grasping too loosely the reins of his own party. Now he was isolated
and alone.

There was, however, one thing Adams could do. He could bring the undeclared
war with France to an end. No war, no Napoleon. Of course, such an action would
split his own party down the middle and throw the upcoming election to Jefferson.
Yet do it he must. Going over the head of Pickering, his disloyal secretary of state,
Adams wrote to William Vans Murray, U.S. minister to The Hague, and ordered him to
Paris at once. The president was willing to settle the French quarrel immediately—
single-handedly if he must. He may not be master of his own house, but he was still in
charge of U.S. foreign policy.

Hamilton and the High Federalists were dumbfounded, of course. They saw Adams' move as the workings of "a vain, jealous, and half-frantic mind." But it was nothing of the kind. By careful design, the federal Constitution had apportioned certain powers in certain ways, on the assumption that too much power in too few hands spelled trouble. In moving to block Hamiltonian, John Adams was behaving exactly as the Founders intended him to. The separations of power, the checks and balances were put there for the purpose of thwarting tyranny and protecting freedom. And here they were in action, working beautifully.

It was just such scenarios that occupied the mind of James Madison at the Constitutional Convention in Philadelphia. At the time, of course, the war with France and the political turbulence accompanying it were still more than a decade in the future. But Madison knew that sooner or later such conflicts would occur. They were inherent in human nature.

They were also inherent in the new federal government. In the old Confederation nothing like this could have happened. Lacking sovereignty, that government could have embarked on a foreign war only with the greatest of difficulty; and as for power, the Confederation never had enough of it to squabble over. The new government, by contrast, was to be both sovereign and vigorous, with all the means necessary for waging war. It had to be approached with utmost caution lest it slip out of control. "In framing a government which is to be administered by men over men," wrote Madison, "the great difficulty lies in this: you must first enable the government to control the governed; and in the next place oblige it to control itself."

Accordingly, the Founders now turned to the issue of control and faced it squarely. How, they asked themselves, could this high-powered, fully sovereign government be made to operate as an instrument of liberty?

Public Virtue in the Constitution

Their first answer to the question was still *public virtue*. True, there had been some setbacks for public virtue during the Confederation period. Factions had gotten out of hand in several state governments, and self-interest had now and then decayed into plain selfishness. Yet the fundamental faith of the Founders remained undimmed. "It must be assumed that the people will have sufficient virtue and intelligence to select men of virtue and wisdom," said Madison, "or no theoretical checks, no form of government, can render us secure."

But how, exactly, did one insure public virtue's survival? Surely there was no way to write *that* into the Constitution. The very nature of public virtue defied accurate description, and the problem of preserving it was elusive in the extreme. Much of the task simply fell to the citizen, each according to his own conscience.

A New Understanding of Virtue

During the Revolution, the discussion of virtue had often been inspired by the classical republics. Theirs, we recall, was a virtue that emphasized iron discipline and rigorous self-denial. "I labor to procure a free constitution," said John Adams,

and if my children do not prefer this to ample fortune, to ease and elegance, they are not my children, and I care not what becomes of them. They shall live upon thin diet and wear mean clothes, and work hard with cheerful hearts and free spirits. Let them revere nothing but religion, morality, and liberty.

This ascetic and unsmiling concept of virtue was most easily maintained during the war itself, when threats posed by the enemy were close at hand.

Yet it was this sort of virtue, apparently, that most easily decayed. As the threat of the British dissipated, so too did the intensity of Americans' patriotic commitment, and the narrowest sort of self-interest took its place. It was the politics of self-interest, more than anything else, that so appalled the Founders during the Confederation period.

However, time and distance were gradually imparting a new perspective to the virtue/self-interest dichotomy. On reflection, many of the Founders had begun to understand that the classical kind of virtue, with its spartan simplicity and tinges of fanaticism, could never win against the self-interest so prominent in human nature. In the long run, it would lose every time.

Perhaps the more profitable thing to think about was not virtue *versus* self-interest but virtue *and* self-interest combined. If the energetic, commercial society was a good thing, as the Founders were coming to realize, one must assume such a society to be *acquisitive* in nature, not self-denying. It would feature promoters, speculators, entrepreneurs, and all manner of self-interested behavior—some of it undoubtedly to an extreme.

The question was: did such behavior necessarily produce corruption? Many of the classical republicans might well say yes. But the more contemporary, Enlightenment thinkers would probably disagree. The Founders themselves, as noted earlier, were men of self-interest who had not become corrupt. It was possible, in the context of American values and the General Religion, to maintain a high sense of patriotic responsibility while at the same time pursuing material gain.

Ending Patronage

One key to the virtue puzzle was the idea of independency. In order for the republican citizen to remain virtuous in a world of self-interest, he had to be his own boss. If he could not, for some reason, control his personal actions, it was unlikely that he could meaningfully participate in the political process. Self-government literally had to begin with the self.

Thus, logically, the way of life associated with patronage had to be brought to an end. The republican citizen needed to put aside the flattering and groveling associated with patronage and stand on his own two feet. *Dependency* had to give way to *in*dependency.

Accordingly, Americans like Thomas Jefferson proposed a new sort of relationship to replace the patronage connection. The friendship connection, they suggested, was much preferable, for it would be based on human dignity. With the friendship connection, one would not have to go to a superior, hat in hand, and beg favors; one could stand proud and self-reliant. If there was a position to be filled, let it be filled by the most qualified candidate, and if there was a favor to be granted, let it go to the most truly deserving. The only aristocracy in a republic, wrote Jefferson to Adams, should be an "aristocracy of talent and virtue."

These, of course, were not constitutional propositions. The Founders imagined, however, that the Constitution could be designed in such a way as to be free of patronage in its own operation, and thus to discourage patronage in society. The electoral college, for example, was supposed to work that way. Its electors would be chosen solely on the basis of merit. They would convene as total strangers. They would be free to vote their consciences. And the man they elected president would not be in a position to reward any of them with political plums. Without—it was hoped—cliques, factions, parties, or personal connections, the electoral college would be the nearest thing imaginable to Jefferson's aristocracy of talent and virtue.

Constitutional Provisions

Then, too, if public virtue could not precisely be mandated in a constitutional text, perhaps it could be promoted psychologically. The Founders reasoned that one drawback of the state governments had been their inability to bring public virtue forward. The virtue itself had been present in the populace—the success of the Revolution attested to that—but the most virtuous citizens had not been attracted to government service. After all, what patriot wanted to be known for his affiliation with a faction-ridden state regime, or, on the

national level, with a government of impotence? Because the new federal government would be neither tyrannical nor impotent, that in itself might draw the virtuous to its banner.

Beyond this there were at least two devices that might aid in bringing public virtue forward. The Founders made sure that both of them were utilized.

The Representative Principle. No large republic, of course, could operate in the way that the Athenian democracy had. Because it was physically impossible for all citizens to play a direct role in the governing process, they necessarily had to work through elected representatives.

But there was more to the representative principle than that. Representatives might be men of the people; they might reflect the values and interests of their constituents; but they were not just anyone off the street. In the very process of being elected, representatives were set apart from their fellows, endowed with a certain prominence, and given sobering tasks to perform. Owing to these circumstances, it was believed that they were more likely to behave virtuously.

And possibly, they were more likely to be virtuous in the first place. After all, given an educated, responsible electorate, would the voters knowingly elect a scoundrel? Probably not. Even today, when many ethical standards are relaxed, we still impose a rigid morality on our politicians. We roundly condemn them for engaging in practices—such as influence peddling—which we take for granted elsewhere.

The principle of representation, then, did not contemplate government by everyone—it contemplated government by the wise and the virtuous.

Methods of Indirect Election. The same was true for the methods of indirect election the Founders placed in the Constitution. If, let us say, the people as a whole were to elect a single representative to exercise the powers of government, it is possible that, for one reason or another, the choice might be made unwisely. If, on the other hand, the people were divided into districts, each of which elected a *separate* representative, it stands to reason that at least some of the districts would make a better choice. Furthermore, if these representatives gathered together and elected a representative of their own, he would be even further removed from the tendency to make mistakes.

It was another principle inspired by the classical experience. In the Athenian democracy large factions had been swayed by the eloquence of a demagogue. In time, the passions he had aroused would cool down—usually after it was too late—and the people would sorely regret their haste. The Founders hoped that by using representation in place of direct democracy, leaders at the top of government would be insulated from the passions and tumults below.

There was something else about indirect election. On the lowest level, a person of merely local reputation—and presumably local outlook—could be elected. If I have to please only the voters in my own neighborhood, I might easily clear that first hurdle. However, on the second and third levels, the process becomes more difficult. If I am to gain election there, my purely local reputation does me no good. Only those known throughout the nation could repeatedly survive electoral playoffs.

Such devices helped insure that none save the truest of patriots would be able to secure high office. The Founders supposed that many good, worthy people would find their way into Congress. To find their way into the Presidency, however, they must be cut to the measure of a George Washington.

The Blessings of Liberty

Virtue in government was, of course, more than the virtue of elected officials. More importantly, it was the virtue of the people themselves—public virtue. For preserving this kind of virtue, the Founders had little to offer. Some of them, in fact, supposed that the virtue of the people could never be sustained in the long run: citizens would tire of their public responsibilities, would grow complacent about their liberty, and would absorb themselves in private matters. The cry for "bread and circuses" during the decline of the Roman Empire seemed to suggest how public virtue ended up.

Other of the Founders were more optimistic. Based on a different reading of human nature, this group believed that rational people who enjoyed the blessings of liberty would never lose their bearings. After all, they pointed out, the Puritan forefathers had known prosperity and comfort, and in the end, far from going soft, had been all the more determined to remain free. It was possible, then, that republicanism was psychologically self-sustaining. It was the sort of question that only history could answer.

Auxiliary Precautions

At their most hopeful, the Founders did not suppose that freedom could be guaranteed by virtue alone. They realized that all people would not be virtuous some of the time and that some people would not be

Suffragettes campaigning for the 19th Amendment:
All have a chance to change the rules. (Library of Congress)

virtuous any of the time. "A dependence on the people is, no doubt, the primary control on the government," wrote Madison, "but experience has taught mankind the necessity of auxiliary precautions."

Auxiliary precautions was Madison's term for those structural controls of human action worked out by the Enlightenment philosophers. Given the large republic with its uncertain hazards, given a potent national sovereignty, and given the danger of human capriciousness, the Founders were determined to make the Constitution's controls as strong as possible. They wanted a backup system that would be little short of foolproof.

At their disposal was the entire inventory of Enlightenment ideas together with their own historical experience. Also, in their recent decade of experimentation, they had learned for themselves something of what did and didn't work. Finally, they had developed the rule of law as a kind of calculus for their constitutional engineering. They had come to understand that in a republic the law alone must rule, and that governmental structure must be consciously designed to eliminate the wills of men. The question now was, what specific structural controls would best insure that outcome?

Consent

If one could institutionalize the rule of law one principle at a time, the best place to begin would be with the principle of consent. Consent was basic to the very notion of republican government and was prominently featured in the Declaration of Independence. If the government was not acceptable to the people it governed, then all else made little difference.

And consent was indeed where the Founders began. To a man, they agreed that the government on their drawing board must be popular in character. Yet to them the term *popular* did not mean *democratic,* for as we have seen, they fully shared the Enlightenment's suspicion of democracy. In a total democracy (like ancient Athens), the people themselves grasped the reins of power, and factions of them sometimes made off with the whole chariot. In a merely *popular* government, by contrast, the voice of the people, while always audible, did not drown out the voice of wisdom, experience, or common sense. What the Founders really believed in was government by the *virtuous.*

Original Consent. To begin with, the Founders wished to secure consent for the form of government they were proposing. In chapter four we termed this *original* consent. During the Revolution, when state governments were first being organized, it was assumed that consent to a new form of government might be registered by the retiring colonial assembly. But Massachusetts thought otherwise. One cannot properly ask an old government to consent to a new one, said the Massachusetts republicans; one must *go back to the people* for such authority. Accordingly, a special convention was called and the new frame of government put to a vote.

The Founders now followed the Massachusetts example. They did not ask the existing state governments to ratify the new Constitution; they asked the people themselves to do so. The citizens of every hamlet and crossroads must get together, debate the proposal pro and con, and then individually make up their minds. Only thus would the government be fully republican.

For the same reason, the Founders included a workable amendment process. It was conceivable that *this* generation might consent to the Constitution and some *future* generation might not. The power of amendment gave every generation its say. The old Confederation was virtually amendment-proof. When twelve of the the thirteen states had agreed to modify the government so as to allow for limited taxation, the plan was squelched by Rhode Island's lone dissent. The new Constitution, by contrast, would be amended repeatedly. The process was admittedly complicated: two-thirds of the Congress and three-fourths of the states would have to agree to any proposed modification. But once this true consensus for change was achieved, the change became law. As a consequence, all Americans, including ourselves, have had a chance to approve the rules of the game.

Periodic Consent. Not only must the *form* of the government win consent, so too must the officers who would staff it and the policies it would pursue. We termed this second kind of consent periodic. With periodic consent in mind, the Founders determined that congressional elections must be held every two years, presidential elections every four years, and senatorial elections every six. (The terms of the senators were staggered so that every two years a third of the senate seats would come up for reelection.) The significance of such short terms is easy to miss. But consider that one of the Founders, Alexander Hamilton, favored the notion of a president serving for life. The others, it seemed, wanted far closer and far more continuous contact with the people.

Filters of Consent. Having ensured popular government, the Founders now sought to ensure against democratic. One way to achieve this would have been by placing restrictions on the right to vote. Most states had such restrictions themselves, usually based on property ownership. The Founders, however, decided not to add any new ones of their own. Accordingly, if the states maintained the existing requirements for voting, those became the federal requirements too; and, if the states did away with them, so did the federal government.

Instead, the Founders proposed a subtler way to hold back democracy: they would process consent through a set of filters. One such filter, already mentioned, was the use of representatives to convey the popular will. Another was the indirect election. Members of the Senate, for example, were to be chosen not by the people directly but by the legislatures of the various states. Choosing the president was even more indirect. The people would first vote for electors, apportioned according to state population. These, in turn, would convene in a special electoral college—like the college of cardinals that elects the pope—to cast their individual votes. By design, the process was to be so convoluted that the people would not know until the electors had finished their work who was even being considered for president.

The staggered elections and overlapping terms of office constituted a final kind of filter. Rather than leaving the entire government up for grabs at a given point in time, the Founders worked to insure that only bits and pieces of it would be exposed. For the House of Representatives, where the close scrutiny of the people seemed important, elections had to be held

SEPARATION OF POWERS

Placing the rule making and rule enforcing powers in different hands.

every two years. For the Senate, where greater remoteness was favored, the term was lengthened to six years. A four-year term for the Presidency essentially split the difference.

Consent laid the foundation for popular government and supplied the central element of the rule of law. Yet consent by itself, even filtered and purified, did not insure freedom, as the experience of the states had clearly shown. The Constitution had to provide against the day when a majority faction might seize the government and try to impose its own will. If the law was truly to rule, it had to be impossible to misuse the law.

Separation of Powers

The first and most important auxiliary precaution employed by the Founders was called separation of powers. In order to appreciate how and why it was used, we must catch a glimpse of its historical evolution.

Separating Rule Maker and Rule Enforcer. Back in twelfth-century England, when Henry II was consolidating the Norman conquest, the English judicial system was merely an arm of the king's authority. As Henry would travel about the realm, he would be asked to settle disputes between private parties, and in his capacity as sovereign he would do so. But the caseload, as we might say today, soon grew to the point where Henry, with other things on his mind, delegated most judicial business to a group of appointed judges. The judges were not independent of the king—they were his personal henchmen. Their use in the situation was merely a matter of convenience.

Now suppose, for a moment, that Henry, who had his share of enemies, decided he wanted to get someone. Controlling the law as he did, the job would not be too difficult. For example, in the case of Thomas à Becket, the Archbishop of Canterbury who managed to become a thorn in the king's side, Henry simply mentioned to a couple of his courtiers that it would be well to have Becket out of the way, and the courtiers went out and murdered him. The king found himself at odds with the church, to be sure, but not with the law. His own personal judges wouldn't dream of bringing him to justice.

Over the centuries, however, that situation gradually changed. The royal judges became used to working on their own and applying the law to particular cases. They forgot they were the king's hired men and became, instead, a power in their own right. Almost incredibly, they began to render decisions, when the requirements of justice so demanded, *against* the interests of the king.

For instance, in 1535 there was another celebrated case in England. Another Henry (Henry VIII) was on the throne, and another Thomas (Thomas More) was in the chancellery. And once again the two were

SEPARATION OF POWERS

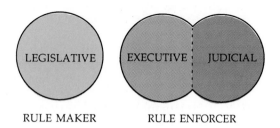

RULE MAKER   RULE ENFORCER

The traditional separation of Rule Maker and Rule Enforcer was modified by dividing the Rule Enforcer into two separate bodies (top) creating a three-way separation of powers (bottom).

THREE-WAY SEPARATION OF POWERS

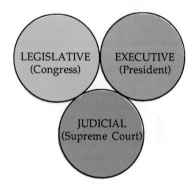

on a collision course. When More, an ardent Catholic, refused to condone Henry's divorce of his childless wife, the king decided to get him too. But thereafter the two cases diverged. So powerful had the law become in England—and so independent the judges—that until Thomas More violated some specific legal rule, there was nothing at all his antagonist could do to him. The law had become a bastion of liberty.

Philosophers of the Enlightenment noted both kinds of examples. They concluded that whenever the rule-making and

Judicial Independence

The Founders, in their wisdom, made federal judges as independent as possible. How did this independence affect their behavior? A tantalizing clue is offered by the career of Earl Warren, U.S. chief justice from 1953 to 1969, and one of the most influential jurists of all time.

Even in the beginning, Warren-watchers might have noted that beneath the man's political exterior resided a markedly different sort of individual. For instance, Warren the politician, always going with the flow, had once been a virulent race-baiter. In the aftermath of Pearl Harbor, he had taken the lead in rounding up California's Japanese and sending them to concentration camps. After the hysteria died down, however, the other Earl Warren peeped out. "Whenever I thought of the innocent little children who were torn from home, school friends, and congenial surroundings, I was conscience stricken," he wrote. At the end of the war, Warren suddenly emerged as a champion of Japanese-American civil rights.

In most matters, however, politics held Warren's inner man in check. As a young right-of-center district attorney, he realized, for example that it was most impolitic to appear soft on Communists, unionists, or violent criminals, and in the famous *Point Lobos* case, he showed just how hard he could be. He held the three defendants—all union men accused of murder—all night in his office, denied them counsel, and later stacked the jury against them. He was widely accused of playing to the McCarthyite frenzy of the day.

rule-enforcing functions were kept in completely separate hands—as in the case of Thomas More—it was appreciably more difficult to misuse the power of government. The principles of generality and prospectivity, so central to the rule of law, were far likelier to be respected when those who made the laws could not enforce them, and those who enforced the laws could not make them.

Besides, when the powers of government were separated, a curious new psychology took hold. The rule maker, jealous of his own authority, often refused to cooperate with the rule enforcer and vice-versa. Each of them eyed the other warily, suspicious of his every move, for the self-interest of each was at stake. It was a classic case of divided power leading to a desirable outcome.

Three-Way Separation of Powers. In the English experience only two powers were recognized: rule maker and rule enforcer. Parliament made the laws and the courts enforced them. Gradually, however, philosophers of the Enlightenment came to recognize a third kind of power, the executive. We speak of the executive (the president) today partly as a rule-maker—he presents a legislative program to Congress—and partly as a rule-enforcer—he arrests criminals and brings them to trial. However one views the nature of executive authority, it has become the greatest single power in government, and with respect for that fact, the Founders decided to separate it too. In the American system, then, there was to be a complete separation of powers and it was to extend to all three branches of government.

But that was the political Warren, the eager young man on the make. What about Warren the chief justice—now well insulated from politics? In the strangely similar case of *Miranda v. Arizona* (1966), he turned loose a patently guilty Ernesto Miranda (along with other defendants) because:

> In each [case], the defendant . . . was cut off from the outside world. In none of these cases was the defendant given a full and effective warning of his rights at the outset of the interrogation process. In all of the cases, the questioning elicited oral admissions . . . which were admitted at their trials.

Judicial independence, then, turned Earl Warren inside out. The moment he was free from the constraints of electoral politics, the long buried man of conscience began to come forth. Within a year of his appointment, the new chief justice had persuaded the Court to unanimously strike down school segregation—and that was only the beginning.

Chief Justice Earl Warren: Independence turned him inside out. (Library of Congress)

Drawing from the experience of the states, the Founders did not concern themselves with merely proclaiming that the powers should be separate. Rather, they sought specific ways to *make* them so. That the separation of powers should be a practical, working reality became the central feature of American constitutional design.

In the first place, each branch of government was laid out to be independent of both the others and as self-sufficient as possible. Each had its own budget. Each hired its own personnel. Each saw to the qualifications of its own officers. If the executive and legislative branches should happen to be quarreling—not a remote possibility—the executive could not hit below the belt by turning off the lights in the capitol building.

Each branch had to have its own separate will, in other words. It also had to have its own separate constituency. For the executive and legislative officers, different groups of voters must take part in different elections at different times. Thus, the president would be chosen in the quadrennial elections, congressmen in the biennial elections, and senators by an indirect and round-about process in the various states.

The judicial branch, the critically important rule enforcer, was made completely and utterly independent. Federal judges, once they were appointed and confirmed, held their offices for life. Their salaries were insured against possible reduction. Nothing was permitted to disturb their responsibility to the law.

TOTAL SEPARATION OF POWERS

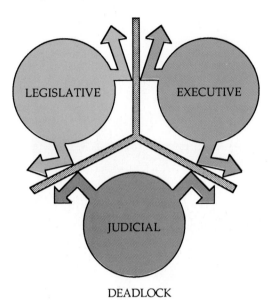

DEADLOCK

With total separation of powers, there is the risk of deadlock (above) or that one of the powers will obtain total control (below).

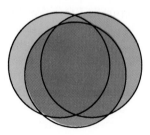

TYRANNY

The accumulation of all powers, legislative, executive, and judiciary, in the same hands, whether of one, a few, or many, and whether hereditary, self-appointed, or elective, may justly be pronounced the very definition of tyranny.
—James Madison

An Energetic Executive. Having separated the three branches of government, the Founders turned attention to the question of how much power to invest in each of them. There was an argument (based on colonial experience with the British governors) for making the executive weak. His term in office might be severely limited. His powers of appointment might be restricted. His very office might be pluralized and assigned to a committee. That way, presumably, the executive's tyrannical ambitions would be curbed at the outset.

Here again, though, the Founders had learned much from their own experience. Weakness in the executive branch of state government had not promoted the rule of law; it had only promoted legislative tyranny. The lesson seemed clear. Executive and legislature must not only be separate; they must have roughly comparable power.

What about the republican argument, often repeated, that the executive should be pliant to the will of the people (as expressed through the legislature)? Here, the shadow of Athens again flitted past. Executives, thought Hamilton, should not be pliant; they should not bend to every breeze of popular passion. They should, rather, be accountable. Their performance should be judged, and judged closely—but only from a perspective of time and distance. In the short run, it may be necessary for an executive to put his foot down against some passing enthusiasm. In the long run, after sober reflection, everyone—including some sheepish congressmen—may thank him for it.

Accordingly, the executive was deliberately made "energetic." He was given a four-year term of office and ample powers of appointment. Most importantly, he was given the veto power. If a bill was passed which he judged to be against the true public interest, it was in his power (and certainly in his duty) to quash it. With the veto power he could also protect his own independence from an imperial-minded Congress, and thus maintain the separation of powers. On the other hand, Congress could also protect itself from *him*, for the veto power was a qualified one and could be overridden by a two-thirds vote of both houses. What the veto did was enable the president to mobilize his virtue as well as his power, and to appeal in a systematic way to the virtue of Congress.

The vigorous, energetic executive was a necessary part of the vigorous, energetic national government.

Checks and Balances

Separation of powers was highly effective at promoting the rule of law. With each branch of government operating independently of every other, the laws of the nation would in all likelihood be made and enforced blindly. By itself, however, separation of powers tended to create deadlock. Suppose, for example, that in some hypothetical government two wholly separated powers find themselves in political disagreement. What danger appears? Each power may flatly refuse to cooperate with the other, bringing the business of both to a standstill. Besides, in order to break the deadlock, each of them may try to corrupt, subvert, or even destroy the other.

The case of President Andrew Johnson showed just how it could happen. Johnson, a Southerner and a Democrat, succeeded to the Presidency on the death of Abraham Lincoln and found himself facing a Congress of northern Republicans. In the ensuing test of wills neither side would budge. So extreme grew the passions that Congress passed an entire legislative program and Johnson vetoed every jot of it.

Andrew Johnson: Without checks and balances the affair may have ended badly. (Library of Congress)

Had there been no provision in the Constitution for such an impasse, the affair may have ended badly. Even as it was, Congress became so angry with the president that it tried to remove him from office.

One remedy for such deadlocks was checks and balances. These were also examples of divided power. They operated on the same assumption of self-interest as the separation of powers did. Yet checks and balances were different in that they divided *the same kind* of power between two authorities.

Take the power of appointment, for example. It would have been easy for the Founders to bestow this authority on one officer alone, such as the president. But if the president went on a rampage with it, Congress could only fight back with a deadlock. So the Founders divided the power of appointment, giving part of it to

Advise and Consent

For those who have not experienced it, the psychology of divided power is difficult to describe. It is a curious blend of hostility and friendliness, cooperation and obstruction. Allen Drury's 1959 novel, *Advise and Consent*, attempts to explore that psychology in detail. In the story, the U.S. president, himself a rather doubtful character, has nominated the even more doubtful Robert Leffingwell to be secretary of state. The novel goes on to probe the minds and hearts of the senators who must now either confirm or oppose the nomination.

In the following excerpt, the president has just told Senator Orrin Knox that the Soviets have stolen a march on the United States and landed men on the moon:

"It is against that background," [the president] said quietly, "that I must ask you to permit Bob Leffingwell to be confirmed."

Senator Knox stared at him thoughtfully.

"How do I know you're telling me the truth?" he asked calmly, and the President looked at him in some disbelief.

"Do you think I would fabricate something as lurid as that?" he inquired dryly.

"You might," Orrin said. "But," he added quickly, "I don't think you are. I fail to see, however, why it should change my attitude about your nominee. If anything, I should think it would make me even more determined that he not be confirmed."

"I feel he is what we need in this situation," the President said with a quiet insistence. "It is inconceivable to me that you would stand in his way under the circumstances. I am asking you as a patriotic American to permit him to assume the office."

"Well, by God," Senator Knox said sharply, "so now it's patriotism, is it? Well, let me tell you, Mr. President. To me it's patriotic to do what I deem best in my own judgment for the country; it isn't to give in to you and let you ride roughshod over everything decent just because you claim it's patriotic and imply that those who oppose you are unpatriotic. What kind of a damned slippery argument is that?"

"Senator," the President said, "do you have any conception of what I have just been telling you?"

"I have a conception," Senator Knox said shortly. "I also have a conception of what is decent and honorable and best for the country which I think is just as good on the moon as it is on earth or Venus or Mars or any other place we're going to go to. And my conception has no room for Bob Leffingwell and his wishy-washy attitudes toward the mortal enemies of the United States. Why, good Lord. You know as well as I do exactly what they're going to start doing tomorrow. They're going to start pressuring us as they never have before. And you want an obliging stooge like Bob Leffingwell to deal with *that*? What kind of conception do *you* have?"

In the end, of course, all is well for the United States, even though one Senator, Utah's Brigham Anderson, who is being blackmailed in order to secure his vote of confirmation, winds up condemning the nomination and committing suicide.

CHECKS AND BALANCES

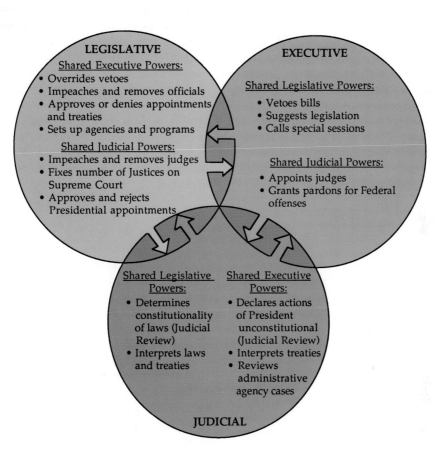

LEGISLATIVE

Shared Executive Powers:
- Overrides vetoes
- Impeaches and removes officials
- Approves or denies appointments and treaties
- Sets up agencies and programs

Shared Judicial Powers:
- Impeaches and removes judges
- Fixes number of Justices on Supreme Court
- Approves and rejects Presidential appointments

EXECUTIVE

Shared Legislative Powers:
- Vetoes bills
- Suggests legislation
- Calls special sessions

Shared Judicial Powers:
- Appoints judges
- Grants pardons for Federal offenses

Shared Legislative Powers:
- Determines constitutionality of laws (Judicial Review)
- Interprets laws and treaties

Shared Executive Powers:
- Declares actions of President unconstitutional (Judicial Review)
- Interprets treaties
- Reviews administrative agency cases

JUDICIAL

Interesting Paradox: The same kind of powers must be shared to maintain separation of powers.

the president and part to the Senate. (The president could nominate candidates for high-level office but the Senate would have to confirm them.) They similarly divided the power to make war (the president could conduct the war, but only Congress could declare it) and the power to conclude treaties.

Dividing the same power between two different branches imposed a more cooperative psychology. No president seeking to fill a high vacancy would care to have one nomination after another hacked up by the Senate. As a consequence, he would take care to nominate only those who stood a good chance of confirmation. And for its part, the Senate would not particularly enjoy playing the hatchet man. It would be disposed to act favorably on any serious nomination.

To illustrate the effect that checks and balances could have, let us return to the hypothetical deadlock outlined above. Two powers of government—let us say president and Congress—face each other in a grim stalemate. We will now add a check and balance arrangement by giving one of them an executive veto and the other a legislative override. (Both, of course, are essentially the same kind of power.) The result is startling. The respective powers still remain separate, but they suddenly find reasons to cooperate. The legislator, with one eye on a possible veto, only wants to pass bills that he seriously expects to be ratified, and the executive, with one eye on a possible override, resorts to his veto only sparingly.

The American System

These three elements—*consent, separation of powers,* and certain *checks and balances*— carefully combined in the support of public virtue, comprise the heart of the American constitutional system. We can see how that system was intended to operate by considering another hypothetical case.

Suppose there is a dominant faction in the U.S. Congress that sponsors a tyrannical piece of legislation. The bill in question singles out a religious minority—we'll call them the Druids—for unfair treatment. At risk is the principle of generality and, ultimately, the entire rule of law.

Admittedly, there is a good chance that even if signed into law, the legislation may not really be dangerous, for it would have to be enforced by the courts of the land— not by the anti-Druid Congress that passed it—and the courts might refuse to cooperate. Separation of powers, in other words, might neutralize it right off the bat.

But this bill never gets signed. The reason? The man who happens to be president recognizes its tyrannical dangers. He also recognizes that he won the recent election by only a few votes, and that Druids voted heavily in his favor. Both self-interest and public virtue incline him to view the bill askance and veto it. Now the question is whether the veto will be overridden.

That is always a possibility, of course, and in this case a lot of anti-Druid lawmakers are threatening loudly. But the president, in his veto message, appeals eloquently to congressional virtue. What have we come to, he asks, that we should persecute a religious minority the way Hitler did? That hits home. When a vote to override the veto is taken, there are enough virtuous legislators to block it.

Thus stymied, the lawmakers go back to the drawing board. Some features of the bill could be saved, they conclude, if the tyrannical ones were eliminated. They redraft the bill in an unobjectionable way and send it back for repassage, confident that this time the president will sign it. The system has acted—virtually automatically—to preserve the rule of law.

Inherent Devices

In addition to the Constitution's main controls, outlined above, there were a number of other ones which simply inhered in a constitutional system. Chief among them were:

Enumeration. By using a written constitution, the Founders could make use of the principle of enumeration. Certain powers

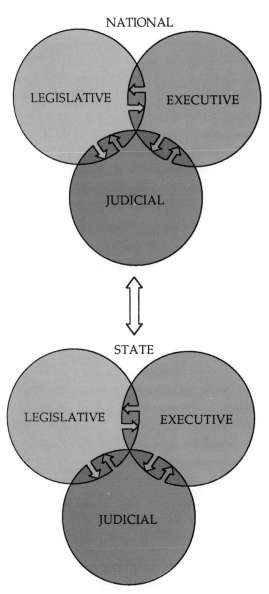

FEDERALISM

NATIONAL

The division of power between the National and State government.

could be assigned to the federal government and certain others to the states. And any power not specifically enumerated could not legitimately be claimed.

Elections. By making frequent use of the electoral process, the Founders also insured an active role for the people. It was not enough for the people merely to consent to the government passively; they must be actively involved in shaping it, staffing it, and above all, watching it. And that was a role Americans could play with gusto. Electioneering came to mean far more to them than simply settling abstract questions—it was the nation's first great participator sport.

Federalism. At first, few thought of federalism as anything more than a necessary compromise. But federalism, too, was a division of power, not between one branch of government and another, but between state and federal establishments. And it worked like the others did. State authorities, jealous of their prerogatives, would assuredly keep watch on the national government, and the national government would just as assuredly keep watch on the states.

Redundancy

Even with all the above in place, the Founders were far from complacent. After all, there was little in their experience or learning to suggest that republics would succeed easily. So, for good measure, they added further devices, accepting the redundancy as necessary.

Bicameralism. Congress was made bicameral—given two separate houses. (This would have been done even without the

BICAMERALISM

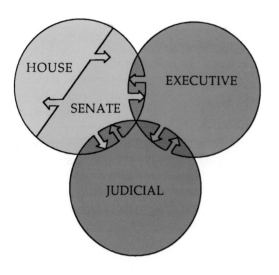

A two-house legislature, each endowed with a different character to check the other and maintain balance within.

Great Compromise.) Furthermore, each house was endowed with a different character, so that what might appeal to one would not necessarily appeal to the other. The House of Representatives, more democratic in nature, was designed to address the here-and-now, reflecting concerns and interests of the moment. By contrast, the Senate, distinctly more aristocratic, was not supposed to bend to every passing breeze, and most Senators have not done so. If there has been a pattern in the interaction of the two chambers, it has been that the House has passed bills that seem timely and popular, and the Senate, with its greater detachment and longer perspective, has killed them.

Powers of Investigation and Impeachment. Not quite like a check, nor yet like separation of powers was the authority of Congress to conduct investigations. This power was virtually unlimited, and its exercise has covered everything from weevils to Watergate. Some congressional investigations have seemed pointless or inane, and a few have actually been dangerous. (The McCarthy investigations of the early 1950s, which aimed to root Communists out of the government, created public hysteria instead.) Yet, on balance, the investigative power has been valuable. It has enabled the Congress to base its legislation on solid research. It has helped to keep the public informed and to unmask the very abuses the Founders feared. And it has served to remind the executive that he does not govern alone.

As an extension of the investigative power, Congress was given the authority to *impeach* high officials and remove them from office. So if, in spite of everything, a tyrant did come to power, Congress could return him to private life. It was up to the House of Representatives to impeach (indict) the errant officeholder, and up to the Senate to try him. Happily, the power has not been widely used. Andrew Johnson, impeached by the House in 1868, came within a single vote of conviction in the Senate, but that proceeding was politically rather than morally inspired, and its outcome did much toward keeping the impeachment process in bounds. The case of Richard Nixon was different. Had he not resigned under pressure, Nixon may well have been expelled from office—in precisely the way the Founders had planned.

Judicial Review. Several of the state governments employed a device known as judicial review. Justices of the state supreme

Chief Justice John Marshall: Deserved to be ranked with the founders. (Library of Congress)

court were given the authority to decide on the constitutionality of other government actions. So, if the state legislature passed a questionable law or the governor issued a dubious order, the judges could examine its constitutional legality. If pronounced unconstitutional, the action had no effect.

Such power, of course, was potentially dangerous. If given to either the executive or legislative branches, it would almost certainly be abused. But the judiciary seemed little inclined to such abuse. Lacking other authority, the judges could not use judicial review to further their own legislative program or persecute political enemies. And the fact that they were more or less above the fray of politics encouraged an objective point of view. Most judges have used the power safely.

Judicial review was not written into the federal Constitution, at least not in so many words. Yet the practiced lawyers who sat

in Philadelphia may well have supposed it to be there by implication. As long as constitutions depended upon the meaning of specific words, someone, somewhere had to decide what indeed was constitutional. The Founders quite possibly believed that judicial review was inescapable.

And so it was. In 1801, in *Marbury v. Madison*, the most important decision ever handed down by the U.S. Supreme Court, Chief Justice John Marshall, who deserves to be remembered as one of the Founders himself, gathered up his courage and declared a federal law unconstitutional. He chose his case shrewdly and awarded judgment to the very group that might otherwise have challenged his bold action. As a result, judicial review won public acceptance and remains with us still. Of all the redundant devices envisioned by the Founders, it has become the most widely discussed, the most controversial, and very likely the most significant.

The Finished Product

It was with a palpable sense of relief that the Constitutional Convention came to a close. Thirty-nine of the delegates affixed their signatures to the document they had argued and fretted over throughout the summer. A few, like Edmund Randolph, concluded with bitterness that they had compromised too much, but Franklin spoke for the majority when he said, "I consent, Sir, to this Constitution because I expect no better, and because I am not sure that it is not the best." It was mid-September now and cool breezes were wafting in off the Delaware. Carriages rattled into the dusty square and bore the Founders off to their distant homes. When a Mrs. Powel asked whether it was a republic or a monarchy

Executive Tyranny!

With the benefit of hindsight, we see the Constitution today much as its supporters (the Federalists) did: as a well-crafted, carefully balanced preserver of republican freedom. But how did it look to the doubters? In a single word, threatening. Not benefiting from our hindsight, the Anti-Federalists could see only tyranny in the Constitution's provision for a strong executive and vigorous central government.

James Lincoln of South Carolina was typical. "From a well-digested, well-formed democratic you are at once rushing into an aristocratic government," he cried. Pennsylvania's James Warren agreed. "The Constitution will result in an immediate aristocratic tyranny," he said, "that from the difficulty, if not the impracticability of its operation, must soon terminate in the most uncontrolled despotism!" George Mason of Virginia had still another set of doubts. "The executive and the Senate form a combination that cannot be prevented by the representatives," he fretted. "The executive and legislative powers thus connected will destroy all balances."

What point were the Anti-Federalists missing? Just this. A government with the proper structural controls can be vigorous and powerful and yet still maintain the rule of law. Indeed, it *must* be vigorous and powerful *in order* to maintain the rule of law. "A weak constitution," said Madison, "must necessarily terminate in dissolution. . . . Tyranny has perhaps oftener grown out of the assumptions of power [under] a defective constitution, than out of the full exercise of the largest constitutional authorities." That, as it turned out, was the view sanctioned by hindsight.

Anti-Federalist Edmund Randolph: Feared the power of the new government. (Library of Congress)

that the convention had decided on, Franklin replied that it was a republic, and added: "If you can keep it."

Government under the Constitution

1. People of the whole nation are sovereign—federal union divides exercise of sovereignty between central government and states.
2. Independent executive—chosen by electors.
3. Separate federal court system, with power to consider Constitutional questions and resolve disputes between states.
4. Congress may "lay and collect taxes, duties, imposts and excises."
5. Congress has power to regulate commerce with foreign nations, among the several states, and with Indian tribes.
6. Congress is composed of representatives who have definite tenure—House is chosen by popular vote, Senate by state legislatures.
7. Constitution may be amended with approval of 3/4 of the states.
8. Congress has implied as well as specific delegated powers.
9. The central government exercises its powers directly upon the people, and concurrently with state governments.

The Founders had done everything they could think of to insure that Americans would indeed keep their republic. They had employed every conceivable device for containing, controlling, fragmenting, and diffusing power. The finished product struck some as "all brakes

Government under the Articles of Confederation

1. States are sovereign.
2. No independent executive.
3. No federal courts—national laws are enforced by state courts.
4. No taxing power in Congress.
5. Congress has no power over interstate or foreign commerce.
6. Congress is an assembly of delegates chosen by state legislatures—delegates may be recalled at any time.
7. Articles may be amended only by the consent of all of the states.
8. Congress has only specific, delegated powers.
9. The central government cannot act directly upon the people.

and no engine," but no apologies were offered for that. For the Founders, it was far more important to bring the vehicle of government under control than to use it for setting speed records.

What the Founders had really done was draw up a document that perfectly embodied the Enlightenment's understanding of man. Human nature, as the Enlightenment philosophers had noted, was capable of both virtue and vice. The American Constitution had, in the words of James Madison, "separated man's virtues from his vices," encouraging the former and controlling the latter. Time alone would tell whether it succeeded.

We the Peo

...sure domestic Tranquility, provide f...
...nd our Posterity, do ordain and establi...

Section. 1. All legislative Powers her...
...Representatives.

Section. 2. The House of Representati...
each State shall have the Qualifications requi...
No Person shall be a Representative...
...nd who shall not, when elected, be an Inhabi...
...Representatives and direct Taxes shal...
...umbers, which shall be determined. by addin...

8

The Bill of Rights

Original constitution which later included Bill of
Rights (Library of Congress)

The Haun's Mill Massacre

Though she was no constitutional scholar, Amanda Smith could understand why certain freedoms, such as freedom of religion, needed more protection than government ordinarily afforded. As the bullets whined past her ear on that October day in 1838, she learned, rather pointedly, that religious persecution was not something out of the Old World or the dim past. It was alive and well in the United States.

The Warren Smith family had become converts to Mormonism in the early 1830s. They left Kirtland, Ohio, in the fall of 1838, when the church there came into difficulty, and headed for the new Zion in western Missouri. When they arrived, they found Caldwell County ablaze with passion and prejudice. The Old Settlers, as they called themselves, had been wreaking frontier violence on Mormon immigrants for several years; and the Mormons, weary of turning the other cheek, were beginning to retaliate. Bushwhacking and barnburning on both sides had escalated to the point where Governor Boggs, who had borne the persecution of the Mormons with remarkable calm, now suddenly declared war on them. "The Mormons," he wrote to John B. Clark of the state militia, "must be treated as enemies and *must be exterminated* or driven from the state." As the Smith party entered Caldwell County in late October, a state militia force under Col. Thomas Jennings was on its way to carry out the governor's orders.

The target they selected was the outlying settlement of Haun's Mill. Jacob Haun had built a small gristmill on the wooded banks of Shoal Creek at the edge of the Great Prairie, and other Mormon settlers had added a sawmill, a blacksmith shop, and a cluster of log houses. Smoke was curling from the chimneys and children were laughing and playing when the Smith party arrived on Tuesday afternoon, October 30, a mellow Indian Summer day. Haun and the others came out to greet them, while the Smith children, six in all, climbed down from the wagon and ran off to play. The residents were armed and noticeably nervous. Had the travelers seen any trouble?

No sooner had the horses been unhitched than Jenning's militia appeared, 240 strong, cantering out of the dust in military formation. Instantly there were whistles and yells for the women and children to run for the woods, and the settlers sprang for their rifles. David Evans swung his hat in the air and cried for peace—a peace of sorts had been formally arranged only two days earlier—but the heedless militiamen drew themselves into a three square formation and unlimbered their rifles. At a signal from Jennings, they opened fire.

Amanda grabbed the nearest of her children and dashed across a plank over the mill pond. As the women scrambled along the bank and up a small hill, the invaders shot at them like partridges, yelling and whooping when they scored. A young girl running next to Amanda flung her arms in the air and tumbled over a log as a bullet struck her. A part of her torn dress hung over the log, and the militiamen, supposing it to be the girl herself, gleefully peppered away at it.

But most of their fire was directed toward the blacksmith shop, where the men had taken refuge. Large chinks yawned between the logs in the building's sides, and through these the figures inside were clearly visible. Although they waved their hats frantically and repeatedly cried for quarter, none was given. Indeed, when old Thomas McBride stumbled out, wounded, and threw down his gun, one of the militiamen

A cartoon depicting Governor Boggs'
"Extermination Order": A blemish on the history of
liberty. (Library of Congress)

hacked him to pieces with a corn cutter. One after another, the others died too. It was like shooting cattle in a pen.

As a finish to their work, the Missourians entered the blacksmith shop to loot the bodies and give each an extra bullet. Under the bellows, trembling with fear, they found ten-year-old Sardius Smith, Amanda's oldest son, and apparently the sole survivor. His seven-year-old brother, wounded in the hip and desperately playing dead, overheard the conversation.

"Don't shoot," said one, "it's just a boy."

"It's best to hive them when we can," came the reply. "Nits make lice." And with that Sardius Smith had his brains blown out.

As the sun set red across the western prairie, Amanda Smith crept out of the bushes to find her dead husband and her dead and wounded children. Her money had been stolen, her wagon emptied, her horses driven off. "Whole damages," she reported sardonically, "are more than the state of Missouri is worth."

"I started the first of February for Illinois," she ended her narrative, "without money, (mob all the way), drove my own team, slept out of doors. I had five small children; we suffered hunger, fatigue and cold; for what? For our religion, where, in a boasted land of liberty, 'Deny your faith or die,' was the cry."

This wasn't Paris during the St. Bartholomew's Day Massacre or Castile at the height of the Inquisition; it was Missouri, famous today for winning football teams and Harry Truman. And Amanda Smith's only offense was being a Mormon.

Following the Constitutional Convention was a national debate over ratification. It was carried on in every town and hamlet, at busy crossroad taverns, on city street corners, and in backcountry meeting houses. As the Founders had intended, Americans came together and discussed the proposed new government, pro and con. Judging by the kinds of questions they raised—notably in a series of newspaper essays titled *The Federalist*—the debate was conducted on an extremely high level.

For the disciples of John Locke, it was a stunning instance of life imitating philosophy. In a strictly theoretical way, Locke had postulated that members of a community could assemble together and determine the form of their own government, and here, a century after Locke's writings, republicans were doing just that.

The Demand for a Bill of Rights

One clear message to come out of the ratification process was that the Constitution needed a bill of rights. That notion, too, ultimately came from John Locke. For, when he had discussed liberty in his *Treatise on Government*, Locke had not referred to separations of power or checks and balances, but to "natural rights." Man's rights to life, liberty, and property were endowed upon him by nature, Locke asserted, and government's only job was to protect them.

It was a peculiarly English idea. In the course of their history the English had talked a great deal about rights. The Magna Carta was essentially a recitation of rights. So was the English Bill of Rights, written under Locke's influence. Americans especially identified with the latter document, which they viewed as a part of their own

heritage. When they began writing their state constitutions during the Revolution, they frequently appended bills of rights to them.

Why the Constitution Did Not Include a Bill of Rights

At the Constitutional Convention the Founders had considered formulating their own bill of rights. But this brought them to ponder certain difficulties in the Lockean, rights-oriented approach to freedom. There were, first of all, some technical problems which bothered the lawyers among them. And beyond these was at least one major philosophical difficulty. In order to understand the American Bill of Rights, we need to have a secure grasp on the various objections they considered.

Technical Difficulties

Although the idea of natural rights was common enough, there was little agreement as to what such rights actually were or how they could be secured effectively. Three immediate problems seemed to stand in the way:

The Problem of Legal Definition. The first problem was that of casting any right into precise language. Take, for example, Locke's right to life. What, exactly, do those words mean, and where do they apply? Do convicted murderers have a right to life? Do enemy soldiers? Does an unborn child? If a madman comes at me with a knife, does he have a right to life which I somehow respect? In drafting the mechanics of the Constitution, language could be used with specific legal meanings in mind. In drafting a bill of rights, language often just got in the way.

Technology Versus Rights

One argument for the existence of implied rights in the U.S. Bill of Rights is that the Founders couldn't have imagined all the ways that later technology might be used to intrude upon rights. Electronic surveillance, for example. In James Madison's day there was no such thing, of course, but we have since raised it to a high art. In a world of satellite communications, eavesdropping antennae and computerized decoders, it is possible for us to listen in on telephone conversations around the world. Not coincidentally, the issue of privacy, which may not have seemed important in Madison's day, has suddenly become so.

Or consider some recent advances in chemistry. The perfection of sodium pentothol and other "truth serums" has made it possible to abridge rights in ways hitherto unimagined, for a single injection can make a victim spill everything. Other kinds of chemicals might conceivably be added to, say, a municipal water supply to create various kinds of disposition—langor, hostility, euphoria—in the populace. Such dispositions might also be produced, perhaps more easily, by skillful manipulation of the mass media.

The list goes on and on. Nuclear power and nuclear weapons-testing have created unimagined civil dangers, as has research into chemical and biological warfare. Genetic engineering raises the apocalyptic specter of man-made monsters. Recent forms of pollution—such as the toxic waste dumped into the Love Canal—give a whole new meaning to phrases in the Fifth Amendment.

If all of this sounds Orwellian, it was George Orwell who first called our attention to it. In *Nineteen Eighty-Four*, we recall, truth was continually victimized by the Thought Police, and Big Brother's TV cameras snooped everywhere. Science-fiction writers have taken it from there, inventing every imaginable invasion of rights from mass produced embryos (*Brave New World*), to emotional repression (*Fahrenheit 451*), to robotic tyranny (*Blade Runner*). Perhaps the ultimate derogation of rights was imagined in a story by Orson Scott Card, in which a victim was sentenced to die "by every means known to man." Each time he was executed, his existing consciousness—including the pain and horror of the execution—would be taped and programmed into another mind, and the whole thing would be repeated over again.

There is, then, something truly to be said for a concept of human rights that transcends the Founders' own listing of them. After all, the worst thing they could think of was an illegal tax on tea.

The Problem of Inclusion and Exclusion. A second problem appeared whenever someone tried to tally up rights into a specific list. What if my list includes ten rights and yours includes fifteen? Does this mean there are five rights, all of them possibly fundamental, that I never even thought fundamental, that I never even thought about? (How many rights that we both never thought about?) And, if so, do I lose those five rights forever just because I didn't put them down?

The Founders worried a great deal about this. Any specific listing of rights, they feared, would be accepted by the people as complete and definitive. But what if somehow they left out a right? Or, more probably, what if someone figured out a way to violate rights which were previously taken for granted? None of the Founders would have thought of including the right to drink pure water in the Constitution, but in our own time, when flouridation has become a public health issue, some people may wish they had.

The Problem of Enforcement. Finally, how, exactly, was a bill of rights supposed to be enforced? In a word, how were rights *against* government to be protected *by* government? With the Constitution's structural controls, there was usually the principle of self-interest at work, insuring that Johnny would cut the cake evenly because Billy got first choice of the pieces. With rights, the problem was different. One could explain to Johnny that Billy had an equal right to the cake—but then what? Would the boy holding the knife consider that argument sufficiently compelling?

Was the Idea of Rights Opposed to Government?

Growing out of the technical difficulties was a broader, deeper, and, for some, more troubling concern. James Madison believed that there was something faintly unruly about the whole idea of natural rights. Since these were the rights that people had enjoyed while living in a state of nature, the question was whether they were compatible with an ordered society. In a state of nature, freedom, for example, would seem to be more or less absolute. A person could do basically anything he wanted to as long as it didn't infringe upon the rights of someone else. In an ordered society, by contrast, the right to freedom

simply could not be absolute, no matter how liberal the government. There would always have to be restrictions and trade-offs based on the necessity of living together.

While all this was clear enough to Madison, it was not always clear to his contemporaries. Some of the more literal-minded of them supposed that a right was a right—period. If I have a right to liberty, it stands to reason that neither society nor government can infringe on it to the least degree. This sort of thinking cautioned against committing rights to paper in a specific legal document. For once the words were out there for all to see, they tended to take on an ideal quality. Interpreted too broadly, a bill of rights could move society beyond liberty and toward license.

Rights and the French Revolution

The hazards of a rights-oriented approach to freedom were nicely illustrated by the French Revolution, which was just then unfolding. Like the Americans, the French had been reading their Locke, and in August of 1789, the French National Assembly adopted its soon-to-be-famous Declaration of the Rights of Man. This document proclaimed that "Men are born, and always continue, free and equal in respect of their rights," which were defined as "liberty, property, security, and resistance to oppression."

When it came to putting the declaration into practice, however, the French ran into trouble. Just what did the words "liberty, property, security, and resistance to oppression" mean? How were these rights to be enforced? And, toughest of all, to whom did they apply?

They did not, apparently, apply to members of the aristocracy, who in 1792 were dragged from their prison cells and butchered in the streets. Nor were they available to the king, who met death on the guillotine a year later. The Girondins, the moderate party of the Revolution, discovered that the Rights of Man did not apply to them either, for when the Jacobins gained power in the Committee of Safety, they immediately began ordering Girondin executions. At last, it became clear that not even the Jacobins were safe. Robespierre, in a frenzy of suspicion, put Danton to the blade. Marat was assassinated. And in a final poetic twist, Robespierre himself was sentenced to death. It began to dawn on Frenchmen that the Rights of Man, so nobly enshrined in their declaration, did not protect anyone.

In the meantime, however, those same unenforceable rights were nothing less than dynamite among the masses, who in their innocence and desperation took them at complete face value. Why, they had a right—a *natural* right—to liberty. And they had an equally valid right to resist oppression—and to punish all oppressors. It was easy to see why they began falling into ranks behind the radicals.

Rights or Rule of Law?

Such difficulties accounted for much of the Founders' skepticism. They believed in human rights, true enough, but they were not certain that such rights could be adequately defined, enumerated, or enforced, and they wondered where a focus on rights might ultimately lead.

Moreover, several of them questioned the wisdom of going beyond the existing Constitution. If constitutional government worked, if it truly established the rule of law, then what, they asked, was the need for a bill of rights? Bills of rights, in the Lockean sense, were something to be declared against a *king*— a way of limiting the exercise of royal sovereignty. With constitutional self-government, by contrast, sovereignty remained with the people themselves. And what people, exercising their own sovereignty, would think of abridging free speech or peaceful assembly? In a sense, the Constitution itself was their bill of rights.

However, there were points to be made on the other side as well, and the Anti-Federalists lost no time in making them. After all, constitutional government, even with its many safeguards, was still the government of the majority, and there were always those cases where the powerless individual or the unpopular minority were at risk. (The rule of law, remember, is an ideal to be striven for, not a fact to be taken for granted.) Subsequent history would record several occasions in which not only the Constitution's structural controls but even a strongly worded Bill of Rights failed to protect some victims.

Besides, the Anti-Federalists were still highly suspicious of the proposed government's power. Anything that promised to limit—or better, to trim back—the scope of its authority looked good to them indeed. And a boldly drafted bill of rights seemed able to do just that.

Accordingly, the Federalists (those in favor of the Constitution's adoption) agreed to the inclusion of a bill of rights. They urged, however, that the Constitution be adopted in its present form, and that the bill of rights be added afterward by the amending process.

Drafting the Bill of Rights

Once committed to a bill of rights, the Founders strove to make it effective. They did not want a document which, like the Declaration of the Rights of Man, could not be enforced, and they most certainly did not want a document which would turn liberty into license. What they wanted was a set of amendments which, in real and practical ways, would expand the compass of freedom without cutting back the authority of free government. It was a tough order.

James Madison, fittingly enough, was the one commissioned to fill it. As a newly elected representative from the state of Virginia, he was given the task of sifting through the various proposals for a bill of rights and determining how the final document should be drafted.

His strategy for dealing with the difficulties before him was to draft the bill with civil rights, rather than natural rights in mind. Natural rights would be sweeping and abstract in tone—like Jefferson's "life, liberty, and the pursuit of happiness" in the Declaration of Independence—and they would savor of the absolute. Civil rights, on the other hand, would be stated more tentatively and carefully, emphasizing the need for restraint and self-control. Civil rights were the kind of rights one could enforce in the courts.

Broad Versus Narrow Drafting

Whenever legal language is used to draft a piece of legislation (or in this case a constitutional amendment), a basic choice must be made. One can use narrow, concrete, specific language, or one can use broad, general, abstract language. If I wished to confer a certain right on my students, I would have to make the same choice. I could say: "All students have a right to fair treatment"—which is pretty broad and general. Or I could say: "All students at this university, properly registered, enrolled in classes that I teach, if they reasonably believe they are receiving unfair treatment

by me or by the teaching assistants I employ, are entitled to a hearing by a panel of arbitrators consisting of one professor, one student, and one member of the outside community"—which is pretty narrow and concrete.

Each approach has its pros and cons. The narrow, concrete approach is not rhetorically stirring, and it is severely limited in scope. Not *all* students are entitled to fairness, it says, only a *few* students are, and it hedges fairness with all sorts of restrictions. But it has the wonderful quality of enforceability. Those who meet the qualifications are likely to get action if the issue winds up in court.

Contrast this with the broad, general approach. It asserts that *all* students have a right to fair treatment, a pretty bold declaration. But how would *it* stand up in court? Right away the lawyers would begin to quibble about the meaning of its wording. They would ask what "fair treatment" means. Fair to whom? Fair by what standards? Fair in the short run or fair in the long? And to what "students" does it apply? My students? Someone else's students? Students around the world? The case might well be thrown out of court.

Narrow, Specific Rights

One way of making the bill of rights civil in character was to emphasize the narrow and concrete in drafting the various amendments. And, whenever he could, Madison did exactly that. The Third Amendment is a good example. It reads:

No soldier shall, in time of peace be quartered in any house, without the consent of the Owner, nor in time of war, but in a manner to be prescribed by law.

Madison could have written: "All people have a right against quartering," but that would have raised some sticky questions.

So instead, he used good concrete terms and several qualifiers, and in the end left room to maneuver with the phrase: "in a manner to be prescribed by law." It was like saying that *some* students have *some* rights to fairness.

Many of the items on Madison's final list were like that. They were not rights in the broad, natural sense—what the French would have called the Rights of Man—but rather points of particular sensitivity to Americans. The following list includes most of them:

The Right to Bear Arms. Madison did not suppose that all people had a right to tote guns on all occasions. Bearing arms, as addressed in the Second Amendment, was a right only because of the historical role of colonial militias in securing and maintaining independence.

Freedom from Unreasonable Search. Colonial history was reflected in the Fourth Amendment, too. Everyone remembered the loosely worded search warrants of the British customs officials and the abuse to which they had been put. The Fourth Amendment declared that searches must be conducted reasonably, and went on to sketch out a reasonable process.

Freedom from Expropriation. Governments had a habit of helping themselves to private property if there was a pressing need, sometimes paying for it and sometimes not. Washington's army was forced to do so on occasion, and while they technically paid for the goods they confiscated, it was often in depreciated paper currency. Madison did not deny the right of government to exercise *eminent domain*, as it was called, but he stipulated in the Fifth Amendment that all property taken must be justly compensated.

Rights of the Accused. English law respected the rights of accused persons as did few other legal systems. However, as we have seen, the British were willing to make an exception in the case of colonial smugglers, who were denied the right of jury trial. The Founders wanted no repeat of that mistake. Accordingly, in the Fifth to Eighth Amendments, they spelled out the traditional protections of English law in black and white. No one should be held for a capital offense except on the formal indictment of a grand jury. No one should be tried for the same crime twice. No one should be forced to testify against himself. Accused persons had a right to a speedy and public trial, to be informed of the nature and cause of the accusation against them, to confront hostile witnesses, to obtain—forcibly if necessary—witnesses in their favor, to have the assistance of counsel, to have their guilt or innocence determined by a jury of their peers. "Excessive bail shall not be required," continued the Eighth Amendment, "nor excessive fines imposed, nor cruel and unusual punishments inflicted."

Broad, General Rights

So much for the specific, concrete rights. Now Madison had to deal with some broad and general ones. Freedom of speech, freedom of religion, freedom of privacy, free use of property—there was no way to cast such concepts as these into narrow-gauge language. When it came to a subject like religion, one could not say that some people should enjoy some freedom some of the time.

Here he confronted the dilemma of draftsmanship most acutely. To declare any of these rights in broad, general language would be to arouse a hornet's nest of difficulties, as we have seen above, yet there was no other way to declare them. Take freedom of speech, for example. To Madison, free speech meant free *political* speech—the right to stand up and criticize the government. But Madison could never use that qualifier in framing the First Amendment, for to do so might weaken other kinds of free expression. So, when it came to putting free speech into so many words, he had to say in effect: "All people have a right to speak freely, period."

But do they? For an answer, let's return to the analogy of the professor who says "All students deserve fair treatment." The language is fraught with ambiguities. We don't know what "all students" refers to and we don't know what "fair treatment" means. Nevertheless, here comes a student armed with a copy of the professor's declaration. He has not been treated fairly, he says—by his *girl friend*. The professor gently explains that that kind of unfairness was not what he had in mind. The student, however, has an interesting comeback. "It doesn't matter what you *had in mind*," he replies, "It only matters *what the words say.*"

And his point is well taken. Broadly phrased declarations of right tend toward the absolute. Madison may have intended to free only political speech, but his words tended to liberate *all* speech. As a result, we struggle mightily with the First Amendment today, not so much in the realm of political utterance, but in the realms of libel, sedition, and obscenity. What began as a narrow right, clearly defined, ended up as a right almost without limits.

When narrowly drafted rights wind up in court, they are subject to some misunderstanding. The lawyers can quibble about the meaning of "quartering" or

"house" in the Third Amendment. But when a broadly drafted, abstractly stated right winds up in court, a great deal more is at stake. Momentous questions will swirl around the meaning and application of free speech—and the way those questions are resolved will affect the very nature of our society.

As we review the broad declarations of the Bill of Rights, we should keep this fact constantly in mind.

The Five Great Right

Freedom of Religion

Ancient societies, including republican ones, all had their official churches, and few supposed that the world should be otherwise. After all, if people were to live together in peace and harmony (and duly respect their rulers), state-sanctioned religion seemed essential. The tradition carried through more than a thousand years of Christianity and survived well beyond the Protestant Reformation.

Some Protestant theologians, however, began to wonder about official churches. Suppose a saint—someone with a close personal relationship to God— found himself stuck in a corrupt and degraded state church somewhere. Quite clearly, it would be better for him to pull out and seek his own worship.

So began the dissenting tradition. Dissenters were those who, for one reason or another, could not abide affiliation with a state church. Understandably, state churches did not take kindly to them. In the name of religious unity, dissenters could be disemboweled, hanged from tree limbs, or roasted alive. Nevertheless, once the process of dissent got started, it proved almost impossible to stop. This was especially true in the American colonies, where dissenters congregated in large numbers. Soon there were dissenters from the dissenters, and then dissenters from *them*. Even where a given group was numerous enough to control the local government (and thus become a state church themselves), they still had to deal with the otherwise minded. Slowly, painfully, it became clear that complete religious freedom was the only thing that made sense.

When we examine these roots of American religious liberty, we catch a glimpse of what disestablishment did and did not mean. It did not mean hostility to religion. What it meant, rather, was that religion should be a thing of the individual mind and heart, not something for the state to impose and the politicians to wrangle over. And, on a more practical level, it meant that in a land of diversity, all religions must tolerate and respect one another if they themselves wished to be tolerated and respected.

Disestablishment also had important republican significance. As Jefferson and Madison, the pioneers of disestablishment, concluded, whenever church and state were tied together, the influence of the church could not independently promote virtuous behavior in the public. Only when church and state were separate and autonomous could the church operate as a true moral force.

Points of Difficulty with Religious Freedom. In the actual drafting of the First Amendment's religion clause, all of this was absent. There was no way for Madison to explain what religious freedom was supposed to mean or not mean. Nor could he insert qualifiers to insure that the right

kinds of freedom were achieved. He had to settle for the shortest and simplest wording possible: "Congress shall make no law respecting an establishment of religion, or prohibiting the free exercise thereof." This was the wording of a broad, universal, and well-nigh absolute right—and as such it was laden with ambiguity.

Here were only a few of the trouble spots. Did the words of the amendment mean that the government should be hostile toward religion, that it should expunge all references to God in public discourse? Clearly Madison had no such thought in mind. But the wording could be read that way.

Secondly, how far was the separation of church and state supposed to go? Could religious meetings be held in public buildings? Could school children be required to recite prayers—or even to sit in silence—every day? If the government rendered aid to private schools, could it render the same aid to parochial ones? Or, on the other side, how much interference in church affairs did the First Amendment allow? Could churches be regulated like other institutions? Could their investments be taxed, their books audited? If church-owned colleges refused to sponsor, say, coed dorms, could the government take them to task?

Finally, in permitting the "free exercise" of religion, how much did society have to put up with in the way of unorthodox, antisocial, or criminal behavior? If Mormons wanted to practice polygamy, could the authorities forbid them to do so? If the followers of Sun Myung Moon engaged in mind-control, and those of Jim Jones tortured dissidents, was that any business of the government? Somewhere, of course, lines had to be drawn. But where?

The Price of Religious Freedom

Freedom of religion means more than having a Catholic cathedral on one corner, a Lutheran chapel on the next, and a Jewish synagogue across the street. Where there is true religious freedom there will also be a vibrant, colorful, and sometimes rowdy religious fringe. Americans know that well enough. They see the Hare Krishna monks on the sidewalks, read ads on kiosks for Eckankar, and peruse articles in the *National Enquirer* about swamis, gurus, and fortune-tellers. It is entertaining to think that Los Angeles County has an official witch on the payroll, that San Francisco's Glide Church features rock music and light shows, or that a group called "The Celestials" believes Mt. Shasta is an intergalactic UFO base.

Yet religion of the fringe poses painful dilemmas for democratic society. There is, for instance, simple nuisance to think about. The Hare Krishnas can raise a frightful racket with their chants and drums. Other groups panhandle shoppers on the sidewalks or confront them with hellfire preaching. Among the beliefs of a Philadelphia cult called MOVE was the importance of depositing refuse on the street. But nothing compares with the nuisance created by a self-styled maharishi called Rajneesh Bhagwan Shree, whose followers moved in on the Oregon farming community of Antelope, registered as voters, and proceeded to reshape the town in their own image.

Contemporary depiction of Shaker worship: The price of religious freedom was religious diversity. (Library of Congress)

Or there is the issue of fraud. Much of the astrological, fortunetelling, and prophesying activities of the fringe religions—for which millions of dollars change hands yearly—would be fair game for bunko squads in another setting. Many evangelical churches engage in high-pressure solicitation through their radio and television stations. Still others trade in miracles. A Portland woman recently sued the Church of Scientology for $39 million for falsely promising to alter her personality and raise her IQ.

A number of religious groups run afoul of fundamental mores. Polygamy, complex marriage, and outright free love have eroded family values and created chaos in domestic relations. (Who inherits what when everyone is married to everyone?) The use of drugs is claimed as necessary to some religious observances, and in the case of the Navaho Indians, drug laws have had to be altered accordingly. Some cultists have denied their children education, deprived them of medical attention, or forbidden them to participate in citizenship.

The question of mind-control raises another raft of issues. L. Ron Hubbard's practice of "dianetics"—a sort of do-it-yourself psychoanalysis—was in constant legal trouble and pronounced "a serious threat to health" by the American Medical Association, but after Scientology was converted to *The Church* of Scientology, its problems all but disappeared. Followers of the Rev. Sun Myung Moon are widely accused of brainwashing recruits, but this is mild compared to the starvation, beatings, and torture inflicted by other groups. Such was the degree of mind- control achieved by Jim Jones over his followers in Guyana, that when he ordered them to commit suicide they willingly obeyed.

Churches, of course, get into politics, too. This seems tolerable in the context of Republican versus Democrat or liberal versus conservative, but what about in the context of white versus black? Certain fundamentalist groups have encouraged racism among whites, while extremist black sects, such as Louis Farrakhan's in Chicago, have fostered the same sort of hatred in reverse. Then, too, Irish-American Catholics have gathered money for the IRA and Indian-American Sikhs have solicited funds for the Punjab—knowing full well that the result would be death and destruction.

And occasionally religions of the fringe have gone all the way. Anton LaVey's First Church of Satan may be harmless enough with its theatrical bohemianism, but some forms of devil worship indeed call for bloodletting. A teenager murdered his foster parents after claiming to have received satanic orders to do so, and in a spectacular Utah case, two self-proclaimed prophets embarked on a murder spree after God supposedly presented them with a hit-list. In Idaho, a group calling itself "The Covenant, the Sword, and the Arm of the Lord" is wanted for multiple homicides.

Such difficulties are not experienced where there is no religious freedom. In Saudi Arabia, to name just one example, there exists a near-perfect religious harmony. Non-Muslims are welcome in the country, under carefully controlled circumstances, but their religion is not: all baggage is subject to inspection at the Riyadh Airport, and foreign religious items (such as family Bibles) are routinely confiscated. The only problem is that where there is no religious freedom—excesses and all—there is no other kind of freedom either.

How Free Should Free Speech Be? The Daniel Schorr Case

At sixty, CBS news correspondent Daniel Schorr, silver-haired and distinguished-looking, cut a figure of journalistic responsibility second only to Walter Cronkite. In truth, however, he was not quite the same benign uncle. For, in the fall of 1976, amid the passions of the presidential election, Schorr suddenly stunned the country by releasing to a New York newspaper the text of an extremely sensitive congressional report. The Pike Report, resulting from an extensive investigation of U.S. intelligence activities, was so damaging to the pride and prestige of the CIA—which was faulted (among other things) for plotting the murder of foreign dignitaries—that the House had voted to suppress it. Schorr, moreover, was wholly unrepentant. He would not answer questions of the House Ethics Committee; he would not produce a copy of the report; and he would most certainly not reveal the source by which he obtained it.

There had been pirated documents before, the most famous of them being the Pentagon Papers of the Vietnam era. But there was a difference in the two situations. Because the Pentagon Papers had shed light on a war that was already intensely unpopular, there was a clear sense that the public interest had been served by their publication. Here, by contrast, many Americans were uneasy. Some of Schorr's most ardent defenders worried about the impact of the Pike Report on the intelligence community's morale and its ability to do its job. National interests were at stake on both sides of the issue.

For his part, Schorr saw only one of those interests: free speech. At issue, he complained, "was not my right to report, but the public's right to know." The national security interest Schorr waved aside. "I believed in national security," he said, "but

Freedom of Speech

As in the case of religious freedom, free speech was not something people had taken for granted. Even in history's most liberal regimes, the idea of speaking out against the government was defined as sedition, treason, or worse. And if the outspoken citizen wasn't hauled up on criminal charges, he might well be sued for libel.

Conditions in America altered this situation, too. With many different peoples and a diversity of value systems, who was to say what constituted proper speech? (Was it sacrilegious, for example, for a Protestant to ridicule the Virgin Mary?) And, as far as libeling the politicians was concerned, the American attitude was that politicians ought to behave themselves.

But the really crucial connection in America was between free speech and republicanism. According to all readings of republican theory, it was the people who must ultimately be in charge of things. The people, not just the politicians, must have a grasp on the issues, must be capable of judging officials, must be the final arbiters of policy. Public virtue literally had no meaning if the people were uninformed or were afraid to speak out.

not in the debasement of national security for cover-up." Others in the journalistic community weren't so sure. An editorial in the *New York Times* condemned Schorr for "selling secrets." At the annual Gridiron Dinner, the correspondent found himself not a roaster but a roastee. And CBS, after agonizing over the situation, finally decided to suspend him from its news staff. (He subsequently resigned.)

Where did the public come down? Ditheringly in the middle. When the House Ethics Committee moved toward a confrontation with Schorr (with the possibility of jail for contempt), the public rallied to his defense. Yet polls showed that Americans also feared the power of the press, power that in this case might have caused real injury. In the end, it came down to a question of whom was mistrusted most, the government or the media.

Daniel Schorr: freedom of speech or the abuse of? (UPI/Bettmann Newsphotos)

The Founders realized that freedom of speech could not be absolute, even in a republic. "No one," as Oliver Wendell Holmes put it, "has the right falsely to shout fire in a crowded theater." Yet, once again, they recognized the impossibility of trying to spell out in legal language the difference between permissible and impermissible utterance. So important was the value of free speech, and so broad were its implications, that they made the language of the amendment simple, short, and seemingly absolute: "Congress shall make no law abridging the freedom of speech, or of the press; or the right of the people peaceably to assemble, and to petition the Government for a redress of grievances."

Points of Difficulty with Free Speech. In the concept of free speech there swirled a similar host of ambiguities. One set of difficulties concerned sedition. At what point did criticism of the government—so necessary in a republic—become incitement against lawful authority? Was it permissible to stand up on a soapbox and cry: "Down with the government!"? Was it permissible to discourage young men from

"Right of the People . . . to Petition the Government for a Redress of Grievances." (UPI/ Bettmann Newsphotos)

enlisting in the army? Was it permissible to urge one's fellows to stockpile weapons, or to steal and publish an embarrassing classified document? These were only a few of the tough questions.

A second set of problems concerned libel. Clearly it was wrong to defame a private citizen, but what constituted "private"? A governor, of course, was not private, but what about a police chief? What about a police*man*? What about a movie star? A television personality? A football coach? And what, if any, standards of truth should apply? If I do not like the governor, am I free to allege that he is homosexual? Free speech can mean nothing if every controversial utterance is punished as a libel, but it can also mean nothing if it is used to protect slander.

And then there was obscenity. What was it, precisely, that made a given expression obscene? "I can't define it," one judge is reported to have said, "but I know it when I see it." But that was the excuse for banning such literary monuments as *Ulysses* and *Huckleberry Finn*. Common agreement on where to draw the lines seemed impossible.

The Right to Privacy

On first reading, the Fourth Amendment seems to address only the narrow, practical problem of unreasonable searches and seizures. But the more people read and thought about the amendment, the more certain they became that there was something else written between its lines.

In order to glimpse that deeper meaning, we must know about another quirk in the English legal tradition. To the English there was something almost sacred about the idea of home. It was regarded as a kind of sanctuary from the world, a place where the ordinary rules did not apply. There were cases on record in which hunted fugitives were regarded as untouchable once they crossed their own thresholds.

With that concept in mind, let us reread the Fourth Amendment. "The right of the people to be secure in their persons, houses, papers, and effects, against unreasonable searches and seizures, shall not be violated." Wasn't this really a way of saying: "People have a right to their privacy?" We can catch other glimpses of the same right by carefully reading the First Amendment—which guarantees the privacy of religious beliefs—and the Fifth Amendment—which protects accused persons from self-incrimination.

Division over the right to privacy (UPI/Bettmann Newsphotos)

The Doctrine of Implied Rights. The problem is, of course, that in order to detect some blanket right to privacy in these three amendments, we have to search not for *words* as such but for *implications*. How would the Founders regard this notion of *implied* rights? They may well have accepted it. One of their worries, we recall, was that any specific listing of rights would be regarded as complete and definitive. That the courts were willing to look for implied rights suggested a willingness to view the Bill of Rights as inclusive and open-ended, an unfinished and unfinishable guarantee of liberty.

Points of Difficulty with the Right to Privacy. Like the other broadly stated rights, however, the right to privacy had its ambiguities. What, exactly, did the concept include? Were people free to lead strange, irregular, or immoral sex lives in the privacy of their homes? Could they introduce their children to offbeat lifestyles and alternative value systems? Could they indulge in the use of harmful substances? Were they free to practice birth control, and if ordinary methods failed, were they allowed to seek abortions? Could men beat their wives or intimidate them in subtler ways, and if so, could wives seek retribution? In short, how much privacy could a republic handle?

The Tragedy of Isidore Zimmerman

Is all the fuss and bother of criminal procedure really necessary? Most of us have asked the question at one time or another, usually after reading of some new outrage in which an obviously guilty criminal got off on a technicality. Here, for balance, is an outrage of a different sort.

On an April evening in 1937, six gunmen held up a small restaurant on New York's Lower East Side. A police detective, Michael J. Foley, inopportunely appeared on the scene, and as he went for his firearm, one of the six gunned him down. All six were subsequently arrested, and in the process of being questioned, one of them, for his own reasons, falsely accused Isidore Zimmerman of supplying the gang's weapons.

The accused, a serious-minded twenty-year-old from a prosperous Jewish family, stoutly protested his innocence. There was considerable reason to believe him. The thug who fingered him had never, to anyone's knowledge, intentionally told the truth about anything, and during the investigation, evidence pointing to Zimmerman's innocence actually came into the prosecutor's hands. The prosecutor, however, did not want to be soft on criminals, and if Isidore Zimmerman was even known to this group, a criminal he must be. In any event, the evidence was suppressed and Zimmerman was convicted.

For nine months Zimmerman lived on Sing Sing's death row while one at a time his supposed accomplices died in the electric chair. His turn came in 1939. His head was shaved and religious rites already administered when, two hours before the scheduled execution, Gov. Herbert H. Lehman, considering the fact that Zimmerman had only supplied weapons, commuted his sentence to life imprisonment. No one at Sing Sing felt sorry for him, of course; he had gotten off mighty lucky. So they took it out on him in various small ways: solitary confinement, a bread and water diet, occasional beatings. Somewhere along the way he lost an eye as well.

This went on for twenty-four years before the Zimmerman case came to the attention of a lawyer named Maurice Edelbaum, who on his own expense had it reopened, retried—and reversed. In 1962, at the age of forty-four, Isidore Zimmerman went free. But he had paid heavily. He had lost his chance for a career. His health was

And, on the other side, what constituted an invasion of privacy? Were people obliged to receive junk mail or to put up with nuisance phone calls? Could the government send auditors to poke about their businesses, check up on their investments, keep tabs on their bank accounts? When was it permissible to use wire taps on a citizen's phone? Or to open his mail? Or to ask questions of his neighbors? Was the right to privacy lost if a person joined the Communist party, visited Cuba, spoke out against the government? The list of questions went on and on.

The Right to Fairness

In the Fifth to Eighth Amendments, as we saw above, the Founders listed a number of items specific to criminal procedure. By the same logic with which a broad right of

permanently broken. He was unable to have children. And, worst of all, several members of his family had died believing that he was guilty of murder. He had trouble repressing the feeling that the State of New York owed him something.

Getting New York to agree, however, was no easy matter. In the first place, the state could not be sued without its own permission, which had to be granted by a special act of the legislature. Several times the New York Assembly passed such a measure, but the governor (himself a billionaire) vetoed each of them as an unseemly expense. It was not until 1981 that the permission was finally signed into law. And then the suit itself, with its legal and technical difficulties, dragged on desultorily for two more years. Meanwhile the petitioner, with no education and rapidly deteriorating health, worked as a doorman in a New York hotel.

Finally, in June of 1983, Zimmerman, now sixty-six, won his suit against the state and was awarded $1 million for his pain and suffering. After paying his expenses, he was left with $660,000, a sum so paltry that it was termed "the second miscarriage of justice" by *Newsweek*. How did Zimmerman celebrate? He bought a car and took a trip to the Catskills for a few days. It was virtually the only pleasure he had ever known. Four months later he died of a heart attack.

Why all the fuss and bother?—Isidore Zimmerman (UPI/Bettmann Newsphotos)

privacy could be implied from the First, Fourth, and Fifth Amendments, a broad right of fairness could be implied from these. Such a right would hold that the treatment of all persons charged with crimes ought to be measured against some general standard. Thus, where the Bill of Rights does not specifically require, say, a reading of rights to persons placed under arrest, the courts have nonetheless determined that such a recitation must be given.

Points of Difficulty with the Right to Fairness. Broad and abstract standards of fairness bring us to face ambiguity once again. Is it fair to trick persons of low intelligence into making a confession? Is it fair to fill the prisons with disproportionate numbers of blacks and Latinos? If the wealthy can hire the best attorneys to defend them in court, is it fair to appoint so-so attorneys for the poor? Come to that, is the death penalty fair? Quite apart from the question whether it is "cruel and un-usual," can it possibly be administered evenhandedly among the various races and social classes?

There are fairness questions on the other side, too. Is it fair to turn loose a criminal merely because of some hangnail technicality? Is it fair to throw out substantive evidence simply because it was improperly obtained? Must we apply easier standards to those who are stupid, or poor, or black just because they are already disadvantaged? In other words, must fairness apply only to criminals—is there no such thing as fairness to society?

So there are a variety of values that must somehow be balanced, often precariously. Most people can recite stories of the notorious criminal who got off. There are other stories, equally dismaying, of the convict who was proven innocent after twenty years at hard labor. Often the question of fairness boils down to: how much disorder can society put up with in the name of freedom? For perfect order can be maintained only by tyrannies.

Due Process of Law

In chapter four we referred to the procedural guarantees listed above as due process of law. That wording actually appears in the language of the Fifth Amendment. It is an ancient phrase, dating far back in English legal history, and its traditional meaning is simply that accused persons cannot be punished unless proper procedures have been followed in convicting them.

Within the past century, courts have discovered a second meaning in the phrase *due process of law*. This meaning applies not to courts conducting criminal trials but to legislatures enacting laws. If Congress passed a law, say, requiring employers to buy health insurance for their workers, an employer, pointing to the Fifth Amendment, might contend that he was being deprived of property (the money for insurance premiums) without due process of law. The legislature, in other words, cannot pass laws which would have the effect of taking his property.

If you accept this interpretation of the phrase "due process of law"—and not everyone does—its effect is to sharply curtail the power of government. The wording of the Fifth Amendment (repeated in the Fourteenth Amendment) that "no person shall be deprived of life, liberty, or property without due process of law" thus comes to mean precisely what Locke and the natural rights philosophers originally intended: that government cannot interfere with our private affairs.

Points of Difficulty with Substantive Due Process. This *substantive* (as opposed to *procedural*) reading of the due process clause has far-reaching implications indeed. Most government regulations curtail liberty in some way, and many of them take away property. Could government regulate the hours of workers without technically restricting their liberty? Could it require safety devices on machinery without depriving someone of property? If the due process clause were interpreted broadly enough, it could virtually destroy the power to govern.

Costs and Benefits of the Bill of Rights

By emphasizing *civil* over *natural* rights, Madison hoped to make the Bill of Rights compatible with constitutional government. Many Anti-Federalists agreed that he did just that. Far from cutting back the authority of the Constitution, they charged, the Bill of Rights was nothing but window dressing.

They were wrong. The Bill of Rights has come to assume a monumental and expanding role in our public affairs, and has profoundly affected constitutional government. Although the rule of law remains the foundation of American liberty, by itself it has not always been sufficient. The skeptics were undoubtedly correct in demanding a declaration of rights as a backup system.

On the other hand, the rights-oriented approach to liberty has come at its price. The ambiguities it has inserted into the Constitution have tended to make the governing process muddy and vague. Constitutional government depends in large measure on agreement among the citizens, and that, in turn, depends on spelling out the rules of the game clearly. Where the Bill of Rights is concerned, the rules often seem unclear, uncertain, and quite beyond the average citizen's grasp.

The Bill of Rights has also affected constitutional development. The Founders expected their work to develop and change over the years, as we will see in the following chapter, but they expected it to do so in a rational, orderly manner. In some ways the Bill of Rights defeated that hope. Whole areas of constitutional law have appeared almost by magic on account of some favored view of this or that phrase, only to disappear just as suddenly. The due process clause, for example, has been both the darling of the left and the darling of the right, depending on how its wording was interpreted.

Then, too, the Bill of Rights has had its impact on public virtue. Just as separation of powers or checks and balances promote certain kinds of public psychology, so too does the idea of rights. The psychology of rights has often been that of the embattled minority fighting for its place in the sun. And the battle has necessarily been waged not only against government but against the whole of society. Since rights can never be absolute for everyone, it follows that more rights for one group may in fact mean fewer rights for another. (If minorities are given the right to be served, then restaurant owners lose the right to refuse service.) In both tone and tactics, the struggle for rights has come to resemble that endless factional free-for-all the Founders so abhorred.

Rights Versus Self-Government. As Madison feared, the history of the Bill of Rights has been one in which the rights themselves have steadily expanded, becoming ever broader, more abstract and more absolute. For some Americans this represents nothing less than the onward march of freedom, and the Bill of Rights has accordingly taken on almost mythic proportions.

But the idea of expanding individual rights *against* popular government would strike many of the Founders as odd. For them there was something supremely noble in the idea of self- government: it demonstrated man's ultimate capacity for virtuous conduct. Their idea of self-government, we recall, literally began with the self and grew out of the order of the individual soul. If the government of the people showed the same restraint, justice, and compassion as the orderly soul did, why would special rights need to be proclaimed against it?

The answer may be that in the modern world the idea of rights has come to be at odds with the idea of the orderly soul. For some, the contemporary notion of rights has come to mean unlimited self-expression. Instead of the individual governing himself in a restrained and virtuous way, he should, rather, "grab for the gusto," in one graphic phrase, or "let it all hang out." Such a notion of freedom, of course, is perilously close to the Founders' idea of licentiousness.

So, whatever else the Bill of Rights has brought us, it has not brought repose. But, then, repose was never republicanism's promise. The difficulties of self-government are ongoing, as the Founders well knew, and the task of resolving its dilemmas will literally never end.

The Living Constitution

Current justices of the supreme court (Wide World
Photos)

177

The Supreme Court Makes a Dramatic Turnabout

Linda Brown, age eleven, a plumpish, bright-eyed youngster with a bashful smile, had always longed to attend Monroe Elementary with her white friends. Only five blocks from her home in Topeka, Kansas, the school stood like a citadel of forbidden desire. For Linda, like millions of other black children in 1954, was condemned to an all-black, racially segregated school far from home. To get there, she had to walk through the railroad yards, catch a school bus, and bump along for twenty-one blocks. So when lawyers for the NAACP came seeking plaintiffs for one of their school desegregation cases, Linda Brown happily signed on.

In theory, *Brown v. The Board of Education of Topeka* had already been decided long ago. For the U.S. Supreme Court, like other courts in the Anglo-American tradition, was supposed to be bound by its own precedents, and for the *Brown* case there was a fairly clear one on the books. Back in 1896 the Court had considered not school segregation, precisely, but a close cousin: segregation in public transportation. Louisiana's Jim Crow laws strictly prohibited blacks from riding in the same railroad coaches as whites, and when Homer Adolph Plessy, holding a first class ticket, boarded a passenger train in New Orleans and insisted on sitting in the for-whites-only coach, he was arrested, forcibly ejected from the train, and locked up in the parish jail.

Plessy v. Ferguson, too, had been a test case, and black leaders at the time had feared it as such. "It is of the utmost consequence that we should not have a decision against us," wrote Albion Tourgee to an associate, "as it is a matter of boast with the court that it has *never reversed itself* on a *constitutional* question." They were stunned when the decision came down. Plessy was found guilty and the law pronounced valid. The provision in the Louisiana statute for "separate but equal" facilities for the two races did not, said the Court, violate the Fourteenth Amendment's requirement of equal protection of the laws.

By 1954, however, much had changed. The personnel of the Court had changed, of course, but, more importantly, the world itself had changed. The *Plessy* decision had faithfully reflected the world of 1896. At that time most American blacks could not vote. Most were ill educated. Most endured a kind of twilight existence in American society. National magazines published jokes about "Rastus" and "Liza." Ragtime composers wrote songs titled "Mammy's Chocolate Soldier" and "All Coons Look Alike To Me." And in an advertisement of the day, a little white girl addressed her black playmate with the words: "Why doesn't your Mamma wash you with Fairy Soap?"

Since that time, what a transformation there had been. There had been the Harlem Renaissance of the 1920s. There had been Richard Wright, and Ralph Ellison, and Langston Hughes. There had been Jackie Robinson in baseball, Duke Ellington in jazz, Sidney Poitier in the movies, and Joe Lewis in the ring. There had been *The Invisible Man, Black Like Me, Porgy and Bess, Ebony*. Blacks had gone north to work in the war plants, and their children were graduating from Harvard and Yale. Kenneth Clark, the distinguished sociologist, John Hope Franklin, the distinguished historian, and Ralph Bunche, the distinguished diplomat, were all black. And, most importantly, northern blacks could and did vote.

A dramatic turnabout and a dramatic experience for Linda Brown: the girl with bows in her hair on the back row (Topeka Capital-Journal)

Nothing better illustrated the new reality than the brilliant black attorneys who had joined the NAACP's legal staff: Charles Houston, James Nabrit, William R. Ming, Spottswood Robinson III. And, of course, Thurgood Marshall. Marshall combined the savvy of an accomplished trial lawyer with the suaveness of a down-home politician. With a small fortune at his disposal, he began carefully laying the groundwork for a series of desegregation cases. For assistance, he reached out to the whole of the intellectual community, black and white—psychologists, sociologists, anthropologists, historians, constitutional lawyers—bringing scores of them together for marathon sessions of brainstorming. When the Court let it be known, early in the *Brown* arguments, that it might reconsider the meaning of the Fourteenth Amendment, Marshall put forty scholars to work on the problem.

Hearing the *Brown* case on the high bench were Justices Hugo Black, Robert Jackson, Frank Murphy, and Wiley Rutledge, all of them appointed by Franklin Roosevelt. And sitting beside them were Felix Frankfurter and William O. Douglas, appointed more recently but with even stronger ties to liberal Academe. Quite clearly, the sympathies of the justices lay with the cause of the black plaintiffs.

Sympathetic or not, however, they still had to face the problem of *Plessy v. Ferguson*. That case had clearly stated that "separate but equal" facilities were constitutionally legal, and Southern school districts, fearful of what might happen, were hastening to bring black schools up to par. In June of 1953, after six months of pondering, the Court called in counsel on both sides and handed them a long list of questions about the original purpose of the Fourteenth Amendment. What the justices were really asking for was some valid historical rationale for reversing the *Plessy* decision.

Marshall's researchers went to work. In the next few months they subjected the Fourteenth Amendment to intense historical scrutiny. But the results were ambiguous. Yes, a case could be made that in drafting the amendment, the framers had intended to sweep away all forms of segregation. But something of a counter-case could be made as well. Marshall and his people were back on square one.

In all the debating back and forth, however, the members of the Court were convinced more than ever that segregation had to go. The new chief justice, Earl Warren, who had taken personal custody of the *Brown* case, was not overly concerned with narrow technicalities. For him, the real questions of the law were: Is it right? Is it just? Is it fair?, and school segregation flunked all three. Urged on by Warren's dynamic leadership, the justices decided to overturn the *Plessy* decision anyway, with or without a legal argument—and to do it unanimously.

On May 17, 1954, in the Supreme Court's vaultlike chamber, the chief justice, in a quiet, emotionless voice, began reading the *Brown* decision to a packed and hushed audience. Before the reading was complete, reporters were slipping out and racing to the telephones, for the tenor of the opinion was clear. "In the field of education," he said, "the doctrine of 'separate but equal' has no place. Separate educational facilities are inherently unequal. Therefore we hold that the plaintiffs are, by reason of the segregation complained of, deprived of the equal protection of the laws guaranteed by the Fourteenth Amendment."

And *Plessy v. Ferguson*? It may have been good law, but it was bad policy. "Whatever may have been the extent of psychological knowledge at the time of *Plessy v. Ferguson*, this finding is amply supported by modern authority," Warren said. "Any language in *Plessy v. Ferguson* to the contrary is rejected." And so it was that the Constitution's Fourteenth Amendment was neatly turned inside out.

Having achieved the ratification of the Constitution and the Bill of Rights, the Founders' work was complete. Was it, though, complete for all time? Thomas Jefferson, for one, did not think so. Constitutions were written by a particular people in a particular circumstance, he supposed. When either the people or the circumstance changed, the best constitution might be left high and dry. And this Philadelphia document was no different. If it lasted twenty years, or roughly a generation, that was all Jefferson expected of it.

Most of the other Founders hoped for better. It was true that particular circumstances changed, they allowed, but human nature did not seem to change much, nor did the fundamental patterns of politics. If a constitution was based on the right understanding of things, there was no reason to suppose that it couldn't last indefinitely.

Building Elasticity Into the Constitution

Both sides were perhaps partly right. The question of a constitution's longevity really depended on adapting the document to inevitable changes in circumstance—but that was no easy trick. For when it came to committing constitutional ideas to paper, on the one hand, and dealing with change, on the other, an extremely difficult dilemma presented itself.

The Dilemma of Constitution Writing

There are two different ways to use legal language, as we learned in chapter eight. One is to employ clear, precise, concrete words to convey meanings as accurately as possible. The other is to employ vague, general words to encompass some sort of abstraction. Each alternative has its strengths and weaknesses, as we saw. Let us now apply those strengths and weaknesses to the problem of constitutional design.

Narrow Drafting, Narrow Construction. Suppose I wanted to write a constitution that would be clear, precise, and easily understood. I would, of course, choose my words carefully. If a vague or fuzzy term came up, I would throw it out in favor of one more concrete and specific. I would never say something like: "The government shall have the power to do good," for such a statement would be fraught with ambiguity. Instead, I would say: "The government shall have the power to raise an army, build roads, and deliver the mail."

Furthermore, I would hope that you, in interpreting, or construing, my words, would act in a similar spirit. For instance, where I had written the word "army," I would hope that you would not read some broader term, such as "armed forces," and proceed to build a navy. Had I wanted to authorize the building of a navy, I would have said so. "Narrow draftsmanship," as the lawyers say, "requires narrow construction."

Our narrowly drafted, narrowly construed constitution is now complete. It is a model of linguistic clarity. Those who consider ratifying it will know in advance precisely what they are getting. And fifty years hence we will not have to worry about someone twisting the meaning of its words to authorize something we didn't want in the first place—such as a navy.

But there is a slight problem. What if the world somehow changes? What if, for example, fifty years from now the people who are living under our constitution find themselves desperately in need of a navy? It is pretty clear that they can't have one, isn't it? So, what must they do? One possibility would be to subvert the constitution: build the navy anyway, paint the ships brown, and call them tanks. A second alternative might be to declare the constitution obsolete and write another one. And a final, last-ditch option might be to stage a revolution. Societies confronting this sort of problem have resorted to all three remedies.

Broad Drafting, Broad Construction. Let us suppose, then, that we learn from our mistake. Nevermore will the constitution be narrowly drafted and narrowly construed. It will be liberally sprinkled with broader, vaguer words intended to bestow flexibility. The defense clause will not limit its authorization to building an "army"; it will allow for anything under the heading of, say, "military forces."

Are we safe now? From subversion or revolution, yes, we probably are. But our new, loose-jointed constitution may face other dangers. Suppose that in fifty years a politician comes along who wants to build a new kind of military force, one never heard of before. The soldiers in this outfit will be trained and equipped to handle civil disobedience, and will take an oath of personal loyalty to the chief executive. People start getting nervous. They turn to the constitution. But the constitution authorizes "military forces," *any kind* of military forces, and these storm troopers seem to qualify.

The new document's broad drafting and broad construction pave the way for all sorts of constitutional development, perhaps, but for precisely that reason they don't operate as a real constitution. The words on paper cannot adequately restrain human behavior.

How the Founders Handled the Dilemma of Constitution Writing

These difficulties were not new to the Founders. They discussed them at great length. Moreover, they had their own experience with the Articles of Confederation to draw upon. That document had been narrowly drafted and made all but unamendable. When it was written, in 1777, the assumption had been that the national government would not require the power of taxation, so that power had been carefully excluded. Later on, when almost all of the states changed their minds, the constitution proved too rigid to alter. The Articles of Confederation were entirely successful at tying the hands of government—but they only survived a decade.

Amendability. With the fate of the Articles fresh in mind, the Founders began with a no-nonsense view of amendability. The power of the people to amend the Constitution in the future would provide their first and most obvious recourse if some aspect of it turned out to be unsatisfactory. And that happened. By the time the

United States had held its third presidential election, it became clear that something was woefully amiss with the balloting system. Owing to the advent of party politics, presidential and vice-presidential candidates were winding up with the same number of votes in the electoral college. (All electors of a given party would cast their two votes for the party's presidential and vice-presidential candidates respectively.) With the Articles of Confederation such a difficulty may have been fatal. With the new Constitution it was easily remedied by the Twelfth Amendment.

Draftsmanship. Amendability could not solve all the problems, however, especially those of growth and adaptation; some would have to be dealt with in the drafting process. Here the Founders had gained sophistication. They had come to realize that in constitutional language there had to be both rigor *and* flexibility. In some matters the words on paper had to act as a barrier of steel, while in others they must be as stretchable as a rubber band. These opposing qualities must be skillfully balanced if the document was to have the deterrent power of a constitution and still be adaptable to the real world. The ideal, as they realized, was to produce a "living" constitution.

In the first place, the Founders decided to keep the document brief. They would not try to spell out the fine points of government with details which might soon become antiquated. Much of the filling-in would be left to the elected officials themselves, drawing on their own experience and wisdom when putting the Constitution into practice.

On the other hand, what the Founders did commit to paper they tried to formulate as carefully as possible. They held long discussions over the use of this word or that, quibbling over seemingly insignificant distinctions. And what was carefully drafted they expected to be just as carefully construed. They wanted their words to operate as a real deterrent.

Yet to this rule there were some notable exceptions. Here and there, in fact, vague words and phrases were actually inserted into the Constitution by design. Once in a while this was caused by disagreement: if the Founders could not settle a difference, they sometimes conspired to bury it in ambiguity. More often, though, the ambiguity had a higher purpose. If the Constitution would have to be stretched in the future to cover unforeseen situations, it was well to provide certain stretch-points in the language of the text.

Stretch-Points

The "Necessary and Proper" Clause. The first stretch-point, and the one receiving the most discussion at Philadelphia, was found in Article I, Section 8. After enumerating the powers of Congress, the article added the power:

To make all Laws which shall be necessary and proper for carrying into Execution the foregoing Powers, and all other Powers vested by this Constitution in the Government of the United States.

From what we have learned about language, we can see that the words "necessary and proper" are not exactly models of concreteness. What parent would use such terms to control the behavior of a child? To some children it might seem necessary and proper to burn down the schoolhouse.

Which was more or less what occurred to Jefferson when he read the words in question. For, construed broadly enough, the "necessary and proper" clause might permit the government to do almost anything. As an example, the Constitution granted the government the power to coin money—plus whatever it deemed necessary and proper to accomplish that end. Was it necessary and proper to set up a mint? To operate a gold mine? To regulate the price of gold? To regulate the prices of things that gold could buy? Once one began extending hazy meanings, it was hard to know where to stop.

In real life, for example, Alexander Hamilton, Washington's secretary of the treasury, believed that those words gave him the authority to establish a national bank. Such banks, in the eighteenth century at least, were not infrequently viewed as hydras of corruption and handmaidens of tyranny, for they wielded enormous economic and financial power. That the U.S. Constitution, with its carefully limited powers, could be put to such a use was little short of horrifying to many Americans. Yet, clearly it could be.

The "General Welfare" Clause. Article I, Section 8 contained another ticking bomb. "Congress shall have power," it read, "to provide for the general Welfare of the United States." It would be hard to draft a broader statement than that. However, like so many others, it could be read two different ways. On the one hand, the words could be taken to mean that Congress might dish out welfare whenever and however it pleased. On the other hand, they could also be read something like this: Congress may never assist a *single* state or region—it must act only in *the general* welfare.

Which of those alternatives did the Founders intend? We will never know. So far, at least, we have interpreted the general welfare clause to mean only the latter. Thus, Andrew Jackson vetoed the construction of a federal highway on grounds that it would lie wholly within the boundaries of a single state and thus failed to serve the *general* welfare. But times could change. Some future generation might conclude, for example, that the general welfare clause authorizes socialism.

The Commerce Clause. Loose draftsmanship was also evident in the commerce clause, which reads: "The Congress shall have power to regulate Commerce with foreign Nations, and among the several States, and with the Indian Tribes." The word *regulate* could mean almost anything, as could the word *commerce*. Taken together, they might be used to legitimize any sort of government intervention into the economy.

Here again, though, there was method behind the Founders' apparent madness. Throughout their discussions they were painfully aware of the potential difficulties of federalism. Some kinds of authority—such as the war making or the law enforcement—were easy to divide between state and national governments. Others were not. And the authority to regulate commerce clearly fell into the latter category. The problem was that many commercial activities were neither intrinsically national nor intrinsically local in character. Take roads, for example. Suppose there is a winding dirt road that runs between two frontier towns. Few would argue that such a road would be anything but local in character, or that the commerce passing along it should be subject to any but state regulation. But the road in question links up

with other roads, so that ultimately a traveler on it could wind up in the next state. So while one user of the road is just moseying down to a neighbor's house, another is making his way across the country. By whom should the road be regulated?

In the all-important area of commerce, then, where the boundaries between state and national authority were almost indefinable, and where critical battles would be fought over the hand of government in private affairs, the commerce clause left a great deal to be settled in the future.

The Bill of Rights

If there were a few stretch-points in the text of the Constitution, several others were added by way of amendment. In particular, there were those swamps of ambiguity found within the Bill of Rights. As we saw in chapter eight, every one of the "five great rights" presented bottomless uncertainties in the application of public power.

This situation would become further complicated later on, when another constitutional amendment, the Fourteenth, would be interpreted to mean that the Bill of Rights must also apply to the states. The Bill of Rights was originally written to curb only the *national* government. After the Fourteenth Amendment it would become the duty of the national government to enforce the Bill of Rights against the states. As a result, every question about free speech, free religion, and the like would constitute a possible new stretch-point for the expansion of federal authority.

Judicial Review

The question remained as to how the Constitution's points of uncertainty should be dealt with. Obviously, someone had to sit down and determine precisely what each of them meant. But who? A great deal depended on the answer. Whichever officer, agency, or branch of government was given authority to resolve constitutional ambiguities stood to exercise conspicuous power over all others. Curiously, however, the Founders never singled one out. If a disagreement came up about the meaning of constitutional language, they left wide open the question of how it should be resolved. In so doing, of course, they created the final, and most far-reaching, ambiguity of them all.

What they probably intended, and what became the earliest practice, was that each branch of the government would work out the uncertainties for itself. Thus, when Congress passed the Alien and Sedition Acts, Jefferson, who regarded them as unconstitutional, vowed that when president he would never enforce them. That sort of government-by-face-off worked well enough to keep the powers at loggerheads, but in terms of constitutional development, it left much to be desired. There could be no agreement about where to draw the lines as long as the president was drawing them in one place, the Congress in another, and the courts in still a third, nor could there be an orderly way to redraw them later on.

Marbury v. Madison

All of this was changed by *Marbury v. Madison*, the Supreme Court decision that brought judicial review into being. In the election of 1800 Jefferson's Democratic Republicans were swept into office and John Adams' Federalists were swept out. As a parting shot, Adams appointed a prominent Virginia Federalist, John Marshall, to be chief justice of the Supreme Court. At the same time, the Federalists created and filled a number of other judgeships, the president working far into the night of his last day in office. If they could not control Congress or the Presidency, they reasoned, at least they could entrench themselves in the judiciary.

The Jeffersonians had their doubts about the legality of all this. But when Jefferson instructed his secretary of state, James Madison, not to deliver commissions for the "midnight appointments," one of the appointees, William Marbury, took the matter to court. Marshall and his fellow justices heard the case in February of 1803. Politically, of course, the chief justice was all for confirming the appointments in question, but he spotted a flaw in Marbury's suit for a writ of mandamus. Although an act of Congress (the Judiciary Act of 1789) authorized the issuance of such a writ, the Constitution did not. Suddenly, Marshall saw a great deal more at stake than a few partisan judgeships.

In writing his opinion on the case, Marshall explained the above facts. He then went on to argue that the Supreme Court—and it alone—could pronounce acts of the Congress unconstitutional. Of his several arguments, the most effective dealt with the function of the courts. In applying the law to specific cases, Marshall said, the courts were obliged to determine exactly what was and was not valid law. If an act was passed in violation of the Constitution, it was not valid law and could not be treated as such. Marshall's logic was not entirely flawless, but his bold seizing of the occasion was a master stroke. The Jeffersonians, who gained the nullification of the midnight appointments, did not challenge the ruling, and judicial review stuck.

Why the Judiciary?

Beyond the politics and legal reasoning of *Marbury v. Madison*, there were some sound justifications for judicial review. The judicial branch of government was the weakest of the three. It had, as Hamilton argued, neither sword nor purse, only judgment. Were the legislative or executive branches to acquire the power of determining constitutionality, the three-cornered balance might easily be upset. A president, for example, who could declare acts of Congress null and void might not be held accountable to anyone. But the judiciary seemed relatively safe.

The judiciary was also the most isolated branch of government, and the most securely sheltered. With their guaranteed salaries and lifetime tenure, the judges were immune from political reprisals—they didn't have to call a "ball" a "strike" just to please the bleachers. The president, by contrast, might be afraid to strike down a popular piece of legislation, especially in an election year, and members of the Congress might feel even more vulnerable. Review of government actions made good sense constitutionally, and the judiciary was the logical authority to undertake it.

Supreme Court: Isolated from ordinary concerns and standing above the fray of politics. (Library of Congress)

From Judicial Review to Judicial Reinterpretation

It was judicial review, by and large, that made orderly constitutional development possible. For, as they passed on the constitutionality of this or that government action, the justices of the Supreme Court did not simply call each as they happened to see it, they acted according to a set of established legal doctrines—doctrines which themselves were slowly evolving. Thus, the growth of constitutional law was both reasonably flexible and reasonably coherent.

For an analogy, consider the development of the English common law. Back in the time of Henry VII, some five hundred years ago, the common law was securely in place and working well. Today the same body of law is still operating effectively. In the meantime, England has dismantled feudalism, gone through the Protestant Reformation, established (and lost) two global empires, pioneered the industrial revolution, survived two world wars, taken up democracy, and experimented with socialism. How did the common law deal with all that? Each time the judges found themselves facing a new situation they expanded the law to cover it. In theory they were bound by existing legal precedents, and in most decisions they followed those precedents to the letter. But in that occasional oddball case, where the precedents didn't quite fit, the judges would have to do a little tinkering. Thus, the common law, while still remaining remarkably stable, could grow and adapt to change.

American judges came to do roughly the same thing. In theory, they too were bound by precedent in their interpretations of the Constitution. If a case came up involving, say, the general welfare clause, the judges were supposed to look back at the precedents before deciding it. And usually they did just that. But, if their search revealed that times had changed in some way, that new problems had arisen, or that new constitutional doctrines had come forth, there was always a possibility they might depart from the precedents. Thus, in a very real way, the Constitution itself could develop.

The Role of the Judges in the Reinterpretation Process

What kinds of personal qualities would lead a Supreme Court justice to reinterpret the Constitution? In the first place, judges

were political animals. Perhaps they were not office-seekers as such, or even avid partisans, but they were men of public affairs in the broad sense and were usually identified with a specific political persuasion. And, of course, they were appointed with all of that in mind. True, a liberal Democratic president may not always nominate fellow Democrats to the court, but he would very likely nominate fellow liberals. That is why Americans typically greet changes on the high bench with great interest. They know that much is riding on its ideological makeup.

Even more importantly, perhaps, Supreme Court justices were intellectual animals. They were raised within a certain milieu and trained by a certain methodology, and the learning and values of their world could have a decisive influence on them. Accordingly, even when the Supreme Court has not been sensitive politically, it has often been sharply attuned to intellectual and social trends. The skepticism of an Oliver Wendell Holmes, the compassion of a Louis Brandeis, and the logical incisiveness of a Felix Frankfurter have shaped the development of the Constitution far beyond the decisions they themselves rendered—for their influence helped mold the broader legal environment.

Finally, Supreme Court justices were citizens of the Republic, each with his own vision of its meaning and destiny. Often they were individuals of extraordinary sensitivity, and their position on the high court afforded them a unique opportunity to make virtue count. For if the United States was truly to live by the rule of law, if the integrity of its justice and the quality

Judges as Political Animals

Despite the fact that they are shielded from the tug and pull of daily politics, judges remain political animals. Nothing illustrated that truth more vividly than the notorious court- packing fight of 1937. At immediate issue was the commerce clause and the way it was being interpreted by the Supreme Court. More broadly at issue was the entirety of Franklin D. Roosevelt's New Deal.

The Court that year was redolent with politics. Four of the justices—the Four Horsemen as they were called—had been appointed by conservative presidents, and they entertained backward-looking, almost libertarian, views of the Constitution. Thus, as far as James McReynolds, George Sutherland, Willis Van Devanter, and Pierce Butler were concerned, the commerce clause did not authorize any sort of economic tinkering by the government, Depression or no Depression. And when the case of *Schechter Poultry Corporation v. United States* came before the Court in 1935, the Four Horsemen, together with a couple of "swing justices," used it to pronounce the New Deal's National Recovery Administration (NRA) null and void.

Beside the Four Horsemen, however, there sat three political liberals on the Court. Louis Brandeis, Harlan Fiske Stone, and Benjamin Cardozo had not themselves been appointed by Roosevelt, but their background was progressive and their sympathies generally lay with the New Deal. Embracing a more nationalistic interpretation of the Constitution, they dissented from the majority opinion in the *Schechter* case and others like it. If Roosevelt wanted to use the commerce clause for the purpose of social engineering, thought they, that was his business.

The two swing justices, Owen Roberts and Charles Evans Hughes, were under extreme pressure from both sides. If they continued to vote with the Four Horsemen,

of its compassion were to remain an inspiration to its people, if it was to continue to be governed by wisdom and moral precept, then the Supreme Court, perhaps more than any other institution, had to lead the way. For it was the custodian of the Constitution.

Judicial Reinterpretation in Action

Just how the judges could reshape the Constitution according to time, place, and circumstance can be illustrated with a convenient example. Take, for instance, the commerce clause, mentioned above as one of the Constitution's stretch-points. Let us focus on its specific ambiguities, and how various justices might reinterpret them in the light of changing conditions.

The commerce clause reads:

The Congress shall have Power to regulate Commerce with foreign Nations, and among the several States, and with the Indian Tribes.

So worded, the clause has three principal points of ambiguity. The first is the word *regulate*. This term could be interpreted to mean anything from perfunctory supervision (as police regulate traffic) to total

the New Deal was in deep trouble. It was undoubtedly with that fact in mind that Roosevelt himself, in an unprecedented foray into judicial politics, took on the Supreme Court head to head. Referring to its justices as "nine old men," the president proposed a major overhaul. The Court, said he, ought to be expanded by as many as six justices (his own appointees, of course) in order to better keep up with its workload.

At this there was a hue and cry throughout the country. Even though Roosevelt's proposal was well within constitutional boundaries (Congress has authority to adjust the size of the Court), it was patently disingenuous and it contravened the idea of judicial independence. The president himself soon saw his folly and backed down. For their part, the two swing justices underwent a profound change of heart. Sensing that the Constitution itself might be on the line, they suddenly began voting with the liberals and upholding New Deal measures. Some wag termed it "the switch in time that saved nine."

A cartoon illustration of Franklin Roosevelt's "Court Packing" scheme: A hue and cry throughout the country. (Library of Congress)

control (as the Politburo regulates Soviet industry). The second is the word *commerce*, which could mean anything from "goods physically in transit," on the one extreme, to "general business activities," on the other. The third ambiguity is found in a word that is missing. Should the clause be read to say that Congress shall have *sole* power over interstate commerce, or only *some* power? *Sole* power would mean that the states had no concurrent right of regulation, even with respect to commerce that was essentially local in character. *Some* power would bring forth yet another set of questions dealing with the meaning of "some."

A States' Rights Interpretation of the Commerce Clause. Let us suppose that some time ago, when the United States was still rather young, the Supreme Court decided that the national government was becoming far too meddlesome, and that the rights of the states must be vigorously reasserted. How, using the commerce clause, could this be accomplished?

The strategy would be to search through the clause's language and find that missing word. The justices would argue that even though the Constitution had given the commerce power to the national

Influence of the Great Legal Minds

Reading the opinions of the present-day Supreme Court, one runs across certain recognizable influences. For, in the process of assembling their thoughts—indeed, in the process of *acquiring* their thoughts—Supreme Court justices inevitably look back to their own heroes, the great justices of the past. As a result, some legal propositions seem truer than others, depending on what Louis Brandeis, or Benjamin Cardozo, or Felix Frankfurter, or Oliver Wendell Holmes happened to think of them.

Brandeis was a Wilsonian progressive. He distrusted big government, on the one hand, and big business on the other. Known early in his career as "the People's Attorney," he defended, often without pay, progressive-minded state laws that limited working hours and guaranteed a minimum wage. No traditionalist, he was especially imaginative in his procedure: if there was no good *legal* argument to be made in a client's behalf, he hauled in sociology, psychology, or just plain horse sense. The "Brandeis brief" is still used by legal activists today.

Cardozo, too, influenced the legal profession before joining the Court. As chief judge of the New York Court of Appeals, he was responsible for shaping and reshaping much American law. While respecting the power of precedent, he was never afraid to break new ground, especially where ethical considerations were concerned. So great was his moral influence on the Supreme Court that he is said to have converted it from a court of law into a court of justice. Felix Frankfurter of the Harvard Law School had a similar impact. The Court's concern for meticulously fair criminal procedure was in large measure due to his influence.

But the justice to whom the Supreme Court has most often looked back is Oliver Wendell Holmes, Jr. Son of a celebrated poet, young Holmes grew up in New England, fought in the Civil War (where he was seriously wounded), and then, willy-nilly, took up the law. After a long and fruitful career, mostly in the academic and intellectual side of the law, he was named to the Supreme Court, where he enjoyed an equally long career before retirement at the age of ninety-two.

government, it apparently had not done so exclusively. After all, the clause doesn't say "Congress shall have *sole* power to regulate Commerce," so perhaps the Founders only meant *some* power. And perhaps they left some power to the states.

That is a lot of "perhaps-ing." Yet a landmark case was argued in just this way. In the late 1840s, an era of ardent states' rights sentiment, a series of lawsuits known as the License Cases came before the Supreme Court. Three New England states had decided to tax and license the sale of alcoholic liquors within their own borders. Ordinarily that would pose no problem, but the liquors in question happened to come from Kentucky and Tennessee, and federal attorneys argued that the state action amounted to regulating interstate commerce.

Not long after his appointment, Holmes became known as the Great Dissenter, for he was often in disagreement with the Court's majority. Yet many of his dissents came to provide the basis for change. The most famous of them, in *Abrams v. United States* (1919), was that the expression of an unpopular opinion—such as opposition to the recent World War—was protected by the First Amendment unless it presented a "clear and present danger" of criminal action. The theory of the American Constitution, as Holmes saw it, was that "the best test of truth is the power of the thought to get itself accepted in the competition of the market."

Holmes had an even greater influence on jurisprudence. Living at a time when formal logic counted for everything in the law, he once again dissented. "The life of the law has not been logic: it has been experience," he wrote. "The felt necessities of the time, the prevalent moral and political theories . . . have had a good deal more to do than the syllogism in determining the rules by which men should be governed." If this was true, it followed that courts should mind their own business and leave it for legislative bodies to make laws, and further, that within broad constitutional limits, legislatures should be free to make whatever laws the people wanted. Where his colleagues on the Court habitually struck down all sorts of legislation, Holmes, dissenting yet again, became the apostle of judicial restraint.

Supreme Court Justice Oliver Wendell Holmes: A broad influence on the profession. (Library of Congress)

In writing the majority opinion, Chief Justice Roger B. Taney (an outspoken states' rights advocate) examined the commerce clause carefully and determined, sure enough, that a word was missing. "It appears to me to be very clear," he wrote, "that the mere grant of power to the general government cannot be construed to be an absolute prohibition to the exercise of any power over the same subject by the States." Accordingly, Taney concluded, if New Englanders wished to license and regulate the sale of Kentucky whiskey, it was fully within their power to do so. The effect of the decision was to cut back markedly on the scope of federal authority, and to enhance that of the states.

Supreme Court Chief Justice Roger B. Taney: A great deal of "perhaps-ing". (Library of Congress)

A Libertarian Interpretation of the Commerce Clause. There are some people for whom any regulation, federal *or* state, is bad medicine. Let us suppose that a group of such libertarians were to gain control of the Supreme Court and now want to reduce the scope of all authority. Again using the commerce clause, how would they go about it?

The answer lies in interpreting the word *commerce* as narrowly as possible. A broad interpretation of that term might include all sorts of things, but a very narrow one might be limited to something like: "transporting commodities from place to place." With a narrow enough definition in mind, one might argue that Congress' authority under the commerce clause was limited to regulating only the physical transportation of goods across state lines.

In 1895, the Supreme Court heard the case of *U.S. v. E.C. Knight Co.* The Court majority consisted of property-conscious conservatives who abhorred all regulation of business. They had already struck down a good deal of state regulation (on other constitutional grounds), but now they had the federal regulators to deal with. In 1890 Congress had passed the Sherman Antitrust Act, outlawing the practice of monopoly, and here in court was an avowed monopolist, American Sugar Refining Company, which controlled no less than 95 percent of the sugar market. The company shipped its product across every state line and sold it in every town and county in the U.S. But did that amount to *interstate commerce*?

No, said the Court, it didn't. "Commerce," as Chief Justice Fuller explained in the majority opinion, "succeeds to manufacture, and is not a part of it." In other words, since the defendent's monopolistic practices involved *manufacturing* rather than *transportation*, regulating them by means of the Sherman Act was beyond the scope of the commerce clause. Congress could regulate trains that hauled the sugar to market but it couldn't regulate the company that loaded them.

A Nationalistic Interpretation of the Commerce Clause. E.C. Knight was an extreme case, but what about the *other* extreme? Suppose the Supreme Court wished to *maximize* national authority. Suppose— just to make the example farfetched—that the activity to be regulated wasn't even commercial in nature. Suppose it was the enforcement of civil rights. How would the court proceed?

The Fuller Court: "Commerce" was not manufacturing. (Library of Congress)

The trick would be to read the term *commerce* very broadly, and to assert that anything even remotely affecting commerce would be fair game for federal regulation. In the 1964 case of *Katzenbach v. McClung*, the Supreme Court, seeking to justify Congress' authority to pass the Civil Rights Act of that year, employed just such reasoning. The offender was Ollie's Barbecue in Birmingham, Alabama, known for its southern soul cooking and its lily-white clientele. (Blacks could eat there only if they used the take-out service.) Since there was no other authority in the Constitution to pass civil rights legislation, the government made use of the commerce clause, arguing that by policing Ollie's racial policies it was really just "regulating commerce." But Ollie's was not located near a bus terminal, a train station, or a freeway exit, and virtually none of its patrons were interstate travelers.

Nevertheless, said the Court, the commerce clause still applied. Ollie's may not have catered to the traveling trade but "a substantial portion of the food [it] served" did come through interstate commerce. The Court, by extending the meaning of the word *commerce*, was stretching the commerce clause like a giant rubber band and giving Congress the authority to regulate domestic social relations. Similar extensions, of course, might be made into other areas as well, for almost anything under the sun affected commerce in *some* way.

The House that Jack Built

Right after the Great Depression, when government intervention into the economy was still an issue of first importance, an independent-minded farmer by the name of Roscoe Filburn decided to bring such intervention to a halt. He took Roosevelt's Agricultural Adjustment Administration to court with a case he figured he couldn't lose. The AAA was telling him how much wheat to plant, he complained, and it clearly had no authority to do so. For, the wheat in question was not sold on the open market, but consumed—as feed for cattle and poultry—on the premises of his Ohio dairy farm. Not the most hypocritical bureaucrat in Washington could claim to be regulating interstate commerce by regulating *him*.

But Filburn lost. A Supreme Court now staffed with Roosevelt-appointed justices was not about to quibble over what did or did not amount to interstate commerce. If Filburn consumed his wheat at home, reasoned the majority, well, that was just so much wheat he didn't have to buy down at the feed store. And, of course, the less wheat the feed store sold the less it had to order from its supplier. And so on. Eventually Filburn's wheat had its effect on interstate commerce. Sometime, somewhere, some trucker would have to load on a bushel or two less wheat because of Filburn's self-sufficiency. Like the dog that chased the cat that killed the rat that ate the malt in "The House That Jack Built," there was a chain of connections that led surely, if circuitously, back to the Constitution.

Of these three views of the commerce clause, which is correct? Many Americans would give the answer that all three are correct, each for its respective time. In 1847—as the argument goes— Roger Taney's view was the right one; in 1895 Melville Fuller's was; and in 1964, Earl Warren's. For it is widely believed that in the American constitutional system there is no immutable truth—that the Constitution is what the Supreme Court says it is.

To this argument, however, there is a reasonable next question. Is such a constitution still a *constitution*? Does it still possess that magical power to shape and control human action? Granted that time must bring change, granted that different courts will have different points of view,

and granted there is no practical appeal beyond the Supreme Court—still, if the Constitution is only what the Court says it is, then we no longer need a Constitution. All we need is a Court.

The Danger and the Opportunity of a Living Constitution

As a counterweight to the idea of constitutional *flexibility*, the Founders insisted on the obverse idea of constitutional *limits*. For example, Hamilton, writing in the *Federalist*, addressed the question of whether the Supreme Court, in exercising judicial review, might become a sovereign power in its own right. He concluded that it

A cartoon illustrating judicial tyranny: Remote but possible. (Library of Congress)

would not, because the justices—"without force or will of their own"—would naturally play the role of custodian, guarding and protecting the Constitution from attempts in the other branches to subvert it. The power of the Court would remain a passive one.

This view lays a heavy stress on the justices' personal qualities. To be a true custodian of the Constitution's spirit, while at the same time allowing for adaptation and change, requires virtue of a very high order and very special character. Above all else, it requires the virtue of *reverence for the law.*

Judicial Legislation

Historically, the Supreme Court, as Hamilton predicted, has exercised its power in largely passive ways. Even when it outraged liberal reformers by declaring reform legislation unconstitutional, it was reacting to what the justices saw as dangerous innovation in the legislative branch.

Beginning with the Warren Court in the 1950s, however, this situation changed dramatically. For the Court itself became a source of innovation, beginning with *Brown v. the Board of Education.* Educational policy had always lain within the exclusive domain of state legislatures. In handing down the Brown decision, the Court was in effect making new laws in regard to education.

In the abortion decision, *Roe v. Wade,* the Court became even more imperial. The problem was not whether abortion was good or bad, or whether states should or should not allow it. The problem was that such questions had always been decided by legislative bodies. By announcing the Roe decision, the court was once again making law.

In both these matters, the justices unquestionably acted out of high and sincere motives. After more than thirty years of school desegregation, there is a broad consensus among Americans that "separate but equal" was indeed unequal and socially disastrous to boot. The willingness of the Court to lead out in civil rights has been widely ascribed to the virtue of the justices. Earl Warren, for example, when faced with legal difficulties in the Brown case, pushed ahead with it anyway simply because he felt segregation was wrong.

Yet the virtue behind judicial legislation is clearly not that of reverence for the law. Rather, it is reverence for general

Judicial Legislation

Where does the Constitution say that school segregation is unlawful? Or that prayers may not be permitted in the classroom? Or that representation in state government must be apportioned on the basis of one person, one vote? The short answer is: nowhere. There is, however, a longer answer, which critics call *judicial legislation*. The classical example is the landmark Supreme Court case of *Roe v. Wade* (1973)—the abortion decision.

However one felt about abortion personally, it was easy enough to sympathize with the plight of "Jane Roe." Drifting from an unhappy childhood to an unfulfilled adult life, the girl represented in the court records by that pseudonym had already been ill used by the world before the night in October 1969, when she and two companions, walking down a lonely Georgia road, were met by three drunken men and brutally raped. The rape itself was traumatic enough, but learning that she was pregnant was far worse. (Her former husband had once beaten her for becoming pregnant, and the child had been taken away by her mother.) She seemed a good candidate to challenge the Texas statute outlawing abortion.

Meanwhile, two young Dallas attorneys were looking for just such a candidate. Since graduating from law school at the University of Texas, classmates Sarah Weddington and Linda Coffee had remained active in the local pregnancy counseling center. Under Texas law, the center could not counsel abortion, and that fact severely limited its options. The only thing to do, concluded the two lawyers, was challenge the law in court. In March of 1970, they learned of the existence of Jane Roe. Even

moral precepts. Saying that you believe in the dignity of man (often voiced in the desegregation debates) or the value of choice (often voiced in the abortion debates) is not the same as saying you believe in sticking to the Constitution.

Accordingly, judicial legislation, no matter how high-minded, had two significant costs. The first was in terms of the rule of law. When the courts make the laws, the laws lose a certain amount of consent (no one elects the justices) and take on a new uncertainty. Abortion is lawful today, perhaps unlawful tomorrow, depending on

factors we can scarcely glimpse. For people who seriously want to run their own lives, such uncertainty can be destructive.

The second cost was in terms of democratic self-government. Put simply, when the judges make the laws, the people don't. (One reason *Roe v. Wade* remains so controversial is that antiabortionists believe the decision could not have survived a popular referendum.) It was the Founders' clear intention that the people of Massachusetts should decide whether to integrate their schools and that the people of Texas should decide whether or not to

though a court decision could not come in time to help the girl personally (she would have the baby long before the issue was settled), the case needed a real plaintiff, and Jane was willing to sign on.

The case itself was a labyrinth of applications, forms, hearings, appeals, briefs—and expenses. Though the original registration was only one hundred dollars, over the months the tab steadily mounted. Sarah Weddington wound up stumping the state for financial support and quitting her job to devote full time to preparation. But things were moving. From the Federal District Court in Dallas, the case steadily worked its way up the ladder of appeals. By December of 1971, Weddington, who had never yet argued in court, found herself standing before the highest bench in the land.

However well crafted Weddington's arguments, the case turned in the end on Court politics. Five of the justices—most of them liberals from the Warren Court—simply believed that abortion was right, and after reargument the majority was raised to seven. Justice Harry Blackmun, who wrote the majority opinion, stood his justification on the implied right of privacy found in the First, Fourth, and Fifth Amendments. And what about the right to life—something the Fourteenth Amendment stated very clearly? That, said Blackmun, who had spent a week of research in the Mayo Clinic library, posed no difficulty, for an unviable fetus was not technically alive.

All of this was not good enough for dissenting Justices Byron White and William Rehnquist, who saw it as an invasion by the courts into the realm of lawmaking. Said White: "In a sensitive area such as this, involving as it does issues over which reasonable men may easily and heatedly differ, I cannot accept the court's [determination]. This issue, for the most part, should be left with the people and to the political process." In other words, according to White, the Court was legislating.

allow abortion. To contend that both groups would make such decisions in error is not to speak highly of their intelligence, virtue, or capacity for self-government.

Just What Is a "Living Constitution"?

The advent of judicial legislation gave ominous new meaning to the dictum that the Constitution is what the Supreme Court says it is, and touched off a vigorous debate about the proper role of the judiciary. That the Constitution should remain "living" is

accepted by both sides. Where they disagree is in the meaning of the word "living."

Original Intent. One side of the debate, prominently voiced by Robert Bork, a noted legal scholar, runs something like this. Judges must apply the law, not their own personal values. In order to find the law, a judge must investigate the intentions of those who originally made it. Thus, when an important decision is to be made by the Supreme Court, the justices ought first to find the principle or value that was originally intended to be protected and act accordingly.

For the people on this side of the debate, the Constitution does not attempt to frame a general theory of human experience. It does not try to tell us something about, say, the dignity of man that courts can generally apply. It is a historical document, written in the eighteenth century and addressed to specific concerns. If we wish to add new concerns to its text, we should do so by way of amendment.

Lodestar of Our Aspirations. The other side of the debate, prominently voiced by Justice William Brennan, holds that we must not try to hew to the historical meaning of the Constitution because the Founders' frame of reference was too narrow and included too many outdated prejudices. After all, when the Constitution was ratified, blacks were not free, women could not vote, and politics was not democratic. The wisdom of the Founders was sufficient for their time—but that time has passed.

Accordingly, what the Constitution has come to mean for us is a broad commitment to justice, brotherhood, and human dignity: it is the "lodestar of our aspirations." Thus, when faced with a constitutional question, the justice does not look to the outdated views of the Founders, he asks

what the words of the Founders have come to mean in our time. The Constitution, in other words, *does* advance a general theory of human experience.

This, of course, is the old debate between Jefferson and Hamilton in new dress. Jefferson would stress rigidity and ask that we reinterpret the Constitution with the intentions of the Framers in mind. And Hamilton would stress flexibility and see the Constitution as the "lodestar of our aspirations."

There is a possible way of bringing the two sides together. What might be emphasized is not the Founders' *original intent* but rather their *original aspirations*. And those aspirations, quite clearly, were for liberty as self-government. They wanted liberty, yes; they wanted man to be free from tyranny and anarchy. But they also wanted him to *govern* himself—to restrain his appetites and control his behavior. They wanted the order of popular government to reflect the order of the individual soul. There was something general about that aspiration. It did have to do with justice, dignity, and the brotherhood of man. But it also had to do with the rule of law and the virtue of self-restraint.

In other words, while the Constitution should remain living, it should also remain a constitution.

Part 2

Economics

The American political system has much to do with answering the "America Question" referred to in the main Introduction. So, too, does the American economic system. Indeed, politics and economics are often close relatives. Both arise from fundamental propositions about human nature; both must be concerned with tyranny, anarchy, and freedom; and both ultimately apply to the happiness and well-being of society. Whatever may be said of self-interest and public virtue in the political realm may be said in the economic as well. For example, despite the fact that self-interest rules economic society, it would be impossible to maintain such society without a respect for law, a willingness to abide by contracts, and a regard for the welfare of others.

Unsurprisingly, then, we learn that the same eighteenth-century debate that produced new ideas about government also produced new ideas about economics. Hume, Locke, and Montesquieu, the political philosophers, had their economic counterparts in Smith, Ricardo, and Malthus. Most of them, in fact, knew each other, corresponded energetically, and kept up a brisk trade in tools, ideas and methods. What was termed "political economy" was to them one thing.

Once again, the developing English colonies of North America played a significant role in the European debate. In these colonies could be found graphic examples of economic tyranny, economic anarchy, and economic freedom. The "tyranny" in question was called *mercantilism*—the idea that economic life needed to be carefully managed by the government. Because powerful English merchants had an interest in American tobacco, sugar, indigo, and naval supplies, they saw to it that Parliamentary laws effectively monopolized all trade in such products. These Navigation Acts, as they were called, never seemed to operate in the favor of American producers quite as much as the London merchants. But, then, as Lord Cornbury used to say, what else were colonies for?

As for economic anarchy, the colonies witnessed that in abundance whenever mercantilism was misapplied. For example, the English politicians who decided that struggling Jamestown was to be made a world center of glass blowing, or that Georgia was to become the silk-making capital of the empire, turned out to be courting disaster, and not much better could be said for the endless pulling and hauling over the possession of colonial monopolies. The messiness of political patronage had its counterpart in the economic world.

Yet, side by side with tyranny and anarchy in the colonies could be found examples of economic freedom. New England merchants presented one such example. Because New England's products, with the exception of naval supplies, never meshed into the empire's broader trade patterns, the merchants of Boston and Salem and Newport were pretty much left on their own: they could trade in whatever goods brought them a profit and at whatever prices they thought fitting. This activity proved to be the basis for some handsome personal fortunes but, even more importantly, it proved to be the region's economic salvation. Complex transactions in foodstuffs, molasses, rum, manufactured goods, and, alas, African slaves, attested to the business acuity of the New England traders, and helped put the colonies on a paying basis.

As in Europe, colonial economic and political questions were closely intertwined. The event that touched off the American Revolution, the so-called Boston Tea Party, was a result of *economic* as well as *political* oppression. It seemed that powerful British politicians, used to managing the colonies' economic affairs as they managed the political, decided to impose a monopoly on the transatlantic tea trade, effectively cutting American merchants out of a lucrative enterprise. In striking against the new monopoly, the colonists were standing up for economic liberty—what Adam Smith would call "market economics"—as well as political liberty. (Smith's economic manifesto, *The Wealth of Nations*, was published in 1776, the year of American independence.)

Just as the Americans felt their way along in the perfection of republican government, so too they felt their way along with the new economics. Reading Adam Smith, drawing lessons from their own history, trying a variety of economic experiments, they set theory against practice very carefully. Sometimes they felt that state-managed, mercantilistic enterprises were best. Alexander Hamilton's Bank of the United States, modeled after the all-powerful Bank of England, represented just such an approach, and Hamilton had other such developments on his agenda. At other times, Adam Smith's notion of the entirely unfettered marketplace had greater appeal. The contest between these two approaches lay at the root of many early political battles.

Ultimately, Americans came down on the side of Adam Smith and the market system. Indeed, some came to feel so strongly about the virtues of the market that they characterized it as nothing less than the handmaiden of liberty. If the United States had a written constitution embodying the idea of republicanism, they said, it had an unwritten constitution embodying the idea of "free enterprise." Whether or not that was true (and some disputed it vigorously), it was true that for much of its first two centuries the United States would cling tenaciously to the market system.

It behooves us to know how that system works.

10
The Political-Economic Problem

Concepts:

Scarcity
Opportunity Cost
Efficiency
Equity
Freedom
Economic Systems
Command or Planning
Market

Stark contrast of poverty and wealth highlights the
Political-Economic Problem. (Culver Pictures)

Mortal Choices

Jamie Fiske and Brandon Hall had much in common. Both were vivacious, playful infants. At about ten months, both got sick and needed the same treatment—a liver transplant. Today, Jamie and Brandon have very little in common. Jamie is alive and well, playing and laughing. Brandon is dead.

Jamie lived because her father, a hospital administrator, knew where to go for help and had the resources to get it. When it became clear that Jamie needed a new liver to survive and livers for transplant were scarce, her father went on the warpath. He telegraphed one thousand hospitals, called Ted Kennedy and Dan Rather, and took out ads in major newspapers. He even made a personal request before two thousand members of the American Association of Pediatricians, singing Jamie's favorite song for them: "You are my sunshine, my only sunshine, you make me happy, when skies are gray. You'll never know, dear, how much I love you, please don't take my sunshine away."

Eventually the three major television networks aired the appeal for a liver, and a suitable donor, an Alpine, Utah, boy who died in a train accident, provided the liver to save Jamie's life. America was proud that someone had come to the aid of a dying little girl.

What many Americans did not know was that Jamie's case wasn't rare. Each year, hundreds of people die because there is a severe shortage of kidney, liver, and heart donors. This shortage exists because few Americans bother to fill out donor cards, and doctors are afraid to ask bereaved parents or next of kin for permission to remove organs of their deceased loved ones. Meanwhile, a new drug, cyclosporin, has significantly improved the odds of surviving a transplant operation, and hence the demand for organs has gone up. In 1987, only 700 of approximately 5000 needy patients received a liver transplant. Of the 15,000 needy heart patients, only 1000 obtained hearts.

Brandon Hall was just one of the many children for whom there is no donor. The son of poor parents, Brandon's case never made it to the "CBS Evening News," and his dad didn't get to sing for pediatricians. With no liver available, he died.

There is an emerging debate within the American medical establishment on the problems of increasing the supply of organs and choosing the fortunate few who will receive transplants. Many medical authorities look upon public virtue as the answer to the organ shortage. A poll by the *New York Times* reported that 70 percent of Americans would be willing to donate part or all of their bodies. However, only 15 percent of Americans have filled out donor cards. Apparently, potential donors may say they are willing to give up their organs, but without incentive they won't actually commit to do it. "If there's no profit, people don't produce things," says economist Marvin Brams. "Why should we expect people to give up an organ for nothing?" Compounding the problem, doctors are frequently unwilling to remove organs when the deceased has a donor card for fear the consent may not be valid. Still, many medical administrators hope that public virtue will solve the transplant problems for them. If not, government may solve the problem through legislation.

Another faction is advocating a free and open market in which organs could be bought and sold. This group would substitute self interest for public virtue. If the sale of organs were allowed, then the incentives would increase the supply of organs and reduce, or even eliminate, the scarcity. This group claims that organ sales would be a source of income for poor Americans who now often provide organs free for the more wealthy.

There is, however, much opposition to such a plan. Opponents of legal sales of human organs counter that a free market would make the poor a source of spare parts for the rich, auctioning off life to the highest bidder, and encouraging families to use the body parts of a deceased loved one to buy a new car or take a trip to Disneyland. This group believes that public virtue through voluntary donation of organs is the solution to the organ shortage.

The consequences of a market for organs are controversial and not entirely clear. Proponents of the market system point to five significant benefits. First, the federal government spends $2 billion annually providing dialysis for people with kidney ailments. Since a free market would provide the way to obtain kidneys for those on dialysis, taxpayers would save some of the $2 billion expenditure. Second, a free market would reduce friction between doctors and patients, and doctors and relatives of patients. As things now stand, doctors must request organ removals at a time when people are least prepared to think rationally. Third, the success rate of organ transplants would probably increase, because doctors would have a wider choice of organs rather than being forced to take whatever is available. Fourth, the money earned could be used to pay medical costs or funeral expenses of the donor or help families who may have lost their breadwinner. Fifth, and most important, more lives would be saved.

Some transplants, particularly of kidneys, can be performed with a live donor. Proponents of the market system argue that people should be allowed to sell a kidney if they so desire, even though this can be life-threatening if their remaining kidney fails. Writing to a congressional committee considering a ban on the sale of organs, Larry Carter of Surrey, British Columbia, argued that allowing him to sell his kidney would provide the means to obtain the degree in environmental management he wanted. "My kidney is the only capital resource I still possess that can be marketed in order to provide me with a chance of gaining access to educational and employment opportunities. I am far more able to sacrifice one kidney, rather than sacrifice the most productive years of my life."

Despite Carter's lofty goal, his statement is cannon fodder for those who oppose the sale of organs. Those who are against a market for organs claim that the possibility of selling a kidney or an eye for a high price would be an incentive for poor people to pillage themselves for the benefit of the well-to-do. No one likes the image of an indigent selling a kidney in return for drugs or alcohol. Milton Friedman, an economist who usually advocates free markets, fears that an organ market would encourage murder. In fact, he points out, two men were convicted of murder in the nineteenth century for killing to provide cadavers to medical science. It is also claimed that paying for organs would cause diseased organs to enter the market because of the incentive for donors to lie about their medical histories.

If society does decide against a market for organs, the problem of how to allocate scarce organs will have to be confronted. According to the American Medical Association, organs should be allocated according to "who needs it the most and who is most likely to do well with the new organ." Unfortunately, when more than one patient is about to die, it is not easy to decide who needs it most. With cyclosporin, most recipients now do very well with the transplanted organ.

Some doctors suggest that organs should continue to go to the children whose parents sought out the organ. Since it takes money to seek after an organ, this system may favor the rich as much as a market. Other options include lotteries or giving the organ to the person who has waited the longest. While these options remove the influence of wealth, they are hardly less capricious and have other disadvantages.

For the moment, there is no accepted solution to the organ shortage. As usual, politicians and medical authorities hope that public virtue will solve the problem for them. So far, that hasn't happened. It is likely that the growing success of organ transplants will force society to choose a system to increase the supply of donated organs and allocate them for use. The choice is unlikely to be easy.

The Nature of the Problem

The root cause of the political-economic problem is *scarcity*. Scarcity intensifies self-interest, which creates the potential for serious conflict. Indeed, the conflict among groups or individuals pursuing their economic interests, perhaps the most common type of conflict in society, can easily escalate into violence. Revolutions and civil wars often have economic overtones. Strikes, conflicts over water rights, property disputes, and attempts at monopolization are a few of the types of economic conflict that have been marked by violence throughout history.

For survival, societies or countries must choose a method or system to control and harmonize economic self-interests. The choice of an economic system is a political decision since it must be made collectively by the whole society. The political-economic problem may be defined as the problem of choosing an economic system to coordinate or harmonize the economic interests of individuals or groups within the society. A society may decide to make a single decision and adopt an economic system that resolves all economic conflicts in the same manner. However, societies are more likely to consider the issue over and over again as each new economic problem arises.

The development of medical procedures to transplant organs (hearts, livers, kidneys, etc.) presents an example of society once again confronting the political-economic problem. Donor organs are tragically scarce. Thousands of people die each year in the United States because of the scarcity of organs for transplantation. This scarcity creates the problem of conflicting self-interests. The interests of donors and recipients are in conflict with one another, as are the interests of different recipients. The interest of the doctor waiting anxiously to transplant an organ is in dramatic conflict with the doctor struggling to save the life of the potential donor. We see evidence of this conflict all around us. Potential organ recipients offer money for kidneys or livers. Doctors struggle to agree on procedures for transplants. Appeals are made on television for livers to transplant into young children near death. Eventually, society must confront the problem and develop a system to deal with the conflicting interests. The problem is a direct result of scarcity. If there were millions of organs available for transplantation, no tension would exist.

If you doubt the role of scarcity in creating self-interest, just consider the difference in the behavior of motorists out for a leisurely drive compared to motorists

THE ECONOMIC PROBLEM

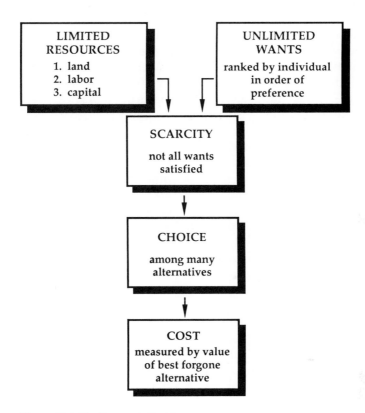

Figure 10.1: The Economic Problem

leaving a concert or a football game. Sunday drivers on an uncongested road are considerate and polite, often letting others go ahead of them. Those same motorists are transformed into candidates for the Indy 500 by the congestion following a concert or sporting event, often cutting off other drivers and challenging the right of pedestrians to remain on earth.

Wants and Resources

Scarcity comes from the interplay of our wants (both as individuals and as a society) and our resources. (See Figure 10.1) There

is a rich variety of resources available to satisfy our wants and needs. The earth possesses great richness in agricultural land, forests, rivers, oceans, minerals, ores, fuels, and other natural materials. Yet, natural resources, usually referred to as land by economists, contribute the least to the value of our consumption in a modern economy. Tools, buildings, machines, and land improvements, known to economists as capital, contribute somewhat more to production than natural resources. Together, capital and natural resources of all kinds account for less than 40 percent of the value of production. Labor, the effort that individuals apply to the process of production, is by far the most important resource available to satisfy the wants and needs of individuals or groups.

These resources (land or natural resources, capital, and labor) combine together to produce goods and services. Through time, better technology has been developed so that more goods and services can be produced from the limited resources available. Most human progress has come about, not because more resources are available, but because we have learned to produce more from the resources at hand. In our modern world with literally thousands of different goods and services, it is easy to overlook the amount of human creativity poured into the process of transforming resources into these goods and services. The automobile you drive is simply a product of the earth you see on a Sunday outing, combined with extraordinary human effort and creativity. That creativity is largely expressed through capital or tools that extend the productive powers of land and labor so that cars, stereos, modern homes, medical care, and other material wonders are possible. Such technological creativity is not often as evident or appreciated as a painting by Rembrandt or a play by Shakespeare, but is no less impressive over the long course of human history.

In spite of the abundant resources available and the dazzling technological progress through time, there has never been enough to go around. With finite or limited resources, goods and services are limited. Unfortunately, our wants are not limited. Man has an insatiable appetite for more. If we have enough of one good, there is always something else on our list. For this reason, economists use the term "wants" rather than "needs" when referring to our economic condition. Our biological needs could easily be met by a fraction of the productive potential of a modern economy. The shock and sense of tragedy concerning conditions of famine in Africa reflect the fact that our economy meets our biological needs quite easily and is largely focused on goods and services to satisfy less urgent desires.

"Needs" also suggests that our purchases or economic behavior will be quite inflexible. "Wants" would appear to be more descriptive of the choice process because our choices seem to vary a great deal with the cost of various alternatives, as well as our income. If the latest model sports car had a price tag of fifty cents, most of us would feel an absolute compulsion or need to have one. If, on the other hand, a basic small car cost $100,000, most of us would turn to bicycles, walking, and buses for our transportation. The word "wants" seems to convey this sense of flexibility better than "needs."

Cause and Consequence of Scarcity

The interaction of our unlimited wants and our limited resources produces scarcity and forces us to choose among competing alternatives. We would all like a new car, a trip to Europe, a new suit, a better tennis racket, or filet mignon for dinner. But we are constrained by our income or wealth, by time, and by the prices asked for goods and services. These limits or constraints force us to make choices. For example, a typical U.S. household had an income of about $27,000 in 1985, spending about 20 percent of its income on food, 8 percent on clothing, 22 percent on shelter, and 10 percent on recreation. In all likelihood, such a family would like a better house, a newer car, and more elegant clothes, but the constraints of a $27,000 income and the prices charged for goods and services force the family to choose among the various alternatives.

Our economic lives are basically focused on two activities. We are continually trying to reduce the pressure of the constraints on our choices by raising our income and accumulating wealth. However, constraints are always there no matter how high our income or vast our wealth because we always prefer more. Consequently, we are forced to make choices about the allocation of our income. We constantly review these choices to see if there is a way to achieve more satisfaction from the limited income available.

Scarcity creates intensified self-interest because it forces choice. If Jamie Fiske receives a liver transplant, it means that Brandon Hall will not receive a transplant and may die. If the government chooses to increase taxes to pay for an expanded educational system, private citizens will not be able to buy the stereos, cars, or VCRs they intended to purchase with the income that has now been taxed away by the government. If society chooses to clean up the environment, there will be fewer goods to enjoy. If Congress and the president decide that the United States should spend more on defense, then other choices such as education, medical care, or houses may have to be forgone. Choice is uncomfortable and difficult, for it means that some interests of some individuals will not be met. The political-economic problem is to choose an economic system that will harmonize the conflicting interests that arise because of the difficult choices forced on all of us by scarcity.

Opportunity Cost

The act of choosing brings cost into the world. For a moment, imagine a world without choice—an Eden. Every possible good thing in life is available without giving up any time or expending any effort. In such a world no choice is necessary. Since nothing is given up in order to have something else, there is no cost in Eden. Were we to live in such a world, then all goods and services would be free and conflicting self-interests would be nonexistent. But we do not live in Eden. In almost every situation imaginable, we pay for our choices by giving up alternatives. The real cost of a choice is measured by what is given up when that choice is made. This concept of cost is called opportunity cost. The opportunity cost of a choice is the value of the best forgone alternative. Opportunity cost is the only definition of cost that will consistently be correct and lead to rational choice making.

Suppose Congress were considering three alternative uses for an appropriation of $50 billion: twenty-five new Trident submarines for defense, an increase of $50 a month in basic social security benefits, or grants-in-aid of $10,000 for five million college students. Congress must rank the three alternatives in order to make a choice. Suppose that their ranking is, first, improvement of social security benefits; second, increased funding to higher education; and third, increased defense spending. The opportunity cost of improving social security benefits is the value of the *next best* alternative—more funding of higher education.

In many instances, the opportunity cost may be directly measured by the money spent for a particular choice. When we buy

The Opportunity Cost of College

The economic value of the college diploma has been much debated. While college graduates do earn more once they have left college, those who forgo the college experience get four more years of earnings and don't have to pay today's hefty tuition. Is it worth it economically to go to college?

On the surface, the earnings advantages of being a college graduate are quite substantial. In raw earnings, a person graduating from college today can expect to earn about $1.6 million in the rest of his life. A high school graduate, on the other hand, will earn about $1.1 million. That means that the college graduate earns over $10,000 a year more than the high school graduate.

The opportunity cost of going to college can be awfully high, however. The typical college education will cost the student about $60,000, assuming $5,000 a year for tuition and books and $10,000 a year in earnings that are lost while attending school. Housing, food, clothing, and other typical expenses are not included in the opportunity cost of an education because this consumption would still exist if the student were not going to college. If a high school graduate did not attend college and invested his savings in an annuity at 4 percent interest, it would give him an annual income of a little less than $3,000. So, the college graduate comes out ahead by about $7,000 a year, but not by nearly as much as it might seem at first.

To complicate matters further, economists note that the difference between the high school graduate's income and the college student's income is deceptive. The person who typically goes to college would probably have made more money without a college education than the person who typically does not. So, the college graduate does earn $7,000 a year more than the high school graduate, but if the college graduate hadn't gone to college, he would have made more than the typical high school graduate anyway. How much of the $7,000 difference is due to college and how much is due to his own abilities?

The bottom line seems to be that the opportunity cost of going to college is higher than most people realize. However, for people with ambition, the opportunity cost of not going to college is even greater. By not going to college they will be giving up a higher income, even if the difference isn't the full $7,000 a year. Of course, college may involve a lot of consumption as well as some investment. A visit to a college campus some fall afternoon to see the big game with an arch rival would convince many that college is worth it even if it doesn't increase incomes at all.

a loaf of bread at a cost of one dollar, we do not need to know the exact alternative had we not purchased the bread. Rather, we think of the cost in terms of the dollar paid. However, there simply are many situations where the opportunity cost cannot be measured by the dollar expenditure. For example, most individuals use airlines for long-distance travel rather than the bus, even though the cost of a bus ticket may be only half as much as that of the airline ticket. This preference for the airplane would seem irrational if we only consider the ticket price in opportunity cost. Obviously, there is another dimension to the opportunity cost of travel, that of time.

Since people value their time, or their time has alternative uses, the cost of travel includes the ticket price *and* the value of time used to travel. Travel by bus involves a lower ticket price but a higher opportunity cost of time for most people. Consequently, people are more likely to travel by airline than by bus.

Choices about whom to marry, whether or not to go to college, or whether we should eat that extra piece of pie, are all examples where dollar expenditure is not the key element of opportunity cost. The liver for Jamie Fiske was donated without a monetary cost. From a view of opportunity cost, however, the cost of the liver transplant for Jamie must include the value of life to the person who would have received the liver had it not been given to Jamie. The principle of opportunity cost has application in every situation that involves choice where it is necessary to sacrifice some alternative in order to obtain the alternative we prefer.

The principle of opportunity cost must be intuitively understood to make rational choices. But it is human nature to deny the cost of our choices. We continually search for ways of making choices costless. Con games and fraud are based on our weakness for the nonexistent costless alternative. Political campaigns are often filled with promises of more public services while taxes will be reduced. In our personal lives, we often try to fool ourselves into believing that our choices are costless. The midnight raid on the refrigerator is rarely viewed in terms of the extra calories it will pack into an already expanding waistline. Diet plans draw billions of dollars away from consumers by promising "You will lose weight while eating everything you want." The opportunity cost of play rather than study or work is rarely

calculated. Unfortunately, nature quickly brings us back to reality by confronting us with the cost of each and every choice. Thomas Carlyle, the great historian, labeled economics as the "dismal science." Because economists remind the world of the cost of each and every alternative, this label of the "dismal science" has stuck. Society does not want to be reminded that the opportunity cost of saving a beautiful little girl from death by giving her a liver transplant is the joy and fulfillment that another child would have received from a liver transplant.

Cooperation and Conflict

As soon as there is contact and interaction among individuals, pursuit of self-interest by one individual may affect the position of other individuals. Thus, the self-interest of each individual is highlighted and brought into focus. At times, it may be in the self interest of individuals to cooperate. Work may be accomplished more easily in teams. Two men carrying boards are more than twice as productive as a single man trying to balance boards and carry them. Trade will often be in the interest of individuals so that individuals may specialize in particular activities and trade with one another. But at other times, it is inevitable that the self-interests of individuals will conflict. A gain for one will be a loss for another.

When an individual is alone, there is no issue of ownership or property. The individual can use all the resources available, managing their use to the best possible level. Once there are more than a few individuals in a society, questions of ownership of property become very serious indeed. Resources, and the rights to use particular resources, must be allocated. Conflict over the ownership and use of

The Boston Tea Party

The American revolution was in part tormented by economic conflict. In general, the colonists wanted an economic system with fewer controls on free exchange. The incident in Boston Harbor illustrates the intensity of feeling that an economic conflict often generates.

Captain William Rotch of the *Dartmouth* was in a spot of trouble. When in London several months earlier, he had been warned against carrying tea to the colonies, as other merchantmen before him; but somehow he had agreed to take the stuff on board anyway. Now, in December of 1773, he was in Boston with his controversial cargo—and was about to touch off the American Revolution.

Arriving on the twenty-seventh of November, Rotch was greeted by an irate citizenry, led by one Samuel Adams, and ordered to turn around and sail back to England. He would have been happy to comply, but there was a hitch. Thomas Hutchinson, the governor of Massachusetts, was just as irate, and he wanted the tea landed. According to the law, Captain Rotch had exactly twenty days to make up his mind, after which time the matter would be taken out of his hands. It was a rough twenty days.

He first tried dallying. Tying the *Dartmouth* alongside Griffin's Wharf (where she was soon joined by two tea-laden sister ships), the skipper hoped that the storm would soon blow over. On December 11, however, he was again summoned by the "Committee of Correspondence," as Adams' group called itself, and asked to explain his delay. He could not set sail without a clearance, he said. *Then get one*, came the reply.

There followed a game of cat-and-mouse over the matter of the clearance. Time and again Rotch went to see the collector of customs for the permit in question, and time and again he met with bureaucratic stalling. For his part, Governor Hutchinson quietly blocked the exit of the *Dartmouth* for good. He moved two cruisers into

Boston Tea Party, December 16, 1773: How Americans came to prefer coffee. (Library of Congress)

position at the mouth of the harbor and ordered Castle William to fire on any ship that sailed without a clearance. Not wishing to be blasted into matchwood for what seemed like an abstract principle, Rotch gave his crew liberty and tried to make himself scarce.

Things came to a head on December 15 when Rotch received a final refusal from the customs house. There was only one recourse left open to him, and that was a direct appeal to the governor. Sam Adams wanted to make sure that every legal means was exhausted before resorting to Plan B. He made arrangements for Rotch to seek out Governor Hutchinson on Thursday, December 16, the *Dartmouth's* twenty-first day in port.

It was perhaps symbolic of his isolation that Thomas Hutchinson had fled to his country estate at Milton. Hutchinson, ironically, was a Massachusetts man himself, one of the few royal governors to be appointed from colonial ranks. So he had to make good. As far as he was concerned, this was the final test of British authority in North America: either the tea would be landed and the empire would rule, or the tea would be destroyed and the mob would rule—there was no middle course. Hutchinson had been deserted by the Massachusetts Assembly and even by his own council. Complaints from the various towns were piled high on his desk, and ever since the Boston Massacre the military had been useless to him. He was possibly the loneliest man in the world.

The crowd milling about the Old South meetinghouse on Thursday afternoon was 7000 strong and in no light humor. Throughout the afternoon, men stood around in small groups, swinging their arms and stamping their feet to shake off the winter chill. "Who knows," said one of them, "how tea will mingle with salt water?" and there was a roar of applause. For, pending the return of Captain Rotch from seeing the governor, Plan B was to go into effect. It had been hatched in a back room of the *Boston Gazette* by Sam Adams and others, and it frankly called for violence. The hour of decision was at hand.

By five o'clock the sun had set and the church was dimly lit with candles. A motion was made and unanimously approved: come what may, the tea would not be landed. Rotch arrived a half hour later with the governor's formal refusal. It was the voice of Sam Adams that broke the ensuing stillness. "This meeting," he said, "can do nothing more to save the country."

Within seconds a war whoop was heard outside and fifty men, thinly disguised as Mohawk Indians, passed by Old South and headed for the wharf. Along with thousands of other Bostonians suddenly in a holiday mood, Rotch trailed after the "Indians" to watch the fun. "Ugh!" was the watchword, of course, countersigned by a "Me know you." Just who really saw whom that night would forever be disputed in Boston, but the tribe clearly included some prominent citizens. One witness claimed to have recognized John Hancock.

While the throng stood watching in the frosty moonlight, the self appointed stevedores did their work. Three hundred and forty-two chests of tea from the British East India Company were hauled to the decks of the three ships, smashed open with hatchets, and emptied into Boston Harbor. The next morning the stuff lay in windrows along Dorchester beach, where the waves had driven it ashore. Americans have preferred coffee ever since.

Thomas Hutchinson was dumbfounded when he heard the news, though he had done as much as Sam Adams to bring the Boston Tea Party about. In any event, he had his test of the king's authority; it remained only to see if Boston would pay for the damage. Captain Rotch carried notice of the affair back to London in the *Dartmouth*—for he was free at last to clear Boston for home.

land and other resources is inevitable unless there is a government or some final authority to decide questions of ownership. Even with government to restrain people, violence over property rights has been commonplace. Violence between European settlers and natives was almost always sparked by unresolved disputes over property rights. Homicide by shovel is enshrined in the folklore of the West because of conflict over water rights. Even if violent conflict does not occur, the interplay of self–interest of various individuals may have adverse effects.

The interaction of individuals creates possibilities of conflict and cooperation. Conflict may exist whenever the interaction of two individuals will make one or both of them worse off. Cooperation may exist whenever the interaction will make both individuals better off. An economic system is needed to resolve the potential conflicts between individuals or groups and to achieve any possible cooperation between individuals or groups. The choice of an economic system is a collective choice that must be made by the group or society. It is a political decision with economic implications. Writers in the nineteenth century referred to the study of the problem of what economic system is best as "political economy" because of the political and economic dimensions of the problem. Therefore, in this text, the problem of what economic system to choose is referred to as the political-economic problem. Once again, this problem is defined as the problem of choosing an economic system to coordinate and harmonize the economic interests of different individuals and groups in society. This decision is the most important economic decision that we make

through government. It affects our prosperity and our freedom. Indeed, the decision about economic systems represents the central division between the Soviet Union and the United States, or East and West.

Basic Economic Questions

Any economic system has to decide certain basic economic questions. First, the system must decide what goods and services will be produced. How much of the economy's resources will be devoted to producing food, clothing, rock 'n roll records, education, etc.? Every choice has an opportunity cost. A society that allocates most of its resources to food may end up with naked but well-fed people—not a pretty picture. Why should resources be devoted to producing rock 'n roll records when there is malnutrition or starvation? It should be obvious that the question of what goods and services to produce is complex and difficult to answer since there are thousands of alternatives meeting quite different wants in society.

Second, an economic system must decide how to produce the goods and services chosen. The varied resources of an economy—natural resources or land, capital, and labor—can be combined in different ways to produce the different goods and services desired in an economy. For example, in a developing country of Asia, rice may be grown in small plots (an acre or two) with a great deal of manual labor and little, if any, machinery. Animal power may play a fairly important role in the production process. Rice grown along the Sacramento River in California would be produced in a much different way with quite large fields being cultivated with large tractors and other farm equipment, and almost no labor. Each method of production may be the best method for that particular economy given the resources available. Just as there are many alternative goods and services, there are a substantial number of production methods available for each good or service produced in an economy. Furthermore, the production method used in one part of the economy must be coordinated with the approach used in another part of the economy. If rice farmers wish to use more tractors and chemical fertilizer in the production of rice, then the manufacturers of tractors and fertilizer must respond, which means that the steel industry and the petrochemical industry must meet the needs of producers of tractors and fertilizer. Their decisions affect still other sectors of the economy. The decisions about how each good and service is to be produced must be coordinated with all of the other production decisions in the economy. That is, all of the production decisions must be made consistently.

The third and final question that must be answered by the political-economic system is for whom the goods and services of the economy will be produced. The question of *for whom* has two parts. First, will most goods and services be produced for consumption now, or will resources be used to increase the goods and services available for consumption later? If the decision is made to consume more now, then natural resources are used up and most capital and labor is used to produce goods for current consumption, such as food, clothing, autos, and TVs. If society decides to create more consumption for the future, then some natural resources are saved for future use. Capital and labor are partially devoted to creating more machines, tools, and equipment for the future so that the ability of the future economy to produce consumption goods will be increased. Of course, every economy balances the two alternatives by consuming a part of the output of the economy now, while at the same time creating more capital for future production.

The second part of the "for whom" question deals with the distribution of the goods available for consumption. For whom *today* are the goods and services going to be produced? Once the economic pie has been baked, are the slices going to be the same size? Or will some slices be much larger than others? Our first reaction might be to argue for very similar slices since equal treatment is a part of good manners. Unfortunately, the "for whom" question is complicated by the fact that the size of the economic pie may be related to the way we cut the pie. It may be that a society that decides to have an equal distribution of consumption or income will find that the economic pie is smaller because of less incentive to work and save to produce economic growth. Thus, the question of "for whom" is complicated because it is connected to the other questions that must be answered by the economic system.

Every economic system must answer these three basic economic questions:

1. What goods and services will be produced in the economy?
2. How will natural resources, capital, and labor be combined to produce the goods and services chosen?
3. For whom will the goods and services be produced?

The economy and the political-economic system will be judged by how well these three questions have been answered. It is necessary to have criteria to judge how well the economic system has answered these questions. We can measure the success or failure of a political economic system by how well it meets the basic goals or objectives of society.

Basic Goals for the Political-Economic System

There are two fundamental economic goals that any society has for its economy. First, each society would like to obtain as much value as possible, in terms of goods and services produced, from the resources that it has available, while increasing the ability of the economy to produce in the future. We label this goal efficiency. Second, each society would like the goods and services available for consumption to be distributed fairly. This goal of economic justice may be labeled as equity. To these two economic goals, a political or social goal of freedom might also be added. These three goals are the criteria by which the political-economic system may be judged. Any system that is superior in all three of these criteria would clearly be preferred over the alternatives. If one system is better in terms of one criterion while another dominates when the economy is considered by another alternative, the choice is more complicated. Suppose, for example, that one economic system is more efficient and fair (equitable), but does not give as much freedom to its people. What choice would or should be made?

Efficiency

Efficiency is a primary preoccupation of economists. The intuitive notion of efficiency is simply that an economy is doing as well as possible. An efficient economy is not necessarily a rich economy. It is possible that an economy may have a fairly low standard of living because of few resources and still be efficient. On the other hand, an economy blessed with abundant resources may perform at a very inefficient level and still have a high standard of living. This means that one must carefully measure efficiency by considering the resources of an economy and their use.

If economists were analyzing an economy at a particular time to evaluate its efficiency, they would look for the following conditions:

1. Full employment of resources.
2. Production of the most desired or right amounts of each good or service.
3. Production of each good or service at the lowest possible opportunity cost by using the right combination of resources.

Full Employment of Resources. The most obvious sign of inefficiency in an economy is unemployment of some resource that should be brought into the process of production. If a worker wants to work but is unable to find employment, the economic pie is not as large as it could be. If tools, buildings, or machines are idle, the result is the same as if workers were unemployed. On the other hand, it will make economic sense to save some natural resources for future use. This means that some storage of natural resources will be efficient and should not be considered unemployment of resources. Unemployment of resources is an important source of inefficiency in many economies. An increase of 1 percent in the unemployment rate of labor in the U.S. economy causes a loss of about $75 billion, enough output to provide scholarships of $10,000 for every full-time college student in the U.S. Twenty-five percent of the labor force was unemployed during the Great Depression of the 1930s, resulting in a loss of perhaps a half trillion dollars of output.

Of course, some temporary unemployment is desirable. There is a small amount of unemployment in the economy due to adjustments from one job to another or because some individuals have just entered the labor force to look for employment. Most experts believe that this sort of unemployment (about 4 percent to 6 percent of the labor force) is not a serious inefficiency since some time is needed to place workers in new jobs.

The Right Goods and Services. However, full employment of resources is not a guarantee of efficiency. Suppose that all resources in an economy were fully employed producing a single product such as T-shirts with a picture of Whitney Houston on the front. Only someone with bizarre tastes would argue that such an economy is efficient. If satisfaction of consumer preferences is a goal of the economy, then resources must be fully employed producing the right combination of goods and services. That combination of products will depend on the preferences of the individuals in society, the distribution of income among these individuals, and the costs of production of the goods and services. Producing the right combination of goods and services is extremely complex and difficult in a modern economy. There are thousands of different goods or services available in the United States to over eighty million households with different preferences. To come close to the correct mix of production requires a great deal of information. Clearly, a great deal of inefficiency can exist in an economy even though all resources are fully employed.

Lowest Possible Cost. Full employment and the right combination of products is not sufficient to guarantee efficiency. The economy must also produce each good and service at the lowest opportunity cost. This criterion requires that the best technique be used and that natural resources, labor, and capital be used in the proper proportions for production of each good. For example, it may be best to produce food with a great deal of land and capital but very little labor to achieve the lowest opportunity cost. On the other hand, land and capital may not be very useful in the production of educational services, so a great deal of labor should be used in that production process. Each good or service will be different. As in the case of the problem of producing the right combination of goods and services, the achievement of production at the lowest possible cost is a complex and difficult criterion of efficiency to meet.

The Push to Efficiency. No economy ever reaches full efficiency, but there are strong forces pushing a society toward that goal. Elimination of inefficiency means that everyone may be better off, or, at the very least, some individuals in the society may be enriched without taking anything away from others. Thus, the elimination of inefficiency provides a "free lunch" to society, giving a strong incentive to find and eliminate such inefficiencies. As long as inefficiencies exist, cooperative actions that will make individuals better off are possible. Consequently, individuals or groups search for "trades" or agreements that help both parties to the agreement. Unfortunately, economic systems and governments sometimes prevent individuals or groups from making exchanges that will move an economy closer to the goal of efficiency. Once all inefficiency has been squeezed out of the economy so that the economic pie is as large as possible, there are no more agreements or trades that will improve the economic position of the individuals. The only way to improve any person's position in an efficient economy is to take something away from someone else.

To sum up, an economy is efficient when resources are fully employed to produce the right combination of goods and services at the lowest possible cost. In terms of the basic economic questions referred to earlier, an economy will be efficient if it has properly answered the basic questions of what goods and services to be produced and how best to produce them. Until an economy has reached efficiency, there will be trades and agreements that could be made between individuals that will benefit both of them. Once an economy has reached full efficiency, the only way to improve the economic position of one individual is by reducing the economic well-being of another individual.

Equity

Efficiency is only one of the important economic goals within an economy by which a system may be judged. People not only want the economic pie to be as large as possible (efficiency), they also want the pie to be fairly divided (equity). In other words, people want the third basic economic question of "for whom" the goods are to be produced to be justly answered. Economics has very little to say about equity because it is basically a matter of individual values and opinions. No one can really claim authority to speak for the community as to what is fair or unfair. Hence, the debate over equity is active and confusing with no emerging consensus.

We may consider economic justice, or equity, from two very different views. One view is usually summarized as equality of opportunity since most people believe that there should be a more or less equal chance for everyone to succeed economically. This view of economic justice would relate closely to some of the principles of the rule of law such as generality, equality, and impartiality. If individuals are to run an economic race with different prizes depending on where they finish, everyone should start the race at the same place and run under the same conditions. Concern for equality of opportunity would lead to equal access in education, anti-discrimination laws, and removal of artificial barriers to any individual's economic progress. However, equality of opportunity would not require that the rewards from the economic race be similar. Some might be very rich because they were very good at the economic game, while others would be poor. As long as all felt assured that the economic game was fair in terms of equality of opportunity, equity would be reached. The great difficulty with the concept of equality of opportunity comes in application. How can society ever assure equality of opportunity? More will be said about this problem in a later chapter.

The other view of economic justice, or equity, focuses on outcomes or prizes of the economic game. Are economic rewards fair, or are some incomes much too large or small in relation to others? A few would argue for equality of result, but this view has never attracted much political support in the U.S. Most individuals believe that economic rewards should not be equal—either because some individuals need more (larger families or difficult circumstances), or because economic rewards should be tied to performance. For most people, equity or fairness does not mean equality. Economic justice is often discussed and debated, but rarely resolved.

Freedom

Freedom, the third criterion used to judge a political economic system, has been discussed extensively earlier in this text. If an economic system affects freedom, the most likely effects are on specific economic freedoms such as the freedom to make trades or exchanges, to use property as desired, or to form business enterprises. Some analysts have argued that economic freedoms are relatively unimportant compared to political freedoms such as freedom of speech, the right to vote, or protection of due process. Others have argued that economic freedoms cannot be separated from other types of freedom—that freedom is a whole cloth. While there may be some freedoms that are regarded more highly than others, all freedoms have value.

Economic Growth. The goals of efficiency and equity can be expanded to include economic growth. Economic growth occurs because the current generation sacrifices consumption and satisfaction to create capital and to save resources for future use. It should *not* be the goal of a society to make economic growth as high as possible because that would require that those alive now sacrifice *everything* for the future. Instead, the growth aspect of efficiency adds two more criteria:

1. The right division of production between goods and services for current consumption and capital goods to increase future economic capacity.
2. The devotion of some resources to the development of new technology and better methods of production.

The amount that each generation should save to create capital for the next generation is difficult to calculate since the basic decision reduces to how much consumption one generation will sacrifice for the consumption of a future generation. The pace of technological change in an economy compounds the problem since the rapid development of new methods of production has ensured a higher and higher standard of living through time.

Measurement of the Performance of an Economic System

Measuring Efficiency

There is no simple way to measure economic efficiency. A relatively efficient economy will still be quite poor if it has few resources. However, if resources are

MEASURING ECONOMIC PERFORMANCE

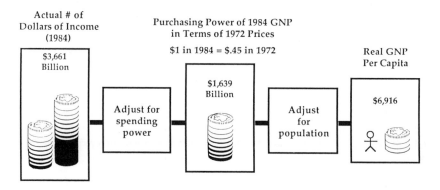

GNP Must be adjusted for inflation and population before comparisons can be made with other countries or previous years.

Figure 10.2: Measuring Economic Performance

similar in two economies, the levels of efficiency in the two economies could be compared by comparing the levels of income. It must be remembered that measuring efficiency by comparing two countries' incomes assumes that the resources of the two economies are similar. The most common measure of income or standard of living on a national scale is real gross national product per capita. Gross national product (GNP) is the value of the goods and services produced in a year that can be put to some final use in consumption, investment, exports, or provision of government services. Basically, GNP is a measure of the value of the economic pie for a given year in an economy.

Once GNP has been computed, two adjustments must be made before GNP can be related to the level of living in an economy. Figure 10.2 shows the adjustments needed to move from GNP to real GNP per capita, the usual measure of the standard of living. First, any difference between two GNP estimates being compared

that is due to price differences must be eliminated. Suppose, for example, that we wish to compare the GNP of the United States in 1969 to that of 1979. The decade of the seventies was a period of inflation in the United States. Therefore, much of the difference in GNP in 1979 compared to 1969 is due to price increases rather than increases in the real quantity of goods and services. This problem of price differences, whether it involves the same country in two different years or two different countries, is solved by expressing the two GNPs being compared in terms of the same set of prices. This adjustment converts GNP into what economists call real GNP which is based on prices in a given year (1982 in Figure 10.3).

Second, any difference between the two GNP statistics being compared that is due to population difference must also be eliminated. India has a relatively large GNP, but that does not tell us very much about the economy of India in comparison with other countries until adjustment is made for population. It is common to divide real GNP by population to get the average size of the economic pie per individual. This basic measure of economic performance is referred to as real GNP per capita. Figure 10.4 illustrates the change in ranking as we adjust GNP for population. Table 10.1 gives real GNP per capita for selected countries for 1982 expressed in terms of U.S. dollars.

Unfortunately, comparisons of real GNP per capita for two economies do not tell us the full story of how close each economy is coming to the goal of efficiency. Natural resources and the amount of capital per worker will vary widely among economies. Even the amount of labor is difficult to compare between two economies because some labor forces are better educated than others. A tourist from a modern developed economy may observe agriculture in a poor country and erroneously conclude that the peasant farmers are very inefficient. However, such farmers are often making the best possible use of resources in their economy. Detective work is necessary to find the actual level of efficiency in an economy. One must look for clues. What is the level of unemployment of resources? Are resources unproductive in one sector of the economy

NOMINAL VS. REAL GNP IN THE U.S. 1970-1987

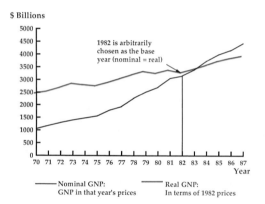

Figure 10.3: Nominal vs. Real GNP in the U.S.

Countries ranked by GNP ($millions)		Countries ranked by Real GNP per capita	
United States	3,946,600	United States	$16,690
Japan	1,327,900	Kuwait	14,480
Germany (Fed Rep)	624,970	Japan	11,300
China	265,530	Germany (Fed Rep)	10,940
India	175,710	Saudi Arabia	8,850
Nigeria	75,300	Nigeria	800
Saudi Arabia	25,050	China	310
Kuwait	21,710	India	270

Figure 10.4: Countries Ranked by GNP

Table 10.1 Measures of Economic Performance for Selected Countries

Country	Real GNP Per Capita (1985)	Annual Growth Rate of GNP Per Capita	Central Govn't Expenditure as a % of GNP	Poorest 20%	Richest 20%	Richest 10%
India	290	1.7	16.7%	7.0%	49.4%	33.6%
Mexico	2,080	2.7	24.9	2.9	57.5	40.6
Israel	4,990	2.5	43.9	6.0	39.9	22.6
Japan	11,300	4.7	17.8	8.7	37.5	22.4
West Germany	10,940	2.7	30.7	7.9	39.5	24.0
United States	16,690	1.7	24.5	5.3	39.9	23.0

Sources: World Development Report for 1987

while very productive elsewhere? Are there unexplainable shortages or surpluses of certain goods? Are individuals spending much of their time in wasted motion lining up for consumption goods? Given the level of education, health, literacy, and resources in an economy, how does real GNP per capita in a country compare with similar countries?

Measuring Equity

Measurement of equity or economic justice presents as many problems as the measurement of efficiency. There are no good measures of the extent of equality of opportunity. More attention has been given to measuring the distribution of income and wealth than to measuring opportunity. Table 10.1 gives some indicators of the distribution of income—the percentage of all income that the poorest one fifth of the population receives, the percentage of all income that the richest one fifth of the population receives, and the percentage of income the richest tenth of the population receives.

The distribution of income is quite unequal in most countries. The richest fifth of the households usually have an income ten to thirty times greater than the income of the poorest fifth of the population. Poor countries tend to have more inequality than richer countries. Unfortunately, some countries such as the USSR, Switzerland, Saudi Arabia, and China do not publish statistics on the distribution of income.

One common misconception is that households or individuals who are poor in one year are also poor in other years. This view is summed up in the slogan "the rich get richer and the poor get poorer." On the contrary, it appears that the rich get poorer and the poor get richer through time. Obviously, economic mobility is an important part of economic equity, since economic mobility is a reflection of equality of opportunity. Suppose that an economy appears quite unequal, with the richest 20 percent of all households receiving 40 percent of all income. Our view of how well that economy is reaching the goal of equity would depend, in part, on the degree of economic mobility possible in that economy. Unfortunately, there is not very much evidence about the extent of economic mobility in different countries. Nevertheless, economic mobility remains a very important aspect of economic equity.

In summary, remember the three basic criteria by which to judge an economic system: efficiency, equity, and freedom. These criteria may also be used to judge smaller issues within the society, as well as the entire economic system. For example, the system devised to deal with organ transplants could be judged from the point of view of efficiency (Are all of the organs that people wish to donate being used?), equity (Are the choices as to who will receive organs fair?), and freedom (Are any freedoms being violated by the system being used?). When we judge an economic system or part of the system using more than one criterion, there may be alternatives that score high in terms of one criterion but not another. This means that we will have to decide which criterion is most important to us and consider trade-offs of one goal for another. One economic system may give better performance in terms of equity by sacrificing efficiency and freedom. Indeed, this trade-off is quite likely. A nation may find that attempts to achieve more equality (which many associate with equity) causes inefficiency. For example, high tax rates on profits and high incomes in order to transfer food, housing, and medical care to the poor may reduce incentives to save, work, and manage resources carefully. Some action to reduce inefficiency in an economy may impose restrictions on the freedom of some people within the society. The three goals of the economic system may often be in conflict.

Alternative Economic Systems

The most important economic decision made by the political process is the choice between two basic economic systems.

1. Command or Planning System—based on authority. Examples would include China, the USSR, Yugoslavia, and, to a lesser degree, France and Great Britain.
2. Market—based on free or voluntary exchange. Examples would include Hong Kong, the United States, Canada, and parts of Latin America.

No actual economy today is based entirely on either of these two types. Instead, every economy is a blend of both command and market, with emphasis on one or the other as the primary means of solving the political-economic problem.

Command or Planning System

In a command economic system, the government uses highly centralized economic planning to achieve cooperation and harmonization among the conflicting economic interests within the society. The rules or decisions of the planners, based upon their reason and intelligence, are accepted because these rules are ultimately backed up by the power of the state. Chairman Mao, father of the Communist revolution in China, was often quoted as saying that all power comes out of the barrel of a gun. The gun may be the ultimate coordinator of self-interest in a command economy. Most of the time the gun is well hidden so that economic matters are settled in routine ways by government bureaucracy. Governments characterized as socialist or communist are normally command economies. Fascist states would also commonly choose command type economic organization. While some command economies are operated by oppressive governments, central planning also characterizes a significant aspect of the democratic economies of France or Great Britain. Alternatively, oppressive governments, such as some dictatorships of Latin America, have chosen to use a market system of economic organization instead of the command form of organization.

In a modern command or planned economy, all major economic decisions are made by planners, even though they are likely to retain some market elements of the economy. Goals or production quotas are set by central planners for the production of goods and services in the economy. They also set prices for most goods and services. In socialist economies such as the Soviet Union, private property is very limited and most capital is owned by the state. The basic decisions of what goods to produce, how to produce them, and who will receive them, are all largely determined by the central planning bureaucracy of the government. (Currently, the Soviet planning system is being reformed under the leadership of Mikhail Gorbachev.) The allocation of production between consumption goods and capital goods to promote economic growth is likewise determined by the planners. The central planners set goals for each industry, the planners for each industry then give goals to each division of that industry, and finally each factory is given production quotas.

In principle, planning is quite simple. Just as the owner of a business in a market economy makes plans for the business, the central planners in a command economy treat the whole economy as if it were a

Kids for Sale
Available — One strong, healthy, white baby boy. Make inquiries at toll free no. (800) 555-0654. Fee negotiable.

If such an ad were to appear in any large city newspaper, there could easily be more than one hundred responses in a given day. Although the number of illegitimate births in the United States has increased from about four hundred thousand in 1970 to about six hundred thousand in 1980, more women are keeping their babies and so there are fewer babies left to adopt. According to the North American Council on Adoptable Children, no more than one hundred thousand children were estimated to be available for adoption during 1984.

The shortage of children available for adoption has driven some childless couples and other individuals who are seeking children to desperate measures. Some make up resumes and send them to family members, friends, lawyers, doctors, and anyone else who might be of service in helping them find a child. Others go to places like Arty Elgart's Golden Cradle in Pennsylvania, where the quick delivery of babies without a lot of fuss is promised. Arty runs his adoption agency in conjunction with his auto supplies distributorship.

Arty's independent private placement agency is part of the "gray market," which includes well-meaning people like friends, relatives, doctors, and lawyers who assist people in adopting children outside of recognized agencies. The gray market, as opposed to the black market, is legal in all but six states that only allow the placement of a child for adoption by licensed agencies, except in the case of a biological parent who places a child with a stepparent or close relative.

The "black market" refers to placements that are made for a profit by baby-brokers, or others whose motives are less than altruistic. Because there are so few babies available, couples are often willing to pay anything from ten thousand dollars to fifty thousand dollars to arrange an adoption. David Rorvik, in an article in *Good Housekeeping*, stated that brokers secure their prey by offering the mother-to-be cash and other inducements such as an all-expenses-paid pregnancy in Florida or the Bahamas. Rorvik tells of a seventeen-year-old unwed mother (he calls her Jane) who was persuaded by a baby-broker to give up her baby in return for a four-hundred-dollar-a-month living allowance prior to delivery, a two-week vacation in Florida, and a five-hundred-dollar gift. When Jane began to have second thoughts about the deal and expressed them to the broker, he spoke threateningly about possible lawsuits to recover the money she had already received and to pay for the anguish she would cause the adoptive parents. Jane was unaware that there are no laws to protect an adopting couple from losing both money and the child they wish to adopt until the mother has signed her final consent. The mother is under no obligation to give her child up for adoption even if a couple has paid all her expenses. Jane went along with the agreement, experiencing an increasing amount of concern and longing for her baby. When she awoke after delivery to find her baby had been given away, she wept for hours. The vacation in Florida and the five hundred dollars were just cheap reminders of what she had lost.

The couple that paid in excess of twelve thousand dollars for Jane's baby may also face serious problems. Jane can challenge the adoption on the grounds that she was coerced into giving up her baby. A court also has the discretion to deny an adoption if the judge feels that either the mother or the middleman was paid an exorbitant fee. Some couples, so fearful that their adopted child will be taken away from them, have neglected to go to court to finalize the adoption. The result is that the child is left in legal limbo and its chances of being taken away from its new parents are enhanced.

Another problem that adoptive parents working within the black market have to contend with is the possibility that the child will be born with a physical or mental handicap or be of a mixed race. A social work supervisor of a large agency in Chicago said that she knew of a couple that paid a one-hundred-thousand-dollar medical bill for a Down's Syndrome child that they eventually chose not to adopt.

In contrast with the gray and black markets, couples who apply to licensed agencies are often told that they will have a two- to six-year wait, and those over age forty are often turned away. Jane Edwards, Executive Director of Spence-Chapin, one of New York City's largest private adoption agencies, reports that although there are about two thousand calls for white babies a year, there are only about thirty seven to place. Licensed agencies strive to protect both the child and the parent and are much less risky than the black and gray markets.

According to Shirley Wheatley, Adoptions Coordinator for the State of Idaho, agencies must complete an adoptive-home study long before a child is placed in a home. Licensed agencies supervise a placement for at least six months to be sure the parent-child bonding is apparent and everyone is happy. In independent placements, however, a petition to adopt is filed immediately and a report to the court is required within only thirty days of the placement. Recently, a social worker in Idaho discovered a case where a mother had independently placed her infant in another home where child abuse was taking place. The state has filed a child-protection action against the couple and the child has been placed in foster care.

To some people, licensed adoption agency involvement in the adoption process seems overly cautious and fraught with delay. It has been argued that an open-market system would better meet the needs of the children and those willing to adopt them. Buyers, they insist, are usually people of means who might offer the babies a much higher standard of living. Also, both the natural parents and the adoptive parents are spared the humiliating inquiries they are often subjected to at adoption agencies. The mother will have her medical expenses paid by the prospective parents and the parents' privacy will be protected. So, who would be hurt? Possibly everyone involved. Babies wind up in homes where they are unloved and perhaps beaten. Mothers lose their children when they may very well still want them. New parents wind up with children who are diseased and find themselves out thousands of dollars in the process. The only sure winner seems to be the middleman. While there may be some advantages to free-market adoptions, those advantages do not seem convincing to most people. In the end, society is unwilling to make babies a commodity to be bought and sold.

single business. They direct resources, plan investments, set prices of products, and market goods and services. While planning is conceptually very simple, execution of the plan is difficult due to the vast amount of detail that must be integrated into the plan.

Individual self-interest is restrained in a command form of economic organization through enforcement of a socially accepted system of rules. For example, the manager in a planned economy might like to price his product higher in order to generate more revenue for his production unit. The planners above the manager will restrain the manager's self-interest and set the price in accordance with the overall objectives of the economy.

Market Economic System

The market form of economic organization takes a different approach. In this system, self-interest is allowed to operate freely and unrestrained, except for the prevention of fraud, theft, or coercion. There are no other direct controls on individual behavior in a market economy. Instead, the market system relies on the movement of prices and profits (the main incentives of a market system) to change individual actions and coordinate the self-interests of individuals. In a command system, the government tries to achieve all the possible gains from cooperation by careful planning. In a market system, cooperation is sought by allowing individuals to make voluntary exchanges or trades. Since individuals will only make voluntary agreements when all parties expect to gain, such agreements are a way of finding most of the situations where cooperation is possible. A market system of economic organization is also known as capitalism, a term laden with emotion just as is socialism.

In one sense, the market system is not organized at all, since no one is directly in charge or responsible for the operation of the economy, nor are there any rules of economic behavior beyond the laws against fraud, theft or coercion. In another sense, the market system is the more complex and subtle alternative because it relies on indirect means to solve the political-economic problem. We will describe the operation of a market system briefly in the next two chapters.

Economic Systems and Transplants

How would each of the two economic systems, command and market, be applied to the problem of organ transplants? The market system would be based on voluntary exchange of organs between donors and recipients on any terms that the two parties could agree to. Donors or their heirs would be viewed as "owning" their organs with the right to sell them. A market for organs would soon develop with organs being purchased and sold just like other commodities. As the price of organs rose, there would be an increase in the number for sale. If a liver, which now has a legal value of zero to the donor or heirs of the donor, were to have a value of perhaps $10,000, it is likely that many more livers would become available for transplant. This market system of organ transplants would appear, on the surface, to be more efficient than the current system. The market would probably search out all possible exchanges of organs given the market price. But would the market for organ transplants be equitable? Clearly, individuals with more money would have an advantage. They would be able to pay the price required to get an organ for transplant while most of the poor might not be able to afford to purchase an organ for transplant. Perhaps the market system would violate some individuals' sense of equity. Certainly, the market system would have a great deal of freedom, since anyone who did not wish to donate an organ for transplant would not be forced to do so.

What about a command or planning system for organ transplants? A government agency or planning group would work out the conditions for organ transplants. There would probably be rules as to who was eligible to receive organs based on criteria set up by the planners. Individuals would be encouraged to donate their body parts for use. They might be paid for doing so or they might be forced to do so at death. It is unclear whether the planned system for transplants would be as efficient as the market. It would depend on how well the planners designed and operated their system. The planning system might be more fair than the market, although planning systems often favor those with political influence just as a market system favors those with wealth.

The example of organ transplants illustrates how difficult the political-economic problem can be. The adoption issue described below is an extreme case where most people do *not* believe the market solution is at all attractive. But many situations are not clear-cut. As one studies these two forms of economic organization in more detail, there are some cases where the market system clearly appears to be superior. In other cases, planning seems to be the best alternative. Unfortunately, in many instances, the choice between the two alternatives is difficult and clouded by uncertainty. Yet the choice has to be made. All societies are faced with the difficult political economic problem. Which of the

alternative economic systems best coordinates and harmonizes individual self-interests while achieving economic efficiency, equity, and freedom? Each of the alternatives has real advantages. The command system concentrates power at the top so that quick decisions may be made in response to difficult problems. The market system exploits incentives in order to accomplish most economic tasks while leaving each individual free to pursue his or her goals.

It is likely that most societies will solve the political-economic problem by a mixture of the two systems. Often, the question is reduced to the amount of each system that should be incorporated into the economy. Some societies, such as the United States, choose to rely primarily on markets, with the addition of some planning for particular problems. Other societies emphasize planning and use markets sparingly. Few people are purists on the matter. Even the most ardent socialist would find state ownership of every plot of land, every restaurant and shop, suffocating. So the issue of which system is best is likely to be decided case by case rather than by one sweeping decision. Indeed, the choice between markets and planning is decided every day in a democratic republic like the United States. Should a community zone land for certain uses? A choice for planning. Should the trucking industry be deregulated? A decision for the market. Such decisions are made every day by city councils, state legislatures, federal agencies, Congress, and the president. To make such decisions wisely, it is necessary to understand how markets and planning processes work given human nature. That is the purpose of the next few chapters.

11
The Miracle of Exchange

Concepts:

Miracle of Exchange
Law of Comparative Advantage
Transactions Cost

Exchange makes both parties better off. (Jon Jacobson)

Auto Restrictions

When the French proletariat stormed the Bastille, Marie Antoinette and her retinue were so unprepared that the throne was lost with hardly a fight. No one has accused the American "monarchy" of GM, Ford, and Chrysler of being as foolish and passive as the French rulers, but with Japanese cars assaulting Detroit, American automakers could easily have been thrown from the automaking palace. But, thanks to some friendly Congressmen and a willing President Reagan, the Detroit automakers were able to stay in power. Between 1980 and 1984, Congress and the President agreed to ask Japan to limit its sales in America to slightly less than two million cars. That buffer helped American car manufacturers make some very hefty profits in 1983 and 1984, after it looked as though bankruptcy might occur for some of them in 1981 and 1982.

In March of 1985, however, President Reagan announced that the U.S. would no longer seek any restrictions on Japanese imports. Those large profits accumulated by the auto companies in 1983 and 1984 no doubt contributed to Reagan's decision to free up the American market. The restrictions were lifted "for the benefit of all the world's consumers," said the President. However, Washington voiced immediate protest when the Japanese announced that they would indeed increase their auto exports to the United States.

The relationship between the availability of Japanese cars and the price consumers must pay for any kind of car has been a cause of much controversy. According to researchers at the Wharton School of Business at Penn, any small car sold between 1980 and 1984 cost a thousand dollars more than it would have cost without any restrictions on Japanese cars. Other statistics seem to indicate an even larger difference. For example, a new Honda Accord loaded with extras sold for $11,000 in Houston, but for only $7,500 in Hiroshima. And even at $11,000, the consumer would normally have waited several weeks before getting his car.

Strangely enough, the restrictions on Japanese imports even worked to the advantage of the Japanese. Since they could only sell two million cars a year, the Japanese car manufacturers concentrated on selling only their high-profit, top-of-the-line models. And they were able to sell those cars at a much higher price than they would have charged had there been more competition.

It would seem that the lifting of the restrictions on Japanese cars would be a boon for Americans, since the increased competition will lower prices on existing models and force Japanese and American manufacturers to offer new low-priced economy models. But, back in Detroit, the complaints are loud. With the Japanese being able to sell all the cars they want in America, the concern is that American automakers will again fall on hard times, and hundreds of thousands of American autoworkers may again lose their jobs. Auto dealers forecast that the reduced prices on Japanese cars could very well "blow open the car market" and force American automakers to engage in price wars similar to those that have so ravaged the airline industry. Chrysler announced a $500 rebate plan on new cars the same week President Reagan curtailed the restrictions. Price wars would be bad news for autoworkers, since layoffs would surely follow.

It is even speculated that a wide-open automobile market could force America right out of the car-making business. "This is a sad day for all America," said Chrysler Chairman Lee Iacocca when he heard that no more quotas would be imposed on the Japanese. "The American middle class standard of living is seriously at stake," said Owen Bieber, president of the United Auto Workers.

PERCENT OF AUTOS SOLD IN THE U.S. (1987)

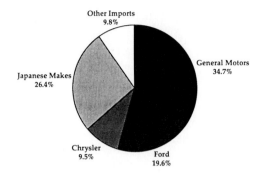

Sources: *Standard and Poor's Industry Surveys;*
Business Week, 7 March 1988.

Figure 11.1: Percentage of Total Autos Sold in U.S.

Why are American automakers unable to compete with the Japanese? It is estimated that, including benefits, the typical American autoworker will soon be making about thirty dollars an hour. With Japanese labor less costly, American manufacturers start out at a disadvantage. This higher labor cost would not be decisive if American technology were superior, but it is not. It takes an American manufacturer about twenty to thirty extra hours of labor to produce a car. With those kinds of obstacles, the scenario of even General Motors going bankrupt isn't so farfetched. "The fact is," said Secretary of Labor William Brock, "Japan builds cars cheaper and better."

Is the possible loss of thousands of American jobs in the automobile industry worth the benefits of less expensive cars for the consumer? The traditional notion among economists is that lower prices more than compensate for the loss of jobs. Lower car prices achieve two objectives. First, low prices increase the "utility," or satisfaction, of the consumer, enabling him to buy more of the goods he wants for the same amount of money. And second, they stimulate output and employment in other industries, since consumers now have more money at their disposal to buy other goods besides cars.

On the other hand, the loss of thousands of good, high-paying jobs causes widespread problems. Many autoworkers are beyond the stage in their lives where they can easily move and retrain. Many would not be able to sell their homes and move. Some are just too old to want to move. Retraining is expensive, and most could never find jobs that pay as well as the assembly line. Perhaps more important, sudden unemployment causes personal depression and discouragement. Hence, allowing an unlimited number of Japanese cars in America benefits all Americans somewhat, but it hurts a few Americans—those who work in the auto industry—tremendously. Naturally, the autoworkers were and are more vocal than are consumers, since their stakes are so much higher. The political process has responded to the pressure from the auto industry. Yet the competition from Japan and others continues. Similar stories could be repeated for other industries such as steel, copper, and textiles. Foreign trade will continue to threaten some Americans while benefiting others.

Markets and Free Exchange

The tensions found in the Japanese challenge to the U.S. auto industry are typical for most economies across time and space. Governments are continually petitioned to prevent trade that is damaging to some interests within the economy. These choices between controlled or free exchange, between government or private decisions, the question of when and how government should intervene, have been a major issue throughout history. Each generation of Americans has been forced to make that crucial decision, and ours is no exception. Sometimes we speak as if we belonged to the first generation to face such choices—that foreign competition or government control of exchange are modern problems and that free markets were the rule of all earlier generations. This illusion may quickly be dispelled by an examination of U.S. history. One of the key colonial complaints before the Revolution was British interference with colonial trade through the Navigation Acts. Tariffs have protected American textiles and other manufactures since 1820. There has always been a tension between desires for freedom in exchange and pressures to use government to control exchange for the benefit of politically powerful groups.

Since one of our major goals is to understand what is possible in a free society, it is obviously very important that we understand the strengths and limitations of free exchange in a market economy as an alternative to government control in economic affairs.

The market system is based on the idea of capturing all the situations where self-interests do not come in conflict with one another. (If you doubt that self-interests may coincide, tour any college campus on the first warm spring day and watch the couples on the grass.) The capturing of self-interested actions that are mutually beneficial is done through the process of exchange or trade between two persons or businesses whose self-interests coincide. For this reason, a market system of economic organization is often described as one where free and uncontrolled exchange is the basis of most economic activity. To the extent that exchange is controlled by government prohibiting trade or prescribing the terms of the exchange or defining the quality of goods that are to be produced for exchange, the economic system has moved from a market economy toward a system of command or central economic planning. We can judge how closely a particular economy resembles the market system of economic organization by the amount of control government exercises over exchange. The eighteenth-century word to describe a pure market system was a French phrase first used by the Marquis d'Argenson, *laissez faire*, meaning roughly to "let alone." Thus, the idea of the phrase *laissez faire* was to simply allow every exchange that people wanted to make to be carried out.

It should be obvious that we are using "self-interest" and "voluntary exchange" in a very broad sense. We include not only the purchase or sale of goods and services but most interaction between individuals—decisions involving marriage and divorce, the number and spacing of children, where to live, how much education to acquire, church attendance, involvement in travel, culture, politics, etc.

There is an assumption, fundamental to the market system, that runs through this chapter or any description of the virtues of a market economy. Each individual's valuation of the goods and services involved in exchange is accepted as valid. If an individual is willing to pay $25 for the latest clothing fad, say t-shirts with authentic grass stains on them, we may feel that is foolish but we accept the fact that they value the item at $25. We reject the idea that we could make them better off by preventing them from making the purchase. In other words, value is determined by the individual rather than being imposed by society.

Exchange Makes Both Parties Better Off

The most basic idea of exchange is that an exchange or trade carried out under conditions of good information and lack of deception makes both parties of the exchange better off. This key observation about the exchange process is well illustrated by the following passage from Mark Twain's *Adventures of Tom Sawyer* in which Tom Sawyer and Huck Finn are involved in very serious exchange.

"Say—what's that?"
"Nothing but a tick."
"Where'd you get him?"
"Out in the woods."
"What'll you take for him?"
"I don't know. I don't want to sell him."
"All right. It's a mighty small tick, anyway."
"O, anybody can run a tick down that don't belong to them. I'm satisfied with it. It's a good enough tick for me."
"Sho, there's ticks a plenty. I could have a thousand of 'em if I wanted to."
"Well why don't you? Becuz you know mighty well you can't. This is a pretty early tick, I reckon. It's the first one I've seen this year."
"Say Huck—I'll give you my tooth for him."
"Less see it."

1. Mark Twain, *The Adventures of Tom Sawyer*, American Publishing Co., Hartford, Conn., 1876, pp. 67–68.

Tom got out a bit of paper and carefully unrolled it. Huckleberry viewed it wistfully. The temptation was very strong. At last he said: "Is it genuwyne?"
Tom lifted his lip and showed the vacancy.
"Well, all right," said Huckleberry, "it's a trade."
Tom enclosed the tick in the percussion-cap box that had lately been the pinchbug's prison, and the boys separated, each feeling wealthier than before.[1]

This passage illustrates the basic ingredients of the exchange process quite well, except for Twain's language in the last line. An economist would prefer that Twain write the last line as "the boys separated, each being wealthier than before." The miracle of exchange is that both parties are made better off by trade even though no additional goods have been produced. By simply changing ownership of goods, both parties are made wealthier. It is very easy for individuals or countries in the difficult but ordinary business of economic activity to forget this basic conclusion about free exchange. The phrase "ripped off" is a common one in modern society. Yet, for most of the exchange that takes place on a daily basis, this phrase is wrong since both parties of the exchange ordinarily gain. From the points of view of the individuals involved, exchange that is voluntary, based on good information and does not involve fraud will benefit all individuals in the exchange.

Suppose you go to your favorite fast-food restaurant for dinner this evening and decide that you will order a hamburger. It is likely that you have made that type of exchange dozens of times in the past. You are perfectly aware of the characteristics of the hamburger: the special sauce, the crunchy sesame seeds, the small piece of meat drying out somewhere inside the bun, and so forth. When you give the restaurant the $1.50 required to buy the hamburger, an exchange has taken place. The restaurant is better off because they value the $1.50 more than the hamburger (an intelligent estimation). But miraculously, you are also better off because you value the hamburger more than the $1.50. If you did not, the exchange would never take place, since it is made on a voluntary basis.

This same principle applies in the exchange between the auto dealer selling a new Honda and the buyer. The dealer values the $11,000 paid for the car more than the car itself. The consumer values the car more than the $11,000. One of them may gain significantly from the exchange and the other very little, depending on the bargaining process. But both of them gain. Should the government prevent this exchange, the standard of living of both the consumer and the auto dealer would fall.

Motives for Exchange

Exchange or trade occurs because individuals or countries value goods differently. This difference in valuation makes exchange very useful as a means for rearranging ownership of goods so that everyone will own the goods they value most highly. The United States is able to produce a great deal of rice. However, the citizens of the United States commonly eat very small amounts of rice, about nine pounds per year per person, while the United States produces over six million metric tons. The Japanese, on the other hand, value rice highly and eat about 280 pounds per person per year. Because the United States values rice less than television sets and Japan values some of its television sets less than rice, an exchange can be made that makes citizens in both countries better off.

The second major reason for exchange taking place is the differences in opportunity costs of production. Differences in the quality of land, availability of ores and minerals, population, education, technology, and even attitudes toward work create differences in the costs of production. Standards of living are raised as individuals, businesses, and nations specialize in particular areas of production and then exchange or trade with each other for consumption. Thus, it is not only relative value that leads the United States and Japan to trade rice for television sets, but differences in the costs of production. Both countries would be worse off if trade were prohibited. Japan cannot produce rice as inexpensively as the United States, nor can we compete with their ability to produce television sets.

Law of Comparative Advantage

One of the principal implications of free exchange is specialization. In a modern economy, most firms specialize in the production of very few products. Individuals are even more specialized and usually concentrate on one small aspect of the production of some good or service. This process of specialization is guided by opportunity cost. For most goods or services, our own opportunity cost of production is higher than the price of the good in trade. For at least one good or service, our own opportunity cost of production (or some aspect of production) is less than the prevailing price. Thus, we specialize in the good or service where we have a low opportunity cost, and we exchange for the many goods or services where our opportunity cost of production exceeds the market price.

An everyday example will help clarify the process. Suppose you have decided to have pizza for dinner. You can purchase a pizza for $8 at a local restaurant. If you produce the pizza at home, you calculate the opportunity cost of the pizza to be $10 including the value of time and cost of ingredients. In this case, you would exchange for the pizza because others can produce pizzas at a lower opportunity cost than you. Your gain from exchange will be the difference between your opportunity cost of production ($10) and the cost through exchange ($8) or a gain of $2. If, on the other hand, your opportunity cost to produce the pizza is only $5, then you should produce the pizza at home. Indeed, you should go into the pizza business since your opportunity cost is less than the prevailing price. If you can make pizza for $5 and sell it for $8, your gain from exchange will be $3 on each pizza. We implicitly think through this same sort of calculation on each item we purchase or produce for ourselves.

It is important to remember that opportunity cost is defined by the available alternatives rather than the absolute level of a person's skill or abilities. A surgeon may be a wonderful chef but rarely cook his or her own food because a medical practice makes the opportunity cost of cooking too high. A university president may be a marvelous teacher but not teach any classes in the university because of responsibilities elsewhere. The good news for most of us is that average or lower abilities do not eliminate us from participation in the economic game. A person with meager cooking skills can find employment as a chef because of few employment alternatives. Of course, the wage may be meager as well. Another person with a few

rudimentary skills repairing cars may find employment as a mechanic's helper if he does not have better skills in other areas.

The point to be emphasized is that there is some work that each resource in the economy can do at a low opportunity cost. Suppose that Susan is more able than John at both accounting and law. For example, assume she can generate an income of $100,000 as an accountant and an income of $90,000 as a lawyer while John could generate an income of $80,000 as either an accountant or a lawyer. Fortunately for John, she cannot do both. When she chooses accounting over law because her opportunities are greater in accounting, employment in law is open for John.

The effect of opportunity cost on specialization and trade has been summarized by economists in the Law of Comparative Advantage: Every individual, group, or nation can produce at least one good or service at lower opportunity cost than others. To maximize their standard of living, they should specialize in the production of such goods or services. As long as opportunity costs differ for various individuals or groups, specialization and trade will be beneficial to the parties involved.

Specialization is the primary feature that distinguishes a modern economy from a more traditional or primitive economy. Specialization dramatically increases the productive power of an economy as individuals and firms learn how to do repetitive tasks better. Technological change or invention usually comes from specialists in firms who have much to gain from reducing the cost of production by a few pennies because they produce millions of units. Just as individuals and businesses specialize, countries also engage in some specialization and trade which, in turn, allows individuals and firms to become even more specialized. The process appears to have no end.

Implications of Specialization and the Law of Comparative Advantage

Full Employment of Resources. First, the law of comparative advantage generates a tendency in an economy toward full employment of all resources in their most preferred use. We will see later that market economies have built-in forces that sometimes generate unemployment of labor and underutilization of capital. However, by and large, the law of comparative advantage does operate, and full employment is close to the norm. This tendency toward full employment follows from the principle of opportunity cost. Since everyone will be the low-cost producer of something, each is able to specialize in the production of that particular good where he has the lowest opportunity cost. This principle explains why the engineer who designs a car employs someone else to repair it and why authors of textbooks on typing do not type their own manuscripts. On the other hand, the operation of the law of comparative advantage explains why there is so much mediocrity in the world, since the operation of this economic principle implies that it is a rare circumstance when the best people are actually carrying out the work. Most individuals are in their particular jobs because they are low-cost producers rather than because they have particularly high levels of competency in that area.

Not only does the law of comparative advantage imply full employment, the law implies that as individuals pursue their self interest, there will be full employment of resources in their best possible use. Planned economies, which do not necessarily allow the principle of comparative advantage to operate, often achieve full employment, but such economies have a difficult time employing resources in their best use.

Widest Possible Gains from Exchange. The second implication of the law of comparative advantage is that its operation generates the widest possible gains from exchange or trade. Consider the complex process of production for an automobile. An automobile contains thousands of parts. It contains many different types of materials such as steel, aluminum, chrome, rubber, glass, and plastic. Over fifty thousand businesses supply various parts of an automobile in the United States. It draws on the skills of engineers, computer programmers, tool and die makers, accountants, secretaries, skilled assemblers, and other labor. Yet this very complex object can be purchased for approximately five months' of income for a typical U.S. family. The gains from trade and specialization involved in that automobile are truly astounding. The gains are similar for all other goods we consume. In the absence of this process, we would all be back in caves—being self-sufficient and poor. The process of specialization and exchange, perhaps more than any other single factor, is responsible for the modern material civilization we all enjoy and take for granted.

Economic Interdependence. The third implication of the law of comparative advantage is that it generates a great deal of economic interdependency. Trade links nearly every individual in the U.S. economy with a vast network of others. We are also linked to individuals in virtually every other part of the world. Even the most simple manufactured objects involve trade on several continents. Complex objects involve exchange with hundreds of thousands of other individuals on various parts of the globe. Consequently, we are all completely at the mercy of one another for our standard of living. This interdependency is at times frightening and causes people to move back toward self-sufficiency. However, a moment's reflection tells us that true self-sufficiency would necessarily require us to live very poorly. This fact means that most of us are willing to accept interdependency as a necessary evil in return for the standard of living that we enjoy because of specialization and exchange. It may also be argued that our economic interdependency links countries together politically and reduces chances of war and violence.

Role of Competition

Individuals choose to trade or exchange for a good as long as the price of the good is less than their own opportunity cost to produce the good. If you could produce the pizza for dinner at an opportunity cost of fifteen dollars, the restaurant could charge you any price up to fifteen dollars and still induce you to trade. This fact raises an important question. What prevents one person or business from taking virtually all of the gains from trade and leaving the others at a very low standard of living, unable to capture significant benefits from economic interdependency? The basic force that distributes and controls the gains from specialization and exchange is economic competition. When we think of economic competition, we should not make

comparisons with athletic or political competition where winners and losers are clearly identifiable. Instead, economic competition usually involves many households and businesses so that no one is competing directly against any other particular household or business.

Economic competition exists when, because of the large number of buyers and sellers, the participants in the exchange process assume the price or terms of the exchange is beyond their control. A wheat farmer does not calculate how much the price of wheat will fall if his wheat is held off the market because the price change would be measured in millionths of a penny. Similarly, an individual consumer does not calculate how much the price of bread rises because of his or her purchase of a few loaves. In the economic arena, we compete against everyone and, therefore, no one in particular. In the real world, where there are hundreds or even thousands of different firms and millions of consumers, we are usually in a situation where no single individual or business firm is able to set the terms of exchange. Instead, there is competition among potential buyers for any particular seller's product and vice versa. It is this economic competition that establishes bounds and order in the process of trade or exchange and prevents the abuses that one might otherwise expect to occur. Economic competition prevents businesses from raising prices at will. Competition controls the quality of goods and the wages paid to labor or the interest rate that is charged. It is a misconception that either party in an exchange sets the terms of exchange when there is economic competition.

The importance of economic competition can be illustrated best by considering a case where there is only one seller who has *monopoly* power. (Monopoly means "one seller.") A monopolist will try to capture all of the gains from exchange. If the monopolist could read the buyer's mind, he or she could charge the buyer a price just below the buyer's opportunity cost of producing the good, or the maximum price that the buyer would be willing to pay. The monopolist would receive the entire gain from the exchange. Economic competition performs the important function of distributing the gains from exchange widely.

Pure Market System

We can now define a market system. A pure market system is characterized by competitive free exchange, in which all exchanges that people wish to make are allowed and competition prevails so that no single individual or firm has control over the terms of exchange. This "model" of a market system is an ideal that is not always met in the real world, but one which describes the important characteristics and tendencies of a market economy.

Transaction Costs

Up to this point in our discussion, we have assumed that exchange could take place between two parties with no cost involved. In reality, this is not true. There are transportation costs involved with exchange that takes place over geographical distances. There are costs in terms of time and travel directly in making the exchange. For exchanges that are more complex, such as home purchases, there are legal costs such as contracts and agreements. These costs, associated with the process of trade or exchange, can be lumped together as transaction costs. If the transaction costs are sufficiently large, an exchange cannot take place because the gains from exchange are less than the costs of making that transaction.

Money

Money, which has existed since recorded history, is the single most important invention that has reduced transaction costs and promoted trade or exchange. Economists define money as the medium of exchange. By this mysterious phrase, they mean that money splits the exchange process into two parts. Individuals exchange money for good A. The recipient of the money then exchanges the money for another good B. The exchange is really good A for good B, but in this way money acts as a "medium" that all exchanges go through. Suppose that an economist is hungry and would like a hamburger. If there were no money, the economist would have to search the community to find a fast-food restauranteur who wanted to hear a lecture on economics in exchange for a hamburger. That coincidence of wants (economist who wants hamburger, restaurant owner who wants economics lecture) is very unlikely and would greatly inhibit exchange. Money severs the need for a coincidence of wants and makes it possible for each person to specialize in production, convert his goods into money, and then use money to buy the goods he desires. It may well be that money rivals the wheel as mankind's greatest invention.

Almost every kind of object has been used as money. Precious metals, such as gold, silver, or copper, have commonly been used because their value per pound is quite high, they are easily recognizable, and they can be easily divided into small quantities with identical properties. Therefore, if one wanted to travel it was not necessary to carry great quantities of precious metals in order to have something of value that would be widely accepted. Anything widely accepted in exchange may be used as money. It is reported that large, immovable rocks have been used as money on certain Pacific islands. Cows have been used in some cultures. Beads were used by some Indian tribes. Cigarettes served as money in prison camps during World War II. Animal skins, grain, tobacco, and gunpowder were all used as money during the early colonial period when the more official money, the king's coinage, quickly flowed back to Britain to buy finished products. The only requirement of money is that it be readily accepted by various parties in the economy in exchange.

In the U.S. economy, as in most other economies today, special paper is used as money because it is light and inexpensive to produce. We define the money supply in the United States today as coins, currency, and checking deposits (also known as demand deposits) drawn on banks, since these are the items used in most exchanges. Gold and silver no longer function as money because they are not commonly accepted in exchange. Credit cards are not money either because one does not exchange the credit card for goods and services. Rather, the credit card is used to postpone payment for a short time. When payment is made, currency or checking deposits are the actual money used. As you can see from Figure 11.2, checking or demand deposits are by far the most important component of the money supply in the United States today.

COMPONENTS OF MONEY IN THE U.S. (1987)

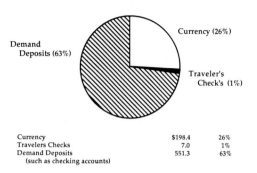

Currency	$198.4	26%
Travelers Checks	7.0	1%
Demand Deposits (such as checking accounts)	551.3	63%

Figure 11.2: Components of Money in the U.S.

Transportation

Man's other great invention, the wheel, has also played an important role in the reduction of transaction costs and, therefore, the promotion of exchange or trade. In the past, transportation costs were extremely high and this limited the amount of exchange or trade that could take place. If, for example, it cost several dollars to travel one mile or to transport a ton of products one mile, then trade or exchange would be limited to a very small geographical area for most goods and the degree of specialization could not be very extensive. Inexpensive transportation expands the limits of the marketplace so that individuals separated by very large geographical distances may trade with one another. Reduction in transportation costs also increases economic competition by bringing more buyers and sellers into the market.

The history of economic development in the United States is closely linked to technological changes in transportation that have greatly reduced the costs of transporting goods from one place to another. In colonial times, a shipment by land from Boston to western Massachusetts cost more than a shipment by sea from Europe. The wheel, the sail, the steam engine, the railroad, the canal, the internal combustion engine, airplanes, pipelines, and supertankers are all important signposts in the reduction of transportation costs through history. The completion of the Erie Canal in 1825 reduced shipping costs from twenty cents per ton to two cents per ton. The river steamboat reduced the number of days it took to travel from New Orleans upriver to Louisville, Kentucky, from thirty days to five days and reduced the average cost of freight from twenty dollars to six dollars. It was these enormous reductions that now make it possible for each of us to be involved economically with buyers and sellers in every part of the globe and gain so much from trade.

Middlemen, the Law, and Communications

There are other aspects of a modern economy that contribute to the reduction of the costs of exchange. Middlemen, such as brokers, wholesalers, jobbers, and retailers, are essentially in business to perform the function of reducing transaction costs by maintaining inventories, providing information, and generally easing the costs of exchange. Such individuals and businesses are often viewed as parasites who do nothing for their income. This is an erroneous view since no one is forced to use their services. If middlemen cease to perform the functions of assisting in the exchange process, they are quickly circumvented by the consumer and the producer.

The legal system helps to reduce transaction costs by defining and protecting property rights and creating and enforcing contracts or legal agreements. Many transactions could not take place without such agreements. The courts reduce the uncertainty and hesitation parties may feel about important or complex exchanges by providing an unbiased arbitration of any disputes that may arise concerning exchange. When the legal system becomes too expensive, cumbersome, and time-consuming, its usefulness for reducing transaction costs is limited.

The communications industry provides information through advertising so that people are able to engage in exchange more easily. Finally, the technological wonder of our age, the computer, should greatly reduce transaction costs over time. We are already seeing its use in stores, banks, and communications networks in ways that substantially reduce the costs of transactions and increase the possibilities for exchange.

The history of American economic development is in part the history of the innovations designed to reduce transaction costs so that exchange could take place over wider and wider areas leading to more and more specialization and a higher standard of living. One of Adam Smith's most famous phrases in the *Wealth of Nations* is "the division of labor is limited by the extent of the market." By this, he means that specialization can only take place when there are enough people participating in exchange. As the market widens, more specialization and exchange can take place. Transaction costs are the main barrier to larger and larger markets. For this reason, reduction in transaction costs is a basic cause of economic growth and prosperity. Any development that might increase transaction costs would be a serious threat to the economy.

Role of Government

Thus far, the market system has been described without any government. There are valid and important roles for government to play in a pure market system that complement and support the exchange process. Regardless of the gains from free exchange and adoption of a market system, this system is not an argument for economic anarchy. The first economic function of government in a pure market system is to prevent coercion and fraud in economic matters. The benefits from specialization and exchange can only be certain if all exchanges that take place are voluntary and based on reasonably accurate information. If one party involved in a trade has to be coerced, we can be sure that exchange is only benefiting the other party. A mugging or a con game does not fit the definition of free exchange. The first obligation of government in an exchange economy is to prevent such coercion or fraud.

A second function of government in an exchange economy is to provide money, the medium of exchange. It is possible to have money provided by various private organizations; however, there are benefits to having a single form of money provided and controlled by the government. As we will see in later chapters, the government often abuses this function of providing money by creating too much money and generating inflation which reduces the usefulness of money. Nevertheless, it seems likely that inflation could be even worse if government were not in control of the supply of money within the economy—making money even less useful.

A third function that government has often assumed in exchange economies is to subsidize or create the transportation and communication networks that reduce transaction costs, enabling exchange to take place over wider areas. In the nineteenth century, for example, the state and federal governments subsidized the building of canals and railroads in order to bring various parts of the country together in an exchange network. Today, the government supports extensive systems of roads, and subsidizes airport construction, port facilities, and space satellites in order to maintain the transportation and communication network that is so important in the reduction of transaction costs. In 1987, governments in the United States spent over $26 billion on subsidies to transportation.

A fourth function of government is to define property rights within the economy. When two parties participate in an exchange, they are actually exchanging goods with a given set of rights associated with each good. If the property rights associated with the good are changed, then the value of that particular good also changes. One can see this clearly by considering our laws with respect to automobiles. Under current definitions of property rights, it is illegal for someone to drive an automobile without the permission of the owner. The owner has the right to lock the car. Most cars are now fitted with a key ignition, and the police enforce the rights of the owner over his car. Auto theft is a serious crime. Consequently, automobiles exchange for significant amounts of money.

Suppose we were to change our laws, making it illegal to lock automobiles or build cars with key ignitions or take any precautions to prevent theft. Suppose further that laws were passed allowing anyone who wished to go somewhere to simply use the nearest car, driving it to their destination. Under that set of property rights,

Who Owns the Air?

A hundred TV channels at your fingertips with a remote-control clutched tightly in your hand—clearly, this is the American dream come true. Every episode of M*A*S*H would be on within a single week. One could watch Ron Howard as li'l Opie fishing at nine o'clock, spending his "happy days" on Blueberry Hill at ten, and see his directorial talents in "Splash" or "Gung Ho" at eleven. If these programs seem too mainstream, there are always the Playboy and other channels directed to the waterbed motel group. Technology in the form of satellite dishes cluttering up backyards and roofs of apartment houses has made this dream come true.

Unfortunately, subscriber television companies like HBO and Showtime, as well as cable companies selling the delights of ESPN, CNN and CBN, view the owners of satellite dishes as thieves who steal their products, just as a shoplifter steals a shirt from the local department store. Dish owners, vigorously denying that any theft is involved, question anyone's right to prevent them from picking a loose signal out of the air. After all, when did HBO et al. obtain property rights over the air?

The conflict between the dish owners and the pay-TV industry is an example of the age-old conflict over property rights that exists in every society. What can be owned? What rights pertain to ownership? These questions must be resolved by government, either through court decisions which apply old rules to new cases, or by laws that clarify and resolve new property rights issues. Resolution of a conflict is unlikely to make everyone happy, so Congress has approached this conflict with all of the enthusiasm that most of us bring to the latest PBS special on dental plaque.

There are perhaps two million owners of satellite dishes in the U.S. Some analysts believe the market could approach 50 million within a few years. These television addicts constitute a powerful lobby since they did not lay out $1500 to $3000 to watch local news and reruns of "Three's Company." On the other side, subscriber companies like Showtime and HBO claim to be losing over a billion dollars in sales because of unauthorized use of their product. Clearly, government action is needed. Congress put the burden of defending their product on the pay-TV companies by legalizing backyard satellite dishes in 1984. The companies responded with plans to scramble their signals and sell decoders to paying customers. These plans made dish owners unhappy, and they are lobbying against the use of scramblers and decoders. Electronics stores are busy selling decoders to dish owners who are fighting back. A free television lunch is evidently addicting.

We haven't heard the last word in the battle in the airwaves and space. Technology has a way of upsetting the status quo with regularity.

the value of the automobile would quickly be reduced to near zero, even though the appearance of the car and its other physical qualities are unchanged. Thus, an important function of the government in an exchange economy is the definition and enforcement of property rights relative to different goods and resources within the economy.

A fifth function of government in an exchange economy is to enforce the exchange agreements that have been made between various parties. In any economic situation where self-interest is important, there will be disputes over the exact terms of the exchange and the compliance of each party to those terms. The government, through the courts and the judicial system, plays a role in arbitrating those disputes so that the exchanges can continue.

Role of Virtue

Exchange is clearly a powerful tool for the resolution of the conflicting self-interests discussed in previous chapters. A beautiful feature of the exchange process is that it searches out all situations where self-interests work together. Thus, free exchange uses self-interest to accomplish the common good and reduce the need for conflict resolution to a minimum. At the same time, an exchange system could never work if most individuals did not possess some modest level of virtue. The virtue most required to allow a market system to function with minimal government interference is simple honesty. Honesty significantly reduces transaction costs, thereby increasing specialization and exchange. If store owners believed every customer was

a cheat, supermarkets could not exist. Individuals trust total strangers in exchanges made every day. Most economic exchange assumes that others are generally honest. If this assumption cannot be made, the exchange system is severely threatened. If virtue dies, the market form of economic organization will also die.

Restrictions of Exchange

In spite of the attractive features resulting from an exchange economy, no society has ever been completely comfortable with unbridled free exchange of goods and services. People have always used government for purposes other than supporting and complementing the exchange process. Governments, responding to interest groups and political pressures, have been used to restrict and limit exchange. The following examples illustrate just a few ways that we use the government to limit the process of exchange and, therefore, to limit the benefits that we receive from trade:

1. We impose tariffs—which are taxes on foreign goods coming into the country—or quotas—which are limits on the amount of foreign goods that can come into the country. For example, today the tariff on women's knit blouses ranges from 37.5 percent to 90 percent, depending on the qualities of the blouse. Maple syrup has a tariff of six cents per pound. The U.S. government has recently negotiated quotas or informal agreements restricting imports of autos and steel. The effects of tariffs and quotas are to decrease the availability and raise the price of goods to consumers, thereby reducing the gains from trade.

2. The government licenses various occupations in order to prevent entry by some individuals who would like to practice that occupation. This licensing limits exchange, raises the cost of services to consumers, and increases the income of individuals possessing licenses. The stated intent is to protect consumers from abuse or their own bad judgment. State governments license hundreds of workers including accountants, cosmetologists, dentists, elevator installers, insulation workers, lawyers, landscapers, parking attendants, refrigerator repairmen, swimming pool servicemen, and well drillers.

3. The government often prohibits any exchange taking place in certain goods. Examples of this type of governmental restriction of exchange include prostitution, gambling, pornography, certain drugs such as heroine and cocaine, and, for the years from 1921 to 1933, alcoholic beverages. The intent is to impose a social standard even if it infringes on the choice of some.

4. The government often sets the terms at which exchange can take place. For example, the government sets a legal minimum wage, declaring that no one is allowed to exchange his labor for less than that wage ($3.35 per hour with an increase being proposed). At other times, the government might set a ceiling on interest rates so that no one is allowed to borrow money at an interest rate above a certain level. Any form of wage and price control involves this type of restriction of exchange. These include rent controls and all agricultural support programs. The intent of these laws is to transfer purchasing power or wealth from one side of the market to the other (i.e., from consumers of dairy products to producers).

5. Local governments often restrict the uses of land in certain areas of the city or county through zoning laws. These zoning laws, then, are restrictions on the exchange possibilities for that particular piece of land. Certain areas of the city are zoned for commercial use, others for residential use by single families, and still other parts of the city may be zoned for apartments or condominiums. These zoning restrictions represent another form of intervention with the free exchange process.

6. The government often regulates the quality of particular goods or services. For example, one is not allowed to purchase an automobile that does not have seat belts, even though a very small fraction of the population consistently uses seat belts while driving. In fact, many state government have passed legislation mandating the use of seat belts just as earlier legislation compelled the installation of belts in automobiles. One is not allowed to purchase children's sleepwear that has not been treated with certain chemicals to prevent the spread of fire.

7. The government often regulates the conditions under which labor or goods are exchanged. For example, the Occupational Safety and Health Administration (OSHA) regulates the dangers of the workplace. The Environmental Protection Agency (EPA) regulates the amount of pollution that industries may put into the air or water. The Food and Drug Administration (FDA) regulates the labeling and availability of many products.

These regulations have the appearance of being for the general good of the society, and indeed they may be. However, we need to keep in mind that each of these rules or regulations prevents two parties from voluntarily engaging in an exchange that both parties believe would make each better off. Therefore, none of these regulations can be viewed as an unmixed blessing. Each restriction of exchange must necessarily reduce the benefits to be gained from the exchange process.

Motives for Restriction of Exchange

Government Paternalism. There appear to be three basic reasons why citizens use the government to restrict the exchange process in a market economy. First of all, citizens as a group often believe that they have an obligation to prevent damage from occurring to individual citizens because of their own mistakes. This causes the government to act in a paternalistic manner to prevent certain exchanges from taking place. The government licenses doctors to prevent individuals from being treated by incompetents. We prohibit the purchase and sale of heroin to prevent addiction to that particular drug. We require that the makers of children's sleepwear treat the clothing with fire retardant in order to prevent injury to children through burns. All of these actions are motivated by the assumption that the government has an obligation to prevent individuals from making mistakes. This assumption is in conflict with the assumption of the exchange process—that each individual knows best what is in his or her self-interest. It is one of the paradoxes of modern society that these paternalistic regulations of exchange have grown at the very time that the population has become more and more educated and the communication system more and more developed so that we are aware of many of the possible dangers to us.

Unfair Effects on Third Parties. A second motive for restriction of the process of trade is that innocent individuals or groups not directly involved in the exchange are often unfairly damaged because an exchange takes place. Suppose, for example, that an individual goes out to a bar and exchanges money for liquor until thoroughly drunk. At that point, the individual too often demonstrates his drunk-driving skills by plowing into another car or knocking down some unwary pedestrian. One can argue that the pedestrian or the driver of the other automobile is an innocent third party who is unjustly damaged because we allowed the exchange of money for liquor to take place in the bar. This type of reasoning prompts the government to restrict or prevent exchanges that damage third parties.

Redistribution of Income. Often particular groups or individuals in an economy use government to restrict exchange in order to increase their income. If the government levies a tariff or imposes a quota on auto imports, American consumers purchasing either domestic automobiles or foreign automobiles suffer because of the increased price of both foreign and domestic cars. On the other hand, American manufacturers of automobiles (General Motors, Ford, Chrysler, and American Motors) are clearly going to be better off if the tariff or quota is imposed. The auto workers will also benefit from this restriction in trade. Here is an example where the corporations and the workers of those corporations have a mutual self-interest. We are often treated to the sight of the head of the United Auto Workers and the heads of the automobile companies going arm in arm to Congress to appeal for trade restrictions on foreign automobiles and then returning to Detroit to haggle over the next labor contract.

Should Seat Belts Be Mandatory?

In the summer of 1984, New York passed the first mandatory seat belt law in the United States. With the passage of this law, not only will installation of seat belts be required for all cars sold in the U.S., but it will be illegal to drive without a fastened seat belt in New York. Governor Mario Cuomo signed the bill just one day after being involved in an automobile accident in his limousine. Cuomo said that his seat belt saved him from harm.

On the other hand, seat belt laws requiring drivers and front-seat passengers to buckle up have failed to pass in ten other state legislatures. Public opinion in Illinois, one of the states to reject mandatory seat belt legislation, was generally as expressed by legislative aide Frank Williams: "You don't tell me what to do in my automobile."

No one disputes the potential of seat belts to save lives and reduce the number of injuries suffered in car accidents, but many would question the right of the government to enforce compulsory seat belt laws. It is argued that such laws constitute an invasion of personal freedoms, most notably the right to privacy and the freedom to make exchanges without government interference. As a man's home is his castle, so also might be his car. There are times when it might be more convenient to go without a seat belt, or briefly remove it, some say. At any rate, no one should be denied his choice.

These arguments have not been impressive to the federal government. Alarmed that only 12.5 percent of Americans use seat belts, Elizabeth Dole, then secretary of transportation, announced in 1984 that two-thirds of the states must pass mandatory seat belt laws by April 1989. If the states do not comply, then automakers will be compelled to equip new automobiles with passive restraints, such as air bags or seat belts that automatically wrap around riders when they close the door. Along with the regulation came a promise that the government would launch a $40 million campaign annually, one-half to be funded by the auto industry, to promote mandatory seat belt laws. By the end of 1987, these efforts appeared to be working since 31 states had passed mandatory seat belt laws.

The Dole plan was downright offensive to those who oppose mandatory seat belt laws. A failure to wear seat belts hurts no one except the person who is without the seat belt, they say. It is a victimless crime, and strong arguments can be made that victimless crimes should be legal. Laws requiring citizens to wear seat belts are clearly paternalistic and run counter to the fundamental freedoms so important to Americans. What Americans do in their own cars should be their own business.

Those who favor seat belt laws, however, argue that failure to wear a seat belt is not a victimless crime. First and foremost, lost lives are a heavy social cost. The results of avoidable auto injuries are lost wages, lowered productivity, higher medical bills, and expensive welfare outlays. All Americans pay for those who don't wear their seat belts. Lost wages translate into families seeking welfare and food stamps. Lowered productivity means all Americans pay more for the commodities they need. Medical bills that could have been avoided mean Americans have to pay more when they really do need medical care, since the demand for hospital care is increased. Indeed, each death on the highway costs state governments $330,000. Hardly a victimless crime, some say.

How effective are mandatory seat belt laws in places that have them? In Puerto Rico, which enacted a seat belt law in 1974, the results have not been positive. Since it is difficult to enforce the law, few Puerto Ricans bother to buckle up. Seat belt usage has only increased from 4 percent to 6 percent. Elsewhere, the results have been more impressive. In Belgium, for example, seat belt usage is up to 92 percent. Fatality reductions have ranged from 12 percent in Switzerland to 46 percent in Sweden (which also lowered its speed limit). Estimates by the U.S. government are that a mandatory seat belt law in two-thirds of the states would save from two thousand to four thousand lives a year.

That figure is disputed by those who oppose seat belt laws. The National Highway Traffic Safety Administration study on mandatory seat belt laws in some of the Canadian provinces reported that before the laws went into effect belt usage was 21 percent, but by 1983 belt usage had nearly tripled to 61 percent. Strangely, however, deaths did not go down nearly as much as seat belt usage went up. Brian O'Neil, senior vice president of the Insurance Institute for Highway Safety, said with regard to mandatory seat belt laws: "There is some fatality reduction, but the evidence is not as clear-cut and overwhelming as the advocates of belt-use laws would claim."

An alternative to mandatory seat belt laws is air bags. Air bags in cars would achieve even more safety advantages than would seat belts, and they would do so without infringing on personal freedom within the automobile. No one even knows there is an air bag waiting in the dash, prepared to spring out if an accident occurs. However, air bags interfere with freedom of exchange and have the added liability of being very expensive. Estimates of their cost range from two hundred to six hundred dollars. American automakers, already pressed by foreign competition, are not excited about laws that would require them to make cars that much more expensive. Automakers much prefer mandatory seat belt laws, since it takes the pressure off them to install air bags.

The only perfect solution would be that all Americans buckle up of their own volition. That would seem impossible, however, since no amount of advertising or hype has convinced them to do so. Therefore, as long as people drive cars, some will die in them, and the debate about seat belts and air bags will continue.

The benefits from restricting exchange are often concentrated on a few individuals, while the costs of restricting exchange are usually borne by a large number of individuals. The effect of this imbalance is to make one group of individuals try very hard to influence the government to impose trade restrictions. These restrictions impose costs on consumers that are greater than the benefits enjoyed by producers and workers. Nevertheless, each individual damaged by the restrictions is hurt so little that he or she brings little or no political pressure to bear on the government to allow free exchange. Most restriction of trade or exchange involves the redistribution of income among various groups within the economy. The government often succumbs to the pressure from special-interest groups to impose exchange restrictions for their benefit.

Government plays a mixed role in the typical modern exchange economy. On one side, government performs vital support functions to keep the exchange system in operation by providing money, enforcing agreements, and defining property rights. On the other side, government is constantly limiting exchange by laws and regulations primarily motivated by the self-interests of different special-interest groups or "factions" within the economy. To the extent that a government restricts exchange, the economy is moving from a market system toward a command or planning system. City councils, state legislatures, and Congress are faced with this decision every day. Should they enact laws to restrict free exchange or should they allow the exchange process to control economic activity?

The Miracle of Exchange

The ordinary nature of exchange and the political confusion surrounding governmental attempts to control exchange may hide the crucial role that specialization and exchange play in our lives. Exchange produces an initial benefit for all involved, as goods and services are reallocated to households and businesses that value them most. Exchange is also crucial to the process of specialization that is responsible for large increases in productive power. Specialization often leads to technical change which further increases the economy's capacity. The process of specialization and exchange is, in some ways, the golden goose. Society is unlikely to kill the golden goose with one fatal blow. But there is a tendency for the process to go unappreciated by the general public, and consequently, the goose may die from a thousand small cuts. A tariff or quota on a few goods here, a price control there, a few new reasonable regulations or licenses—gradually the exchange possibilities shrink until much of the potential gain from exchange is lost. The miracle of free exchange is so subtle and quiet that its disappearance may not be missed.

12
The Role of Prices and Profits

Concepts:

Law of Demand
Law of Supply
Equilibrium Price
Role of Profits

Many goods are exchanged in open markets all over the world. (UPI/Bettmann Newsphotos)

Fare Wars

There were haunting visions of a crash-and-burn market when the airlines were deregulated in 1978. Analysts speculated that cutthroat competition would eliminate all but the most hardy competitors. But the dreaded shakeout was not as bad as anticipated. Some airlines have merged together such as Texas Air, Eastern and Continental as well as Delta and Western. Many airlines have had tough negotiations with employees, cut costs, lowered fares, and are now making money.

For consumers, deregulation has been great. Flying is now affordable. In Europe, where the market is controlled, flights from Paris to Geneva, equal in distance to a Dallas flight to Houston, may cost roughly twice as much. A round-trip from New York to San Francisco only cost $238 with a special promotional fare while a round-trip flight from Taipei to Singapore would cost many times that amount. Twenty-two new airlines have entered the market since deregulation while some like Braniff and Peoples' have failed. U.S. Air, Texas Air and American West are examples of the wave of new airlines offering rock-bottom prices. Those new airlines with their lower fares, are attracting a new kind of customer. In 1984, low-price fares attracted 344 million passengers, compared to 240 million in 1977.

In order to finance the lower fares, airlines have been forced , in some cases, to lay off employees or to cut back on wages. The Airline Pilots Association estimates that employee concessions have reached at least $1.2 billion since the government ended its regulation of the industry. Unions claim that 55,000 airline employees have lost their jobs. After suffering a major setback in 1984 as a result of a miscalculation of the effects of frequent-flier bonuses (free rides were amounting to 11 percent of air travel), Pan Am talked of stepping up productivity by 25 percent by having workers perform more than one job and lengthening their workday. Other airlines have introduced profit-sharing and stockholder plans to offset paycuts. Clark Onstad, a representative of Continental, said, "It's a revolution! Our employees have become our bankers of last resort." Delta, while expanding to the tune of $40 million in the Dallas-Fort Worth airport, lost money in 1983 for the first time in 30 years, but, for whatever reasons, proposed no layoffs or delays in equipment purchases. Out of gratitude for having been spared their jobs, Delta employees later reciprocated by taking up a collection to raise $30 million for the Boeing 767s the company had on order. United, once the nation's largest carrier, has not been immune from the pressures of competition. United negotiated with its labor unions to cut wages for new employees while maintaining existing wage rates for experienced workers. The negotiators for the pilots resisted the two-tier salary schedule and imposed a costly strike on United in May 1985. United has since undergone financial reorganization.

The decrease in the number of employees and the fewer services provided by the airlines, as induced by market forces, have led some observers to comment that flying is no longer the luxury that it once was. Jim Street, a spokesman for the Dallas-Fort Worth Airport, said, "I remember when you were going to fly, you put on a coat and tie and the planes were not crowded—nyou could travel in class and style. Today it's like taking the bus." Passengers have been forced to spend more time waiting for a flight. The Federal Aviation Administration, as part of governmental deregulation, removed restrictions on the number of flights that could land at 22 of the busiest airports in the country. As a result, the airlines are taxing airpost capacity to the limit. In June 1984 alone, 40,852 flights were at least fifteen minutes late. This not only means frustrated passengers, but dangerous conditions. In 1987, the government started publishing data on customer complaints and the number of on-time flights for each airline prompting airlines to clean up their act. Although the airlines recognize that delays in many cities have reached crisis proportions, they are not anxious to chance losing passengers by scheduling more flights at unpopular hours.

The search for the cheapest or best flight to any given city may produce some very confusing results. There are frills and no-frills flights, some offering no free baggage checking while others offer lavish transcontinental flights complete with champagne and caviar. There are flights with no stops and flights with half a dozen stops; and while some flights have a multitude of restrictions, others have none. "On a given day, there may be 104 different fares from Detroit to Los Angeles," says Joseph Halissey, senior vp of the American Society of Travel Agents.

Some passengers don't mind the barrage of choices or the wait as long as the price is right. A *Wall Street Journal* editorial on the subject noted that "if any lesson has come from the United States' deregulation of the airline industry, it is that competition opens up travel to people who couldn't afford it when there was less competition." In airlines where there are profit-sharing and stockholder plans for employees, passengers have reported much better service.

Airline executives have different theories about how to survive and even thrive in the competitive industry but most stress cautious flexibility. "The problem is that when a new carrier comes in and you allow them a price differential, they take the market away," says C. E. Meyer, president of TWA. "You either have to meet their price or get out." The "stake out your turf" school would have airlines hold on to business by lowering fares where it will damage a rival the most and oneself the least. Cutting prices in crowded markets is dangerous because of the chances of sparking a full-blown price war. All airlines fear the onslaught of a major price war that would hammer profits and might force some to go out of business. A vice president of United has remarked that "the entire industry is walking on eggs."

In summary, it looks as though the friendly skies have indeed become friendly for consumers, who now have plenty of options to choose from at lower prices. The airlines may have to bend a little because of competition and consumer demands, but many are already learning how to turn a healthy profit. The calamities predicted when air travel was left to market forces have not materialized.

The deregulation of airlines is a good illustration of a market in action. Prices, profits, and competition all played their critical market roles in the expected fashion. The strength and weaknesses of a market form of economic organization cannot be understood and appreciated until these roles are clear. The exchange process is regulated and coordinated by the movement of prices and profits. The gains from exchange are dispersed through economic competition.

Organization of a Market Economy

Once the exchange process involves more than a few people, markets develop so that the trading or exchange becomes more organized and can be accomplished with lower transactions costs. Figure 12.1 illustrates the organizational structure of the exchange process in a market economy. Whether we consider economic, political, or social decisions, the family is the basic

THE MARKET ECONOMY

Market for Goods and Services

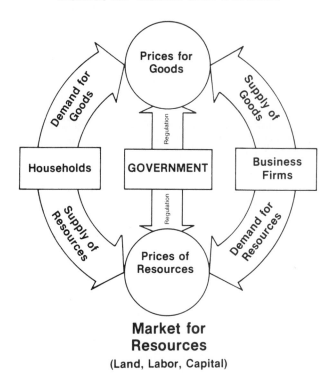

Market for Resources

(Land, Labor, Capital)

HOUSEHOLDS OR FAMILIES

1. Household demand for goods is the basic source of motivation.
2. Households determine what goods are produced (consumer sovereignty)
3. For whom (distribution) determined partly by household decisions of (a) who and how many of family offer their services in the market. (b) how many hours spent in leisure vs. working.
4. When to consume vs. save determined by households.

GOVERNMENT

1. Defines property rights
2. Enforces contracts
3. Prevents fraud and coercion
4. Regulates exchange

BUSINESS FIRMS

1. Businesses seek to maximize profits (the difference between selling price and costs of production).
2. Businesses supply goods to consumers.
3. Businesses must hire factors of production from resource market in order to supply goods.
4. Businesses determine how resources are used in production.

Figure 12.1: The Market Economy—Market for Goods and Services

decision-making unit. Most exchanges take place within families or involve families interacting with other decision-making units. In the United States today, there are about 90 million households. Most of these households are family units with either one or both parents present. However, a growing number of U.S. households, now about 22 million, are comprised of single individuals living alone.

The basic economic objective of these households is to try to use their resources in order to produce as much happiness or satisfaction as possible for their members. Every household owns some labor time that it can exchange in the marketplace for income. Whenever we take a job, we essentially exchange labor for goods and services. For example, in 1987 the 90 million households of the United States provided 121 million workers for the labor force, working billions of hours. However, households do not choose to sell all the labor time they might, since the average worker only works about forty hours per week when there are 168 hours available. This means that much of the labor time is used outside the market system in home production, leisure, activities, or other pursuits, such as sleeping. In addition to labor time, households also own land and capital which they either sell or rent to business firms in the resource market.

The major objective of household activity in the resource market is to gain income in order to enter the market for goods and services. These goods and services purchased in the marketplace are then combined with household time and with goods and services produced in the home to achieve the highest level of happiness or satisfaction possible. In 1987 these households received a total income, after taxes, of nearly $3.2 trillion. They chose to spend $3.0 trillion on goods and services and to save the remaining $200 billion.

Businesses, unlike households, are not interested in achieving as much happiness as possible. Contrary to the image that corporations often try to promote in their advertising campaigns, boards of directors and chief executive officers of corporations do not sit around planning ways the corporation can make consumers and workers happier. Instead, the primary objective of businesses is to generate as much profit as possible for the firm. There are over sixteen million firms in the United States. They are usually classified into three categories: proprietorships (businesses owned by a single individual), partnerships (businesses owned by a few individuals, each of whom is liable for the activities of the business), and corporations (owned by large numbers of stockholders whose liability for the business is limited to the value of their stock). In the modern economy, corporations are the dominant form of business organization. All three types of firms share the common objective of attempting to gain as much profit as possible. *Profits are defined as the difference between the total revenue from sales and the total cost of production.* In 1987, total business profits were approximately $273 billion before taxes. In order to make a profit, businesses must produce goods and services households wish to buy. Businesses produce goods and services by hiring or purchasing resources in the markets for labor, land, and capital.

The interaction of households and businesses creates a circle of economic activity. Within that circle of activity, households receive income from the sale of their resources; they then use this income to buy goods and services. The purchase of those goods and services generates revenue for businesses, which in turn use their revenue to buy the resources of the household. This circle of economic activity is, therefore, coordinated through the goods and services markets and the resource markets. In this way, households and businesses interact with each other in the process of exchange.

The government does not play the central role in this idealized model of a market economy that households and businesses play. Rather, the government creates the environment in which households and business firms interact with each other. In reality, the role of government is, of course, much larger—due in part to the difference between our idealized model and the complex world of political power.

The question remains as to what controls this economic activity. What ensures that there will be enough blue shirts and not too many red shirts? What determines that there will be the right number of civil engineers and the right number of French-pastry chefs? In fact, these are the three basic questions discussed earlier that have to be answered in any economy. (1) *What* goods will be produced and in what amount? (2) *How* will these goods be produced? How much labor, capital, and land will be used in the production of these particular goods? (3) *For whom* are the goods to be produced? How is the economic pie to be divided? When should consumption take place—now or in the future? In a market system these basic economic questions are not decided by an individual authority or central committee. In a sense, no universal decisions are made. Instead, the issues are solved through the reaction of millions of individual households and businesses to changes in prices and profits. In fact, the market system is often called "the price system" because of the central role that prices play in this particular form of economic organization.

Basic Propositions

In order to understand the role of prices and profits in a market economy, we will examine four basic economic propositions:
(1) The Law of Demand
(2) The Law of Supply
(3) The Equilibrium Price
(4) The Role of Profits
These four propositions describe the basic operation of a market system. It is the combination of these four propositions that causes the market system to allocate resources efficiently and to answer the basic economic questions of what, how, and for whom.

Law of Demand

As the price of a good or service rises, individuals will buy less of that good, assuming no other influence on demand has changed.

It is important to understand exactly what the law of demand is and is not. The law is a statement about the effect of price changes *holding all other factors that might influence demand constant*. If the price of running shoes fell at the same time that incomes rose, the purchases of running shoes could well increase because of the effect of income on the market for shoes. If it becomes a fad to wear a sequined glove on the left hand, the purchases of such gloves could go up in spite of a price increase. The law of demand refers to price changes alone.

Adam Smith

Adam Smith, the father of economics, was born June 5, 1723, in Kirkcaldy, Scotland. His own father had died several months before. Smith was the quintessential *Mad Magazine* scholar. He was pale and skinny, had poor vision, and never married. Smith was chronically absent-minded, and it was said that he was often "absent in the company of friends and sociable when alone." He was frequently seen wandering the beaches of Kirkcaldy muttering to himself. If alive today, he no doubt would have thick, horn-rimmed spectacles, a calculator on his belt, and six 2 pencils.

Adam Smith: *Mad Magazine:* Zaniness and unparalleled brilliance.

Despite his peculiarities, Smith's influence on the two hundred years that have followed him cannot be overstated. His book, *An Inquiry Into the Nature and Causes of the Wealth of Nations,* published in 1776, has dominated economic thought like no other book has ever ruled over a discipline. The *Wealth of Nations* is nine hundred sometimes laborious pages of history, sociology, politics, philosophy, and economics, and could be subtitled "Everything There Is to Know about Anything in the Eighteenth Century." But more important, the book articulates the principles and identifies the issues that still color our economy today. *The Wealth of Nations* describes how markets work, belittles government intervention in the affairs of men, sings praises to free trade, chides free public education, and explains how public virtue and self-interest work together to provide for the betterment of all men, both princes and paupers.

To appreciate *The Wealth of Nations,* it is helpful to understand Smith. He began formal higher education at Glasgow University at the age of fourteen. Three years later he received a scholarship to study at Oxford. Smith loved Glasgow and hated Oxford, for reasons that would later greatly affect his thinking. At Glasgow, teachers were paid according to their skills. Lecturers had a profit motive. At Oxford, teachers were paid a standard salarywith no incentives, and their lectures were stale and uninspiring. Smith would later write that governments should pay for school buildings, and students should pay for teachers. The importance of incentive was forever impressed upon him.

After leaving Oxford, Smith spent two years looking for employment, finally receiving a post as a lecturer in Edinburgh. Soon thereafter, he was invited to join the faculty back at Glasgow, where he would spend eleven years. During that time he published his first book, *The Theory of Moral Sentiments.* Smith's critics who claim that he was nothing more than a friend of the rich and an advocate of "survival of the fittest" surely have not read *Moral Sentiments*. The book is about good old fashioned kindness and paints a picture of men who care as much for others as for themselves. Writes Smith: "How selfish soever a man may be supposed, there are evidently some principles in his nature which interest him in the fortunes of others and render their happiness necessary to him, though he derives nothing from it except the pleasure of seeing it." The book was so popular that busts of Smith soon appeared in Glasgow bookstores.

In 1764, Smith's life turned in a way that would later turn the world of economics. The professor was invited to tutor the young Duke of Buccleuch and to travel with him through Europe. This post had two significant effects. First, it gave Smith the opportunity to meet with the best minds of the continent and share ideas with them. Second, Smith was paid three hundred pounds a year for life, an extravagant sum that would allow him to spend time in Kirkcaldy writing *The Wealth of Nations*. It took Smith thirteen years to write the book. Ironically, it was published in 1776, and like *Moral Sentiments*, it was an instant success. He rode the wave of its popularity to the position of commissioner of customs in Scotland, even though the job required him to collect the tariffs that he had lambasted in his book. Smith held the job until almost the time of his death, July 1790.

The stories of the man's odd nature and absent-mindedness are both legion and legendary. Two stories are especially illustrative. At a dinner one evening, Smith broke into a tirade against a prominent politician and statesman of the day, criticizing both his policies and his character. He quickly recanted, however, when he remembered that one of the statesman's closest relatives was his dinner partner. And as commissioner of customs, Smith would often forge the signature of a prior commissioner when handed official documents. His clerks would then remind him that he had been made the commissioner several months before and had the authority to sign for himself.

But it was his brilliance and not his forgetfulness that made him famous. The economic policies Smith advocated 210 years ago are still argued today, and the opinions of most economists of the 1980s descend from him. Smith explained how the self-interest of men, if left unfettered by the government, could work to increase the wealth of all men:

> It is not from the benevolence of the butcher, the brewer or the baker that we expect our dinner, but from regard to their own interest. We address ourselves, not to their humanity, but to their self-love, and never talk to them of our necessities but of their advantages.
>
> . . . Every individual is led by an invisible hand to promote an end which was no part of his intention. By pursuing his own interest he frequently promotes that of the society more effectually than when he really intends to promote it.

Of government planning and intervention, Smith said that "Great nations are never impoverished by private (but) by public prodigality and misconduct. For kings and ministers are themselves always, and without exception, the greatest spendthrifts in the society." Smith advocated a limited yet important role for government that included national defense, police protection, and public works. It did not include meddling with prices and profits. "To prohibit a great people from making all that they can of every part of their own produce, or from employing their stocks and industry in a way that they judge most advantageous to themselves is a manifest violation of the most sacred rights of mankind."

Smith's vision of markets, and the role played by competition in increasing a society's wealth, is continued today by many scholars. His epistles against protectionist tariffs and quotas are still cited in Congress. His writings on taxation, in which he advocated fairness, simplicity, and restraint, have not lost any of their applicability. In sum, his work "set the prescription for the spectacles of generations."

Smith was a man whose knowledge encompassed his generation. He had read all the great authors who preceded him. He knew and had conversed with many great contemporaries, men like Franklin, Hume, Rousseau, and Voltaire. His powers of observation were astute, and his books are full of anecdotes that teach the concepts of free markets. In fact, it was this power that accounted for his absent-mindedness, for when Smith focused on an idea his mind was irretrievable. His prose was uncluttered but forceful. There are few men whose impact on academic thinking has been more pervasive.

The law of demand is the most well-verified law of economics. After literally hundreds of independent tests, no researcher has found substantial evidence that the law of demand is violated with any consistency. In every instance, an increase in the price of a good, where all other factors influencing individuals to purchase that good have been controlled (including income), has induced individuals to purchase less of that particular good and substitute an alternative for it.

For some goods, such as gasoline, food, and utilities, an increase in price induces a fairly small reduction in the quantity purchased, particularly for short periods of time. For goods such as clothing, recreation, and most manufactured goods, an increase in price induces people to buy considerably less. And in many industries, an attempt by only one firm within the industry to raise the price will cause that firm's sales to virtually disappear (e.g., one bowling alley, one clothing store, etc.).

However, the most important point is that in all cases individuals respond to an increase in price by purchasing less of that good and substituting other goods in its place. The events within the airline industry show how lower prices increase the quantity demanded. When the government deregulated airline fares in 1978, increased competition forced airlines to lower their fares.

The law of demand is so obvious and straightforward that in one sense it is hardly worth discussion. However, we often forget that the law of demand is constantly in operation. For example, the oil embargo imposed by the OPEC nations in 1973 drastically reduced the supply of oil to the United States, generating what the press quickly called the "energy crisis." As politicians, journalists, and commentators discussed the energy crisis, their basic assumption was that Americans would consume the same amount of gasoline regardless of the price. It was felt that people would not conserve unless forced to do so by the government. Roderick Cameron, Director of the Environmental Defense Fund, expressed a common view: "We have to start thinking about cutting demand for energy with things like an excise tax on big gas-gulping cars." In other words, he felt, as did many others, that gasoline price increases alone would not do the job.

Programs were initiated to force the automobile companies to produce smaller more efficient engines and smaller cars because many forgot the law of demand and insisted that the American public would never make such a change voluntarily. Discussions were held concerning the need for mandatory rationing of the available supplies of gasoline because there was no way to induce people to consume less. Presidents Nixon, Ford, and Carter all appeared on television at various times in their administrations, pleading with American citizens to conserve because it was their patriotic duty. In other words, they felt that public virtue rather than self-interest was the only possible solution to the energy crisis.

However, prices gradually rose and the law of demand came into operation. Over time, individuals began to purchase more efficient and smaller cars (most of which were foreign made). Individuals began to drive less and to conserve gasoline as it became more expensive. In 1973 the consumption of gasoline per automobile in the U.S. was 736 gallons. By 1985 the consumption per automobile had fallen to 525 gallons. Economists have researched the relationship between the price of gasoline and the amount purchased, and have found that, in general, a 10 percent rise in the

price of gasoline will cause people to buy about 3 percent less. Once again, the law of demand is in operation.

The most basic implication of the law of demand is that prices can be used to ration scarce goods and resources. As the price of a good rises, individuals and businesses economize on that good. As prices fall, these same groups are induced by the decline in price to purchase more of that good. This means that price in a market economy can perform the important operation of rationing scarce goods.

An important property of the law of demand is that the response to a price change will be greater over time—response to an increase in energy prices is greater when people have time to trade in large cars, insulate homes, buy more energy-efficient appliances, and make other changes to economize on energy use. The law of demand implies that prices are a powerful device for social control. Individual behavior can be manipulated through changes in the prices of various goods. A tuition increase lowers the number of applicants to a university. An increase in the penalty for a crime reduces crime. An increase in medical fees causes people to see their doctor less and even to seek home remedies. These examples are but a few of the daily expressions of the law of demand.

Law of Supply

As the price of a particular good or service rises, businesses will produce more of that good.

The law of supply is as important as the law of demand. Prices act as a reward to sellers. As this reward increases, sellers are induced to supply more of their particular good.

It is easy to see the law of supply in operation in the labor market. During the 1960s and early 1970s, very few individuals graduated with degrees in engineering in the United States. The effect of these choices was to gradually increase the wage engineers were making. For example, only 46,900 engineers graduated in 1975. As the wage increased in the late 1970s and early 1980s, college students flooded into engineering programs, so that eighty thousand graduated in 1982, in response to the large increase in the starting wage. Earlier policy makers predicted that there would be a crisis in the American engineering professions because students no longer were interested in this type of occupation. Rather, students wanted to enter the socially relevant occupations, such as law, politics, and government service. However, as the wage of engineers rose, the policy makers were once again proved wrong for ignoring the law of supply.

Again, we can expect the effect of a price change on quantity supplied to be greater the longer the time period. Over time, the higher prices associated with the so-called energy crisis not only decreased the quantity demanded by consumers, but acted as a powerful incentive for firms to find new sources of energy and more efficiently extract oil from old wells.

Equilibrium Price

In free markets, the price for a particular good will move to that price, called the equilibrium price, where buyers want to purchase the same amount that sellers wish to sell.

The genius of the market system is that the interaction of the law of supply with the law of demand moves price to the level at which consumers are willing to buy just the amount producers are offering for sale. In economics, this price is called the equilibrium price. We can understand why the market system moves prices to an equilibrium by considering what happens if the price is too high or too low.

Consider a hypothetical example where the price of record albums is very high ($50 for the typical LP). At this price, sellers are ecstatic. They produce large numbers of records. However, consumers have shifted their demand almost entirely to other goods (they buy cable and watch MTV). Consequently, a large surplus of records builds up on the market. Sellers find they are not able to sell the amount they would like to at $50 a record so they begin cutting the price. In other words, the surplus acts as a weight that drives the price downward. Now suppose, instead, that records were selling for 50 cents an album instead of $50. Buyers are ecstatic. Everyone wants more albums, but few are offered for sale, and shortages develop. Sellers soon find they can charge a little more than 50 cents. In fact, buyers are offering them more and the shortage acts as a lever to move the price upward.

These market forces, producing surpluses when price is too high and shortages when price is too low, stop once the price reaches the point where buyers and sellers desire to exchange the same amount. So the market system will either gradually or quickly, depending upon circumstances, adjust the price of each good to its equilibrium price where the amount buyers wish to buy just equals the amount sellers desire to sell.

The importance of this characteristic of the market system is difficult to exaggerate. It is this characteristic of seeking the equilibrium price that allows the market system to ration scarce commodities by

MARKET EQUILIBRIUM

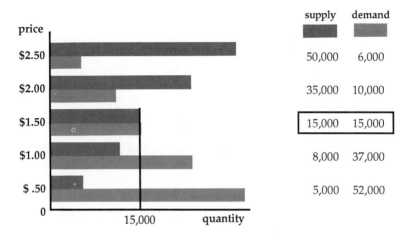

	supply	demand
$2.50	50,000	6,000
$2.00	35,000	10,000
$1.50	15,000	15,000
$1.00	8,000	37,000
$ .50	5,000	52,000

In a market, the price will move to an equilibrium ($1.50 in this chart) where quantity demanded equils quantity supplied.

Figure 12.2: Market Equilibrium

moving prices in the direction required by product availability and changes in resource costs. Thus, without coercion, or even governmental edict or control, behavior changes in the desired direction.

Consider the following hypothetical case. Assume the pizza market is working just fine. The price is at equilibrium. Assume now, that a medical research team discovers that a steady diet of pepperoni and anchovy pizza will cause significant weight reduction (pepperoni and anchovies combine to produce a natural starch blocker). Buyers now wish to purchase more pizza. Consequently, a shortage immediately develops. Sellers sharply increase the price of pizza. As the price rises, consumers begin to economize somewhat on pizza—the amount consumers wish to buy falls as the price rises.

Figure 12.2 illustrates these three basic propositions of economics. As the price rises from $.50 to $2.50, the quantity demanded falls from 52,000 to 6,000 units while the quantity supplies rises from 5,000 to 50,000. The operation of the market will push the price to $1.50 where the quantity supplied will equal the quantity demanded at 15,000 units. While all of this seems very simple, the operation of these three propositions achieves rather easily what planners struggle with endlessly in a planned economy—the right price.

Role of Profits

High profits in a particular industry cause businesses and resources to be attracted to that industry while losses cause firms and resources to exit an industry.

It is not enough that prices are simply moving up and down in a market system. Consumers may respond to prices, but business respond to profits. It is therefore necessary that we have changes in profits and losses as prices change. Profits are the key economic signal to firms as they move resources into and out of various industries. Profits act as the magnet that attracts businesses to particular activities. As profits rise in a particular industry, usually because of an increase in the demand or because of a reduction in the cost of producing the good, firms in that industry expand their size in order to capture more profit. Furthermore, new firms enter the industry to take advantage of the abnormally high profits that exist in that particular sector of the economy.

On the other side, as losses are incurred, firms depreciate their productive facilities and leave a particular industry for more attractive alternatives. For example, lower air fares in the airline industry lowered profits for the many different carriers. As a result, several of the airlines got out of the business. Other carriers tried to lower labor and other costs so their profits would be comparable with the profits they could make in other industries. Profits are a key ingredient to moving resources from one sector of the economy to another.

Consider the pizza market again where the price has risen because of the weight reducing power of a combination of pepperoni, anchovies and cheese. As the price increases, firms in the pizza business make abnormally high profits. New firms and resources are attracted, over time, into the pizza market because of these profits. As new firms enter increasing the supply, price falls until finally the price of pizza once again reaches an equilibrium at some new price (below the initial sharp rise but perhaps above the old equilibrium), with consumers and producers once again satisfied with the situation. The important point is that the movement of prices and profits prompts the movement of resources and promotes changes in consumer behavior.

Economic Interactions

We illustrate the interrelationship of the four economic propositions by considering the following typical chain of economic events: (1) Buyers desire to shift their consumption toward a particular good because of some change in taste. (2) A shortage develops for that good. (3) Price rises. (4) The rise in price causes buyers to reduce the amount of that good they wish to purchase (the law of demand). (5) The rise in price generates profits, causing existing firms to produce more (the law of supply). (6) The abnormal profits in this industry cause new firms to enter the production of this good (the role of profit). (7) Output increases until the abnormal profits in this industry disappear. (8) The market for this particular good is back in equilibrium.

The role of prices and profits in a market system can be summarized under the following three functions: (1) Prices ration scarce goods and valuable resources. If, for some reason, a good or resource increases in scarcity, the price of that good will rise in order to ration the available supply. As certain minerals, or fuels, or other key elements of the economy begin to diminish in availability, the price of that resource will rise, creating an incentive to economize on its use. Goods that are fixed

If You're So Smart, Why Aren't You Rich?

Economists and others who should know something about the economy are often viewed with suspicion because they don't seem to make money in the markets that they love to praise. If economists are so smart and understand how markets operate, why aren't they making a killing in the stock market, or in gold, or the bond market? The answer to this question tells us a lot about how markets operate.

On Friday, April 22, 1988, traders met at the New York Stock Exchange on Wall Street in lower Manhattan to buy and sell stocks, which are shares of the ownership of corporations. This particular stock exchange, the largest in the U.S., is part of a worldwide market in stocks. There are stock exchanges all over the world where traders buy and sell the stock of distant companies. There are similar markets for anything else that can be bought and sold, although most markets are not in locations as well defined as the stock market. At the start of the day, IBM common stock was selling for $112.38. (By tradition, stocks are quoted in terms of eighths of dollars, so that a broker would have said that the stock was quoted at 112 and three-eighths. It makes it more mysterious but doesn't change the essence.) On that Friday, 1,100,000 shares of IBM stock changed hands. Obviously sellers thought the price of $112.38 was too high and the price would fallover time. Buyers thought the price was low and made purchases through their stockbroker. At the end of the day, the price had risen to $113.75 for a gain of $1.37 for anyone owning a share of IBM. Surely, stockbrokers, economists, and others who study "the market" could predict whether prices of stocks or other assets will go up or down and thereby make a fortune. Sadly, the answer is that they can't.

At any given moment the price of a stock, a piece of land, an ounce of gold, or any other commodity reflects all of the known information about that asset. This information includes not only what has happened but also what people expect to happen in the future. In other words, all the information on April 22, 1988, that affects recent, current, and future performance of IBM is embodied in the price of $113.75 During that day, some people decided that IBM faced a rosier future than was implied by a stock price of $112.38, so they bought the stock and drove the price upward.

It is important to understand that the price reflects the best guesses about the future as well as what is current. If an event that occurs in the future will have a

in supply, such as paintings by Rembrandt or antique clocks, will be rationed in a market system entirely by the price which moves up or down to ration that given supply. Tickets to a popular play or sporting event will increase in price until the available number is rationed. (2) Prices and profits act as incentives to change individual or business economic behavior. A higher price is a reward to a seller and a penalty to a buyer. (3) Prices and profits send signals to households and businesses that influence their future plans. If a particular wage rises, some households and individuals respond to this signal by entering that occupation. When profits

positive effect on a company's product, that impact will be built into the price as soon as it is known. The stock market doesn't wait for an event to happen before making an adjustment. Changes in prices will occur as soon as any new bit of information surfaces. The IBM stock price of $113.75 reflects the views of millions of private individuals, managers for "institutional" investors such as pension funds and insurance companies, and corporate finance officers. And the same can be said for the price of every other commodity and stock.

How can someone beat the market? It's really very simple. You simply have to be smarter than all of these other people. Certainly, knowing a little economics will not do the trick. If it were that simple, then all the stockbrokers, insurance companies, banks, mutual funds, and investment houses would hire an economist and a computer and make a killing. What is needed to beat the market is something called "inside information." Inside information is secret knowledge about a company or some government action that will change the price of a stock as soon as it is known. For example, if you worked in the Pentagon and knew that the government was going to award a multi-billion dollar contract to Lockheed instead of North American Rockwell, you could make a fortune by buying Lockheed stock. In fact, you would probably buy the stock on the margin, which means you have to put up a fraction of the value of the stock to make the purchase. You could also make money by selling Rockwell stock, even though you do not own any. This trick, called "selling short," is accomplished by borrowing the stock from a brokerage, selling it, and then buying the stock later after the price has fallen, to repay the brokerage. All of these clever transactions will return enormous profits if you have inside information. There is only one small problem. It is illegal for most people who have inside information to act on it.

Beyond inside information, is there any way to beat a market that obviously contains enormous quantities of information? Probably not. If you follow the advice of most financial advisors or brokers, you will on average make about the same amount of money as you would if you threw a dart at a listing of stocks. Some strategies do better for a period of time just because of luck, but no strategy has outguessed the market over a long period with varied conditions. Of course, millions of investors are still trying and new schemes are proposed every day. Someone may be able to beat the market. Just remember that if they do, they probably will not sell you the secret in a book for $19.95, since they could make billions, not millions, with such a secret.

change, businesses respond to that signal by shifting resources in or out of that particular area of the economy.

In summary, prices and profits perform the same function in a market economy that government planners perform in a command economic system. Economic planners attempt to ascertain the desires of households, determine what goods and services ought to be produced, allocate resources to the production of the various goods and services, and then distribute the output of the economy to households in a manner consistent with the values of the planning system. In the market system, the preferences or desires

MOVEMENT FROM THE FARM TO THE CITY

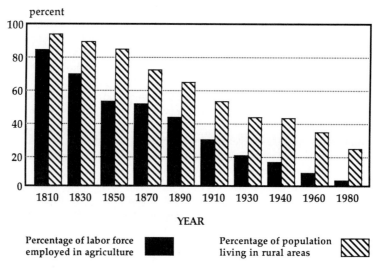

Figure 12.3: Movement from the Farm to the City

of households are expressed through the upward and downward movement of prices, profits act as signals or incentives that move resources from one part of the economy to the other, and the prices of resources owned by various households determine the distribution of income, which in turn determines who receives the goods and services produced by the economy.

Applications

The operation of prices and profits in a market system can best be seen by examining specific situations in which they are allowed to fulfill their function in the system, as well as situations in which, for one reason or another, the government has prevented prices or profits from functioning. The first example, involving the market system and American agriculture,

illustrates how prices and profits reallocate resources. This example is strong evidence of the allocative power of a market system.

You Can't Keep Them Down on the Farm

Figure 12.3 gives the percentage of the labor force employed in agriculture from 1910 until 1980. The overwhelming majority of today's Americans were born and raised in urban areas. However, a significant portion of their parents were born and raised in rural areas, and most would have at least one grandparent who was born and raised on a farm. Figure 12.3 dramatically demonstrates the urbanization process over the past 150 years.

How has this occurred? Has there been planning, which has gradually moved people from the farm to the city, or has this been accomplished through the market

In 1850 more than 1 out of every 2 workers was in agriculture: Today less than 1 out of 30. (Library of Congress)

mechanism? The process of urbanization starts with a simple biological fact—people can only eat so much. The economic importance of that biological fact is that as incomes grow, people spend a smaller and smaller proportion of their income on food. Suppose you were given ten thousand dollars today. Even the most obvious candidate for Weight Watchers would probably spend a fairly small portion of that increase in income on food.

One of the tasks of a growing economy is to shift workers from agriculture to other areas of the economy. A market economic system accomplishes this shift of resources by rewarding those people working in manufacturing and services with higher wages and penalizing those working in agriculture with lower wages. Over the past 180 years, wages in agriculture have been consistently below wages in other parts of the economy. This wage difference has induced movement of workers from agriculture and rural life into urban areas to take better paying jobs.

Literally millions of families and individuals have moved from farms into urban life over the past two centuries. This movement has been induced and controlled by market forces.

There have been no government programs to move people out of agriculture into urban occupations. In fact, the government, through its subsidy to agriculture, has tried to inhibit the process of urbanization. These government subsidies are a bit like holding back the tide with a six inch wall of sand and have had relatively little effect. The movement out of agriculture has continued in spite of the fact that rural life has been extolled and glamorized within the United States. While many individuals would prefer to live in small communities or in a rural area, the wage difference between urban employment and rural employment has simply been too large to allow people to stay on the farm.

Minimum Wage or No Wage

One of the best ways to understand the operation of prices in a market economy is to examine government intervention that prevents prices from reaching equilibrium. The government sometimes imposes price ceilings to prevent prices from rising. Price ceilings have been imposed in the form of rent control in some large U.S. cities. At other times, the government imposes price floors to prevent prices or wages from falling below certain levels. The federal government has imposed some price floors for agricultural commodities to increase the income of specific groups of farmers. Perhaps the most important case of a price floor is the minimum-wage law, which places a floor of $3.35 per hour. While the congressional motivation for such legislation was good, the legislation has had unintended effects that frustrate legislative intent.

In 1935 the U.S. Congress passed the first minimum-wage legislation. The intent of this legislation was clear. It was to help poor workers have at least a subsistence wage that would guarantee some possibility of a decent standard of living. Since that time the minimum wage has increased until it now stands at $3.35 per hour. (Congress is considering raising the minimum wage to $4.50 an hour.) What is the long-term effect of this legislation which was passed with the best of intentions? Essentially, a minimum wage interferes with the operation of a price—the wage. Minimum-wage legislation sets a limit or floor so that the wage cannot fall below a certain level.

How would we apply the four economic propositions outlined in this chapter to minimum-wage legislation? The first three propositions concerning demand, supply and equilibrium are relevant. In the labor market the law of demand applies as it relates to businesses. As the wage rises, businesses choose to hire less labor. They find it convenient and profitable to substitute machinery or highly skilled labor for the unskilled laborers generally affected by minimum-wage legislation. The law of supply applies to the individuals who are selling their labor in this market. As the legal wage rises, more and more people choose to supply more and more hours of work. The effect of minimum wage then is to reduce the quantity of labor that businesses choose to buy and increase the quantity of labor that individuals, especially unskilled young workers, wish to supply. In short, a surplus of labor is created. More people are looking for jobs than businesses are willing to hire at the minimum wage of $3.35 per hour. If the market

Rent Control

You are not likely to see this ad in the *Los Angeles Times*. "For rent, nice one-bedroom apartment in Santa Monica, near the beach, quick access to the freeway." In 1979, Santa Monica instituted a tough rent control law for existing housing. The rent control board sets rents, approves demolition of buildings, and arbitrates eviction cases. The experience of Santa Monica with rent control is a good case study of what happens when prices are prevented from reaching their natural equilibrium.

Rents in Santa Monica have risen much slower than inflation since rent control was instituted. With rents below equilibrium, shortages have developed. Ads indicating that apartments are available are rare. Apartments go to friends of the landlord or tenants who learn that an apartment is being vacated. Some apartments are rented through agencies that charge very high fees. Since owners may have several hundred applicants for each apartment vacancy, they can pick tenants carefully. Consequently, the apartments tend to go to "yuppies" (young urban professionals) who have stable, high incomes. Rent control has certainly not made Santa Monica a haven for the poor. One Santa Monica landlord estimated that his tenants' incomes had risen by 150 percent in the five years since rent control was instituted.

Landlords are responding to rent control in a predictable manner. They are spending less on the maintenance and upkeep of buildings. Sales of apartment buildings have declined since rent control was instituted. The Santa Monica Board of Realtors estimates that apartment buildings in Santa Monica sell for about $200,000 less than comparable apartment buildings in other locations (*Los Angeles Times*, April 8, 1984). Obviously, not many developers are anxious to build new buildings in Santa Monica, even though new apartments are exempt from control at present.

Opinion on rent control falls along predictable lines. The April 8, 1984, *Los Angeles Times* quotes a renter as saying, "It's a wonderful law." Landlords hate it. Politicians of all stripes favor the law because there are more renters than landlords. The poor person paying higher rents in Watts or East LA probably wonders why he is paying more to live in a run-down neighborhood than yuppies are paying to live at the beach. But patience is needed here. If rent control remains effective and stringent, Santa Monica will become as run-down as some other neighborhoods of the Los Angeles basin, though it will still have a wonderful beach.

---

were left alone, the wage would fall until the number of people who wanted to work would just equal the number of people businesses chose to employ. However, the minimum wage prevents proposition three, the achievement of equilibrium, from occurring because of the floor below which the wage is unable to fall. Consequently, the surplus of labor continues.

The above example and its conclusions follow from our description of efficiently operating prices within a market system. Obviously, there are other causes of unemployment among the youth, the unskilled, and racial minorities. However, data on unemployment among these groups suggest that the laws of supply and demand, combined with the idea of an

Table 12.1 Percent Unemployed in 1986

All Workers	7.0%
Males	6.9
Females	7.1
Whites	6.0
16–19 years old	15.6
20–24 years old	8.7
Blacks	14.5
16–19 years old	39.3
20–24 years old	24.1

Source: *Statistical Abstract*

equilibrium price, explain the impact of minimum-wage legislation upon employment within these markets. Table 12.1 illustrates the surplus labor and unemployment rates for various groups of individuals within the economy. It is clear that the groups with the highest rates of unemployment are young unskilled teenagers. Unemployment among young blacks reaches the disastrous level of nearly 40 percent.

The minimum-wage law has two effects on the unskilled workers for whom the legislation was designed. First, those who are able to find jobs work at a higher wage and are made better off by the minimum-wage legislation. Second, another group of workers is unemployed because of the legislation. They are clearly worse off by this action. How are other groups in the economy affected? Businesses are worse off because they are unable to hire unskilled labor at a lower wage. Skilled labor benefits since businesses will now find it profitable to use a skilled laborer where they might have employed two or three unskilledworkers had the minimum-wage legislation not been in effect.

Many economists believe that the very high rate of unemployment among young blacks is due in part to minimum-wage legislation. Businesses find that they can hire all the unskilled labor they wish at the minimum wage. In fact, there is a surplus of applicants. Since businesses can then choose among the various applicants, unskilled jobs tend to be rationed according to some characteristic other than wage. Perhaps the businessman chooses his young relatives, or teenagers living nearby, or teenagers that have the characteristics that he values in terms of appearance and education and, perhaps, skin color.

The example of the minimum wage illustrates a pattern that is often replicated when the government prevents prices and profits from performing their function in the market economy. The control of prices and profits creates a distortion that is usually reflected in either a surplus or a shortage. This distortion by the government makes some people in the economy better off, while damaging a larger but less represented group. Finally, there are usually unintended side effects from government intervention in the market system. These side effects often hurt the very groups that the government is trying to help.

Markets and Information

Like many things, the full advantages of the market system can best be appreciated by considering a world without it—a socialist world. Suppose you were appointed as chief planner in charge of shirts for a socialist country that did not have the benefit of observing and learning from surrounding market economies. Unless you are indifferent to consumers, you need to know their preferences for different styles, sizes, and colors of shirts. You will want to know how consumers will respond to different prices you might charge. What kind of buttons will be best, and again, in what size, color, and material? What combinations of wool, cotton, and various polyesters should be used? (The answer to this question will in turn influence production in agriculture and petrochemicals.) Obviously, shirt production should be coordinated with the production of pants, ties, jackets, skirts, and other closely related goods. What wages should be paid to workers? Again, the answer depends on what is happening elsewhere in the economy. The questions go on and on. In short, as chief planner in charge of shirts, you would need enormous amounts of information, much of which is not available even in a modern computer world.

The genius of the market system, with its reliance on prices and profits, is that it eliminates the need for one person or group to possess most of this information. Individual decisions of thousands of businesses and millions of households generate the required information in the form of prices, wages, and profits, which is communicated to those more directly affected by the decisions. The information transmitted through changes in prices and profits changes consumer behavior and reallocates resources. If households have a

sudden shift of preferences toward blue shirts, prices will rise for blue shirts, inducing a response from businesses and households without any individual consciously collecting the information about the change of preferences—a collection that would be essential in a socialist or planned economy. A bumper crop of cotton automatically lowers the price of cotton, leading to a substitution of cotton for other materials in clothing without conscious collection and analysis of information by planners. In others words, the market system with its central role for prices and profits minimizes the information needed to keep the economic system in operation. It is our experience that most economic planning in the world is done by planners who observe prices operating either in other countries or on the black market. Planning in a world totally without markets would be much more difficult than it is in today's socialist economies.

This praise of the market system is not meant to imply that markets are perfect. Far from it. Actual market systems contain a number of weaknesses that will be reviewed in the next chapter. However, both in our ideal model and in practice, the market system has considerable potential for controlling self-interest and allocating resources efficiently. Without this system, the necessary scope of government must be substantially increased and the task of securing liberty is significantly more difficult.

13
When Markets Fail

Concepts:

Market Weaknesses
Imperfect Information
Public Goods
Externalities
Monopoly Power
Recession
Economic Injustice

Pollution: One example of a market failure.
(Dubuque Telegraph-Herald, Dubuque, Iowa)

A Day with the *TIMES*

The *New York Times* is the newspaper of record in the U.S. America's elite like to sit down, especially on Sunday, and read the *Times* from the front page with its coverage of foreign events, however distant, to the Sunday magazine where articles compete with provocative fashion and lingerie ads. The *Times* reflects the concerns and attitudes of America's elite. News in the *Times* spawns next year's legislation. Perhaps reading the *Times* will show how the U.S. economy is perceived and how the market system really works—not in the ideal, but in the messy real world we live in.

Page 1

President Reagan offered a compromise to Congress on the deployment of MX missiles. The president, who wanted to build one hundred MX missiles, has agreed to pause after deploying fifty missiles. Supporters of the MX argue that it is needed to upgrade our land-based nuclear capability and to put pressure on the Soviets to negotiate. Opponents counter that the MX is vulnerable to attack and may destabilize the balance of weapons between the U.S. and USSR.

National defense has taken 5 to 10 percent of the U.S. output for the past forty years. Decisions about national defense could not be more vital to our future. Yet, the market system is of little practical use in resolving national defense spending problems. In fact, it is difficult to imagine how a market economy could deal with defense. Certainly, private companies are unlikely to provide defense, and private households are unlikely to purchase defense. The market seems to fail in this area.

Page 1 Again

The growth of the economy has fallen to a 0.7 percent annual rate, raising fears that the economy is headed into a recession. Some financial analysts are afraid that the strong dollar, which makes exports from the U.S. too expensive for foreign buyers, will cause an increase in unemployment. Unemployment is already above 7 percent and does not seem to be falling, even though the economy has grown substantially over the past year.

One implication of the law of comparative advantage is full employment. Yet, unemployment persists in most market economies, including that of the U.S. How can a market system be working effectively if there is unemployment? Unemployment implies that the labor market is not working efficiently. Each percentage point of unemployment in the U.S. costs about $75 billion in lost production.

Page A17

Air pollution is damaging our national parks—ruining lakes, poisoning fish, spoiling scenic vistas, and threatening wildlife and vegetation. The main culprits are sulfur dioxide and the acid rain associated with sulfur emissions. Acid rain is a serious threat to lakes and streams as well as the fish who depend on clean water for survival. One researcher is quoted as predicting "sulfur in the soil constitutes a time bomb to aquatic life in our streams." Environmentalists are calling for stronger laws to protect the national parks.

Are markets really working if pollution presents such a serious problem to the environment? Do we really want to produce as much pollution as we do, or would we, as a group, prefer to devote more resources to cleaner air and water? After all, pollution is a result of economic activity. The market economy doesn't appear to handle environmental problems very well.

Page 1 — Business Section

Antitrust officials of the government express concern about court decisions regarding hostile takeovers of one corporation by another. The concern over takeover rules has been prompted by the activities of rogue entrepreneur T. Boone Pickens, who is trying to gain control of Unocal, a large oil company. Apparently the courts are concerned that takeovers will concentrate excessive economic power in the hands of the few. The antitrust officials of the government are fearful that court rules will inhibit economic efficiency.

Do market economies put too much power in the hands of a few large corporations and rich entrepreneurs? The benefits of a market system are based on economic competition, but does such competition exist in the real world? The market economy is based on the benefits accrued from voluntary exchange. Do the individuals exchanging money for cigarettes really benefit from an exchange that causes illness and death? Billions of dollars are spent in a market economy to control individual tastes and preferences. Perhaps individuals do not really determine their own expenditures; maybe Madison Avenue does. Newspapers report failures of the market system every day. Waste and confusion about national defense, unemployment, pollution, businesses that manipulate and destroy, goods that kill, wretched poverty side-by-side with incredible wealth—all are perceived as indictments of the market system. The alternatives may be even worse, but the market form of economic organization seems to be far from perfect.

The power of the market system to search out all beneficial exchanges has been described and emphasized in chapters ten and eleven. In the 210 years since Adam Smith laid down his pen after writing *The Wealth of Nations*, economists have rigorously worked out the operation of a market economy, demonstrating that markets reach the goal of efficiency if the proper conditions are met. They have also demonstrated that a market economy can reach full efficiency with *any* distribution of income, so the issues of efficiency and equity can be separated. Unfortunately, the conditions necessary to guarantee complete market efficiency are stringent, including the following:

1. No buyer or seller may act as if he has any power over prices.
2. Each buyer and seller must have full information about prices and costs of all goods and services in the economy.
3. Businesses and households must be certain about all the information in the economy.
4. Property rights or contracts must be defined in such a way that third parties are unaffected by exchanges of others.

Obviously, these conditions are not going to be met in reality, so the more practical issue for a society interested in choosing a political-economic system is the degree to which a market economy is efficient and fair. We will see that the market does rather well when compared to the alternatives, though it is far from perfect. In this chapter, we review some of the main weaknesses of a market economy and the steps the government can take to improve the operation of this system.

The Role of Prices and Exchange

The genius of the market system lies in its use of voluntary action and freely determined prices to discover and promote all beneficial exchanges. The weaknesses of a market economy occur because exchanges take place that are not beneficial from a social point of view, or because other beneficial exchanges are passed up. These misallocations of exchange occur because the prices determined by the markets for particular goods, services, or resources are not the prices that produce the best set of exchanges in the economy.

The problem of acid rain provides an example of a market setting an incorrect price. Most sulfur emissions (the cause of acid rain) come from electrical generation and heavy industry, such as steel. The market price for the products that cause the problem does not reflect the costs of the acid rain. In this case, the equilibrium price determined by market forces is too low and does not promote efficiency in the economy.

The problem of unemployment provides another example where beneficial exchanges are missed in a market economy.

Unemployed labor could be used by entrepreneurs to produce additional goods and services, producing revenue to pay the workers and profit for the business. The labor market does not bring the potential employees and employers together for the mutually beneficial exchange. In this case, the equilibrium wage is too high to achieve an efficient use of labor in the economy.

In each instance of market weakness or failure, the problem may be analyzed in terms of incorrect prices or a breakdown in the exchange process. The diagnosis of why the market system does not produce the "right" price or generate the correct set of exchanges will point policy makers toward steps that government might take to improve the operation of a market economy. Any time government intervenes in the economy, a decision has been made to substitute planning for the market. Whether or not government planning corrects the market breakdown is always open to question.

Government and Market Weaknesses

Government's basic role in a market economy is limited to a few essential functions, including defining property rights, enforcing contracts, preventing fraud, and providing money for exchange. However, the existence of market weaknesses puts pressure on officials to intervene in the market economy and inject some government planning into the poorly functioning market. Government intervention in modern market economies is quite extensive, as shown in Table 13.1. Much of this intervention is in response to the market weaknesses or failures discussed in this chapter. Each market problem has put

Table 13.1 Central Government Revenue as a Percentage of GNP in Market-Oriented Democracies (Revenue Includes Taxes and Government Borrowing)

Country	1972	1985
United Kingdom	34%	38%
France	34	42
FRG (West Germany)	25	29
United States	20	24
Switzerland	15	20
Japan	11	12

Sources: World Development Report 198; Statistical Abstract 1987.

pressure, through the political process, on government to respond and, if possible, correct the market failure. Unfortunately, there is a tendency for the political process to ignore the problem after the government has intervened in the economy to solve a problem. It is possible that the government intervention will not in practice solve the problem but, instead, actually make the problem worse. Government control of prescription drugs provides just such an example.

As modern medicine has developed and become more scientific, it has been successfully argued that the ordinary individual and the ordinary physician are not competent to judge the quality of prescription drugs. The government has taken an increasingly active role in regulating drugs to insure that the sale of such drugs (exchanges) is actually beneficial for consumers. This trend toward regulation has received added impetus from time to time as approved drugs are found to have harmful side effects. One of the most significant examples of tragic side effects from drugs occurred in the 1950s with the sedative thalidomide. Thalidomide was safe for most people but produced birth defects when taken by pregnant women. Children with deformed limbs were the tragic consequence of permitting this drug on the market. Congress, through hearings and legislation, pressed the Food and Drug Administration (FDA) to do a better job of regulating prescription drugs.

It seems self-evident that government intervention in the prescription drug market is desirable. There are, however, unintended and adverse consequences from this government regulation. Regulation adds cost to the drugs. Companies must spend additional resources testing drugs to meet FDA regulations. Companies must wait much longer after developing a drug to market it, adding additional cost. Sam Peltzman, an economist studying government regulation, estimates that complying with FDA regulation adds 10 percent to the cost of prescription drugs. Many people would say a 10 percent increase in price is a small price to pay to improve the quality and reliability of prescription drugs. Unfortunately, life is not that simple.

As the regulator of prescription drugs, the Food and Drug Administration can, and does, make two types of errors. First, regulators may allow bad drugs onto the market, creating problems such as the thalidomide tragedy. Second, they may also prevent good drugs from entering the market for use by consumers as soon as possible. This second kind of error is just as lethal for individuals needing the drug as the first error is for those who take an unsuitable drug. Professor Peltzman estimates that the net effect of FDA regulation has been to increase the death rate rather than reduce it. The purpose of this example is not to convince everyone that the FDA should be immediately abolished.

Rather, it should sensitize us to the possibility that government intervention may not correct a market weakness, but worsen it.

There are three steps in analyzing market weakness or failure. First, find the source of the market breakdown. Are exchanges taking place that should not? Or are there exchanges that should take place that are not forthcoming? Is the market price too high or too low? Second, define the necessary government policy to correct the market problem. Third, evaluate the success of the government in implementing the policy that will correct the market weakness. There is a temptation for participants in the debate over the best economic system to talk in ideal rather than real terms. In reality, the market system is not perfect. Nor is government action to correct market failure likely to be perfect. Instead, each market breakdown requires close scrutiny. At times, government can do a great deal to correct a particular market deficiency. At other times, government intervention will actually worsen the problem, so that the best policy is acceptance of the market weakness.

Common Market Weaknesses

There are six general areas of market weakness or failure:

1. Imperfect Information
2. Public Goods
3. Externalities
4. Monopoly Power
5. Recession or Depression
6. Economic Injustice

The first five of these weaknesses involve inefficiencies within the market system. The sixth is the belief that the market system of economic organization produces an inequitable distribution of income and wealth. Naturally, opinions differ on the seriousness of each of these areas of market imperfection.

Imperfect Information

The Problem. A voluntary exchange makes both parties to the exchange better off if those involved in the exchange are acting on good information. If those involved in the exchange do not have adequate information about the products involved or the terms of exchange that are common in the market, then it is possible that they will miscalculate and the exchange may be harmful to one or both of the parties involved. Suppose a teenager goes into a grocery store to buy a pack of cigarettes. Will that exchange benefit both the grocer and the teenager? Many would argue that the teenager is unaware of the consequences of cigarette addiction, unaware that a lifetime of smoking increases the probability of lung cancer and reduces life expectation.

Information is often difficult and costly to obtain. Which car should we buy? Are prices for a home computer going to fall or rise? Is the new radial keratotomy procedure to correct myopia safe and effective? There can be no question that imperfect information causes exchanges to take place that do not benefit all parties, and prevents truly beneficial exchanges from occurring. Critics of a free exchange system can always point to examples and instances where consumers have been cheated in the marketplace. Consumer advocates such as Ralph Nader and David Horowitz command wide audiences, pointing out examples of market failure based on poor information of either workers or consumers. Popular television shows like "60

Minutes" or "20/20" reach their greatest audience appeal when they uncover some unscrupulous business practice damaging to benighted, uninformed consumers or workers. Obviously, exchanges take place that are not mutually beneficial. The real issue is whether such exchanges are so systematic that the usual remedies of the market system are not sufficient to solve the problem.

How does the market system approach the problem of poor information? Many exchanges are repetitive. We purchase gasoline, food, clothing, and personal services such as meals or haircuts on a regular basis. This means that both parties to the exchange have an incentive to treat each other in a manner that makes future exchanges more likely. A grocery store that mistreats its customers will fail quickly. Restaurants that provide bad meals soon lose their clientele (unless located near a college or university).

However, some exchanges involve technical information that consumers do not normally have. In these instances, intermediaries to help consumers naturally develop in the market system. We employ the services of a physician to diagnose illness and tell us what purchases of medicines and therapy will make us better. While physicians may not always use their information for their patients' full advantage, they generally act as good intermediaries, helping their patients make advantageous decisions. If a physician fails to perform this role effectively, the patient always has the option of finding another doctor. Since customers always have the power to withhold their business in a market system, businesses, professionals, and individuals performing services have strong incentives to provide customers with good products and good information.

Suppose a company has a superior product that many consumers would purchase (and thereby gain from the exchange) if they only had information about the product. Obviously, the company has a strong profit incentive to provide consumers with information. This information is conveyed through advertising. Advertising expenditures in the U.S. totaled more than $110 billion in 1987—a lot of information. Even an ardent devotee of a market economy would probably not argue that an ad featuring a Hollywood starlet draped across a sports car represents much information. Nevertheless, a great deal of information is conveyed through advertising. Consider how much we have learned about personal computers, videocassette recorders, compact discplayers, and automatic 35mm cameras in the last five years through advertising. Grocery shoppers scrutinize the weekly ads in order to manage their shopping for the week. A vast amount of information about both the quality and prices of products is presented to us through the media without government sponsorship.

Market Failure with Imperfect Information. In spite of all the incentives to provide information and the development of intermediaries such as physicians to help consumers, there may still be exchanges based on poor information. Such exchanges violate the very premise upon which free exchange and the market system is based for they do not benefit both parties to the exchange. Since these exchanges do not promote efficiency or economic welfare and should be eliminated if possible.

Government and Imperfect Information.
Since there may be exchanges that are not beneficial, does government then have a role to play? The traditional governmental method of redress for misinformed exchange has been the courts. For centuries, fraud and deception have been grounds under common law for invalidating contracts and providing compensation to victims. Civil courts provide a way to retain freedom of exchange while still protecting individuals from deception or fraud.

Some exchanges that are not beneficial do not directly involve fraud or deception. Rather, consumers simply do not have all the information relevant to making decisions, and no one in the system has any interest in giving them such information. Consumers of tobacco need to know that there is strong statistical evidence linking cigarette smoking to lung cancer. However, no private individual or group has any strong self-interest motive for providing this information. Consequently, the government has taken responsibility to provide such information. Labeling on food and other packages, warnings about health risks of some products, and television ads encouraging young people not to use drugs, are examples of government provision of information either directly or through laws requiring private individuals and businesses to provide such information. Government involvement in generating information appears to have been quite successful. Consumers seem to gain from the information at a relatively low cost.

In recent years, government has gone beyond providing information to interfere directly in the exchange process on the grounds that consumers and workers are sometimes incapable of making sound exchanges. Laws mandating safety devices such as air bags or seat belts for automobiles, or laws prohibiting trade in certain products such as drugs, reflect an increasing social impulse for government to control the exchange process. Whether this impulse will remain quite limited or represents a significant movement toward more planning in the economy is unclear. Some find it paradoxical that modern democracies feel safe entrusting important electoral decisions affecting life, death, and taxes to ordinary citizens, but that these same governments worry that these same citizens are incapable of buying pajamas without guidance.

Is Government Intervention Successful?
There have been few criticisms of the government's efforts to simply provide information through labeling, government pamphlets or television messages. The criticisms have come when government has taken a more active role of prohibiting exchange because it feels the exchange is based on poor information. The problem is a simple one. Under the guise of preventing bad exchanges, the government also prevents beneficial exchanges. Consequently, the harm done through regulation must be compared to the good done. The analysis of the FDA regulation of prescription drugs discussed above illustrates the problem well, but it is not an isolated case. Government licensing of occupations such as physicians, cosmetologists, accountants etc. is designed to prevent harmful exchange. Unfortunately, the licensing agencies are used to restrict entry and exchange in order to raise the price charged by the licensed group.

To summarize, poor information may lead to exchanges that are not beneficial to the parties involved or prevent exchanges that would be beneficial from taking place.

While the market system has some strong incentives within it to minimize this problem, there is a role that government can play to provide information that will not ordinarily be provided by businesses or individuals following their self-interest. In recent years, government has moved beyond the provision of information to quality and price controls of goods on the grounds that participants in the market do not have the capabilities to act in their own best interest. How far the government will move in this regard remains to be seen.

Public Goods

The Problem. Some market imperfections, such as inadequate information, allow markets to continue to operate even though they do so in a flawed manner. However, in the case of public goods, the market simply fails to operate. For this reason, almost all economists accept the necessity of government intervention to provide public goods that cannot be provided effectively by the markets.

The term *public good* has a narrow and technical definition. It does not refer to all goods provided by government. A public good is a good or service for which consumption by one individual does not diminish the amount of the good or service available to others. Furthermore, it is difficult or impossible to prevent individuals from using the public good. For example, most elementary and secondary education is provided by government in the United States, but education is not a public good. All public goods have the remarkable property of being available for all to consume jointly if anyone should happen to purchase or provide them. The services of

a lighthouse are a good example of a public good. If one shipping company should construct a lighthouse to aid in navigation, that service would be available for every ship in the vicinity of the lighthouse. Furthermore, use by one ship does not reduce the amount of light available for other ships to use.

Many goods have some element of a public good in them. Police protection has an element of a public good in the sense that good service by police may reduce crime in a city, providing protection for all. However, if the police are busy in one area of the city, they are not available for others. So in this sense, police protection fails the test of a public good that consumption by one individual does not diminish the amount available for other consumers. Radio and television signals, navigational aids of all kinds, and, most significantly, national defense are examples of pure public goods.

Market Failure with Public Goods. The failure of markets to provide public goods lies in the nature of such goods. If one individual provides the good, others will be able to reap the benefits without cost. Therefore, each individual has an incentive to let others provide public goods. So no one goes down to his friendly store and buys public goods, because it pays to try to get someone else to make the purchase. This problem of incentive is called the free-rider problem. Consider the lighthouse example. Every ship owner finds the services of the lighthouse useful. However, each owner knows that the construction of the lighthouse will provide services for everyone. So each ship owner hopes that other owners will build and maintain the lighthouse in order that he or she may be a "free-rider," consuming the services of the lighthouse without cost. To the extent that a business or household can consume the public good without paying for it, it is a free-rider with regard to that good. Thus, there is a paradoxical situation in which a business or household would be better off if it made an exchange for the good, but has an incentive to refrain from making the exchange.

If public goods were left to the free market, there would be almost no production or consumption of the goods and many beneficial exchanges would be missed. Consequently, the government must intervene in the economy and eliminate the free-rider problem by taxing everyone.

Radio and television signals represent unique public goods because communications technology may either create or eliminate the free-rider problem. Everyone with an antenna may receive a radio or television signal. Reception and use by one party does not diminish the potential use by someone else. These signals represent the epitome of public goods. Yet, in many circumstances, the market for these signals operates efficiently. For ordinary radio and television reception, the free-rider problem is eliminated by the use of commercial advertising. Commercials are the "price" we pay for reception of the signal. Since we are forced to listen to the commercials in order to receive the signal, it is impossible to be a free-rider in this case. This combination of the commercial with the program eliminates the usual public good problem.

The development of microwave transmissions and satellite dishes for home use has reintroduced the public good problem, especially with television signals for subscription TV like HBO, MTV, etc. In these examples, individuals are required to pay

for the service through a cable hookup. However, individuals, apartment complexes, and hotels owning satellite dishes are able to receive the signal without payment, which recreates the free-rider problem. If more and more households purchase the technology to receive these subscription signals without payment, provision of these signals will be less profitable until the signals are no longer provided. The cable companies are now developing "scramblers" to negate the satellite dish capability. Changes in technology may either intensify or diminish the public goods problem.

National Defense. The most important public good is national defense. Each individual within the borders of a particular country is protected regardless of the amount he has paid for defense. The protection the missiles give to citizens in New York does not diminish the amount of protection available for citizens in California. But each individual has an incentive to be a free-rider—to let others pay for the defense provided. Moreover, there is no way to make people pay as they use the good, as there is with the radio or TV signal. In economic jargon, there will be no revealed demand for national defense even though individuals would benefit from exchanging income or resources for the protection of national defense.

Could national defense be provided by a market system? Suppose that some private firms were created to provide the product—General Defense Corporation, Kellogg's Rockets, McDonald's Tanks. No doubt the Japanese would enter the market with Mitsubishi armored cars—small, well made, and economical. Each of us would encourage our neighbors to purchase national defense in the hope that we could free-ride on their purchase. The market would underproduce these goods, if they were produced at all. The only solution to the problem appears to be government provision of these public goods, levying taxes to pay for them.

Government and Public Goods. Since markets for public goods either collapse or are extremely poorly developed, governments have assumed the role of providing public goods, especially national defense, throughout history. Indeed, governments are almost synonymous with public goods. The primary government solution is to provide the public good directly. There are a few examples of contracting the provision out to private firms, but most public goods are provided directly by government. Public goods are no small matter for most modern societies spend a significant fraction of their income on national defense and police protection.

Is Government Intervention Successful? The fact that the government has assumed the responsibility to provide public goods does not mean that the problems surrounding public goods have been solved. Policymakers have no guide from the public as to the exact quantity to provide. With other goods, consumers reveal their preferences for the good through their purchases or consumption. Shortages or surpluses develop if the wrong amount of a good or service has been produced. However, there will be no observed shortages or surpluses of public goods because no one reveals his demand for the product. Consequently, the quantity of national defense or any other public good provided by government must be determined through reason and debate. (Sometimes government generates a little too much of the latter while ignoring the former.) In the presidential campaign of 1988, Democrats and Republicans differed significantly in their proposals for national defense expenditures.

Clearly, turning public goods production over to the government does not necessarily solve the problem. But the government solution is superior to the market alternative. The good news is that there are very few public goods. The bad news is that national defense, by itself, absorbs about 7 percent of all production in the United States.

Externalities

The Problem. In the *ideal* market world, exchanges only affect the two parties involved in the trade. Everyone else in the economy is left unaffected by any particular exchange. Problems develop when parties not directly involved in the transaction are affected by the exchange. To illustrate, suppose that a student entrepreneur rents a house and stages a party each weekend. The admission price of ten dollars per couple is gladly paid by some local college students for the privilege of seeing and hearing the latest rock videos while feasting on the refreshments available. The music is played at 100 decibels so that all may enjoy the subtle lyrics and harmonic variations of artists such as the Poison or the Boomtown Rats. However, a quiet professor lives next door, working each weekend on his magnum opus—The Economics of Banking in Siena in the Thirteenth Century. The exchange is beneficial to both the entrepreneur and his or her customers, but harmful to the professor. The professor is a third party adversely affected by the exchange.

Love Canal

Environmental damage is surely one of the most tragic and obvious failures of the market system. The Environmental Protection Agency has identified more than five hundred sites throughout the country where businesses have deposited toxic chemicals in the soil. Although the federal government has allocated several billion dollars to cleaning up those sites, the damage has already been done in many instances, and no amount of money can clear up the mess. For example, in 1976 residents living by Love Canal near Niagara Falls noticed a sickening chemical slime seeping into their basements and oozing into their backyards. The stench from the chemical fumes was almost unbearable. Bubbling pools appeared above the surface, conjuring up images of "witches' brew." Homeowners were in a panic wondering what was to become of them and their property.

The mysterious source of this chemical menace was soon diagnosed as the Love Canal itself, where during the 1940s and 1950s 22,000 tons of toxic waste had been dumped by Hooker Chemical and Plastics Corporation. Eighty-two different chemicals had been stored in metal drums and sunk directly into the receding waters of the unused canal or buried in the mud along its banks. Before 1976 there had been no problems, but years of abnormally heavy rain caused the chemical containers to corrode. The chemicals then leaked out and rose to the surface.

When an Environmental Protection Agency study revealed that local residents had suffered chromosome damage because of the toxic waste, President Jimmy Carter declared an emergency in the Love Canal neighborhood and moved for the relocation of some 2500 residents. The Love Canal Area Revitalization Agency sprang into existence with $20 million in funding from the state and federal government. The agency's mission was to relocate families who wished to leave and to buy their homes for an average price of about $35,000. Most residents accepted the offer, even though the price was often well below the cost of their homes. In addition, billions of dollars were claimed as damages in class- and individual-action suits against Hooker. The federal and state governments also filed claims for $650 million to recover their expenditures.

These third-party effects in exchanges are labeled "externalities" because they are costs or benefits that are *external* to the two parties directly involved in the exchange. An externality occurs whenever a third party not directly involved in an exchange either receives benefit or suffers cost because of that exchange. The exchange between the student promoter and his customers generates an external cost for the professor. Examples of external costs would include factory pollution damaging nearby homes, contamination of drinking water by farmers or upstream manufacturing from a city, offshore oil drilling which harms fish and mammals along a coast, blood donations by persons with diseases such as AIDS or hepatitis, and so forth. Other transactions may generate external benefits. In fact, if the professor were

A host of health-related problems among the Love Canal residents have been linked to the disaster. Women in the area suffered miscarriages 50 percent more often than would be expected. There was a high incidence of birth defects. In the southernmost section of the area, 4 out of 24 youngsters were retarded. The psychological strain allegedly caused several divorces and two suicides. Hooker's chemicals have been blamed for just about every abnormality in the region.

An article in *Fortune* reported the rage of nasty anti-Hooker publicity after the disaster, much of which may not have been deserved. Ralph Nader said that the Love Canal incident was symptomatic of "the cancerous, toxic cesspools left by callous corporations." A new author emerged, Michael Brown, who wrote Laying Waste: The Poisoning of America by Toxic Chemicals, and became a regular on the talk-show circuit, denouncing Hooker at every breath. ABC drilled the message home against Hooker in a documentary that centered on the high incidence of disease in the Love Canal area. The *New York Times* condemned Hooker for its "alarming indifference to poisonous particles."

It is not yet clear if the judicial system can provide a remedy to the disaster. Amazingly, Hooker's dumping of the metal containers was consistent with government regulations at the time. Therefore, it is arguable that Hooker was not negligent and should not be liable for damages. It is possible that Hooker could be held liable under the theory that Hooker management knew they were engaged in an abnormally hazardous activity even if they were not negligent. However, problems of causation and conflicting scientific testimony make it certain that it will be many, many years before any of the area's residents will recover damages from Hooker. Love Canal was a market failure that the courts will not easily resolve.

Proponents of government regulation argue that Love Canal is tragic testimony of the need for tighter supervision over market forces. It is not clear, however, that government control would have prevented the Love Canal nightmare. Since Hooker Chemicals had complied with government standards, it appears that governmental control would not have prevented the tragedy. The results of the dumping simply were not foreseeable at the point in time when the dumping occurred. Therefore, the sole lesson of Love Canal seems to be that the weaknesses of market systems can have lasting and tragic consequences.

writing his one great book on the musical tastes of contemporary college students, the parties would generate external benefits to him. Examples of external benefits might include inoculations which reduce the chance that others will contract a particular disease, honey production providing pollination for certain agricultural crops, and citizenship education since more enlightened voting will benefit others.

Market Failure with Externalities. Externalities do not necessarily inhibit exchange. Why, then, do they cause a problem for a market economy? Perhaps the problems can best be seen by considering two examples—one involving external costs and the other involving external benefits.

Return to the student promoter with his weekend parties specializing in loud rock music. Both the entrepreneur and his customers are better off because of the party. For illustration, assume the gain from the exchange after all costs are considered is $60. If this is the case, the parties will continue, since everyone directly involved in the exchange benefits. However, suppose that the professor suffers a loss valued at $100 because the party impedes his great intellectual endeavor. Then, from the viewpoint of the whole society, the exchange should not take place since the benefits only total $60 while the costs total $100. But, ironically, the market will ignore the costs born by the professor because he is not directly involved in the exchange.

External costs allow exchanges to take place that are not efficient in the sense that they do not create net benefits. If there are certain goods in the economy that create external costs, they will be overproduced in a market system because the external costs are ignored. The market price for such goods will be too low from the point of view of the whole society or too low by a criterion of efficiency. This low price, reflecting only the costs of production borne by the producer and not the external costs, induces overproduction.

External benefits create as many problems as external costs for the efficient operation of a market economy, although society tends to focus more attention on the problem of external costs. An inoculation or vaccination provides a clear example of an external benefit. If an individual goes to a physician and pays a fee to receive an inoculation or vaccination against a particular disease such as polio, both the doctor and the individual benefit and are better off because of the exchange. However, third parties also benefit because the treated individual is less likely to communicate the disease to others. Suppose

that a polio vaccination costs $50 in physician's fee, patient's time, and, above all, pain. Only those individuals who value the vaccination more than $50 will be inoculated. Suppose, also, that each vaccination generates $40 in benefits to the rest of society in terms of increased prevention. If George Jones only values a polio shot at $20 in personal benefits, he will not get the shot even though the benefits to society as a whole are valued at $60. In other words, goods or services involving external benefits will be underproduced by a market economy. Notice that George Jones would purchase the vaccination if it cost less than $20. The price of goods involving external benefits is not an efficient price in a market economy. Just as the price of goods involving external costs is too low in a market economy, the price of goods involving external benefits is too high.

Government and Externalities. One of the basic functions of government in a market economy is to define and enforce property rights. Externalities occur because property rights are not fully defined. Some resources, such as air and water, are not owned or are owned in common and misused. If all resources could be fully and explicitly owned by someone, externalities would disappear. Persons suffering external costs would be able to sue for damage, forcing the two parties to the exchange to bear all costs involved in the exchange. If the professor had a clear property right to the air surrounding his house, he could sue the student entrepreneur for violating his air with the sounds of rock music. This suit would force the two parties involved in the exchange to bear all of the costs involved. Similarly, problems of air and water pollution discussed above would tend to disappear if property rights for all resources could be fully and explicitly defined. Unfortunately, definition of resource ownership for air and water is either difficult or impossible. Consequently, the problems caused by externalities cannot be fully solved by clearer specification of who owns what.

Even though property rights are vague, some externalities are eliminated by private arrangement, reducing the problem significantly. Consider, once again, the case of the professor and the student entrepreneur. The gains of the rock video party amounted to $60 for the entrepreneur and his customers, while the losses to the professor were valued at $100. The fact that the loss to the professor exceeds the gain to the students generating the external cost implies that there is room for an exchange to eliminate the externality. If the professor offers more than sixty dollars, the student entrepreneur may be willing to eliminate the parties and the externalities. Externalities that involve very few people can be eliminated through private arrangement.

The more serious problems with external costs or benefits occur when the costs or benefits involve large numbers of people or businesses in situations where property rights are difficult to define. Air pollution of major metropolitan centers cannot be solved by definition of property rights or private arrangements. The copying of motion picture or music videos generates an externality that requires some government action for solution, since it is impossible to enforce the property right of the video's owner and private agreements are unlikely.

The government can reduce the externality problem with taxes, fees, or subsidies that have the effect of making individuals or businesses who generate external costs pay for those costs, or making those receiving external benefits compensate the producers of the external benefits. For example, drivers in Los Angeles and surrounding counties could be taxed according to the amount they drive and pollute the air. (The tax can be collected on gasoline and other fuels.) Such a tax turns the external cost into an internal cost which would now be paid by the correct parties in the economy. Similarly, general taxes might be levied on the segment of the population that benefits from the polio vaccination program. These taxes may then be used to subsidize vaccinations so that the cost to the individuals obtaining the shots only reflects their personal benefits, with society at large paying for the external benefits.

Is Government Intervention Successful?
Government's record in dealing with externalities is mixed. Certainly, the definition and adjudication of property rights by government has helped to reduce the problem of externalities and promote efficiency. Government control of external costs from pollution has been less successful. It is difficult to know what level of pollution is best from the point of view of the whole society. Environmentalists argue for no pollution, but that would mean no output of some goods as well as less jobs in certain industries. Advocates for the polluting industries and the associated jobs argue for leaving the control of pollution to the public virtue of the industry, but that would mean a great deal of pollution with the associated threats to health. Actually, there is an optimal level of pollution where the increment to the external costs just equals the net benefits of the increment to

Rockefeller's Standard Oil: Increased the public's
fears of monopoly power. (Library of Congress)

production. Unfortunately, it is very difficult to know exactly this optimal level of pollution. Consequently, government sometimes regulates too much and at other times too little. Unfortunately, getting things just right is not government comparative advantage.

While government has done a mediocre job of dealing with external costs, it has usually done a poor job of dealing with external benefits. With the possible exception of education, most external benefits in areas such as medicine, the arts and research are ignored or underfunded by government. Consequently, goods and services that have external benefits are underproduced in most economies.

External costs and benefits are likely to remain serious problems in some sectors of a market economy. Fortunately, most economic activity has quite limited external effects. Government policies to correct externalities are actually quite easy to design, but their political implementation is often quite difficult because the individual losses from such policies can be substantial.

Monopoly Power

The Problem. One of the most serious potential weaknesses of a market economy is the possibility that economic power will be concentrated in the hands of a few individuals or businesses. The fear of economic power has been heightened by the development of large corporations with thousands of workers and billions of dollars in assets.

General Motors had sales in 1987 of about $102 billion dollars, profits of $3.6 billion, and a capital stock of $87 billion. It employs 813,000 workers who, with their dependents, might account for a population of three million people. Perhaps General Motors should be invited to join the U.N.: its sales are larger than the GNP of many U.N. member nations, including Ghana, Thailand, Philippines, Chile, and Greece. (Maybe it should be a member of the security council.) General Motors is big, but it is not a solitary giant. IBM usually has more profit. Exxon has more capital and usually more sales. Many foreign firms are just as large as these American giants.

While the size of these large corporations creates some fear and distrust, the real issue is the extent of their economic power and the implications of that power. Economic power is associated with the term "monopoly," which literally means one seller. True monopolies are quite rare and normally confined to utilities such as local phone service, electricity, or natural gas. More often, there are a few large producers or sellers such as the automobile industry that appear to have considerable economic power. (A few large sellers are called an oligopoly.) Table 13.2 shows the degree of economic concentration in a number of industries in the United States, suggesting the possibility of economic power.

Table 13.2 Economic Concentration in Selected Industries

Industry	Percent of Production Generated by Four Largest Firms
Motor Vehicles	93
Breakfast Cereals	90
Cigarettes	84
Aircraft	66
Aluminum Sheets	65
Cookies and Crackers	59
Farm Machinery	47
Cotton Weaving	31
Paper Mills	24
Carpets	20
Women's Dresses	9
Ready Mixed Concrete	6

Source: Census of Manufacturers

Cartels. "People of the same trade seldom meet together, even for merriment and diversion, but the conversation ends in a conspiracy against the public, or in some contrivance to raise prices."

This famous quote from *The Wealth of Nations* reminds us that businesses have strong interests in conspiring to set prices at high levels. The conspiracy by manufacturers of electrical generating equipment during the 1950s illustrates the dangers of price fixing. (See the description in this chapter.) Firms that make such agreements and act together like a monopoly are referred to as a *cartel.* The Organization of Petroleum Exporting Countries (OPEC) has acted as a cartel since 1973. Through an oil embargo and production quotas, the cartel restricted production and dramatically increased the price of oil. No doubt the countries involved reaped enormous profits from the cartel.

GE Brings Good Things to You

The world of electrical turbine generators would not seem to be prime material for Arthur Hailey mystery novels. One doubts that the Mafia would ever try to control that hotbed of corruption, the circuit breaker business. The television programs "Dallas" and "Dynasty" are believable because they are about oil, not electrical insulators, right?

In the 1950s, however, the business of electrical equipment sales very much resembled an Arthur Hailey novel or an episode of "Dallas." There were secret meetings in hotels and country clubs during which business executives plotted how to cheat competitors, consumers, and the government. There were code names for products and aliases for conspirators. There were phony documents and paper shredders. Between 1950 and 1960, twenty-nine major suppliers of electrical equipment engaged in one of the most extensive price-fixing and bid-rigging schemes of the modern American economy. Their conspiracy bilked Americans out of millions of dollars, and demonstrated that even in a free-market economy the markets aren't always very free. The five major conspirators were General Electric, Westinghouse, Allis-Chalmers, Federal Pacific, and ITE Circuit Breakers. General Electric was eventually fined more than $425,000 and three of its executives were thrown in jail, albeit for only thirty days.

The methods those twenty-nine companies used were strange and definitely anticompetitive. Their main objective was to divide up the electrical equipment market and hence keep the competition from lowering prices and profits. Electric utilities regularly requested the companies to submit sealed bids for equipment, the objective being to get the lowest possible price. However, the electric companies agreed in advance which company would submit the low bid, and just how high the low bid would be.

The companies devised three plans to decide which company would win which bid. The most bizarre was known as the "phases of the moon" scheme. Although it sounded strange, it merely meant that the companies rotated turns submitting the lowest bid. Another company would get its turn once the moon changed phases. This scheme was considered safe since it required no communication between the different companies. The second and third plans were a market-share theory and a geographical theory. Under the market-share theory, General Electric was to get 39 percent of the contracts, Westinghouse was to get 31 percent of the contracts, etc. The geographical plan divided the nation into different sectors, and each company received one sector over which it was to exercise control. Each company was free to divide the contracts as it saw fit.

Keeping the bid-rigging scheme secret was no easy matter. Meetings were held on a regular basis in swanky New York hotels, but the company's representatives never acknowledged each other in restaurants or lobbies. Indeed, as a joke, the Barclay Hotel later advertised itself as an excellent host for having price-fixing meetings. "Antitrust-corporation secrets are best discussed in the privacy of an executive suite at the Barclay," the advertisement read. In addition, the conspirators always called each other by their first names, all phone calls were made from pay phones to each other's home phones, company letterhead paper was never used for memoranda, and even the companies' own lawyers were kept completely in the dark. All of the companies had express policies against price fixing, but obviously, those policies were more form than substance.

How was the pricing scheme uncovered? Slowly, reports of bizarre pricing began to filter down to the United States Justice Department. When the Tennessee Valley Authority complained that it was getting identical bids on insulators and transformers, the Justice Department began to search hotel registers for electrical company employees. Once it became clear that executives from all the companies were meeting in the same hotel at the same time, and that indictments would follow, the Justice Department was able to convince some of the perpetrators to tell the whole story in return for clemency. Amazingly, it seems evident that the very top officials of the different companies were unaware of what was going on. The corporation's structures were so decentralized, and the pressure on division managers to generate profits so intense, that lower-level executives masterminded the schemes without ever telling the corporation bosses. Nevertheless, under the legal theory of vicarious liability, the corporations were held liable for the wrongs of their employees and were forced to pay millions of dollars in reparations to the government and to utility companies.

One of the great ironies of the story is that ten years after Westinghouse pled guilty to the antitrust charges, it nearly went bankrupt as the victim of a price-fixing scheme by uranium producers. Westinghouse held a number of contracts to supply uranium to utility companies at a certain price. When the price of uranium escalated because of a successful price-fixing plan, Westinghouse found itself with hundreds of losing contracts. Westinghouse sued to renegotiate the contracts, but a court, perhaps with a long memory, held that Westinghouse would have to take its lumps.

Price fixing is just one example of how markets are subject to abuse. Normally, cartels die of their own weight, since the incentive for companies to break out of the cartel and grab a large share of the market is great. However, when they don't break up, cartels can wreak havoc with the free enterprise system. "What is really at stake here," said Judge J. Cullen Graney, who presided over the government's suit against the electrical conspirators, "is the survival of the kind of economy under which this country has grown great, the free-enterprise system." Market economies are based on the notion that prices and profits determine production and resource allocation. Price fixing skews the market and causes distortions. Conspirators argue, of course, that price fixing is sometimes necessary just to survive. "We need protection from buyers," said F. F. Loock of Allen-Bradley, one of the defendants. Obviously, the government and the judge did not agree.

But just as there are incentives to form cartels to raise prices, there are strong incentives for each member to cheat on the agreement by lowering the price, raising its profits by increasing sales. Cartels and price-fixing agreements are constantly being formed, but their life span is usually quite short. By the 1980s, OPEC started to lose its power. Member governments constantly exhorted each other to maintain the high price, but most governments were producing more than their allotted quota. By 1985, the price of oil had fallen to $25 per barrel from its high of $35 per barrel. In early 1986 oil was less than $15 per barrel. Even the OPEC cartel seems to be unstable.

Market Failure with Monopoly. In a competitive market, no individual or business has significant power over the price of the good or service being exchanged. Businesses may appear to have the power to set prices as they wish, but a price set above the market equilibrium will eliminate virtually all sales for that business. Consequently, the business's true power over price is very limited when there is economic competition. A monopoly or an oligopoly does have real power over the price because of limited competition. This power to control price is a serious threat to a market economy. It is important to understand the nature of that threat.

Exchange continues to take place even though one party has economic power, because exchange continues to benefit the parties involved. Economic power does not imply that monopolists or oligopolists are able to force consumers to buy the product. Businesses are always constrained by the law of demand. However, businesses or individuals with economic power can dramatically increase the gains from trade or exchange by setting a high price for their product. Thus, one of the most important effects of monopoly is to redistribute the gains from trade so that nearly all of the gain is captured by the monopolist or party with power.

If all the monopolist did was redistribute the gains from exchange, economic power would be a problem of equity. Unfortunately, the method monopolists use to capture the gains from exchange creates inefficiency in the economy. This inefficiency comes because the monopolist restricts the production of his product to raise the price, capturing the most gain possible from exchange. When the monopolist restricts production, many exchanges that would be beneficial from society's point of view are eliminated.

The following hypothetical illustration may be useful in understanding why monopoly or market power creates inefficiency. There is ample competition in the pizza market in most cities. If the cost of making a pizza is $10, the forces of competition will eventually keep the price close to the $10 cost of the pizza. Everyone who values a pizza more than $10 is able to purchase one, and all beneficial exchange in the pizza market has been captured. But suppose that organized crime gains full monopoly power in the pizza market by controlling the supply of mozzarella cheese. The economist hired by the mob to analyze the pizza market recommends that they reduce production of pizza by two thirds and charge a price of $20 to maximize their profits or gains from exchange. They do this even though pizzas only cost $10 to produce. Individuals previously buying pizzas now buy hamburgers or chicken, or eat at home. Too few resources are being used to produce pizza and too many resources are being used elsewhere, because the monopolist has

Free trade: One way to control monopoly power.
(Library of Congress)

created an artificial scarcity of pizza. For this reason, economic power creates inefficiency in a market economy.

Government and Monopoly Power. There are two strategies available to government to control economic power.

1. Government may regulate economically powerful firms, forcing them to price and behave like competitive firms.
2. Government may take action to foster competition in order to eliminate the economic power of firms.

Regulation is most often used to control industries that naturally tend toward monopoly. Utilities such as natural gas, electricity, and local telephone service are the most important contemporary examples. Most states have regulatory commissions that control the economic power of utilities by setting the rates for their services. The federal government has also set up agencies such as the ICC (Interstate Commerce Commission) and the CAB (Civil Aeronautics Board) to regulate businesses such as railroads and airlines.

For nearly a century, the federal government has tried to inhibit monopolies and promote competition through laws that have been grouped together under the title of antitrust policy. Monopolies (and groups of firms joined together to act like monopolies) were called "trusts" in the late nineteenth century; hence the name. Antitrust policy began with the passage of the

Sherman Antitrust Act in 1890 which made conspiracy to restrain trade or the creation of monopoly power illegal. This law gave the government power to use the courts to prosecute conspiracies, set prices, and break up companies that had monopoly power. Later laws, such as the Clayton Act (1914) and legislation passed during the New Deal, strengthened the power of government over business. Antitrust legislation essentially requires the government to prosecute businesses it charges with monopoly practices or conspiracy to set prices. This legislation also allows other businesses or consumers to sue for damages from monopoly in the economy.

International trade may be the most effective method of promoting competition to reduce monopoly power. The three largest automobile companies account for nearly all domestic automobile production, with one firm, General Motors, producing the major share. Clearly, the potential for abuse of economic power exists in this situation. A few casual meetings on golf courses in Bloomfield Hills or Grosse Point would be sufficient to set prices at a monopoly level. Fortunately, international competition is intense in the automobile industry. Pressure from Nissan, Toyota, Mitsubishi, Volkswagen, Fiat, Honda, etc., effectively removes the threat of monopoly as long as international trade is left unfettered. Since international trade has grown over the past few decades from inexpensive ocean shipping coupled with widespread economic development, the threat of monopoly has been significantly reduced. Indeed, much economic power exercised today is caused by government actions which create domestic monopoly through protection, or international government cartels such as OPEC that act like monopolies.

Is Government Intervention Successful?

The record of government regulation of economic power is mixed at best. In fact, the businesses being regulated often control the regulatory agencies. Individual consumers have relatively small stakes in the actions of any regulatory agency, so consumer attention to the actions of such agencies is sporadic. However, businesses being regulated have enormous stakes in the actions of the regulatory agency. Consequently, they lobby the agency intensely and often persuade it to take action in their favor. Indeed, government regulatory agencies, created to control monopoly power, have often been used by business to create additional monopoly power by setting high prices and controlling entry into the regulated business. Yet most policy makers and citizens would not want natural monopolies such as the public utilities to go unregulated.

The implementation of anti-trust laws has not been entirely successful either. The use of the courts to control economic power through antitrust laws is expensive and time consuming. (The government recently sued IBM for restraint of trade. The litigation took ten years, after which the government dropped the case because all parties recognized that technological change had destroyed the monopoly that IBM had enjoyed earlier.) Yet antitrust policy remains an important tool to control monopoly. Businesses may change their economic behavior in anticipation of possible antitrust action against them. Antitrust laws may reduce the number of business conspiracies to control prices. The threat of antitrust action against economic power may well be worth keeping, in order to encourage more economic competition.

Karl Marx

The most formidable challenge to capitalism has come from Karl Marx and his followers. Few men have been as well known and yet as little understood as Karl Marx. He remains for the most part an enigma. His theories of social and economic development are so complex they cause even the brightest scholar to wonder at their meaning. His personal life is a story equally mysterious.

Marx was born in Trier, Germany, the son of a Jewish lawyer, Heinrich Marx, in 1818. In Trier, an elegant cosmopolitan city, Marx benefited from both the French and German cultures, it being only six miles from the Luxembourg border. Heinrich Marx himself was a devotee of the French philosophers Rousseau and Voltaire. He believed in the equality of all men and in man's ability to create a better world. The senior Marx eventually renounced his faith and converted to Christianity

Karl Marx: Well known but not well understood. (Library of Congress)

in order to retain a public position. It had been decreed that no Jew could hold public office. His allegiance was not to his fathers, but to the state.

Karl Marx, the direct descendant of a long line of rabbis, thus became a Christian when he was six years old. Karl loved his father and was somewhat attached to his older sister, Sophia, but to the rest of the family he was cold and distant. He had the most profound affections for his neighbors, the family of Baron Ludwig von Westphalen. Baron von Westphalen's daughter, Jenny, first introduced Karl to the Baron. The Baron took Karl under his wing, discussing Shakespeare, Homer, Dante, and the great German writers with him as an equal. They often took long walks together along the Moselle River, where they talked of religion, life, and philosophy. The Baron's voluminous library became Karl's second home. Marx later described this time as the happiest period in his life. At the age of seventeen, Marx went to the University of Bonn to study law. At first Marx enjoyed his studies and the companionship he shared with other students. He got into some minor scuffles, like when he found himself in debt from spending too much on his books, or when he was thrown into jail one night for carousing with fellow students.

After two semesters Marx was granted a transfer to the University of Berlin. A year later he asked for and was given Jenny von Westphalen's hand in marriage. To the outsider this would have seemed a strange mismatch. The beautiful Jenny could have married any man she wished, and yet she chose Karl Marx. The gloomy, brooding Marx, who even his own children later called "The Moor" because of his dark sullen looks, hardly seemed the appropriate suitor for Jenny, the belle of Trier society. It was only because of the Baron's great love for Karl and his liberal, humanist thinking that the marriage was permitted. The union of Jenny and Karl meant a considerable rise in station for the Marx family. While in Berlin, Karl wrote love letters and filled his notebooks with mediocre verse in praise of Jenny. Karl's father wrote him letters encouraging him to see that he always be able to provide for Jenny's support and gave him lots of advice about how he could advance in his career. However, Heinrich Marx's kindly advice went unheeded.

Karl soon became frustrated with his studies of the law, disillusioned by its arbitrariness. He longed for the pure logic of philosophy and its emphasis on unifying ideas. In all German universities the most prominent philosopher of the day was Wilhelm Friedrich Hegel. Schools were alive with debate over his theories. In Hegel's view, change was inevitable. There was always a new idea or "thesis" which naturally produced its opposite or "antithesis." The best elements of the thesis and the antithesis then merged to form a "synthesis." The cycle then continued with synthesis giving rise to another thesis, and so on. Hegel called this process of social change "the dialectic."

Marx became an enthusiastic convert to Hegelian philosophy. Much to his father's chagrin, he decided to train to be a teacher of philosophy. Soon thereafter both Marx's father and Baron von Westphalen died. Marx was left with very little money, and all possibility of any academic career was closed because of the controversial articles that he had written while at the university. He turned to journalism and demonstrated some skill as a writer, soon becoming the editor of the most radical newspaper in Germany. It wasn't long, though, before Marx offended the government's sensibilities and was ordered to resign.

In order to avoid the harsh German censorship, Marx moved to Paris to write for a liberal journal that was to be smuggled into Germany. The first edition of the journal was seized at the German border. Marx quarreled with his co-editor over the second edition and was again jobless.

It was in Paris that Marx developed into a revolutionary. Using French socialism as a reference, Marx was able to refine and to develop his own theories. While there, he also began what was to be a life-long friendship with Friedrich Engels. Engels was the wealthy son of a German manufacturer and had a thorough understanding of industrial society. It may, however, have been Engels' capacity to agree with Marx that proved his most important quality. Where Marx was unyielding and obstinate, Engels was understanding and submissive. Engels was brilliant, but lacking in conviction. A gifted writer, he was able to convert some of Marx's more obscure but profound ideas into clear prose.

Perhaps Engels' greatest influence on Marx was in the area of economics. It was he who first sparked Marx's interest in the subject. After Marx moved to London in 1849, he spent long hours in the British Museum reading economics. Once Marx decided that he wanted to learn about economics, he read everything he could find by both the French and English authors, including Adam Smith. After his study Marx came to the same conclusion Engels did—that all the writings on economics were only meant to rationalize and to justify the present system. Together Marx and Engels authored the *Communist Manifesto*, a revolutionary tract written to establish their goals of a new society. The words "Working men of all countries, Unite," were Marx's cry to the proletariat, or working classes, to throw off the chains of bondage which the industrial revolution had imposed on them. Marx never in any of his writings explained what society would be or should be like after a workers' revolution, only that it would be "classless." It has been up to Marx's disciples to convert his ideas into planned economies. Marx and Engels advocated the abolition of private property, state control of all industry, transportation, and communication, free education, and a progressive income tax.

Marx said that "the history of all hitherto existing society is the history of class struggle." Marx thought that history was the activity of man seeking to achieve his ends, which are inspired and shaped by economic realities. The economic organization of a society determined people's attitudes, behavior, and history itself. Capitalism was just a stage in human development leading to a dictatorship of the proletariat and then to the ultimate egalitarian society.

The proletariat in a capitalist society was said to be "alienated" or separated from direct involvement with production. The worker was just another tool, as were "the means of production," i.e., the instruments needed to do work. The capitalist monopolizes the means of production and is thus able to control the labor market. Marx stated that "laborers have no other value other than that of a simple productive force, and the capitalist treats him accordingly." Marx's attacks upon the capitalists were sometimes vehement, as he once said that "capital is dead labour, that vampire-like only lives by sucking labour."

Because of this view of capital which Marx described in his book, cleverly entitled *Capital*, he thought workers should receive the total value of production. Marx called the difference between the total value and the wage "surplus value." The worker was only paid enough to keep himself alive and working, and the rest was skimmed off the top as profit. Marx believed that capitalism would produce its own downfall by introducing labor-saving machinery to keep pace with competition. This would cause a narrowing of the capitalist's profit base because of the smaller consumer market. The capitalist would then make adjustments and the cycle would continue but would one day lead to the inevitable collapse of capitalism.

Marx's idea was that men could not long endure being treated as mere tools without any independent control over their activities. He lived in a day when many worked eighty-four-hour weeks only to come home to poverty. He himself was miserably poor, having to borrow money continually from Engels to feed himself and his family. Marx was not an effective money manager. He often would pay for his children's piano lessons at the expense of feeding them. His wife Jenny was forced to share a bed with a prostitute in debtor's prison, and she had to beg for money for a coffin to bury her child. For some time Marx could not leave his house because his shoes and coat were pawned.

Before he died, Marx grew tired of the constant bickering among his supporters and said quietly, "I am not a Marxist." His approach had been dogmatic. In his mind, there was no room for disagreement as to the correct principles of Marxism. When Marx's dreams of a pure ideology were shattered, he withdrew from the movement. Today millions of people confess to being Marxists, but there are almost as many variants of Marxism as Marxists. Marx, the revolutionary, left his mark on society in an unprecedented fashion, but whether he would recognize his own architecture in the existing communist regimes is open to debate.

AN HISTORICAL PICTURE OF AMERICAN BUSINESS CYCLES
Fluctuations are recurrent but not periodic (i.e., the peaks and troughs do not occur at regular intervals).

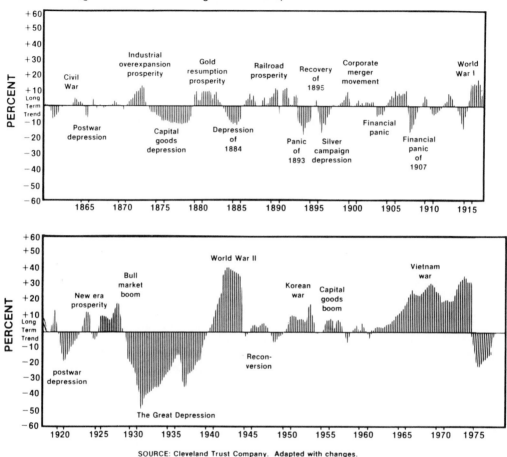

Figure 13.1: An Historical Picture of American Business Cycles

As pointed out earlier, international competition is an important constraint on monopoly power. Yet, governments have sometimes prevented international trade under the guise of job protection and fair play. On balance, government has opposed monopoly power, but that opposition has been faint-hearted at best. Fortunately, true monopolies are rare as is concentrated economic power.

Recession

Market economies have always had cyclical patterns of output and employment. Figure 13.1 charts the boom-and-bust pattern of the U.S. economy since the Civil War. All market economies have similar patterns. A small downturn in the economy, when unemployment is usually less than 10 percent, is called a recession, while a more severe decline is called a depression. Recessions and depressions represent the most serious weaknesses of the market system of economic organization. The causes and remedies of recession are only partially understood, but it is possible to see that the exchange process does not work properly during either a recession or a depression.

In the ideal market economy, prices, wages, and interest rates adjust to economic conditions so that all exchange possibilities are realized. For some reason, these adjustments are not complete during recessions. Workers want to exchange labor for goods but are unable to do so. Merchants want to sell their accumulating inventories but cannot do so at prevailing prices. Capital is idled by the downturn in the economy. A recession is a direct contradiction of the law of comparative advantage which is normally confirmed by economic experience.

The problem of recession or depression is of such vital concern to an assessment of the two alternative economic systems that a subsequent chapter will examine the problem in more detail. There is little doubt that it is the most serious efficiency problem in a market economy. Monopolies or externalities may cost an economy like the U.S. a few billion dollars. The costs of recession and unemployment must be measured in the hundreds of billions.

Economic Justice

The distribution of economic rewards strikes many observers as too unequal in a market economy. The richest 20 percent of all households receive about ten times as much income as the poorest 20 percent of households. Wealth is even more un-equally distributed than income. The poorest half of households hold no wealth; that is, their debts are about equal to their assets. To many observers, this inequality means that the market system of economic organization should be rejected regardless of its advantages in terms of efficiency and economic growth. Indeed, Karl Marx's attack on capitalism is really based on the injustice of a market economy.

Distributions of income and wealth are determined by the ownership of resources and the prices determined by the markets for those resources. Since a market economy determines prices solely on the basis of supply and demand, there is no intrinsic mechanism in a market economy to insure that the distribution of income or wealth is equitable. If young people in a society like to identify with mediocre musicians who wear outlandish costumes, the market will pay successes in this field like princes. If society does not value care and training for the mentally handicapped, the market will pay a pittance for persons trained and motivated to work in this area. In other words, the market is *amoral* in terms of the distribution of economic rewards. Some individuals are content with the distribution of income and wealth produced by the market system. Others find such distributions quite unfair and appeal to government to correct this defect in the system.

Efforts by government to change the distribution of income and wealth through transfer programs such as welfare or social security, as well as subsidy programs of all kinds, have become increasingly important in the past few decades. The next chapter is devoted to consideration of the moral and economic issues involved in economic justice.

EXPENDITURE BY GOVERNMENT ON MARKET FAILURE

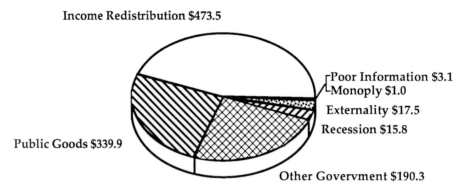

Figure 13.2: Expenditure by Government on Market Failure

Conclusion

In this chapter, we have reviewed some of the weaknesses of a market economy. No system of economic organization is perfect. Defects of a planned economy and strengths of a market economy will be reviewed in a subsequent chapter. But even advocates of the market form of organization recognize these potential weaknesses in the system. There is plenty of room for disagreement about the severity of the weaknesses. It is easy to magnify the problems. However, it is clear that these weaknesses induce increased involvement of government in economic affairs.

Figure 13.2 breaks down the budget of the U.S. federal government in 1984 into categories of expenditures that correspond to each market failure. As you can see from this table, most governmental expenditures are motivated by one of these market weaknesses. It is an open question whether the government intervention to correct these perceived weaknesses moves the economy closer to or further away from its goals of efficiency, equity, and freedom.

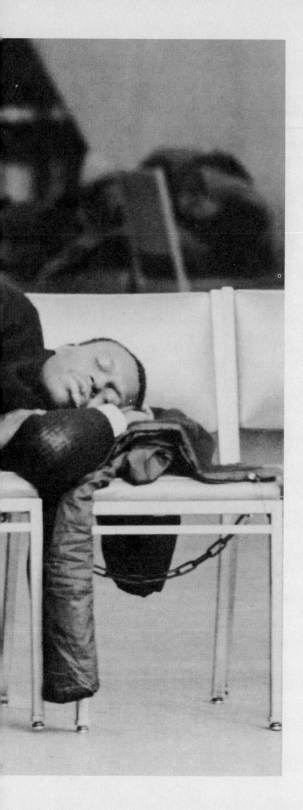

14
The Pursuit of Economic Justice

Concepts:

Equity or Economic Justice
Equality of Opportunity
Equality of Result

The homeless pose a tough question about equity in a market economy. (Wide World Photos)

America's Four Hundred

Forbes Magazine presents an annual list of this nation's four hundred richest people, complete with minibiographies that reveal how each person gained his wealth. The *Forbes Four Hundred* effectively portrays two important facts. First, the rich in America are very, very rich. And second, to be rich in America, or to be poor in America, is not necessarily a permanent condition.

How rich are America's richest? Well, according to *Forbes*, there were 49 Americans with a net worth of more than $1 billion before the stock market crash in October of 1987. The richest American, Sam Walton who owns Wal–Mart stores, was estimated to be worth at least $8.5 billion. If you had one billion dollars earning a modest return of 5 percent, the interest would be $136,986 a day. Even with taxes, you could live well and never touch the principal.

Mere millionaires need not apply for the *Forbes* list. To be ranked as a "Mr." or "Mrs. 400" one has to be worth at least $225 million. In fact, there's not a single pro athlete or rock star on it. Larry Bird and Michael Jackson don't even come close. Having $225 million would be sufficient to satisfy anyone's wildest fantasies. Have you ever wanted to buy 7,500 Mercedes-Benz automobiles? It would be no problem. Would you like your own tennis court in the backyard? With $225 million, you could put 10,000 tennis courts in your backyard. Would you like to feed starving Africans? With $225 million, you could feed 1,320,000 Africans for the next month, according to statistics from the American Red Cross. It is safe to say that if all the assets of the people on the list were thrown into a big pile and then distributed equally to those Americans living below the poverty level—presto!—there would be no Americans living below the poverty level for quite a while.

Of course, it may not be a good idea to take away all the wealth of America's richest people and distribute it to the poor. To do so might destroy the incentive for people to work hard and to earn money, and the end result might be that all Americans would be poor. In fact, the *Forbes* list demonstrates an important point. Wealth in America is most frequently generated by hard work, talent, and luck—not by inheritance. Approximately 60 percent of the people on the list earned their money through their own business ventures, not by inheritance. Consider An Wang, a sixty-five-year-old immigrant from Shanghai, China. Wang came from a middle-class Shanghai family. As he recalls it, "middle class" meant wealth of "maybe $100 American." From those humble beginnings, Mr. Wang amassed a personal fortune of $725 million. Closer to home is Jack Simplot of Boise, Idaho. Anybody who has ever been through Boise has probably seen Simplot's fifty-foot U.S. flag on his sixteen-story flagpole in front of his showcase home on top of the biggest hill in town. Simplot quit school in the eighth grade and went to work sorting potatoes and raising hogs. By the time he was thirty he had made $1 million. He eventually gained the patent for frozen french fries, and is now worth $500 million. "It makes me feel good to know I can walk into a bank and get $80 million just on my name." There is a dispute as to how rich Simplot really is. *Forbes* lists his wealth as a mere $200 million while *Fortune* has him as a billionaire.

FIFTEEN RICHEST AMERICANS FOR 1987

Name	Estimated Wealth	Inheritance	Source
Sam M. Walton	$ 8.5 billion	no	Retailing
John W. Kluge	3.0 billion	no	Media
H. Ross Perot	2.9 billion	no	Computers
David Packard	2.9 billion	no	Electronics
Samuel and Donald Newhouse	4.7 billion	yes	Publishing
Lester Crown	2.1 billion	yes	Industrialist
K. Rupert Murdoch	2.1 billion		Publishing
Warren E. Buffet	2.1 billion	no	Finance
Leslie H. Wexner	2.1 billion	no	Clothing
Jay and Robert Pritzker	3.8 billion	yes	Finance
Edgar M. Bronfman	1.8 billion	yes	Liquor
Barbara Cox Anthony/ Anne Cox Chambers	3.6 billion	yes	Publishing
Ted Arison	1.8 billion	no	Cruises
Adolph A. Taubman	1.5 billion	no	Real estate
Henry L. Hillman	1.5 billion	yes	Conglomerate

MISCELLANEOUS OTHERS

Name	Estimated Wealth	Inheritance	Source
Joe Albertson Jr.	355 million	no	Groceries
Marriott Family	1.2 billion	yes	Hotels
Leonard Skaggs Jr.	480 million	yes	Retailing
Rockefeller Family	2 billion	yes	Oil
Steven Spielberg	225 million	no	Movies
Joan Kroc	1 billion	no	MacDonalds
Ted Turner	465 million	no	Broadcasting
Carl Icahn	525 million	no	Financier
Malcolm Forbes	700 million	yes	Publishing
Donald Trump	850 million	some	Real Estate
Pulitzer Family	520 million	yes	Publishing
Ray Lee Hunt	1.3 billion	yes	Oil
Anheuser Busch Jr.	1.3 billion	yes	Beer
Ralph Lauren	350 million	no	Clothing

Source: *Forbes*

Note: *Forbes* published their list just before the stock market crash in October, 1987. Most of these people were worth considerably less after the crash.

Just as astounding as the rags-to-riches stories are the tales of riches-to-rags. In 1918, *Forbes* compiled a list of the thirty richest Americans. Of those thirty, only six have an heir on the list today. One of the thirty was Charles M. Schwab, who became the first president of United States Steel and gained a fortune of $200 million. Unfortunately, business turned sour for Mr. Schwab, and when he died in 1943 the tax appraisal on his estate listed him with a net deficit of $338,349.

The point of these stories seems to be that while income and wealth are not very equally distributed in America, people don't seem to mind very much because there is always the hope that they themselves could get rich someday soon. And in fact, they probably could. *Forbes* surveyed the 400 people on its list in 1983 and found that virtually all of them agreed that the potential for becoming rich has never been better in America. Wealth in America is not static, they said. It can be earned with just a little luck, or it can be lost with just a little luck. "I always thought I'd end up penniless," said Caroline Hunt Schoelkopf, possessor of an inherited fortune from her father, H. L. Hunt. In America, as Mrs. Schoelkopf makes clear, anything is possible. Of course, Mrs. Schoelkopf fell off the *Forbes* list for 1987.

Inequality

Inequality is the political preoccupation of the twentieth century. More political rhetoric, social legislation, and governmental expenditures are directed toward the perceived social evil of inequality than ever before. The charge that a tax change or social program favors the rich is likely to be the first volley of opponents. Developing countries often choose socialistic forms of economic organization because they accept the view that capitalism allows too much economic inequality. Yet, our views about economic justice are not very well developed. What constitutes economic justice? Should there be absolute equality so that every individual consumes exactly the same amount of each good? What characteristics should be allowed to affect the income (or consumption) of individuals: age, sex, race, occupation, intelligence, education, religion, height, appearance? In the modern world, equality is a powerful norm. A protest of inequality

or discrimination creates an instantly sympathetic political response. Yet, it appears few individuals would be comfortable with a world of absolute equality. Extreme inequality also has little appeal. What principles can guide us in defining economic justice?

The Problem of Definition

Each of us makes our own judgments about the degree of inequality we find acceptable or the rules of the economic game that seem fair to us. Unfortunately, much of our rhetoric about inequality comes from a keen awareness as to our own position on the economic pyramid. A Wall Street banker who lauds the virtues of inequality based on thrift and self-reliance strikes many as hypocritical, as does the indigent who advocates equality while lounging on the park bench. It has been suggested that we should think about economic justice from a "veil of ignorance" behind which we cannot anticipate our own economic position. Would the Wall Street banker sing the same tune if he had absolutely no preconception of his own economic position? Suppose that we had absolutely no idea of any of our abilities, characteristics or background. How much inequality would we desire in an economy that we were about to enter?

We might explore this idea with the following experiment. Suppose that there are six friends, three with blue eyes and three with brown eyes. Each individual puts one hundred dollars into a pool. In a bag, put a blue marble and a brown marble. Now set a distribution of prizes (two hundred dollars for a given eye color and zero for the other, or one hundred dollars for everyone) but do not specify which eye color is to receive the high or low prize.

Ask the individuals to define the degree of inequality they want before they know their place in the distribution. One suspects that individuals involved in such a game would opt for near equality of prizes. If this were the case, it suggests that our justification for inequality may simply be a rationalization of our place in the system rather than an expression of our actual feelings about inequality. The problem with this example is that it assumes that income distribution is generated by chance. It is possible that even behind the "veil of ignorance," differences in income would be allowed if individuals believe these differences are generated by acquired skills, years of training, personal effort, or difficulty or hazards associated with particular occupations, locations, and working conditions.

A type of inequality that almost all individuals would accept is an inequality that makes everyone better off. Suppose that two individuals had exactly the same income of one thousand dollars. Would they both accept a condition that raised one individual to two thousand dollars and the other to five thousand dollars if they did not know which one of them would receive the larger gain? It seems plausible that they would. Perhaps our basic fear of complete equality is that it leads to a lower standard of living for all. If individuals do not accept inequality that increases everyone's income, it means that relative position is extremely important and people will sacrifice standard of living to obtain equality.

Another puzzle in the quest for economic justice is the question of geographical boundaries. Should fairness be defined by the community so that equal incomes of five hundred thousand dollars in Bel Air and equal incomes of five hundred dollars in Watts would be just? Probably not. If the boundaries are not drawn at the community, then where should they be drawn? At the state or national level? There are virtually no poor by world standards in the United States. Yet, the drive for world fairness does not generate much excitement in even the most egalitarian circles. We only think seriously about economic justice at the national level where intense political action takes place. This suggests that much of the concern for economic justice may be political smoke hiding the usual maneuvering for government aid that dominates modern politics.

Another question: should economic justice be defined in terms of the outcome of the economic game, or the rules by which the game is played? In games or sports, we define equity in terms of fair rules, not fair outcomes. In economic matters, a definition of fair rules is difficult. Indeed, it may be impossible to implement fair rules, because so many factors that affect the distribution of income are beyond the control of government or society. This difficulty leads society to concentrate on results. It is as if we defined the fairness of a race by how close the last runner was to the first. If, on the other hand, it is not possible to make the rules of the game entirely fair, should we then make the outcome of the game equal? Are opportunities and results good substitutes for one another?

These questions are not posed for quick and easy answers. They are raised to illustrate that the issue of economic justice is extremely difficult to resolve and rests largely on the personal ideals and values of individuals. The issue of fairness could be ignored except for the fact that, with the possible exception of nuclear war, it may be the most pressing political issue in most

Table 14.1 Distribution of Wealth in 1774 and 1962

Percentage of Wealth held by:	1774	1962
Richest 1%	15%	34%
Richest 10%	56%	62%
Richest 50%	98%	95%

modern societies. The policies that societies implement in their search for economic justice usually have important implications for freedom, economic efficiency, and public virtue. One suspects the answers to the question of fairness will determine the future path of the American society.

The Distribution of Income and Wealth in the American Economy

Scholars have often approached the issues of economic justice by examining the distributions of income and wealth. Income is the amount an individual earns in a given time period—$500 a month, $40,000 per year. At the end of the time period, most of the income will have been spent for consumption. Wealth is the amount an individual has accumulated is assets such as real estate, cash, stocks and bonds. Wealth would be measured at a particular moment in time such as Sam Walton's wealth on September 1, 1988. Wealth and income may be very different. An individual may have high wealth and low income or vice versa although the two often go hand in hand.

For much of American history, there are no data on the distribution of income. There are data, however, on the distribution of wealth (all property and assets owned by a household) at various bench

marks in American history—1774, 1860 and 1962. Table 14.1 compares the distributions in 1774 and 1962. As we can see from the table, wealth has always been unequally distributed in the United States. The poorest half of the population have essentially no wealth. Over the past two centuries, the richest 1 percent of the population has increased its share of total wealth, although the data on wealth are subject to inaccuracies in measurement. The richest 10 percent of the population had about the same share of the wealth in 1774 and 1962. Overall measures of inequality for the two years show very little difference in inequality. It is surprising that the distribution of wealth has changed so little over two centuries while the economy has been dramatically affected by urbanization, changes in education, and changes in the role and extent of government.

We know less about the historical distribution of income because most income data are only available in modern periods. We do know, however, that income is distributed more equally than wealth. While the richest 20 percent of the households hold about 75 percent of the wealth, they receive "only" 44 percent of the income. And while the poorest 50 percent of the households have virtually no wealth, they receive about 20 percent of the income. The historical pattern of income distribution has probably not changed very much over time, and the income distributions of 1774

Table 14.2 Distribution of Income Before Taxes

Year	Poorest Fifth	Second Fifth	Middle Fifth	Fourth Fifth	Richest Fifth	Richest Five Percent
1929	3.5%	9.0%	13.8%	19.3%	54.4%	30.0%
1941	4.1	9.5	15.3	22.3	48.8	24.0
1947	5.0	11.9	17.0	23.1	43.0	17.5
1962	5.0	12.1	17.6	24.0	41.3	15.7
1977	5.2	11.6	17.5	24.2	41.5	15.7
1986	4.6	10.8	16.8	24.0	43.7	17.0

Sources: E.C. Budd, *Inequality and Poverty*, Current Population Reports Series P–60. Definition of income shifts slightly between 1941 and 1947.

and 1962 were probably quite similar, although there may have been a slight increase in inequality from the Revolutionary War period until 1900.

Recent Trends in Inequality

Table 14.2 shows the changes in the distribution of income among all households from 1929 to 1962. The overall distribution is quite stable. The poorest fifth of the population has increased their share of the economic pie slightly while the richest 5% of the population have seen their share of the pie decline significantly. The two great historical events of the twentieth century—the Great Depression and World War II—both reduced the inequality in the U.S. economy. The Great Depression reduced the share of income going to the richest 5 percent of the population by 6 percent. The decline in the income share for the rich was spread rather uniformly to all other groups. World War II also redistributed income away from the richest 5 percent of the households, with most of the gain going to the upper-middle-income groups.

The domestic political life of the United States in the post-World War II period could be described as the drive for equality. In the 1950s and 1960s black Americans challenged the American political system to live up to its ideals and grant them full equality. Civil rights legislation of the 1960s made *legal* equality for black Americans largely a reality. In the 1970s, unequal treatment of women was pushed to center stage in the theater of equality. The Equal Rights Amendment debate ended in defeat, but the major objectives sought by the feminist movement were largely attained through piecemeal legislation without a constitutional amendment.

These two important drives for equality were and are in part motivated by the economic concerns of blacks and women. On average, both groups receive lower income than households where white males are the major income earners. The median income of black families is about 56 percent of that of white families, while the median income of families headed by females is only about half that of the median income of all households. There are, of course, adjustments for education, job experience and duration in the labor force that should be made before comparisons are made between large social groups. Even if these adjustments are made, however, there appears to be a residual discrimination against blacks and women.

These drives for equality were accompanied by increased social programs for all poor—young, elderly, racial and ethnic minorities, women, handicapped, and others. The economic approach to the drive for equality is two-pronged. On one hand, programs such as Headstart, loans for education, and antidiscrimination laws are aimed at the creation of equality of opportunity. On the other hand, programs such as social security, welfare assistance, food stamps, and housing subsidies are directed toward equality of result. A most intriguing question concerns the tangible outcomes of this drive for equality. Has the distribution of income changed in the postwar period? If so, are changes due to more equal opportunities or simply the transfers that the government has made?

There are essentially two types of households covered in the income statistics—families and single households. Families comprise the majority of households. The distribution of income (before taxes and transfers) among families has changed very little in the post-War period. The richest 5 percent of the families received 17.5 percent of income in 1947 and 17.0 percent in 1986. The poorest fifth of the families lost a little ground in the economic race, with their share of total income declining from 5 percent in 1947 to 4.6 percent in 1986. Income among single individuals is much more unequally distributed than the income of families. But the inequality among households with only one member has declined substantially in the post-War period. In 1947, the richest 5 percent of single individuals received 29 percent of the total income of the category. In 1977, their share had fallen to 19.6 percent. The share of households that are families has likewise declined in the postwar period.

The result of all this complexity is that the distribution of income before taxes and transfers is virtually unchanged in the post World War II period. This fact suggests that changes in equality of opportunity have not yet had an obvious impact on the distribution of income. The more equal access to education, anti-discrimination laws, and other measures to create equality of opportunity, have not yet had an effect on the distribution of income. If the government has had an impact, it is on household income only *after* direct transfers through taxes and government programs such as welfare, social security and unemployment compensation.

The noticeable effects on the trend in the distribution of income seemed to be associated with the Great Depression and World War II—both seemed to have made the distribution more equal, Even these two promoters of equality of income did not cause dramatic changes. More than anything else, history suggests that the distributions of both income and wealth are quite stable and resist significant change.

Economic Mobility

Thus far we have considered the distribution of income for a single year. This inequality at a moment in time is very clear to social critics and ordinary citizens alike. If one starts on Park Avenue in Manhattan and moves through Harlem and the South Bronx, the obvious inequality assaults the values and sensibilities of most individuals. A leisurely drive southward from Bel Air and Beverly Hills to Watts would convince few people that the U.S. economy is a reflection of equality of opportunity and fair play. But is this snapshot of inequality at a moment in time deceptive? Don't we need a moving picture that shows the economic mobility of individuals through time? How much mobility exists in the American society? Perhaps the American dream is not of equality in the distribution of income and wealth, but instead of the opportunity to move from rags to riches, as reflected in the stories of Horatio Alger.

We know relatively little about the history of economic mobility within the United States. It is likely that westward migration and the settlement of frontier areas increased economic mobility. Certainly the famous historian Frederick Jackson Turner believed that the frontier generated more equality and economic mobility, imparting a unique character to American society. When the French nobleman Alexis de Tocqueville visited the United States in 1831, he was struck by the fluid nature of the society where individuals would go from poverty to riches and back again in a short span of time.

It is not that in the United States, as everywhere, there are no rich; indeed I know no other country where love of money has such a grip on men's hearts or where stronger scorn is expressed for the theory of permanent equality of property. But wealth circulates there with incredible rapidity, and experience shows that two successive generations seldom enjoy its favors.

Tocqueville felt that this mobility and equality over time gave the American society a distinctively democratic and individualistic character. Quantitative studies of the period before the Civil War indicate that there was more inequality than Tocqueville and Turner imagined; nevertheless, there was economic mobility. Of the fifty-nine individuals who, in 1828, held more than one hundred thousand dollars

in wealth in New York City, only thirty-six, or about 60 percent, still wealthy in 1845. Twelve percent of Boston's wealthy in 1833 were no longer rich just five years later in 1838. It seems plausible that there was a great deal of economic mobility pushing households and families up and down the economic ladder, while the very rich remained less affected. Data on economic mobility in contemporary America is scarce, but the scanty available evidence suggests there is still considerable mobility in the U.S. economy.

Occupational mobility has been studied more often than mobility in terms of wealth or income. These studies indicate that there is substantial occupational mobility in the United States. In the nineteenth century, roughly 35 percent of the sons of blue-collar workers moved into white-collar positions. This type of movement continued in the twentieth century, when about 30 percent of the sons of blue-collar workers moved upward on the economic ladder.

Determinants of Income in a Market Economy

Households receive income by selling or exchanging the resources that they happen to own. If they own extensive resources or unique resources that command a high price, they will likely have high incomes. Of course, most households own few resources—mostly labor—that have value. Rents on land account for a small part of income—about 2 percent. Income from capital is somewhat more important, accounting for about 23 percent of all income. (Some of the income from capital may be disguised rent on land.) But labor income is the most important, accounting for 75 percent of all income. The possession of land or capital comes from savings out of labor income or borrowing to acquire assets. Therefore, the factors influencing labor income, in large part, determine the distribution of income in the economy. Table 14.3 reports earnings for selected individuals and some occupations. The salaries of individuals, which are essentially gossip, should not be taken too seriously. Nevertheless, it is clear that earnings are very unequal and probably inconsistent with most people's values concerning what is really important or essential.

Factors Influencing Labor Earnings

The important determinants of earnings can be considered from a number of views. Most scholars of the subject would include family background, intelligence, education, occupational choice, sex, race, and luck as important influences on earnings.

Family Background. Parents and family characteristics play an extraordinary role in determining the income of their children. The family influences most of the other variables that are considered important factors affecting income. One way to measure the effect of family background is to perform the following experiment: Choose two individuals at random and compare their incomes. Then, draw out a pair of brothers or sisters and compare their incomes. Repeat the experiment many times and measure the difference. Social scientists have performed such experiments and find that brothers or sisters have similar incomes. In fact, this common family background is the most important determinant of earnings, accounting for as much as 35 percent of the inequality in

earnings. The family influences earnings through a variety of avenues including education, intelligence, occupational choice, and values about work and effort.

Intelligence. It should be no great surprise that IQ or intelligence affects earnings, accounting for perhaps 30 percent of the differences in earnings. Intelligence affects the level of education attained, the choice of first occupation, and the extent of upward mobility once an individual is on the job. IQ is largely determined by the family, genetically and environmentally, so the strong association between intelligence and economic success offers more evidence of the importance of family background.

Education. Education, especially higher education, has a positive effect on earnings, even if one accounts for family background and intelligence. Maybe people actually do learn something useful in college. Individuals with four years of college have earnings 20 percent higher than individuals with similar family backgrounds and intelligence who do not go to college.

Occupational Choice. Occupational choice plays only a small part in the distribution of earnings after the influences of intelligence, family background, and education are removed. However, there are notable aspects of occupational choice. Some occupations such as garbage collection, underground mining, and steel construction pay well because the work is either distasteful or dangerous. Other jobs such as lifeguard may pay poorly because the work is quite pleasant. These wage differences are thought of as compensating differences. The existence of compensating differences means that some inequality is an

Table 14.3 Who Makes What?

SELECTED INDIVIDUALS (Not a ranking of the top earners)

William Cosby Jr.	Actor, comedian, author	$57 million
Michael Jackson	Singer/dancer	31 million
Bruce Springsteen	Singer	27 million
Madonna	Singer, actress	26 million
Whitney Houston	Singer	24 million
Sylvestor Stallone	actor, writer	21 million
Lee Iacocca	CEO, author, TV personality	20 million
Johnny Carson	Talk Show Host	20 million
Jim Davis	Cartoonist for Garfield	16 million
Marvin Hagler	Boxer	15 million
Ray Leonard	Boxer (beat Hagler)	10 million
Oprah Winfrey	Talk Show Host	8 million
Bruce Willis	Actor	8 million
U2	Rock Musicians (4)	29 million
Jane Fonda	Actress/Exerciser	5 million
Bernard M. Fauber	CEO of K-Mart	3.4 million
Kareem Abdul Jabbar	Basketball player	2.5 million
Magic Johnson	Basketball player	2.5 million
Ozzie Smith	Baseball player	2.3 million
Ivan Lendl	Tennis player	2 million
Dale Earnhardt	Race-car Driver	1.7 million
John Akers	CEO of IBM	1.5 million
Eric Dickerson	Football player	1.4 million
Roger B. Smith	CEO of GM	1.4 million
Jose Santos	Jockey	1.2 million
Steffi Graf	Tennis player	1.1 million
Charles S. Locke	CEO of Morton-Thiokol	938,000
Curtis Strange	Golfer	912,000
Betsy King	Golfer	505,000
Sam M. Walton	Storeowner	349,000
Lewis Feild	Cowboy	144,235

Categories

800 Leading Business Executives	$706,000
U.S. President	200,000
Supreme Court Justices	115,000
Cabinet Officers	99,000
Senators	95,000
Government Workers	29,000
Store Clerks	16,000
Teachers	23,000
Accountants	41,000
Attorneys	45,000
Physician (General Practice)	75,000
College Professor	45,000
Registered Nurse	19,000
Minimum Wage Worker	6,700

Sources: *Sport Magazine, Statistical Abstract, Forbes Magazine*

illusion, because differences in earnings reflect the differences in the nonmonetary aspects of different jobs. Even though some occupations have much higher mean incomes, there is always considerable variance in income within any occupational group. Perhaps 10 percent of physicians earn less than a third of the mean income of physicians. The income of lawyers will cover the full range of incomes, high and low. Occupation in and of itself does not guarantee a particular income.

Race. Unfortunately, large differences between the average income of whites and the average income of minorities persist in the U.S. For 1986, the median income of black households was only 58 percent of the median income of white households. Much of this difference is accounted for by unemployment. The black-white ratio increases to 73 percent when full-time male workers are compared. Another part is accounted for by education, since whites have chosen or had better access to education, although the monetary return to blacks who do invest in education has been lower than the return to whites. The data suggest that market discrimination is declining in the U.S., but it persists. Blacks would earn less than whites even if other variables such as education, experience, and personal characteristics were the same.

Sex. The earnings of women are about 62 percent of the earnings of men for full-time employees. Again, adjustment for age, experience, and education remove some, though not all, of the difference. Women are entering the labor force at much higher rates than in the past. Fifty-five percent of women chose labor force participation in 1987, compared to 35 percent in 1960.

Indeed, 56 percent of married women were in the labor force in 1987, compared to 32 percent in 1960. Even though women are increasing their market work a great deal, they appear to be reducing their non-market work (work in the home) very little. This means the gains to women from entering the labor force are probably not as large as the gains to men, since married women are now contributing more market income and still doing most of the non-market work.

Households with a female adult present, but no male, are among the poorest in the U.S. Such households had a 1986 median income of $13,827, compared to a median income of $32,923 for married couples. Male householders, no wife present, earned a median income of $21,129. So far, the women's liberation movement combined with antidiscrimination legislation has not been able to achieve economic parity for women. Some scholars suggest that the current generation of young women will achieve earnings parity with men if they stay in the labor force. Time will tell.

Luck. Random events and luck play an extraordinarily powerful role in the distribution of income. Social scientists armed with the latest computer technology and statistical methods find that they cannot explain more than 60 percent of the variance in income or earnings with variables such as education, intelligence, age, family background, and individual characteristics, including sex and race. In other words, much of the inequality that we see in the world is due to no factor under the control of either the individual or the government. It is simply luck.

Markets and the Distribution of Income

A market system of economic organization does not produce a particular level of inequality in the distribution of income and wealth. The distribution of economic rewards in a market economy depends on the ownership of resources, and the demand and supply conditions for those resources. A market economy with widely shared ownership of land, capital, and labor would produce a distribution of income or wealth that was close to equality. Since the ownership of land and especially capital is quite unequal—many households own no land or capital—the market system often produces distributions of income and wealth that likewise are not very equal.

However, there are forces within a market economy that level incomes. If a particular occupation happens to be well paid, people enter that occupation, driving down the wage of that occupation and narrowing the distribution of income. When business or capital in a particular industry earns very high returns, these high returns attract other businesses and capital, driving the returns back to a normal level and evening the distribution of income. In other words, any characteristic or behavior that makes some people wealthy will be copied by others. As others acquire the wealth-producing attribute, the income or wealth that accrues to businesses or households with that attribute falls. Thus, the market has a built-in leveling mechanism that helps to produce equality. Unfortunately, there are other forces which move in the other direction and produce inequality in a market economy.

Markets will only produce more equality if people *can* respond to the price signals given in the marketplace. There are many important characteristics that produce high incomes, that cannot be acquired or copied. For example, suppose that a particular wealthy society enjoys watching men run up and down a hardwood floor throwing a round ball into a hoop at each end of the court. Tall men who are well-coordinated would have an advantage at this game. This advantage might be turned into millions of dollars for coordinated men over seven feet tall. Such men will then be at the top of the income ladder. They are rich because they possess characteristics that cannot be acquired. As more people enjoy basketball, the return these men earn on these scarce characteristics of height and good coordination increases because no one else can produce these characteristics.

Inequality increases in a market economy because individuals possess highly valued assets or characteristics in fixed supply, so there can be no market response to the high return. Personal characteristics that earn high returns but cannot be produced include beauty, rare athletic skill, IQ, talent for entertainment, inventiveness, and a high level of entrepreneurial ability. Assets such as rare works of art, patents and land with particular qualities such as a location at Fifth Avenue and 59th in Manhattan are also fixed in supply and likely to earn high returns.

The market has no built-in sense of the value of different activities and assigns no intrinsic value to them. Rewards in a market system are simply a reflection of the incomes, tastes, and preferences of households. If households value rock music highly, musicians producing such music will be highly rewarded while individuals doing work that might seem more valuable to some, such as school teaching, will not be rewarded highly. Thus, part of the complaint about the unfair system of rewards in a market economy is likely a complaint about the tastes and preferences of the population.

Discrimination and the Market System

The economic reflection of general prejudice and bigotry against certain groups is one of the least attractive features of a market economy. The economic disadvantages of women and blacks have been documented above. Statistics on income, earnings, and poverty show serious discrimination within the U.S. society. Discrimination of some kind is inevitable in a world where individuals make decisions. Most final choices employers make are conducted on very marginal grounds. When a business has narrowed the potential candidates for a position to three or four people, the final decision will probably be based upon factors most of us would find discriminatory.

It is impractical to outlaw all discrimination. Studies show that many factors including shortness, obesity, and unattractive features reduce earnings because of prejudice against people with these characteristics. But such discrimination does not seem particularly serious to society as a whole because this discrimination does not have a large effect on earnings. The American view of discrimination has certainly changed through time. As a society we have become more and more sensitive to prejudice and its malignant consequences. A later chapter will detail the struggle that many groups have waged to unlock the door of opportunity within this country. Nevertheless a basic issue remains as to what discrimination society wishes to prevent or alleviate through government.

Discrimination based on race or sex seems to have the largest impact on earnings and to be of mostconcern.

Discrimination in the marketplace operates in a variety of ways. Some employers may be prejudiced against certain groups. They may not hire individuals from such groups, or if they do hire them, pay them less. If many employers share the same prejudice, the wage of the disadvantaged groups will be lower than the wage of others. However, the profits of businesses that discriminate will also be lower since they are less efficient in their hiring. One suspects that businesses care more about profits than prejudice, so it is unlikely that the bigotry of businessmen is a major explanation for the low wages of blacks and women.

Market discrimination is more likely to work through prejudices of consumers or fellow workers. A black salesman may not be as productive as a white salesman, simply because of the prejudices of consumers. Consequently, the market will reward that salesman at a lower wage even though that person may work just as hard. Patients may not trust female or black doctors. Similarly, black or female workers may find it difficult to get cooperation from fellow workers, so their productivity is not as high as that of white male workers. Finally, and perhaps most importantly, discrimination in the marketplace may be the result of prior discrimination in education and training.

Government Policies to Redistribute Income

There are aspects of the market distribution of income that many people find morally or socially unacceptable. Few people would defend the role that discrimination plays in the determination of market earnings. While many people would accept a role for luck to play in the distribution of income, there is question as to how extensive that role should be. Of course, criticism of the market distribution of earnings, income, or wealth is based on value judgements. If such criticisms are widely shared, political pressure will build to change the market distribution of economic rewards by government intervention. Unfortunately, once the government accepts responsibility for the distributions of income and wealth, interest groups or factions will attempt to secure government favors, thus redistributing income or wealth to themselves. Since many factions will be competing with one another, perhaps Madison's view of the effectiveness of a large republic in controlling factions will prevent serious injustices.

Government efforts to redistribute income can be grouped into two categories. There are those programs and laws, such as public education and antidiscrimination laws, that are designed to provide more equality of opportunity. In contrast, there are programs and laws, such as social security and rent control, that might be considered attempts to provide more equality of result.

Government and Equality of Opportunity

Education. Government efforts to provide more equality of opportunity have a strong political appeal today in the U.S. Over $225 billion was spent in the U.S. by government on education with about 70 percent of these expenditures for elementary or secondary education. Certainly, the provision of more opportunity for the disadvantaged is a major motivation for these expenditures.

Antidiscrimination Laws. Since the 1960s, the U.S. has passed numerous laws aimed at eliminating economic discrimination. The Civil Rights Act of 1964 prohibits employment discrimination on the basis of sex, religion, race, color, or national origin. This law also created the Equal Employment Opportunity Commission to combat discrimination. The Equal Pay Act of 1963 prohibits wage discrimination on the basis of sex. The Employment Act of 1968 prohibits discrimination on the basis of age. The Rehabilitation Act of 1973 prohibits recipients of federal contracts from discriminating on the basis of physical or mental handicap.

These and other laws have undoubtedly had some impact on equality of economic opportunity, but the extent of their impact remains unclear. Much of the inequality of opportunity comes before a person enters the labor market. Educational opportunities, in spite of public education and subsidies for students from low-income families to attend college, are far from equal. A college degree from a local community college does not have the same value as a B.A. from Harvard or Yale. Family background, which is largely beyond the influence of government, has a profound impact on opportunities. Thus, laws and government programs have a positive, but limited, impact on equality of opportunity.

Results of Government Efforts to Improve Equality of Opportunity. The results of government efforts to improve equality of opportunity should appear in the pre-tax distribution of income and in the differences in earnings for various groups. The evidence is not encouraging. From Table 14.2, it is clear that the distribution of income has changed very little over the years that the government has

Table 14.4 Taxes and Redistribution: A Hypothetical Example

	Income	Tax Paid	Taxes as a % of Income	After-Tax Income
Proportional Tax	$ 10,000	$ 2,000	20%	$ 8,000
	50,000	10,000	20%	40,000
	100,000	20,000	20%	80,000
Progressive Tax	$ 10,000	$ 2,000	20%	$ 8,000
	50,000	15,000	30%	35,000
	100,000	40,000	40%	60,000
Regressive Tax	$ 10,000	$ 2,000	20%	$ 8,000
	50,000	6,000	12%	44,000
	100,000	8,000	8%	92,000

made a concerted effort to improve equality of opportunity. The income of the poorest 20 percent of families was 5.0 percent of all income in 1962 and was 4.6 percent in 1986—discernible but not dramatic downward change. Most important government legislation was passed twenty years ago.

To some extent, reformers and politicians sympathetic to redistribution have become disillusioned by the failure of the war on poverty, government programs such as Headstart, and antidiscrimination laws to produce more results. Consequently, efforts have shifted from a focus upon equality of opportunity to emphasis on more equality of results.

Government and Equality of Results

The government can use its budget and tax policies in several ways to drive a wedge between income and consumption. Government can provide goods and services directly to poorer households so that consumption is higher than income. Government can also take a smaller percentage of income in taxes from poorer households so that after-tax income is more equal than before-tax income. Finally, the government can use its regulatory power to redistribute income from one group to another.

Redistribution through Taxes. Taxes may be classified according to the change in the tax rate with income. Table 14.4 illustrates the three possible effects of taxes on the distribution of income. Taxes may be *proportional*, so that everyone pays the same percentage of income in taxes. Proportional taxes would leave the distribution of income unchanged. That is, the after-tax incomes have the same relationship to each other as the pre-tax incomes. Taxes may be *progressive* like the current income tax, so that the percentage of income paid in taxes rises with income. Progressive taxes will narrow the spread of after-tax incomes. Taxes may be *regressive*, where the percentage of income paid in taxes falls with higher income. The sales tax is an example of a regressive tax because lower income families will pay a larger percentage of their income in sales tax than higher income families. A regressive tax will increase inequality by taxing low incomes at a higher rate than higher incomes.

Who Pays This Tax, Anyway?

In an effort to make taxes fair, Congress often looks to the corporate income tax in order to give tax breaks to poor and middle income families. It seems so right to tax rich corporations instead of hard-working, middle-class voters. There is only one small problem with this benevolent act of Congress. No one knows who pays the corporate income tax.

The incidence of taxes is a very tricky matter. Obviously, the point of collection of a tax does not really tell us who pays the tax. What we really want to know is whose income is going down because a particular tax has been levied. This is never a simple question, and with the corporate income tax it appears to be a question without an answer.

The corporate income tax is a tax on the income of the corporation after it has paid its costs. (There is an ongoing controversy over the definition of costs. Does a three-martini lunch or a rented Mercedes Benz really constitute a cost?) But what happens after the tax is imposed? Do corporations raise their prices in response to the tax? If so, then customers of corporations are actually paying the corporate income tax. Are employees paid as much after the tax is levied? If not, workers are paying part of the tax. Perhaps the salaries of top management go down with the corporate income tax. If prices and wages do not change, then the owners of the capital of the corporation pay the tax.

But who owns the major U.S. corporations? Everybody, for much of the commonstock of businesses is owned by insurance policyholders and workers' pension funds. The fact is, no one knows who pays the corporate income tax. So the next time a politician campaigns on a platform of taxing the rich by raising the corporate income tax, be wary. It may be your pocket that is being picked.

Of the major taxes in the U.S. tax system, only the federal income tax and taxes on inheritances and gifts are clearly progressive, redistributing income away from the rich and in favor of the poor. Social Security taxes are regressive because there is a ceiling income (currently $47,000) above which the tax is not paid. Politicians seem to be convinced that the corporate income tax is a progressive tax, even though economists have found no evidence to support that point of view. As yet, the effect of the corporate income tax on the distribution of economic rewards is unknown. In summary, the total impact of taxes on the distribution of income appears to be negligible. In effect, taxes do almost nothing to redistribute income in the U.S.

Redistribution through Government Expenditures and Transfers. Transfers such as food stamps, housing, Medicare and cash through Social Security and welfare payments may also change the distribution of income. Transfer payments by all levels of government to individuals increased fourteen-fold from 1960 to 1984. Most of these transfers do not go to the poor. Rather, they go to the elderly—a group whose poverty

Poverty

In the 1960s, Lyndon Johnson declared war on poverty while we fought an undeclared war in Vietnam. Neither war turned out well.

Poverty is an ambiguous concept at best. The poor in India, or the poor in the United States in 1850, do not closely resemble those families defined as poor in the United States today. Some scholars define poverty so that it refers to one who has less than half of the average income. If the average family income is $20,000, families with incomes of $10,000 or less would qualify as poor. The proportion of the population defined as poor would be unlikely to change under such a rule. (A candidate with presidential aspirations once declared that poverty would cease when everyone had an income above the average. Fortunately, he was not elected!) The government has chosen to define poverty by the income needed to consume certain basic goods. For example, a household with four persons was considered below the poverty level if its

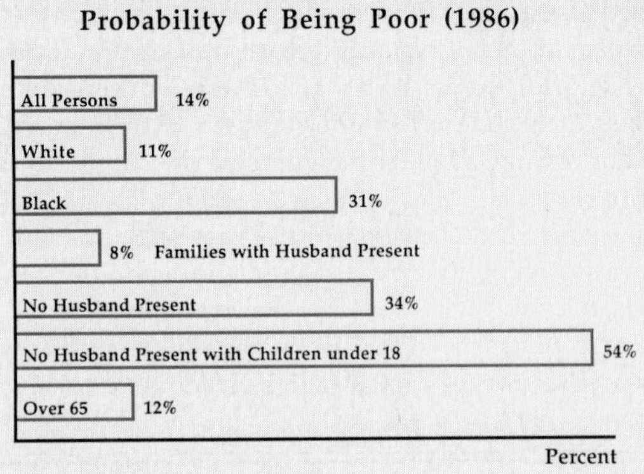

Probability of Being Poor (1986)

All Persons	14%
White	11%
Black	31%
	8% Families with Husband Present
No Husband Present	34%
No Husband Present with Children under 18	54%
Over 65	12%

Percent

Figure 14.1: Probability of Being Poor

income was less than $11,200 in 1986. By these definitions, about 15 percent of U.S. citizens were poor. Regardless of our definition of poverty, certain groups have a much higher probability of falling inside the circle of poverty. Single individual households have twice the probability of being poor as families. Households headed by women are four times more likely to be poor than households with an adult male present. Blacks have double the poverty rate of whites.

rate does not now differ significantly from that of the general population. However, some government programs do transfer income specifically to the poor. In 1978, the poorest fifth of families received about 5 percent of all income. Transfers to them raise this percentage to about 7.5 percent. In that same year, the richest fifth of the families received about 41 percent of income and 39 percent after transfers.

Tax policies in the U.S. do little to change the distribution of income. Federal taxes create a little more equality, which is partially offset by state and local taxes that tend to be regressive. Transfers, which have been growing, do produce more equality, but the effects are not dramatic. Thus, the government makes the distribution of income slightly more equal than it probably would be otherwise. Nevertheless, the effect is small enough that it can only be detected by social scientists working hard to detect the effect. These small government effects on distribution seem to be confined to equality of results. During the post-war period, the United States government has been heavily involved in programs to equalize both opportunity and results of the economic game. As yet, there is scanty evidence to suggest that these policies and programs have had any long-term effect on the distribution of income in the United States—a startling result.

The Big Tradeoffs

In this brief discussion we have raised some of the basic issues surrounding questions of economic fairness. Justice presents the most difficult challenge for any economic system. This has been particularly true of market or capitalistic systems. The rejection of markets in favor of planning by much of the modern world has largely been based on the judgment that markets are intrinsically unfair to large numbers of people. Socialist and communist movements gain public support for revolutionary action and come to power by exploiting the issue of economic injustice. Inequality may be the Achilles' heel of the market system. Yet there is substantial inequality in planned economies as well.

The three major criteria for judging an economy—efficiency, equity and freedom—are very closely intertwined. Equity or economic justice may conflict with efficiency, as in the case of heavy taxes on workers' income or business profits. Governmental attempts to reduce inequality are likely to also reduce liberty or freedom, as in the case of minimum wage laws. In a fundamental way, the United States, like most Western democracies, faces a difficult dilemma. The pursuit of more equality, which seems to reflect people's values about economic justice, also appears to reduce freedom and efficiency. Consider the implementation of antidiscrimination laws. Such laws have been passed to provide equal opportunity for minorities and women in the labor market. The goals of such laws are consistent with most individuals' ideals of equal opportunity. How can we argue for equal opportunity if we allow discrimination in the most important market of the economy—the labor market? Yet, the effect of such laws may well be to reduce economic efficiency and freedom. The freedom to hire whom you wish is clearly abridged by such laws. Efficiency is reduced because resources are no longer allocated solely by the principle of opportunity cost. Compliance costs in terms of government forms, legal fees, and additional bureaucracy, are also substantial. Laws against discrimination illustrate the basic trade-off faced in the drive for equality. To force schools to admit a ration of minorities or women is to reduce the opportunities available to white males. An increase in freedom for one may be a decrease for another. Thus, a society sacrifices some freedom and some efficiency as it pursues economic justice. This harsh reality places our decisions about economic fairness on difficult terms. How much freedom should we give up for a given increase in equity as defined by current standards? Should we sacrifice ten billion dollars in output through inefficiency in order to redistribute five billion dollars to the poor? Again, no easy answers, but necessary questions.

If our ideas of economic justice include not only some limits to the degree of inequality in society, but also an acceptable level of economic mobility, there may also be potential conflict between more equality today and economic mobility over time.

Suppose that the intervention of government in the economy through regulation and taxation reduces economic opportunities to move up the economic ladder at the same time that it reduces the inequality in the society. Would the government in this case promote or retard economic justice? Is it possible that the focus of government on people at the bottom of the economic ladder prevents them from climbing higher on the ladder?

As yet, there are no answers to these questions about the tradeoffs between the different elements of economic justice (more equality now versus more economic mobility) and among the three goals of economic organization (freedom, efficiency and equity). But the questions are important and intriguing. Certainly, equality of opportunity is consistent with economic mobility, while equality of outcome, as measured by income or some other economic variable, may not be. Certainly, government programs that redistribute wealth and income reduce not only economic efficiency but also freedom. The real questions concern the size of these tradeoffs, not their existence. Modern societies have many problems awaiting resolution. Perhaps the most pressing social need is a mechanism to redistribute income in a way that does not reduce freedom, economic efficiency, or long-term economic mobility. Such a mechanism would be general and natural, so that the redistributive process did not rely upon intervention by government in each individual market to further equality. Such a mechanism should also promote long-term movement by the poor up the economic ladder. Until such a mechanism exists, the redistribution of income will remain the "hidden agenda" of politics, and we will continue to face choices between more equality and fewer goods and less freedom.

Bayerische Ban[k]

zahlbar mit Mark

1'000,000,[g]

Eine Milliarde

Vom 1. Januar 1924 ab kann diese Banknote aufgerufen und u[...]
andere bayerische Banknoten oder gegen Reichsbanknoten

München, den 1. Oktober 1923

Bayerische Notenba[nk]

Der Staatskommissär:

Direktion:

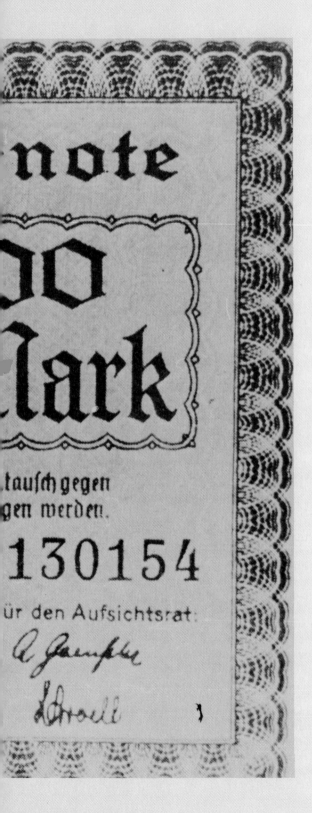

15
The
Government
Temptation

Concepts:

Inflation
Money Supply
Fallacy of Composition

Increases in the money supply are often at the heart of inflation. (Culver Pictures)

Come Back, Evita

The most famous story of all is the one about the wheelbarrow. An elderly woman traveled to the store carrying a wheelbarrow full of money, and then went inside leaving the money and the wheelbarrow outside. When she returned, the money was still there. But the wheelbarrow was gone.

Why would someone have stolen the wheelbarrow but left the money? The time and place was post-World War I Germany, and the cause was an inflation so incredible that a wheelbarrow full of money was worth far less than the wheelbarrow itself. In Germany in 1922, prices rose 5,470 percent. In 1923, prices increased an incredible 1,300,000,000,000 times (1.3 trillion in one year). In other words, if such an inflation were to happen in America, within two years the price of the book in your hands right now would far exceed the preinflation gross national product, and the current huge federal deficit would be less than the price of a simple BIC pen.

This "hyperinflation" turned the German society upside down, and there

Germany 1923: Currency was more valuable as fuel than as money. (Library of Congress)

are many other bizarre tales besides the one about the purloined wheelbarrow. The inflation was so severe that by 1923 contracts and insurance policies written before World War I were literally not worth the paper on which they were written. Employers would pay their employees twice a day, and the money to pay them would be brought in huge trucks. The husbands or wives of the employees would wait for the money and then rush to the store to spend it all. Food and clothing had some permanent value, but cash was good for maybe only a couple of hours. Restaurant patrons would ask to pay for their meals in advance. If they waited until after they ate, it might have cost twice as much. By October 1923, butter cost 1.5 million marks per pound, a loaf of bread was two hundred thousand marks, and a single egg sixty thousand marks.

What caused the inflation? Heavily burdened by World War I debts, Germany resorted to printing money to pay those debts. Eventually, the printing presses were so busy that the German economy was flooded with cash. Presto, with all that money out there, prices went through the roof, and an unstoppable spiral had begun.

Believe it or not, Germany doesn't hold the record for the largest inflations. In October of 1946, prices in Hungary rose 38 octrillion percent! Hungary has the dubious distinction of having printed the monetary note of the largest

Table 15.1 An Example of Argentine Inflation

	1876	1977	1978	1979	1980
Inflation %	334%	347%	160%	169%	139%
Monetary Growth %	192%	256%	124%	170%	145%

denomination—a 100 quintrillion pengo note (that is ten plus nineteen zeros)! That's no joke.

Surely, you say, such inflations are things of the past. No modern economy could ever fall prey to such an inflation. Well, within the last 20 years there have not been any hyperinflations like the German or the Hungarian one, but that isn't to say there haven't been some whopper inflations. Consider Argentina, which some people claim has a Marxist economy, even though the country's financial system bears little resemblance to the Soviet Union's. Rather, these critics say, Argentina's economy runs like it was devised by Groucho, Chico, Harpo, or Zeppo.

In Argentina, prices rise more consistently than your mom's home baked bread. Inflation in Argentina is like taxes in America—absolutely unavoidable. Argentina's annual inflation ranges from about 150 percent to 500 percent, which is enough to make a trip to the market nearly an Indiana Jones-like adventure. If the United States were to experience an inflation like Argentina has experienced in the past six years, a Big Mac would cost more than $1,500, a typical student's rent would be more than $100,000, and a new Honda Civic would be a hefty $6 million. Fortunately, interest rates to get a loan to pay such prices would be quite reasonable, say 250 percent per year.

Inflation like Argentina's obviously causes problems. The government has begun printing 1 million-peso notes, American visitors who plan to stay awhile run out of money sooner than they had expected if they make the mistake of converting all their dollars into pesos as soon as they arrive, and banks must offer interest of 150 percent on savings deposits. There are few depositors, since no one knows when inflation might really take off.

What makes Argentina's inflation most distinctive is its permanence. Unlike hyperinflations, Argentina's inflation simply goes on and on, year after year. The government must promise a huge return on bonds, workers expect hefty pay increases regularly, and, therefore, the inflation feeds itself, like a train that has lost its brakes running downhill. In the process, landowners and debtors get richer and richer, while retirees, creditors, and those on fixed incomes get poorer and poorer.

All efforts to derail the inflation train have been frustrated. Argentines are a proud people who reject belt-tightening measures. When U.S. banks suggest austerity, rebels burn effigies of Uncle Sam in the streets. Heavily unionized and spoiled by very low unemployment rates, Argentines staunchly rebuff any plan to reduce public spending or slow the printing presses. Hence, the government greatly increases the money supply each year, and prices go up right with it (see Table 15.1).

Despite its inflation, don't cry for Argentina. The country is surely one of the most prosperous in South America, is one of the world's largest exporters of beef and grain, has few population or energy pressures, and few workers are unemployed. With all that going for it, consumers may not mind the $1,500 Big Mac.

Three Goals

The first half of the twentieth century was ravaged by three cataclysmic forces--world war, inflation, and the most severe economic depression in more than a century. The fact that all three occurred within one generation from 1914 to 1945 compounded their impact upon people's lives and attitudes. The two world wars are well chronicled, but the effects of the economic forces of depression and inflation, inextricably tied to the world wars, are still with us today.

The hyperinflation of Germany and the chronic inflation of Argentina described above should be convincing evidence that inflation poses a serious threat to any economy. Inflation inverts economic values. Borrowing becomes a virtue while saving is ill-advised. Wealth fixed in terms of the economy's currency, such as life insurance policies, pensions, or money, quickly loses its value, while speculative ventures in real estate, commodities, or stocks, often pay off extravagantly. Money, instead of being useful to make transactions, is shunned because of its continuously declining value. In this inverted economic world, other values like hard work, virtues like honesty and thrift, and respect of others' property and rights are also questioned. What causes this virulent economic disease? Surely the government can protect people from inflation and its effects. Unfortunately, asking the government to protect us from inflation is akin to asking the fox to guard the chickens—the government is responsible for most inflation. The real mystery surrounding inflation is not economic but political. Why do modern democracies have such a strong tendency toward inflation?

Recessions had been a part of the U.S. economy from the beginning, but the 1930s were to drive home the costs of the business cycle with a cruel vengeance. Unemployment in the United States during the Great Depression reached at least 25 percent of the labor force and much of our capital stock was underutilized. The suicide rate increased to over seventeen persons per ten thousand in 1932, the highest rate in the United States in the twentieth century. Countless lives were disrupted and fundamentally changed by the events in the economy of the 1930s. The Republican party was reduced from the majority party to a very small minority in the 1932 presidential election. Over a million voters voted for the radical parties of the left in that same election. Franklin Delano Roosevelt was swept to power with 57 percent of the popular vote and began making fundamental changes in the American society. An object of love and hate in American society, Roosevelt was seen by some as the destroyer of the past and America's traditional values and institutions, while others regarded him as a savior of American democracy and capitalism.

There were clear social, political, and economic lessons from the Great Depression of the 1930s and the transparent connection between Germany's hyperinflation of the 1920s and the rise of Hitler to power. After the Great Depression, the government could no longer play a passive role in the economy. After Roosevelt's vigorous, even though less-than-successful, attack on the depression of the 1930s, no American president could sit quietly in the White House and allow a recession to run its course. Just as the United Nations was created after World War II with the hope of eliminating world conflict and war, national governments turned to the economic problems of inflation and recession with intensity. In the United States, Congress passed the Employment Act of 1946, formally giving the national government three important economic charges:

1. to insure full employment of resources.
2. to maintain stable prices (in other words, to eliminate inflation).
3. to generate a high rate of economic growth.

These three macroeconomic goals embody the main national or aggregate economic objectives. Together they form the most important political aspects of economic policy. The fortunes of congressmen and presidents rise and fall with the economic indicators related to these three goals. Since the 1930s, the Gallup polls have asked citizens what they consider to be the most important social or political problem of a given year. With the exception of the main war years of World War II, the answer has consistently been the high cost of living, meaning inflation, or the problem of economic recession.

These two problems, inflation and recession, have been more important politically than economic growth, but there is mounting concern about that problem as well. Americans are becoming uncomfortable with the economic competition from Asia and Western Europe. One hears comments more and more frequently about the possibility of economic decline in the United States and a consideration of which government policies will promote economic growth most effectively. The next presidential election, as the last, will no doubt be significantly influenced by the current administration's record on these important economic issues.

It is, therefore, worthwhile to consider each of these economic problems in turn: What are the causes of inflation, unemployment, and economic growth? What can the government do to solve the problems associated with each? And, why does the government have so much difficulty in each of these particular areas? This chapter examines the issues related to inflation, and the succeeding chapters look at recession and economic growth.

Definition

Inflation is defined as generally rising prices. Inflation is *not* high prices. Once prices stop rising, inflation stops. To have inflation, the average of prices must be rising, since at any given time in the economy, some prices are rising while others are falling. So it is the average that is important in the definition of inflation.

Some prices, such as the prices of milk, gasoline, housing, or clothing, are important in the economy because households spend large portions of their income on such goods. Other prices, such as the price of impressionist paintings or the price of dancing lessons, matter very little. Consequently, the simple average of prices is not as good a measure of inflation as an average of prices where each price is weighted by its importance in typical consumption. Economists and statisticians construct price indexes that are weighted averages of prices in the economy. The most commonly reported price index is the Consumer Price Index (CPI). One year (currently 1967) is arbitrarily given a value of 100 and all other years are measured in terms of the prices of that year. For example, the CPI was nearly 328 in 1986, meaning that prices in that month were

U.S. EXPERIENCE WITH INFLATION SINCE 1750

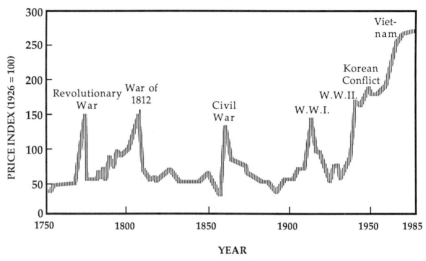

Figure 15.1: U.S. Experience with Inflation

about 328 percent of prices in 1967. Some prices, like energy, had risen a great deal since 1967 while other prices, like clothing, had not risen as much. Other important price indices that reflect inflation are the producer price index and the implicit price index used to adjust GNP. If inflation is a serious problem in the economy, it will be reflected by increases in all of these indices.

Historical Patterns of Inflation

Current generations have lived with the problem of inflation throughout most of their lifetimes. There are ebbs and flows, but there has been a constant, often accelerating, increase in prices since World War II. Recent experience gives an impression that prices stay the same or rise, but never fall. A longer historical perspective shows us that this is not the case.

In Figure 15.1 the level of prices in the United States is charted from 1750 to the present. As can be seen in this figure, inflation is not inevitable. There have been long periods in the history of the United States when the average level of prices fell over time (deflation). Of particular note is the period after the Civil War from 1865 to 1896. In this period, prices fell by approximately 2 percent per year. And while a situation of falling prices may sound attractive to those of us from an era of inflation, individuals and businesses of that earlier period found deflation to be as irritating as we find inflation today.

Figure 15.1 also clearly demonstrates that much of the inflation of the past has been associated with war. During the Revolutionary War prices rose by 262 percent, during the Civil War and World War II by identical amounts of 230 percent, and during World War I by 213 percent. Probably the most striking and serious feature of this chart is the change in the pattern after World War II. After every war except World War II there was a considerable period of deflation in which prices were brought back down to earlier levels. However, after World War II prices have continued to rise for the past forty years. For the first time in American history we are faced with prolonged, peacetime inflation.

Possible Causes of Inflation

Market Forces

Any temporary increase in market demand for *all* goods and services in the economy could cause inflation. In reality, increases in demand are not a very good explanation for inflation since increases in demand for one good or service are normally offset by reductions in demand for other goods and services in the economy. If people decide they want to wear green shirts instead of blue ones, the price of green shirts will rise and that of blue shirts will fall. Thus, the average of prices should not change very much and there should be little inflation.

A temporary decrease in supply of a significant number of commodities in the economy could cause inflation if demand remains unchanged. For example, the Arab oil embargo in 1973–1974 caused serious dislocation in various economies. The fall in oil supplies and the decline of output in related industries caused some inflation

since demand did not fall as much as supply. However, supply changes are not the major cause of inflation since supply reductions in one area of the economy, say agriculture due to adverse weather, are not usually related to changes in another part of the economy, say steel. Indeed, one of the famous slogans of economics is that "supply creates its own demand." This means that increases in supply usually increase incomes so that general demand rises as well. Conversely, declines in supply will normally reduce incomes and, therefore, general demand in the economy.

Unions or Corporations

Both workers and management are often blamed for inflation. Journalists and politicians often refer to the wage-price spiral as a cause of inflation. Unions negotiate higher wages, causing management to raise prices, causing unions to negotiate higher wages. Politicians and journalists sympathetic to organized labor reverse the causation. This kind of argument may be responsible for a small part of the inflation in an economy, but is probably not a valid explanation for the sustained inflation that many countries have had for the past two decades. Each union tends to be negotiating with particular companies so that the forces of competition keep the process in check. If Ford caves in to the United Auto Workers, General Motors has incentives to drive a harder bargain. Even if both succumb to UAW pressure, foreign competition, a fact of life in most industries today, will discipline the process over time. Workers and management always want higher wages and prices, so it is difficult to explain variations in inflation by the wage-price spiral.

Since the wage-price pressures are more or less constant within an economy, and other economic forces such as competition and the demand for money by businesses and households control these pressures, some factor other than a wage-price spiral must account for most inflation. Most economists believe the prime cause of inflation is the growth of the money supply in the economy.

Growth of Money Supply

Most economists believe that sustained inflation is caused by consistent increases in the supply of money by the government or monetary authority. In order to see why the relationship between money and inflation is so strong, consider the colonial economy as Washington and members of the Continental Congress attempt to pay for their relatively expensive argument with the British. The economy consists of a few hundred thousand families living on the eastern seaboard. While the new nation was able to borrow some from the French, neither its credit nor its taxes were able to approach the total expenditure of the Revolutionary War. Thus the individual states and the Continental Congress began printing "continental" dollars to pay for the supplies and wages of their soldiers.

Let us assume that before the Revolutionary War, each household in the economy maintained a certain quantity of money (say ten dollars on average). They kept this money on hand rather than in property or other assets in order to make transactions, buy goods and services, or meet other financial obligations. As explained in chapter ten, they find it convenient to trade with one another and use money in this process of exchange.

At this point, let us assume a particularly large payment is made by the Continental Congress for back wages and supplies. Their new printing press allows them to catch up, and effectively double the amount of Continental dollars that each household has. If each family were holding ten dollars before, they would now have twenty dollars in money since, on average, the amount of money would double for each household in the economy.

What will happen as the supply of money in this not-entirely-fanciful economy is doubled? Clearly, when people first notice the increase in money, they will congratulate themselves on their good fortune. They are now "richer"—they have twice as much money as they had in the past and they all feel wealthier. After some reflection, each household will probably decide that it does not wish to hold all of this new money. Consuming more goods is probably preferred to holding money; so each household decides it wants to spend this good fortune that has befallen them. For example, if each household now has twenty dollars in money, it might decide that only ten dollars in money is needed, and it will spend the extra ten dollars that the Continental Congress has sent it.

A common fallacy of thinking is the fallacy of composition which consists of assuming what is true for the individual is also true for the whole. In economics, individuals can often take actions not available to the whole economy and vice versa. Such is the case with money. Each individual can exchange money for goods or services, but the whole economy cannot transform money into anything else. Each household has a perception that it can exchange money for the goods and services produced in the economy. Each household

Confederate currency: the worst case of American inflation yet.

will attempt to make that exchange. However, let us assume that all are already employed and no one is willing to work more hours per day or build more factories. Thus, while there is new money there are no more goods than before, and as a group these households are incapable of exchanging the additional money for more goods and services. In other words, what is true for the individual (he can have more goods by reducing his balance of money) is definitely not true for the group (the aggregate economy is not producing more, therefore, more cannot be purchased).

We now have each household in the economy attempting to convert money into goods and services. Since this is not possible, something must yield to the pressure. What will that something be? The answer is, of course, prices. Prices of existing goods and services rise until households decide they want to hold the amount of money that has been injected into the economy. If prices rise sufficiently, households will decide they really need the

twenty dollars of money on average in order to make the normal transactions they wish to make. The twenty dollars will purchase just about the same amount that the ten dollars would purchase before the rise in prices.

This story describes the basic phenomenon leading to inflation. As the money supply is increased, households and businesses, finding themselves holding more money, decide to spend a portion of that increased money supply. Production does not rise or is already at capacity; thus, in the aggregate, households cannot exchange money for goods. Prices rise until households and businesses decide they are holding the proper amount of money for their circumstances. Most sustained inflation, that is, inflation of more than a few months duration, is caused by increases in the supply of money in the economy.

There are two exceptions to this tight link between monetary growth and inflation. In rare situations, households and businesses may want to hold more money

Inflation and the Confederacy

From the firing on Fort Sumter to the surrender at Appomattox, Southerners displayed their bravery on the battlefield and their economic ignorance in the financial markets. At the time of Lincoln's second inauguration, prices in the South were eighty times their level at the time Lincoln first assumed office. About 60 percent of the revenues of the Confederacy came from printing notes or money. At first, Southerners held the new currency because they thought it was the patriotic thing to do. As prices rose, they thought prices were simply too high and they held their new currency. But the light finally began to penetrate. This money was losing its value and it would continue to lose value. Confederate notes were shunned like typhoid or malaria. Sharp businessmen did not lend unless repayment was in something that held its value, like gold or some commodity. Debtors tried to pay debts with Confederate notes, but many creditors refused to take them. Workers refused to accept money for wages and began to insist on payment in food or other commodities.

The government had few alternatives to the printing press. Few wealthy individuals or banks wanted to lend to rebellious states that looked like they would lose. There was little to tax in the South. Consequently, the government turned increasingly to the printing press. Each note or piece of paper money was individually signed. By July of 1862, seventy-two employees were signing notes, but the note-signing bureau had to be increased to 262 employees a year later. There was such a shortage of printers, engravers, and other necessary employees that the secretary of the treasury recommended that counterfeiters be allowed to turn in counterfeit money for Confederate bonds. Then the counterfeit money could be stamped as valid money and reissued to pay government bills. In 1864, Union armies threatened Richmond, so the printing press had to be dismantled and moved south. Some of the note signers refused to move and other employees were lost. These difficulties meant that the government could not print money at the same rate as earlier, which caused some break in the inflationary spiral that was afflicting the South.

Amazingly, most Southerners did not understand the cause of the inflation. Many blamed speculators, the ready villain during inflations. Others blamed the North, the blockade runners, drought, or government procurement agents. Somehow, they failed to understand that the government was printing more and more money to be used to buy fewer and fewer goods as the war progressed. The government did not, of course, tell the people the true cause of the inflation, although C. G. Memminger, secretary of the Confederate treasury, understood the process perfectly. In order to stop the inflation, the government instituted price controls and appointed a price commissioner but failed to give him any power. Newspapers would advertise goods listing the official price and the actual price of the product.

The inflation did not hit everyone the same. Laborers lost heavily since wages increased much more slowly than inflation. Cotton prices rose very slowly because the Union blockade confined cotton sales to the South. The price of goods that had been imported from the North or Europe before the war skyrocketed. Blockade runners did not carry food and sturdy clothing, but rather, Yankee trinkets and manufactures.

Like most hyperinflations, things got worse near the end. In the last four months of the Confederacy, prices doubled. Defeat brought the inflation mercifully to a close, ending the worst case of inflation in American history . . . yet.

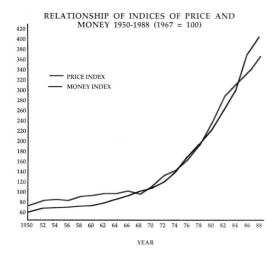

Figure 15.2: Relationship of Indices of Price and Money

for transactions or other purposes than they currently possess. In that case, the government can increase the money supply without causing inflation, because the new money will not be spent. The other exception is based on unemployed resources. If labor or capital is idle in the economy, the increase in the money supply may stimulate increased output of goods and services instead of increased prices. Thus, the link between the money supply and inflation is not exact, though it is strong.

The Evidence for the Different Explanations of Inflation

As you might guess, government planners, monetary authorities, and politicians are reluctant to accept the blame for inflation. Instead, they almost always find some other excuse, including the rise in oil prices, bad weather and food shortages, the demands of unions for wage increases, the setting of prices by greedy corporations, avaricious consumers, or the deficit in the federal budget. In order to see why none of these factors can be the basic cause of a sustained inflation, it is useful to recall the definition of inflation. We define inflation as rising general prices. Whatever phenomena generate inflation, they must have a continuous, steady impact on prices, causing them to rise.

Price of Energy. An increase in the oil price that does not continue cannot be a suitable explanation for inflation. It may lead to a once-and-for-all increase in prices throughout large segments of the economy, but this is not the same as a continual rise in general price level. Further evidence that inflation cannot be caused by the rise in oil prices can be seen by comparing the rate of inflation in the United States with that in Switzerland. The argument generally takes the following form: During the 1970s, oil prices increased seven times (from $5 per barrel to $35 per barrel), and since the United States must rely on expensive imported oil for 20 percent of its total consumption, that combination accounts for the 80 percent increase in general prices in this country since 1971. If oil is the culprit, how do we account for Switzerland, which imports all of its oil and yet had an average annual inflation rate of less than 5 percent while the U.S. had a rate of over 8 percent. The reason that Switzerland enjoyed the lower rate of inflation is that the Swiss restrained the rate of growth of their money supply to less than 4 percent. While the U.S. allowed their money supply to grow by about 7 percent. Key price increases may cause some temporary inflation, but they are not the primary cause of most inflation.

Corporations and Unions. The demands of unions and price tactics of corporations also fail as a basic cause of inflation. Unions always want wage increases just as corporations always want price increases. It is difficult to understand how these institutions could be the initial cause of inflation when their demands are so constant, and yet inflation moves up and down with the changes in the supply of money. We experienced inflation in this country before there were corporations or unions. We have had inflation when corporations and unions were powerful and when they were weak. And we have had no inflation or even deflation when they were powerful and when they were weak. Labor unions cover less than 25 percent of nonagricultural employment. The prices of unionized sectors of the economy do not generally behave much differently than prices elsewhere. The evidence is not strong for the wage-price spiral as a cause of inflation.

Federal Deficits. For a time, it was thought that federal deficits and the national debt were a potential explanation for inflation. This kind of argument disappeared in the 1980s as federal budget deficits soared to unheard of levels with substantial increases in the national debt and declining inflation. Deficits may put pressure on the Federal Reserve to expand the money supply. However, the Fed, as the Federal Reserve is called, often resists this pressure or responds to other factors in the economy.

Other Causes. Similarly, bad weather and spendthrift consumers are common phenomena, but do not correlate well with inflation or deflation. This is not to argue in favor of bad weather, OPEC, deficits, or unreasonable demands of unions, corporations, or consumers; but rather that whatever may be their harm, they do not seem to be the primary causes of inflation.

Growth of the Money Supply. Figure 15.2 illustrates the high correlation between inflation and the growth of the money supply in the United States over the past few decades while Figure 15.3 illustrates the link between monetary growth and inflation for various countries. The link is not completely firm since inflation rates may be slightly higher or lower than the rate of money supply growth. The evidence of a link between the money supply and inflation over long periods of time is, however, very strong. But who, if anyone, controls the money supply?

Government Control of the Money Supply

In most economies, it is the government that controls the quantity of money generated in the society. This government control over the money supply is usually exerted through a central bank of some kind.

Federal Reserve System

In the U.S. economy, the quantity of money is basically controlled by the Federal Reserve System. The Federal Reserve System was created in 1913 with the aim of giving the United States a central bank which would create an elastic currency. The Federal Reserve was to expand the money supply when economic conditions threatened the stability of banks and to reduce

RELATIONSHIP BETWEEN MONEY GROWTH AND INFLATION

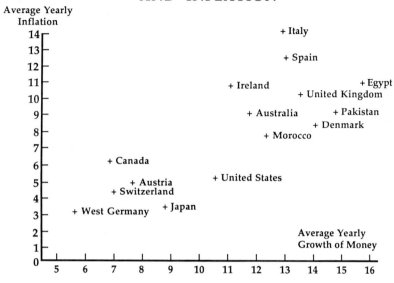

There appears to be a positive relationship between the growth of money supply and inflation based on fifteen year (1970 - 1985) averages for fifteen countries.

Figure 15.3: Relationship Between Money Growth and Inflation

the money supply when there was too much speculation or inflation in the economy. The Federal Reserve System has the power to issue money, lend to banks, clear checks for banks, and generally supervise banking activities. Figure 15.4 describes the basic organization and functions of the Federal Reserve System.

This division of power into twelve districts, reminiscent of a confederacy of central banks, created some power struggles in the 1920s, especially between New York and Washington. Consequently, the general transfer of power to Washington during the New Deal of the 1930s included the shift of most of the power of the Federal Reserve to the Board of Governors in

Washington who have some independence from congressional and presidential political pressure. In this regard, they function much like the independent judiciary, the Board of Governors being similar to the Supreme Court.

Open Market Operations. The most important work of the Federal Reserve System is carried out in New York City where Federal Reserve employees buy and sell government bonds in an effort to control the supply of money in the economy. When the Fed *buys* government bonds from banks, the banks have more money (fewer bonds) to lend to the public. Eventually, the money supply is increased and interest

Organization of the Federal Reserve System

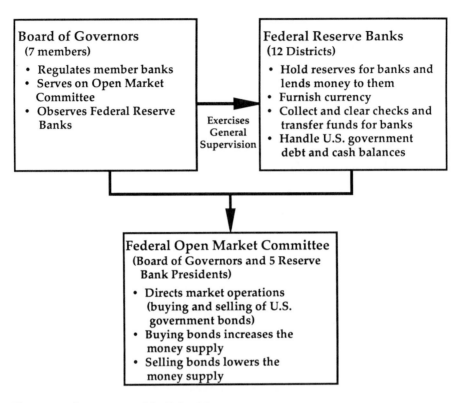

Board of Governors
(7 members)

- Regulates member banks
- Serves on Open Market Committee
- Observes Federal Reserve Banks

Exercises General Supervision

Federal Reserve Banks
(12 Districts)

- Hold reserves for banks and lends money to them
- Furnish currency
- Collect and clear checks and transfer funds for banks
- Handle U.S. government debt and cash balances

Federal Open Market Committee
(Board of Governors and 5 Reserve Bank Presidents)

- Directs market operations (buying and selling of U.S. government bonds)
- Buying bonds increases the money supply
- Selling bonds lowers the money supply

Figure 15.4: Organization of the Federal Reserve System

rates have a tendency to fall temporarily. When the Fed *sells* bonds in the New York bond market, it draws money out of the economy. Banks, then, have less money to lend, and the money supply decreases. In this case, interest rates may temporarily rise. The buying and selling of bonds to control the money supply is called open market operations.

The Fed can also control the supply of money in the economy through changes in the interest rate it charges the banks that borrow from it, and changes in the reserves required for banks to hold. The details of the management of the money system by the Federal Reserve are quite complex and need not concern us here. The central point is that the Federal Reserve has the capacity to control the supply of money in the economy over extended periods of time. It may not be able to control week-to-week fluctuations, but it certainly has the power to meet quarterly or yearly targets for money-supply growth. Thus, the power to determine the long-term pattern of inflation is largely in the hands of members of the Board of Governors of the Federal Reserve System. Responsibility for inflation or the lack of inflation should largely be laid at the feet of the Board of Governors.

The Politics of Inflation

If there is agreement that inflation is largely caused by the government increasing the money supply, why does the Fed or the government continue to allow, let alone generate, inflation through the creation of additional money? The answer is found in examining the various effects of inflation on the economy. Not everyone loses from inflation. Consequently, there are pressure groups with political power who gain from inflation. In order to understand the political forces leading to the creation of money and the resulting inflation, it is necessary to find out who benefits from and who loses through inflation.

Winners and Losers with Inflation

Moneyholders. One large group always loses from inflation. Anyone holding money loses part of its value from inflation. If you hold one dollar of your wealth as a dollar bill, that dollar loses value at the rate of inflation. If the inflation rate is 10 percent per year, then 10 percent of the value of the dollar is gone after one year. If the rate is 50 percent, then half of the dollar value is lost in one year. A 10 percent inflation costs each person in the U.S. economy an average of nearly $160 per year. The only way for individuals holding money to escape this loss from inflation is to stop using money. If a serious inflation is expected, households and businesses try to reduce their use of money for exchange. Since inflation cannot always be anticipated, unanticipated inflation creates additional losers, but it also creates a group of beneficiaries from the unexpected rise in prices.

Creditors. The primary victims of an unanticipated inflation, for which adjustments have not been made, are creditors—those individuals or firms that have lent money to other people. Suppose, for example, that an economy has not experienced recent inflation and you have lent someone one thousand dollars at an interest rate of 4 percent. Now, for whatever reason, the government increases the money supply, leading to an inflation of 10 percent in the economy. Given this new circumstance, the interest rate of 4 percent does not cover the decline in the purchasing power or value of money that will be paid back. Since the individual who has borrowed from you will be able to pay back dollars that have depreciated in value, you will receive only $940 ($900 in principal and $40 in interest) in real purchasing power for the one thousand dollars you loaned. This means that the *real* interest that you will receive on your loan will be a negative 6 percent (4 percent minus 10 percent inflation). An unanticipated inflation hurts creditors such as banks, thrift institutions, savers, and insurance companies.

Debtors. Obviously, the unanticipated inflation which makes victims out of those individuals or businesses who lend money, benefits those who borrow money. Debtors are able to borrow money at what are essentially negative rates of interest. A hyperinflation like Germany experienced after World War I will wipe out the debts of borrowers and eliminate many of the assets of creditors. An unanticipated inflation creates a significant amount of wealth for debtors who borrow funds to invest in assets that increase in value with the inflation, and then pay back their debts with depreciated dollars.

Politics at the Fed

Just before Christmas in 1985, while others were worrying about that last-minute gift or discussing the latest and most unlikely star of the National Football League, a three-hundred-plus-pound running back and defensive tackle named William (the Refrigerator) Perry, nine rather nondescript men and one woman surrounded a table in Washington, D.C., to polish the minutes of their two-day meeting. Their meeting would not make the evening news. Indeed, anonymity seemed to suit their purposes. The minutes, not published for four months, would be so contorted by bureaucratic and technical language that no one would know what they had decided after the minutes were published. Yet, the actions of these ten people would affect every person in the U.S. and a great many people elsewhere. Who were they? And what was going on? The meeting, held December 15 and 16, was the regular meeting of the Open Market Committee of the Federal Reserve. No important element of the government, including the CIA, is as misunderstood by the general public as the Federal Reserve System. To grasp the importance of the meeting, we must understand the basic framework of the Federal Reserve System.

The Federal Reserve, originally organized in 1913, reflects Americans' distrust of Wall Street by carving the country up into twelve districts with a bank operating somewhat independently in each district. The banks are in Boston, New York, Philadelphia, Cleveland, Richmond, Atlanta, Chicago, St. Louis, Minneapolis, Kansas City, Dallas, and San Francisco. In reality, these banks are relegated to housekeeping details of the monetary system, such as burning old money. But, once every month or two, some of the presidents of these regional banks get an opportunity to exercise real power.

Most of the power of the Federal Reserve is in (where else) Washington, D.C., in the hands of the Board of Governors of the Federal Reserve. The seven members of the Board are appointed by the President and confirmed by the Senate for fourteen-year terms. One of the seven is appointed to a four-year term as Chairman of the Board of Governors. It has become fashionable for reporters to refer to the Chairman of the Fed (as it is typically called) as the second most powerful man (it has yet to be a woman) in government, even though not one reporter in five hundred could tell you what the Fed actually does. Chairman Paul Volcker, appointed by President Carter and reappointed by President Reagan until 1987, dominated the Fed for a number of years,

You should note that fully *anticipated* inflation has no effect on borrowers and lenders. The financial market will build the anticipation of inflation into the interest rate, so that neither lenders nor borrowers are greatly affected by the inflation that occurs. One of the basic reasons that current interest rates are high is the expectations we hold about future inflation. In the example above, an anticipated inflation of 10 percent would likely lead to an interest rate of 14 percent, thus returning a real rate of interest of 4 percent to the lender.

accumulating considerable prestige in the process. Recently, four Reagan appointees to the Board—Preston Martin, a California banker; Martha Seger, an economist from Michigan; Manuel Johnson, a supply-side economist; and Wayne Angell, an economics professor from Kansas—have begun to challenge Volcker's power. It appeared that they might be winning because Volcker had lost a couple of minor votes. Then, Preston Martin, whom many considered as Volcker's replacement as Chairman, suddenly resigned, reportedly because the White House refused to assure him that he would be the next Chairman of the Fed.

This Board of Governors shares one very powerful decision with the presidents of the regional banks in what is called the Federal Open Market Committee. This Committee is composed of the seven Governors, the President of the Federal Reserve Bank of New York, and four of the other eleven presidents of district banks on a rotating basis. This Committee, operating with relatively little scrutiny, basically controls the money supply of the United States. It does this by buying and selling bonds, mainly of the U.S. government. When the Committee wants to increase the money supply, it buys bonds in the New York bond market, which increases the reserves of banks throughout the country. These reserves are lent to businesses and consumers, causing the money supply to increase. To reduce the money supply, the Open Market Committee sells bonds to take money out of the economy. The Fed takes these actions in secret and later publishes the minutes of its meetings. In order to prevent market traders from knowing what the Fed is doing, the Fed buys and sells massive quantities of bonds every month. (In December, 1985, it made purchases and sales of nearly a hundred billion dollars.) Each meeting of this Committee has the potential for inflation or recession, although the Committee can easily change its decisions.

What did the Committee decide in its pre-Christmas 1986 meeting? Not much really. It instructed its operators in the bond market to "decrease somewhat the existing degree of pressure on reserve positions" (April 1986, *Federal Reserve Bulletin*, p. 251). Translated into ordinary language, this means it intended to increase the money supply a little faster than earlier. One member of the Committee dissented.

So it goes in Washington, D.C. Young congressmen in $500 suits and $25 haircuts, but without the power to influence any economic trends, compete with one another for footage on the evening news while quiet bankers and economists sit around a small conference room making absolutely vital economic decisions in as much secrecy as they can. One wonders if Thomas Jefferson would have approved.

Inflation-Related Industries. Some industries benefit particularly from unanticipated inflation. The demand for automobiles and especially for real estate is particularly sensitive to the availability and cost of credit. An unanticipated inflation reduces the cost of borrowing so that these industries do particularly well when inflation is high but interest rates are still low because of incorrect expectations about inflation. Conversely, a low rate of inflation and high interest rates, such as the period from 1981 to 1984, have a devastating effect on such industries.

The Government and Inflation

Is there any party who benefits from inflation whether it is anticipated or unanticipated? The answer is yes—the government. The government gains from inflation in a variety of ways. In order to understand the government's relationship to inflation, a short review of government finance is helpful.

Government Finance. The government may finance its expenditures in three ways. It may *tax* households and businesses. In 1987, the federal government collected about $854 billion dollars in taxes. The personal income tax (nearly $400 billion) and various social security taxes ($303 billion) are the primary sources of tax revenues. Taxes are painful for politicians because they are painful for voters. Politicians dislike voting for tax increases and rush to vote for tax reductions. Consequently, they often choose to spend more than they are willing to raise with taxes, creating a budget deficit. For example, the federal government spent just over $1 trillion in 1987, but only raised $854 billion in taxes—creating a deficit of about $150 billion.

If the government runs a deficit in its budget, politicians must choose between two alternative methods of financing that deficit. The government may *borrow* funds from households and businesses or it may *create money*. Each of the alternative methods of covering a deficit carries a serious liability.

Governmental borrowing from the public causes an increase in interest rates, which, in turn, creates distress in the housing and auto markets and other interest-sensitive industries. Further, governmental borrowing may become so extensive that lenders become concerned about the ability and the will of the government to repay its debts. Perhaps the government will simply repudiate its debts. Finally, governmental borrowing increases future expenditures and, most likely, future taxes because the government will have to pay interest on the debt as well. Interest payments by the federal government were over $137 billion dollars for 1987.

On the other hand, creating money causes inflation. But when governments are under severe financial pressure, inflation seems like a small price to pay in order to avoid tax increases, high interest payments, and economic distress for key industries. In fact, the inflation often creates additional benefits for the government.

Inflation and Taxes. Until the tax legislation passed in 1981, government could raise taxes through the process of inflation. Since the personal income tax system of the United States is progressive, the government is able to raise taxes by inflation moving every individual up into higher percentage tax brackets. Inflation increases incomes, though not purchasing power. An increase in income moves a household into a higher tax bracket so that the household pays a higher proportion of its income to the government in spite of the fact that the purchasing power of that income is constant or may even have fallen. There are other aspects of the tax code, such as the treatment of capital gains and personal exemptions, that provide opportunities for government to profit from inflation. The government is able to increase its share of total income even though real purchasing power for the entire economy is no higher. With many tax systems, government can actually raise taxes through inflation without politicians facing a vote to raise taxes. Indeed, inflation makes it possible for politicians to vote for tax reductions every few years while relying on inflation to raise taxes over time.

Government and Debt. At the end of the 1986 budget year, the U.S. Treasury had a debt of $2.125 trillion, enough to keep you awake at night if you had to pay the interest. Actually, the Treasury owes $575 billion of this debt to other government agencies, such as the Federal Reserve, which owns a mere $191 billion of the debt. The government, like any other debtor, gains from an unanticipated inflation. Inflation reduces the burden of this debt.

Politics and Inflation

We can see that there are "factions," or special-interest groups, supporting inflation. Debtors, the government, and particular industries that benefit from subsidies to debtors, such as the housing industry and, to a lesser degree, the automobile industry, have a stake in seeing that inflation continues. Therefore, these groups put pressure on government to expand the money supply so that inflation will take place. This pressure is never directly stated as a plea for inflation; rather, it is stated indirectly as a plea for the Fed to provide a stimulus to the economy through low interest rates or readily available credit. The government, since it has an interest in promoting inflation, is all too ready to respond to these particular constituencies. From time to time, individuals injured by inflation will gain the upper hand politically and force the government to slow down the rate of money growth. It remains

to be seen if they will be successful in permanently reducing the rate of inflation in the United States.

If inflation is anticipated or expected by everyone in an economy, the effects on the economy are quite small, with no one particularly benefiting or losing from the inflation. In fact, the only real winner from an inflation that everyone knows is coming is the government. The government gains since it is able to create the money, spend it, and compel others to accept the money as payment for goods and services. Anyone who is caught holding money will lose from the inflation.

Possible Reforms

Since government is the principal culprit in the problem of inflation, discussing government solutions to the problem of inflation is similar to a discussion of how burglars can reduce the rate of neighborhood crime. Some suggestions have been made that might help solve the long-term problem of inflation in the economy. Most suggestions take away government's incentives to increase the money supply.

Indexation

One way to remove such incentives is through a process called *indexation*. Indexation makes *real* government expenditures and receipts independent of the rate of inflation. If this is done, the government receives little gain from inflation. Most receipts and expenditures could be indexed. Currently, personal income tax brackets and some transfer payments such as social security are indexed against inflation.

Government debt could also be indexed to remove additional temptations to inflate. The government could be required to pay a set amount of interest on government bonds, plus the rate of inflation. For example, an individual who lends $1000 to the government at 4 percent interest would receive $40 in interest each year plus whatever increase occurred in the rate in prices. If inflation were 10 percent, the individual would receive 14 percent, or $140. If the inflation were 5 percent, the individual would receive only $90.

Money Growth Rule

Other proposals would impose a constitutional rule that the government could only increase the money supply by a given percent, such as 3 or 4 percent per year. Historically, we have been able to add production of goods and services at about that rate per year (3 to 4 percent). If the increase in money is equal to the increase in goods, there is no inflationary pressure. Inflation results from increases in the money supply that exceed our ability to produce goods and services. As an example, if the money supply increases 10 percent, while we only add 4 percent more in goods, an inflationary pressure of 6 percent is created. A constitutional rule would take away much government flexibility relative to the supply of money in the economy. Some of those concerned about inflation have proposed that we return to a gold standard, where the gold supply would determine the quantity of money in the economy, rather than the amount of currency in checking accounts, as determined by the Federal Reserve.

The purpose of these proposals is to restore some discipline to the monetary authority. Inflation is a clear case of *government* failure, not market failure, and results from special-interest groups' influence and government's having the power to print money. History suggests that the monetary authority will succumb to political pressures as long as those pressures are at all intense. If citizens want services or expenditures from government but are unwilling to be taxed for those expenditures, the monetary authority will bow to the pressure and create money to finance government activity. In previous times, the pressures were most intense during war. Therefore, the monetary authority only generated inflation of significance during wartime. In the post-World War II period, the political pressures in most developed democracies have involved not only national defense, but also full employment, large quantities of social services, and the redistribution of income from some groups to others. These political pressures have evidently caused the monetary authority to give in to pressures from certain factions and to increase the rate of money growth. It seems doubtful that any solution that fails to recognize the self-interest of government and the effectiveness of political pressures is likely to succeed. Inflation is likely to remain an attractive temptation to which governments succumb with frequency.

16

The Market Curse

Concepts:

Recession
Fiscal Policy
Monetary Policy

Economic downturns can make even the wealthy
become the homeless. (Culver Pictures)

You Can't Win for Losing

The nature of the market economy is harsh. Like so many sports heroes, when a market economy is good, it is very, very good, and when it is bad, it is very, very bad.

In 1981 and 1982, the American economy was very, very bad. President Reagan cut government expenditures, and the Federal Reserve Board squeezed the money supply. As a consequence, interest rates climbed to an almost incredible 20 percent, new investment came to a standstill, and America's employers were forced to lay off workers.

A variety of indicators demonstrates just how bad the economy was. New housing constructions declined throughout 1982, and productivity increases were marginal, if not nonexistent. The Gross National Product, that all-important statistic of general economic health, actually declined, in inflation-adjusted dollars, by $20 billion between 1981 and 1983. It was the first such decline since the 1930s.

But it was the unemployment rate that most clearly emphasized the economy's woes. When President Reagan took office in January of 1981, the unemployment rate was 7.5 percent. But by December 1982, the rate had climbed to 10.6 percent, the highest since 1940. Such an increase in unemployment meant that more than three million Americans had lost their jobs, most of them in the high-paying automobile, steel, mining, and general manufacturing industries. In shocking comparison, the unemployment rate had been as low as 3.4 percent twelve years earlier, and had been 5.8 percent just three years earlier.

The unemployment rates for minorities were particularly stunning. The rate for black workers reached 18.6 percent, and for black teenagers, an astronomical 46.1 percent; for single women with children, 13.3 percent. Since government expenditures on income support programs had been cut, at least nominally, unemployment translated into economic suffering for millions.

When a market economy takes a turn downward, it chooses its victims arbitrarily and without concern for who deserves to suffer and who doesn't. Consider Reginald Andrews, a twenty-nine-year-old father of eight from Manhattan. In December 1982, Andrews was among the 10.6 percent who didn't have a job. His phone was disconnected, he didn't have a car, and food was scarce. That Christmas there would be no presents for the children. He had, by his own estimates, filled out more than one thousand job applications in the past year.

On December 20, 1982, Andrews was waiting for a subway in downtown Manhattan after a job interview. As he waited for the right train, a blind man, seventy-five-year-old David Schair of the Bronx, attempted to board a different train. Schair got confused, and instead of walking into the car he walked right between two cars. He fell down the crack and lay moaning as the subway car prepared to depart. If the train departed before he moved, it would have crushed him. Andrews leaped to save him even though the train was only seconds from starting to roll. He climbed down the crack, grabbed Schair, and pulled him into the narrow crawl space under the edge of the train platform. Unless the train stopped, Andrews would now be crushed, because there was only room for one body. Fortunately, a screaming woman caught the conductor's attention, and the train was stopped just after it had started to roll. "I wasn't thinking about the danger," said Andrews, "just that, hey, somebody needs help." He tore ligaments in his leg in the process.

The next day Andrews became a hero. He had to limp down five flights of stairs every time someone called, since the nearest phone was in a grocery store at the bottom of his building. One of his congratulatory calls came from Ronald Reagan, who wanted to thank him "for all Americans." "I thought he was Rich Little," Andrews said. When Reagan found out that Andrews had been coming from a job interview, he asked for the name of the employer. "Give me their phone number," he said, "I want to call and give you a reference from me."

With that kind of high-powered support, Andrews got the job working for a frozen foods business. Tragically, however, the business lost its lease within a month and Andrews was again unemployed. When the *New York Times* checked on Andrews three months later, he was earning $100 a week by hanging out at grocery stores and helping to unload produce trucks. "I'm still behind in my rent. I'm back right where I was before," he said. "I'm not uncomfortable in this position, because I'm so used to being there."

When the economy recovered in 1984, Andrews' financial situation improved. But his story paints a picture that is at once sad and revealing. The market economy can be cruel and unmerciful, and its victims can be among the most courageous and capable of society. There are no lifetime guarantees in the market economy, and as the business cycle rises and falls, many millions of Americans rise and fall with it.

Of the three problems covered in the Employment Act of 1946 (inflation, recession, and economic stagnation), recession poses the greatest challenge to a market economy. Inflation is largely a question of political will. That is, inflation can be controlled if the government can exercise self–discipline and limit the growth of the money supply. As we will see in the next chapters, market economies have a good record of economic growth. Recession or depression is another matter. This problem of economic instability, reflected in recession, poses a profound challenge for we do not, as yet, have the economic knowledge necessary to prevent cyclical movements in a market economy. This lack of knowledge is costly because recessions and depressions impose real hardship on their victims. The fact that fluctuations in employment and output are smaller and, perhaps, less costly in a planned economy is an advantage that socialists and communists emphasize with vigor. Economists and policy makers have made progress on the control of recession since the Great Depression. There are lessons to be learned here even if the solution evades our grasp.

Definition and Measurement

Whenever the actual level of output in the economy falls significantly below the output that the economy can produce with full employment of resources, the economy is in a recession. A depression is simply a very severe recession. We usually measure the extent of the recession or depression by the amount or percent of the labor force unemployed.

UNEMPLOYMENT RATES 1900 - 1988

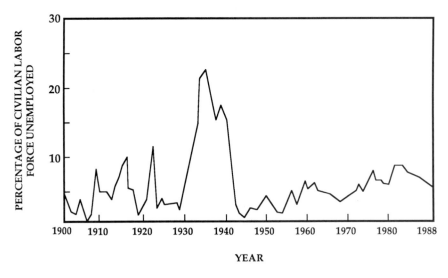

Figure 16.1: Unemployment Rates 1900–1988

The population can be divided into three categories:

1. Employed—Includes all full- and part-time employees. For example, in February, 1988 there were 116 million people employed.
2. Unemployed—Includes all individuals over sixteen years of age who are not in school and actively seeking work. Unemployment statistics are based on surveys in which individuals define their own employment status. In February of 1988, there were 6.9 million people unemployed. The employed and the unemployed comprise the labor force, which was 122.9 million people in that month.
3. Not in the Labor Force—Includes everyone over sixteen years of age who is not in school and is not employed or actively seeking employment. In February, 1988, 62.6 million people were in this category.

Figure 16.1 shows the variability or "cycles" in unemployment over time. Some unemployment is inevitable because people are shifting to new jobs or have recently entered the labor force. If most unemployment is *voluntary* or short term so that exchange in the labor market is working smoothly, the economy is not in a recession. When large numbers of people are *involuntarily* unemployed, indicating that exchange in the labor market is being frustrated, the economy is in a recession. Table 16.1 compares the economy in a period of boom, near full employment (1984), to the trough of a recession (1982). It is difficult to date a recession precisely, but it is not difficult to see that the economy of 1984 was much better than the economy of 1982.

Cost of Recessions
and Depressions

The cost of a recession in terms of lost output swamps all other inefficiencies in the economy. It has been estimated that the U.S. economy lost over a trillion dollars due to unemployment during the last decade, which was a period of relative prosperity. A deep depression can inflict catastrophic costs on a society. The most severe depression of the twentieth century was the period from 1929 to 1940. This period, called the Great Depression, started with the crash of the stock market in 1929 and slipped to its worst depths in 1933 when 25 percent of the work force was unemployed. The stock market lost over 80 percent of its value. Real per capita income in 1933 was the same as it was in 1907. The lost output during the 1930s may have been as high as two trillion dollars in today's prices or 3.5 years' income during the 1930s.

A depression does not affect everyone equally. More personal statistics from the Great Depression convey the individual tragedies that always accompany a cyclical downturn in the economy. There were 130,000 business failures, including nine thousand banks. The four thousand bank failures during 1933 alone are ten times the number of bank failures for the following forty years total. During the tragic year of 1933, 50 percent of the mortgaged farms were delinquent in their payments and, therefore, subject to foreclosure. And, perhaps most devastating of all, foreclosures on private homes were occurring at the rate of one thousand per day. But these statistics, powerful as they are, do not convey the full attack, the psychological as well as material devastation, that the Great Depression heaped upon the American

economy and people. Most who went through the Great Depression were affected by it for the rest of their lives.

Causes of Recession
and Depression

Both the timing and frequency of recessions indicate that they are to some degree inevitable in a market economy. Unlike inflation, which historically has been closely correlated with war or political forces putting pressure on central banks to increase the money supply, recessions and depressions appear to be the result of random shocks to the economy that cannot be readily blamed on government action. This explanation of recessions as natural market phenomena does not, however, totally absolve the government of responsibility. There exists a fair amount of evidence that a number of these recessions, such as the depression of the 1930s, have been worsened by government action.

Nevertheless, market economies have a pattern of cyclical economic behavior (see Figure 13.1)—a period of full employment and rapid economic growth followed by a period of unemployment and economic stagnation. To date, government policy makers have not discovered a way to completely eliminate this cyclical movement of output from the economy. Thus, the frequent unemployment of labor and capital remains one of the most telling criticisms or weaknesses of the market system. The explanation of the business cycle or recession remains the largest unresolved intellectual problem in economics. The fame of the most notable economist of the twentieth century, John Maynard Keynes, rests on his proposed solution in the 1930s to the problem of recession. While Keynes made

Table 16.1 Statistical Profile of a Recession

Year	Months	GNP Growth	Unemploy-ment	Consump-tion	Invest-ment	Gov't. Spending	Money Growth	Interest Rate
1980	Oct–Dec	4.3%	7.4%	$941	$210	$283	1.0%	17.5%
1981	Jan–Mar	9.0	7.4	954	220	286	2.0	19.5
	Apr–Jun	0.7	7.4	957	221	284	1.0	18.7
	Jul–Sep	3.6	7.4	963	220	287	0.7	20.0
	Oct–Dec	− 5.9	8.3	958	216	290	2.2	17.6
1982	Jan–Mar	− 4.6	8.7	954	205	290	1.7	16.3
	Apr–Jun	− 0.8	9.3	959	200	287	1.1	16.5
	Jul–Sep	− 0.9	9.8	964	194	293	2.1	15.0
	Oct–Dec	0.5	10.5	976	178	301	3.2	12.5
1983	Jan–Mar	3.3	10.2	983	191	294	4.0	11.0
	Apr–Jun	9.4	10.0	1006	213	292	2.8	10.5
	Jul–Sep	6.8	9.2	1016	231	292	1.0	10.7
	Oct–Dec	5.9	8.4	1032	250	289	0.8	11.0
1984	Jan–Mar	10.1	7.8	1044	286	289	2.7	11.2
	Apr–Jun	7.1	7.4	1064	284	302	2.0	12.3

Note: Percentages are in annual rates. Dollar amounts are in billions of 1972 dollars.
Source: Economic Reports of the President

significant contributions to our understanding of the problem, it would not be unkind to conclude that he did not bring us very close to a solution to this vexing problem.

The basic puzzle of recession concerns the persistence of *involuntary* unemployment. Why can't people find jobs during a recession? If a market is working properly, a surplus should make the price fall until the surplus is eliminated. Unemployed labor, which is a surplus in the labor market, should make the price of labor, wages, fall until all unemployment is eliminated. Furthermore, the law of comparative advantage tells us that the opportunity cost of unemployed labor should be very low, which should lead to the employment of that labor in some specialty. Basic economic principles tell us that unemployed labor should not persist. But it does. This is the basic puzzle to be solved.

Put differently, why doesn't the wage fall until everyone who wants to exchange some of their labor for income is accommodated? Thus, price and wage flexibility to control exchange, the genius of the market economic system, fails us in the labor market during recession. And, unfortunately, the labor market is by far the most important market in the economy while perhaps the least effective.

Current economic analysis tells us that wages do adjust to control labor exchange and eliminate unemployment, but the process is very slow. This sluggish response in the labor market means that the economy cannot respond well to economic shocks such as the dramatic increase in oil prices in 1973, sudden changes in governmental tax policy, or a large reduction in the money supply such as the decline from 1929 to 1933. The ideal market response to these shocks would be wage and price changes that would leave the economy at full employment. Unfortunately, prices and wages do not change as rapidly as they should, and output falls, causing unemployment.

Any unexpected event represents a potential economic shock to the economy. Because the economy does not adjust quickly or properly, the effect of most of these unexpected events is to reduce the total or aggregate demand of the economy. As demand falls, prices and wages should adjust by also falling. Unfortunately, prices and wages tend to be "sticky" or somewhat fixed because of contracts and business plans. Instead of prices and wages adjusting, people are laid off from their jobs and some businesses close or suspend production. Thus, the combination of a decline in demand and inflexible wages and prices produces a recession. In other words, output is forced downward in response to the decline in aggregate demand because prices and wages are slow to adjust to the new economic conditions. Recessions occur because the response to economic shocks is in terms of *quantity* adjustments rather than *price* adjustments—sales, output, employment, and plant utilization all decline. If prices and wages would adjust quickly, some individuals or companies would be hurt by the adjustments, but the economy would stay at full employment of resources.

Components of Aggregate Demand

The fact that a depression or recession is usually caused by a sharp and sudden decline in aggregate or total demand focuses attention on the components of aggregate demand. If economists or government policy makers could detect approaching declines in demand, perhaps something could be done to prevent the changes in aggregate demand that ignite recession.

We can think of total spending as resulting from three sectors: households consume, businesses invest, and governments appropriate government expenditures.

Consumption. Household consumption is largely determined by the incomes of households. To a lesser degree, it is also influenced by interest rates, expectations about the future, and the wealth of the households. If interest rates rise, households borrow less for consumption. If households become pessimistic about the future, they may choose to spend less and save more in anticipation of bad economic times. If the wealth of households somehow increases, they will probably choose to spend more even if their income has not increased. No doubt disposable income (income after taxes) is the most important influence on consumption. Household consumption uses up about 94 percent of disposable income. Household consumption tends to be quite steady and less volatile than the other components of aggregate demand. Table 16.1 indicates that consumption did not fall significantly during the last recession in 1982 and 1983.

Business Investment. Business investment includes all the expenditures by businesses that are not translated directly into consumption goods and services for households. Investment (which *does not* refer to stocks and bonds) includes activities such as the construction of new plants and buildings, the purchase of new equipment and machinery, and increases in inventories.

John Maynard Keynes

"Keynes' intellect was the sharpest and clearest that I have ever known. When I argued with him, I felt that I took my life in my hands, and I seldom emerged without feeling something of a fool." —Bertrand Russell

Bertrand Russell was not the only intellectual heavyweight who felt trepidation when entering the ring with John Maynard Keynes, for Keynes could make almost anyone seem like a fool. By age four, Keynes had figured out the economic meaning of interest, and by age five, he was asking questions about how his brain worked. And by age sixty-four, when he died, Keynes's knowledge had nearly encompassed his generation.

Keynes' interests were so vast that he regularly entertained and overwhelmed the elite of world society. His friends and acquaintances ranged from Max Planck, the originator of quantum mechanics, to Virginia Woolf, the idiosyncratic British novelist,

John Maynard Keynes: Stood economics on its head yet again.

to Franklin Roosevelt and Winston Churchill. He was a member of the most elite intellectual circle of England, the Bloomsbury set, with the Woolfs, the Webbs, G. B. Shaw, and Lytton Strachey (who had some rather unkind things to say about Keynes in his chronicles of Edwardian England). Keynes' wife was a renowned Russian ballerina. Indeed, Keynes would one day write a collection of biographies of twentieth-century dignitaries based on his personal observations of them.

But it was Keynes the economist and not Keynes the social butterfly who changed the way the world's governments do business. What Adam Smith had been to the eighteenth century and what Karl Marx had been to the nineteenth century, John Maynard Keynes was to the twentieth century. Before Keynes, governments looked upon unemployment and inflation as unfortunate but unavoidable side effects of free enterprise. But Keynes showed that governments could do something about those problems without turning the keys to the city over to the Marxists. Governments, according to Keynes, had within their grasp the means to alleviate poverty without becoming paternalistic.

John Maynard Keynes (it rhymes with Mains) was born in June of 1883, which, strangely enough, was the year Karl Marx gave up the ghost. This year of passage was about the only thing the two had in common. Marx was bitter and a bore, sober, unattractive, and poor. His main theme in life was "Capitalism Doomed." Keynes, on the other hand, was a preppie. He wore the nicest clothes and the broadest smile. He loved life and sailed through it. He earned a hefty fortune, sold tickets at his own theatre, and collected modern art. No doubt he was the architect of "Capitalism Viable."

Unlike most preppies these days, though, Keynes actually attended a prep school. He was a student like few others: perfect grades, captain of the debate team, and unusually insightful. A letter to his father describing a headmaster's speech illustrates his youthful understanding. "It was the usual stuff. Ought to show our thankfulness; remember dignity of school; if anything done must be of best; as always before."

Keynes would later graduate from Kings College in Cambridge. Professors there begged him to become a full-time economist like his father. Fortunately, he consented and, after a short stint working in India, returned to teach at Cambridge. It wasn't long before Keynes was appointed editor of England's preeminent economic journal, a post he would hold for thirty-three years.

Keynes spent the rest of his life enjoying triumph after triumph. He earned a huge fortune trading foreign currency and commodities, he wrote scholarly books, he helped save England from financial collapse during both World War I and World War II, he became the tutor of prime ministers and presidents, and he married a beautiful ballerina. Keynes' busy schedule forced his wife to give up dancing professionally, but she did not give it up altogether. Visitors at the Keynes' home reported a certain pounding and thumping on the floors above. Mrs. Keynes was practicing her art.

In spite of all his successes, it is generally agreed that Keynes somehow avoided becoming a jerk. He was filthy rich and could be arrogant and sarcastic, particularly toward those who thought to be his peers. But he could also be very patient with slow-thinking students. He loved humor and the arts.

It was in 1936 that Keynes published *The General Theory of Employment, Interest, and Money*. It stood economics on its head, much as Smith's *The Wealth of Nations* and Marx's *Capital* had done before. *The General Theory* came to be the bible of modern liberalism. Buried amid its deserts of calculus and differential equations rested three simple and all-important premises: (1) An economy in depression might well stay there indefinitely; (2) Prosperity depends on investment; and (3) Private investment is undependable. From these three premises follows a logical conclusion—governments can abort depressions by doing their own investing. Economic downturns can be stopped by governments willing to invest or who persuade the private sector to invest. Wrote Keynes:

> If the treasury were to fill old bottles with banknotes, bury them at suitable depths in disused coal mines which are then filled up to the surface with town rubbish, and leave it to private enterprise on well tried principles of laissez-faire to dig the notes up again . . . there need be no more

unemployment and with the help of the repercussions, the real income of the community would probably become a good deal larger than it is. It would indeed, be more sensible to build houses and the like; but if there are practical difficulties in the way of doing this, the above would be better than nothing.

The idea may seem ridiculous on its surface, but theoretically it is altogether plausible. During depressions consumers have no excess money to save. Interest rates rise because of the savings shortage, and businesses won't invest because of the high interest rates and because consumers don't have money to spend anyway. Hence, the economy will sit permanently in depressions. But governments can stop this vicious cycle by investing. And to Keynes, this type of government intervention was not at all Marxist, but a necessary evil to save capitalism.

> Whilst the enlargement of the functions of government . . . would seem to be a terrific encroachment on individualism, I defend it, on the contrary, both as a practical means of avoiding the destruction of the existing economic forms in their entirety and as the condition of the successful functioning of individual initiative.

Most government policy that endeavors to adjust the economy, therefore, comes partially from Keynes. Tax cuts, government work programs, and big defense budgets all have as a partial purpose the flattening of the business cycle. "I am a Keynesian," said Richard Nixon. He is not the only one, by any means.

Ironically, Keynes also advocated that governments reduce spending when the economy returns to full speed. Keynes argued that if heavy government spending continued once the economy had regained its footing, inflation must surely result, and Keynes loathed inflation. "By a continuing process of inflation, governments can confiscate, secretly and unobserved, an important part of the wealth of their citizens. . . . There is no subtler, no surer means of overturning the existing basis of society than to debauch the currency." His advice has not been as heeded in this regard, as economists agree that runaway government spending contemporaneous with a vibrant economy can surely cause inflation.

Keynes died in April of 1946. He had been weak and ill for several years, but that had not stopped him from counseling world leaders who sought out his advice about how to finance a war.

Keynesian economics dominated economic thought for three decades after Keynes' death. Gradually, newer developments in economic theory and the clear difficulties in implementing Keynesian prescriptions for the economy overshadowed the more simple version of Keynes' theory. Today, few economists would support Keynesian economics without reservations. But all would acknowledge a large intellectual debt to this most notable economist of the twentieth century.

Business investment is affected by interest rates in the economy, expectations about the future, and governmental tax policies toward business. As interest rates rise, businessmen find that some planned financial projects appear unprofitable, and they reduce the amount of investment they originally intended. As business planners become more pessimistic about the future of the economy, they also reduce their construction of new plants and equipment. If government taxes a larger share of profits, fewer investments in new capital are attractive to business.

Investment tends to be quite variable because business expectations and other factors change the timing of business investments. From the first quarter of 1980 to the depth of the latest recession in the fourth quarter of 1982, business investment fell by 20 percent and then rose by 64 percent. Fluctuations in business investment are clearly one source of instability in a market economy, but the investment itself is also the lifeblood of any economy.

Government Spending. Government spending is under the direct control of the Congress and the president and can be varied according to their wishes. It is difficult to predict the exact path of government spending. Some budget items, such as unemployment compensation and welfare payments, increase during a recession. Tax revenues are hard to predict because of fluctuations in household income and business profits—the two main sources of taxes. If an adjustment is made for inflation, government spending changed very little during the past recession.

Typical Business Cycle of Recession and Expansion

If one or two of these areas of spending decline and prices do not fall, then it is possible for the economy to be thrown into a recession or depression. Conceivably the recession might result from sharp change in any sector; however, if we look at the three, business investment seems to be the most volatile.

In order to understand a natural business cycle, we must first examine the nature of business decisions. Unlike consumer and government decisions, which are based largely on current income, prices, and interest rates, business decisions always involve time, risk, and uncertainty. A business firm or entrepreneur may make an investment decision today involving $10 million to $50 million to build a new plant or add production capacity to an existing plant. This project may take two to five years to build, and not start producing until completed. Thus, the costs are almost entirely up front with revenue from sales some years away. Profits are, therefore, even further into the future. Hence, today's decision ultimately rests on expectations of market conditions some four or five years into the future and continuing for the next several years. Imagine yourself being held responsible for making that judgment relative to the expenditure of $20 million of someone else's money. Is it any wonder that entrepreneurs who do this well are paid salaries of several hundred thousand dollars per year?

There is no certainty in the process, but there is surely one obvious rule. Don't have this expensive project on-line and at full production just as total demand and, therefore, the economy begin to slip into a recession. If you expect a recession, hold off. How would a recession be anticipated? The obvious case occurs when the economy is already in the early stages of decline. Barring that, if there have been four to six good strong years of growth and you know anything about periodic cycles or downturns in the economy (which average about one every six years), you may want to hold off until there is additional information. While this may appear to be no better than astrology, it is the stuff (the risk and uncertainty) that constitutes business decision making.

If enough firms, in making their investment decisions, read the signs in the way suggested above, investment declines, which causes a decline in employment, wages, and salaries. If there are no offsetting price declines, the fall in investment spending reduces aggregate income which in turn causes a decline in consumer demand, leading to further decisions to reduce business investment, which causes employment and income to fall even further. We have a snowballing effect which turns a small decision by a few firms into unemployment and recession.

Again, an integral aspect of this problem is the reluctance of workers, producers, bankers, and other economic participants to take pay cuts. If there were immediate reductions in costs (wages, material costs, interest rates, etc.), the recession could conceivably be stopped in its tracks. If costs declined far enough, employers would proceed with their investment plans, regardless of the possibility of a small decline in demand. However, it seems to be a natural instinct of each of us to resist a decline in that price which is our

income (wages, the price of stereos, the price of houses, profit level, interest rate charged, etc.). Eventually, competition and falling demand may force us to take wage cuts or lose our income and jobs altogether, but in the meantime the reluctance to take these cuts leads to increasing postponement of investment plans, the loss of some jobs, and declining output—a series of quantity adjustments rather than price adjustments that add up to a recession.

The recent recession of 1982 and 1983 followed this pattern. High interest rates and uncertainty about the future of the economy caused business investment to decline quite quickly from autumn 1981 until autumn 1982. Unemployment rose from 7.4 percent to 10.5 percent. Consumption stagnated and would probably have fallen without the stimulus of a tax cut. In the spring of 1983, investment increased and the economy began to grow and move out of recession, relieving the Reagan campaign planners for the 1984 election.

Other Factors Contributing to Recession

Not all recessions are caused by declines in aggregate or total demand. There can also be shocks to the economy on the supply side, such as a steep increase in the price or availability of a key resource like oil, or bad weather that limits agricultural production. Agriculture-based economies often have recessions that are supply induced by bad weather, but industry-based or service–oriented economies are more likely to have recessions based on the demand-side problems of the economy.

The analysis of this chapter has ignored the international dimension of the economy. A sudden fall in the demand for the exports of an economy can also cause recession. During the Great Depression of the 1930s, the U.S. passed a high tariff which adversely affected world trade and helped spread the depression of the U.S. to the rest of the world. As economies today become increasingly interdependent, recession in one country has a negative effect on the economies of others. Alternatively, an increase in demand for the products of a country can pull it out of recession.

Government Policies to Combat Recession

Government policies designed to reduce the effect of recession or depression must attempt to offset the reduction in spending by household consumption or business investment that causes the recession to begin. The government has two types of economic policies that can be used to stabilize total demand or total spending—fiscal policy, which involves government expenditures and taxes, and monetary policy, which involves the money supply and interest rates.

Fiscal Policy

Assume the government knows that aggregate demand is going to fall in the coming year if the government does not change its policies. Government policy makers can use public expenditures and taxes to offset or eliminate the expected decline. Government spending can be increased so that total demand will not fall, even though consumer spending or business investment might fall. If policy makers do not want to increase government expenditures, they can reduce taxes on household income to stimulate consumption, or cut taxes on business investment to encourage more investment in the economy.

The fiscal policy prescribed for recession requires the government to spend more and tax less—in other words, run a deficit in the federal budget. Figure 16.2 shows the surpluses and deficits in the federal budget for the past three decades. Politicians seem to enjoy running deficits in the budget, since they have chosen to do so for all but five years since 1950. There has been no budget surplus in the past twenty years. Most economists suggest that fiscal policy be applied consistently over the business cycle—deficits in recessions, balanced budgets in normal years, and surpluses in the budget in years with increased inflation. Politicians find this diet to be low in political sugar and have chosen to ignore it.

Monetary Policy

The other potentially stabilizing government policy is monetary policy, which involves the action of the Federal Reserve System upon the money supply and interest rates. In times of recession, most economists would recommend that the Federal Reserve increase the money supply and push down interest rates. Since the Federal Reserve System has the power to increase or decrease the amount of money in the economy, it can also temporarily influence, although not completely control, interest rates. For example, the Federal Reserve might be able to temporarily reduce interest rates by injecting large quantities of money into the economy. Lower interest rates would cause households and businesses to increase their spending in

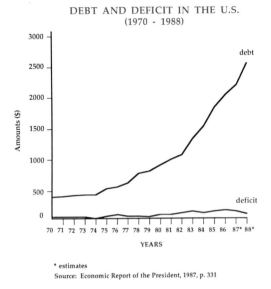

DEBT AND DEFICIT IN THE U.S.
(1970 - 1988)

* estimates
Source: Economic Report of the President, 1987, p. 331

Figure 16.2: Debt and Deficit in the U.S.

Problems of Implementing Government Policies

These measures to combat recession appear to be so simple that the question is raised as to why the government is unable to eliminate recession from the economy. There is a set of complicating factors that makes the practice of these prescriptions much more difficult than it appears. Policies designed to combat recession are not immediately effective, but take time to work through the economy. Government planning, like that of businesses, must always be done with an eye toward the future rather than the present. Therefore, the most difficult aspect of government policy is to collect information and forecast the future economy and then make changes today to offset that projected future.

Collecting Information. The difficulties of applying stabilizing policies can perhaps best be seen by looking at the actual process. The first step is to obtain data about the current state of the economy and then use that data to forecast the future. It takes government officials in the Departments of Labor and Commerce about a month to forty-five days to develop an accurate picture of the economy as it exists at a given point of time. For example, due to the lag in information, it was September 1988 before we knew the true state of the economy in July 1988.

Forecasting the Economic Future. The second step is to use this delayed information to forecast the future. Beyond eighteen months, forecasts are really no better than guesses. All forecasts have a degree of

reaction to lower interest rates. Furthermore, households and businesses will try to spend the increased money supply and, thereby, stimulate the economy.

During 1981 and the first nine months of 1982, the Fed was concentrating on controlling inflation. Consequently, the money supply was restricted to very little growth during this period. This action by the Fed probably initiated the recession of 1981 and 1982. The restrictive monetary policy of the Fed combined with inflationary expectations caused interest rates to be abnormally high during this period. High interest rates and worries about the economy caused investment to fall between the third quarter of 1981 and the fourth quarter of 1982 pushing the economy into a recession.

error, since the forecast must accurately predict the aggregate behavior of millions of households and businesses. Economists are sure that GNP will be positive in the next year. They are reasonably sure that GNP will be within five percent of the previous year's GNP. Beyond this expert knowledge, there is substantial guessing about the course of the economy. Our ability to forecast the economic future is only slightly better than our ability to forecast the weather a week from now. In general, the more positive the expert is about the future of the economy, the less confidence one should have in the predictions.

Deciding on a Policy. Step three requires the president and the Federal Reserve to decide on the appropriate economic policy. Government decisions take an excruciatingly long time even when economic events are moving rapidly.

Suppose the president decides that the economy is headed into recession in a year or two, so that a tax cut or an increase in government spending is appropriate fiscal policy. He then makes these recommendations to Congress. A tax proposal goes to the House Ways and Means Committee which takes it under deliberation. If we are fortunate, the Senate Finance Committee will act at the same time, but all tax measures must originate in the House Ways and Means Committee. In most instances, it takes Congress a long time to deliberate tax policy. For example, the tax cut proposed by President John F. Kennedy as a remedy for the mild recession of 1960 was not enacted until 1964, when the recession had already passed.

Obviously, if Congress takes that much time to respond to recommendations by the president, rather than acting to remedy the economic conditions that the president had in mind when making the request, these policies may do no good at all, or even have adverse effects as they fuel the next inflation rather than alleviate the current recession. There are similar problems with policies involving government spending—they may be delayed in enactment and even more difficult to shut off once the recession is over.

The Federal Reserve can change the rate of growth of the money supply in the economy more quickly since it does not require congressional approval for such action. Because the Federal Reserve is an independent agency, the policies of the Fed, Congress, and the president often conflict. That is, the monetary policy may be directed at control of inflation while the fiscal policy is combating recession.

Implementing the Policy. Once the decisions have been made, the programs must be implemented. An increase in government expenditures may be implemented very quickly if the program simply involves transfers to households. However, governmental construction projects, such as highways and dams, require years for planning and construction. The problems of implementing changes in the money supply are even greater, for a change in the money supply today will have its effect on the economy anywhere from a year to two years into the future. These types of lags and imperfections in the implementation of economic policy create enormous difficulty for the government in its attempt to eliminate the recessionary cycle in a market economy.

Forecasts or Flim-Flam?

George Stigler, a Nobel Laureate in economics, once boasted that he could produce an accurate economic forecast. He predicted that GNP would be positive, not negative, and that the level of GNP this year would be near the level of GNP last year. Many economists have made small fortunes forecasting future economic events for government and business. Societies have always wanted someone to predict the future whether by reading tea leaves, analyzing of the entrails of a goat, or forecasting the economic future with 1,000 equations and a large computer.

How good have the forecasts been? They appear to be a lot like weather forecasts. Short-term forecasts are reasonably accurate because the economy does not change quickly. Long-term forecasts (a year or more) are not very good. But, just like the local TV weatherman, economic forecasters are extremely good at explaining why some unanticipated event caused their forecast to go awry. In the spring of 1983, the typical forecaster predicted that GNP would be $3.46 trillion in the first three months of 1984, but it was actually $3.55 trillion—an error of $90 billion. The forecaster will point out that this is less than a 3 percent error. However, it is better to ask how well the forecaster predicted the change in GNP over a one-year period. When viewed in terms of changes, the average forecaster underestimated the change in GNP by 26 percent. During this same period, forecasters overestimated the change in prices by 38 percent.

Interest rates rose by 12 percent in that year, but forecasters predicted a rise of about 1 percent. The unemployment rate fell by 25 percent from February of 1983 to February 1984. Forecasters expected only a 7 percent decline.

On the whole, forecasts of the economy have not performed well. Why should they? An economy is constantly bombarded by random events such as oil embargoes, weather failures, strikes, and unanticipated governmental policy changes. Predictions are going to be very tentative at best. Economic theorists now know that the parameters of the equations forecasters use to predict the economy will be consistently wrong if businesses, households and other economic actors have access to the same information government and the forecasters have. Furthermore, prices such as interest rates contain a distillation of the known information at a point in time. There is no reason to believe that forecasters will be able to predict changes in such prices successfully.

If forecasts are so full of error, why do hard-headed businessmen and government officials pay high prices for such forecasts? Because some information is almost always preferred to none. Buying a forecast is also buying a scapegoat if things go bad. As long as the future matters to us, we will go on looking for prophecies.

Here is a good generic economic forecast. GNP will be positive, as will interest rates. There will be some unemployment (probably less than 50 percent). Prices, however, may rise or fall.

Inconsistency. Another difficulty in reducing the effect of recession on the economy is the short time span of most political decisions. In the United States, politicians have very near time horizons because of the two-year intervals between elections. They tend to be impatient with policies that promise results three, four, or five years into the future. Consequently, they constantly search for quick and painless fixes to economic problems that face the country. The remedy for inflation discussed in the last chapter involves slow rates of growth of the money supply, that may cause high interest rates for a time. The monetary prescription for combating a recession is just the opposite. The money supply should grow quickly, interest rates should be low, and government should spend more than it takes in. All too often the political system is faced with a choice between controlling inflation or combating recessionary tendencies in the economy, a choice politicians find extremely difficult. Administration after administration comes into office promising to combat recession and inflation at the same time, finds it is unable to do so, and eventually chooses economic policies that contain inconsistencies—one phase of the policy may be anti-inflationary, the other acting to increase demand.

Political Pressures. Recession and inflation have significant political consequences. Presidents are swept into office because of the poor economic situations confronting their predecessors. Franklin Roosevelt, John F. Kennedy, and Ronald R. Reagan won their elections largely because of weaknesses in the economy against which they could conduct a vigorous campaign.

Jimmy Carter. (Library of Congress)

Herbert Hoover. (Bureau of Printing and Engraving) Political casualties of economic malfunction.

The Great Depression as a Case Study

The Great Depression illustrates the complexity of the recession or depression problem. While cyclical movement in the economy may be inevitable and cannot be blamed on government policies, it does not follow that the Great Depression was simply a phenomenon that illustrates the weakness of the market system. Examining government policies during this decade has convinced many economists that the government turned a mild recession into a severe depression by its action. From October 1929, when the stock market crashed, to April 1933, the Federal Reserve System allowed the money supply of the economy to fall 30 percent. To give you some idea of the magnitude of the decline in money and the failure of banks, if this were to happen today in the same proportion it would mean the disappearance from the economy of $165 billion of our $500 billion, and the closing of almost 6,000 of our 14,000 banks (with their checking and savings accounts uninsured). Thus, at a time when the economy needed monetary growth, or at least stability, the Federal Reserve delivered a body blow to an economy already in trouble because of the stock-market crash and other recessionary forces. The effect of this reduction in money supply greatly intensified the decline in output and threw the economy into the worst depression of American history. It is hard to imagine a worse monetary policy than that pursued by the Federal Reserve during this period.

Was fiscal policy better? A little. Federal expenditures grew significantly from 1929 to 1934, while spending by state and local governments grew slowly. There was less growth of expenditures after 1934. The big mistake in fiscal policy was the increase in taxes at all levels of government. Roosevelt is often viewed as the first president to use Keynesian economics. But the fiscal policies of his administration did little to move the economy out of a deep depression. It seems fair to conclude that monetary policy made a deep depression out of a recession and that fiscal policy did little to rescue the economy from the mistakes of the Federal Reserve.

In 1932, as Roosevelt was running against Hoover, the unemployment rate in the economy was about 24 percent. The depth of the Depression made the election of 1932 a foregone conclusion. Roosevelt won with 472 electoral votes compared to Hoover's 59 electoral votes.

Kennedy campaigned against the unemployment and slow growth caused by the recession of 1960—a period which, for obvious reasons, Eisenhower and Nixon refused to call a recession, preferring instead to call it an "economic pause."

In 1980, Reagan was able to campaign against the results of Carter's economic policies. Unemployment in 1980 stood at 7.1 percent, while inflation was at an annual rate of 13.5 percent. Reagan was very critical of Carter's economic policies, criticism that the public was ready to accept.

Once in office and faced with political reality, it is often the case that little of what was promised is actually delivered. For example, if the problem is perceived to be inflation, the prescription calls for some combination of reducing the money supply, higher interest rates, lower government spending, or higher taxes. There is not one among the list that does not negatively affect an important part of the economy. No one likes tight money and high interest rates, least of all the housing, construction, and timber industries. While it might be popular to propose reducing government spending, another way to state the consequences of that proposal is to suggest, "Let's do away with thousands of jobs in the space industry, or eliminate the water and reclamation projects in the Mountain West." How many congressmen support reducing government waste, only to balk at any cutbacks affecting their own districts? Government waste often seems to be defined as "all government spending outside my district." And finally, which President or congressman wants to return to the voters having just gone on record to raise their taxes by 10 percent? Much of the economic policy debate in Washington is simply a search for nonexistent answers to very difficult questions.

Responses of Households and Businesses.
Even if all the political problems of implementing monetary and fiscal policy could be swept away, these policies still may not be very effective. The purpose of fiscal and monetary policies is to control or at least influence aggregate demand. It is possible that households and businesses offset the government actions in very rational ways from their individual points of view. If government spends more, households and businesses may spend less so that demand is left unchanged in the economy. If government cuts current taxes to stimulate consumption, households, believing that future taxes will rise to pay for the interest and debt incurred by the government, may

not increase consumption even though their take-home pay has increased. If the Federal Reserve increases the money supply to reduce interest rates, households and businesses may revise their expectations about inflation upward and reduce savings, thereby forcing the interest rate up instead of down. In other words, if households and businesses are as smart as the government policy makers (a reasonable assumption), then monetary and fiscal policy may not be able to influence aggregate demand very much.

An Unresolved Problem

Recessions are clearly a weakness of a market economy that, in the past, has exacted a high cost from time to time. Market economies have suffered recessions in all countries under the range of economic conditions—agrarian and industrial, big government and virtually no government, democracy and dictatorship, historically and in modern times. As societies came to expect government to solve more and more problems, the responsibility for eliminating recession was likewise given to government. Politicians, who by disposition and taste love power, are always ready to tackle new problems. Economists, confident in the power of Keynesian economics or the criticisms of it, convince politicians that they possess the tools to deal with recession effectively.

Our historical experience with the control of recession has had a chastening effect on both politicians and economists. The Great Depression illustrated how government could turn a recession into disaster. Since World War II, the economy has alternated between moderate inflation and moderate recession. Each administration has said that it could do better, but has been unable to demonstrate any convincing ability to solve the problem. We may now be at a point where we can avoid disastrous policies, but the unemployment of 10.5 percent in 1983 should be ample evidence that absolute control of recession still eludes market economies.

However, the search for control of recession and depression continues. The market economy does too many things well to be rejected because of its cyclical nature. Yet, recession imposes unacceptable costs in the form of unemployment, bankruptcy, and vanished dreams. Economists will continue to search for economic understanding of recessions. A Nobel Prize is waiting for anyone who can significantly further our knowledge about the problem. Politicians will continue to promise economic panaceas and experiment with new policies because reelection and political power are waiting for the political party that deals successfully with recession—the market curse.

Profile of a Recession

In its April 6, 1981 issue, *Time* heralded a new eight year high in the Dow–Jones average at a value of 1015 and decided that the economy was more healthy than many supposed. The economy had been growing since 1975 with the exception of the election year, 1980. But inflation had been at double digit rates for three years and interest rates were at historic highs. Some thought a recession was coming. They were right. In the summer of 1981, the Fed stepped on the monetary brake—money growth stopped and interest rates went still higher to 20 percent. In the last three

months of 1981, GNP fell at an annual rate of nearly 5 percent. Unemployment increased by over a million workers. By December 14, 1981, *Time* had changed its optimistic tune of the spring, "With each passing day, the industrial landscape is increasingly marred by padlocked factory gates and smokeless smokestacks." Fortunately for the Reagan administration, the economic slump had come soon enough that they could blame it on the Carter administration.

Through most of 1982, the economic slide continued. The recession was now world-wide. Canadian Prime Minister Trudeau warned, "We are moving from crisis to catastrophe." (He was right for he would soon be moving from his office.) In the U.S., unemployment continued to climb and topped 10 percent in the fall of 1982. Comparisons were made (stupidly) to the Great Depression. All during the fall, the evening newscasts were filled with stories of discouraged unemployed workers. Pessimism and gloom were everywhere. Business investment in the fall of 1982 was only 80 percent of what it had been a year earlier.

In 1983, the economy slowly improved. Over the spring and summer, GNP grew at a very high rate as it often does at the end of a recession. By fall, unemployment was down to 8 percent and interest rates were half what they had been two years earlier. At the end of 1983, *Time* headlined "Cheers for a Banner Year."

The recession of 1981–1982 had been like many others of the past—not anticipated by most, very costly to some, and blamed on the other guy by politicians. Most Americans were just glad it was over.

17

The Promise of Economic Growth

Concepts:

Economic Growth
Causes of Economic Growth
Capital–Labor Ratio
Technological Change
Entrepreneurship

America's economic growth has created one of the largest middle classes in history. (Jon Jacobson)

The Sand Island Success Story: A Parable

Sand Island lies somewhere off in the western Pacific, let us say, not far from the coast of Japan. It is not a real place, but the stories we are going to tell about it are all, in their own way, true. Everything that happens on Sand Island has also happened in the real world of market economics.

Life on Sand Island went along unchanged for centuries. The thousand or so inhabitants lived in little grass huts and ate mangoes and bananas that grew wild. Theirs was not a bad life, but sometimes they wished for better. When the occasional ship would put in at Sand Harbor, the islanders observed that others enjoyed many things that they themselves lacked. But what could they do? With no marketable commodities to speak of, their prospects of prosperity did not seem very bright.

Then, one day, a Sand Islander with a good deal of imagination and drive—they called him "Get-Up-and-Go"—hit upon an idea. "Why not sell sand?" he asked. The island sand was clean, white silicon, ideal for making cement. In Japan, which was not far away, there were a number of large cement plants, and most of them used inferior sand brought in from the Gobi Desert. Under the leadership of Get-Up-and-Go, Sand Islanders arranged for a cargo ship to stop by every couple of weeks, and this they filled with sand from their own beaches, every able body manning a garden shovel and working furiously. They sold the sand to the Japanese cement plants and used the money it brought in to buy things they wanted. Soon Sand Islanders were wearing Seiko watches, listening to Sony Walkmans, and putting around the island on Yamaha three-wheelers. They had begun to experience economic growth.

Once they had tasted prosperity, Sand Islanders wanted more and more of it. But, after that first spurt of growth, their economy remained static. The problem was one of volume. Even with all the islanders shoveling as hard as they could, they could only shovel so much sand. True, as the population increased there were more shovelers— but there were also more mouths to feed, and more users of those wonderful Japanese goods. They just couldn't seem to get ahead.

Eventually, Get-Up-and-Go came up with an answer. They must buy themselves some bulldozers to load the sand. That way, instead of loading one ship every two weeks, they could load several ships every day. The bulldozers they needed were big ones—Caterpillar D–10s equipped with five-yard scoops—and very expensive. Since there were no banks nearby, the only way to get the machines was by pooling their own resources and buying them. Of course, some islanders did not *want* to pool their resources; they wanted to keep buying gadgets and gizmos with their money. But by promising them fabulous returns on their investment, Get-Up-and-Go was able to convince them to save their money and buy Caterpillars with it. Eventually they purchased four or five.

Now life really changed on Sand Island. Since the bulldozers could load hundreds of times more sand than all the shovelers put together, the sand ships came and went in a steady parade, and soon money was pouring into the island. Get-Up-and-Go was now the wealthiest man in the western Pacific, but others were doing okay, too. Some were bulldozer operators or mechanics. Others were store owners, homebuilders, autodealers, and TV-repairmen, for the island, with its new-found prosperity, now enjoyed all these amenities. True, a few people—those who could do nothing but shovel sand—were thrown out of work by the new machines, but even living on welfare, they did better than they had as shovelers. Nobody complained.

The island even had a college now. Sand Island Tech was a small institution, not lavish, and its faculty of engineers was heavily weighted toward what we might call "sand sciences." They came up with many new uses for sand: sandpiles, sandpaper, sand-filled kitty-litter boxes, and the like. They even worked up sand castles made with glue and shipped them off to American curio shops. Everything that improved the market for sand improved the fortunes of Sand Island.

One day, however, one of the professors at the college made a startling discovery: Sand Island was running out of sand. It seemed that the prosperity they were enjoying was costing them the very ground beneath their feet, and soon both the prosperity and the ground would be gone. Everyone began to worry, even Get-Up-and-Go. If Sand Island was going to be saved, someone would have to come up with a truly brilliant innovation.

And someone did. One of the professors at the college had been tinkering with silicon, the substance created by melting sand under high temperatures, and one day he discovered how to produce electronic microcircuits on small silicon chips. It took a while for the professor and his colleagues to iron out the wrinkles in making these "semiconductors," but when they did, what an invention they had. They called it the "computer."

Get-Up-and-Go went to work immediately. Soon he had organized such a welter of activity in designing, building, and programming computers that the island was informally renamed "Silicon Island." Of course, it took a lot more investment to set up and staff all those factories and laboratories—it was like buying hundreds of new bulldozers—but once the investment was made, the industry growing out of it was quiet, clean, stable, responsible, and extremely profitable. Moreover, since it utilized so little actual silicon, it put an end to the large-scale depletion of the island's resources.

Sand Islanders now lived very well indeed. Giant corporations built steel-and-glass towers here and there on the island and surrounded them with boutiques, restaurants, and tree-shaded boulevards. There was a baseball team, an opera house, several theaters, and a first-rate symphony orchestra. Sand Island Tech became Silicon University, a pioneering institution in electronics and aerospace technology. And the people themselves built palatial homes overlooking the island's lovely white beaches. After all, sand had gained a special place in their hearts.

The Sand Island success story brings the importance of economic growth into direct focus. Economic growth considers long-term changes in the average level or standard of living for the citizen of a particular country. While Americans have grown accustomed to almost constant improvements in their level of prosperity, there are numerous historical and contemporary examples of economic retardation or stagnation. In fact, economic growth has been common only for the past two centuries, and then only in certain parts of the world.

Not only is growth not automatic, but stagnation looms as a constant and persistent threat. Again, there may be a tendency for Americans to take their high standard of living, their political and economic power, their social and political stability for granted. The history of great civilizations suggests a cyclical pattern: a zestful youth and complacent middle age followed by relative decline. Is this inevitable, and, if so, where is the United States in this process?

Ankeny and Ambala

Few industries illustrate the blessings of economic growth as dramatically as agriculture. One hundred and fifty years ago the farmer in a typical American farm town, Ankeny, Iowa, for example, and the farmer in a small Indian town, Ambala, for example, lived similar lives. Both plowed, planted, and harvested their crops by hand, and struggled to earn a subsistence living. But after 150 years of steady economic growth, the farmer in Ankeny enjoys a life of comfortable work, leisure, and high consumption that the Ambalan farmer cannot even envision.

The farmer in Ambala is severely handicapped by the size of his acreage. Because of Hindu inheritance patterns in which the children each receive an equal share of the land, Ambala's farms have grown smaller and smaller. Today, the typical farm is merely 2.5 acres. In Ankeny, however, the average farm is somewhat larger than 400 acres.

The process of farming for the Ambalan has not changed much over the centuries. The Ambalan farmer tills his field using an ox and a wooden plow, and then plants his seeds by hand. The method is slow and deliberate. Once he has planted, the farmer is dependent upon the monsoon to irrigate his crops. If there is a drought, much of the crop will be lost. The farmer uses tree branches to help protect the young crop from the wind and the rain. He cannot afford fertilizer, either commercial or natural. The dung of his cows is made into chips and then used as fuel, so it isn't available to provide nutrients for the crops. When it is time to harvest (if there is any crop to be harvested), the Ambalan uses a sickle to cut the crop, then bundles it by hand and wraps it in sacks. Much of it may be spoiled by a rainstorm. With luck, he will have a few bushels of wheat, rice, or corn, of which two-thirds will be needed to feed his family, and one third will go to market.

The rolling hills near Ankeny are home for a different kind of farmer, one who takes advantage of 150 years of rapidly improving technology and prosperity. The Ankeny farmer buys modern tractors direct from the John Deere factory located in town. He also has cultivators, seeding equipment, fertilizer spreaders, chemical

Definition and Measurement of Economic Growth

There is no perfect measure of economic growth. In most instances, we think of economic growth as an improvement in the average standard of living for a particular economy through time. Our best, though imperfect, measure of this type of economic growth is the increase in real Gross National Product (GNP) per capita. (That is, total output adjusted for price and population differences.) Since GNP is the output of goods and services in an economy, it forms the basis for making judgments about the ability of a nation to satisfy material needs and desires. However, two adjustments need to be made. The first is an adjustment for inflation. If an economy has the same physical output in two different years, there should be no change in the standard of living. However, if prices have doubled, GNP will also double, since it is measured in terms of product prices at the time of measurement. In order to adjust for inflation and measure

sprayers, combines, trucks, and storage and drying equipment. Chances are, the Ankeny farmer is capitalized to the hilt. The typical farmer in Iowa will have more than $150,000 of equipment. Every stage of the planting and the harvesting is done by machine, and the sun is more likely to rise in the west than the Ankeny farmer is to use a sickle to harvest. In America, farmers own $111 billion of farm machinery, including an average of 2.5 tractors per farm.

Using all that machinery, the Ankeny farmer is remarkably productive. The Ankeny farmer can produce over 100 bushels of corn from each acre, and he labors about three hours to do it. Just 30 years ago, the Ankeny farmer needed 34 hours to produce that amount, indicating how far American agriculture has progressed. The farmer in Ambala labors hundreds of hours for each bushel of corn, and his 2.5 acre farm produces far less than 100 bushels. The greatest difference between the Ambala farmer and the Ankeny farmer is their standard of living. The typical Iowa farmer earns about $18,000 a year. The Indian farmer, on the other hand, earns maybe $250.

The stark contrast between American prosperity, brought to us by steady economic growth, and the poverty of the third world helps explain the tragedy we all felt when the nations of northern Africa suffered from a severe drought in 1983–1985. The drought, which inspired forty popular music stars to produce "We Are the World" and the "Live Aid" Concert, was a calamity that Americans could not imagine. With food so abundant, the American economy concentrates on satisfying superfluous wants. With pet rocks and videocassette recorders and Cabbage-Patch dolls all selling like hot cakes in the store, it is sometimes hard to believe that there are people elsewhere who cannot even buy, well, hot cakes.

The farmer in Africa is very similar to the farmer in Ambala. When the storms failed to deliver, there were no complex irrigation systems or wells to provide water. One hundred and fifty years ago, no doubt a drought would have brought similar consequences to the Ankeny farmer. But economic growth has brought the Ankeny farmer to the point where he no longer is completely a victim of the elements. Clearly, the process of economic growth, and understanding how to accelerate it, is the key to saving the starving children of Africa and to providing hope to the farmers of Ambala.

only changes in physical output, we use the same prices for both periods—generally the prices of the first, or base, year. Thus, real GNP will measure only output (real) changes, not inflation. The second adjustment concerns population. Since we are interested in the standard of living for the average person, we need also to adjust GNP for the growth in population that the GNP must serve. Thus, in our measure of real GNP per capita, the *real* refers to the adjustment for inflation, and the *per capita* refers to the adjustment for population. (See chapter 10 for more detail.)

American Economic Growth

Let us first examine our past with reference to this process of economic growth. The early colonists were so poor that they could not adequately feed themselves. During the first fifteen years, almost 80 percent of the colonial populations of Virginia, Massachusetts, and Maryland died from starvation, disease, childbirth, or

Indian attacks. Death rates were as high as 252 per 1,000 per year (one of four died annually) compared to today's rate of 15 per 1,000. As late as 1640, thirty-three years after the first arrivals, as many as 50 percent were dying prematurely from fevers and other diseases. In most respects, however, these rugged colonists were not much worse off than had they stayed in England, Scotland, France, Holland, or Spain.

Both logic and evidence suggest that there could not have been broad, sustained economic growth in the world's major countries before the middle of the seventeenth century. Our first estimates of economic well-being come from that period (around 1650 to 1700) and are so low that to project backwards in time at the rate most European and North American countries have grown since 1750 implies a level which could not have sustained populations of the size that actually existed. Rather than pushing later growth rates back in time, economic historians believe there was little sustained economic growth before 1750. While there were undoubtedly periods of relative prosperity, these were followed by recurring plagues, years of destructive wars, domestic dislocations, political instability, and other calamities that contributed to centuries of economic stagnation.

Thus, it was not prosperity that met the early colonists, but in most cases deprivation and death. Why did they continue coming? Partly because conditions were not much better in Europe. In addition, once the period of starvation was over, the colonists hoped for greater religious and political freedom, and the prospect of greater personal and economic independence through the opportunity to own land. It is hard for us to imagine what the ownership of land meant to poverty stricken, land-starved Europeans in the seventeenth and eighteenth centuries. In Europe, owning land not only made one wealthy, but it also made one part of the elite, privileged class.

Table 17.1 shows changes in the U.S. real GNP per capita from 1710 to 1980. The prices are fixed in terms of 1972 prices, and population is as shown for each year. While other countries have enjoyed higher rates of economic growth over short periods of time, none has enjoyed this kind of growth for such a sustained period of time. This means that the United States enjoyed the highest standard of living in the world from the late nineteenth century until the 1970s.

The lessons from the American experience are that economic growth matters—in fact, few things matter more—but its consequences are spread over long periods of time and hardly perceptible in periods as short as a year or two. Imagine the new opportunities that occur as a nation's total income increases more than 20–fold. The politics of resolving the conflicts among interests groups is obviously easier to conduct if the economic pie is growing. Social programs financed from economic growth are accepted more gracefully by the electorate than programs funded by a reduction in the standard of living for most of the population.

On the other hand, there are no quick, easy roads to prosperity. The 270 years that it took to increase the income of the average American twenty-four times is, rather than slow and faltering, the longest, most rapid sustained growth we have on record. And what rate of growth is implied by this impressive record? This growth has been produced by a less than 2 percent increase

Table 17.1 Real GNP Per Person, United States

Year	Real GNP (Billions of 1972 $)	Population (millions)	Real GNP Per Person (1972 $)
1710	$ .090	0.33	$ 270
1840	9.4	17	550
1870	34.1	40	852
1900	123.6	76	1,626
1929	315.3	122	2,584
1960	737	181	4,072
1970	1,086	205	5,298
1980	1,474	228	6,465

Source: Constructed from data in the Statistical History of the United States

in income per year per person. That unimpressive sounding annual rate of growth, viewed from a longer perspective, enables each generation of Americans to be twice as well-off in terms of total national income as the preceding generation. Thus, growth is extremely important, but it takes perseverance, patience, and no shortcuts.

Causes of Economic Growth

There are five necessary ingredients in the production of goods and services. As these ingredients grow or decline, they influence the rate of economic growth. (1) Labor is by far the most important input to consider. Labor accounts for two-thirds to three-fourths of the value of output. (2) Capital, the tools, machines, and equipment created by humankind to increase production, is another important element in the process. (3) Natural resources provide the material base that labor and capital use for the process of economic growth. (4) Technological change makes possible more and more production from the limited available resources. (5) Entrepreneurship consists of the skills of management, creativity, and the ideas used in the production process.

Labor and Population Growth

From July, 1986 to July, 1987, the U.S. population increased by about 2,177,000 persons. If GNP or output had remained constant at its 1986 level, GNP per capita would have fallen by about 1 percent. The labor force also increased because of graduates from high school and college, along with a few others, were entering the labor force, increasing its ranks by about two million persons.

The rate of economic growth is essentially determined by the outcome of a race between increases in population and increases in the other four factors in the process. Suppose there is a fixed amount of capital and natural resources in an economy. Assume further that the technology does not change, nor is there any change in the entrepreneurial skills of businessmen who are combining the resources. Population growth, with no increase in the other four factors of production, causes the amount of capital and natural resources per worker to fall. In such a case, output will rise since there are more workers, but output per worker and real GNP per capita will fall. Labor due to population growth contributes to output, but not to sustained economic growth defined in terms of the average standard of living. If population grows, there must be changes in the capital stock, natural resources, technology, or entrepreneurship, for economic growth to occur. Population or labor growth increases output but reduces real GNP per capita, while increases in the other forces in the growth equation increase both output and real GNP per capita.

The Malthusian Trap. Most economies, bound by population growth, are on a constant treadmill where additions to capital, discovery of new natural resources, technological change, or new methods of organizing business must overcome the natural increases in population that occur. Thomas Malthus, a British economist who followed Adam Smith, thought that this treadmill effect in the economy would always end in defeat, that man was destined to a life of poverty. Malthus theorized that an increase in wages would cause people to marry sooner, have more children, and live longer. Thus, the population would increase, driving the wage back toward a subsistence level that would just support the population. In this sense, Malthus saw the common man as being in a trap from which there was no escape. This theory worked rather well up until Malthus put it down on paper at the end of the eighteenth century. During the Middle Ages, events such as the Black Death and other plagues had reduced population and raised wages for a time. Soon after wages rose, population would increase, causing wages to fall back to a subsistence level.

Fortunately, the trap was being destroyed by changes in England and elsewhere in the eighteenth and nineteenth centuries. Malthus did not foresee the liberating effect of changes in technology combined with capital investment. As technological change exploded during the nineteenth century, it became clear that technology and capital accumulation could overcome the negative effects on economic growth of population increases and potential depletion of natural resources. Consequently, the process of economic growth focuses on investment that increases the capital stock of the economy and on technological change.

Capital

Capital consists of all of the man-made elements used in production, such as tools, machines, and buildings. Capital investment occurs in the economy because households choose to save rather than consume. If all our resources are used to produce consumer goods, and these are consumed, obviously there can be no production of tools, or capital goods. In order for capital goods to be produced, households must consume less than they produce (save), converting this surplus into capital goods. In the market system, saving occurs because there is an incentive for individuals to forgo consumption now in order to have even more consumption later. The price that induces people to postpone consumption by compensating individuals who do so is the interest rate. If the interest rate is 10 percent, an individual who gives up $1 of consumption today is able to consume $1.10 one year from now. Thus, the interest rate plays a crucial role in the process of economic growth.

The ratio of capital to labor is critical to the process of economic growth. As the capital–labor ratio rises, output per worker and real GNP per capita also rise. Since capital depreciates and wears out, an economy must invest some savings just to keep the capital–labor ratio constant. Moreover, new labor is constantly entering an economy because of population growth. As this new labor enters, investment is again required to keep the capital–labor ratio constant. Even more savings and investment are required if this ratio is to grow and cause growth in the standard of living. Consequently, an economy that saves a large portion of its income and invests it in new capital may expect a higher rate of economic growth than an economy with a low rate of savings. As shown in Figure 17.1, the U.S. put about 11 percent of its GNP into capital formation in 1986 while Japan, the country the U.S. fears most economically, invested 28 percent of GNP. If these percentages persist, there is little question as to who will win the economic race.

Technological Change

Technological change is the key ingredient in the process of modern economic growth. Without such change, the inevitable increases in population and the depletion of natural resources will make any significant increase in the standard of living impossible. In spite of the importance of technological change in the growth process, we know very little about the causes of such change.

At times, technological change appears to be accidental or random, as illustrated by Goodyear's development of rubber, or Roentgen's discovery of X-rays. Even in these cases, however, years of work preceded the accident on Mrs. Goodyear's stove, and it took Miles Goodyear's experience to recognize that smelly substance as galvanized rubber, rather than an awful

Whitney's cotton gin: Made the south boom before the Civil War. (Library of Congress)

mess needing to be cleaned up. Most technological change, however, is planned and influenced by the prospects for large financial rewards. Watt's development of the steam engine was funded by investors desiring a better engine to pump water out of mines. Eli Whitney solved the problem of separating cotton fibers from the seeds that had plagued cotton production for years. Thomas Edison was the first major inventor in the United States to understand that much technological change could occur in research labs simply through trial and error and repeated attempts to develop a particular new technology.

Today the government, private industry, and universities invest large sums of money in the creation of new knowledge and its application through new technology. Research labs and technological inventions are commonplace in a modern economy. Yet, this narrow definition of technological change does not explain the broader aspects of what we might call technological improvement. Investments in human beings through education, better health, and on-the-job training are also important contributors to the process of economic growth and may be lumped under the broad category of technological change. Whatever the motivation or reasons for technological improvement, we must emphasize that it plays the central role in the process of economic growth.

Entrepreneurship

The role of entrepreneurship, or business creativity, in economic growth is a controversial and much debated issue. Some scholars believe that business creativity is crucial to the process of growth, and that less-developed countries have difficulty improving their economic performance due to a lack of business creativity or entrepreneurial ability. Still others who have studied the matter believe that each society will generate enough entrepreneurs as long as the other ingredients of economic growth are present. Whenever an economy has slow growth or begins to decline in economic performance, the lack of business creativity is usually cited as the reason.

Since the concept of entrepreneurship is difficult to measure, it is hard to evaluate the importance of entrepreneurial spirit to the economic growth process. For example, the rapid rate of growth in the Japanese economy, as contrasted with a slower growth rate in the United States, is currently being explained by a difference in management style between Japanese and American firms. Experts suggest that the Japanese have better labor-management relations, use long-term planning, and utilize labor more effectively. A fundamental problem with these explanations is that they do not explain why the business practices of the United States worked well in the 1950s and 1960s when the United States experienced impressive economic growth and then suddenly became less effective in the 1970s when the United States' economic growth rate declined. The correct view of the role of entrepreneurship is probably somewhere in between the views that it is crucial and that it is unimportant. Entrepreneurship is necessary for the process of economic growth but will not carry an economy that does not have the key ingredients of high rates of capital investment and significant technological progress.

Institutions and Economic Growth

Each of the basic economic institutions of society plays an important role in the growth process. Each institution has the capacity to promote or retard growth.

Households

Households are the central players in the growth process. Since no single household can be of much importance, their cumulative role is usually overlooked. With almost no direction from the state, and relatively small influence from the marketplace, households have been responsible for providing the native or immigrant populations which have ultimately provided our labor force. Decisions regarding the age of marriage and the spacing of children primarily determine our native-born population. Family investments in the type, quality, and amount of education have largely determined the skills of our workers. The extent of participation in the labor force by males, females, and children is primarily a family decision. Decisions regarding leisure, home production, market production, and saving are strongly influenced by families. Families transfer traits, attitudes, skills, and even wealth, all of which influence economic growth. Too often we assume that important decisions must have central direction. The decisions taking place within households and families are among the most important made in any society, and yet they are almost entirely decentralized, taking place in millions of individual households.

The powerful role households have played in American economic growth should not be minimized. Neither, however, should we overlook the possible negative influences stemming from this source. Households provide population increases which, if not matched by increases in capital and technology, reduce per capita growth. Negative examples are to be found in India, Bangladesh, China, and elsewhere. If households choose to increase consumption at the expense of savings, this will negatively effect capital formation. If families substantially reduce their investment in education or increase their hours of leisure, economic growth will decline. In such cases, we must ask whether these changes are adverse shifts in household attitudes and desires, or if they are induced by changes taking place in the marketplace, or the result of government action.

Businesses

While households generate economic growth through their supply of savings and a skilled and educated workforce, business firms also play an important role in the growth process. Business controls the process of investment that increases the capital–labor ratio and puts new technology to productive use. If businesses are aggressive and internationally competitive, they foster economic growth. If they are content or spend most of their efforts protecting themselves from competition, they impede growth. Businesses play the central role in the process of research and development that creates new technology. Business innovation is a complex process, not well understood, but certainly vital to a growing economy.

Market Economies and Economic Growth

The primary role that markets play in promoting economic growth is the organization of specialization and exchange. Markets search out all efficient exchange. This exchange, in turn, promotes specialization, which is the basis of most economic growth. As specialization occurs, workers become more productive because they repeat tasks and learn to do them better. Furthermore, specialization leads directly to technological change since the rewards for new technology increase with specialization.

The market has been the primary institution influencing the manner in which resources have been used in the United States. Differences in the relative prices of labor, land, and capital have heavily influenced their changing uses over time. We have mentioned the role of the market in the large and important shifts from agriculture to manufacturing and services. Accompanying this shift have been those from rural to urban America, from home production to market (commercial) production, and the increasing specialization and mechanization of labor. This transformation of America has largely accounted for its impressive record of economic growth and results primarily from the interplay of market incentives and household decisions.

We have discussed at length the efficiency of competitive markets in determining the efficient use of limited resources. Efficiency and economic growth are virtually synonymous. There are, however, several ways in which markets may not contribute positively to growth. Monopoly power limits market efficiency and inhibits the creative drive for new and better products. Negative externalities impose costs upon other industries and use resources in ways that do not maximize the return from them. One of the most serious charges against the market allocation for growth is that consumers, and therefore markets, tend to overvalue present consumption and undervalue future consumption. Their undervaluation of the future leads to the overuse of resources in current production and depletion of resources for future generations. The essence of this argument is that we are using up our exhaustible natural resources—petroleum, coal, and other mineral resources—too rapidly. The blame for this problem, to the extent that it is real, is shared by households and the marketplace, which reflect consumer demand.

Planned Economies and Growth

Planned economies have certain advantages in promoting economic growth. They can control the rate of capital formation more easily and direct the economy's resources toward capital investment at the expense of current consumption if that is desired. For example, the USSR has achieved quite respectable rates of economic growth. However, this economic growth has been achieved by reducing consumption considerably and investing a large portion of output in new capital.

Planned economies can also encourage rapid technological change by compelling units of production to adopt the latest techniques. They may also direct resources toward those sectors of the economy considered to be most important for growth. Planned economies have also demonstrated an ability to trade effectively with market economies by concentrating bargaining power in government agencies.

The weakness of planned economies lies in their inability to structure incentives properly through appropriate prices and wages. Too often, the economic growth of planned economies is frustrated by the misallocation of resources, so that the sacrifice of consumption to produce capital goods does not return as much benefit as it would in an efficient economy.

Government

The U.S. government has also played a positive role in the record of economic growth. Undoubtedly, the single most important contribution of the government to growth has been the provision of a stable political environment operating under the rule of law. Business decisions are made with a careful eye to the future. Those decisions will be dramatically altered for the worse if it is unclear whether or not there will be stability, inflation, and possibly even government confiscation of profits and/or property. The U.S. Constitution and government have provided the type of stable political environment which is supportive of economic growth. The lack of intervention itself has enabled the market and families to do what they do best—efficiently allocate resources.

We have looked at the role government has played to increase competition and reduce monopoly through antitrust legislation; to encourage positive externalities such as education, health, dissemination of information, research, and transportation; and to provide public goods in the absence of markets for defense and security. These contribute positively to growth by increasing the efficiency and, therefore, the income of the economy. Governments, including the U.S., have often provided capital that private business is unable to provide. Capital such as transportation networks, communications, dams, and harbors has been provided by governments at both the federal and state levels. Government has also provided much of the funding for research and development of new technology that is vital to the growth process.

On the other hand, modern governments may actually be an impediment to economic growth. A short time–horizon afflicts most modern governments causing them to emphasize equity and market regulation. Governments often have adverse effects on incentives through a high level of taxation of individual income and business profits. Recall the important role of changes in prices, wages, and profits in determining the use of resources. For more than a century before 1900, federal taxes were no mare than 3 percent of income. Today, taxes take about 30 percent of income reducing the incentives to work, save and invest.

At the same time, federal, state, and local governments, through their expenditures, now determine the use of more than 30 percent of our total resources—instead of the 3 to 7 percent of the nineteenth century. Thus, the question of efficiency in government is far more relevant to the question of aggregate economic growth than it was previously.

U.S. Government and Capital Accumulation. The government currently influences the level of consumer and business savings—and thereby investment—through a number of its policies. The monetary authorities not only determine the money supply (and rate of inflation), but also influence, at least temporarily, the level of interest rates. Easy monetary policies that increase the money supply may benefit some industries through temporarily low interest rates. However, saving is discouraged by such a policy since interest rates are the reward for saving. Consequently, any government policies that affect interest rates will ultimately affect the rate of economic growth. For a number of years, the government restricted the interest that banks could pay to savers. No doubt this policy reduced savings in the U.S. Fortunately, this policy has been changed so that small savers can now receive a market rate of interest on their savings.

The government also affects savings through social security programs and decisions about the government budget. Social security programs yield income to the retired. Since one of the motives for saving is to provide income after age sixty-five, social security programs may reduce the incentive to save. Also, social security contributions are extracted from current taxes rather than private or public savings. Therefore, no capital is created by the social security program. If the social security system did not exist, individuals would save more of their income and invest in the capital market, enhancing the prospects for economic growth.

Evaluating the Twin Deficits

From 1945 to 1980, the United States exported just about as much as it imported. During that period, government expenditures often exceeded tax collections, but the deficits were small relative to the whole budget. The 1980s, however, have seen a major change in these trends. Both the federal budget and the national balance of payments have been flooded in red ink. The financial markets would tense up and shudder each month when the report on the trade deficit was issued. Politicians traded in their foreign cars (Mercedes and BMW for Republicans; Hondas and Toyotas for Democrats) and tried to pretend that they understood the "twin deficits" and their importance.

The budget deficit is pretty simple. The government loves to spend and hates to tax. Consequently, there is usually a "deficit" in the federal budget. For example, in 1986, the federal government took in $769 billion in taxes and spent $990 billion with a deficit of $221 billion. The international trade deficit is a little more complicated because it involves merchandise flows, services that are invisible, and capital flows. Basically, it worked out as follows for 1986. The U.S. exported $373 billion worth of goods and services, mostly agricultural products. We imported $499 billion giving us a deficit in our balance of payments of $126 billion.

The trade deficit has been a blow to the American confidence. Why don't foreigners want our goods? Have we lost our ability to compete? It was no accident that Bruce Springsteen's song "Born in the USA" was extremely popular in the 1980s. Not wanting to bear bad news, most politicians suggest that the blame lay with the Japanese and other countries who had the bad manners to sell us goods we wanted to buy. But why blame anyone? A trade deficit just meant that the U.S. was consuming a lot more than it was producing--what every red-blooded American consumer wants. Actually, the blame for the trade deficit, if there was any blame, belonged closer to home for the large trade deficits were, in part, a result of the large budget deficit.

Perhaps more important are the government deficits that occur almost annually. When the government has a deficit in its budget, caused by government expenditures being larger than revenues, it must borrow funds to cover the amount of the deficit. In doing this the government takes savings away from their potential growth-enhancing use—capital investment. For example, total savings in the U.S. economy were about $680 billion in 1986. About $450 billion of this amount was needed to keep the capital stock constant because of depreciation. This left about $230 billion for new capital, assuming that government did not borrow to finance its expenditures. However, the federal government borrowed about $205 billion in 1986. Fortunately, state and local governments ran a surplus and added about $57 billion dollars to savings. Further, foreign investors contributed about a $190 billion dollars more in funds to the U.S. economy

Budget deficits contribute to trade deficits in at least two ways. First, as the government increases spending, it increases demand generally. Since demand for imports is a part of total demand, the volume of imports also expands. Increased U.S. demand for foreign goods without a proportional increase in foreign demand for our goods results in a trade imbalance.

The second relationship between these deficits is less direct, but more important. To finance a budget deficit, the government has to borrow a lot of money ($221 billion in 1986). When the government steps up to the loan window at the bank and asks for a loan of $221 billion, interest rates in the U.S. go up above the world interest rate. Foreigners attracted by high interest rates trade their currencies for dollars to buy U.S. securities. This increases the value of the dollar relative to other currencies which, in turn, makes U.S. goods expensive compared to foreign goods. As a result, exports decline and imports increase. Eventually the process turns around. The dollar fell in value in 1987 and by 1988 exports were on the rise.

In practice, it is difficult to assess how much impact the budget deficit has had on U.S. trade imbalance. However, there is a definite relationship. C. Fred Bergsten, a treasury official in the Carter Administration, voiced a common sentiment when he asserted that the trade deficit and its negative effects could be eliminated "only by cutting the budget deficit by $150 to $200 billion." Although this will not be easy, it is potentially less harmful than imposing a tariff or allowing large exchange rate fluctuations.

One beneficial effect of the flow of foreign capital to the U.S. has been its impact on U.S. investment. The U.S. invests a smaller fraction of GNP than most countries. Without foreign capital, we would have negligible accumulation and very little economic growth.

than Americans invested in foreign economies. (See the discussion of the twin deficits for an explanation of how foreigners have helped finance our federal budget deficit.) These savings flows combined with the government deficit left the U.S. with an increase in the capital stock of about $220 billion in 1986. While this sum may seem like a lot compared to your monthly allowance as a kid, it does not represent a high rate of investment for an economy as large as that of the U.S. The government, like businesses and individuals, often finds itself in a position where its goals for the immediate future conflict with the long-range goal of economic growth.

Figure 17.1 shows the use of GNP by the U.S. and Japan. Clearly the United States is not investing as much of its income as Japan. Instead, the U.S. is emphasizing private consumption (70 percent of GNP including imports) and public consumption of government services (19 percent of

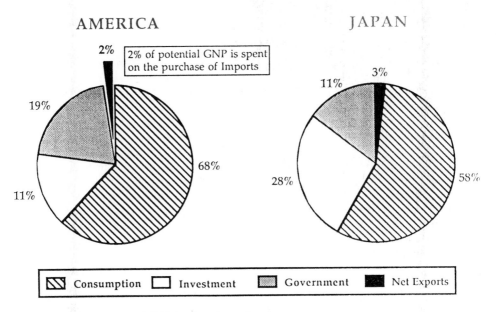

Figure 17.1: Components of GNP for America and Japan

GNP). Japan, on the other hand, consumes relatively little and invests 28 percent of its output. If this pattern continues, the United States can expect slower growth than countries such as Japan that are currently sacrificing higher rates of consumption for investment in their futures.

Is Growth Good?

Economic growth should not be viewed as the only objective of an economy. Remember that growth requires sacrificing of current consumption so that future consumption may be higher. Clearly, there is a limit as to how much the current generation should sacrifice so that future generations will be richer.

Economic growth can also put pressure on the environment. Precious resources may be depleted more quickly by

higher growth unless technological changes economize on those resources. Growth may increase the conflicts over pollution and harm to the environment. Wilderness areas may be threatened by certain kinds of economic growth.

Economic progress can be a painful process. In some ways, growth spawned by technological change is a process of "creative destruction." Old industries are destroyed as new ones are brought into existence. The development and mass production of the automobile brought significant growth to the U.S. economy, but it also brought economic woe to countless livery stables, carriage makers, leather harness makers, farmers growing alfalfa and barley, and horse breeders. Growth can be painful. Currently, there is concern that the industries such as autos and steel that dominate the Northeast and Midwest are

Table 17.2 Real GNP Per Capita

Country	Year 1970	Year 1980	Year 1986
United States	$11,187	$16,009	$17,417
Canada	10,030	12,549	13,686
West Germany	11,116	13,309	14,769
Japan	6,961	13,786	16,416
France	8,639	12,188	12,822
Soviet Union	5,295	7,682	8,190
Sweden	13,572	13,813	15,274
Switzerland	14,292	20,628	21,876
United Kingdom	5,873	8,752	9,781

Source: *Statistical Abstract.*
Note: International comparisons are sensitive to exchange rates.

in decline, causing stress in these politically powerful states. The issue involves a decision about growth. It is possible that a decision to help these states reduces the rate of economic growth in the U.S. as a whole. These kinds of painful decisions are as old as the phenomenon of sustained economic growth. (See the insert on the Luddites.)

The Future

The bottom line is a very impressive record of performance by the American economy in the past. In addition to the 24–fold increase in per-capita income—a doubling of purchasing power every generation—life expectancy at birth has increased from about thirty-five years at the time of the Revolution to seventy-five years today. The larger per capita GNP of today is produced with considerably less labor than the smaller GNP of our ancestors. It is estimated that the average work week was nearly seventy hours in 1840, sixty hours

in 1890 (six ten-hour days per week) and only thirty-five hours today, an increase in our leisure time of over twenty hours each week.

Clouding our pride in the past is concern for the future. Are we, as a nation, pursuing policies and undergoing a transition that will make this country less prosperous compared to other nations? And what might be the economic, social, and political consequences of such a decline in America's economic status around the world?

While the United States enjoyed the highest standard of living of any country in the world from around the late nineteenth century until the 1970s, it now appears that other countries are surpassing the United States. Table 17.2 shows real GNP per capita for selected countries. While a number of countries have higher real GNP per capita than the United States, Americans still seem to enjoy a larger supply of consumer durables such as housing, automobiles, and refrigerators. Though it may not be clear whether other

There's a Little Luddite in All of Us

In 1972, a Redding, California, man was enjoying a San Francisco Giants-Houston Astros baseball game, with the Giants enjoying a six-run lead. When the Giants blew the lead and lost the game, however, the man took out his frustrations. He planted eight bullets right into the TV screen. The repairman said it couldn't be fixed.

The urge to destroy machines is not unique to Giants' fans. Many fans of the Chicago Cubs have felt similar urges, not to mention just about anyone who has worked with modern technology. How many of us have been tempted to pound our computer keyboard or kick our dishwasher? Yet no act of violence toward machines quite matches the activities of the Luddites, a group of nineteenth-century British textile workers who responded to the fear of losing their jobs by destroying their employers' machines. The Luddites were not acting out of stupidity or misinformation. From their perspective, economic growth was a curse, not a blessing, and machines were causing them to lose their jobs.

Historians do not agree on the origin of the name "Luddite." What is clear is that the group wrote letters to employers telling them that their machines would be destroyed and signed them "King Ludd of Sherwood Forest," or "Ned Ludd." At first, the group went to the British Parliament to seek relief from unemployment. The advent of better and faster machinery was causing many textile workers to be laid off. When Parliament did not respond, a group of hosiery workers, who had machines in their cottages, destroyed them. The group was directed by leaders who were always masked and never identified, and public opinion was on their side. Such acts of machine wrecking continued until 1816.

The movement gained some following in continental Europe. French workers tossed their wooden shoes (known as sabots) into machines so they would break down (hence the word "sabotage"). However, since most factories outside the textile industry were heavily guarded, the Luddites were unable to spread their influence. By 1816, the British government had sent twelve thousand soldiers to guard the textile facilities, and many Luddite leaders had been hanged. The movement had been aborted.

countries have passed the United States in overall standard of living, it is clear there is a serious question about the economic future of the United States. One suspects that economic growth will become a more dominant political issue as the twentieth century ends.

Economic growth does not have the same political impact that inflation and recession have. It is by nature a slow process, more difficult to make into a serious political issue. But its effects upon our lives are perhaps even greater in the long run than either recession or inflation.

As the industrial revolution ends and the technological revolution accelerates, the memory of the Luddites becomes more poignant, and the prospect of a sort of revival becomes a possibility. The emergence of robots threatens to replace many factory workers, and acts of violence by American workers against Oriental and Latino immigrants who are willing to work for low wages are documented. The lesson to be learned from the Luddites and from contemporary accounts of violence against low-paid immigrants is quite clear. Changes in economic distribution can cause violence, and economic growth causes changes in the economic distribution. While British society as a whole benefited from the advent of machinery, the textile workers suffered. The distribution of wealth was changing. Likewise, the employment of low-paid immigrants benefits society as a whole since it reduces the costs of production and consumer goods are less expensive. But, whenever there is growth there is change, and violence can be expected.

Antagonism toward economic growth may be expressed by many groups within society. Economic growth requires the proper utilization of natural resources, so environmental groups protest. Such protests are a result of a rational self-interest. The Sierra Club is primarily composed of well-to-do white-collar workers who like to escape to the mountains for a weekend of backpacking. They have a vested interest in the status quo and resist change. On the other hand, unemployed workers are less adamant in opposing the use of natural resources. For example, the United Mine Workers of America actively support the construction of a coal-slurry pipeline across the western United States. The pipeline would decrease the cost of coal and make coal a more viable economic alternative. The jobs of coalminers would be more secure. However, the pipeline is opposed by environmental groups since it would "scar" lands which have been heretofore untouched by development. Once again, the message is clear. Economic growth rarely benefits everyone, since it changes the distribution of rewards.

Figure 17.2 shows the effects of differing growth rates on the level of income through time. These should be viewed as differences in real purchasing power rather than inflation. Just like airplanes starting from the same point on slightly different courses, the differences in incomes widen and widen. If the median family income in the U.S. of about $27,000 in 1985 were to grow at an unrealistically high rate of 4 percent, median family income would be nearly $200,000 after 50 years of growth in the year 2035; $121,000 with 3 percent growth, just over $73,000 with 2 percent

THE EFFECT OF ECONOMIC GROWTH
ON MEDIAN INCOME

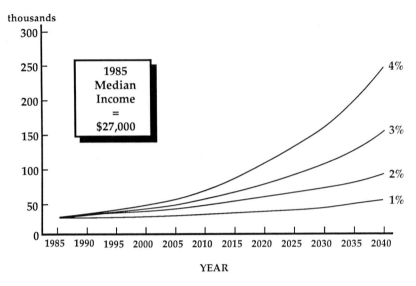

Figure 17.2: The Effect of Economic Growth on Median Income

growth and only $44,500 with 1 percent growth. Changes in economic policies that could lead to changes in long–term growth matter profoundly and should be considered very seriously. Unfortunately, short–term expediencies generally triumph over long–term considerations.

We can see that economic growth matters dramatically over the long sweep of economic history. High rates of economic growth expand the options available to an economy or society in a significant manner. The problems such as crime, pollution, poverty, and discrimination, that concern us so much today, can be dealt with much more effectively if the U.S. economy experiences rapid growth. It seems clear that one of the most important policy issues facing each of us and our elected representatives is the pace of this growth. Ironically, little attention is paid to this crucial issue.

18
Which Economic System?

Adam Smith and Karl Marx: two different views of economic systems. (Library of Congress)

Meeting of the Minds

Imagine that Adam Smith, Karl Marx, and John Maynard Keynes have been summoned by President Thomas More, president of Utopia, a newly formed country. More's central concern is choosing an economic system, and he is unsure as to which system is best. He has summoned the best minds of the ages to help him make this crucial decision.

MORE: Karl and John, I am delighted to meet you. Thank you for coming. I am sure that it has been an inconvenience, but I desperately need your help. I am expecting Adam Smith momentarily. I have sent someone to find him. I understand that he is a bit absent-minded and once fell into a tanning vat while walking.

(More's daughter Sarah leads Adam Smith into the room.)

SMITH: Ah, I found you. So sorry to be late. I got to thinking about the slave trade between West Africa and the Americas and its effect on the price of British cloth and lost track of both time and place. Now, Thomas, why have you called us here? We are all busy, you know.

MORE: I need your advice. We are a new country with no constitution or traditions to guide us. Our goals are freedom and justice. Of course, we would not mind being prosperous as well. We have definite ideas about government. We certainly want to have the rule of law and are very impressed with separation of powers when combined with checks and balances. James Madison was here a fortnight ago. He was a tremendous help, and his wife Dolly was most charming. We have invited them back for the grape festival in the fall.

But I must tell you. This economic business is most puzzling. I cannot make any sense out of it. Economists talk in such abstract terms and use the worst jargon imaginable. John, you are the worst offender with terms like "marginal propensity to consume" and "liquidity preference."

KEYNES: Thomas, sometimes you have to use new language to be precise and rigorous.

MORE: But the language! I would almost prefer talking to sociologists. At any rate, I have invited the three of you here to help me solve our basic economic problem. What kind of economic system should we have here in Utopia? Adam, I read your book, *The Wealth of Nations*, with great interest. You make a compelling case.

SMITH: Thank you, Mr. President.

MORE: Call me Thomas. Do you really think that a *laissez-faire* system will work for us?

SMITH: I did not use that particular term. But I do believe that a system of markets is consistent with natural law. There is a beauty in the way that the instruments of production are guided to their best use in a market system. How did I put it? Here it is.

> The rich only select from the heap what is most precious and agreeable. They
> consume little more than the poor; and in spite of their natural selfishness
> and rapacity, though they mean only their own conveniency, though the sole

end which they propose from the labours of all the thousands whom they employ be the gratification of their own vain and insatiable desires, they divide with the poor the produce of all their improvements. They are led by an invisible hand to make nearly the same distribution of the necessaries of life which would have been made had the earth been divided into equal portions among all of its inhabitants; and thus, without intending it, without knowing it, advance the interest of the society, and afford means to the multiplication of the species. When providence divided the earth among a few lordly masters, it neither forgot nor abandoned those who seemed to have been left out in the partition. These last, too, enjoy their share of all that it produces. In what constitutes the real happiness of human life, they are in no respect inferior to those who would seem so much above them. In ease of body and peace of mind, all the different ranks of life are nearly upon a level, and the beggar, who suns himself by the side of the highway, possesses that security which kings are fighting for.

MARX: What utter nonsense! Adam, I sat for years in the British Museum reading your work. I thought you were intelligent. Don't you understand that the market system exploits workers, ripping bread from the mouths of children to satisfy capitalist greed? Have you no sense of compassion for the masses? How can you defend a system that is so inequitable? Of course, you did not have the benefit of my work. No doubt you would change your mind if you read *Capital*.

KEYNES: My dear Karl, no one has read *Capital* all the way through.

MARX: John, you spent too much time with that artsy Bloomsbury set and not enough time with real people.

KEYNES: Now see here, Karl!

MORE: Calm yourselves, gentlemen. I take it that there is some disagreement on what we should do here in Utopia.

MARX: The solution is clear, Thomas. I spelled it all out in *Capital*. There are progressive stages in the economic development of any society. Feudalism was the first stage, but Utopia went through that stage two hundred years ago. For the past two hundred years, capitalism has dominated the scene. Now it is time for socialism, which will lead gradually to full communism where true utopian dreams are realized. If you choose socialism now, the future will revere you as a great leader of vision. If you choose capitalism, you will be labeled as a reactionary puppet of the bourgeoisie.

KEYNES: Karl, some of your analysis was interesting and provocative, but your language is so extreme. Your argument really isn't convincing; but then, neither is Adam's. The truth is that the "invisible hand" has a touch of arthritis, especially when it comes to the problem of unemployment. On the other hand, a total rejection of markets and capitalism is much too extreme. You know, Karl, the actual examples of socialism, like Russia and China, have been disappointing.

MARX: (impatiently) I know. I know. Those Soviet planners have given me a bad name. I wish I could be associated with some other country, like Sweden or France.

MORE: This is wonderful! I invite the three greatest economists of history here to settle a basic economic question, and I receive three answers. I'm glad I did not invite any others. Let's get back to basics. Here in Utopia we want to achieve three basic goals. We want to be free. We also want to be prosperous so that we can enjoy the good things of life. Therefore, we want our economy to be as efficient as possible with a high rate of economic growth. Finally, we want justice, including economic justice. Now, which of the alternatives will achieve our goals?

MARX: My friend, you want a socialist economy. Socialism will achieve the economic justice that you desire. Under socialism, there are no capitalists to exploit the workers. All production will belong to the workers. With socialism, everyone will be employed; capitalism leaves part of the masses unemployed. I predicted that the ranks of the unemployed would get larger and larger. In fact, this army of the unemployed instigates the revolution.

KEYNES: Of course, your prediction did not come true, Karl. Unemployment is a serious problem in capitalist economies, but I am not sure that the problem is getting any worse. Anyway, I explained how government could control unemployment in *The General Theory*.

MARX: (laughing) If government can control unemployment, why is it still a problem?

SMITH: I think we are getting confused here. Thomas, you have three goals, correct?

MORE: Yes, and we want to meet all three goals.

SMITH: What happens if one alternative works better in meeting one goal and another is better at fulfilling the other goals? What will you do in that case?

MARX: This will not happen, because socialism will be superior in every regard.

SMITH: But if it does happen?

MORE: I do not know. Look, this is very frustrating. I was hoping that you would give me a clear answer. I much prefer talking with Jimmy Madison about political affairs.

KEYNES: You know, Thomas, you don't have to choose one alternative—capitalism or socialism. You can mix the two. You could use markets when they work well and substitute government planning for markets that do not work as well. Then you could meet all three goals. It's really rather simple.

SMITH: I doubt that it is that simple. Men pursue their self-interest regardless of their employer. The fact that a man is employed by government does not exempt him from his own self-interested passions. By the way, Karl, capitalists are also capable of public virtue and acts of sympathy. Did you read my *Theory of Moral Sentiments*?

MARX: I didn't like it as much as your other works.

MORE: Let me state my impressions so far. Adam, you say that we should rely on markets to organize our economy because markets effectively control self-interest. You claim that markets are efficient. You, Karl, on the other hand, claim that capitalism will produce increasing unemployment and that capitalism is unfair. You paint a glowing picture of socialism in which government planners make the decisions that markets make under capitalism. Now, John, you seem to believe that both Adam and Karl claim too much for their respective systems. You believe that actual socialism is considerably different from the idealized socialism that Karl described and, similarly, that capitalism does not always work the way Adam describes it. John, you advocate a mixed economy with elements of capitalism and socialism. But I am confused about how one knows when to use markets and when to use planning. You seem to have too much confidence in the ability of political leaders to make these critical decisions. Gentlemen, you all seem to be a little too impractical for Utopia. We need a system that works.

SMITH: Markets have shown that they work.

MARX: Markets work fine if you are rich. They suck the lifeblood from the poor. Adam and John are both bourgeois puppets with little sympathy for oppressed workers. Socialism is the only sensible answer. I can't understand why you cannot all see that.

KEYNES: Karl, you never learned any manners, did you? I will wager that no one in England invited you to tea. I'm beginning to doubt your intelligence. Of course the English are the only ones who really understand economics.

MORE: I think I will resign.

Introduction

The choice of an economic system is the most important economic decision any society makes. This choice not only affects the path of economic growth and prosperity, it also weighs very heavily on other aspects of society such as political freedom, cultural development, the arts, and even religion. Consequently, this economic decision requires careful consideration and debate within any society.

Decisions about economic systems are rarely made self-consciously. They are usually made on a case-by-case basis with political pressures dominating any regard for first principles. But every society, political body, or government official brings a set of prior beliefs about economic systems to the choice-making process. Some will come convinced that markets almost never work and that government planning is the answer. Others believe that free

markets are the answer to all economic issues. Still others bring a mixed view, believing that markets work sometimes, but that government must often redress the problems created by market imperfections. Inertia and history dominate most decision making. Markets are likely to be used where they have been used in the past, just as government planning is likely to be used where it has served in the past. But when a new problem presents itself, prior belief or ideology is bound to be important.

John Maynard Keynes once said,

The ideas of economists and political philosophers, both when they are right and when they are wrong, are more powerful than is commonly understood. Indeed, the world is ruled by little else. Practical men, who believe themselves to be quite exempt from any intellectual influences, are usually the slaves of some defunct economist. Madmen in authority, who hear voices in the air, are distilling their frenzy from some academic scribbler of a few years back.

This statement is especially appropriate to describe decisions about economic systems. The voices of both Adam Smith and Karl Marx are clearly heard across the centuries. In fact, the present political division between East and West, with its threat of nuclear destruction, is largely based on fundamental differences in economic ideologies. If this choice is so volatile that it may help to destroy the world, we had better be clear about the issues and the options before us.

The Constitution and Economic Systems

What does the U.S. Constitution say about economic systems? Very little. The Constitution tells us a great deal about political structure and process. It defines certain rights. But it says almost nothing about the choice of an economic system. What it does say about economic matters is so vague and ambiguous that the courts have been able to arbitrarily interpret the economic clauses to suit the pressures of the day. It is fair to say that the Constitution places almost no restrictions on government where economic matters are concerned.

Preamble

The preamble of the Constitution spells out the intent of the Constitution. That intent has little to do with economic issues. Uppermost in the minds of the Framers were a better union of the states, justice, tranquility, common defense, general welfare, and liberty. We may construe only two of these objectives as economic. "Justice" might have included economic justice, but it is doubtful. It is more likely that the Founders were concerned with political justice and due process of law, for they did

not design any mechanisms to deal with economic justice in the body of the Constitution. The phrase "promote the general welfare" probably did have an economic connotation. Here the words "general welfare" denote government activities for the good of all, rather than subsidies to particular deserving individuals. The Founders' view of liberty could also have included support for private property and free exchange.

Revenue Powers

Most of what the Constitution does say about economic matters is contained in Article I, Sections 7 and 8. Here the revenue powers of the federal government are defined. All tax bills are to originate in the House of Representatives. All taxes are to be uniform throughout the country. This means that states or citizens of particular states cannot be punished by punitive federal taxes. Taxes were not to be directly imposed upon citizens. For this reason, an income tax passed to finance the Civil War was found to be unconstitutional. The income tax was made constitutional by the Sixteenth Amendment, ratified in 1913.

Interstate Commerce Clause

Most of the economic regulatory power of government is based on one important, yet vague, clause in the Constitution. Article I, Section 8 reads: "The Congress shall have Power. . . . To regulate Commerce with foreign Nations, and among the several States, and with the Indian Tribes." This clause, known as the interstate commerce clause, is the basis for most government intervention in the economy, since any powers not enumerated in the Constitution were reserved for the states and the people. If this clause did not give the federal government authority over economic matters, then it had no authority. Consequently, there has been endless litigation over the meaning of this clause. The words "regulate" and "commerce" have been interpreted and reinterpreted to meet the perceived needs of society for the past two hundred years. Today, the interpretation is broad enough that the federal government is nearly free to regulate the economy as it wishes.

Specific Powers

Section 8 of Article I does give the government certain specific economic powers. Congress may coin money and regulate its value. While the government is very skillful at coining or creating money, it is still learning how to control its value, so this clause may have been a bit premature. Congress was also given the power to impose a uniform set of weights and measures—very useful to promote trade. It was given the power to establish post offices and post roads and promote creative and technological progress through patents and copyrights. These powers constitute the important specific powers given to the government on economic matters. Obviously, they are very limited and reflect the economic realities in the 1780s, rather than some grand design for absolute management of the economy.

Freedom of Trade

Taxes or duties on exports from the U.S. were prohibited, but duties on imports were allowed. This particular combination illustrates the lack of economic sophistication of the Framers. An import duty or an export duty is actually a tax on trade. In practice, it does not matter whether the tax

is on imports or exports; the effect is exactly the same. Southerners realized this before the Civil War, arguing that tariffs on imported manufactures were the equivalent of a tax on the cotton that they exported from the South to England.

One of the more important clauses in the Constitution prohibits states from imposing special taxes on goods crossing state lines (Article I, section 10). Before the Constitution was ratified, states were engaged in small trade wars with one another. Taxes were being imposed on goods coming from other states in order to encourage local industry. The Constitution prohibited these tariffs and turned the United States into a free trade area within its boundaries. Thus, California may inspect fruit or vegetables entering the state to prevent disease, but it may not levy a tax on Florida oranges. The courts have jealously guarded this clause and kept states from imposing significant restraints on free trade among the states. This clause is probably the most beneficial economic clause in the Constitution since it guarantees the unimpeded flow of exchange among the states.

Bill of Rights and Amendments

There is only one clause in the Bill of Rights that deals with economic issues. The Fifth Amendment provides some protection for property. "No person shall . . . be deprived of life, liberty, or property, without due process of law; nor shall private property be taken for public use, without just compensation." The Founders believed strongly in private property and expected it to be secure. A strict interpretation of the Fifth Amendment would make it difficult to nationalize capital in order to move the U.S. closer to a planned economy.

The Thirteenth Amendment outlaws slavery and involuntary servitude. Modern students do not usually consider slavery an economic matter, but Southern planters did. Slaves were valuable property, accounting for perhaps one-third of the income of white Southerners. The definition of most property rights other than slavery was implicit in the powers of the courts. This definition of property rights, one of the most important governmental powers, is spread throughout the court system with no particular court having jurisdiction. Of course, judicial review gives the Supreme Court ultimate power over property rights. The Thirteenth Amendment is the only case where property rights are specifically defined by the Constitution.

The Eighteenth Amendment was an attempt to restrict the exchange process by prohibiting exchange of alcoholic beverages. By experience, it was soon learned that the Constitution was not a particularly effective device to deal with unsavory exchange. Black markets for liquor were commonplace. A majority of citizens turned into potential criminals, and the experiment failed in spite of laudable motives. The Eighteenth Amendment was repealed by the Twenty-first Amendment.

Why is the Constitution Silent on Economic Systems?

Certainly, the Constitution gives no economic blueprint to future generations. The Founders did not possess uniform views on economic issues. Their divisions became apparent as soon as Washington's administration began its work. Alexander Hamilton was essentially a mercantilist. He proposed an elaborate system of tariffs and subsidies to encourage manufacturing and the commercialization of the economy. He advocated a national bank to exercise some control over financial matters. Thomas Jefferson, who soon became Hamilton's antagonist within Washington's cabinet, opposed the encouragement of manufacturing and advocated free trade. Any specific economic guidelines in the Constitution would have elicited the opposition of the very factions the Constitution was designed to control. No doubt the Founders thought it wiser to leave economic affairs to senators, representatives, and presidents.

There is within the Constitution implicit support for a market economic system. The Founders believed in private property, the foundation of a market economy. They accepted free exchange with a few limitations, largely on foreign trade. They were most fearful of government intrusion into the lives of citizens. There is no reason to believe that they would have welcomed the extensive role of government in a planned economy. Indeed, some of the Founders such as George Washington had probably been brought to the revolutionary cause by English involvement in the colonies' economic affairs through the Navigation Acts and other mercantilist measures. The Founders were not presented with a clear choice between the two basic alternative systems. Had they been, it is reasonable to beleive that they would have chosen a market form of organization even though they did not embody any strong wording on this matter in the Constitution.

The real debate over economic systems had not been engaged at the time of the founding. Karl Marx and Frederich Engels issued the *Communist Manifesto* in 1849, sixty-two years after ratification of the Constitution. Robert Owen and utopian socialists did not arrive on the scene until the nineteenth century. If the Constitution had been debated and written fifty years later, it might have had much more to say about economic matters. As it is, the question of which economic system is left open for each generation. Presumably, these decisions about the economic system will be more informed decisions if we know how well each of the alternatives—markets and planned economies—attains the basic goals of efficiency, equity, and freedom.

Goals and Economic Systems

The general performances of market and planned economies may be compared by judging how well each economic system meets the three basic objectives of efficiency, equity, and freedom. In principle, each type of system could meet each objective perfectly. Market economies could be fully efficient if the right conditions existed so that none of the weaknesses or failures discussed in chapter thirteen were relevant. Economies planned by omniscient planners would also be efficient. There is a tendency for advocates of each system to describe it in ideal terms. That is not the purpose here. Rather, our intent is to compare *actual* planned economies to *actual* market economies in order to judge which alternative does best in terms of each goal. We will concentrate on the U.S. and the USSR, the two superpowers who typify the two alternatives.

Two problems must be kept in mind. The observation and measurement of any economy is imprecise. This means that judgments about that economy are never completely accurate. Therefore, some of the criticism or praise of the two alternatives may be in error. While some economies will be classified as planned (e.g., the Soviet Union's and East Germany's) and others as market economies (e.g., those of the U.S., Japan, and the U.K.), there are no pure examples of either type. The economy of the Soviet Union has a market element just as that of the U.K. has considerable planning. This imprecision in classification means that some of the blame or praise given may be misplaced. Perhaps part of the praise given to Soviet planning may be due instead to their reliance on some market mechanisms, or the signals and information they receive from market economies. Similarly, praise of market economies may actually result from the judicious use of government planning in those economies. In spite of these problems, some judgment of the alternative economic systems is necessary because the decisions about economic systems will not wait until everything is known about the alternatives.

Efficiency

Which system is most efficient? Neither system comes close to full economic efficiency, so the choice is between two rather flawed alternatives. The definition of efficiency is crucial to the judgment. The democratic tradition of the West implies a certain kind of efficiency—efficiency based on individual preferences and desires. In other words, the efficiency of an economy is based on how well it meets the preferences of individuals. Is the economy doing the best it can for individuals in the sense that no one in the economy can be helped without taking some goods and services away from others? This notion of efficiency is clearly individualistic, presuming the government or the state to be the servant of individuals, not superior to them. To some degree, countries within the Soviet bloc may not accept this individualistic notion of efficiency. Instead they may prefer a collective definition which bases efficiency on how well the economy meets the goals of the state. In this discussion, we will assume the individualistic idea of efficiency and judge the economies on this basis.

Consumer Sovereignty. One of the hallmarks of market economies is the distribution of power. Most power in a market economy is in the hands of consumers. No single consumer has any power over price, quality, the spectrum of goods produced, or the level of service in the economy. But as a group, consumers determine the goods and services produced, the quality of those products, and the way the economy responds to their demands. In a planned economy, most of the power tends to be in the hands of producers rather than consumers. This power of consumers in a market economy is referred to as *consumer sovereignty,* indicating consumers are economically sovereign, just as the people are ultimately sovereign politically in a democracy.

Perhaps the power of consumers is best illustrated by the difference in personal treatment when shopping for an item of clothing, such as a suit, versus a government transaction, such as securing a license plate. In both instances money changes hands, but the general treatment and atmosphere is different in each case. If a person goes to a department or clothing store to purchase a suit of clothes, the experience is normally comfortable and reassuring. There are no lines for purchase and the clerk is usually helpful, hoping for a sale. The merchandise is attractively displayed in a variety of styles, colors, and sizes. The purchase can be made quickly with minimum effort. If the garment has a flaw that is discovered after purchase, an exchange or refund is normally made without difficulty.

Contrast this process with that of getting license plates from the local government office. Lines are common. The staff may or may not be helpful, depending on their mood. There will undoubtedly be forms to fill out. The license plate comes in one size and one color. Imagine the response if you request a salmon-colored license plate to match your car. No one fit to drive a car would think it wise to return a defective license plate. One simply makes do with that unhappy circumstance. In short, when buying a suit, you have power; when buying a license plate, you do not. Markets give consumers power, while planned economies normally favor producers.

The lot of consumers in the Soviet Union is difficult for Westerners to absorb or comprehend. Journalists' stories seem unbelievable, almost absurd. Most people in the Soviet Union leave for work carrying an "avoska"—a mesh bag used to bring home the day's catch from shopping. Shopping is a bit like foraging in more primitive societies. Carrying large amounts of cash is a necessity. Everyone must be ready to purchase, for one never knows when a particular good buy may be available. Availability is more important than price. Queuing, or lining up, for good merchandise is so common for consumers that lines have a magnetic quality in the Soviet Union. One's first impulse is to join a line, since it must mean that something extraordinary is for sale.

Most ordinary purchases are made through a process of three lines. First, people line up to look at the merchandise, learn prices, and make a selection. Second,

Soviet collective farms: Unable to feed the Soviet people. (Library of Congress)

a queue forms in a separate part of the store to pay for goods and obtain the receipt. Finally, there is a line elsewhere to present the receipt and receive merchandise. Long waiting lists may exist for durables such as autos (still quite scarce), washers, or refrigerators.

The quality of goods is varied. The word "brak" is commonly used to describe goods that are junk or fall apart. Imports from the West have the highest value, with blue jeans the leading symbol of our standard of living. Goods from Poland, East Germany, and Czechoslovakia are prized above Russian production. The fact that Russians purchase unexpected good buys for kin and friends, knowing the sizes and desired colors of all, tells us a great deal about the position of consumers in their society. Foreigners and the elite shop at special stores carrying higher quality goods as well as Western merchandise.

A market system of economic organization appears to be superior to planning as a method of meeting consumers' desires. The profit motive puts power into the hands of consumers because businesses cater to consumer tastes and anticipate buyers' moods and wishes. Most planned economies seem to have difficulty translating consumer preferences into goods and services. No doubt planned economies are improving their production of consumer goods. Yet the gap between planned and market economies in this regard is not narrowing. In fact, as economies become more service oriented, planned economies may have even more difficulties since service workers have little incentive to respond to consumers.

Allocation of Resources

Which system is most efficient at allocating resources? Advocates of a market economy cannot point with pride to performance of capitalist economies under the stress of the oil embargo in 1973. Socialists must have some doubts about their ideal when Soviet Agricultural production has often been so low that staples are often imported, and the consumption of meat, vegetables (other

Russian Economic Humor

Humor often tells us a great deal about reality. The Russian sense of humor conveys some of the frustration that ordinary people feel concerning the economic system and the government. Here are a few examples taken from *Paris Match*, David K. Shipler's *Russia*, and Hedrick Smith's *The Russians*.

The System: Capitalism, Socialism, and Communism are having a conversation. Socialism leaves to do an errand and does not return for three hours. Capitalism asks, "What took so long?" Socialism replies, "I had to buy some kolbasa (sausage like salami) and there was a line." "What's a line?" asks Capitalism. "What's kolbasa?" asks Communism.

A young Soviet sociologist is sent abroad to study capitalist methods of production. Upon his return, a colleague asks, "So! Did you go all over?"
"Yes; I went to Rome, Paris, London, and New York."
"And what did you see there?"
"I saw the decline of capitalism."
"And what did you think?"
"That it's a beautiful way to go."

Queues to Purchase Goods: Two friends meet in a Moscow cafe.
"Ivan, you should hurry. They are distributing potatoes."
"Where?"
"In Minsk."
"How can I get some?"
"Easy. Take the train to Smolensk."
"Why Smolensk?"
"Because that's where the queue ends."

Poem of Andrei Voznesensky
    I am 41st for Plisetskaya,
    33rd for the theatre at Tagonka,
    45th for the graveyard at Vagankovo.
    I am 14th for the eye specialist
    21st for Glazunov, the artist,
    45th for an abortion
    (When my turn comes, I'll be in shape),
    I am 103rd for auto parts
    (They signed me up when I was born),
    I am 10,007th for a new car
    (They signed me up when I was born).

Planning: "What's the difference between a fairy tale and a Soviet economy plan?"

"A fairy tale begins with 'Once upon a time . . .' while a Soviet plan begins with 'There will be a time. . . .'"

Propaganda: A man goes to a clinic, looking for an eye-and-ear doctor. "We don't have an eye-and-ear doctor," said the receptionist, "only an eye doctor and an ear-nose-and-throat doctor."

"I need an eye-and-ear doctor," the man insisted. "I keep hearing one thing and seeing another."

"Winter came and went; then came summer. Thank you, Lenin, for all that."

Stealing and Corruption: "If you want a two-hump camel, you must order a three-hump camel. The system will shave off the extra hump."

"I think," says Ivan to Volodya, "that we have the richest country in the world."
"Why?" asks Volodya.
"Because for nearly sixty years everyone has been stealing from the state and still there is something left to steal."

(Satirical letter published in a Soviet magazine)
Dear customer, In the leather-goods department of our store, a shipment of five hundred *imported* women's purses has been received. Four hundred and fifty of them have been bought by employees of the store. Forty-nine are under the counter and have been ordered in advance for friends. One purse is in the display window. We invite you to visit the leather department to buy this purse."

A worker leaves a factory pushing a wheelbarrow containing a huge sack. A guard says, "Tell me, what's in the sack?"
"Sawdust. My foreman says I may take some home whenever I wish."
"Let's see!" The worker empties the sack. It is indeed sawdust.
The next day the same thing happens, and so on.
On the night before the guard is to retire, he says confidentially to the worker, "Listen, tomorrow I'll be gone. Now you can tell me the truth. I'm curious to know what you were stealing."
"Wheelbarrows."

Shortages: Two writers meet. "I've just written a new book," says the first.
"Good. What about?"
"A young man meets a young woman."
"Ah! A novel."
"They're in love."
"Ah! A love story."
"They marry and find an apartment."
"Oh! A fairy tale!"

than potatoes), fruit, milk, and eggs is usually well below the stated norms of the Soviet Union. Since both systems are less than perfect, the issue of efficiency is a relative one.

The case for the superior efficiency of planning can be summed up in one phrase—full employment. Planners can quite easily insure full employment of labor, capital, and other resources. Therefore, the inefficiency of unemployment that plagues market economies is absent from most planned systems. Unfortunately, full employment does not mean efficient employment, since resources may be misdirected in the economy. As noted earlier, planning requires incredible amounts of information and, ironically, a planned system does not produce the same useful information that a market system produces. Market prices embody information about costs, preferences, even the future. Most of this information is much harder to glean in a fully planned economy.

Market economies seem to allocate resources more efficiently than planned economies, except in times of recession, when there is widespread unemployment. Market economies require little centralized information. The information embodied in prices, profits, and costs is used efficiently in a market economy as signals for households and businesses who make the everyday economic decisions. Coordination in a market economy is accomplished through prices and profits, which keep the coordination inexpensive. Indeed, the costs of coordination within a market economy appear to be a small fraction of such costs in most planned economies.

The glaring inefficiency of market economies is unemployment. If 10 percent of resources are idle, then the economy is clearly inefficient, even if the employed

resources are allocated perfectly. If market economies were able to solve the recession problem with the aid of government, they would clearly be more efficient than planned systems. As long as the business cycle remains a serious problem, a nagging doubt about the relative efficiency of markets remains. Still, most economists who study the differences between the two economic systems have concluded that market economies are more efficient at allocating resources than planned economies.

Incentives

Resources in an economy may be efficiently placed and, yet, there will still be inefficiency because of poor incentives. Market economies seem to be superior at structuring incentives. Owners of businesses have a claim on profits—whatever is left over after all costs have been paid. This claim on the profits is a powerful incentive to manage the firm efficiently. Most important managers in corporations have some claim on profits so that they also have compelling incentives to do their jobs well. Stockholders can sell or buy stocks depending on their judgment of management's performance, adding another incentive to the market system. Possible dismissal from the job is a powerful incentive for workers.

Most of these incentives are missing in a planned economy. Workers are unlikely to be fired from their jobs. Managers have some incentive to perform well, but their motivation is more that of a government bureaucrat than a corporate manager. Consequently, planners struggle to improve incentives in their economy. Government gives plants or production units quotas, and workers and managers receive extra compensation if the quotas are filled. Of course, defining quotas is difficult. The story is told of the window-glass industry in the USSR. The quota was first given in terms of tons of glass, so the production units made glass so thick that residents could not see out of the windows of their apartments. Next the quota was given in terms of square meters of glass produced. In this case, the production units made glass so thin that it broke upon installation. Quotas are not a satisfactory replacement for profits as incentives.

The incentive problem within a planned economy is aptly illustrated by the Soviet experience with private plots owned by peasant farmers. These private plots are a small fraction of agricultural land—less than 1 percent. However, the farmer is able to keep all production from the private plot for his own use or sale. Therefore, the private plots are worked very hard and account for an estimated 27 percent of total Soviet agricultural output. Incentives matter.

Growth. In spite of the many consumer problems in planned economies, growth rates have been reasonably high. Soviet growth is difficult to measure because of secrecy and data scarcity. Therefore, any comparisons of U.S. and Soviet growth are subject to wide degrees of error. But for the past thirty years, Soviet growth appears to have been above U.S. growth—a 4.9 percent annual rate of growth of GNP for the USSR compared to 3.5 percent for the U.S. Growth rates in earlier periods were even more impressive—5.4 percent from 1928 to 1940, 5.7 percent for the 1950s. The growth of only two market economies—Japan and West Germany—has been more impressive than the Soviet Union's growth in the postwar period. However, there appears to be a systematic decline in the rate of Soviet

growth—5.7 percent in the 1950s, 5.1 percent in the 1960s, 3.1 percent in the 1970s, and 2.0 percent in the 1980s. It is a trend that concerns Soviet officials. In 1958, Soviet leader Nikita Khrushchev, confident of the future growth of the Soviet Union, boasted that the USSR would bury the U.S. economically. That boast now seems hollow, since Soviet GNP per capita is still less than half that of the U.S.

Consumers have paid a heavy price for the growth achieved by the USSR. Productivity has grown faster in almost all developed market economies than in the Soviet Union. Thus, the Soviet Union has achieved its growth by denying consumer goods to its population and investing heavily in capital. Soviet planners allocate about one-third of Soviet output to capital investment. Japan, the only other industrialized country to invest at such a high rate, enjoys a growth rate much higher than the USSR because it also has a high rate of productivity growth.

Equity or Economic Justice

Which of the two alternatives best meets the criterion of economic justice? Since economic justice cannot be a precise, value-free concept, any conclusions about the economic justice of the two alternative economic systems must be based on the values individuals hold concerning equality and economic mobility.

Equality. Both market-oriented and planned economies have a surprising degree of inequality. Table 18.1 ranks countries according to a common measure of income inequality called a Gini Index. The index involves a complex statistical computation which tries to summarize the inequality within an income distribution.

Soviet Capitalism?

There is a new show on Soviet television called "Spotlight on *Perestroika*." (*Perestroika* means "restructuring.") The show, as combination of "60 Minutes" and Geraldo Rivera, investigates the failures of the Soviet economy. Reporters rush into factories to investigate conditions and ask workers why they are not working. One big story tried to figure out who was to blame for spoiled tomatoes in Moscow. What is *Perestroika* and will it change the Russian economy?

Mikhail Gorbachev hopes that January 1, 1988 will be a turning point in Soviet history. On that day, the first stage of his economic restructuring was started. According to the Soviet leader, his program is designed to transform the Soviet economy from an "overly centralized command system of management to a democratic system based mainly on economic methods." Gorbachev's chief economic advisor Abel Aganbegyan says that by late 1990 government planners will set prices of only 1,000 key items and allow the rest to be determined by the market. This would be a radical change—in 1987 the government mandated prices of 500,000 goods.

Perestroika presents Soviet citizens with new economic realities. Workers who are accustomed to secure jobs, set wages, and subsidized food prices will be paid on merit and operate in markets where prices are determined by supply and demand. Factory managers will be increasingly free from the control of central-planning bodies like GOSPLAN. And for the first time, unprofitable industrial plants will not be protected from bankruptcy, and Soviet citizens will have access to checking accounts.

In implementing this program, Gorbachev must successfully clear several hurdles. He has already weathered opposition from conservative bureaucrats who, while accepting the changes, think that he is moving too quickly. He has also received resistance from the 100,000 employees of central planning agencies—half of whom would lose their jobs if the new program is successful. The biggest hurdle *Perestroika* must face is the Soviet Union's lack of experience with market mechanisms. Plant managers adept at following the orders of central planners may not be adept at setting production schedules, purchasing raw materials, ensuring quality control, and distributing cash incentives to workers.

Perestroika is a revision of traditional Soviet socialism but certainly not a rejection. Gorbachev argues that he is reviving the socialism practiced by Lenin which rebuilt the Soviet economy after World War I and encouraged private enterprise. He says that current Soviet economic stagnation is "alien to socialism."

A nineteenth century Russian historian said that Czar Peter the Great wanted the serfs to remain as slaves but act like free men. Now Gorbachev is asking the ordinary Soviet citizen to show initiative and accept risk—in other words, act like they live in a market economy. But, he still wants them to accept the domination and discipline of the Communist Party. An economic saying of the West comes to mind. "There ain't no such thing as a free lunch." Gorbachev will probably find that his reforms will not come free either.

Several leaders before Gorbachev, notably Kruschev and Brezhnev, attempted economic reforms without notable success. Only time will tell whether tradition-oriented Soviet society can successfully respond this time to such fundamental change.

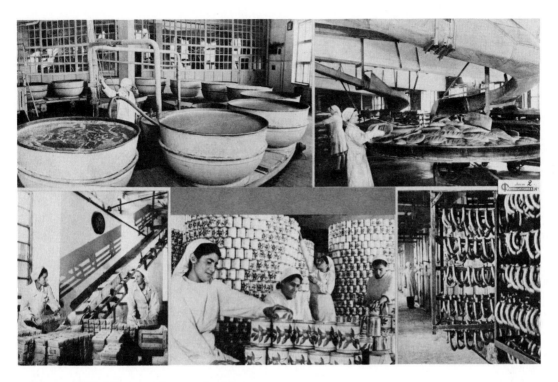

Equality in USSR: Women perform much of the manufacturing and heavy construction. (Library of Congress)

Table 18.1 Distribution of Income in Selected Economies

Country	Planned or Market	Government Redistribution Programs	Gini Index
Denmark	Market	heavy	.23
Sweden	Market	heavy	.27
Rumania/Bulgaria	Planned		.27
East Germany (GDR)	Planned		.28
United Kingdom	Market	heavy	.30
Poland	Planned		.33
Hungary	Planned		.33
Canada	Market	light	.34
USSR	Planned		.34
Yugoslavia	Planned		.35
West Germany (FRG)	Market	heavy	.35
U.S.	Market	light	.36
France	Market	heavy	.37

Source: C. Morrison, "Income Distribution in East European and Western Countries," *Journal of Comparative Economics*, 1984.

Two Germanies

It is always difficult to compare the strengths and weaknesses of market and planned economies. While the U.S. produces more goods and services per capita than the Soviet Union, one cannot logically conclude that free markets are, therefore, more productive or efficient. The United States has a much better climate, a one-hundred-and-fifty-year headstart in industrialization, rivers that do not freeze over, and capital unravaged by World War II. The two countries have so little in common that almost any productivity comparison is suspect.

For that reason, East and West Germany may provide the most accurate test of economic systems. The two nations have similar climates, rebuilt their economies at the same time, and draw workers from the same culture. Neither country is particularly rich in raw materials. They provide an excellent comparison.

From the consumer's vantage-point, West Germany has the advantage. Per capita, West Germany produces twenty times more cars than East Germany, four times as many bicycles, nine times as many televisions, and four times as much beer. There are twenty-one million cars in West Germany and only two million in the East. More than 90 percent of West German homes have bathing facilities, while amazingly only about 50 percent of East German homes have the same. About the only consumer good that East Germans produce more of is pianos. Also, the average East German sees an average of five movies a year, while the West German sees only two. (This difference may be due to the quality and availability of television in East Germany.) Per-capita GNP in East Germany is about 80 percent of that in West Germany.

The closer the index is to zero, the less inequality. As the index moves toward one, inequality increases. By this index, Denmark has the most equal distribution while France has the most unequal distribution.

Table 18.1 demonstrates that conclusions concerning superior economic justice of one system over the other are difficult to justify. Both market and planned economies have inequality, and neither system clearly distributes income more equally. Most market economies temper market distribution with government programs. Planned economies have found it necessary to use more material incentives than socialist ideals warrant. As a consequence, both systems produce inequality, although the range of income is usually wider in a market economy. However, the middle class is also bigger in most market economies.

Economic Mobility. There is no systematic evidence concerning economic mobility. Anecdotes from the USSR suggest

Perhaps more revealing is the amount of time that a worker must labor to be able to buy various commodities. The West German worker works fifty minutes to earn enough to buy a kilogram of butter; the East German, two hours. To buy a kilogram of coffee, the West German labors two hours while the East German must work fourteen hours. Most of these differences result from differences in productivity between the two countries. The per-acre yield of farmland is twice as high in West Germany.

The planned economy of East Germany does have its benefits. The official unemployment rate in East Germany is zero, while the West German rate approaches 10 percent. A typical West German pays 20 percent of income as rent; housing in East Germany is poorer, but with subsidized rent averages only 5 percent of income.

Education and health care may be better in East Germany. Life expectancy is nearly the same in both countries, with lower infant mortality rates in East Germany. A higher percentage of East Germans go on to college, nearly half of the students female. Only a third of West German females go on to college. East Germans are especially proud of their sports programs. Per capita, no country in the world wins as many medals in the Olympics as the East Germans.

What do all these figures mean? Not very much. They probably do not tell us very much about people's happiness in the two Germanies. East Germans consume a little more liquor than West Germans. They also divorce more frequently. But which group is happier? We know that many East Germans vote with their feet. The border between the two countries is heavily guarded; yet, many East Germans have risked harm to come west. Are they trading their security in East Germany for slightly better material opportunities in West Germany? Or, is freedom so meaningful to them that they will pay this potentially high price?

considerable rigidity in the educational system of the Soviet Union, which translates into economic immobility. There are four educational tracks in the Soviet Union—vocational school for manual and skilled workers, the *tekhnikum* which leads to middle-level technical jobs and foreman positions, the normal secondary school which leads to college or university, and special schools for the elite. Workers' children are likely to end up in the vocational schools, but it is certainly possible for them to move up the educational ladder. The children of the communist elite are much more likely to be in positions of influence and economic advantage. For example, in one Russian city, 73 percent of persons classified as elite had parents who were also part of the elite. Fifty-nine percent of workers had parents who were also workers. Most of the other workers had parents who worked on collective farms. There are clear intergenerational patterns in Soviet society. Of course, the same can be said of most market societies. The children of wealthy capitalists or well-educated parents have distinct advantages in a market economy. Family background is important in most societies, regardless of economic organization.

Freedom

The ranking of alternative economic systems is not in doubt when we consider the criterion of freedom. The market alternative clearly provides more freedom. Private property and other economic freedoms, such as free exchange, are much more prevalent in market economies. Furthermore, other liberties, such as freedom of speech, travel, religion, and assembly, are usually more extensive in market economies. Some scholars, such as F. A. Hayek, argue that freedom is made out of whole cloth, so that restricting so-called economic freedoms will lead inevitably to a loss of all freedom. Others argue that this is not true—that economic freedoms can be curtailed without serious jeopardy to our political rights. Regardless of one's view on the separability of freedom, it seems clear that the market does provide more freedom than its primary competitor.

Systems and Goals

Which system meets the three goals of efficiency, equity, and freedom best? The picture is somewhat muddled. On the whole, market economies appear to be more efficient than the centrally planned economies, although the difference is probably not as dramatic as most nonsocialists might believe. Productivity growth has been higher in market economies; planned economies have only achieved comparable growth through very heavy capital investment. Market economies have established a clear superiority in meeting the wishes of consumers. The only area of efficiency where planned economies are superior is the full employment of resources. But, all things considered, market economies are somewhat more efficient.

Both market and planned economies have distributions of income that are very unequal. That fact does not imply that these distributions are inequitable or unfair. The distribution of wealth is more unequal in market economies, permitting a wider ownership of private property. Planned economies appear to provide more economic security, while market economies offer more economic opportunity. However, the difference in the distribution of economic rewards between the two types of economies is surprisingly small given the rhetoric with which socialist writers have condemned inequality within capitalism. Class feelings seem to be prevalent in the USSR in spite of the official allegiance to equality. Hedrick Smith cites a Soviet workers' saying of the 1970s. "As long as the bosses pretend they are paying us a decent wage, we will pretend that we are working."

The choice between markets and planning might look something like this:

1. Efficiency—Give the edge to markets, although unemployment in market economies makes this choice more difficult than it would otherwise be.
2. Equity or economic justice—May be a tossup or a slight edge to planned economies. Market economies have used government intervention to eliminate most of the difference between the two alternatives.
3. Freedom—Market economies are clearly superior, but neither system inherently guarantees any kind of freedom.

Meeting of the Minds Again

(Six months later, Thomas More calls Adam Smith, Karl Marx and John Maynard Keynes back to see him and hear his decision concerning an economic system for Utopia.)

MORE: Thank you all for coming once again. I wanted to share my decision with you and get your reactions. I hope you will all be good sports about this. (They all agree.)

MARX: Let's hear it. I am most anxious.

KEYNES: Please go on, Thomas.

MORE: It is clear that this decision about an economic system is the most difficult that I have had to make as president of Utopia. The economic system affects so much of our daily lives. There is no perfect system, and I have had a hard time accepting this fact. I want the best for Utopia, and I kept looking for the perfect way to organize an economy. I finally realized that I had to accept one of Adam's most basic principles. Men are self-interested, even here in Utopia. I cannot escape the fact that this self-interest must be controlled. There are really only two alternatives. On the one hand, we could use markets to control interest in the ways that Adam described so beautifully in his books.

SMITH: Why, thank you, Thomas.

MORE: Alternatively, we could use the power of government. Karl, after much thought, I came to the conclusion that it is very difficult to control government power. Wherever it has been used for economic matters, it has been abused.

MARX: But if you have the right people in charge. . . .

MORE: You cannot count on the people here in Utopia being superior to government officials elsewhere. Therefore, we are going to base our economic system on free markets. They provide us with the best chance of managing self-interest without inducing tyranny.

MARX: I am sorry to learn of this decision.

MORE: Wait. I am not finished. We are under no illusion that markets are perfect. We understand the cyclical problems that persist in market economies. We know that markets have certain tendencies that produce inefficiencies. As difficult as it may be, we intend to follow John's advice and use government planning to correct as many of these market deficiencies as we can. However, John, we plan to scrutinize government carefully. If a program to correct a market failure, such as externalities, is not working, we are willing to eliminate it and accept that cost as part of our decision to use markets. We are not afraid to use government to control economic matters. But we know government is not a panacea.

KEYNES: A wise policy.

MORE: Karl, you may feel that all of your work and writing has been in vain. Not so. You have made us much more sensitive to the issue of economic justice. Here in Utopia we are not going to allow the advantages of a market economy to seduce us into acceptance of inequity. We plan to use the power of government to come as close to economic justice as possible without sacrificing the power of markets. We are not going to interfere in each market to promote equity. We are not going to destroy incentives to redistribute income. Instead, we will search for taxes, educational programs, and a welfare system that minimize the damage to efficiency. We are willing to trade some efficiency for economic justice, but we want the price to be as low as possible.

Karl, we really decided to base our economy on markets because of our love of freedom. A market economy allows every individual and family to pursue their own vision of what is best for themselves and the country. We want to give them that freedom, and we hope they use it wisely.

Gentlemen, thank you for your help.

Part 3

History

In Parts I and II, we considered two distinct (though related) sets of ideas and practices, the American political and economic systems. As we saw, these were not mere abstractions pulled out of the air; they were the products of long, and sometimes painful, historical experience.

Historical experience is the experience of change. Simply put, history changes everything. There was never a society— including ancient Egypt, where change was glacially slow—that was impervious to time. Thus, over the centuries, we have seen nations rise and decline, empires spread and wither, ideas flourish and decay. We have seen religious movements such as Buddhism, Islam, and Christianity extend their influence dramatically. We have seen global shifts of power from north to south and east to west. We have seen forms of government come and go—monarchies, republics, democracies—and we have seen economic systems mutate drastically. In our own time, the world has undergone seismic alterations.

Lest we forget history's relentless motion, we might well consider the experience of our cousins, the English. Students visiting the quiet villages of present-day England could ponder the fact that in the time of their grandparents London was the seat of a world-wide empire, mightier than ancient Rome. Yet, in the days of Queen Elizabeth I, not so very much earlier, England was not only not yet an empire, it was not even a fully coherent national state. The great power of the world at that time was Spain, which was preparing to launch the invasion of the century against Elizabeth's broken-down, ramshackle, debt-ridden government. Enter history. Within the space of a lifetime, the Spanish Armada had failed, Spain's might had crumbled, and Elizabeth's struggling island kingdom had taken Spain's place as the world's imperial colossus. History is full of surprises.

The question of history—and where it is leading us—is especially important to the United States. For here, as the Pilgrims noted, change occurs with special swiftness. The simple act of crossing the Atlantic, physically distancing themselves from Europe, brought Americans many kinds of change at the outset. The creation of republican government and the implementation of market economics entailed similarly momentous changes. Then the nineteenth century, a veritable dynamo of change, generated endless new developments for the United States. Everything from physical expansion to machine technology to political democracy to radical social change would sweep through the American experience—and American life would be altered by them all.

Where has history taken us? Where will it take us next? And how has it, how will it, affect the design and function of what we have broadly described as the work of the Founders? These issues, tightly intertwined, are perhaps most important of all to our answering of the America Question.

19
From the Constitution to Politics

Concepts

Two-Party System
Winner-take-all
Proportional Representation
Coalition Blackmail
Coalition Politics

"County Election" (From the collection of the
Boatmen's National Bank of St. Louis)

The Election of 1800

Although there had been presidential elections before in the American republic—three of them to be exact—there had never been anything like this. It was fortunate, some said, that Washington had passed away the year before, for he would have abominated the very sight of it. He had repeatedly warned his countrymen against "the spirit of party," and now here it was in full flower.

There were plenty of issues to galvanize opposition to the ruling Federalists. Jay's Treaty with England, Hamilton's controversial financial program, the war scare with France, the specter of a standing army, and, touchiest of all, the notorious Alien and Sedition Acts. These the Federalists had rammed through Congress expressly to silence political opposition—First Amendment or no First Amendment. As a result, for speaking "falsely and maliciously" against the government, twenty-five persons had been arrested, fourteen indicted, and ten (including a U.S. congressman) tried and convicted, all of them admirers of Thomas Jefferson.

Jefferson, as vice president, was oddly enough a part of the government himself. Before the Twelfth Amendment was passed, the vice president was the presidential candidate receiving the second highest number of electoral votes; thus, he naturally represented the opposition. And Jefferson had certainly done that. Every time the Federalists had touched off a new controversy, the Virginian's facile pen had been set to framing objections. Soon everyone who was discontented, aggrieved, or just politically ambitious came to see Jefferson as a rallying point.

The Federalists were amazed at how well Jefferson's Democratic-Republicans could organize. Almost overnight, it seemed, there were committees within committees, networks of correspondence, carefully coordinated propaganda campaigns. And the new party's agents were everywhere. "Every threshing floor, every husking, every work party on a house-frame or raising a building, the very funerals are infected with bawlers or whisperers against [the] government," complained Fisher Ames. In Congress, too, every debate turned into an election skirmish. The House, wrote one observer, was like "a conclave of cardinals, intriguing in the election of a Pope."

As the idea of political opposition was new to them, the Federalists were dumbfounded by it all. They fought back stridently, viciously, as though on the brink of Armageddon. If Jefferson was elected, shrilled Hamilton to Jay, it would mean "the OVERTHROW of the GOVERNMENT . . . a REVOLUTION, after the manner of BONAPARTE." Worse even than that, an anonymous pamphleteer moaned: "Murder, robbery, rape, adultery, and incest will be openly taught and practiced, the air will be rent with the cries of distress, the soil will be soaked with blood, and the nation black with crimes." But the Democratic-Republicans could sensationalize too. One editor referred to the President as "old, querulous, bald, blind, crippled, toothless Adams."

There were other quirks in the campaign that might seem familiar today. When Jefferson dispatched his Philadelphia friend, Dr. Logan, to Paris to see if the French quarrel could be patched up, a poem in the Federalist press accused him of wanting to make time with Logan's wife. When Republican congressmen rose to speak against the Alien and Sedition Acts, Federalists in the House chamber were smitten with such a coughing fit that the speakers could not be heard. Elbridge Gerry, a prominent

An early political cartoon: Not always a politics of
decorum. (Library of Congress)

Massachusetts Federalist, dramatically switched parties and ran for governor. And a
tunesmith knocked out the country's first political song:

> Rejoice, Columbia's sons, rejoice
> To tyrants never bend the knee
> But join with heart with soul and voice
> To Jefferson and Liberty.

Religion was hauled into it too. Jefferson, who had helped disestablish the
Anglican church in Virginia, was depicted as an atheist, an infidel, and a worshipper
of the devil. The *Gazette of the United States* emblazoned an issue:

THE GRAND QUESTION STATED

At the present solemn moment the only question
to be asked by every American, laying his hand on his heart,
is "Shall I continue in allegiance to

GOD—AND A RELIGIOUS PRESIDENT;

or impiously declare for

JEFFERSON—AND NO GOD!!!"

Scare tactics or not, the Democratic-Republican juggernaut lumbered forward. Leaders in every state tirelessly plotted strategy and tallied up votes. In New York City, which would prove crucial, Aaron Burr swept the local elections with his own jerry-built political machine and, as a reward, was placed on the ticket as vice president. And almost daily, Jefferson himself, over dinner at the Francis' Hotel in Philadelphia, held councils of war with Republican congressmen. "A little patience," he assured them, "and we shall see the reign of witches pass over, their spells dissolved."

When the votes were counted, the Democratic-Republicans had won handily, and Thomas Jefferson became the third president of the United States. The Federalists were left in a daze. With the turn of the century, it seemed, a new world was dawning, at least in American politics, and if they were to be a part of it, they had better forget Washington's admonitions about the "spirit of party" and roll up their sleeves.

There was something almost classical about the United States Constitution as a body of ideas. Written in the elegant script of the eighteenth century and preserved under glass, it seemed almost Olympian in its detachment. Citizens who stand before it today may wonder whether a document so remote and aloof could possibly be addressed to the realities of life. To reassure ourselves on that point, we have only to observe the Constitution in practice— where it loses its aura of majesty and comes to be called "politics."

Implementing the Constitution

The difference between theory and practice became evident at the outset, for putting the Constitution into actual operation brought forth surprises. A few features of the document worked only awkwardly. Others did not work at all and had to be changed. And everywhere the power of precedent became manifest. For example, when George Washington read in Article II, Section 2 that "The President shall have

Power, by and with the Advice and Consent of the Senate, to make Treaties," he assumed that the Senate was to "advise" him on treaty negotiations in progress. However, he soon changed his mind. The first time he sought senatorial advice, he got such a deluge of conflicting opinions that he resolved never to seek it again. His successors have all followed that precedent.

With the power of precedent in mind, we can appreciate how much depended on the virtue of those early officials. For, in spite of the Constitution's barriers, officeholders were free to mold the document substantially simply in the way they chose to implement it. For this reason alone, the United States was fortunate to have George Washington as its first president. His good sense, self-restraint, and sincere patriotism made for the right kind of precedents.

Even so, there were developments resulting from the implementation of the Constitution that Washington himself found appalling. Politics was one of them. The first president, along with many others, looked upon politics as the bane of republican government, and seriously hoped that the United States could get

The Power of Precedent

How should citizens address the president of the United States? We know now, of course, but only with the benefit of hindsight. In 1789, when the first president took office, no one knew the answer and the question was vigorously debated. After all, in a seemingly small matter such as titles and forms of address, precedents could be established which might push the evolution of the presidency toward, say, monarchy. The question was not insignificant.

John Adams, for one, believed that the American president should possess as much dignity as any European monarch. "If the *state and pomp* essential to this great department are not, in a good degree, preserved," he wrote, "it will be vain for America to hope for consideration with foreign powers." Accordingly, Adams proposed that the president be addressed as: "His Highness the President of the United States and Protector of Their Liberties."

George Washington as president: The precedents were far reaching. (Library of Congress)

That was a mouthful, especially to those who believed that the genius of republicanism, ancient *and* modern, was to be found in its plainness. Indeed, after the Revolution it was quite fashionable for a time to dress without adornment, to avoid fancy speech, and to build houses of dignified simplicity. (Catching the fulness of this spirit, sculptor Horatio Greenough would execute a statue of Washington clad in a Roman toga.) When the republican Mr. Jefferson heard about Adams' proposal in Paris, he repeated Ben Franklin's assessment of that worthy: "always an honest man, often a great one, but sometimes absolutely mad."

The advocates of republican simplicity won the day. The chief executive was called simply "The President of the United States" and addressed even more simply as "Mr. President." For his part, Adams was injured by the affair, for it was now whispered that he secretly desired monarchy. If so, he must have disliked the title someone hung on *him*: "His Rotundity."

along without it. But what he termed "the spirit of party" was abroad in the land, and there was little he could do to stifle it. Indeed, the rough-and-tumble politics that we take for granted today came forth while Washington was president.

The Political System Takes Shape

In colonial America, political parties, as such, did not exist. When an issue came along, people of various minds would take a stand on it according to how they felt, and after it was resolved, they forgot about it. This chaotic factionalism was changed by the Revolution. So ardent and deep-rooted were the passions excited by the struggle against Britain that the identities of *Patriot*, on the one hand, and *Tory*, on the other, could not be sloughed off overnight. But commitments of such depth produced an unfortunate side effect. The partisans on either side were so convinced of their own rightness, and so doubtful of the other's, that they tended to see dark implications in political disagreement. For a Patriot, of course, a Tory was a traitor, and it worked just as well the other way around. That political opposition could be both loyal and legitimate gained credence very slowly.

Hamilton and Jefferson

After the Revolution, Patriots and Tories faded away. However, in the 1790s, during the administrations of George Washington and John Adams, circumstances combined to create another division, almost as indelible. The most important of these circumstances was the emergence in Washington's cabinet of two prominent voices which, on most issues, were diametrically opposed.

Alexander Hamilton: Government for the rich and the wellborn. (Library of Congress)

Alexander Hamilton. Born out of wedlock in the West Indies and raised by a doting uncle, Alexander Hamilton had the outsider's fascination with power and privilege. And he was so gifted that General Washington handpicked him for his aide-de-camp during the war. Although their relationship was not without its abrasions (Hamilton resigned over an imagined slight), General Washington remained impressed with the younger man's ability, and when elected president in 1788, he appointed Hamilton secretary of the treasury.

Notwithstanding his American patriotism, Hamilton greatly admired British institutions of government, which he had hoped the Constitution might emulate. When it failed to do so, he remained undaunted—for there was still that business

Thomas Jefferson: Government for the ordinary citizen. (White House collection)

of implementation to think about. As secretary of the treasury (at that time the most powerful position in the cabinet), Hamilton could do much to shape the way the Constitution actually worked.

What Hamilton wanted was a vigorous, centralized government allied with the rich and the wellborn. Thus, in a series of rather dauntless reports, he advocated policies—such as funding the national debt at par—which would both extend the reach of federal power and enhance private fortunes. (Wealthy speculators had bought up certificates of the national debt for a few cents on the dollar. Under Hamilton's plan, they were paid the face value of their bonds.) As for the limitations imposed by the Constitution, Hamilton unfailingly advocated "loose construction" of constitutional language. What were words for

anyway, he asked, if not to be stretched here and there in the interest of good government?

Thomas Jefferson. Ironically, Hamilton's chief opponent in the Washington cabinet was everything that Hamilton himself could have wished to be. Thomas Jefferson, the secretary of state, was wealthy and wellborn, internationally respected, and politically popular. Through a combination of personal inheritance and shrewd manipulation, he had become master of Monticello, a five- thousand-acre estate in the Blue Ridge Mountains, and architect of its graceful manor house. As a scientist Jefferson had won European acclaim; as a political philosopher, he was favorably compared with John Locke; and as a prose stylist, he had been picked to draft the Declaration of Independence.

Where Hamilton gained his inspiration from the English monarchy, Jefferson's came from classical antiquity. Thus, in contrast to Hamilton's vigorous, centralized government, Jefferson advocated a small and decentralized one; and in contrast to Hamilton's faith in finance and industry, Jefferson believed in the life of the soil. Republican government could not survive, he said, if it harbored great concentrations of power.

Their ultimate disagreement was over constitutional construction. Where Hamilton, seeking to build a powerful government, construed constitutional language broadly and loosely, Jefferson, seeking to restrain such a government, construed constitutional language narrowly and strictly. Jefferson was horrified by Hamilton's reports—which he took to be blueprints for tyranny. It was as simple as that.

Two Germinal Issues

Many of the issues that arose during Washington's first administration enabled Hamilton and Jefferson to crystallize and clarify their respective views. Two, however, were especially important.

The Bank Question. Hamilton proposed that the government, in cooperation with private financial interests, establish and operate a national bank. Credit facilities were limited in the new republic—state banks were small and inadequately financed—and a large, well funded, and politically prominent banking facility would perform a useful function. It would also, of course, immeasurably benefit the rich and the wellborn.

The problem was that nowhere in the Constitution was there authorization for such an enterprise. But for this difficulty Hamilton was more than ready. Taking his longest reach yet, he argued in a memorandum to the president that since the government did have authority to collect taxes and coin money, and since the operation of a bank could be deemed "necessary and proper" to carrying out both of those functions, the proposed bank was therefore constitutional. Suddenly, the *necessary and proper clause* of the Constitution (discussed in chapter nine) took on a jolting new relevance.

Before making up his own mind, Washington solicited an opinion from Thomas Jefferson, who, in reply, minced no words. In his view, the proposed bank would be an exploiter of farmers, a fountain of corruption, and a possible harbinger of monarchy; but even more dangerous was the constitutional argument necessary to sustain it. If something so far afield as a national bank qualified as

"necessary and proper," Jefferson argued, virtually any scheme under the sun could do likewise.

Jefferson's argument did not persuade the president, who eventually gave the bank his blessing, but it did make an impression on others. For many Americans, Hamilton was beginning to reflect ambitions of napoleonic size, and when they thought about ways of thwarting him, the name of Thomas Jefferson—and the activity we know as politics—increasingly came to mind.

The French Question. In 1789, the year George Washington took the presidential oath of office, the French Revolution embarked on its career of violence and bloodshed. The themes of the struggle—republican freedom, natural rights, an end to privilege—were familiar enough to most Americans, and the passions they ignited added new heat to U.S. politics. One reacted to the news from France according to how one felt about the issues between Hamilton and Jefferson.

Nor was that all. Revolutionary France, soon at war with Great Britain, strove desperately to win American diplomatic support. French republican editors and organizers flocked to the U.S. to stoke up popular enthusiasm, and before long they were boldly mixing into politics. Recalling that *they* had supported *our* Revolution, they now asked pointedly whether *we* intended to support *theirs*. That, in essence, was the French question, and it began to burn like a slow fuse.

It was over the French question that the Jeffersonians and Hamiltonians came into open conflict. Domestic politics was one thing, the partisans sneered at one another, but allegiance to a foreign power was quite another. Each side saw the other as verging close to treason: the Jeffersonians were pictured as wild-eyed Jacobin sympathizers, while the Hamiltonians were put down as lackeys of the English crown. And newspapers on both sides poured forth an ascending spiral of invective. One office-holder complained that he had been described "in such exaggerated and indecent terms as could scarcely be applied to a Nero, a notorious defaulter, or even a common pickpocket." And this was George Washington.

The Parties Form

In so tense and agitated a situation, it did not take long for real parties (as opposed to passing factions) to emerge. The Hamiltonians, seeking to identify with American patriotism, called themselves Federalists—after the original supporters of the Constitution—while the Jeffersonians, in what to our ears seems a curious mixing of terms, became the Democratic-Republicans. Historians disagree whether the parties were organized from the top down by their respective leaders, or from the bottom up by the rank and file. What was important either way was that people were willing to be organized.

Historians do agree on other things about the early parties. Not yet the age of political democracy, there was little in the way of mass participation or popular appeal in either of them. In background, if not always in demeanor, politicians were still supposed to be gentlemen, and their important decisions were supposed to be made in candle-lit drawing rooms. Accordingly, the command center of each party was not a popular convention, as we would expect today, but a caucus of high officials—representatives, senators, perhaps a cabinet officer or two—who assembled periodically to make nominations, formulate issues, and lay out campaign strategy.

The voters themselves typically came from the wealthier, better educated, and better-informed classes. The idea was that people of property had a greater stake in society and thus naturally should make its important decisions. Besides, political activity took time and money. Merely to keep abreast of the party's thinking required long hours of poring through turgid essays in party-run newspapers.

The Election of 1800

The crucial year for the new political system was 1800. Jefferson had resigned from the cabinet back in 1793 and three years later had run for the Presidency himself. The Federalists had run John Adams against him, and the latter had narrowly won. But the real power in the Adams administration had been Hamilton, who had held no office as such—he was much too unpopular personally—but who had commanded widespread party loyalties and always gotten his way. For Jefferson's supporters, 1800 was to be the year of reckoning.

The campaign was a vicious one. The French Revolution had by now run completely out of control and Franco-American relations had deteriorated to the breaking point. Furthermore, in order to silence the French propagandists, Congress had passed the notorious Alien and Sedition Acts—prescribing stiff penalties for merely criticizing the government—and Adams had enforced them ruthlessly. The Jeffersonians viewed these acts as utterly unconstitutional and a threat to the republic. And for their part, the Federalists equated opposition to their own policies with disloyalty to the United States. There was not much room for give and take.

On election day, the Jeffersonians won decisively. Jefferson himself was elected president, and his Democratic-Republicans swept both houses of Congress. The outcome was a bitter pill for John Adams, but it was a substantial victory for republicanism. For it demonstrated that power could change hands in a free society—not just from one officeholder to another but from an entire political persuasion to its opposite. Henceforth, the party out of power would no longer be seen as disloyal.

There was another dividend in the election. It became obvious that, far from disrupting the workings of the Constitution, political parties strengthened them. When the Democratic-Republicans captured both the Presidency and Congress, the Federalists entrenched themselves in the Judiciary, and each party made sure that the Constitution's structural controls worked with a vengeance against the other. If those controls were originally powered by self-interest, politics in effect made them turbocharged.

The Two-party System

What began during that seedtime was not only politics, it was two-party politics. This became clear only in time. Third parties occasionally came and went on the American scene, and small splinters were always flying off in angry sparks, but the operative number always seemed to be two. When the Federalists folded up in the eighteen-teens, the old party of Jefferson, after a period of turmoil, effectively broke in two. A new Democratic party coalesced about the person of Andrew Jackson, while

Some Important Terms
Plurality:
The largest block of votes cast.

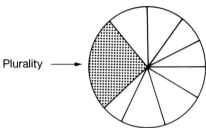

Plurality →

Majority:
More than half of all votes cast.

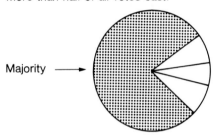

Majority →

the American, or "Whig," party took the Federalists' place. Those two battled it out for some twenty more years, until the tumults of the 1850s left the Democrats divided and the Whigs in a shambles. But by 1856, after another season of realignment, two parties were back in the field. Democrats and Republicans have been jousting with each other ever since.

"Winner-Take-All"

In order to understand why there should be two parties and only two, we must look to the rules, written and unwritten, of the American political game. In the Constitution were to be found several provisions which materially shaped the character of political contests. Consider, for example,

Parties in a Proportional Representation System:

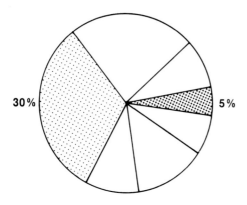

30%   5%

Any party that can capture some measurable fraction of the vote can exercise influence in the government.

the single-member legislative district. If a state could elect, say, ten members to the U.S. House of Representatives, the ten were not to be chosen at large by the state's entire population; rather, each had to be elected by a separate voting district. There might be any number of interests in a given district—and any number of potential parties—but when the dust settled, only a single candidate was chosen. This has been called the principle of winner-take-all.

Winner-take-all was applied beyond the Constitution, too. Take, for example, the way votes were counted in the electoral college. If a certain state had, say, ten electoral votes, the Founders assumed that these could be cast for any number of presidential candidates depending on the individual electors. In practice, though, electors began to do a very different thing. The single candidate who won the state's popular vote was awarded all ten electoral votes. The winner, once again, took all.

The corollary to *winner-take-all* was *loser-take-nothing.* If some party were to poll a very respectable 49 percent of a district's popular vote (and a single opponent were to poll the 51 percent remaining), it would wind up electing no one to Congress and casting no votes for the Presidency. In 1936 Alf Landon polled 38 percent of the popular vote in the United States but gained just eight electoral votes (out of 531) for president. In American politics, it does not pay to come in second.

The application of the winner-take-all principle made the two-party system virtually obligatory. In order to see why, we must digress for a moment and see how an alternative political system might work.

Proportional Representation

In many other democracies, votes are not counted by the winner take-all principle but instead by the principle of proportional representation. In such systems, a typical voting district, instead of electing only one member to the legislature, may elect, say, ten. The election is held, the votes are tallied, and the seats declared filled according to the proportion of votes cast for each participating party. If Party A polls, say, 40 percent of the vote, it will gain four of the district's ten seats. If Party B polls 30 percent, it will gain three seats. And Party C, polling only 10 percent of the vote, even gets a seat of its own. Indeed, in such systems everyone comes away with *something.* Any splinter group that can poll a certain minimal fraction of the vote will wind up with power commensurate to its size.

Coalition Blackmail. And it may wind up with even more. Let us suppose that an election is held and the seats of the assembly distributed among some fifteen

Parties in a Proportional Representation System

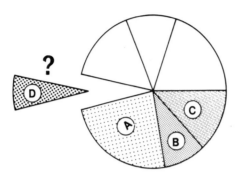

Coalition Blackmail:

A tiny splinter party may be as influential as a major party.

The patterned parties A, B, and C are trying to assemble a coalition in Parliament. In order to achieve this they must have a majority of the vote. A, B, and C are just a little short of a majority and need the support of party D in order to obtain a majority. Party D is therefore in a position to blackmail parties A, B, and C and has more influence than a major party.

contending parties. Since no single one of them has anything like a majority, it cannot by itself organize a government. (That is, it cannot control the selection of executive officers, nor insure the passage of its program.) In order to do that, two or three parties must get together and form a ruling *coalition*.

But there is a hitch. Coalition partners A, B, and C, with 20, 15, and 12 percent of the seats, respectively, are still a couple of seats shy of a majority. As it happens, though, there is a very small party with just three seats that may—just may—be willing to join them. Its price? It will accept three cabinet posts, one for each of its deputies, and the posts had better be important ones. Otherwise no deal.

How Votes Are Counted in the American System

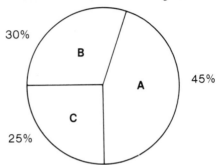

If party A gets 45% of the vote, how much influence do B and C have?

Winner take all!

If party A consistently gets a plurality of the vote, the only way for parties B and C to beat A is to band together. At the end of the process, there will be two parties vying for majorities rather than multiple parties vying for pluralities.

The American Party System

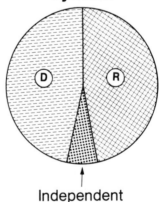

Independent

The Democratic and Republican Parties each consistently pull a little less than one half of the votes. This means that each is within striking distance of a plurality. Whether or not this plurality is achieved is influenced by the independents. The independent segment contains both liberal and conservative elements and therefore does not vote as one group.

FAR   LEFT   MIDDLE   RIGHT   FAR
LEFT   RIGHT

ideological   **ideological**

half and half   **half and half**

practical

The ends of the political spectrum (far left, far right) tend to be dominated by principle. Those in the middle tend to be practical and will compromise on all but the most important issues. Those on the left and right tend to be a mixture of ideology and practicality.

This sort of blackmail, which occurs regularly in systems of proportional representation, underscores the difference between those systems and the American. With proportional representation, small parties are paid handsomely to stay in business, and a large number of them do. For, with luck, every party, including the tiniest, has a chance to wield influence far beyond its numbers. It is a game of "loser-take-all."

The Two-Party Logic

In the American system, the political logic was very different, as the politicians soon learned. If there were, say, three parties in the field and Party A polled 45 percent of the vote, Parties B and C felt the force of that logic immediately. If they were to continue dividing 55 percent of the vote between them, they would also continue to lose elections, and in America, remember, there was no benefit for losers. Their only salvation, therefore, was to get together into a single party capable of beating A. Such logic worked almost irresistibly to make the parties combine together until there were only two.

This simple mechanism has kept the two-party system on track and functioning in America right down to the present. It explains why various third party movements have so far all failed, and why upon the death of a major party some other has

Distribution of Voters

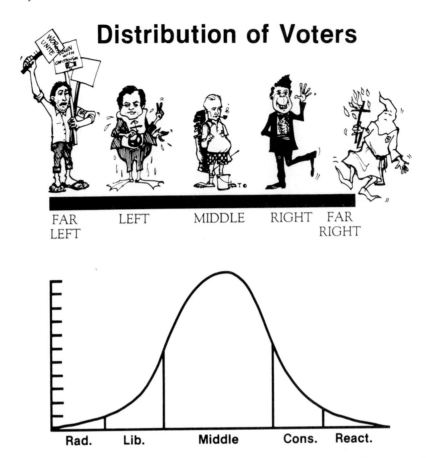

FAR   LEFT   MIDDLE   RIGHT   FAR
LEFT   RIGHT

Rad.   Lib.   Middle   Cons.   React.

This curve represents the distribution of votes. Most of the voters wind up in the middle, comparatively fewer voters are either liberal or conservative, and even fewer are at the far extremes. If a party needs to capture a large plurality or a majority of the voters, it must move to the middle.

arisen to take its place. It may have been a historical accident that Hamilton and Jefferson first squared off against each other— but it is in the very nature of the system that the two-party quarrel still echoes today.

Implications of the Two-party System

The two-party system—as opposed to the multiparty systems of the other democracies—has had an enormous impact on the course of American political life. Simply looking around us today we can gauge some of its more important effects.

1. It Is a Politics of Practical Results

There are, broadly speaking, two different kinds of political behavior. *Ideological* behavior emphasizes the importance of doctrine and principle. When a true ideologue encounters a problem, he does not concern himself with practical solutions nearly so much as with adherence to a set of abstract

FAR   LEFT   MIDDLE   RIGHT   FAR
LEFT   RIGHT

The normal position of the parties
in American politics

Although both the Republican and Democratic Parties are slightly shifted ideologically, both must straddle the middle in order to achieve pluralities.

ideals. As the old expression goes, he would rather be right than be president. Practical political behavior, on the other hand, emphasizes the importance of results. The practical politician, as he appears in so many cartoons, would rather be president than be right. When he encounters a problem, it is with a far greater sense of flexibility as well as a more easily assuaged conscience. If he has to bend and crimp his principles a little in order to get the thing solved, well, what else is politics for?

As we survey the political spectrum, we encounter both kinds of behavior. On the far left and far right (positions we usually designate as radical and reactionary, respectively), we find the ideologues, the politicians of principle. We know them by their rhetoric, which is typically high-flown and doctrinaire, and by their essential unwillingness to compromise. In the middle, by contrast, we find the practical politicians, whom we also know at a glance. Their rhetoric is by comparison a little muddled, perhaps, but we can count on them to compromise almost anything. And finally there are the intermediate positions, the liberals on the left and conservatives on the right, who have a little of each behavior in their makeup. Like the ideologues, they often speak earnestly of principle—but in the interest of solving problems (or getting elected) they will sometimes find a way to yield.

Each of these behaviors, ideological and practical, is brought out differently in different political systems. For example, the

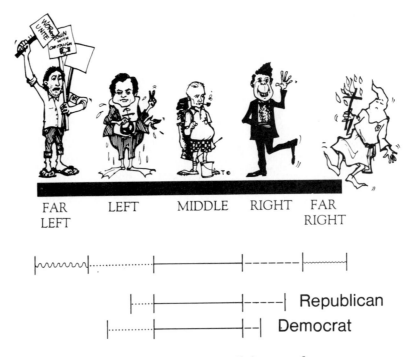

Both parties are coalitions of
left, right, and middle elements

The Republican and Democratic Parties are coalitions of right, left, and middle elements. There are liberals as well as conservatives in both parties. The bulk of both parties, however, consists mostly of the middle elements.

multiparty systems described above clearly encourage ideological behavior. The various small parties in such systems cannot really hope to control the government in the way that Democrats or Republicans do in the United States. Rather, what they try to do is faithfully represent a certain point of view and make it as influential as possible. Left or right, each party has its own credo, often put forward with great passion, and to the extent that the electorate— or coalition blackmail—provides an opportunity to voice that credo, they do. The total picture is a clash of competing ideologies.

In the two-party system, by contrast, there is a far different chemistry at work. In a situation where winners get everything (and losers get nothing), no party can survive on a narrow ideological basis, because on such a basis it cannot win elections. In order to remain in the American political game, parties can settle for nothing less than electoral majorities. And where are those to be found? Certainly not out on the ideological fringes. On the far left or far right there are plenty of doctrines, to be sure, but not many voters. The voters, alas, are for the most part practical-minded people, more concerned about

Of Politics and Pumping Gas

The service station analogy, mentioned in the text, was a contribution of the American economist Harold Hotelling, who may or may not have had firsthand experience at pumping gas. Hotelling's Paradox has at least one corollary worth exploring. Suppose that on a very foggy night a motorist pulls into one station and asks directions for finding the other one. A less-than-candid attendant may choose to conceal the fact that his competitor is right across the street, and may submit instead that he is far, far down the road.

Politicians do the same thing. In the merciless and never-ending two-party conflict, a favored strategy is to depict one's own position as being in the middle but the opposing party's as being far out on the fringe.

Candidate Barry Goldwater: Extremism was no vice. (Library of Congress)

Politicians do the same thing. In the merciless and never-ending two-party conflict, a favored strategy is to depict one's own position as being in the middle but the opposing party's as being far out on the fringe.

It happened with a vengeance in 1964, when Lyndon Johnson was running for reelection against Barry Goldwater. Neither candidate was a centrist, exactly, Johnson being as confirmed in his liberalism as was Goldwater in his conservatism. The question was, which of them could best represent himself as being in the middle.

With that in mind, Goldwater goofed badly. At the Republican convention in San Francisco, he allowed himself to say, "Extremism in the defense of liberty is no vice . . . moderation in the pursuit of justice is no virtue." That was all it took for the Democrats to blast him with great effectiveness as an "extremist." There were even some jokes about it. When a Goldwater billboard intoned: "In your heart you know he's right," one Democratic wag replied: "Yes, he's too damned far right!"

The clincher came with the famous daisy commercial, one of the most effective—and devastating—bits of political advertising contrived in this century. Vietnam was heating up, and Goldwater somewhat obliquely suggested that if worst came to worst, nuclear weapons might conceivably have to be used there. The Democrats made no comment. They simply showed television viewers a picture of a little girl holding a daisy, then cut abruptly to a nuclear explosion. The voters flocked in droves to Lyndon Johnson.

And when the dust had settled, Johnson embarked upon the Great Society, the most ideologically oriented program since the New Deal. He also, by the way, sent a half million troops to Vietnam. All of which illustrates, once again, that if the fog is thick enough, a really convincing gas pumper just might bring it off.

The Freeze Factor at Work

Of the several presidential elections that could be used to illustrate the freeze factor, that of 1884 deserves a special place of honor. Although the Republicans were numerically superior, they were rather badly divided, and a reform faction known as the Mugwumps actually voted for the Democratic candidate. As a result, the political balance was about even.

It made for a memorable campaign. "The public is angry and abusive," wrote Henry Adams. "Every one takes part. We are all doing our best, and swearing like demons. But the amusing thing is that no one talks about real interests." It was true. Corruption, the

Campaign broadside for Blaine: Plenty else to talk about. (Library of Congress)

tariff, civil service reform—all pressing issues of the day—received but scant attention as the campaign unfolded, for both candidates were fearful of alienating the voters in their own parties.

Fortunately there was plenty else to talk about. Speaking on behalf of the Republican candidate, James G. Blaine, the Rev. Samuel D. Burchard blasted Democrats

tackling their problems than sticking to their principles. To win in two-party politics, a party has to shoot for the middle.

Indeed, *both* parties have to shoot for the middle. That may seem dubious as a logical proposition, but think about it for a moment. Suppose there were a ten-mile stretch of road with potential customers scattered along it, and you wanted to find a place for a service station. In order to draw business from the entire stretch, you would place your station right in the middle, five miles from either end. Now, where would someone else build a *second* service station in order to compete most effectively with the first? Work it out on paper. The second station has to go right across the street.

So it is that American politics steers unerringly between the extremes. Its two broadly based, centrist parties have a built-in affinity for the only voter who can put them over the top—the man in the middle. With his hopes, his fears, and his prejudices clearly in their sights, they concern themselves less about doctrinaire abstractions and more about getting problems solved.

2. It Is a Politics of Compromise and Adjustment

In proportional representation systems there is often little reason for compromise. True, the various parties forming a coalition must yield a bit in order to work together, but beyond that, each can remain true to its founding principles. As a whole,

as the party of "Rum, Romanism, and Rebellion"—which played very interestingly in Irish-Catholic New York. For their part, the Democrats got wind that Blaine was speaking at a dinner attended by two hundred of the nation's wealthiest men. This was announced in the New York *World* by a half-page cartoon of "Belshazzar Blaine and the Money Kings" gorging themselves in luxury while hungry Americans shivered outside in the cold.

But the really juicy items were the scandalous ones. Digging into Grover Cleveland's background, the Republicans learned that he had probably fathered an illegitimate child. Blaine had a shady past too. He had earlier been implicated in a series of underhanded railroad deals and stood more or less convicted by his letters to one Mulligan. At the bottom of one missive he had even written: "Burn this letter!"

So, as the campaign heated up, both sides took to chanting in the streets. The Republicans, in reference to Cleveland's unacknowledged offspring, chanted:

"Ma! Ma! Where's my Pa?"
He's gone to the White House, ha, ha, ha.

And the Democrats, in reference to the Mulligan Letters, chanted:

Blaine, Blaine, James G. Blaine
The continental liar from the state of Maine
—"*Burn this letter!*"

Cleveland narrowly won. The voters, apparently, felt better about bastardy than they did about graft. It was not a high moment in U.S. politics.

---

ideologically oriented parties find compromise difficult—for it threatens their very reason for existing.

In the two-party system, by contrast, compromise and adjustment begin at home, *within* the parties. In order to capture electoral majorities, each party must welcome all comers. Along with the middle of-the-road voters, there will be liberals and conservatives, even radicals and reactionaries, all waving their placards together. They can quarrel with each other if they want to, and sometimes they do, but if they truly want to win elections, such conduct is not well advised. Thus, at the Democratic National Convention, liberal Ted Kennedy warmly embraces conservative Earl Long, and their Republican counterparts do the same.

The two parties readily compromise, too. Settling for half a loaf becomes a way of life with them. Thus, bills started through the Congress by one party end up with amendments to please the other; plums are passed out to foes as well as friends; and lopsided victories are shunned as un-American. Politicians can battle fiercely on the campaign trail, but once in office they typically become friends.

Compromise and adjustment have important implications for public virtue. In the idea of compromise, though never quite stated, is the notion of a truly *public* interest. However energetically the parties may oppose one another, however earnestly they may seek victory for themselves, there comes a point in the formulation of public policy where each must acknowledge the dignity of the other. Where politicians become so vehement in their dividedness that they cannot continue to communicate—as in the recent past of Lebanon or El Salvador—republicanism cannot last.

3. It Is a Politics of Inherent Stability

Proportional representation systems are generally not noted for stability. Not infrequently, the government of the moment depends on the cooperation of several coalition members, any one of whom could pull out and send the government crashing. So it is that Italy, for example, has gone through forty-four governments since World War II. Then, too, multiparty systems are haunted by the possibility that ideologues on one side or the other may somehow gain the whip hand. In Menachem Begin's Likud coalition in Israel, for instance, small parties on the religious right consistently hindered the government in its efforts to find peace. And in many such systems, oddly enough, some of the parties even aim to destroy the establishment itself.

Once again, American politics provides a striking contrast. Rather than having factions on the loose as separate parties, the two-party system makes all groups, including factions, climb into the same bed. To be sure, they often make strange bedfellows, as we have seen, but somehow the bed must hold them. This is accomplished by formulating the party's program as broadly and generally as possible. By itself the feminist vote, the black vote, or the labor vote might be narrow and self-seeking, but by the time they come together in the Democratic party they advance the welfare of millions. Thus, just as Madison's large republic diminished the

Why the Parties Cannot Afford to Take Strong Ideological Positions:

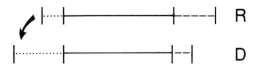

The Republican party has decided to take a strong ideological position on a conservative issue. This will cause them to lose the liberal elements in the Party. The liberal element will jump ship and join the Democrats. This may make it impossible for the Party to win elections.

influence of any particular faction, the large political party reconciles differences and promotes the common good.

4. It Is Often a Politics of Deadlock

So far in our comparison, the two-party system looks good. The contrast, however, is not always so flattering. Whatever else their flaws, multiparty systems do offer the voters meaningful choices. In the France of Francoise Mitterrand, for example, one can vote for candidates ranging from the Gaulist party on the far right to the Communist party on the far left, and know that in the complex arithmetic of government the vote will count. The politics of America, on the other hand, is often that of Tweedledum versus Tweedledee. For that reason alone, many voters refuse to participate.

And there is another problem. Even with choices so narrow, the two-party system is prone to deadlock. This is because the parties, in their mad scramble after the same voters, often wind up so evenly matched that they immobilize each other. At work is a mechanism we might call the freeze factor.

Gary Hart: marital infidelity (UPI/Bettmann Newsphotos)

"I Didn't Change, The Democratic Party Did"—Ronald Reagan (UPI/Bettmann Newsphotos)

Suppose, for example, that in a certain campaign the public opinion polls show the two parties running neck and neck. Everyone, of course, carefully avoids saying anything that might upset anyone. But sooner or later some question of ideology will nonetheless be raised: How does Candidate A feel about abortion? The candidate rustles nervously in his chair. He may in fact have a position on the question, and he may even be willing to share it publicly. But the freeze factor seizes him in its icy grip. He reflects on the fact that many voters *in his own party* disagree with him. By taking a position—any position—with the balances hung so finely, he might alienate just enough of the ideologues in his own ranks—and transfer their votes to his opponent—to throw the election the other way. So instead he freezes up.

When the freeze factor settles in, two-party politics moves off the issues entirely and into some diversionary mode. One alternative is for the candidates to sling mud. Most political closets have their skeletons if one looks for them, and the public always loves to see the bones. So the campaign suddenly delves into dark and shadowy personal matters—public intoxication, marital infidelity, contacts with the underworld. Such diversions may heighten voter interest, but they often lose political relevance.

Swapping Issues

In the ideological world of European politics, it would be unthinkable for a party to embrace some position once held by its opponent. After all, parties are supposed to stand for something, yesterday, today, and tomorrow.

Not so in American politics. Where the two parties are hardheaded, practical minded, and basically middle-of-the-road, it is comparatively easy for them to rummage through each other's garbage cans for usable issues. Indeed, it is almost as though they sometimes sat down and just swapped. A few memorable examples:

It was the Hamiltonians (forerunners of the modern-day Republicans) who started the tradition of loosely construing the Constitution in order to augment national power. The Jeffersonians (forerunners of the modern-day Democrats) believed in strict construction in order to curb national power. Today those positions are reversed.

In the days of Andrew Jackson, Democrats were anything but big spenders: they were known as the party of small, lean, frugal government. Jackson himself went so far as to veto construction of a national highway through the Appalachian Mountains, believing it to be an unwarranted extension of federal power. Today, of course, the Democrats are blasted as the party of "tax and tax, spend and spend."

Throughout much of the nineteenth century, Democrats, not Republicans, were the hawks in foreign affairs. They were the ones, generally speaking, who wanted to fight Mexico and expand American territory into the West. In today's world, they are usually regarded as the doves.

Republicans got their start as the party of civil rights. The left-wingers of the 1860s were to a man Radical Republicans, some of whom embraced the idea of full and complete racial equality. Democrats, by contrast, had a reputation for racial prejudice.

Finally, even very short memories can recall the day when it was the Democrats, not the Republicans, who were famous for unbalancing the budget. Indeed, no one called them to account more vociferously than presidential contender Ronald Reagan.

Considering such historical flip-flops, it is little wonder that, say, Wayne Morse could start out as a Republican and wind up as a Democrat, or that Ronald Reagan could start out as a Democrat and convert to a Republican. "I didn't change," Reagan has protested more than once, "The Democratic party did."

A second kind of detour is into the realm of the mindless. Rumor suddenly has it that candidate A is the tool of . . . fill in the blank. Anything from big business to some international conspiracy has been listed as the evil puppeteer. In the presidential election campaign of 1928, photographs were circulated of the Democratic candidate, Al Smith of New York, standing before the mouth of an enormous excavation. In fact, this was the Holland Tunnel beneath the Hudson River, completed during Smith's term as governor. The caption on the photo, however, alleged that it was a tunnel being dug through the earth to the Vatican, so that the Catholic Smith, if elected, could receive his orders directly from the pope.

A third possible diversion is into the world of illusion. Pictures of politicians are worth more than the proverbial thousand words because they convey their messages silently, without argument. Believing his constituents respected hard work, Calvin Coolidge stood before the camera to dig ditches, plow fields, and pitch hay—always dressed in a three-piece suit. Soon after that, political image-making was taken over by Madison Avenue and developed into a high art. The admen marketed John Kennedy to the public as the Ivy League intellectual, the South Pacific war hero, the Hollywood-style heartthrob, and the clear-eyed man of destiny—all by means of simple pictures.

None of this is fortunate for republican government. Few citizens will take their public responsibilities seriously if they believe it is pointless to do so. If the system does not offer meaningful choices, if it clouds and confuses the issues, if it trivializes the political process, and if it fails in the end to make much difference one way or the other, the people will soon lose interest in participating.

5. It Is a Politics of Self-interest

Human nature being what it is, self-interest abounds in any political system. Still, some systems play to it more pointedly than others. In the ideological politics of proportional representation, self-interest is obliged to share the stage with various conceptions of virtue advanced by the parties of principle. The parties of the far right and far left especially, whatever else may be said for them, are often sincere in their public-spiritedness. If nothing else, their assertions of what is right and good and truthful act as a brake on runaway self-interest.

In the two-party system, on the other hand, there is no similar braking mechanism. The politics of the middle tends exclusively to be one of self-interest. At its best, say critics, it is a politics of distribution, cutting up the public pie among dozens of hungry house guests, and at its worst it is a politics for the politicians only, a politics of horse trading, logrolling, pork barreling, and the like. Either way, it addresses man exactly as it finds him—caught up in himself.

Politics Beyond the Two-party System

Two broadly based, practical-minded, often uncourageous parties reaching for the same voters with indistinguishable appeals can add up to a politics of frustration, and many of the frustrated have turned away in anger. The following constitute some of the ways that Americans have stepped outside of the two-party system:

Political Machines. Throughout much of the nineteenth century and on into the twentieth, it was common for certain groups to organize private political parties called machines. These enabled their patrons to use the political process more directly to their own advantage. Where the national parties were ramshackle conglomerations of divergent interests, the machines were local in character and narrowly focused. Yet for specific segments of the electorate—such as Irish or Polish immigrants—they were a godsend. By routinely supporting the machine and its candidates, the voters could win for themselves not good government exactly, but an array of tangible benefits, from improved law enforcement to better garbage collection. Political machines were often corrupt

Why third-party movements fail:

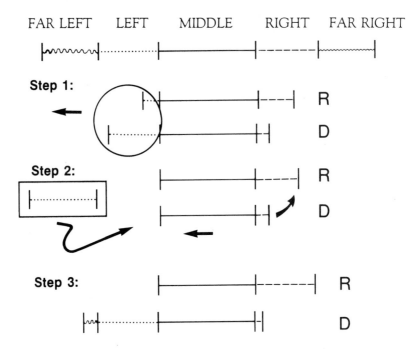

Step 1: Parties of the left are dissatisfied and leave the two-party system and form a third party—the Liberals.

Step 2: The Liberals are now separate. The Democrats and Republicans are without liberal elements. Both parties make a pitch to receive the support of the new third party. The Democrats shift left to accommodate the Liberals causing the Democratic conservatives to join the Republicans.

Step 3: There is a new alignment as the Democrats pick up the third party, the Republicans pick up the conservatives from Democrats and the Democrats are left with the liberal and radical elements.

and they played a dangerous game. For while the machine bosses feathered their own nests at the expense of the general public, they made a lengthening parade of enemies, and sooner or later they were put out of action. We will discuss political machines at greater length in chapter twenty-one.

Pressure Groups. The modern-day answer to the old-time political machine is the pressure group. It, too, is able to circumvent the two party system for the benefit of certain voters, but where the constituents of the political machines tended to be ethnic in nature, those of the pressure group tend to be either interest-oriented (farmers, laborers, businessmen, professionals) or issue-oriented (civil libertarian, anticrime, pro-abortion). And pressure groups carry a larger toolkit. Where the machine bosses had to control government directly, usually on the city or county level, pressure groups can campaign, lobby, propagandize, finance, or simply bully the politicians.

Where the two differ most strikingly, however, is in the matter of political loyalty. Political machines were indelibly Republican or Democratic in character, and rarely if ever did one change sides. Pressure groups, on the other hand, never commit themselves before getting the best deal possible. Thus, the Teamsters Union, anxious about deregulation of the trucking industry, supported Democrat Jimmy Carter in 1976, then switched sides to support his opponent in 1980. Pressure-group politics is the last word in pragmatism.

The leverage of pressure groups is vastly enhanced by the freeze factor. In situations where the two parties are balanced almost evenly, an uncommitted pressure group can be a loose cannon on the deck. Individual officeholders are especially vulnerable. A congressman from, say, western Kentucky must think very soberly before voting on mining legislation, for he knows that the miners in his district are numerous, well organized, and politically active. After all, that is how pressure groups got their name.

Third Parties. Ideological personalities never quite rest comfortably within a two-party system. They see the endless compromises as a betrayal of cherished principles and the haggling of the politicos as a waste of time. Even the team players among them yearn to break out of the posturing and deceitfulness and stand up for their true beliefs. The only recourse for such elements has been the third party, a kind of temporary, though recurrent, aberration from the two-party system.

Third parties have occasionally scored impressive gains against their major-party rivals. Most noteworthy was the career of

the Peoples' party at the end of the nineteenth century. Dissatisfied farmers for the most part, the Populists, as they were called, grew weary with the inability of the two-party system to deal with their problems. They were suffering from overproduction, a high tariff, monopolistic gouging, and an assortment of natural catastrophes, and the freeze factor had left ordinary politics icebound. So they revolted.

At the height of their power in 1896, the Populists captured several state governments and sent dozens of their candidates to Congress. The two-party logic eventually overcame them, however, and they joined the Democrats in supporting William Jennings Bryan for president. Although Populism ceased to be an independent force after that—and although Bryan lost the election—the Populist revolt was not in vain. In order to recapture the errant radicals, Democratic politicians had to bestir themselves and act. Within the next few years, a revived and revitalized Democratic party was able to achieve most of what the Populists had wished for.

Coalition Politics. Occasionally in their history Americans have confronted issues so broad and far-reaching that ordinary politics could not grapple with them. The Great Depression of the 1930s was such an issue. The experience of the Depression affected so many people so deeply, that it tended to scramble the traditional party alignments. In place of the normal give and take between Republicans and Democrats there emerged a single, all-engrossing issue: the role of the federal government in meeting the emergency. Those who believed that the government should assume

Bryan's Populists swallowing the Democratic Party:
In accordance with two-party logic. (Library of
Congress)

an active responsibility in combating the
Depression lined up on one side, and those
who believed otherwise lined up on the
other—regardless of party affiliation.

Earlier in the chapter, we used the term *coalition* to describe the cooperation of dissimilar groups in a multiparty government.
The politics of the Great Depression had
something of the same character, for those
who supported Roosevelt's New Deal—
Republicans as well as Democrats—comprised a kind of coalition. Whenever issues
of ideology happen along in American
politics, there will always be a temptation

for liberals, be they Democrats or Republicans, to respond one way, while conservatives, be they Republicans or Democrats,
respond another. Such an alignment is the
essence of coalition politics.

The Future of the Two-party System

Difficulties and all, the two-party system
has proven itself to be both resilient and
resourceful. As if to demonstrate that a final
judgment cannot yet be passed on it, the
system has recently begun to show a new

look. At about the time of John F. Kennedy, the major parties started reorienting themselves toward stronger, clearer, and more distinct ideological positions. Thus the Democratic party of Kennedy, Johnson, Humphrey, and McGovern moved appreciably to the left of center while the Republican Party of Goldwater, Nixon, and Reagan moved appreciably to the right. For the old-time politicos this was a little unsettling, but for the republic it was clearly a boon. Voters could go to the polls at last and make real choices.

What had happened? A little of everything. Third-party revolts on the left and right—especially George Wallace's American party movement of the 1960s—helped pull the politicians off dead center. Ideological coalitions began forming once again over the soul-searing issues of civil rights, abortion, and the war in Vietnam. Voters of the baby-boom generation clung tightly to the idealism of youth. And a new spate of economic problems seemed to defy the old practical solutions.

Still, there was much of the familiar old politics within the new. For all his conservatism, Ronald Reagan still endorsed the old liberal agenda of welfare, civil rights, and environmental protection—to say nothing of deficit spending! What this tells us is that the mechanisms of the two-party system are still functioning in the 1980s more or less as they did in the 1790s, when Hamilton and Jefferson first squared off. Americans have come to accept that system, with all its faults, as an articulate expression of themselves. It is, quite simply, the Constitution in daily life.

20
The Democratic Transformation

Objectives

The New Democracy
Strengths of Democracy
Weaknesses of Democracy
Politics and Popular Culture

"Verdict of the People" (From the collection of the
Boatmen's National Bank of St. Louis)

The Tweed Ring

When the New York County auditor was killed in a sleighing accident in March of 1871, his replacement, William Copeland, found that some of the Manhattan Borough ledgers were kept locked away. Curious, he contrived to steal a look at them one day. To his utter amazement, they contained, in neatly penned figures, the untold story of the Tweed Ring. It made for pretty lively reading.

The story began innocently enough. William Marcy Tweed, a sometime chairmaker, saddler, bookkeeper, and fireman, at last found his true calling in politics, and in 1851 became a member of the New York Board of Aldermen. Among the "Forty Thieves," as the board was often called, he learned much. By 1863, when he was made Grand Sachem of Tammany Hall—the granddaddy of American political machines—he was ready to apply his knowledge.

The problem, as Tweed saw it, was to get the right few people into the right few slots in New York City government. His control of Tammany Hall helped a great deal, for with Tammany's enormous voting power, he could deploy officeholders like pawns on a chessboard. Eventually he saw to it that Peter "Brains" Sweeny was made city chamberlain, Richard B. "Slippery Dick" Connolly was installed as comptroller, and A. Oakey "O.K." Hall was elected mayor. With himself as president of the Board of Aldermen and commissioner of public works, things were finally in the proper alignment. Indeed, it was like getting three bells in a row on a Las Vegas slot machine.

For the Tweed Ring, as the four of them came to be known, could certainly make the money gush forth. Any contractor who wanted to do city business understood at the outset that he must pay a 65 percent bribe. This posed no problem to *him*, of course, for once the contract was awarded he could turn around and submit a 65 percent overcharge, and the city would faithfully honor it. By such means, the cost of the county courthouse exceeded the architect's $250,000 estimate by a stupefying $12 million. (Itemized, the bill looked even crazier: one carpenter's work for one month cost the city $360,747.61.) In five years Tweed and his friends stole $200 million.

Could they be stopped? Not very easily. With $200 million jangling in their pockets, the ring was capable of unexampled bribery. Legislators were in their pay. Judges were in their pay. Law enforcement officers were in their pay. (When Copeland showed the secret ledger to Sheriff James O'Brien, the latter concluded that his cut hadn't been large enough, and tried to shake down Tweed for more.) And of the newspapers, some eighty-nine locals were directly controlled by Tweed through the use of city advertising.

Besides, New Yorkers rather liked Tweed. He was large—three hundred pounds—soft-spoken, plain mannered, clean living, sanctimonious, and unctuously polite. He made sizable, and well- publicized, donations to every charity in the state. He held some forty public offices, including state senator, and appeared to be a very busy man. He had what we would today call a good public image.

And he had Tammany Hall. The Irishmen of New York did not know about Tweed's shenanigans, and they did not care to learn. They knew only that the Boss liked them, spoke their language, came to their celebrations, marched in their parades, supervised their naturalization as American citizens (150 in a batch, with no questions asked), fixed up their legal troubles, and staunchly defended their causes. When election time rolled around, they sent the Tammany ticket back into office again and

Thomas Nast's depiction of the Tweed Ring: The
bottom line was astronomical. (Library of Congress)

again, regardless of what they heard about graft and corruption. "As long as I count
the votes," Tweed said to the would-be reformers, "what are you going to do about
it?"

What indeed? Tweed and the Ring continued on their merry way. The Boss, a
little tastelessly, bought himself a $15,500 diamond stickpin to wear in his cravat. He
acquired a handsome house. And when his eldest daughter was married, he threw a
wedding bash to rival that of royalty. (Indeed, the money spent on gifts would have
literally purchased the crown jewels of England.) And still the four of them won
continual reelection, though some voters wondered how they could live so well on
their meager city salaries.

Ultimately, Tweed had bigger plans. If he could control the Democratic party in
New York State, why couldn't he control it in the rest of the country as well, and make
himself president? In 1869 he made a serious, and nearly successful, attempt to do just
that. If only he could keep those nasty reformers from snapping at his heels. Every
time one of them would allege some new wrongdoing on the part of the ring, Mayor
Hall was cued to reply: "It will all blow over." He even repeated the phrase after the
secret ledger came to light. "The gusts of reform are wind and clatter," he intoned.
"Next year we shall be in Washington."

By the beginning of the nineteenth century, the American system— constitutional and political—had proved to be a rousing success. The Constitution actually worked as it was intended to, an attempt at tyranny had been thwarted, and power in the government had changed hands peacefully. This record, and the confidence it inspired, had a liberating effect on Americans, persuading them to look to the future and carry on with their constitutional development. From this point, in fact, they would be on the high road to democracy.

By the term *democracy*, we don't refer to a government like that of ancient Athens, where all citizens took an active daily part, but rather to the political style of the United States today, marked by universal adult suffrage, minimal restrictions on office holding, and popular participation in public affairs. The essential characteristic of modern democracy is that important decisions are made by the people as a whole rather than by some privileged elite.

Was democracy a novel development for the United States? Democratic elements had existed on the American scene long before 1800. In many of the early colonies voting had been broad and inclusive, and even in the mature colonies, though there were undeniable restrictions, voting was, in practice, widespread. In colonial Virginia, for example, more than 90 percent of the adult males could go to the polls.

By itself, voting did not add up to democracy as we know it today. What was missing in colonial America was the sense that ordinary people could really *participate*. If we were to go back to colonial Virginia and watch an election in progress, we would be struck by how undemocratically the system actually worked. To begin with, a candidate for the Virginia House of Burgesses would be expected to announce for the office by putting on a barbecue for his constituents that might cost several thousand dollars and require the work of several hundred slaves. And on election day, he would find it necessary to treat the voters—all of them—to a free drink or two. Not only that, he would sit upon a dais in the public square and greet them individually as they stepped up to orally record their vote, calling each by name and thanking him for his support. Politics clearly was a gentleman's game and only gentlemen were expected to play it.

The Democratic Revolution

In time, these assumptions began to change. As Americans in the new republic reflected upon their own experience, democracy made ever more sense. The Constitution itself made a democratic contribution, for it was difficult to accept that document's idea of popular government and still exclude some citizens from taking part. The fact that the Founders themselves did not draw lines— and instead left voting requirements up to the states—was testimony that they trusted the people.

Then, too, the world of the new republic was increasingly the world of the common man. Owning his own land and directing his own life, the common man in America stood in marked contrast to the rootless indigent that he often was in Europe. In America it was the common man, not his social betters, who was taming the land, tinkering with inventions, and dreaming up new business schemes. It seemed increasingly out of keeping that he should be denied a full voice in politics.

Finally, the very meaning of America was changing. With time and perspective, the events of the American past, brief as it was, were coming to assume almost mythic proportions. The search for freedom, the republican revolution, and the writing of a working constitution all pointed toward some sort of cosmic design. And somewhere off in the future seemed to hover the design's final element—true democracy.

A New Style of Politics

Politics did not change overnight, however; the democratic transformation was both gradual and subtle. The prime mover for change was the two-party system itself. The parties quickly learned, for example, that they could create small margins of advantage for themselves by widening the electorate here and there. (Wouldn't *you* vote for the candidate who made it possible for you to vote in the first place?) Even more importantly, the parties learned that effective mobilization of their human resources was the surest route to success. It was well to have competent leadership at the top of the organization, but it was even better to have dedication and enthusiasm among the rank and file. In a relentless game of one-upmanship, the two parties hit upon one device after another for energizing the political process.

Political Societies. Americans had already shown themselves to be joiners. They joined lodges, fraternities, and clubs of every description. While some of these were supposedly secret—with high signs, passwords, and droll little induction ceremonies— their real purpose was to pass the time pleasantly. The Bucktail Society of New York also had its passwords and high signs, and its members playfully pinned bucktails to the lapels of their coats. But the Bucktails came to have an objective beyond good fellowship: electing their members to public office.

And, with increasing frequency, they succeeded. Hardly any of them could be called gentlemen in the elitist sense—they were mostly white-collar professionals—but that didn't seem to matter. What counted on election day was only the number of votes they could muster, and with voting restrictions becoming ever more relaxed, the Bucktails' tally of successful candidates in city and county government kept rising. With a little political muscle, it seemed, it was possible to elect the commonest sort of people.

A New Rhetoric. For one thing, it was the commonest sort of people who often gave the best speeches. They had nothing to prove by employing the high-flown rhetoric of the genteel classes, so they used clean, hard, kinetic prose instead. The simpler the words (and the ideas behind them), the easier they were to understand and remember. There were, to be sure, a few snake-oil peddlers who found careers for themselves in the new politics, but there were some truly brilliant orators too. In a day before electronic media, when lung power alone could make a person heard, there were democratic stump speakers who could not only hold, but could hypnotize, an audience of thousands. The organlike voice and rolling cadences of Daniel Webster, for one, put listeners in mind of a Demosthenes or a Cato.

The success of democratic oratory did not please everyone. For some there was an uncomfortable parallel between American political rhetoric and the demagoguery of ancient Athens. However, if the opposing party was making use of the exciting and the emotional in its campaign speeches, what else could *your* party do but follow suit? Soon the orators were everywhere: on the street corners, at the whistle-stops, and in gospel tents out on the frontier. Indeed, the farther west one traveled, the more of them he encountered—and the more entertaining politics became.

Political Wingdings. Something else the voters liked were those lavish ox roasts from colonial days. Only now they were held in more democratic surroundings, and were paid for by the party rather than the candidate. Election campaigns took on a carnival atmosphere. The voter could wander about and be treated to as many free drinks as there were candidates on the ballot. He could then watch a parade. Along would march the office seekers, waving and hallooing, followed by a brass band, placard bearers, some sort of totem symbol (in one case a ten-foot hickory pole with a live eagle tied to the top), and a cheering section decked out in, say, bucktails. The procession would sing songs, shout slogans, and tramp up a fearful dust.

There were as many different versions of the political wingding as there were busy minds in the contending parties. Some candidates made their mark by shaking hands and others by kissing babies. Some were comics. Some were clowns. Most were "good old boys" of one kind or another. Common to all of them was the realization that elections were now being decided by the ordinary people—and that it paid to be seen as one of them.

Conventions. The place to see everything at once in the new politics was a political convention. These replaced the old caucus system of nominating candidates. Where

Andrew Jackson: More important for what he believed than for what he did. (U.S. Capitol)

the caucus had been a business of the party's high leadership, and had been conducted quietly over cigars and sherry, the convention was a business of the entire party membership, and was typically raucous in the extreme. Amid a circuslike atmosphere—occasionally complete with a big top—delegates would convene for up to a week of politics and merrymaking. The supporters of this candidate or that, armed with placards, slogans, and mandates from the voters back home, would converge on the convention town by the trainload—determined not to leave empty-handed.

The showdown among the various groups might take place in smoke-filled hotel rooms, where democratic compromises would wearily be hammered out, or on the convention floor itself, where sign-waving delegates would attempt to outsing, outshout, and outlast one another in an Armageddon of noisemaking. After hours, the conventioneers could stroll

Andrew Jackson's plantation, The Hermitage:
Politics was still dominated by gentlemen. (Library
of Congress)

among the sideshows, visit the town's restaurants and theaters, or congregate with one another informally. It was an experience capable of converting someone from a political bystander into one of the party's true believers—and often it did just that.

Jacksonian Democracy

No single group or party created all of these changes. Some were initiated by Jefferson's Democratic-Republicans, others by political clubs like the Bucktails, and still others by particularly imaginative candidates. But there was one man who became the visible symbol of them: Andrew Jackson.

"Old Hickory," as he was affectionately known to his followers, was not really a man of the people. His Tennessee plantation, The Hermitage, was something out of *Gone With the Wind*, and the man himself could be as frostily aloof as a titled aristocrat. Nevertheless, Jackson had been a border captain, an Indian fighter, a cotton planter, and a man of affairs. He had fought duels on the frontier, executed spies in Florida, and, in the War of 1812, routed a British army in the Battle of New Orleans. When Americans today think of Uncle Sam, that is more or less the idea people had of Andrew Jackson.

Like almost everyone else in the 1820s, Jackson considered himself a Democratic-Republican, for the old Federalist party was all but a memory. When he ran for the Presidency in 1824, however, he was defeated by what he took to be a cabal of aristocratic interests. (Owing to the fact that no candidate received an electoral majority, the election was decided, as the Constitution requires, by the House of Representatives; and two of the candidates, John Quincy Adams and Henry Clay, joined

Electioneering, Jacksonian Style

What was it like to run for office in the days of Andrew Jackson? One indication is given in the autobiography of Davy Crockett who, as the song says, "went off to Congress and served a spell." Just why he chose to do so is unclear, for as he admitted, "I knowed nothing more about [government] than I did about Latin, and law, and such things as that."

Nevertheless, in the fall of 1821, Crockett "set out electioneering." He began in Heckman County (North Carolina), the farthest reach of his frontier district. "Here," he reported, "they told me that they wanted to move their town nearer to the centre of the county, and I must come out in favor of it. There's no devil if I knowed what this meant, or how the town was to be moved; and so I kept dark, going on the identical same plan that I now find is called *'noncommital.'*" He was learning fast.

Next the candidate got wind of a squirrel hunt at Duck River. Since he was the best squirrel hunter around, he figured he had an advantage. And sure enough, when the "scalps" were tallied up at the end of the day, Crockett's team had won. Before the celebration could begin in earnest, however, the voters asked him to make a speech. He had never spoken before, nor did he have the faintest idea what to say. "I know'd I had a man to run against who could speak prime," he said, "and I know'd, too, that I wasn't able to shuffle and cut with him." And so did the opponent. "He didn't think for a moment that he was in any danger from an ignorant backwoods bear hunter."

The speech began with a flourish of bravado. "I got up and told the people I . . . had come for their votes, and if they didn't watch mighty close I'd get them too." Then, suddenly, he faltered. "I choked up as bad as if my mouth had been jamm'd and cramm'd chock full of dry mush." But no matter: he told an anecdote instead. It seemed there was once a fellow on the roadside beating on an empty barrel, and when a passerby asked him why, he replied that although it had once contained cider, he couldn't seem to get any out. "I told them that there had been a little bit of a speech in me a while ago, but I believed I couldn't get it out." The audience roared with approval.

After a few more homely stories, the candidate remarked that he was "dry as a powder horn" and put off toward the liquor stand. A majority of the crowd trailed along behind. "I felt certain this was necessary, for I knowed my competitor could talk government matters to them as easy as he pleased. He had, however, mighty few left to hear him."

And so it went. Although the thought of speaking "set my heart to fluttering almost as bad as my first love scrape with the Quaker's niece," in fact he never had to go through with it. Stories, jokes, a timely anecdote here and there, and the sheer boredom of his audience "afforded me a good apology for not discussing the government."

And the final outcome? "I was elected, doubling my competitor, and nine votes over."

Andrew Jackson destroys the Bank of the United
States: Politics was as valuable as it was
entertaining. (Library of Congress)

forces to beat Jackson. Adams later made
Clay his secretary of state.) So incensed
were Jackson and his supporters by the
"corrupt bargain" of 1824, that they began
to dissociate themselves from the political
mainstream. By 1828, when Jackson was
elected at last, they were already calling
themselves Jacksonian Democrats.

First as an amorphous movement and
then as a distinct party, the Jacksonians institutionalized many of the changes that
had already taken place. Thus, while there
were still gentlemen—like Jackson himself—in positions of party authority, beside
them were increasing numbers of farmers,
mechanics, tradesmen, and urban professionals. While Jackson was in office, the last
of the voting restrictions disappeared and

male suffrage became the rule. Politics
grew ever more spontaneous, exciting, and
frenetically participatory, and the Jacksonians took full advantage.

As president, Jackson was more important for what he believed than for what
he actually did. He believed that human
possibility was endless if the barriers to its
development could be removed. For him,
government was not the answer—it was
the problem. With its Hamiltonian monopolies and elitist point of view, the federal
establishment, as Jackson saw it, was
always standing in someone's way. Accordingly, Jackson, even more than Jefferson before him, was interested in
keeping the central government small,
lean, frugal, and tightly under control.

Changing the Politicians' Tune

What difference does voting make on the behavior of the politicians? All the difference in the world. For a case in point, take that of Alabama Gov. George Wallace. As a democratic politician, he has undergone a veritable sea change, and it corresponds rather closely with the ability of black Alabamans to vote.

Wallace gained his first headlines in 1959 as the lowly state judge who stood up to the Washington bureaucrats. When ordered by the Civil Rights Commission to turn over voter registration lists, he angrily refused to do so and was cited for contempt. Overnight "the fighting little judge" became a figure in state politics, and in the following election he won the governorship by the largest vote in Alabama history.

A year later, in 1963, Wallace became a national figure as well. Battling integration

Alabama governor, George Wallace: "I was to blame for a lot of it". (Library of Congress)

Whenever he saw officials throwing their weight around, Old Hickory instinctively went for his gun.

As in his famous bank war, for instance. In the early 1830s Hamilton's old Bank of the United States was still around and very much in business. To Jackson, the bank, with its wealthy patrons, its monopolistic powers, and its free-wheeling political influence, symbolized every evil he could imagine. The bank was coming up for periodic rechartering in 1836, and Jackson was determined it would not succeed. To stop it, in fact, he was prepared to go to any lengths. He lobbied strenuously

among his supporters in Congress. He withdrew federal deposits and placed them in state banks. He fired members of his cabinet who would not support his position. "It is trying to kill me," he said of his powerful adversary, "but I will kill it." And eventually he did.

Jackson's slaying of the "monster bank" was highly symbolic. It convinced millions of ordinary Americans that politics was as valuable as it was entertaining. By means of political activity they themselves could make a difference: they could take on the rich and the powerful and come out on top. Even though the bank war came

tooth and nail, he seemed to be everywhere at once. Now he was defiantly shutting down the public school system. Now he was challenging President Kennedy's right to send in the military. Now he was clearing his guns for court action. And finally, in a memorable scene on national television, he was standing in the doorway of the University of Alabama and bodily barring the entrance of a black student. The long and short of his message was: "segregation now, segregation tomorrow, segregation forever."

In 1965, however, the new Voting Rights Act was passed, and in the months following, though Wallace and others battled it in the trenches, the act gradually took effect. The number of Alabama's eligible black voters grew inexorably from a few thousand to tens of thousands and then to hundreds of thousands. And it was reasonably clear that they were not going to vote for the fighting little judge.

Unless, of course, he found some other fight. But that was precisely what Wallace did. Abandoning the idiom of racism entirely, he switched to an array of new issues, from federal relations, to eroding values, to crime in the streets. And come election time he courted black voters as heartily as the white: shaking hands, kissing beauty queens, and symbolically burying the past. Of the old-style race-baiting he confessed: "I was to blame for a lot of it."

Nor was that all. The new Wallace appointed blacks to high office. Judgeships, state boards, high-level commissions—even a cabinet-level post—were staffed by the governor's former foes. And the blacks reciprocated. Wallace began polling as much as a third of the black vote, and eliciting the support of such black leaders as Johnny Ford, Mayor of Tuskegee, who had been locked out of public school in 1963 when Wallace's troopers had shut the system down. But why not support him? After all, as Wallace himself said, "No man should be persecuted and hounded . . . just because of the color of his skin."

at a stiff price—it touched off an orgy of speculation and then a resounding crash—the victory seemed well worthwhile.

Strengths and Weaknesses of the New Politics

The various implications of democracy did not manifest themselves overnight. Some, of course, were obvious at the outset but others were extremely subtle. A perceptive young Frenchman by the name of Alexis de Tocqueville traveled widely in Jacksonian America and filled two volumes with his insights. Democracy, he concluded, affected everything in the country from fundamental values to popular culture. Among the positive effects that De Tocqueville and others noted were the following:

The Service of the People. Good things have always happened to those who controlled government, for the rulers have always equated their own good with that of the whole and acted accordingly. One could step out of a time machine anywhere in history and, just by observing how various groups lived, tell who was politically in charge.

The same held true for democracy. When those who were in charge happened to be the people themselves—a rare circumstance—then it was the people themselves who benefited. This was as true for conservative, thrifty societies as for liberal, welfarish ones. It was even as true for comparatively poor societies as for comparatively wealthy ones. If the society in question was truly democratic, then, solely as a matter of statistical probability, its people tended to live longer, to enjoy better health, to gain a superior education, and to have a greater array of choices and opportunities in life. Government of the few is good to the few; government of the many is good to everyone.

Creativity. Democracies were not only more humane, they were also more creative than their autocratic counterparts. Wherever decision making was entrusted to a particular elite, the members of that group tended to become stodgy and tradition-bound. In the Russia of the czars, for example, modernization became an extremely difficult task, because the rulers, liking things just as they were, were not interested in change.

Democracies, by contrast, were hothouses of creativity. Since no particular group could monopolize the creative process, far more people became involved in it. Jacksonian America was a crucible of new ideas in virtually every field. Jacksonian farmers embarked upon scientific agriculture while Jacksonian inventors hastened the Industrial Revolution. Utopians were busy too. At New Harmony, Indiana; Nashoba, Tennessee; and a place outside of Boston called Brook Farm, they tried out everything from voluntary communism to "complex marriage." And there were dozens of new religious movements, including Mormonism, Adventism, and Christian Science. Not since the Enlightenment was there a greater hope of achieving human perfection.

Wisdom. One argument against democracy held that the common people, lacking intellectual sophistication, did not have the wherewithal to make important decisions. Often just the reverse was true: the common people seemed to possess a wisdom that surpassed ordinary intelligence. Although they could (and did) elect both fools and knaves to office, when the chips were down the people had a way of coming up with Abraham Lincolns. Lincoln, as it happened, was a near perfect dark horse in the 1860 campaign, for the obvious candidate of the Republican party was the much-learned and world-wise William Henry Seward. Indeed, Lincoln said so little during the campaign that some Republicans feared him incompetent, and after the election Seward readied himself to take over. (Seward's proposed solution to the secession crisis: provoke a war with Britain and France in the hope that Southerners would suddenly feel patriotic and rejoin the Union.) Only the people, apparently, knew who was who all along.

The wisdom of the people was not the brilliance of the artist or the acuity of the scholar; it was more like plain common sense. (The cracker-barrel wit of a Will Rogers or a Mark Twain still delights us with reflections of it.) Graced with such wisdom, the American people have rarely fallen for sophisms. Where they have been provided with good information, they have generally rendered sound and farsighted decisions.

Public Virtue. Not only could the people be wiser than their betters, they could also be more virtuous. Lacking sophistication,

The Republican convention of 1952: Sign-waving and sideshows. (Library of Congress)

they tended to lack cynicism, and were continually preoccupied with the right and wrong of things. The Founders, as we recall, were concerned with the future of public virtue in America. They supposed that in time it may very well lapse into apathy and egoism, and they wondered how it might be regenerated. Democracy offered an enticing possibility for that regeneration by drawing on a new inner resource.

For the common people were outraged by wrongs, perceived or real, and their outrage was a force to be reckoned with. The Jacksonians, for example, saw evil and injustice all around them and waged war against it on a broad front. Temperance groups wanted to banish drunkenness. Peace groups wanted to banish war. Prisons, orphanages, and insane asylums were radically restructured, and the groundwork was laid for the modern

public school. Even feminism got its start as women, extending the logic of democracy, began to wonder why they too shouldn't have a voice in politics. From the bottom up there bubbled a continuous demand for reform.

Weaknesses

Despite these strengths, democracy had a number of weaknesses, and sooner or later they threatened to bring grief to the republic. The weaknesses were not necessarily those the Founders had anticipated. Sometimes, in fact, they were only the reverse side of democratic strengths.

Leadership. Under the rule of democracy, political elites did not disappear, they merely changed character. The old elites had been inspired by the notion of *noblesse oblige*, the idea that people of a certain rank and station had an obligation to lead. There were dangers in such a system, but there were corresponding benefits. When a young man stepped into a position of public trust, his good name and that of his family were on the line, and it was a bold character indeed who would willingly bring them into disrepute.

Democratic leadership was another matter. What counted in popular politics was not rank and station but raw ability. And all too often, it seemed that those with the ability preferred to work behind the scenes, where anonymity gave them room to maneuver. As a result, the party's real decision-makers were often shadowy figures in smoke-filled rooms whose only qualification for leadership was that they knew the ways of power. Such people were not, by and large, the sort to be held back by noblesse oblige.

In consequence of this change, democracy advanced a markedly different style of leadership. In the day of the Founders, had someone chanced to draw up a list of the most admired and respected Americans then living, virtually every name on it would have been that of a public official. On such lists today, by contrast, there appear the names of scientists, philosophers, humanitarians, activists, even entertainers—but the politicians are remarkably few.

Manipulation. The excitement of democratic politics was less spontaneous than it seemed. Much of it, in fact, was orchestrated from backstage. As a result, there was a troublesome dissonance between appearance and reality. Were the partisans marching through the streets because they truly supported their candidate—or because they had orders to march through the streets? Were the bonfires and songfests really impromptu—or were they being paid for? Did the conventioneers whoop and cheer on their own initiative—or was someone holding up cue cards?

Those who manipulated the voters had little interest in inspiring or enlightening them, for it was much easier to play to their naiveteerstrike'. Accordingly, for every truly spellbinding orator there were two or three charlatans filling the air with bombast. One of them, out in the Ohio country, poured piles of gunpowder on the tree stump behind which he stood, and when his speech needed a little pickup, he would touch his cigar to one. But that was no worse than some verbal fireworks, such as this passage from a speech in the 1848 congressional campaign:

Fellow-citizens, you might as well try to dry up the Atlantic Ocean with a broomstraw, or draw this 'ere stump from under my feet with a harnessed gadfly, as to convince me that I ain't gwine to be elected this heat. My opponent don't stand a chance; not a sniff. Why he ain't as intellectual as a common sized shad. . . . Boys, I go in for the American Eagle, claws, stars, stripes, and all; and may I bust my everlastin' buttonholes ef I don't knock down, drag out, and gouge everybody as denies me!

Taste of this sort permeated Jacksonian politics. In the famous "log-cabin campaign" of 1840, for instance, the Whigs, in what they saw as an appeal to the common man, advertised their candidate, William Henry Harrison, as a person who would happily retire to a log cabin and drink hard cider after his term in office. (They dramatized the point by trundling log cabins through the streets and passing out hard cider by the barrel.) That this tactic was intended to obscure the real issues was all too evident. Said one of the Whig strategists: "Let [General Harrison] say not one single word about his principles, or his creed. Let no committee, no convention, no town

Politics of the Smoke-filled Room

How often is democratic politics stage-managed from some smoke filled room, as legend always seems to have it? Probably not often, but it does happen. The Republican nomination of Warren G. Harding for president in 1920 has become an American political classic, and, for some people at least, it proved the truth of the legend.

Harding was not a complete dark horse: he had been mentioned as a possibility early on. Yet almost no one looked on him as presidential timber. He was an affable, easygoing man, much given to front-porch gossip and back-room poker, precisely the sort of politician one would expect to come out of a small Ohio town. His real advantage was that he was a party regular and seemed easy to control. And everyone agreed that he looked like a president.

President Warren G. Harding: "The best of the bunch." (Library of Congress)

Just as Harding's manager, Harry Daugherty, had confidently predicted, the Chicago convention deadlocked at the start. The three strong contenders—former Army Chief of Staff Leonard Wood, Illinois Gov. Frank Lowden, and California Sen. Hiram Johnson—stalemated one another through ballot after ballot on the first day, until Senator Lodge finally recessed the convention. Late that night, in an assuredly smoke-filled room in the Blackstone Hotel, a group of Republican leaders, mostly senators, debated how to cut the knot. At long last they settled on the senator from Ohio. "This man Harding is no world beater," they later told reporters, "but we think he is the best of the bunch."

At that point, the candidate-to-be, who was asleep in an adjoining suite, was awakened and, still somewhat groggy, led into the room, where he was asked if there was any reason why he shouldn't be nominated. He thought it over but couldn't come up with one. When he went back to bed, it was with the knowledge that he would be the next president of the United States. "Well," said he, "we drew to a pair of deuces and filled."

Not by accident, the Harding administration would go down in history as one riddled with corruption, and the man himself would die, possibly of anguish and disappointment, before its third year. As just one example, campaign manager Daugherty, who would become the attorney general, would be found running a well-lubricated graft ring from his combination brothel and speakeasy on K Street. The man who had cannily predicted that the nominee would be chosen by "fifteen or twenty men, somewhat weary" at "about eleven minutes after two o'clock on Friday morning," forgot to predict what else was sure to follow.

A tapestry inspired by the campaign of 1840: Log cabins, hard cider, hard cider, and votes. (Library of Congress)

meeting ever extract from him a single word about what he thinks now or will do hereafter."

Not only bad taste but bigotry seemed to play well, for both parties indulged heavily in it. During the high summer of Jacksonian democracy, there were crusades against Mormons, Masons, and Catholics. The Irish were put down by pro-English politicians and the English were put down by pro-Irish. Jackson removed the Cherokee Indians from their ancestral lands in Georgia, and his successors fomented war against Mexico. Almost everywhere there were rumors of plots and conspiracies, all of them involving outsiders—and all of them politically useful.

Patronage. Democratic politics was played by a different set of rules, too. Only gentlemen would play for honor and prestige alone; the new politicos preferred to play for power and profits. And patronage enabled them to do just that.

Contrary to the Founders' hopes, patronage had not become extinct in America. In many areas its influence was severely weakened, to be sure, but politics was not one of them. In the political game—and especially the democratic political game—there was a constant temptation to use the power and perquisites of office as a reward for faithful service. John would help Bill get elected, and in return Bill would appoint John to some office. A few politicians, like Jefferson, steadfastly resisted such pressures. When his party swept into office in 1800, Jefferson left competent Federalists undisturbed in all but the uppermost level of government.

Jefferson's successors, though, were ever more sorely tempted. For, as the parties became more and more democratic, they stood more and more in need of a new energy source. After all, how could a party expect its ward heelers and precinct captains to spend endless hours meeting the voters and listening to their complaints if the job's only reward was a sense of virtue? Appointive office, on the other hand, was tangible, prestigious, and universally gratifying. Its hours were short and flexible. It came with a title on the door, an assortment of "perks," and a degree of social standing. And, best of all, officeholding meant power—the ability to intercede in human affairs and make things happen. So great was the demand for office that the politicians eventually gave in and began handing out appointments freely. Andrew Jackson made the practice official by declaring: "To the victor belong the spoils!"

Corruption. In and of itself, patronage was not necessarily corrupt. If it was carried on in the open, if both parties could make use of it, and if it could be kept in bounds by a sense of propriety, patronage could fulfill a legitimate, though very human, function. The problem was that all of those restraints had to be self-imposed—which was a little like asking the fox to police the chicken coop.

And for many politicians that was asking too much. They threw caution to the wind and doled out patronage to the best advantage possible. Our friends the New York Bucktails were a case in point. The more patronage they acquired, the better use they could make of it. Soon they were using it to buy votes outright. After all, what immigrant Irishman, lost and alone in the big city, would not cast his vote for Big Jim O'Callahan if Big Jim bought shoes for his kids, helpd him out of minor legal scrapes, and sent a turkey to the family at Christmas time? By precisely such means, the Bucktails transformed themselves into the notorious Tammany Hall, granddaddy of the political machines.

Given large immigrant populations and the assumptions of democratic politics, political machines worked only too well. The votes they purchased kept their own candidates safely in office— where they could ransack the public treasury. They poked greedy fingers into gambling, prostitution, influence peddling, protection buying, and anything else that seemed profitable. But their favorite shenanigan was straight graft. Before granting a contract to do city business, such as street paving, the bosses would demand a kickback of as much as 60 percent of the contract's value, which the contractor was then allowed to recoup as an overcharge. It was an arrangement that benefited everyone but the taxpayers—and the idea of free government.

A Case Study in Democracy

We can see both sides of democracy at work in the way the Jacksonians dealt with a specific problem. This particular problem was a tough one, and other political systems may have had just as much difficulty in dealing with it. Still, it is hard to escape the conclusion that democracy figured prominently in the way the problem was handled. Indeed, autocratic forms of government facing the same problem—such

Of Politics and Pop Culture

The following essay was written by a historian of modern America. Although it is deliberately unkind to both politics and popular culture, its basic thesis—that democratic politicians must appeal to a "pop culture mentality"—is worth thinking about.

Americans, who watch something like four hours of television every day, often seem not to know where popular culture leaves off and serious politics begins. This is because many politicians, in trying to reach the masses, have learned to appeal to the pop-culture mentality. A few particulars:

Popular culture has taught voters to look for, identify with, and respond to *images*. I switch to Marlboros because I see myself (or would like to) as that suave, virile, ruggedly handsome cowboy who is always squinting into the sunset. Unsurprisingly, then, politicians build images too. There are plenty of Marlboro Cowboys running for office every year, and their managers know just how to pose them in the light of the setting sun.

Popular culture has taught voters to love sports. They follow the home team passionately, keep track of box scores, and spend Monday nights with the NFL. Politicians trade on this too. They make use of athletic metaphors—running, fighting, winning— and conduct their campaigns like sporting events. The "fans," of course, are expected to root and cheer and maybe even throw popcorn. And after the votes are counted, they are expected to go home and forget all about it. After all, it's only a game.

Popular culture has given voters a taste for scandal. Magazines like *True Confessions* and *Hollywood Tattler* ply their readers with salacious gossip while soap operas spin out an endless tapestry of intrigue. Politicians make good use of this taste. They know that allegations of scandal—especially juicy scandal—are surefire attention-getters, and on election day can be translated into votes.

as czarist Russia—solved it comparatively easily, while in the United States it very nearly spelled the end of the republic. The problem was slavery.

Slavery Before the Democratic Revolution

Black slavery, once practiced throughout colonial America, had become an exclusively southern institution by the time of the Revolution. Although it was generally recognized as an evil, it was also, alas, financially rewarding—for northern bankers as well as for southern planters. Along with slavery there was a slave-owning interest, politically very powerful. Yet the Constitution was designed to keep such interests under control, and for a good many years it did so successfully.

Popular culture has taught voters to love melodrama. Familiar heroes and villains permeate our dramatic entertainment, and familiar things happen to them in the end. The politicians know this, too. That is why political issues are so often sensationalized and complex situations reduced to caricature. To many Americans Fidel Castro, Muammar Gaddafi, and the Ayatollah Khomeini are not real people at all—just typical foils for Dirty Harry.

Popular culture has taught voters to love fantasy, and sometimes to blur its distinction with reality. Monstrous, boat-eating sharks, a loveable extraterrestrial, the Nazi-zapping lost ark are not a part of the real world. But neither is continued prosperity with a $200 billion deficit. Or meaningful civil rights without government action. Or nuclear disarmament without a willingness to negotiate. It is no accident that Ronald Reagan's Strategic Defense Initiative was dubbed Star Wars by its critics, for it appeals to the same mentality as the Lucas film.

Popular culture has taught voters to respond to advertising. Peering into the hamburger bun, the little old lady asks "Where's the beef?" and Wendy's doubles its profits. Only naturally, then, Walter Mondale could ask the same question of Gary Hart and wind up with a similar bonanza. (That episode clearly marked the turning point of the 1984 Democratic nomination.) Precisely like advertising, political slogans have long since become bumper-sticker cliches.

Popular culture has taught voters to respond to fads and fashions. Hemlines go up and down. Hairstyles are in and out. Hip turns preppy and preppy turns punk. Similar dynamics govern the fortunes of the politicians. In the 1960s rebellious youth rallied to George McGovern—in the 1980s they prefer Ronald Reagan. Each new cause in democratic politics is presented as the latest bandwagon, with the hope that fashion-minded voters will jump aboard.

Popular culture has taught the voters to believe in peace, love, and happy endings. Imagine how you would feel if Rocky got clobbered or Indiana Jones died of snake bite. Politicians know this very well. Here and there, perhaps, a reckless Walter Mondale might suggest that taxes will have to be raised in order to cut the deficit, but the voters, accustomed to the politics of "feelin' good," will assuredly pay no heed. Why, higher taxes, they say, would be like sinking the Love Boat.

Consider, for example, the issue of expanding slavery into the West. Because cotton planting exhausted the soil, planters were constantly looking for new lands to cultivate, and by 1820 slavery had spread beyond the Mississippi. There was considerable consternation over this. Should a single interest, people asked, be allowed to expand its influence indefinitely? But in this instance the constitutional system performed well, and the politicians were able to work out a compromise. They agreed to maintain a rough parity in Congress between slaveholding and nonslaveholding states, and to limit the future expansion of slavery to the southern half of the West. The Missouri Compromise, as it was called, essentially satisfied everyone.

Slavery and Democratic Reform

Jacksonian America had a far more difficult time with the slavery issue. In the first place, slavery was no longer viewed as just another interest. In 1830 the abolitionists began their crusade against it with the publication of William Lloyd Garrison's weekly, *The Liberator*. Garrison was not popular, even in his native Boston, but he understood the Jacksonian conscience. If power, privilege, and corruption were undesirable, he asked, what could be more powerful or privileged than the owning of fellow human beings—and what could be more corrupt? So it was that the slavery question landed in the mainstream of democratic reform.

Southerners acquired new moral perspectives, too. When slavery was openly attacked, they took a second look at it and also at themselves. Much of what was uniquely Southern was connected in one way or another to the "peculiar institution." The out-of-doors life, genteel society, an emphasis on human relationships, a feeling for home and community—here were the beginnings of a distinctive regional culture. To challenge slavery was not just an exercise in moral philosophy, it was an affront to the Southern way of life.

What was important about these ideas was their democratic nature. They were ideas of the people themselves, not just the politicians. And they were directly connected to basic American values. There was undeniable virtue in the Northern notion that slavery besmirched the American republic, but there was also virtue in Southerners' defense of their homeland. Yet the issue wasn't who was right or wrong: the issue was that deeply held moral convictions, right *or* wrong, were not likely to be subjects for compromise.

Illustration from an abolitionist pamphlet: Why slavery bothered Americans. (Library of Congress)

Slavery and the Politicians

The increasingly strident tones north and south created new opportunities for the democratic politicians. In the North, taking a stand against the continued expansion of slavery was ever more popular. One could win elections that way, and for many politicians that was enough. When Abraham Lincoln ran for Congress on the free-soil platform of the Republican party, it was not out of principle alone: it was also out of political savvy.

Southern politicians did the same thing in reverse. *They* won elections by promising to keep slavery expanding, and, later on, by promising to secede from the Union if the expansion was brought to an end. These fire-eaters, as they were called, are remembered today as irresponsible fanatics, but if the South had won the Civil War, they would have become its Tom Jeffersons and Patrick Henrys. Above all else, they were typical Jacksonians—flexible in their approach to politics where their own self-interest was concerned.

Take John C. Calhoun as an example. His first aspiration was to be president, not of a Southern confederacy but of the United States. He began his career as a congressman from South Carolina and went on to become vice-president under Andrew Jackson. He was admired north and south as a man of exceptional brilliance and might well have become Old Hickory's successor. But his luck turned sour. There was a sticky little imbroglio in the cabinet (involving the reputed virtue of someone's wife) and, from Jackson's point of view, Calhoun came down on the wrong side. He resigned and went back to South Carolina, a bitter and disappointed man, and not long afterward began working on a constitutional theory that would enable the South to secede from the union. It was a classic case of sailing on democracy's shifting tides.

Slavery and the Democratic Downside

What about the dark side of democracy—the hatred and suspicion that seemed to lurk in the Jacksonian mind? Slavery intensified it. The slaves of the South were not fellow Europeans; they were black Africans. Their very presence in white society produced a tangle of anxieties. Racial and sexual taboos reached disturbing new heights where the slaves were concerned, and fear of a slave uprising became almost hysterical.

Under these pressures, Southerners began to react irrationally. They sought to justify slavery by denying the slave's spirituality, his intelligence, his very humanity. Slavery was not an evil, they affirmed, it was a positive good—and anyone who thought otherwise was an enemy. They came to see abolitionists as

John C. Calhoun: Sailing on the shifting tides. (U.S. Capitol)

madmen, and Northern politicians as opportunists and cowards. Republicans they especially despised. If a Black Republican (their term) ever got to the White House, they vowed, they would secede from the Union at once.

Northerners had their paranoia, too. For them, the lurking evil was something they called the "slave-power conspiracy." Almost everything that happened could be charged to it. For example, when Moses Austin led a band of American settlers to northern Mexico in 1819, the enterprise seemed innocent and aboveboard. But later on, when slaveholding Texas broke away from Mexico and applied for American annexation, the whole thing suddenly fit into the slave-power conspiracy. So exercised did Northern opinion become that Texas had to postpone statehood for a decade.

Denouement

Matters came to a head in 1846 with the outbreak of the Mexican War. As a result of the war, the United States acquired the whole of the present-day Southwest, from the Pacific Ocean to the Rio Grande. And an increasing number of Northerners were convinced they knew why. The slave-power conspiracy had outdone itself at last. It had to be stopped.

Almost in a panic, Northern politicians decided on a showdown. In the House of Representatives they introduced (and repeatedly passed) a piece of legislation known as the Wilmot Proviso, stipulating that slavery was to be barred forever in all territories taken from Mexico. The Wilmot Proviso failed in the Senate, where the sectional balance was even, but that merely postponed the day of reckoning. Sooner or later, new states in the Southwest would be applying for admission to the Union, and the deadlock over Texas would be nothing by comparison.

What sense can we make of all this? The Constitution, which had worked so well before the democratic revolution, was not working well any longer. It had been designed to deal with runaway self-interest, and to keep such interest from leading to tyranny or anarchy. But history had posed a different problem for it, a moral problem with no obvious solution, a problem not wholly relevant to self-interest, a problem over which reasonable men could differ.

Democracy was not the cause of the problem, but it proved to be a fearful complication. For with the advent of democracy, the passions and prejudices of the people had to be taken into account. In a democratic world, the differences between the North and the South were no longer something that gentlemen could sit down and work out—they were differences that had to be resolved in millions of minds and hearts.

The Pilgrims had learned that America meant change, and so it did. Developments such as democracy and slavery, unknown in the Old World, altered the existing meanings of things. What *did* patriotism mean to a Southerner living in 1850? Did it mean that he supported the United States, which was increasingly hostile to the ways of his state and his people, or did it mean that he supported his state and his people—and slavery? Only one thing was clear. As the sun set on Jacksonian America, the great republic of the Western world, barely a human lifespan old, was living on borrowed time.

21
Crisis of the Republic

Concepts

Failure of Political Virtue
Failure of Structural Controls
War Changes Constitution
Public Virtue Saves Union

General Lewis Armistead and his Virginians momentarily break through the Union line at Gettysburg: The tragedy of a broken vow. (National Archives)

Pickett's Charge

At ten minutes after two, Porter Alexander's cannons fell silent. The brownish-yellow smoke began drifting from the woods on Seminary Ridge as the men, lying in long rows like toppled fences, scrambled to their feet. General Pickett, his long, brown curls falling about his shoulders, drew his sword and raised it above his head. Garnett's and Kemper's brigades fell into formation first, with Armistead's directly behind them. When the order to march came down the line, General Armistead, his voice never very strong, bawled out with all his strength: "All right now, boys, for your wives, your sweethearts, for Virginia! At route step, forward, *ho!*"

It was an awesome sight. Three divisions, fifteen thousand men, the blue flags of Virginia fluttering softly in the blazing July afternoon, all in perfect formation in a front a mile wide, the sun glinting from their fixed bayonets, advanced majestically into the meadows beyond the ridge. Below them swept the valley, scarred and smoldering from two days of battle and dotted with thousands of bloating corpses— but beautiful nonetheless. And across the valley, along the boulder-strewn croppings of Cemetery Ridge, was Mead's entire army, three corps strong, reinforced and dug in, with Hancock's Second Corps dead in the center of the line.

Winfield Scott Hancock. The best soldier in the Union army and Lewis Armistead's best friend in the world. Last night, while the boys were sitting around the campfires, a tenor had sung the old Irish ballad, "Kathleen Mavourneen," and the memories had come flooding back. Armistead thought of that night before the war, when all the young officers had stood around the piano drinking toasts and singing songs, "Kathleen Mavourneen" among them, and in the end, since some were bound for the blue and others for the gray, had become tearfully sentimental. And how, when the singing was done, Armistead had clasped Hancock's hands and taken a solemn oath: "If I lift a hand against you, friend, may God strike me dead." How tragic it was when a nation made war upon itself.

But Pickett's charge was supposed to bring the war to an end. The Union army had lost battle after battle in Virginia, and General Lee, sensing his chance, had decided to invade the North. Three days ago, quite by accident, the two armies had collided on the outskirts of the Pennsylvania picket-fence town of Gettysburg, and here they were. After two days of brutally heavy, but inconclusive, fighting, Lee had decided to go for broke with a frontal assault at the Union center. If Pickett and his men, in a final supreme effort, could breech the Union line, the Civil War would be over.

Armistead's ranks were thinning and becoming ragged. The federal cannons were pounding them fearfully. Gaping holes opened up where the percussion shells hit, and the solid shot sliced through the brigade like murderous bowling balls. Strewn in the general's path, now, were men doubled over in agony or laid open like sides of beef. A boy with terror-stricken eyes kneeled in the ditch before him, blood gushing from his chest. "Close it up," barked the sergeants, and the decimated ranks bunched together.

As they approached the Emmitsburg Road on the valley floor, Pickett's division had to wheel slightly left in order to close with those of Pettigrew and Trimble. This maneuver enabled the federal artillerymen down by the Round Tops to shoot along the Confederate lines. And Cemetery Ridge—how well named—was still a half mile distant. Through the smoke of the cannonade, Armistead could make out the clump of trees that marked the Union center. General Longstreet had pointed it out to him that morning when they had stood together on the hill. At the time, Armistead had alluded to his oath about Hancock, and had nearly asked to be relieved of command. But Longstreet hadn't understood. "Old Pete," as they called him, was always the outsider, and had never known the warmth of soldierly comraderie. Besides, this suicidal attack was not his idea; he had vehemently opposed it. When Armistead last saw him, Longstreet was sitting morosely on a rail fence behind Alexander's guns, tears streaming down his face.

Up ahead a line of blue soldiers emerged from the tall grass with a roar of musket fire. The first skirmishers. Garnett's line visibly faltered, and his right began to reel backward. Garnett himself was on horseback, in violation of Pickett's express orders, for he intended to die that day. His honor had been impugned at Chancellorsville, and in the Confederate army honor meant everything. Within minutes his black mare would come galloping back, riderless.

Soon Armistead's own brigade began to falter. The ranks were nearly formless now; more than half of the men had been blasted out of them. And the worst was yet to come. The federals were loading double cannister for short-range work and soon the air would be alive with flying shrapnel. More soldiers doubled up in the grass. More screams and moans. More bodies. A cannonball zipped past, cartwheeling blood. The lines crumpled, reformed, crumpled again. Armistead was still a full thirty yards from the stone wall of the cemetery when he looked around to see, with finality, that the attack had failed.

Yet still he moved ahead. He took off his black felt hat and stuck it on the point of his sword. "Virginians!" he screamed, "With me! With me!" There were no lines any longer, just a mass of gray-clad men, some kneeling to shoot, some milling about in confusion, some falling back to the rear, many littering the field. A hundred of them swung behind Armistead as he headed for the wall. Behind it was a line of blue-clad soldiers, their muskets blowing out death. Suddenly there was jolting shock in Armistead's right thigh. Blood gushed onto his gray pantleg. He kept going.

The heads behind the wall moved back. They were running at last! Someone sounded the rebel yell. Armistead, hobbling badly, somehow climbed over the wall. He had done it! The attack had failed, but Brigadier General Lewis Armistead had succeeded. Another powerful blow, this time in the chest. More blood. The Yankees weren't running after all; they were on the brow of the hill, kneeling and firing. Armistead leaned on a cannon to steady himself; the world was beginning to swim before his eyes.

Then there were blue soldiers all around him, one of them, a young officer, cradling him in his arms. Armistead spoke. "Is General Hancock . . . would like to see General Hancock."

A voice replied: "I'm sorry, sir. General Hancock has been hit." Armistead closed his eyes. Himself a widower, he had addressed a package of his personal effects to Mira, Hancock's lovely wife, in the event of his own death. And now both of them! He opened his eyes. "Will you tell General Hancock. . . . Can you hear me, son?"

"I can hear you, sir."

"Will you tell General Hancock, please, that General Armistead sends his regrets. Will you tell him . . . how very sorry I am. . . ."

The shattered remnants of Pickett's three divisions staggered back, flags torn and drooping, to Seminary Ridge, where Robert E. Lee met them with stoical composure. General Longstreet was still sitting on the rail fence, like a man made of wood. The Confederate army had sustained twenty-five thousand casualties in three days of battle. And it had lost the Civil War.

Senator Charles Sumner: "Hit him again!" (Library of Congress)

In its early years, the American Republic was fortunate to be graced with both peace and prosperity. Unlike the fiery birth of the French Republic, American institutions could develop in an atmosphere free from conflict. This helps explain the buoyant optimism and unbounded self-confidence often noted by foreign travelers. Americans heartily believed in their system.

But how well would their system work when the chips were down? What if there were a serious thrust toward tyranny? What if the virtue of the people suddenly collapsed and self-interest ran amok? Skeptics in Europe—and there were a great many of them—pondered such scenarios for the United States. Republicanism was not proven, they said, until it had surmounted a real challenge.

By 1850, it was alarmingly clear that the challenge had arrived. The American Republic was about to face a disorder of greater magnitude than the worst doubters had imagined, a crisis jeopardizing its very existence. Here, then, was the awaited moment of truth. Would democratic republicanism indeed survive? Would it remain morally sound? Would it recover its famed self-confidence? These and other questions were soon to be answered by history.

The Traumatic Decade

The 1850s presented the United States with a decade of turmoil and trauma. It began with the request of California for statehood in 1850 and ended with the election of a "Black Republican" to the Presidency ten years later. The malaise was manifest everywhere and in every form. The mechanisms of government ground into deadlock. The two political parties were riven and shattered. Civility vanished from public discourse, with fisticuffs in the House of Representatives, a caning in the Senate, and challenges to duels in the Capitol cloakrooms. And out in the Kansas Territory there was a brush-fire civil war, as pro- and antislavery elements bushwhacked one another in the name of freedom.

Unfortunately, this particular travail was not one the Founders had anticipated. Still, the Constitution's combination of virtue and auxiliary precautions represented the best that man had yet devised for dealing with human difficulties. So it is important for us to ask how the Constitution and its mechanisms fared.

Political Virtue

Far from holding the republic together in the crisis, virtue helped tear it apart. This was because virtue meant different things

The Brooks-Sumner Affair

By 1857 there were indications everywhere that the United States was falling apart. Out in Kansas a mini-civil war was raging, and on every street corner there was agitated discussion of the North-South impasse. But the critical symptom of the Republic's pathology was to be found in the halls of Congress, presumably the last bastion of decorum. There, so it seemed, all civility was quickly coming to an end.

Senator Charles Sumner of Massachusetts, for instance, had visibly discarded his. When a Senate colleague, Andrew Pickens Butler of South Carolina, made a pro-slavery speech concerning Kansas, Sumner answered him in an eight-hour oration, the tone of which is suggested by this passage:

> Were the whole history of South Carolina blotted out of existence, from its very beginning down to the day of the last election of the senator . . . civilization might lose—I do not say how little; but surely less than it has already gained by the example of Kansas against oppression. Ah, Sir, I tell the senator that Kansas, welcomed as a free state, will be a ministering angel to the Republic when South Carolina, in the cloak of darkness which she hugs, lies howling.

Said Stephen A. Douglas, who usually knew what he was talking about, "That damned fool will get himself killed by some other damned fool."

Douglas may or may not have been thinking of Representative Preston Brooks, young, chivalrous, hotheaded, intensely Southern—and Andrew Pickens Butler's nephew. Family honor, of course, was a value strongly held in the antebellum South, and Brooks brooded sleeplessly for two days before deciding that his must be vindicated. The following afternoon he strode purposefully down the aisle of the Senate to Sumner's desk, seized a gutta-percha cane, and began shattering it over the Massachusetts Senator's head.

Whether he sustained six blows (the Southern count) or thirty-six (the Northern), Sumner lay wounded and bleeding when Brooks marched back out, and did not resume his work in the Senate for three and a half years. The deed was blasted from every Northern pulpit, of course, and Sumner became an instant martyr to the fiendish Slave Power. For his part, Brooks was touted as a Southern hero. Through the mail he received dozens of canes to replace the one he had lost, including a gold-headed one with the inscription: "Hit him again!"

to Northerners and Southerners. In the North it meant love of freedom. Northerners came to recognize slavery as a monstrous contradiction of the republican ideal, and to see in its continued expansion the death knell of free government. It was simply not possible, as Lincoln observed, for slavery and freedom to coexist indefinitely.

In the South, virtue meant love of country. When Virginia seceded from the Union in 1861, Robert E. Lee, who was no defender of slavery, tearfully resigned his commission in the United States Army and threw in with the Confederacy. "I cannot fight against my country," he said. Whatever their faults, the Southern states *were* country to their citizens, slaveholders and nonslaveholders alike, and to turn against them over a thing like slavery would have been like turning against the United States today over its racism.

So political virtue gave way. There was no possible conception of it that would have saved the Union from its fate. The Founders had supposed that only one moral truth could exist in public affairs, and that all worthy citizens would agree on its meaning. Here there were two moral truths, and the Founders themselves would have had difficulty in choosing between them.

Auxiliary Precautions

The Founders, however, had planned carefully for such a day. They had worked out an elaborate series of *auxiliary precautions* that would come into play if and when virtue faltered. Of course, these devices had been designed to prevent tyranny and anarchy, not to resolve moral dilemmas. The question was, how well would they work here?

Structure. The structural controls of the Constitution, its carefully separated powers and intricate checks and balances, did work to a certain extent. They at least helped to forestall the final showdown. For the South felt reasonably safe in the Union as long as it controlled key elements of the federal machinery. It could not control the House of Representatives, for the population of Northern states soared ahead of that of the Southern, but it held its own in the Senate and exercised a near monopoly on the Supreme Court.

That left the Presidency. Such were the workings of two-party politics that no one could be elected president without truly national support, which in practice meant that presidents were either Southerners themselves—Jackson, Polk, Taylor—or else Northerners who were friendly to the South—Van Buren, Pierce, and Buchanan. The Democratic party, which elected most of the presidents, was adept at compromising sectional differences in the interest of party unity.

What would happen, though, if the South ever did lose the Presidency? Actually not much. With its voice still strong in the Senate and its own people sitting on the Supreme Court, the South could not truly have been threatened. Southerners, however, failed to see it that way. For them, the possible loss of the Presidency came to symbolize a nameless terror, and when Lincoln won the election of 1860, they began filing out of the Union.

Federalism. Federalism not only failed to help the situation, it materially made it worse. Federalism meant that the individual states were as sovereign within their own jurisdictions as the United States of America was in its. This should have been comforting to the South, for it meant that, come what may, slavery was fully protected within the borders of the Southern states.

Federalism, however, had a tragic flaw. Constitutional thinkers like John C. Calhoun had wondered whether it really was possible to divide sovereignty between state and nation. What would happen, for instance, in a serious confrontation between a state government and the national? The full sovereignty of both could obviously not be affirmed; one or the other would have to give way. Calhoun believed—and Southerners generally followed him—that the one to give way must be the federal government. Indeed, when Congress passed a tariff bill intensely disagreeable to South Carolina, Calhoun argued that the latter could legally *nullify* the law within its own borders, and if necessary, even secede from the Union.

There was another view possible, however, and most Northerners happened to share that. It may have been true that the states were once completely sovereign, this view held, but when they became part of the Union, they lost that complete sovereignty for good. So, if it came to a showdown between federal and state authority, the *state* would have to be the one to give way. When South Carolina nullified the Tariff of 1828, no less a Southerner than Jackson himself made ready to lead an army to Columbia and enforce the law.

The ambiguity of federalism helped to keep the North and South on their collision course. For Southerners supposed that if worse came to worst, they could always exercise their right of secession, while Northerners, dismissing such a right, were equally confident that the South could not. It would be hard to imagine a more dangerous misunderstanding.

The Supreme Court. It was the Supreme Court which was supposed to resolve such issues once and for all, and in 1857 all eyes turned hopefully toward it. The precise question was this: could Congress forbid the further expansion of slavery into the territories? If it could, then perhaps the issue could be resolved politically one way or the other. And if it could not, well, then the issue was already resolved. Both sides had elaborate arguments to support their respective positions.

A case was cooked up with the appropriate background. The facts of *Dred Scott v. Sanford* were complex and involved, but the principle enunciated in the decision was unambiguous. Slaves were property, said Chief Justice Roger Taney for the Court majority, and the Constitution held that no person could be deprived of his property without due process of law. Congress, therefore, could not forbid a man to take his slaves into the territories any more than it could forbid him to take his horses.

But the *Dred Scott* decision did not lay the issue to rest. Northern Republicans, implacably opposed to the further spread of slavery, stated flatly that they would ignore the *Dred Scott* doctrine, and Democrats, anxious to hold their increasingly fragile party together, found loopholes for getting around it. After all the fanfare, the Supreme Court solved nothing.

The Political Process. There was still hope that the two-party system, with its legendary inventiveness, could somehow come up with the answer. The rewards for success promised to be substantial—total dominance of national politics—but so did the penalties for failure. The Whig party failed. It broke in half and sank like a torpedoed freighter. That left the Democratic party to try.

Stephen A. Douglas: Believed in a democratic solution. (National Archives)

John Brown: Confirmed the deepest fears. (Library of Congress)

The wizard of the Democratic party was a Senator from Illinois who, standing but five feet two inches tall, was respectfully known as the Little Giant. Stephen A. Douglas knew that if the party was to be held together (and he himself elected president) some formula had to be found that would please the North as well as the South. Douglas called that formula *popular sovereignty.*

The idea was simple. Whether or not a given territory should have slavery should not be determined by Congress at all, said Douglas, but by the settlers themselves. If the settlers of the Nebraska Territory wanted slavery, then slavery in Nebraska should be both constitutionally lawful and morally okay; if the settlers of the Dakotas did not, well, that was their business. There was much to be said for popular sovereignty. It was simple, straightforward, and eminently democratic. It took no moral

stand one way or the other and thus presumably offended no one. Best of all, it seemed able to hold the party intact.

Popular sovereignty was tried out in Kansas. Slaveholder and nonslaveholder alike were welcome to settle there until the slavery question was decided by referendum. Northern abolitionists were anxious to win a favorable decision, so they pooled their resources and financed (as well as armed) any and all settlers who agreed with them. Southerners more or less did the same thing. Soon there were all kinds of settlers in Kansas, pro- and antislavery, holding referenda, writing constitutions, and challenging one another's actions. Kansas had two complete sets of territorial government.

And then the shooting started. There was a little sniping here and bushwhacking there, and then a few drunken pro-slavers shot up the antislave town of

Lawrence. Finally, it was murder in cold blood. A New England settler, who often heard the whisper of strange voices, got his sons together, armed them with cavalry broadswords, and galloped into the pro-slave settlement of Pottowatamie, where they systematically butchered the male inhabitants. The political attempt to save the republic was pretty well finished off by John Brown.

The Final Countdown

Where did the many attempts to deal with the slavery problem finally lead? To increasing bitterness, frustration, and madness. This became evident in 1859, when John Brown, not satisfied with his butchery in Kansas, put an even more grandiose plan into action. He and his followers would capture the federal arsenal at Harpers Ferry, Virginia, seize a cache of weapons, and foment a massive slave uprising. When the attack fizzled, Brown was taken prisoner, tried in a Virginia court, and sentenced to death. Both in the courtroom and on his way to the gallows, he spoke eloquently of his purpose in freeing the slaves.

Brown was quite obviously insane and should have been treated as such. But Virginia chose to try and execute him instead. As a consequence, Northern pulpits rang with praise for the man, going so far as to compare him with Christ, and Northern armies would march along singing his name. This, in turn, confirmed the South's deepest and most irrational fears: abolitionists were indeed madmen and Northerners were indeed abolitionists. Here was the downside of democracy at its most disconcerting.

The John Brown affair enabled radicals on both sides to gain control. Southern fire-eaters gathered up the pikes with which Brown was to have armed his rebel slaves and showed them all over the South. By the following summer, when the Democratic party met for its convention in Charleston, the Southern Democrats were ready to stand up and file out before a cheering throng of spectators. Splitting the Democratic party, of course, virtually insured the election of a Republican president.

Thus, in the end, almost every aspect of the system broke down. The problem was not poor design—it was history. Slavery was indeed a contradiction of republican freedom, and there was no obvious way to eradicate it peacefully. All that remained was war.

Decision on the Battlefield

In the winter and spring of 1861, a moment of truth arrived for all Americans. It arrived first for Southerners. Then, as now, the people of the South were noted for their patriotism. Theirs, after all, was the tradition of Washington, Jefferson, and Madison, and thoughts of abandoning the republic which they themselves had created were painful in the extreme. But Southerners were no longer thinking rationally: the question of the Union and its meaning in their lives was answered by the primal emotions.

Northerners were in a quandary too. Initially many of them were tempted to let the erring sisters go in peace, and only after a great deal of soul-searching did they change their minds. The question they came down to, after months of tumultuous debate, was not economic or constitutional so much as spiritual: whether indeed the government of the people, by the people, and for the people would perish from the earth. And by early summer, Northerners, by and large, were ready to say no.

A Rocky Start

As a wartime leader, Abraham Lincoln proved to be not only a brilliant strategist—probably the equal of any general in the field—but an operator second to none. In an intricate game of cat and mouse, he maneuvered the South into firing the first shot, at Fort Sumter in South Carolina. After that, however, the Northern war effort was characterized by everything one would expect from an unmilitary democracy: waste, corruption, bungling, political intermeddling, and defeat after defeat on the battlefield. For the first two years of the war the North lost every major battle on the eastern front.

It is only against this background of discouragement that we can appreciate how well the American system still worked. Once the South was out of the picture, the North pulled itself together, formulated a clear national purpose, and set the machinery of government back to work. That it could master the martial arts, harness the energies of a diverse population, search out the right military leaders, solve staggering problems of production and supply, and wage war effectively on several different fronts, attests the vigor of both republican democracy and the market system.

Yet the South also distinguished itself. Lacking resources, manpower, and an industrial establishment, it nevertheless performed incredible feats on the battlefield. In the Battle of Second Manassas, to cite just one example, Robert E. Lee and "Stonewall" Jackson divided their already inferior forces, executed a baffling series of maneuvers, and crushed a bewildered John Pope, while "Jeb" Stuart's cavalry raided the Union bases. Pope then joined the ranks of cashiered federal commanders and Lee carried the war into the North.

Abraham Lincoln: A war for all mankind. (National Archives)

Public Virtue and the Union Cause

It was the South's battlefield miracles, in fact, that endowed the Civil War with its highest meaning. For it became woefully apparent that if the Union was to be saved, it was not to be saved easily. There was no Northern Robert E. Lee. Northern manpower and industry seemed more than offset by Southern skill and pluck. And the powers of Europe had set their teeth against the Union cause. It was truly a dark hour for the Republic.

It was in that hour, somehow, that the people of the North reached the crucial decision of American history. They decided to save the Union anyway—come what may. There were, of course, exceptions. Some Americans, propelled by self-interest, took advantage of the war and used it to improve their own fortunes. Others ignored the war, hired substitutes to fight in their place, or collected their enlistment

Aftermath of a Civil War battle: Willingness to pay the ultimate price. (Library of Congress)

bounty and deserted. And still others traded with the enemy, sold information, or took political advantage of the government. But a great many chose the other way. If the Union was to be saved, they concluded, it would have to be saved by extraordinary virtue.

The Politicians. Northern Democrats, for example, might easily have profited from the war. After all, they had been the compromisers and pacifiers. In his historic debates with Abraham Lincoln, Douglas had said over and over that Republican narrowmindedness over the slavery issue would surely reap the whirlwind. He was now free to say "I told you so."

Instead Douglas worked himself to death—literally—to swing the support of his party behind the war effort. Under his leadership, most Democrats declared politics adjourned and joined their adversaries in a wartime Union party. Afterward,

their loyalty to the Union would be largely forgotten, and it would be the Republicans who were remembered as its saviors. During the next seventy-five years, there would be only two Democratic presidents.

There were Republicans of virtue too. Two of the more noteworthy were Charles Sumner, who survived his near-fatal caning to become a leader of the Senate's Radical Republicans, and Thaddeus Stevens, his counterpart in the House of Representatives. Both were accused of profiting from the war and, later on, of being harsh and vindictive toward the defeated South. But each in his way was a man of terrible conscience, and the real reason for their radicalism was to insure that the war for human liberty would not be fought in vain.

Still, no political contribution could compare with that of Abraham Lincoln. As a Republican free-soiler, Lincoln had helped stir up the passions that drove the South from the Union, and he suffered

The Radical Republican Mind: Thaddeus Stevens

Ever since the days of Reconstruction, the Radical Republicans have been a puzzle. Who were these people, anyway, who were at once so high minded and so venomous, so idealistic and so practical, so respectful of American institutions and so eager to alter them? Take just one Radical Republican, for instance, Representative Thaddeus Stevens of Pennsylvania, the group's unquestioned leader.

He was not much to look at. Above his long, pockmarked face sat a wig—an *obvious* wig—often slightly askew. His eyes were bright, scintillating, sometimes (people said) flashing with a malevolent gleam. His underlip protruded defiantly. His voice was hollow, devoid of music, and often sharp as a rapier. And he had a limp, produced by a deformed foot, which caused him to bend slightly as he walked. He was intellectually brilliant, often sardonic, usually deadly

Representative Thaddeus Stevens: Put his money where his mouth was. (Library of Congress)

under the knowledge of that guilt. He saw the South as a victim of historical circumstance, not as an evil slave empire, and although he prosecuted the war relentlessly, he never gave in to vindictiveness. Above all, he sought to endow the struggle with transcendent human meaning. It was not just a war for the Union, he said, it was a war for all mankind.

Ordinary Citizens. The virtue of the politicians was not without its rewards, as postwar elections would show. The sacrifices of ordinary citizens, by contrast, had

to come exclusively from the heart. Thousands of them participated in the host of voluntary organizations that either aided the Northern cause directly, such as the Union League, or served broader humanitarian purposes, such as the United States Sanitary Commission, a forerunner of the Red Cross. The volunteers folded bandages, distributed Bibles, entertained soldiers, and encouraged public support.

Beyond that, of course, the citizens contributed themselves. Illinois, with a population of 1,711,000, sent 259,000 young

serious. But even his humor could be fearful, "[playing] upon men and things like lurid freaks of lightning."

Some explained Stevens' actions as the result of blind hatred. When General Lee had invaded the North in 1863, he had sent a detachment of men specifically to demolish Stevens' iron mill, and friends feared that he never got over it. At any rate, he bitterly fought all proposals for Confederate amnesty. He demanded that Southerners pay the costs of the war. He advocated the confiscation of rebel property. And years later, when others were trying to forget the war, Stevens was still raving about "punishment for traitors."

Others explained his actions politically. He was a partisan Republican and made no bones about it: every time he came up with a Reconstruction policy, he justified it as a way of maintaining Republican ascendancy. "While I am in favor of allowing [the Confederates] to come in as soon as they are fairly entitled," he said, "I am not very anxious to see their votes cast along with others to control the next election."

But there was one other way of looking at Thad Stevens. As a young lawyer he had done a great deal of voluntary legal work for the poor and the helpless. It was possible that when he spoke of making blacks free and equal, that that was exactly what he meant. His hatred of the South may have been nothing more than the hatred of slavery and secession, and his Republican partisanship the only safeguard he knew against further rebellion. And if Stevens wanted to change the Constitution, perhaps it was because he knew only too well that constitutional changes were needed.

In any event, Thaddeus Stevens put his money where his mouth was. He fought for the rights of the freedmen in season and out, demanded land and education for them, sought to give them suffrage, and pushed through the Fourteenth Amendment in their behalf. He lies buried today in an otherwise all-black cemetery, beside the body of his black wife. Quirks and all, his might have been an authentic—and inspiring—story of American virtue.

men off to battle, while the enlistments of other states were comparable. And casualties took a similarly high toll. With roughly a million people killed or wounded in the fighting, most American hearthsides had their empty chair or pair of crutches. One widow in Minnesota lost four of her five sons.

And it all seemed to no purpose. As the Army of the Potomac lurched from one disaster to the next, the North was gripped by black despair. A thousand dead here, five thousand dead there, ten thousand dead somewhere else. It seemed as though the war would never end—that its ghastly slaughter would reel on indefinitely.

That the North was willing to continue under these circumstances was the truest measure of public virtue—the virtue of the people themselves. In the classical republics, we recall, it was the virtue of the ordinary citizen which in the last analysis was called upon to make the system work. It was they who had to stand for the rule of law, they who had to oppose the tyrants and ignore the demagogues, they who, on many occasions, had to take sword in hand and defend their liberty in blood. Modern republicanism could exact the same price.

The Soldiers. The real display of public virtue was on the battlefield. Unlike their Southern counterparts, Northern soldiers were not defending their homeland. Most of them had no particular quarrel with the South or even with slavery. If there was any rational purpose for putting their lives on the line, it was solely to save the Union.

At first it was hoped that the Union might be saved painlessly. If there were a small battle or two, so the idea went, fraternal feelings would reassert themselves and all would be well. By the end of the peninsular campaign of 1862, when General McClellan chalked up some twenty-four thousand casualties in a single week, that notion was pretty well spent. But it was only with the advent of Ulysses Grant that the full horror of the Civil War became manifest. For Grant, unlike his predecessors, thoroughly understood modern war. He knew that it was impossible to outfox Lee—as others had tried to do—and that in the end the war would come down to brutal attrition. He must match Lee death for death, knowing that he could make good on his losses while Lee could not. Like a giant anaconda, he must move frontally at the Virginian and crush him.

What the anaconda policy led to was ghastly and horrendous bloodletting. At the Battle of Cold Harbor, in June of 1864, Grant ordered one of his famous frontal attacks, right into the teeth of Lee's entrenchments, losing twelve thousand killed and wounded in eight minutes. Yet the men, somehow, were willing to abide such madness. They pinned names and addresses to their shirts for the swift identification of their bodies, picked up their rifles, and charged. They were tired of the war and even more tired of losing. The only course they didn't seem to consider was giving up.

The South, too, exhibited public virtue. The valor of Lee's soldiers when driven to the limits of endurance has rightly become legendary. Still, there was an important difference in the two causes and in the way people responded to them. The South was fighting *against* freedom, especially after the Emancipation Proclamation, and *for* the destruction of the Republic. Such contradictions could not help but take their toll. It is significant to note that after the war, 22,298 Southerners submitted reimbursement claims to the federal government for supplies they had made available to the Union armies.

In the end, the North won because of its greater manpower and resources, and because its leadership better understood modern war. The real imponderable in its victory, however, was the determination of its people. Foreign observers, who watched the fighting with great interest, found that determination puzzling. What was at stake here, they asked, but a new-fangled form of government with decidedly strange ideas? What they failed to understand was the power of republican public virtue.

The War and the Constitution

The kind of public virtue that saved the Union was intense, fiery, and patriotic. It was quite possible—if human history was a guide—that the price of such emotionalism might be constitutional government itself. For those who prosecuted the war might reach the point where they would bowl over anything (including the Constitution) that stood in their way. In their hatred and bitterness, they might discard the rule of law for the rule of a vengeful will.

The Battle of Missionary Ridge: The ultimate
expression of public virtue. (Library of Congress)

It could happen like this. The president, facing a desperate situation, declares a national emergency, suspends the Bill of Rights, clamps an iron censorship on the newspapers, and resorts to summary arrest. That, at a stroke, takes care of all disloyalty, all espionage, and all opposition to his policies. He then proceeds to fight the war two-fistedly.

Luckily, however, there was another side of American public virtue that altogether forbade such actions. Lincoln and his advisors carefully trod a whole series of narrow lines between tyranny and wartime necessity. Some of them were as follows:

Constitutional Freedoms. Freedom of speech, of assembly, and of the press were almost completely untrammeled during the Civil War. Reporters went everywhere, saw everything, and freely wrote of it in their papers back home. When there was a disaster on the battlefield, they reported it so vividly that the government immediately faced a public outcry. And there was more. The newspapers reported casualty lists, troop movements, rendezvous points, and identification procedures with such accuracy that Robert E. Lee took to reading them carefully. Nor did they soft-pedal political criticism. Lincoln was blistered by the press regularly and his policies held up

The Battle of Missionary Ridge

How to explain mass suicide? For more than a century, military historians have been wrestling with an episode in the American Civil War that seems, properly, to have no explanation. But it does give us some tantalizing clues to what the war must have meant to its participants.

On November 25, 1863, Union forces were surrounded and, by some reckonings, marked for destruction in Chattanooga, Tennessee. The key to their difficulty was a five-mile stretch of high ground called Missionary Ridge, along which the Confederate forces of Gen. Braxton Bragg were heavily dug in. Bragg considered his position impregnable. His troops, with their bird's-eye view, had been looking down on the federals for more than two months, utterly and airily secure.

Ulysses Grant, fresh from his victory at Vicksburg, had arrived to take charge of the situation. At length he had determined to try an assault on the far left of the ridge, using Sherman's forces from the Army of the Tennessee. As for the Army of the Cumberland, whose recent rout in the Battle of Chickamauga had landed the Union in this mess, they were simply to conduct a kind of diversion, attacking the Confederate rifle pits along the base of the ridge so as to keep Bragg from reinforcing his right. With fresh memories of Gettysburg on his mind, no general, Northern or Southern, would have been foolish enough to try a frontal assault against the ridge itself.

What was planned and what actually happened, however, were two different matters. George Thomas' Cumberland troops, eighteen thousand strong, launched their diversionary attack, moving forward in parade ground alignment. Despite the cannonade from above, the assault was successful, and they carried the rifle pits. But

---

for ridicule. One editor lashed him so mercilessly for not receiving a group of purported Southern peacemakers that Lincoln sent the editor himself to meet them.

Habeas Corpus. Lincoln did suspend the right of habeas corpus, in September of 1862, and resorted to summary arrest. Thereafter, persons who caused the government undue difficulty could simply be locked up, evidence or no evidence. The number of detainees is still uncertain but it clearly ran into the thousands. The president also made use of martial law, subjecting civilians to military justice in some

circumstances. Both policies were of doubtful constitutionality, and after the war the Supreme Court condemned the use of martial law explicitly. On the whole, however, Lincoln wielded his tyrannical powers humanely and with self-restraint. His policy was to prevent, not to punish.

Political Opposition. Mixed in with the loyal opposition to the government were some truly dubious activities. Peace societies, such as the Knights of the Golden Circle, opposed the war so vehemently that they sometimes actually collaborated with the enemy. One such Copperhead (as the

then, suddenly, without orders, the men began pushing onward, up the woody, rock-strewn hillside. Grant, grimly chomping his cigar, watched in stunned disbelief from a small hillock to the rear. He asked General Thomas what was happening, and Thomas asked General Granger. No one knew.

Equally disbelieving was Braxton Bragg. High atop the ridge he watched the blue wave scrambling madly into the underbrush and up the steep hillside. He ordered cannoneers and riflemen alike to pour down the punishment, but the scene had become so unreal that his men seemed transfixed by it. Even though line after line of entrenchments stood between Bragg and the onrushing Yankees, Confederate musket fire was growing tentative and uncertain. Here and there the defenders, still in blank amazement, began to fade back from the firing line and throw down their weapons.

Down below, the race to the top continued in dreamlike silence, the men too winded to shout. One company commander had to grab a soldier's coattails in order to crest the top ahead of him. And on the summit, still fighting for breath, they threw their caps in the air noiselessly while watching Bragg's army in full retreat. Later on, General Granger, in mock displeasure, cantered along the ridge breathing curses. "I am going to have you all court-martialed," he bawled in his drill-sergeant voice, "You were ordered to take the works at the foot of the hill, and you have taken those on top!"

Why did it happen? Perhaps it was the eclipse of the moon two nights before—an eerie omen to the defenders. Perhaps it was because Phil Sheridan, angered by a cannon salvo that spattered his new uniform, told his own men to go for the top. Perhaps it was the effect of all that watching and waiting, or of the humiliating defeat at Chickamauga, or of Grant's decision to give the attack to the Tennessee boys. But perhaps, too, it had something to do with loving the Union more than life itself.

peace-at-any-price elements were known) was Clement Vallandigham, an Ohio Democrat who could find little to praise in the war, the Republicans, or Abraham Lincoln. On May Day of 1863, Vallandigham made a speech in Mount Vernon, Ohio, in which he charged the president with fighting the war not to save the Union but to free the slaves. After Vallandigham was court-martialed and found guilty, Lincoln, more embarrassed than outraged, took the unusual step of banishing him to the South. When the Irishman returned, replete with a false beard and pillow disguise, and once again campaigned against the war, Lincoln simply ignored him.

Treatment of Captured Confederates. Despite the fact that treason may be (and often is) punishable by death, the Union leadership refused to be vindictive toward Southern prisoners. Even the officers and high officials of the Confederacy were essentially forgiven and their punishment limited to political disability, financial loss, or shame. Only one Southerner was executed—for war crimes in the notorious Andersonville prison—and only one was imprisoned. Jefferson Davis, the president of the Confederacy, spent two years in jail.

Looking around the world today, we see nothing even remotely approaching this record. For all its violence and horror,

Clement Valladigham: There was a thin line between politics and disloyalty. (Library of Congress)

the American Civil War gives us a virtually unprecedented example of public self-restraint. No republic could save itself, as Lincoln well understood, if in the process it lost its own soul.

Stillness at Appomattox

When the guns fell silent in the spring of 1865, it was difficult to grasp the enormity of what had transpired. Indeed, more than a generation of cooling passions and subsiding bitterness would be required before Americans could truly comprehend their civil war. Broadly speaking, the war had gone to the very heart of republicanism. For even though the conflict over slavery and its westward expansion had not fit the classical pattern of self-interest leading to tyranny and anarchy, it had demonstrated the perils with which free government must contend. The American Republic had not escaped unharmed, to be sure, but it

had escaped. With courage and imagination, the people had removed an obstacle capable of destroying their nation, and they had done so without sacrificing their own liberty.

On the other hand, the war's price was astronomical. Beyond the loss of life, which was horrendous, whole areas of the South were desolated. Richmond, Atlanta, Columbia, and dozens of smaller towns lay in smoldering ruins. Virginia's once-lovely Shenandoah Valley had been systematically destroyed by Sheridan's troops, and the thousand-mile path of Sherman's march through Georgia and the Carolinas was a blackened waste. Bridges had been blown up, forests burned, levees dynamited, harbors ruined, buildings razed, and a thousand miles of railroad meticulously disassembled. Thirty-two percent of the region's horses were dead, along with 30 percent of its mules, 35 percent of its cattle, and 42 percent of its swine. Southerners had grown accustomed to eating horses, mules, and even rats, which the Confederate president had recommended with hollow cheer. As for capital investment, the South's had not been in machines and factories, which could be rebuilt and put back to work, but in slaves; and the loss at a single stroke exceeded the destruction sustained by Germany in World War II. In all, nearly half of the South's fabled wealth was gone with the wind.

Aftermath

Less visible, perhaps, but no less real were the changes the war brought about. One of them, certainly, was the death of slavery. This was not inevitable. For no matter how guilt-ridden about human bondage, Americans were loath to do away with it. Slaves

Ruins of Richmond, Virginia: Desolation lay everywhere. (Library of Congress)

were property, after all, and if this kind of property could be taken away, other kinds could too. Lincoln himself tried to avoid emancipation, or alternatively, tried to compensate slave-owners for their losses. In the end, though, there was no other way to justify a war of such numbing cost and so the slaves were set free. However reluctant the decision, once it was made it had a strangely exhilarating effect, south as well as north. Like a breath of spring across a wintry landscape, it suddenly enabled Americans to set their values aright.

The freedmen themselves constituted a second change. There were some four million of them, and they were penniless, uneducated, narrowly trained, accustomed to bondage, culturally alien, often sullen, and black. That they constituted an unmeasurable social problem went without saying, yet there were some to whom the problem seemed invisible. Minor differences—Catholic versus Protestant, Jew versus Gentile—had grossly upset many societies. The difference between black and white would from now on be the scourge of this one.

A third change was manifest in the United States itself, which would never be the same again. America could not return to the happy world of Jackson; the scars of the war ran too deep. And soon they would go even deeper. Radical Republicans, fully in charge of the federal government now, would conclude that Southern society had to be fundamentally altered in order to prevent history from repeating itself. Lacking other means of bringing about the desired reforms, the Radicals would use force. The army would be sent into the

Sherman's March to the Sea

When Gen. William Tecumseh Sherman said "War is hell," he was not complaining. War, in fact, was hell, and Sherman was bothered by the fact that noncombatants, and the politicians who represented them, seemed oblivious of that fact. Sherman was a kind of prophet, one who looked into the future and saw the war making of our own day, when not just armies but whole peoples would fight, and do their level best to make it hell.

Sherman himself did that. He conceived the idea of bringing the war home to the Southern people, so they would not continue to suppose that it was only a matter for the concern of General Lee. After the capture of Atlanta in 1864, Sherman marched his army of sixty thousand right through the heart of the South, burning and pillaging as they went. They advanced along four parallel roads and covered about fifteen miles a day. Foragers, known as "bummers," fanned out

General William Tecumseh Sherman: War was hell indeed. (Library of Congress)

South; its officers would be given dictatorial power; and the defeated states would be run as conquered provinces. Worse, the Republican party would clamp a stranglehold on Southern politics—and would maintain it through the manipulation of black voters. Southerners who might have forgotten the war would never forget Reconstruction.

Finally, the role of government itself had changed. Back in Jackson's day, many Americans had been deeply mistrustful of government power and had sought to curtail it at every turn. But in the drama of the Civil War, that power took on new meaning. After all, it was government that saved the day—and big government, to boot. Only a massive, consolidated, Hamiltonian establishment proved capable of prosecuting the war successfully and eradicating the evil of slavery. The precedent would remain snugly in place. And in the future, when the nation faced another crisis, it would turn again to the federal government, almost instinctively.

into the Georgia countryside and gathered commissary goods for the army: horses here, cattle there, chickens, turkeys, hogs, whatever. In theory, this business was supposed to be conducted in an orderly fashion, and a reasonable portion left to sustain each family. But as the ruins of Atlanta fell behind, a holiday atmosphere spread among the troops, and soon they were on a frolic of destruction:

> Dead horses, cows, sheep, hogs, chickens, corn, wheat, cotton, books, paper, broken vehicles, coffee-mills, and fragments of nearly every species of property that adorned the beautiful farms of this country, strew by the wayside. The Yankees entered the house of my next door neighbor, an old man of over three score years, and tore up his wife's clothes and bedding, trampling her bonnet on the floor, and robbing the house and pantry of nearly everything of value.

More thorough yet was Sherman's destruction of Georgia's railroads. First the men would take up the rails from the ties. Then the ties themselves would be pulled up and piled into bonfires. The rails would be laid in the fires until the middle of each rail glowed cherry red, and then, with ten men on each end, it would be wrapped around a tree and left to cool. Then the cars would be burned, the wheels and trucks broken, the axles bent, the boilers punctured, the cylinder heads broken, the connecting rods twisted, and anything still recognizable thrown into deep water. When they were finished, nothing was left except the right of way.

Sherman was, and still is, much excoriated for the wantonness of the destruction. Yet in a left-handed way there was something almost humane about it. He was making war on property as a substitute for war on persons, and he believed that if the war on property was conducted thoroughly enough, it would help bring an end to the slaughter. Probably it did, too. When Southerners came to agree with Sherman that war was hell, they began telling their leaders it was time to stop fighting.

An Altered Constitution

These changes were so deep and pervasive that they were necessarily reflected in an altered constitution. This was true both of the formal Constitution, the one that was written on parchment and preserved under glass, and the informal constitution, the one that existed as a series of unwritten understandings. The American system of 1865 was significantly different from that of 1789.

Federalism. For example, the riddle of federalism was solved once and for all. No alteration was necessary in the constitutional text, for this was one of those informal understandings; but the change was as dramatic as any amendment. The showdown between North and South had been hastened by the uncertainty of whether the state or the nation retained *ultimate* sovereignty. That was now settled. While there would be those in the future who would mourn the passing of states' rights, there

Southern freedmen: Penniless, alien, sullen, and
black. (Library of Congress)

would never again be a serious debate
about secession. The federal government
ruled supreme.

The Fourteenth Amendment. Three constitutional amendments came about as a
direct result of the war. The Thirteenth
Amendment outlawed slavery, which was
so firmly entrenched in Southern society
(and American law) that nothing short of
a constitutional amendment could eradicate it. The Fifteenth Amendment attempted (unsuccessfully as it turned out)
to insure that "race, color, or previous condition of servitude" would not be used as
a basis for denying American citizens the
right to vote. But the truly revolutionary

amendment, the one that would substan-
tively alter the Constitution, was the Fourteenth.

The Fourteenth Amendment grew out
of desire of Radical Republicans to recon-
struct the South. These lawmakers, with
some justification, believed that unless
fundamental changes were made, the Civil
War might well have been fought in vain.
The freedmen, for example, could easily be
reenslaved by means of certain legal
tricks—a few of which the South had already tried—and the political independence that originally led to secession might
reappear in some other guise. A congressional Joint Committee on Reconstruction

worked up a program of legislation designed to effect the necessary changes, but mere laws could always be circumvented by local authorities and even nullified by the Supreme Court. So the Joint Committee recast its program in the form of a constitutional amendment and forced the South to ratify it.

The Fourteenth Amendment introduced several new elements into the Constitution. It began by defining national citizenship—making sure in the process that the freedmen could not be excluded. Then, in a curious, backhanded approach to voting rights, it stipulated that if a state denied any of its citizens the right to vote, its representation in Congress would be reduced proportionally. But the amendment's real muscle was found in this language:

No State shall make or enforce any law which shall abridge the privileges or immunities of citizens of the United States; nor shall any State deprive any person of life, liberty, or property, without due process of law; nor deny to any person within its jurisdiction the equal protection of the laws.

What did all this mean? No one could say for sure. Ambiguous legal phrases, as we recall from chapter nine, could mean just about anything, and here were three of them laid end to end. What they were *intended* to mean was that all Americans should be equal before the law, an old Enlightenment concept. But how the courts would actually interpret them could be— and would be—quite another matter.

The most important of the new phrases was the second one, which we recognize from chapter nine as the due process clause.

It appears in the Fifth Amendment as a kind of all-purpose limitation on the power of the federal government. Here, presumably, it poses the same limitation on the power of the states. It has been given a very broad, and sometimes changing, interpretation by the Supreme Court, and we could fill several volumes on its various applications. But one application is uppermost. The due process clause has been interpreted to mean that the entire Bill of Rights, written to limit the authority of the *federal* government, must now apply to the *states* as well. Thus, where the First Amendment guarantees every American the right of free speech as far as the federal government is concerned, the due process clause of the Fourteenth Amendment guarantees him that same right against the states.

And who was to enforce all of these new rights? The federal government, of course. That, too, was almost certainly in the minds of the Framers. For they not only wanted to protect the rights of the freedmen, they also wanted to change the way the federal system operated. States that could deny the freedom of their citizens, states that could defy legitimate federal authority, and, yes, states that could secede from the Union entirely, had too much independence, thought the Radical Republicans, and it was time to cut it back. As a result of the Fourteenth Amendment, the federal government could impinge directly upon the lives of American citizens—something it could never do before—and protect them from their own state.

How, then, was the Constitution altered? It was now the Constitution of a more powerful and vigorous federal government and of weaker and more dependent states. It contained new rights, the meaning of which was still murky, and new responsibilities. And it was at last a Constitution of all the people, not just a ruling caste. The United States of America had passed through the fire and in a sense been born anew.

The Republican Test

All the trauma, carnage, and sea changes aside, the American Civil War had the curious effect of vindicating republican government. European monarchies, ever nervous about republicanism, had been anxiously awaiting its demise in the United States. Now, reluctantly, they realized that republicanism was far sturdier than they had supposed. Far from succumbing to the anarchy they had expected, it had met its mortal challenge successfully. It had passed the test of history.

It had passed a test with Americans, too. After 1865 the system would be accepted by them as a given. Even though they would face grave perils in the future—the Depression, Vietnam, Watergate—they would never again consider abandoning the work of the Founders. On the contrary, the work of the Founders, freed at last from the incubus of slavery, would grow steadily in the public's esteem until it approached the sanctity of the divine.

22
American Economic Growth

Concepts

The American Dream
Growth as an Historical
Phenomenon
Effects of Growth on Everyday Life

Signs of economic growth (Culver Pictures)

Ragged Dick and the American Dream

Richard Hunter, age fourteen, lived the life of a bootblack in the streets of New York. He had been orphaned as a small child, and since the age of seven had been quite on his own. He was not a model boy. He smoked, gambled, and sometimes even swore. He was careless with his extra earnings, too, spending frivolously for plays at the Old Bowery Theater and liberally treating friends to oyster stews. But he was above doing anything mean or dishonorable: he would never lie or cheat, and his character was manly and self-reliant. He slept in the streets wherever a nook was available, and dressed pretty much in rags. Indeed, he went by the nickname of "Ragged Dick."

On the street one day, Dick spied a well-dressed boy, about his own age, talking to an older man. Overhearing the conversation, he gathered that the strangers were en route to Connecticut where the boy was to be enrolled at a boarding school. Further, the boy could use a guide and chaperone for the day while his uncle conducted some business. So Dick offered his services. It proved to be the turning point in his life.

One of the many books by Horatio Alger: From rags to riches. (Library of Congress)

For the boy, Frank, and his uncle turned out to be extraordinary people. They had a purpose in life, knew exactly what they were doing, and from the beginning sought to make Dick think of better things. "A good many distinguished men have once been poor boys," Frank lectured earnestly. "There's hope for you, Dick, if you'll try."

Dick was taken aback. "Nobody ever talked to me so before," he said. "They just called me Ragged Dick, and told me I'd grow up to be a vagabond . . . and come to the gallows."

"Telling you so won't make it turn out so," Frank replied. "If you'll try to be somebody, and grow up into a respectable member of society, you will. You may not become rich—it isn't everybody that becomes rich, you know—but you can obtain a good position, and be respected."

What must he do? The advice poured forth in a torrent. He must stop smoking, stop gambling, stop sleeping in the streets, stop going to the theater, and stop wasting his money on oyster stew. He must become honest, faithful, kind, moral, and honorable in all things. He must work hard, learn thrift, invest wisely, and above all, find a way to gain an education. Frank and his uncle even set him on the path with five dollars and a suit of Frank's old clothes. "Thank you for your advice," said Dick at the end of the day. "There ain't many that take an interest in Ragged Dick."

With that, Dick undertook to change his life. He gave up his bad habits, took a room at a boarding house, opened a savings account at the bank. Seen no more at the Old Bowery Theater, he went to bed early, slept well, and arose in the morning to eat a good, hearty breakfast. Education, of course, was a bit more elusive, but here pluck made for luck. Dick discovered that a fellow bootblack, Fosdick, was quite well educated—he had been orphaned by a genteel family—and so the two of them worked out an arrangement whereby Fosdick could share Dick's room free of charge in exchange for tutoring him in the basics.

In the meantime, there were a host of adventures in Ragged Dick's life. His bankbook was stolen by a fellow boarder, and by turns he solved the mystery. He outsmarted a pair of swindlers. He roundly drubbed a bully who ridiculed him for "puttin' on airs." And he met Ida. She was a nine-year-old with a silvery laugh, whose well-to-do parents, seeing the change in Dick's life, had invited him out to their stately brownstone for Sunday dinner. He tucked her away in his memory, against the day of his eventual success.

And of that there could be no doubt. What progress he made in a single year! He could read. He could write. He had mastered some grammar, a little geography, and the fundamentals of arithmetic. And he now radiated an air of confidence, for his speech and manners had improved markedly. That quality came in handy the day Ragged Dick got his big break.

He was on a ferry boat at the time, seated near the rail. A six-year-old slipped and fell into the water, and it appeared that he would drown. But Dick, who could "swim like a top," dove in straightaway and pulled the boy out. At that point, the lad's grateful father, as impressed with Dick's bearing as with his presence of mind, promptly offered him a job in his counting house—for triple the going wages. Dick accepted, of course, for ever since that encounter with Frank and his uncle, he knew he was destined to succeed.

"Here ends the story of Ragged Dick," explained his creator, Horatio Alger, Jr. "As Fosdick said, he is Ragged Dick no longer. He has taken a step upward, and is determined to mount still higher." The progress could be followed, if the reader so desired, in a sequel fittingly titled:

Fame and Fortune;
Or,
The Progress of Richard Hunter

Mere kitsch? Far from it. The story of Ragged Dick, told over and over with different titles and characters, was quite possibly the most important piece of literature in nineteenth- century America. For Ragged Dick was every man: every lean and hungry immigrant, every discontented farm boy, every homeless urchin in the crowded city streets. And it went without saying that America was his oyster. In Italy, in Serbia, in Ireland or the Ukraine, the poor were condemned to their poverty; but in the United States of Andrew Carnegie and John D. Rockefeller, poor boys could make it to the top. To be sure, this may not have been statistically true—the data suggest otherwise—but it was true as an article of faith. In Gilded-Age America, as Alger's millions of youthful readers knew, a Richard Hunter could go from rags to riches. It was called the American Dream.

Partly because of its political freedom, partly because of its emerging national character, and partly because of its unique historical circumstances, the United States gave increasingly free reign to the market system. The contest between markets and mercantilism, still very much alive at the beginning of Jackson's presidency, was pretty well settled by the end of it, for events like the bank war sharply undercut the mercantilists. There was an emerging consensus among Americans that market solutions were simpler, fairer, and more rewarding all around.

Indeed, Americans gradually exalted the market system to the status of an economic constitution. Everything that was being said about political liberty applied equally well to market economics, and in a sort of argument-by-analogy, Americans began to assert that unrestrained capitalism, what the French called *laissez faire*, was the logical handmaiden to republican democracy. Freedom in government, they said, implied freedom in the marketplace.

As a result, more than a decade before the Civil War, market forces were allowed freer play in the United States than they had ever enjoyed in the modern world—and the American republic became a kind of showcase for what they could accomplish.

Burgeoning Expansion

Throughout the century following the election of Andrew Jackson in 1828, American economic expansion fairly stunned the world. Never before had growth occurred on so broad a front or so grand a scale, and never had it sustained itself for so long. It wasn't a single explosion but a whole series of them, all seemingly detonated at once.

To begin with, there was a revolution in transportation. The dirt roads and ramshackle ferries of the new republic were speedily replaced by canals such as the Erie, completed in 1825, and by railroads, whose steel bands began crisscrossing the country like spider webs. By 1900 there were four thousand miles of canals in the U.S., enough to float a barge across Russia, and sufficient railroad mileage to encircle the globe ten times. On the American rivers cruised a new kind of vessel, the steamboat, powered by a reciprocating engine and drafted shallow enough to steer through Mississippi shoal water. There were new roads, too, endless miles of them. Leveled, graded, and for the first time adequately drained, they were able to absorb the rush of wagon and carriage traffic that increased by the week. And on the high seas sailed new kinds of ships—everything from the Yankee clippers that sped like greyhounds to Canton and Calcutta, to the steel-hulled steamers that carried mail around the Horn.

Intertwined with the transportation revolution was an agricultural one, equally dynamic. It began in the South, where King Cotton spread its domain from the clay hills of Georgia to the bottom lands of Mississippi. Enough bales of it bulged warehouses from St. Louis to New Orleans to feed the mills of New England and all of Europe too. But the expanding empires of corn, wheat, barley, oats, and sorghum were not far behind. Americans had always raised more foodstuff than they consumed, and with the new transportation they boosted that capacity a dozenfold. Soon corn stretched to the Nebraska horizon, while Minnesota wheatfields were so large that farmers had difficulty harvesting them. Farther west stretched the cattle kingdom

Early locomotive: The transportation revolution led the way. (Library of Congress)

where Texas longhorns grazed by the hundreds of thousands, and beyond that, California—a cornucopia of fruits and vegetables, so vast and so fertile that it would revolutionize the American diet. In less than three decades, the United States became the breadbasket of the world.

At the same time, it became the world's largest workshop. Heavy industry, viewed with suspicion by Jefferson, was nevertheless made necessary by the demands of transportation—all those steam engines and iron rails—and later on by the Civil War. The steel industry, which was the first to feel the effects, mushroomed from a few backyard foundries in Jackson's day to an expansive titan by the end of the war. After that, under the skillful guidance of a young Scottish immigrant named Andrew Carnegie, it grew even more rapidly. Only slightly behind steel was petroleum, also under skillful guidance. John D. Rockefeller's Standard Oil Company grew up with the petroleum industry and soon came to control it. By 1890 his refineries dotted the country, and his retailers could be found everywhere.

Accompanying steel and petroleum was large-scale manufacturing. American toolbuilders had been in the forefront of their craft since 1850, when they dazzled the Crystal Palace Exposition in London by

An Alger Hero in Real Life

Horatio Alger, Jr. might not have sold half as many books were it not for Andrew Carnegie. For, anyone who lacked faith in the American Dream had only to look to him. Though it was true he did not start out literally in rags, he started pretty close, and he quite visibly wound up with riches.

In the little town of Dunfermline, Scotland, the Carnegie family was respectably poor. Hard times in the Lowlands drove them to America in 1848, and they settled in the Pennsylvania boom town of Pittsburgh. Everyone, including thirteen-year-old Andy, the family whiz-kid, had to work in order to make ends meet. Andy started as a bobbin boy in a cotton mill for $1.20 a week, and moved on to become a telegraph messenger. Telegraphy fascinated him and he quickly got the hang of operating the key. In his spare time, like any Alger hero, he plugged away on an education, learning double-entry bookkeeping.

Andrew Carnegie: A tribute to "Ragged Dick". (Library of Congress)

The big break came in 1853. Carnegie came to the attention of Thomas A. Scott, a rising power in the Pennsylvania Railroad, who made the young man his personal

assembling Colt revolvers from inter-changeable parts. (Such were the vagaries of manufacturing that metal parts always had to be custom-made and hand fitted.) In the succeeding years they outdid them-selves repeatedly in the manufacture of everything from trolley cars to threshing machines. The same was true for heavy construction. Whether building a bridge across the Hudson, a dam on the Ten-nessee River, or a canal through the Isthmus of Panama, Yankee know-how proved to be efficient and competitive.

American industry, in fact, reached ever higher levels of sophistication. Just as the Americans learned that precisely tooled parts could be assembled interchangeably, so too they learned that factories located near strategic materials were much more efficient, and that machines deployed sys-tematically on the factory floor were more

telegrapher and then his private secretary. Soon he knew the business so well that Scott could send him off to Europe to market the company's securities, and on the commissions he earned (plus some shrewd investing on his own) he was making fifty thousand dollars a year.

At that point he began investing in earnest. Steel seemed to be the up-and-coming thing, especially for the expanding railroad industry, so Carnegie plunged headlong into the building of a single giant plant, which, in honor of the Pennsylvania Railroad's president, he named the J. Edgar Thompson Steel Works. Not surprisingly, Mr. Thompson was soon buying all of his rails from Carnegie.

That was how his whole career went. It wasn't so much that he knew about steel, it was that he knew about people. He had the knack of picking geniuses to work for him and then finding ways to make them outdo themselves. For example, Charles Schwab, one of his managers, noted how many heats of steel were being turned out by a rival furnace, and simply scrawled the figure in chalk on the plant floor one day. When the workers figured out what the number meant, they became determined to beat it. Almost daily the number kept going up, for Carnegie's "Lucy" furnace was now pitted in a go-for-broke contest with the competition's "Isabella." Soon Lucy's production quadrupled.

Carnegie was always beating the competition. He was a brilliant marketeer. He could anticipate shifts in demand. He kept abreast of the newest and best technology. He knew how to expand in all the right places. Eventually his own ships carried ore from his own mines to his own ports and over his own railroads to his own mills, and when the ore was changed into steel, his subsidiaries turned it into finished products.

By 1901, when Carnegie sold out, the firm was clearing $40 million a year—which was a lot of money in those days. But the man himself remained Algeresque to the end. In his book, *The Gospel of Wealth*, he argued that it was a sin to die rich, for great wealth imposed great responsibilities. And, taking his own advice, he retired to the castle he had purchased in Scotland and began giving it all away. The fact that every little town came to have its Carnegie-endowed library seemed a tribute not only to Andrew Carnegie but also to Ragged Dick.

productively used. The more orderly factory layouts became, the more production could be streamlined and accelerated, until, in the Chicago packing houses, carcasses of the slaughtered animals were actually moving on assembly lines. The most famous of the assembly lines, those at a mammoth plant in Detroit, would roll automobile parts along tightly coordinated conveyor systems and bring them together—every thirty seconds—as Model T Fords.

There were other areas of American economic achievement, dozens of them. U.S. mining, from the Comstock silver of the Sierra Nevada to the blast-and-load operations of Mesabi iron, became the admiration of engineers everywhere. American timbering, from the redwood groves of the Pacific to the coniferous forests of the Great Lakes, swelled into a billion-dollar industry. Yankee builders, grasping the implications of structural

An early steel mill: Muscle-flexing industrial expansion. (Library of Congress)

steel, began altering the face of the modern city with sleek, soaring towers. Merchandisers, such as Sears Roebuck and Marshall Fields, built commercial empires of continental proportions. And the American banking industry, rising above them all, became the financial colossus of the world.

America and the Growth Equation

How can such a performance be explained? Generally speaking, by the happy coincidence of factors necessary for economic growth. In chapter eighteen we saw what those factors were, and considered them in an abstract context. What we want to examine now is how they came together in a specific historical setting—and what that can tell us about the market system in action.

Resources

To begin with, the United States was graced with a breathtaking endowment of natural resources. It possessed more arable farmland than all of Europe, including Russia. Its climate was ideal. Topsoil in the Mississippi Valley lay as deep as four feet, and the prairie grass that sprang from it was

Early Pennsylvania oil field: The beginning of an empire. (Library of Congress)

tall enough to hide cattle. The slopes of American mountains were covered with pine, spruce, and fir, enough of it to forest over France and Germany together. And from those same slopes flowed water for irrigation, power for hydroelectric development, and a ready-made source of transportation.

The American mountains were full of ore, too. It was gold and silver that sent the prospectors from the Sangre de Cristo to the Black Hills, but it was iron, copper and aluminum that would ultimately prove more important. In the Mesabi Range alone there was enough iron ore to build every

steel structure standing today; and there were similar concentrations of copper, lead, zinc, phosphate, and sulfer. U.S. geology also included mammoth deposits of coal, oil so plentiful that it seeped up through the ground in Pennsylvania, and natural gas burning red in the Indiana night. Petroleum reserves along the Gulf of Mexico alone would keep the United States running for a century.

Without this treasure trove American economic prospects would have been dimmer, perhaps, but growth is not brought about by resources alone. There are a number of poor countries in the world

Italian immigrants arriving in 1905: In search of The American Dream. (Library of Congress)

and southern Europe to round up laborers by the tens of thousands. And those numbers were willing to come. The economies of many European countries were slogging along in the doldrums, and living conditions were all but desperate. For many young people, unschooled, untrained, and facing a future of deepening poverty, the prospect of a better life in the United States seemed well worth the risk. Between 1866 and 1915 some 25 million immigrants poured into the U.S. It was the largest migration in history.

This labor force was not only cheap and plentiful, it was of exceptionally high quality. Peasants who had eked out a living in the marshlands of Latvia or the barren hillsides of Sicily were well accustomed to hard work, and the condition of their lives had typically been so dire that anything seemed like an improvement. Many of them, moreover, fervently believed in the American Dream, and eagerly sought the chance to make their fortune. On the whole, they worked hard, learned fast, lived modestly, and took their American citizenship seriously.

with relatively affluent resources, and at least one rich one—Japan—with virtually no resources at all. This fact underscores the necessity of the remaining elements in the growth equation.

Labor

In the beginning, the U.S. was hobbled by a too-meager supply of labor, for with land cheap and abundant, many would-be laborers preferred to own their own farms. But against this difficulty new forces came into play. In the 1830s and 1840s hundreds of thousands of Irish immigrants poured into the United States, victims of the great potato famine, and most of them were only too happy to break with farming. Immigrants being drawn into the shops and mills set the pattern for the future.

A half-century later, when industry was expanding at a breathless pace, large corporations sent their agents into central

Capital

By itself, of course, the labor supply, no matter how abundant, did not make for economic growth. More workers could do more work but they also presented more mouths to feed. In order to achieve growth, the ratio of capital to labor had to be steadily increased—the workers had to have ever more and better tools.

To that end, two things were necessary. First, large holders of capital, such as the great European financiers, had to be persuaded that investing American was a good idea. And increasingly they were. The favorable outcome of the Civil War convinced many of them that the United States

Immigrants came by the thousands (Culver Pictures)

was here to stay, and in the postwar years the return on their American investments began to soar.

Second, and even more importantly, the savings of millions of individuals had to be productively put to use. Here again the United States was fortunate. Ever since the days of *Poor Richard's Almanac*, the twin virtues of industry and frugality had been prized American values, and no less hard-working or thrifty were the immigrants pouring in from Europe. Thus, in his study of working-class mobility, Stephan Thern-strom concluded that almost all laborers, no matter how meager their incomes, managed to lay something aside. It was that money, by and large, that financed the new gantry cranes and open-hearth furnaces.

Entrepreneurship

Common people also supplied the entre-preneurial element of the growth equa-tion. That, too, may have been inherently American. For one thing, ever since the Revolution, Americans had prided them-selves on both their imagination and their derring-do—qualities which were essen-tial to entrepreneurship. The Americans also seemed to benefit from their physical separation from Europe. The Old World, after all, was steeped in tradition, and its established ways of doing things did not lend themselves to bold innovation. In America, by contrast, there was no estab-lished way of running a business enter-prise, just as there was no established way of building a community, and in that atmosphere the entrepreneurs seemed to thrive. Indeed, entrepreneurs may have actually been created by the immigration process itself. For anyone who abandoned the familiar life around him and sailed off into the unknown was, by definition, an entrepreneur, and the emigration process sifted millions of them out of the European populace. Whatever the explanation, travelers agreed that Yankees were a restless, eager, go ahead sort of people, anxious to improve the world and their own place in it. They were entrepreneurs by second nature.

In that golden age of expansion, the entrepreneurial influence was everywhere. There were merchants, for example, who grasped the significance of the new high-speed sailing vessels and used it to marvelous advantage. In New England, a pair of them came up with the unlikely idea of selling American ice to the inhabitants of India. Improvising their own technology, Frederick Tudor and Nathaniel Wyeth loaded ship after ship with large blocks of ice harvested from local ponds and sent them speeding around the Cape of Good Hope. They became millionaires.

Another Yankee, Nathan Appleton, experimented with novel sources of labor. Despairing of finding an adequate number of young men to employ in his Massachusetts textile mill, he hit upon the idea of using young women instead. He recruited the girls from the surrounding countryside, installed them in freshly painted dormitories, and subjected them to strict paternal discipline. These "nuns of industry" soon made the mills of Lowell the most productive in the world.

There were entrepreneurs in the West, too. A young Jewish immigrant in the California gold rush, observing how rapidly trousers wore out in the mines, decided to try making them out of tougher material. After experimenting with canvas, which was a little stiff, he settled on a hardy new fabric from France called *serge de Nimes*, or "denim." Then, after further discovering that copper rivets kept the pockets (usually stuffed with ore samples) from ripping out, Levi Strauss presented the world with its first pair of blue jeans.

Tales of entrepreneurial success could be multiplied indefinitely. In Sacramento four local merchants, convinced they could build a railroad through the forbidding Sierra Nevada, became founders of the Central Pacific and among the richest men of all time. In Virginia City an Austrian immigrant named Adolph Sutro hit upon the idea of digging a giant tunnel to drain water from the Comstock silver mines. And in New York the chairman of the Equitable Life Insurance Company worked out a new kind of insurance policy, one that paid the insured to stay alive instead of dying before his time. All of them struck business bonanzas.

Guided by the entrepreneurial spirit, there were developments in the amassing and use of capital, in the layout of industrial facilities, in the use of transportation, in the employment of labor-saving devices, in methods of accounting and bookkeeping, and in the means of putting goods and services on the market. Marketing, in fact, became an American specialty. One Yankee, seeking to advertise his museum of oddities, hired a man to stand on a New York street corner and act strangely. When a crowd had gathered, the decoy would

Thomas Edison with his phonograph: Small contraptions could make a big difference. (Library of Congress)

start for the museum, drawing many of the curious behind him. This proved to be the debut of American advertising—and of its founding father, P. T. Barnum.

Technology

Technology was an equally unpredictable element in the growth equation. And here again, the Americans outdid themselves. "There is no clinging to the old ways," Friedrich List reported of the United States, "the moment an American hears the word 'invention' he pricks up his ears." By 1850 Yankee inventors had come up with thousands of innovations, many of them aimed at doing jobs quicker, easier, cheaper, and more efficiently. Reporting back home, a visiting team of British engineers breathlessly described new screw augers, trip hammers, chaff cutters, sand sifters, last polishers, rope spinners, and a host of other contraptions. "It may be said that there is

not a working boy of average ability in the New England states who has not an idea of some mechanical invention by which, in good time, he hopes to rise to fortune and social distinction."

And when it came to economic growth, small inventions made a large difference. Eli Whitney's cotton gin, invented in 1793, made the cotton kingdom possible. The cattle kingdom owed a similar debt to Samuel Colt's six-shooter—enabling a few armed cowboys to hold their own on the open range. Farmers everywhere could thank Joseph Glidden for the invention of barbed wire. But this was only the beginning of agricultural technology. Plows were soon being hooked together into gang plows, and seeds were being planted with high-speed drills. As reapers and threshers became feasible, dozens of inventors went to work on them. The ultimate contraption was assembled in 1851 by Cyrus McCormick. The combine-thresher, as it was called, looked and sounded like a factory on wheels, with gears whirring and belts flying; yet somehow it worked. It cut a ten-foot swath through a field of wheat and left neatly tied sacks of grain in its path.

The expansion of industry also depended on the inventors. Out of the railroad shops came the Westinghouse air brake in 1869, revolutionizing the way trains were operated. Only five years earlier George Pullman had invented the sleeping car—and now people really dared to sleep in it. Out of the steel plants came the Bessemer process, named after an Englishman, Henry Bessemer, but independently developed by William Kelly of Kentucky. Heretofore, the making of steel had been a tedious process, better suited to the laboratory than the factory. Now a blast

Mass Production

The invention that most stimulated economic expansion was mass production, generally credited to an inventor-cum-tycoon named Henry Ford. Ford began as another of those backyard toolsmiths. That he designed and built a gasoline-powered automobile in the 1890s was not particularly remarkable. Ford's later Model T was remarkable, however. It was cheap, rugged, and proverbially dependable—democracy on wheels. By 1910 the "Tin Lizzie," as it was affectionately known, had made Ford a millionaire.

What happened next was not entirely Ford's doing. While the Bells and Edisons had been working on inventions that would surprise and amaze, hundreds of anonymous inventors had been toying with ways to streamline production processes. One thing they had learned was to array production facilities in a linear fashion from start to finish. In organizing a slaughterhouse, for example, they would funnel live animals into one end of a long building, slaughter them inside the door, and then hang the carcasses on a movable conveyance that would carry them step by step through the remaining operations.

One day in 1912 Ford's magneto assemblers got a similar idea. They were working upstairs in his Highland Park factory, and each was fully assembling magnetos from scratch. Then, since they were standing shoulder to shoulder at a long table, one of them suggested beginning a magneto assembly at one end of the table and passing it along to the other, each workman adding a new piece or two as the unit slid in front of him. Astonishingly, the five of them tripled their production.

It was obvious, moreover, that what would work for magnetos would work for every other assembly in a Model T. Soon Ford was installing moving conveyor belts left and right, each of them precisely timed and coordinated so that each chassis would roll up to the engine rendezvous just as each completed engine would come swinging overhead and drop into place. The necessary integration of the rivers and streams of moving parts fairly boggled the mind; and a breakdown anywhere in the system could bring the whole thing grinding to a halt. But when the assembly line worked, it worked liked a miracle. Watching it in action moved Aldous Huxley to compare Henry Ford to Jesus.

To be sure, there were others who sneered at Ford's method and compared it to a sausage machine, but Ford had the last laugh. Mass production enabled him to drop the price of a Model T runabout from $825 to $290—while doubling the wages of his employees. Against that sort of competition one automobile manufacturer after another sank beneath the waves, and those who remained afloat had to close-haul the wind. Several of the more seaworthy reorganized themselves into a company called General Motors and put Ford's practices to work. So did everyone else. By the end of the 1920s assembly lines wound their way through the whole of industrial America, and along them whirled everything from chewing gum to steam shovels. If Thomas Edison had changed the world, Henry Ford had changed it again. When the two of them went for their tramps in the woods together, they had much to talk about.

of air was injected into the molten iron, burning off in two minutes the impurities that formerly required days to remove. With the open-hearth method, developed soon afterward, the steelmaking process required a little more time, but its quality was more easily controlled. Both innovations contributed to the productivity of the American steel industry, which between 1879 and 1900 multiplied 150 times.

Out of the petroleum industry came catalytic cracking, enabling refiners to procure a higher yield of kerosene from their crude oil. But kerosene would not be the leading petroleum derivative for long. Already the tinkerers were at work on a new kind of engine, one that would burn gasoline, and by the 1880s the first prototypes were beginning to cough and sputter. The story was endlessly repeated. Printing was revolutionized by Mergenthaler's Rube-Goldberglike linotype machine. Mining was transformed by the development of high explosives, and heavy construction by the advent of the steam shovel. Railyard switching, once the most dangerous business in the world, was made safe overnight by the invention of the automatic coupler.

All of this said nothing for the inventions that transformed domestic life: the telephone, the electric light, the phonograph, the radio, the movie camera, and so many others. A preponderance of these came out of the U.S., too, and they certainly had their rightful place. But it was the technology of production that did most to stimulate growth. By 1900 the steel industry of the United States dwarfed that of all competitors combined. Industrial output had soared from $1.8 billion in 1859 to $5.9 billion in 1879, to $14 billion in 1900, and there was no end in sight. Side by side with

Jefferson's vision of an agrarian republic was Hamilton's vision of an industrial titan.

The Growth Equation and the Market System

Why did the growth equation work so well for the United States? There were, after all, other countries with generous resource endowments, others yet with available capital, and still others with resourceful, hardworking populations. In no single element of growth did the U.S. enjoy a monopoly.

What it did enjoy, however, was a minimum of mercantilistic interference. It is true that market economies were on the rise in many parts of Europe, but in most of them mercantilism was far from dead. In part, mercantilism was a state of mind, and it was shared by shop and mill workers on the bottom of society as much as by government officials at the top. Everyone worried that if central planning were entirely removed from the economy, the result might be chaos. To trust the market system completely, after centuries of mercantilistic experience, required a considerable degree of faith.

That was where Americans held the advantage. In a land where everything else was new, the new economics excited far less apprehension and gained far more solid trust. Human self-interest, the great powerhouse of the market system, was not downplayed in the United States, it was openly and unabashedly revered. In launching a new enterprise, the American entrepreneur did not need to justify it as a virtuous deed—as was often done in Europe—it was enough to say he wanted to be rich. And the same held true for other players in the economic game.

The Breakers, the Vanderbilt mansion in Newport, Rhode Island: 9 chefs, 3 orchestras, and live hummingbirds. (Library of Congress)

Stevan Lazich: High hopes and crushing disappointments. (Courtesy of the Mikita family)

Thus, in the United States, the flood of new inventions could be linked directly to the hopes of their inventors for fame and fortune. The ready market for immigrant labor reflected the dreams of millions for a better life. And the massing of large sums c f capital was not so much a matter of personal virtue (as it is in present-day Japan) as an understanding that saving and investment paid off.

Self-interest, then, was the key. It was a veritable dynamo of energy and creativity. To be sure, self-interest had its downside, as the scandals and corruptions of the day well illustrated. But the American experience was coming to show that, on the whole, self-interest could safely be allowed to operate, and that the result was indeed betterment for all. Accordingly, in Gilded-Age America, the forces of the marketplace were increasingly given maximum leeway. In a word, *laissez faire* was what made the growth equation work.

The Benefits of Growth

The ultimate assessment of growth was how it affected the lives of individuals. If it did not measureably improve their lot in the world, then the work and sacrifice it demanded was hardly worthwhile. We know, of course, that it improved the lot of the already fortunate. Those who have visited Newport, Rhode Island, or New York's Upper East Side have seen evidence of how incredibly wealthy some Americans were. But the test of an economic system, especially in a democratic society, is in the lives of the ordinary.

One way to conduct such a test is with statistics. Here we might observe that growth in real per capita income maintained a fairly consistent velocity in the range of 1.7 percent. This meant that real income doubled roughly every forty years—that every generation, in other words, was twice as wealthy as its predecessor. The chart above illustrates some of

Glitter and Glitz at Newport

What was it like to be very, very wealthy back in the days of the Vanderbilts? Those who spent their summers at Newport, Rhode Island, knew the answer. For there, standing shoulder to shoulder on Ocean Drive and looking out at the placid Atlantic, were the summer palaces—officially termed "cottages"—of the country's idle rich. With musical names like Bonnicrest, Crossways, Beaulieu, Rosecliff, and The Breakers, these forty-room mansions witnessed the most splendiferous social life the American aristocracy could muster.

The object of the game was to see who could put on the flashiest ball of the season, and Newport hostesses vied endlessly with one another to win. First there was the matter of decorations, which were supposed to be as imaginative as they were lavish. The Van Alen's had a huge Egyptian tent constructed and festooned with imported tapestries. Grace Vanderbilt put up a three-hundred-foot carnival midway, complete with barkers. And the Levi Mortons had an outside ballroom made entirely of glittering ice. But nobody outdid the redoubtable Tessie Oelrichs, for whose White Ball one year she constructed a dozen full-scale ships—all in white.

Then there were the favors, which had to be something worth coming for. At Grace Vanderbilt's Carnival, for instance, the guests played mock games of chance and were rewarded with gold cigarette cases for the men and enamel vanity boxes for the women. But Grace's own mother topped that. Down the middle of her elaborate dining table, her carpenters built a long box filled with sand. By each place setting were a tiny gold trowel and rake with which the guests, at their leisure, could dig through the sand for the hundreds of cut gems hidden there.

The cuisine, of course, was ever sumptuous. At least three French chefs were needed for the average Newport gala, but one event at The Breakers required nine, for a single course consisted of four hundred mixed game birds. The nine- and ten- course meals could last up to three hours, leaving the guests in no condition to dance until dawn, as custom required. (Breakfast in the morning was optional.)

And then came the entertainment. For a so-so party a large orchestra was needed, but the really nice affairs required up to three. The dancers whirled through every sort of exotic atmosphere on floors strewn with rose petals. (One fete was bedecked with ten thousand roses, another with imported lotus blossoms, a third with, yes, live hummingbirds.) For the older guests, who often petered out around midnight, there had to be some other diversion as well. Mrs. Vanderbilt licked that problem by having her carpenters put up a complete theater with professional lighting, and hiring the entire company of the Broadway hit *Red Rose Inn* for the night.

Still bored? Well, there was always Mrs. Stuyvesant Fish's annual Mother Goose Ball, where everyone dressed up as a nursery-rhyme character, or Grace Vanderbilt's Louis XIV fling, with its period costumes and vintage champagne, or—if absolutely nothing else would please—Mrs. Elizabeth Drexel Lehr's Dog's Dinner, where the invited guests were all blooded canines. Fare for the evening consisted of stewed liver and rice, fricassee of bones, and crumbled dog biscuits. "It must have been appreciated," Mrs. Lehr recalled, "because Elisha Dyer's dachshund so overtaxed its capacity that it fell unconscious by its plate and had to be carried home."

the areas of human life that were affected by such a growth rate. It documents dramatic changes in infant mortality, longevity, family size, the length of the work week, the percentage of income spent for basic necessities, and income itself. The comparisons must be seen over the long haul in order to be appreciated, but even at that they are remarkable.

Yet statistics tell only part of the story. What we really need to know is how economic growth changed lives—how it affected their texture and quality. We need to know what happened, say, to the typical immigrant around the turn of the century, to his children and his grandchildren, as they struggled to make their way in the new economy. Those who have investigated their own family histories know how vivid such stories can be, and how worthwhile the perspective they impart. One of them, a fairly typical one, is worth relating here in some detail.

The Rise of the Lazich Family

One of the European immigrants crowding the rail to stare up at Miss Liberty was Stevan Lazich. In 1912, when the rusty German merchantman on which he rode swung into New York harbor, he was only sixteen years old, and, except for a brother, Urosh, who was off in the Ohio Valley somewhere, he was alone in the New World. He had but four years of formal schooling, few occupational skills, a scanty knowledge of English, and five dollars in his pocket. Of course, he also had his dreams and ambitions, and a high determination to succeed.

Stevan hailed from Hajtic, a small cluster of farms in the hills of northern Croatia, but his people were Serbs rather than Croatians. His father, Petar, operated a farm that was far too small for the needs of a large family, and in spite of extra work in an adjacent stone quarry, the Laziches were extremely hard pressed. Like many of their neighbors, they thought of sending their sons to America, the land of milk and honey, where they could make money and send a portion of it back home. Urosh was the first to go. Then it was Stevan's turn.

It was not established that the boys were crossing the Atlantic permanently, but in Stevan's case there was a sense of finality about the parting. Standing at the train platform in his first-ever suit and leather shoes (until now he had worn only a knitted sokule, the curl-toed boot), he seemed more a part of the future than the past. His mother, Anna, whom he would never see again, handed him a basket of sausages and sweet bread, and stammered a tearful good-bye. His dog, Liso, broke its tether and loped after the train for miles.

The United States, as Stevan found, was not particularly hospitable to Serbo-Croatian immigrants. When he joined Urosh in Youngstown, Ohio, the two of them passed through a succession of difficulties. They were able to find work on a railroad gang, laying track for $1.50 a day, but their wages were garnisheed by a landlord whose rent they had left unpaid, and it was five months before they saw any money. After that, there were small jobs here and there and large gaps of unemployment in between. Stevan spent the entire winter of 1913–14 out of work.

His first bit of fortune came with the outbreak of war in Europe the following summer and the consequent rise of American steel production. Stevan happened onto a brass identification tag left behind by a former employee of the Youngstown Sheet and Tube Company, and, assuming the name of the departed worker, he was

Table 21.1 Changes in the Standard of Living

	1774	1890	1930	1980
Life expectancy				
Male	*40 years	43 years	58 years	70 years
Female	*40 years	44 years	62 years	78 years
Infant mortality (death in the first year of life)	*1 of 7 children	1 of 8 children	1 of 20 children	1 of 75 children
Family Size	*7 children	5 children	3 children	2 children
Population	3.9 million (1790)	62.9 million	122.8 million	226.5 million
Population per square mile	4.5	21.2	41.2	64.0
Income per capita in 1980 prices	*$470	$1,600	$3,120	$11,500
% of 1980 income	4%	14%	27%	100%
Average workweek	*70 hours	60 hours	50 hours	39 hours
Man-hours to produce 100 bushels of wheat	380 hours	130 hours	70 hours	8 hours
Education	—	4%	29%	75%
High school graduates as a percent of 17–year-olds				
Percent of income spent on food	*65%	45%	29%	22%

*Guesses based on fragmentary data.

able to hire on as a shearman's helper. In this country, so it seemed, success came only with imagination.

And with luck. The labor movement had increased its militancy with the onset of the war, and it was not long before Youngstown Sheet and Tube found itself locked in a bloody strike. Stevan literally walked into the middle of it while attempting to cross a field between angry picketers and a squad of company detectives. As he and his friend, Guro Dodosh, approached the mill's main gate, shots rang out and Guro crumpled to the pavement. Stevan then watched in horror as the enraged crowd cut a swath of destruction through the streets of Youngstown. By the time the federal troops arrived the next day, sixteen people were dead. (Guro Dodosh, who had been hit in the hip, eventually recovered.) In the ensuing

shakeout, Stevan, who had taken no part in the strike, had a chance to move up—to brakeman.

It was better work, more interesting and challenging, but it was also more dangerous. The brakeman rode the ingot buggies down into the pit, where molten steel shot like an orange laser from the open-hearth furnace, and in an inferno of noise and heat he had to perform his job flawlessly. Once, when someone missed a hand signal, he was very nearly crushed between the jangling cars. Yet, hazards and all, it was a day's work, and Stevan stuck with it gladly throughout the war years.

After the Armistice, he got another chance to move up. His superintendant, Mr. King, was heading off to the construction of a new steel mill at Weirton, West Virginia, just below Pittsburgh, and decided to take the best men along with him.

The Weir brothers, founders of the mill, did not want another Youngstown on their hands, and sought to avoid it by keeping out the union. They were willing to pay higher wages—in the beginning at least—but put their foot down on anything that smacked of organization. That was fine with Stevan Lazich, whose policy was to do his job and keep his mouth shut. Resuming his perilous duties as brakeman, he watched his wages rise steadily, from twenty cents an hour at the plant's opening to thirty-three cents an hour a year later.

In 1922, however, there was a period of slack, and the Weir brothers began trimming wages. Stevan and three other brakemen, all of them known as exemplary workers, approached the boss quietly to see if the cutback could be moderated. The foreman was sympathetic but to the superintendant it smelled of incipient unionism. All four "troublemakers" were summarily fired and blacklisted. Stevan Lazich, with $120 in savings and ten years of hazardous experience, was back to square one.

He could have gone elsewhere and started over, perhaps, but he liked Weirton and wanted to stay. There was a thriving Serbian community in the town and an Orthodox church across the river in Mingo Junction. He decided to stick it out and see what opportunities might turn up.

The first one was billiards. With the coming of Prohibition, Weirton's 120-odd bars had officially become poolrooms, and as places for the steelmen to congregate, they were second only to the church itself. Stevan bought a table and some racks on a shoestring investment, acquiring the necessary bootleg contacts in the bargain. He worked the poolroom and speakeasy side by side, buying contraband whiskey in twenty-gallon lots and retailing it at a hefty profit. In a year he was four thousand dollars ahead.

But he disliked breaking the law. So with his acquired capital he bought into the grocery store next door. It was a rickety business, teetering close to the line of failure, and Stevan was not much of a businessman. The steelworkers bought their food (as well as their moonshine) mostly on credit, and when the end of the month came around many of them preferred to settle with their bootlegger first. His partner was a liability, too, spending much of his time in card games, and in desperation Stevan bought him out. The business did not markedly improve, however, and in 1928 it finally capsized.

Meanwhile, Stevan got married. Dessie Tepsic was born in the United States, and in some ways was a typical movie-struck kid of the Jazz Age, but her Balkan roots ran as deep as Stevan's. Her father, Milivoj Tepsic, desiring to avoid the celibacy of his friends, had written to his family in Bosnia and requested a "picture bride." Milica Hajdin, a pretty peasant girl with large, sturdy hands and a boundless capacity for work, had duly hastened forth to the New World and a blind marriage. Now she and Milivoj operated a white-framed boarding house for Serbian workers. Dessie was one of their six children.

Stevan did not propose. He simply spied the girl out and went to her father, Serbian-style, to arrange for the marriage. In such a union there was not much in the way of romance or affection, but there was little time for such things anyway. Stevan's grocery business was lurching toward its final demise. When the end came, in 1928, it would wipe out everything he had accumulated in a decade—including his wife's dowry.

Yet, with immigrant pluck, he and Dessie picked themselves up and started over. His father-in-law signed a mortgage on a truck, a weather-beaten old Federal of World War I vintage, but one that still ran. Stevan threw a pair of coveralls over his white shirt and black bow tie and proceeded to haul anything—coal, dirt, grapes—that would make him a dollar. That kept food on the table for his wife and two children but provided precious little else. The family's existence in America was still woefully precarious.

Then, in the depths of the Great Depression, when success seemed the least likely, Stevan's luck finally changed. He went back into the pool business again, borrowing on an insurance policy to come up with the necessary two hundred dollars in capital, and this time he made a go of it. With the election of Roosevelt in 1932, beer was legalized, so the poolroom could serve part of its alcohol legitimately. Hard liquor was another matter. Even with the repeal of Prohibition the following year, West Virginia elected to remain dry. Since the steelmen universally drank both ways—a shot and a beer—the newly reopened bars of Weirton had little choice but to accommodate them, and Stevan Lazich found himself back in the moonshine business.

And the moonshine business was a tough one. The bar had to be tended day and night. Somebody had to go to Washington on the weekends and scout up whiskey. There were troublesome politicos to accommodate—at one point Stevan had to switch parties—and at least one sheriff demanding the payment of protection money. And every night there were lonely steelmen to talk to, loutish customers to deal with, and several drunks to drive home. Dessie had her hands full, too.

In addition to the children, she had set up a boarding house of her own in a big frame structure on Avenue D; and applying her Serbian standards of housekeeping to her untidy patrons was a full-time job.

The family's prosperity was relative. The children still wore hand-me-down clothing, and Dessie had to stuff cardboard in the soles of her shoes. Yet even at that they were beginning to enjoy things that others in the neighborhood lacked: a telephone, a radio, a Sunday paper. And, finally, a real house. The boarding house on Avenue D, only a block from Stevan's bar, was at best a make-shift affair in a gritty neighborhood. But the dwelling on Pennsylvania Avenue, where they moved in 1935, was Dessie's dream home come true. It was on a tree-lined street in a residential part of town. It had a front porch with awnings, and on warm summer evenings they could sit out in the glider and watch the world go by. The kids had their own bedrooms, too; no more doubling up on the cranky old hide-a-bed. Real prosperity was still a way off, but the Laziches were now making strides.

Their gathering success was dramatized by the fact that all three of the children went to college. In high school they were good students. Mildred, the eldest, took college prep courses and did very well. Her father was fiercely proud of her accomplishments and insisted that she not be crippled by a lack of schooling. She attended West Virginia University and studied education, returning to Weirton to teach. The two boys, Perry and William, followed behind her, both of them majoring in business. The sacrifices for this triumph were little short of spartan, but Stevan and Dessie counted them well worthwhile.

KSL TV anchorwoman, Carole Mikita: The third generation found the dream. (KSL TV. Used by permission)

And indeed they were, for the doors of opportunity began to open wide. Mildred, for example, met and married a young doctor. Like her, William Mikita was a second-generation immigrant. His parents had come from northern Czechoslovakia, near the Polish border, and their story was not markedly different from the Laziches'. Jan Mikita, a short, powerfully built man whose skin was ruddy from the heat of the Weirton blast furnaces, had married Susana Brezuch, a girl of virtually no education but one who was shrewd and canny in business matters. Together they had scrimped and saved, and Susana had performed miracles of financial manipulation in order to send their three children to the university. William had finished high school at sixteen, college at nineteen, and medical

school at the ripe old age of twenty-three. He had served in the Pacific on a destroyer, done a residency in orthopedic surgery, and returned to the Weirton area to set up a practice. He saw Mildred dancing the cancan in a hospital benefit show and learned that she taught chemistry and physics at the local high school. It was love at first sight.

Their life in Steubenville—just across the river from Weirton—reflected little of the want that had shadowed their parents. They inhabited a succession of graceful homes in the outlying suburbs, drove expensive European automobiles, and became members of the local country club. Where Mildred had watched enviously as her childhood friends took singing or dancing lessons, she now saw to it that her own daughters, Carole and Judith, had every such opportunity. And in addition to the lessons there were side trips to the New York theaters, jaunts here and there about the country, and educations at exclusive prep schools. Carole, stagestruck from her first look at a Broadway musical, studied acting in college before becoming a television news anchorwoman. Judith became a professional dancer in Chicago. And both of the boys pursued legal careers, William in Cincinatti and Stephen in Salt Lake City. "Not bad for ol' bootlegger," boasted their grandfather in his still heavily accented English.

The Lazich story is not atypical. Indeed, it is so common that we may lose sight of how remarkable it truly is. But let us stop and think about that.

Carole Mikita and her family live in a pleasant middle-class suburb of Salt Lake City. Their house, a New England saltbox, is surrounded by a spacious yard and has a stunning view of the Wasatch Mountains. It is tastefully decorated, with formal living and dining rooms, a comfortable family area, and separate bedrooms for the children. In the kitchen, where she often prepares gourmet cuisine, appliances range all the way from European food processors to computer-controlled microwave ovens, and beyond the sliding glass doors is a backyard patio and barbecue.

On the Croatian farms of Carole's ancestry there were no formal dining rooms; neither, for that matter, were there electric lights, central heating, or indoor plumbing. People worked in the fields until it was too dark to see, then trudged home wearily to bowls of unappetizing (and often unnutritious) food. Because it was dark and cold in the rest of the house, family members huddled about the fire before retiring to an early bed. After all, they had to rise before dawn to milk the cows—if they were lucky enough to have cows.

In the mornings Carole drives her Saab along the freeway to her office, located in a glass-walled high-rise surveying a vista of fountains and statuary. Her workday transpires in a maze of telecommunications, as newscasts are assembled from bits and pieces of information from around the world. The morning may include an interview with some distinguished personality, or maybe a quick helicopter jaunt to the scene of a recent news event. Back at the studio, she writes and checks her own scripts and prepares to go on camera—where for an hour she must convey the appropriate mix of omniscience, warmth, and good humor.

By contrast, the labor of her ancestors was thankless and grueling. They used wooden plows drawn by oxen, and worked the land with desperate intensity. If

drought, pestilence, or war intervened, deadly famine was the inescapable result. Women were expected to rise before their men, split wood, draw water, and make a fire before beginning the day's real work. Cooking, washing, scrubbing, sewing, and all of the rest was done by hand, not to mention the work of raising nine or ten children. It was a life of hazards, too: Carole's great-great grandmother was gored to death by a rampaging bull.

While driving to work, Carole and her husband listen to music on their respective car stereos. They also attend concerts of the Utah Symphony, plays at the Pioneer Memorial Theater, lectures at the University of Utah, and an array of local recitals. When they travel, as they often do, they haunt the art galleries in search of serigraphs by their favorite artist, Erteerstrike', whose sensual art deco adorns their home. Carole's husband is a university professor: the walls of his study are lined with expensive books, and he boasts a definitive collection of Tolkien memorabilia.

The cultural opportunities of Carole's forebears were nil. They never heard a symphony orchestra, never attended a play, never saw a movie. Nor did they read many books, since there was neither time nor light for reading and since most of them were functionally illiterate. If they ever ventured beyond the farm, it was probably no farther than the nearest village, and if they ever found relief from walking, it was probably on the back of an oxcart. When Stevan Lazich stepped onto a train to come to America, it was the first time he had ever been inside one.

When Carole's brother, Stephen, was still an infant, he was diagnosed as having Werdnig-Hoffmann's disease, a degenerative condition that would leave him virtually paralyzed. (He would have only the partial use of arms and hands.) In the world of the family's ancestors, such a fate would have spelled an early and quiet death—but the American Mikitas did not have to settle for that. Thanks to a combination of medical science, industrial technology, and their own immigrant fortitude, they saw to it that the child led an astonishingly normal life. He went completely through the school system, excelling in his studies, then on to Duke University and BYU Law School, where he was known for his natty dress, eye-catching dates, and mischievous sense of humor. He became a lawyer and political consultant in the office of Utah's attorney general.

Growth and Progress

So it was that Americans confirmed their belief in progress. To them, progress was not just an abstract idea; it was an everyday working reality. The genius of the Americans had been to create political freedom, and then, by means of the market system, to translate that freedom into individual betterment. They learned that when economic opportunity was made generally available, and when government controls were correspondingly relaxed, there opened unguessed resources of energy and creativity. Self-interest could indeed work miracles.

This fact, in turn, affected the way Americans regarded self-interest and its relationship to virtue. For the ancients, we recall, self-interest and virtue were often held to be at odds. Americans, on the other hand, had come to believe that a person could be materially self-interested and still politically virtuous. Now, with the affluence of the Gilded Age before them, they seemed more certain than ever of this faith.

Consider their choice of popular heroes. These were invariably captains of industry who were also—rightly or wrongly—known for their moral qualities. Much of the philanthropy of the Carnegies, the Morgans, and the Rockefellers might be viewed skeptically today, but in the Gilded Age it was taken at face value. Andrew Carnegie explained his own generosity in a book titled *The Gospel of Wealth*, arguing that rich men like himself were only stewards of their wealth, and that they were obliged by God to exercise that stewardship virtuously. The man himself was as good as his word. He retired from steelmaking and systematically gave his fortune away.

What Carnegie was in real life the Alger heroes were in popular fiction. And, here again, virtue and self-interest coexisted peacefully. Like Ragged Dick, most of the Alger heroes won their fame and fortune not solely through economic behavior but partly through Christian. They collared thieves, rescued old folks in trouble, and set a good example to younger kids. In fact, when the Alger stories are analyzed carefully, it was the moral actions of the heroes—finding a wallet and returning it to its owner—that usually opened the big break in their lives. Ragged Dick became a symbol for the age.

And it was an age that needed its symbols. In the face of their mounting prosperity, Americans needed reassurance that self-interest would indeed not undermine their republican virtue. Economic growth—especially on so lavish a scale as this—was a whole new prospect for the United States. It remained to be seen what its final impact on the American experiment would be.

23
Change

Objectives
Growth Brings Change
Urbanization
Technological Change
Scale
Bureaucracy
Interdependence
Mobility
Mass Culture
Nostalgia

The nostalgic past within change (AP/Wide World Photos)

Nostalgia

While celebrating opening night, a successful young playwright is accosted by an old woman who hands him a watch and says: "Please come back to me." He then drives out to an old Victorian resort hotel and figures out how to travel backward in time to the year 1912, when the hotel was bustling and modern, when the old woman was a beautiful young actress, and when the tired and jaded America of the 1980s was still in the blush of springtime. And it is undoubtedly better, that world of the past. Horses clop unhurriedly before stately carriages; women dress elegantly in flowing brocades; and the hotel's guests relax in wicker chairs to savor the beauty of Lake Huron. Returning to the present, by contrast, is so painful that the hero wastes away and dies.

Somewhere in Time is not the only film of post-Watergate America to look backward longingly. There are also *The Way We Were*, *The Great Gatsby*, *Paper Moon*, *Ragtime*, *The Sting*, *The Summer of '42*, *American Graffiti*, and *Places in the Heart*, to name just a few. Or, if you prefer television, there are "Happy Days," "The Waltons," "Little House on the Prairie," and even "M.A.S.H." Broadway, too. Seven productions in the 1982 season had themes, dance routines, or music borrowed from the past, and one of them, *Annie*, chalked up more than two thousand performances. Even our commercials are retrospective. We watch with approval while the Budweiser Clydesdales majestically pull their beer wagon through every sort of bygone landscape. "Those were better times," we sigh.

The word *nostalgia* is defined as a wistful longing for the past. It was coined in 1688 by an Alsatian medical student, who joined together the Greek words for *home* and *pain*, so its original meaning was something akin to *homesickness*. Nostalgia was a condition that Europeans experienced as they scattered themselves around the globe. But Americans hardly felt it at all. Throughout the nineteenth century, they lived eagerly in the present and leaned forward into the future. "We have no interest in the scenes of antiquity," huffed Noah Webster, "except to serve as an avoidance."

No more. Americans of the twentieth century live in a world redolent of nostalgia. Take old movies, for instance. Today's college students imbibe their Buster Keaton, Laurel and Hardy, and Harold Lloyd with something like slavish worship. Revivals are endlessly recycling MGM's musicals, Cary Grant's screwball comedies, Frank Capra's common man heroics, and yet another go-around of Dorothy and the ruby slippers. Our very heroes are the old-time stars, from Humphrey Bogart—"Play it again, Sam"—to Clark Gable—"Frankly, my dear, I don't give a damn"—to Orson Welles— "Rosebud. . . ."

Or take music. FM stations across the country specialize in Frank Sinatra, Ella Fitzgerald, and the music of the Big Bands, and their listeners are often under thirty. For slightly more contemporary memories, Elvis Presley, Chuck Berry, Fats Domino, and other pioneers of rock and roll are still wildly popular—and a radio station in Los Angeles plays nothing but the Beatles. In Hackensack, New Jersey, an empressario named Roger Rudnick puts on a monthly concert known as "'40s in the '80s," complete with usherettes in bobby socks and antique autos parked outside.

Historic preservation plays to the same audience. What American town isn't sprucing up some old landmark for present reoccupancy? Kansas City, Missouri, has restored a 1920s movie palace and a 1930s auditorium. Millions have been sunk into

Denver's Larimer Square, San Francisco's Ghirardelli Square, and Salt Lake City's Trolley Square, all three of them creaky relics. And in Los Angeles, the old Biltmore Hotel has undergone a radical facelifting. One can go back now on Saturday nights and dance to the music of Glenn Miller.

And collectors have gone after almost everything else—dolls, toys, posters, comic books, even original editions of Horatio Alger. The trade in Mickey Mouse memorabilia alone amounts to tens of millions a year. Fountain pens are back in style, along with convertibles, *Life* magazine, and the *Saturday Evening Post.*

What does it all mean? There are a dozen explanations but most of them echo a common theme. "There's a terror of technology, of social and economic conditions that we seem unable to handle," according to historian Ray Browne, "so we look back to times when things were simpler." The author of *Future Shock* agrees. "Mounting evidence that society is out of control breeds disillusionment with science," says Alvin Toffler. "History is a great alternative to the super-industrial environment we don't know how to live in."

Two forms of American nostalgia deserve special mention, for their popularity cuts across all ages, classes, and interests. One is the Hollywood western. Whether it is Hopalong Cassidy with his rhinestone chaps, Roy Rogers on his high-stepping palomino, or John Wayne squinting and blazing away, some cowboy has played some role in the childhood dreams of most American males. Reflecting the frontier and its values, the cowboy seems to have become part of our national consciousness.

The other is *Gone With the Wind.* Its charm, equally pervasive, is more difficult to pin down. However, like the western, *Gone With the Wind* reflects a special sense of the American past. The world of Tara, with its eucalyptus-shaded lane, its broad verandah, its light hearted barbecues, is, after all, the world of the American Founders. George Washington might have lived at Tara, and so might James Madison, Edmund Randolph, or John Marshall. In a sense, *Gone With the Wind* shows us where we started out as a nation, and looking back on it shows us how far we have come. If we become nostalgic about it, perhaps it is because we feel a certain sense of loss between our own world and that of Thomas Jefferson. Perhaps nostalgia really is a kind of homesickness.

American progress was not just quantitative—creating more and better of everything—it was qualitative as well. It changed the basic character of life. No people had ever experienced such growth and prosperity before, and to do so had revolutionary implications. Americans had long thought of themselves as pioneers. When they had originally settled this country, they had braved the unknown, and when they had experimented with constitutional government and democratic politics, they had been on the cutting edge of human experience. Now, toward the end of the nineteenth century, they faced a different kind of pioneering—a forging into the future. And as with their Pilgrim forefathers, no one knew exactly what lay at the far shore.

Growth and Change

What they did know was that the American experience was increasingly characterized by rapid, pervasive, and far-reaching change. Some of the changes

Jefferson's estate at Monticello: A simpler, easier, mellower world. (Courtesy of Bert R. Holfeltz)

grew out of the development of American political institutions. Others came from the changing climate of ideas in the Western world and still others grew out of the increasingly troublesome course of international relations. But the most important changes were powered by the burgeoning growth of the economy.

In the first place, an expanding market economy made change a watchword. After all, inventors and entrepreneurs, as we have seen, were paid handsomely to delve into the unknown, and as a result they came up with new materials, new processes, new forms of organization, new management techniques, new scientific knowledge, and wondrous new gadgets. They also, of necessity, came up with a new understanding of human beings. For, in the dawning world of the twentieth century,

fast foods, credit cards, soap operas, giveaways, and recurrent cycles of fad and fashion would have as much impact on life as telephones and automobiles would.

In the second place, with more disposable income and more available time, consumers themselves were ready for the innovations. Viewing the new goods and services as life enriching, they gained an unquenchable thirst for ever more of them. Thus, in time, the basic, standard products—such as the black-painted Model T Ford—had to be replaced by an expanding variety of alternatives, by yellow Stutz-Bearcats with chrome-plated headers and wire wheels, by red LaSalles and green Lincoln Zephyrs and tan Jordan Playboys, and ultimately by Volkswagen Beetles and Nissan 280–Z's. The new, the novel, the distinctive, and the personal became means both of self-awareness and self-expression.

Change within a Human Life Span

Think for a moment of the life span of a person born in 1820 and living to the ripe—but not really rare—old age of one hundred. At birth he would have been a contemporary of Jefferson and Adams, both of whom had six years left to live. During his lifetime, the West would be settled, the size of the United States increased by half, the gross national product tripled, the standard of living quadrupled, and the population increased tenfold. America would change dramatically from a land of farms and farmers to the greatest industrial power on earth. The railroad would appear, then the automobile, and finally the airplane, which by 1920 would have already crossed the Atlantic. The telegraph would be invented and come into use, as would the telephone, and ultimately, the radio. Television would be a scant six years off. Chemistry would advance from the theory of flogiston—"fire substance"—to the synthesis of organic compounds, while physics would penetrate the secrets of the atom. During these same years the United States would fight four major wars, the first of them with flintlocks, the last with tanks. Darwin would sail off on the *Beagle*, Freud would puzzle over Fraulein Pappenheim's strange neurosis, and the equation $E = MC^2$ would become old hat. At the time of his death in 1920, our hundred-year-old, who had been the contemporary of Thomas Jefferson, would be the contemporary of your grandparents.

Finally, the abstract forces of economic development exerted their own powerful influence for change. If better jobs were to be found in the city, people went to the city and altered the way they lived. If shorter hours and increased pay improved their chances for schooling, they became better educated. And if some cunning invention had the effect of wiping out their trade, they necessarily had to go out and scout up a new one. The world of economic expansion was one of uncertainty and hard knocks, to be sure, but it was also one of exploration and discovery.

From Jefferson's World to Ours

We can gain some idea of the pace of change, and of the size of its impact, by seeing how rapidly the world of the Founding Fathers was swept away after the Civil War. In comparison to our own, the world of Jefferson was striking in its simplicity. Most people lived in the country, close to nature and the soil. The weather was an active force in their daily affairs, and the turn of the seasons visibly affected their lives. It was a world, too, in which most people were in touch with a system of controlling values. There was general agreement that crime deserved punishment, that sin was to be avoided, and that the traditional virtues were indeed virtuous.

Jefferson's world also respected the individual. After all, individuals, guided by rational intellect, had thrown off the yoke of British rule, written themselves a Constitution, and were pioneering the art of self-government. And the government they had created was drawn to human scale. If the president had something to

An early American drugstore: City life had its
seductions. (Library of Congress)

discuss with the secretary of state, he
strolled over to his house after supper and
knocked on the door, and if the State Department needed to be briefed later on, that
was simple too: there were only four employees in the entire organization.

But then, all institutions were small. In
Jefferson's world, a business firm that employed fifty people would be regarded as
outsized, and one employing two or three
hundred would be seen as gargantuan.
Cities were small as well. Philadelphia,
Boston, and New York had populations the
size of Idaho Falls, Santa Fe, and Palm
Springs in the 1980 census. And, just as the
owner of a shop or mill was expected to
know his employees by their first names,

many a city mayor knew his own constituents—all of them—the same way.

The people of Jefferson's world took
pride in their self-sufficiency. Those living
on the frontier necessarily had to fend for
themselves, but even in the more settled
areas a man who could not dig a well, shoe
a horse, or deliver a baby might find himself in trouble. This independence had its
economic costs, to be sure, but there were
corresponding benefits in a sense of self-
mastery. Jefferson's contemporaries did not
complain of uncontrollable forces in their
lives. The very idea of such forces sent
them reaching for their muskets.

What was it that swept the world of Jefferson away? It was not one kind of change
but many. Most of them were economic in

nature and were in one way or another linked together. The more important ones are as follows:

Urbanization

Although they idealized the agrarian way of life, Americans often found real farm work unrewarding. The farmer's day was long, his work hard, and his profits far from certain. With the increasing mechanization of agricultural production, farm prices fell steadily while the cost of machinery inched upward. Farm life could be harsh and lonely too. In *Giants in the Earth*, Soren Rolvaag's novel about early Minnesota, the heroine was driven mad by her never-ending battle with the elements.

For these and other reasons, Americans began leaving the farm for the city. Slowly at first, then with gathering speed, the ratio of rural to urban population began to shift in favor of the latter. In 1790 ten people lived on the farm for every one who lived in the city. By 1970 seven people lived in the cities for every three who remained on the farm. With such demographics at work, it did not take long for towns to become cities, cities to become metropolises, and metropolises to become megalopolises. When the Civil War broke out, there were only six urban centers with populations over fifty thousand; a generation later there were seventy-eight.

Of course, city life had its problems too, especially in the midst of rapid growth. Surviving cityscapes from the Gilded Age look anything but appealing. The streets are dark and narrow, and jammed with a throng of vehicles. Wires are strung about like thick, black cobwebs, and architecture seems to follow the dictum that *too much is not enough*. Urban life was not very healthy either. The city's burgeoning population was often crammed into tenement warrens, its services were rudimentary, and its thoroughfares were open sewers. In New York City alone, horses deposited 2.5 million pounds of manure and sixty thousand gallons of urine onto the streets every day.

Still, the city had its attractions. There were places to shop and dine, places to lounge and stroll, and places to find an evening's entertainment. City barbershops provided free quartet singing and city saloons furnished free lunch. And it was in the city that newfangled things first appeared. There was a machine, for instance, that you straddled like a horse and turned foot-pedals to cruise through the streets; there was a confection that was cold and sweet and served to you in cones; and there was an enthralling new game played with wooden bats and horsehide balls. Most importantly, the city was where the jobs were found, and even when they were not the best jobs, they beat pitching hay.

Whether people found metropolitan life pleasant or appalling, they found it markedly different than life on the farm. For most Americans the world of the city was as new and as strange as Babylon.

Technological Change

At the same time farmers were moving into town, inventors were flooding the marketplace with new gadgets. And, like city life itself, the gadgets could be extremely unsettling. The very humblest of them had the capacity to change the rules of society—sometimes right in the middle of the game.

Frank Sprague's electrical traction motor was a case in point. Directly it made possible the streetcar, but its indirect effects were unmeasurable. For streetcars, by shuttling workers in and out of the city

The Impact of Automobility

Nothing changed the world like the automobile did. In the beginning, motorcars were regarded as curiosities—playthings for the wealthy. But when Henry Ford made them both cheap and dependable, they quickly transformed society. The car changed the house by adding a garage. It changed the city by multiplying its streets and causing them to be paved. It changed rural living by bringing urban stores and amusements to within driving distance. It changed the concept of travel with inexpensive motels and drive-in restaurants. It fashioned new entertainment in the Sunday-afternoon drive and the Saturday-night cruise. It revolutionized social mores by introducing short skirts (for female drivers), drive-in movies, and the pastime of "parking." It consolidated education by means of school buses, streamlined the postal service with rural free delivery, and souped up law enforcement with the high-speed chase. Labor leaders complained that it emptied the union halls, and ministers, that it emptied the churches.

Automobility had its emotional side, too. Auto racing became *the* sport of thrills and chills; and people who felt small and helpless in the modern world could get behind the wheel and make themselves powerful. Cars, according to the psychologists, became objects of art, phallic symbols, and projections of the inner personality. Outraged females even accused the car of man- stealing.

In our own day, automobiles have defaced the landscape with freeways, polluted the air with hydrocarbons, filled the junkyards with rusting scrap, and placed the U.S. at the mercy of OPEC. They have powered American economic expansion, made Detroit into an important city, and brought the United Auto Workers into the front ranks of labor. They have spun off a hundred ancillary industries, from helicopter traffic-spotting to the automatic carwash, and given Disney Studios "Herbie," its biggest star since Donald Duck.

And, long before this year's models were ever on the drawing board, automobiles killed more Americans on the highways than all U.S. wars put together.

---

center, gave rise to the suburb; and the suburb gave rise to rambling houses, spacious yards, garden parties, and bowling leagues—a whole new way of life. Equally revolutionary was George Westinghouse's air brake. An ingeniously foolproof device, the air brake not only continued to operate in the event that railroad brake lines were cut or damaged, it automatically brought the entire train screeching to a halt. Now anyone dared to climb aboard, even little

old ladies with birdcages. People from Nebraska could visit their long-lost relatives from New Jersey, and people in New Jersey could watch the sunrise in Yosemite.

The new devices changed not only the outside world but the inside world as well. Eastman's Kodak gave rise to the picture album, the picture book, and pictures themselves as a way of seeing life. Mergenthaler's linotype machine made printing easier, books cheaper, and all sorts

Railroad advertisement: Anyone dared climb aboard. (Library of Congress)

of information more accessible. The Bonsack cigarette rolling machine vastly expanded the use of tobacco and created a new idea of "cool." And Edison's light bulb (together with forced-air central heating) altered family relationships by enabling children to spend more time alone in their rooms.

Gadget-lovers from the start, most Americans saw the new technology as a blessing. However, as with urbanization, the blessing was not always unmixed. Electric wires strung here and there proved

dangerous as well as unsightly, and thousands were electrocuted by them. The new farm machinery dramatically increased crop yields, but in the resulting glut farmers saw their prosperity vanish. The factories that turned out turbines and dynamos also filled the air with smoke and the rivers with pollution. And automobiles threw harness-makers out of work, as did refrigerators icemen and sewing machines tailors. The most beneficial of inventions harmed someone.

Then, too, the same sort of genius that could invent electric lights and telephones could also invent poison gas and dumdum bullets; and right beside the new consumer marvels came armored tanks, steel hulled battleships, and torpedo-firing submarines. Designed to promote security, the new weapons of war produced just the opposite effect. For, whatever one power came up with, the other powers had to match and surpass. A race in naval armaments led directly to the outbreak of World War I, and a similar race in aircraft development presaged its ghastly sequel. Then it was the atomic bomb, ICBM's, missile-firing submarines, and, most recently, nuclearpowered lasers deployed in outer space. Technology could get out of hand.

Scale

Thomas Jefferson's America was drawn to human scale. As time went by, however, the scale of everything—except people—increased markedly. To begin with, the size of the country was expanded as settlers poured into the West and began trekking toward the Pacific. Already large, the United States soon became a geographical colossus. A citizen residing in San Diego was closer to the Yukon than to the seat of his own government, and a citizen residing in Honolulu was closer to China.

The scale of politics increased even more. As millions of immigrants thronged into Boston, New York, and Chicago, any sense of common identity was overwhelmed. The individual vanished in the political process, his place taken by sprawling ethnic blocs. And with power measured in megaunits, politics itself became numerical. To increase their leverage, groups had to expand their membership. To win elections, parties had to play to the masses. And to hang onto their offices, politicians had to spend less of their time making speeches and more of it counting numbers. Needless to say, the typical mayor no longer knew his constituents by name.

Still, government did not grow as rapidly as industry did. For the Carnegies and Rockefellers were discovering that the best way to increase efficiency was by realizing economies of scale. As a result, production processes grew bigger, faster, and more impersonal. The first locomotives were manufactured in backyard shops, a hum of conversation in the air, but as the locomotives became larger and more complex, the methods of producing them grew ever more sophisticated. Soon large foundries were needed, together with massive bores, lathes, and walking cranes. As the number of workers increased, the plant's friendly chatter diminished. In one factory it was forbidden altogether.

A few figures tell the story. When the Constitution was signed, the largest corporation in the United States numbered some five hundred workers. By 1850, five hundred was no longer even noteworthy, since the cotton mills at Lowell, Massachusetts, employed nearly ten thousand. Fifty years later, at the turn of the century, there were payrolls in the United States of more than a million—more people than lived in Jefferson's Virginia.

The workers themselves felt intimidated by what was happening, for many of them could still recall those backyard shops of their youth. They also felt increasingly unimportant. Where it had once been the case that a good steam fitter could forge and assemble every piece of a locomotive engine, now, in the cavernous Baldwin factory at Philadelphia, each worker performed—over and over again—only a miniscule part of the whole operation. It was neither challenging nor interesting work. And by the day it became ever more regimented. One started and stopped by the blast of the factory whistle and shuffled through the gates with thousands of others. With the arrival of the assembly line, the worker's smallest movements had to be precisely timed and coordinated—sometimes by the use of stopwatches. In the age of machinery there were those who began to feel like machines themselves.

Fighting fire with fire, some workers began to form organizations of their own. Labor unions eased some of the strain, perhaps, but the unions themselves were large and impersonal organizations, and were equally capable of dwarfing the individual. Wherever one looked, it seemed, the scale of things was no longer human.

Bureaucracy

If the size and power of industrial America had an intimidating effect, so did its increasingly bureaucratic style. Bureaucracy was not an intentionally contrived poison; it was a means of coping with life's growing complexity. If that complexity could not be simplified, it was supposed, at

Bureaucracy: The Fourth Branch of Government?

That we all have our run-ins with bureaucracy is attested by the fact that we all have our bear stories to tell. Most of us can report encounters with mindless rules, computer-answered telephones, punch-card polemics, and process divorced from reality. There was, for example, the IRS ruling denying that a woman whose house had been hit by an airplane had sustained any "loss." Or there was the memorandum instructing federal employees what to do in case of nuclear attack: "Go to the nearest Post Office, ask the Postmaster for a Federal employee registration card, fill it out and return it to him." The memo added that "this card will also enable us to forward your pay."

Language, apparently, is part of the problem. One government memorandum, attempting to define *Acts of God*, came up with: "weather and sea conditions greater than one standard deviation above the historical mean for the place and season of a casualty." Jimmy Carter had even worse semantic difficulties: In proclaiming Leif Erikson Day in 1977, he sang the praises of "that courageous Norseperson." (Lampooning Carter's terminology, Congressman Edward Michel sang the praises of "that great President, Harry S. Truperson.") And then there was the computer-written Diner's Club application that was somehow addressed to the General Services Administration in Washington. "Once you actually have our card, Gen. Administration," it promised, "you can easily see for yourself that Diners offers more advantages to a qualified person of your caliber."

Nor are the lawmakers immune. In Helena, Montana, a city ordinance requires night club strippers to wear no less than three pounds, two ounces of clothing at all times. In Spads, Indiana, it is unlawful to open a can of food by firing a revolver at it. And in Oklahoma, the driver of any vehicle involved in a fatal accident is required to give his name and address to the person struck.

Bureaucracy, of course, is always busy. In 1979, the Air Force Uniform Board conducted an elaborate survey to determine "the optional use of umbrellas by male personnel in uniform." Items in the questionnaire assessed the rank of the user, type of weather in which use was made, typical protection afforded by the instrument, and comments tendered by watchful civilians. At bottom, it seemed, was whether "Use of umbrellas detracted from the combat ready image that US military forces should project."

Bureaucrats do come in out of the rain occasionally. One state official, stymied in purchasing the copy machine best suited to his agency's needs, found a way to cut through the red tape. "Who is your boss?" he asked of the state copy machine czar. An answer came back through the telephone. "And who is his boss?" And so on and so on, right up to the governor. Then, with perfect bureaucratic logic, he unsnarled the whole thing: "You can tell Bob to tell Bill to tell John to tell Judy to tell the governor that I got thirty thousand more votes in the last election than he did, and I'm going to buy the copy machine I damn well please." It worked.

least it could be organized and systematized, even at the cost of jamming a few square pegs into round holes. Well-intentioned administrators set about to bring order out of chaos.

Back in the simpler world of Jefferson, things could be done informally (and unbureaucratically) without putting order at risk: bargains could be made, arrangements negotiated, workmen hired, materials purchased, and accounts kept—more or less on a handshake. But no really large organization could work that way. There had to be settled procedures for everything or the managers themselves might lose track. Red tape inexorably made its way into American life.

The work of the bureaucrats was assisted by another spate of inventions. Christopher Scholes' typewriter, first used in the 1870s, opened an enormous breakthrough in processing information, as did in turn the mimeograph, the dictaphone, the Xerox machine, and, yes, the computer. Even mundane gadgets made a contribution: the filing cabinet, the stapler, the paper clip. Cheap paper made the greatest contribution of all.

These innovations made possible the modern office, and the modern office made possible all the rest. For now items of miscellaneous importance—the kind Jefferson would have simply jotted down in one of his leather-bound notebooks—could be meticulously sorted out and filed away. Papers could be signed in duplicate, triplicate, and quadruplicate, coded in different colors, lined with tabs and index markers, and stashed in all the appropriate places. Records could be kept with ever greater care. And with records came rules. The yellow copy must go to the district manager. *What! there is no district manager? Well, then, let's get one. Where else can we send*

the yellow copy? Not all the rules were necessarily absurd, but they were all necessarily mindless—for the very presence of a rule precluded thinking. Thus, all locomotives had to carry a coal-shoveler, even if the engine burned oil; all employees had to wear hard hats, even if they worked at a typewriter; and in the U.S. State Department, correspondence with both China and Cuba was filed together under "C."

It did make sense—of a kind. All bureaucracy did. But it also added to the anonymity and dislocation of life and measureably increased its complexity. For in the bureaucratic world of the twentieth century, housewives would have to master accounting, laborers would have to wade through the Internal Revenue Code, and people with the most ordinary of problems would have to learn to speak to computers. Where the danger of modern scale was that the individual would be overwhelmed, the danger of modern bureaucracy was that he would be dehumanized.

Interdependence

Both the expanding scale and developing bureaucracy of modern life contributed to a feeling of powerlessness. So did economic interdependence. In Jefferson's day it was the boast of many Americans that they relied solely upon themselves—but the progress of market economics soon took care of that. Through specialization and exchange, markets insured ever more benefit from economic activity, but they also insured ever greater mutual dependence. Working in a large factory interlocked with dozens of suppliers, at the mercy of a powerful labor union, and dependent on advertising, selling, and delivery for its continued prosperity, no one could say he stood alone.

Because events routinely proved the contrary. A strike thousands of miles away might completely disrupt a company's work. The strength of the dollar overseas might decimate its sales. A mine accident in West Virginia, a derailment in Nebraska, or a killer frost in California might interrupt its supplies, halt its deliveries, or alter the habits of its customers. The South's decision to break up the Union in 1861 proved the ruin of many *Northern* interests.

Economic interdependence was not all bad. Indeed, possibly more than any other force in the modern world, it promoted human understanding. For, if Christians had to do business with Muslims in order to turn a profit, there was little incentive for them to put down Islam; and the same held true for whites doing business with blacks, Americans doing business with Mexicans, and men doing business with women. The growth of religious toleration in colonial New England had largely been due to the influence of the merchants, who had to live in peace with everyone.

But interdependence could be destabilizing, also. European squabbling about the coal fields of Silesia helped to undermine the Treaty of Versailles ending World War I. Similarly, the Japanese, who had to rely on the United States for supplies of scrap iron, were ready to bomb Pearl Harbor when those supplies were cut off. And in our own day, America finds itself embroiled in the Middle East over the question of oil. If economic interrelatedness could help to forge a single world, it could also help to shatter it.

Mobility

Even before advances in the technology of travel, Americans liked to move about. They headed out west after cheap land, up

An early automobile advertisement: Americans became ever more mobile. (Library of Congress)

north to search for gold, down south to plant cotton, and back east if their luck played out. But with improved technology, they became even more mobile. The opening of the Erie Canal in 1825 sent a flood of traffic up the Mohawk Valley and into the Great Lakes. Passenger trains, soon following the canals, were similarly filled to capacity. And out on the Mississippi the graceful stern-wheelers cruised majestically up and down between the river towns. There were those so enchanted by the steamboats that, like Huckleberry Finn, they rode them aimlessly, watching the country slip by.

Most Americans did not travel aimlessly, however, but in the pursuit of better chances. In Europe, if a man was born a cobbler in Dublin, he was likely to die a cobbler—in Dublin. Not so with the typical Yankee. If improved opportunity was to be found somewhere else, he would likely be on the next train out of town. Economic mobility (moving up or down in society) and geographic mobility (moving from place to place) were in America tightly intertwined.

And both of them altered the familiar patterns of life. The man who moved his family across the country encountered a whole new culture, but the man who moved from New York's Lower East Side to upper Fifth Avenue experienced an equally remarkable change. Both situations obliged people to take life as they found it, and to adapt quickly to their new surroundings. Mobile Americans had to play the chameleon.

That was not a familiar game to Europeans, for whom a sense of place was traditional. Once William Bradford had settled in Plymouth, for better or worse, Plymouth was his home. The same was true for Ben Franklin in Philadelphia, George Washington in Virginia, and Thomas Pinckney in South Carolina. For them home was not just a geographic locale, it was friends and acquaintances, childhood memories, pride in the local team, and, most importantly, the ties of family and kin. To snap all of these connections was like pulling up a sapling by the roots.

But later Americans learned to do just that. "In the United States," observed Tocqueville, "a man builds a house in which to spend his old age, and he sells it before the roof is on; he plants a garden and lets it just as the trees are coming into bearing; he brings a field into tillage and leaves other men to gather the crops; he embraces a profession and gives it up; he settles in a place, which he soon afterwards leaves to carry his changeable longings elsewhere." As a result of all of this moving and removing, Americans created a distinctive new social order, one in which friends, family, and childhood memories necessarily played a diminished role, and in which individuals—*as* individuals—necessarily played an expanded one. Restless, rootless, and cosmopolitan, the individual

in America learned to carry his lifestyle around with him, like the bedouin his tent, and put it down in whatever setting.

The new way of life was not without its advantages. It liberated people from the tyranny of small-town gossips and placed them in situations where ability and drive were all that counted. Then, too, it was interesting. In a world constantly on the move, your new neighbor might be a billionaire, a movie star, or the quarterback of the Dallas Cowboys. (Then again, he might be a junkie, a pervert, or one of the FBI's ten most wanted.) Urban anonymity could bring a heady sense of liberation, and many Americans rejoiced in it.

On the other hand, the new mobility had its price. Anxious uncertainty seemed to grip many Americans in the twentieth century. If there was exhilaration in their changing surroundings, there was alienation and anomie as well. They looked back on the small town of their childhood—its stolid Main Street, its simple amusements, its contrived respectability—and saw in it a lost utopia. The family as an institution also suffered. After all, if neighborhood and community were no longer important in the scheme of things, then what was the value of motherhood or fatherhood?

Mass Culture

Accompanying these developments, and sometimes actually promoting them, was a rapidly changing cultural life. Art and literature, more or less accessible for centuries, suddenly began lapsing into incomprehensibility. To the man on the street, a T. S. Eliot poem made little more sense read forward than backward, and a Kandinski painting might just as well be hung upside down. High culture started losing touch with the common people.

A nineteenth century advertisement: Selling ideas about products.

In the meantime, a new and truly popular culture rapidly took its place. This, too, was a product of the inventors. High-speed printing, able to zip out pictures with four-color accuracy, created the popular book and magazine. Radio seized the imagination with its vividly staged theater of the mind. And Edison's Victrola, scratching out a Rudy Vallee love song or some Scott Joplin ragtime through its flowerlike horn, gave rise to popular music.

But the ultimate expression of popular culture was the silver screen. Another product of Edison's fertile mind, it began as a novelty at penny arcades—flickering pictures of a girl dancing or of a weight lifter hoisting a barbell. Then someone discovered that the dancing girl might peel off a few articles of clothing, and that the weight lifter, through trick photography, might appear to be lifting a locomotive. People sat up to the fact that motion pictures were more than a novelty—they were a means of spinning out magic.

Even in those early days popular culture proved worrisome. Social critic Walter Lippmann, for one, warned that the new mass media created mental images ("stereotypes") which could powerfully affect the way people understood reality. By listening to the radio, for example, a person might come to believe that all blacks were as silly and comical as "Amos and Andy." By reading dime novels about red-blooded Frank Merriwell, it was possible to conclude that life always rewarded the person who tried. And by sitting through enough Valentino matinees, a moviegoer might gain some extremely distorted notions about sex. The trouble with popular culture, said Lippmann, was that it lied.

Nor was it hard to guess why. For, appearances to the contrary, popular culture existed less for the purpose of entertaining, informing, or dramatizing truth than for simply making money. It grew up hand in hand with advertising and the two never parted. Advertising was also learning some tricks. Admen discovered, for example, that it was more important to sell *ideas* about a product than to sell the product itself. Claiming that Himmelfritz Beer was the best in the world might excite consumer skepticism, but showing handsome young couples quaffing down their Himmelfritz carried the subtler—and unanswerable—message that using the sponsor's product made you desirable.

Archie and His Lonely Crowd

Readers of the comic strip "Archie and His Friends" may or may not have noticed that in all outward appearances (except hair color) two of the male characters—Archie and Reggie—and two of the female characters—Betty and Veronica—are virtually indistinguishable from one another. And yet, equally curiously, one member of each pair is definitely understood to be an insider in the world of teenage sociability while the other is more or less outside of it all. (For instance, Veronica is immensely popular with the boys, while Betty is always hunting for dates.) Obviously, there were distinctions among comic-strip characters that were completely invisible to adults.

Reflections on such problems prompted Harvard sociologist David Riesman to ask what it was that made young people of the 1950s tick. After a good deal of research and reflection, he concluded that popular culture was teaching them to be exactly like one another. Instead of internalizing certain fundamental values and using them as a "gyroscope" through life, kids were tuning sensitive "radarscopes" to one another—learning to become members of the crowd. Should one wear a wide belt or a narrow one? Should one turn one's blue jeans up at the cuff? Should one tuck in one's shirt or let it hang out? Answers to such questions were coming to define social acceptability.

And what had become of the old-time values like imagination, daring, and individualism? Suddenly they seemed obsolete. "I would like to fly if everyone else did," confessed a twelve-year-old fan of Superman, "but otherwise it would be kind of conspicuous." Or there was the mother of the musically gifted fourteen-year-old who curtailed his piano practice, lest he get out of step with his friends. "I hope to keep him a normal boy," she said.

Where, finally, did all of this "other-directedness" end? Not with much happiness or fulfillment, Riesman supposed. In his book, *The Lonely Crowd*, he concluded that:

Many of the desires that drove men to work and to madness in societies depending on inner-direction are now satisfied relatively easily; they are incorporated into the standard of living taken for granted by millions. But the craving remains. It is a craving for satisfactions others appear to attain, an objectless craving.

It was a pretty bleak picture: youngsters sitting forlornly in front of the television and wishing themselves to be part of the Pepsi Generation. And altering their individuality over the years to be like Elvis, and then like the Beatles, and then the Rolling Stones, and then Michael Jackson, and then Prince. . . . And *still* winding up a loser—like Jughead.

Madison Avenue grew so adept at psychological persuasion that it was soon drawn toward politics. By the 1960 presidential campaign it was obvious that a candidate must look out for his skin color, his television profile, and his projected warmth and sincerity, for like Himmelfritz beer, he was being marketed on the strength of his *image*. As one adman observed, the candidate resembling a forthright young sheriff (John Kennedy) was destined to win that election, while the candidate resembling a crafty railroad lawyer (Richard Nixon) was destined to lose.

The power of the media seemed especially disconcerting when applied to values. Observing details in the background of magazine stories, researchers discovered that attitudes toward racial minorities or sex roles changed in popular literature *before* they changed in society. It was possible, in other words, that readers were actually altering their values in response to what they read in *True Confessions* and the *Police Gazette*. Suddenly it seemed terribly important that Jimi Hendrix favored the use of drugs, that "Charlie's Angels" went in for casual sex, and that Boy George dressed like a woman. For, whatever else was clear, it was certain that in modern America the moral consensus of Jefferson's day was rapidly breaking apart.

A Changing World of Ideas and Values

The changes described above took place in a world of changing ideas and values. Along with the new lifestyles came a new understanding of life itself. In the world of Jefferson there was great respect for the rational mind, which was held to be the greatest of God's creations, and for Truth, which was still spelled with a capital T.

Darwin and Freud. Charles Darwin's work was to have a devastating impact on these assumptions. Darwin's discoveries, published in 1859, led him to conclude that man, far from being a special creation of God, was merely a higher animal evolved from lower ones. Through a process of natural selection, Darwin argued, weaker and less efficient species tended to die out, their place taken by stronger and more successful ones. Moreover, chance mutations in the genetic code, if they enhanced a species' survivability, were likely to become the basis for new evolutionary forms. Man could be viewed as a sort of cosmic accident.

The implications of this idea were far-reaching. For one thing, constant struggle with winners and losers was seen to be a part of the natural order. This seemed agreeable to the Carnegies and Rockefellers, who in building their giant enterprises had devoured their competitors, but it proved cold comfort to the poor and disadvantaged. Instead of advancing higher moral concepts, Darwinism seemed to backtrack to the jungle. It also undercut respect for human reason. In the evolution of man, said the Darwinists, reason was a late development. If it was the highest form of biological activity, it was also the newest and least experienced. This explained why, in critical situations, man abandoned his reason and fell back on the primal impulses.

The idea that man was just an animal, and possibly a vicious one at that, was given further credence at the turn of the century by Sigmund Freud. His psychoanalytic investigations revealed a world of the mind hitherto unknown. In the subconscious, said Freud, swirled all sorts of strange thoughts and desires, many of them related to the libido. Neurotic or psychotic behavior gave an indication of how frightful some of these impulses could be— but even normal persons, in their dreams, tapped into the dark world below. (Who, for example, hadn't dreamed of being unclothed in a public place?) Man the animal, it seemed, was driven by forces utterly beyond his comprehension.

Republican Values. Darwin and Freud were only two sources of the new thought—there were several others—but they had a sizable impact on republican values. After all, if man was but an animal, and his reason often subordinate to his obsessions and compulsions, what was there to say for the Enlightenment's notion that he could rationally discover truth? Come to that, was there any real truth for him to discover? Some Darwinists—not all of them—argued that evolution explained away the existence of God, with the result that Christian truth, once thought to be divine, was only human wisdom. And even the "self-evident truths" of John Locke seemed open to question. Was it really true, the skeptics asked, that all men were created equal, or that they were capable of self-government? In the world described by Darwin and Freud, such propositions seemed doubtful.

The new skepticism had an obvious impact on the idea of virtue. If the General Religion wasn't True—with a capital T— then Virtue (with a capital V) was not going to merit any heavenly reward, and perhaps vice made just as much sense. Truth was increasingly viewed as being partial, subjective, and relative. One person's truth was not necessarily another's. One society's truth did not apply everywhere. One age's truth did not encompass all time. And, by similar logic, virtue could be broken down, fragmented, and split into competing concepts. *Your* virtue may be in obeying the law, while *my* virtue may be in violating it.

Self-interest, too, took on new meaning. With increasing prosperity and multiplying choices, self-interest became tinged with the irrational. Why stop with one house? Why not have two—or ten? Why drive a Ford when there were Rolls-Royces, or eat steak when there was caviar? And beyond material consumption there was the consumption of experience— travel, leisure, entertainment, glamor, excitement. In a world where truth was relative and standards relaxed, self-interest could run into self-indulgence.

Not all Americans—nor even a majority—were affected by these developments, but their influence was substantial. Along with urbanization, technology, and the other changes sweeping through the Gilded Age, the world of ideas began to change as well. And values took on a new flexibility.

Change and Nostalgia

What, exactly, did all of this mean? For those who believed in the cult of progress, every new development was necessarily for the better. In his influential 1887 novel, *Looking Backward*, Edward Bellamy, imagining America in the year 2000, envisioned a world in which (in addition to automobiles zooming along at forty miles an hour and airships crossing the country in only a few days) Americans had banished poverty, promoted social harmony, and secured the good life for all. There was, however, another sort of literature to come out of Teddy Roosevelt's America, one more ambivalent about the future. With the publication of Owen Wister's *The Virginian* in 1902, America saw its first real example of nostalgia.

If we look closely at the most popular themes of nostalgia, they furnish clues to our real feelings about rapid change. For in nostalgia can be found visions, often highly idealized, of what we believe we have lost.

In the western, for example, we see a world marvelously free of bureaucracy, in which individuals solve their problems unassisted. Cowboys never have to go to court to resolve a difficulty, nor do they ever have to contact a government agency, fill out forms, or see someone's secretary. In those palmy days gone by, we see people having counted as people.

The cowboy's world is also one of airy personal freedom. When the hero rides off into the sunset, he generally rides alone. And he carries with him no worries about meeting mortgage payments, figuring out income taxes, or participating in the PTA. Believably or unbelievably, man in American nostalgia is depicted as a nearly disembodied free spirit. In the Clint Eastwood westerns, the hero doesn't even have a name.

In the lore of nostalgia, little people, acting alone, often confront some big establishment and in the end defeat it soundly. Here it is a solitary reporter against the mob. There it is an honest cop against the crooked politicians. Somewhere else it is a broken-down lawyer against the megafirm. In today's world of outsized institutions, the little person may not seem to count for much, but when Jeremiah Johnson decides to take on the entire Crow Indian nation, we know in advance who will win.

Human relations are often warm and loving in American nostalgia. Watching "The Waltons" or "Little House on the Prairie," we learn that the world was not always as cold and impersonal as it may seem today. For back in that misty past people bore one another's burdens, shared each other's joys and sorrows. Without prosperity to distract them, they recognized that people, not things, were what counted in life.

The world of American nostalgia is often the world of the small town—the community. For even with their boosters and their busybodies, the Grover's Corners and Gopher Prairies of the American imagination have both a fetching innocence and an abiding sense of togetherness. From *The Music Man* to *American*

Grafitti, there is something ineffably American about the small-town experience. It is as if all of us once marched in the River City Boy's Band.

Hardly anything in the world of nostalgia is hard to understand. There are problems, to be sure, but they are not problems to defy the wit of man, and in the end they are always solved. Orphan Annie has to locate Daddy Warbucks and all will be well. Or Dorothy and her friends have to get to the Wizard of Oz. In the imagined past, life was surpassingly simple.

So, what does nostalgia add up to? It strongly suggests that change in our recent past has taken place too swiftly for us to cope with psychologically. For what seems to lie hidden in much of the nostalgia is none other than the lost world of Thomas Jefferson. The verities, the values, the senses of permanence and place, the abiding respect for humanity and the high premium placed on individual freedom would all be familiar to the Founding Fathers.

Jefferson's world is gone now, swept away in a cyclone of change. The question is, what difference, if any, does that fact make for us? The optimistic answer holds that nothing of real importance has changed. Human nature today is still essentially as it was, and the institutions designed in the eighteenth century are still well able to cope with it.

There is, however, a pessimistic answer, too, one indicated by the strength and pervasiveness of our nostalgia. This holds that life may indeed have been altered by the onrush of change, and altered in fundamental ways. Is the American citizen of the present day still virtuous in the right ways? Is his self-interest still a benign (or constructive) force? Do the controls of the market system, on the one hand, and the political system, on the other, still moderate the hazards of the human predicament? Or is change about to bring forth some fresh challenge?

Faced with these two possibilities, Americans at the turn of the century looked into the future with a new sobriety. The United States was coming of age, as was plain to see, and the republican experiment was taking on new implications. For most Americans, change was still synonymous with progress, and their traditional optimism yet prevailed. But for a minority of gathering size and strength, the time had come to reassess the old meanings of things.

24
The Perils
of Prosperity

Portrait of an immigrant family in new quarters
(Culver Pictures)

The Erie War

The great hidden asset of the Erie Railroad was that it provided the missing piece to three different puzzles. If Cornelius "Commodore" Vanderbilt, owner of the New York Central, could get hold of the Erie, which ran up the Hudson River Valley and westward to the Great Lakes, it would enable him to monopolize virtually all rail traffic into New York City. If John S. Eldridge could gain control of the Erie, he could hook it up with the line his firm was building between Boston and the Hudson River, enabling him to carry freight all the way from Massachusetts to Chicago. And if Daniel Drew, the Erie's major stockholder, could keep his hands on the line, which once upon a time had been prosperous, he could continue milking it for gigantic profits while running it gradually into ruin.

All of this enormously interested Jay Gould. He was a small, quiet, sloe-eyed man with an immense, flowing beard. Unlike Vanderbilt, who made outrageous public statements—"Law! What do I care about law? Hain't I got the power?"—unlike Drew, who spouted scripture and spit on the floor, unlike almost any of the tycoons of Gilded-Age America, Gould worked in the hush of secrecy. "There was a reminiscence of the spider in his nature," Henry Adams recalled. "He spun huge webs, in corners and in the dark." And in the spring of 1867, he began spinning a web for the Erie.

At the railroad's annual meeting that year there was a major shakeup. Vanderbilt, who had been buying Erie shares by the carload, became the principal stockholder, but Eldridge continued as president and Drew retained his seat on the board. The Commodore watched the two of them closely, fearful that they might do something to thwart his plans. He even went to one of the judges in his pay—there were literally dozens of them—and secured an injunction forbidding the board of directors to issue further stock. (The more stock there was available, the more Vanderbilt would have to buy in order to retain control.) But he did not watch the diminutive stranger with the great black beard who also, it seemed, now sat on the Erie's board. He should have.

For Gould immediately went to work. Noting that himself, Eldridge, and Drew controlled the board's executive committee, he hit upon a crafty ploy. Vanderbilt's injunction forbade only *the board's* action—it said nothing at all about *the executive committee's*. Accordingly, as soon as the Commodore's back was turned, the three of them issued $10 million in convertible bonds, and then began changing them over into stock. Soon more and ever more shares of Erie stock were flooding the market, and Vanderbilt, in desperation, had to keep buying them up. The Commodore was an extremely wealthy man, but the titanic expense of purchasing one hundred thousand shares of his own stock was almost too much for him. Besides, the watered stock was rapidly losing value and even imperiling Vanderbilt's credit. Crowed one of the conspirators gleefully: "If this damned printing press doesn't break down, we'll give the old hog all he wants of the Erie."

Then Vanderbilt struck back. Approaching another friendly judge, he secured a citation of contempt against his wayward partners and issued a warrant for their arrest. Once again, however, Gould sniffed out a loophole. The citation was only valid in New York. So, packing up the company's records, files, and newly acquired cash, they loaded everything onto a ferry and rowed across the river, where they finagled themselves a law making the Erie a New Jersey corporation. They then set up headquarters at Taylor's Hotel, posted several small cannon outside, and hired a squad of Jersey City policemen to protect them from Vanderbilt's thugs. The Commodore was livid.

But the standoff could not continue indefinitely. (For one thing, the Erie's officers could not set foot in New York.) What Gould and Drew really needed was some sort of legislative action legalizing what they had done. Accordingly, Gould filled a satchel with money and headed for the New York state capital at Albany. He set himself up in the posh Delavan House and began interviewing the state legislators one at a time, counting out banknotes in heavy wads. Of course, Vanderbilt was just down the street doing exactly the same thing. One legislator, his pockets bulging with seventy-five thousand dollars from the Commodore, came out of the Delavan House with one hundred thousand dollars from Gould. What a wonderful time it was to be in politics.

After considerable pulling and hauling, Gould's bill passed. But obviously something more amicable had to be worked out or the Erie War would sizzle along indefinitely. When spies reported to Gould that Drew had secretly made contact with Vanderbilt, Gould decided to negotiate a settlement. The parties haggled back and forth and finally signed a peace treaty. Vanderbilt was given $3.5 million for his controlling shares of the Erie, together with a million-dollar bonus for his trouble. Eldridge was similarly paid off. At last, the Erie, now known derisively as the "scarlet woman of Wall Street," belonged to Jay Gould.

But the Commodore wasn't quite finished yet. He could still ruin the Erie with some old-fashioned throat-cutting, and he began sharpening up his razor. He lowered the New York Central's freight rates on cattle from $125 to $100 per carload. Gould, unflustered, cut the Erie's to $75. Vanderbilt went down to $50. Gould dropped to $25. On and on it went, until Vanderbilt's railroad was hauling cattle from Buffalo to New York City for *one dollar* a carload. When the Erie's rates suddenly shot back up, the Commodore actually thought he had won. Only later did he learn that Gould had bought up every steer he could find in upstate New York and shipped it off to market at Vanderbilt's expense. Said he in bitter resignation: "It never pays to kick a skunk."

None of them noticed, in all the fuss, that the American people were somehow losing respect for the market system.

Reform has always been a part of the American experience. Back in Andrew Jackson's day, the reformers took on everything from the school system in New England to the practice of slavery in the South. And after the Civil War, angry farmers in the Midwest, suffering severe economic dislocations, launched a virulent reform movement known as Populism. None of this should surprise us. The seeds of reform sprout naturally in democratic soil, and in almost every generation, including our own, some of them have flourished.

Even so, the reform movement that came into flower at the turn of the century was unique. Unlike Populism, it was not the result of economic misfortune, for it transpired in a season of prosperity. And there was something curious about the reformers too: they were generally of urban origin, comparatively well educated, often

Theodore Roosevelt: Progressive reform as a way of coping with change. (Library of Congress)

well-to-do, and more than occasionally people of consequence—not generally the sort who want to turn the world inside out.

Historians have puzzled over the problem and have come up with several different explanations for it. Common to all of them is the notion that people will react in some way to rapid change in their society. Undoubtedly it was change, more than anything else, which lay behind the phenomenon we remember as *progressivism.*

The Progressives

Progressivism was the watchword in American politics for a good twenty years. There were progressives identified with both major parties—Theodore Roosevelt

was a Republican progressive and Woodrow Wilson a Democratic one—and they ranged across the political spectrum. There were progressives in state governments, too, and in countless local establishments. Their programs came in a wide diversity and addressed hundreds of different reforms. Yet, fundamentally, the progressives thought of themselves as kindred spirits.

Though generalizations are sometimes risky, a great many progressives clearly hailed from the upper middle class, claimed professional status, and were associated with some sort of traditional elite. Bankers, lawyers, accountants, professors, and newspaper editors were well represented in their ranks, along with leaders of what we might call the social establishment. They were the kind of people who felt the winds of change most keenly. It has been suggested, in fact, that they may have felt personally threatened by those winds, and that the real purpose of their reforms was to seek out a safe harbor. Whether or not that was true, the progressives did seem ambivalent about the changes taking place around them.

Take Teddy Roosevelt, for example. No one looked toward the twentieth century more eagerly than he. He took up motoring when most people still gaped at the automobile in awe, and went flying when airplanes still resembled kites. As president, his domestic policies made a sharp break with the past, and his foreign policies anticipated the world of the 1950s. When the political organization he founded in 1912 was called the Progressive party, the name seemed entirely appropriate. Yet Roosevelt also associated himself with the past. He lived the life of

New York's Lower East Side: Noisy, crowded, and dirty. (Library of Congress)

an Oyster Bay aristocrat, wrote books about the old West, and spent a few years in Nebraska as a cattle rancher. When he was elected president of the American Historical Association in 1885, that seemed appropriate too.

Undoubtedly, the progressives, like other reformers, acted out of various kinds of self-interest. As people of means, they had a stake in American society, and were often eager to protect their investment. On the other hand, much of their activity could only be described as public virtue. It is impossible to read the writings of the progressives without concluding that they truly feared for the American Republic and believed that all the courage and patriotism they could muster was needed to save it.

But save it from what? Generally speaking, from the perils of prosperity. For, while it was true that economic growth had brought many advantages to the United States, it had brought some disadvantages as well. As we saw in the previous chapter, all change was not necessarily for the better, and in spite of the American belief in progress, there was a discernible gathering of anxiety about the future.

Progressivism and the Muckrakers

The anxiety was markedly increased by a turn-of-the-century style of journalism known as muckraking. This was a product of the revolution in media that made printing cheap, photographs reproducible, and readers ever hungrier for the

Granddaddy of the Muckrakers

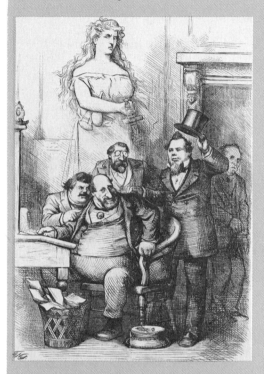

Thomas Nast's depiction of Tweed Ring: "Let's stop them damn pictures." (Library of Congress)

If the muckrakers had a spiritual godfather, it was a political cartoonist by the name of Thomas Nast. For, long before the first investigations of Standard Oil, Nast showed the world what investigative reporting was all about and what it could accomplish. The big trophy on Nast's wall was none other than Boss Tweed.

In 1869 the Tweed Ring seemed to have everything going its way: the police were well in hand, the newspapers were quiet, the public was apathetic, and the money was rolling in. Somehow, though, a publishing firm by the name of Harper Brothers (publishers of *Harper's Weekly*) got it into its head to do battle with the Ring, and young Thomas Nast was elected to lead the charge.

Nast was a competent artist, but his real gift was his mordant sense of irony. Now he depicted Tweed as a vulture picking over the bones of democracy, now as a buffoon playing blindman's bluff with Justice, now as a lustful

dramatic and sensational. With the latter circumstance especially in mind, muckrakers—we would call them investigative reporters today—turned out an endless parade of scandalous exposés. Such popular journals as *Forum, McClures,* and *The Atlantic Monthly* engaged in particularly aggressive muckraking, though almost every publication dabbled in it. In addition to crusading journalists, muckrakers included such prominent novelists as

Frank Norris and Upton Sinclair, such political thinkers as Henry George, Lincoln Steffens, and Henry Demarest Lloyd, and even an assortment of artists and photographers. Lovely or unlovely, muckraking proved to be a going concern—for in every corner of American life there seemed to be plenty of muck to rake up.

In politics, for example, the muckrakers described the callous depredations of the big-city bosses. Of course, political

Caesar throwing Miss Liberty to the Tammany Tiger. In all of the cartoons, Tweed was wearing his air of sanctimony, and in many of them he was sporting his outsized diamond stickpin as well. Nast knew how to manipulate symbols in all the right ways.

The effect of Nast's work was devastating. It kept Tweed's misdeeds constantly before the public eye, and it made the public itself feel vaguely guilty. But the cartoonist's most important contribution was to render Tweed and the others into laughingstock and thus make them seem beatable. Tweed himself understood this well. "Let's stop them damn pictures," he said to his henchmen. "I don't care what the papers say about me—my constituents can't read; but damn it, they can see pictures."

In the interest of stopping the pictures Tweed was ready to play hardball. His first ploy was to reject all of Harper Brothers' bids for schoolbooks, and to destroy $50,000 worth of Harper's books on hand. That came so close to ruining the company that Fletcher Harper had to threaten resignation in order to keep the crusade alive. For his part, Nast just drew another cartoon: of Tweed knocking a textbook from a child's desk.

So the Ring turned its tactics directly on Nast. They threatened his career. They threatened his life. They even tried bribery. Nast sat through the negotiations in mock good faith, running the amount of the bribe up to $500,000, exactly one hundred times his salary at Harper's. Then he stood up and strode majestically out of the room. Said he: "I made up my mind . . . to put them behind bars and I am going to put them there."

And eventually he did. Under the pressure of Nast's relentless hectoring, a blue-ribbon committee was appointed to investigate the Tweed Ring. Soon members of the Ring were falling over one another to testify. Such were the standards of the day, however, that Tweed himself was the only one who went to jail. And even at that, his life was well provided for, with a tastefully appointed cell, an array of creature comforts, and daily carriage rides about the city. Occasionally, he even cruised wistfully past Harper Brothers.

machines were nothing new: Tammany Hall in New York dated back to the days of Aaron Burr. What *was* new was the spreading influence of the bosses and the widening circles of their corruption. Josiah Flynt wrote a graphic series of articles on the subject in the pages of *McClures*, and in reading them, many Americans were jolted out of their complacency.

And then there were the slums. These had been bad enough in the days of the Jacksonian reformers, but of late they had become much worse. In the recent decade alone, millions of immigrants had poured into American cities, and there was no accommodating them in the nicer neighborhoods. As a result, tenement ghettos sprawled across New York's Five Points and Boston's Fort Hill district like a blight. And the Lower East Side, once a bazaar of ethnic humanity, had become a jungle of airless flats, rat-infested alleys, and dark, brooding misery. Anyone who gazed upon Jacob Riis' photographs of tenement life,

With millions of immigrants came overcrowded
slums (Culver Pictures)

or read the poetic captions he appended to
them, found it increasingly difficult to believe in the American Dream.

The muckrakers took aim at other targets. They were horrified by the conditions under which many people worked,
by the injustice meted out to racial and
ethnic minorities, and generally by the life
of the lowly. Organized crime caught their
eye and so did organized labor. They
searched nervously for threats from abroad,
for subversions at home, for every manner
of wrong and wrongdoing. But one evil
fascinated them more than all others. In the
breadth of its scope, in the heft of its power,
and in the darkness of its insidious malig-
nancy, nothing could compare to *the trusts.*

The Trusts

Big business, as we have noted, had become
a proud symbol of the postwar republic.
The very idea of American achievement
was embodied in megacorporations like
Standard Oil, U.S. (formerly Carnegie)
Steel, General Electric, Westinghouse,
Western Union, American Telephone, Ford
Motor, International Harvester, Du Pont
Chemical, the House of Morgan, and any
of a dozen major railroads. Their stories
were a part of the American story and their
successes validated the American Dream.

However, big business had another
side, a much less appealing one, which was
illustrated repeatedly by its attempts at

John D. Rockefeller: Brass-Knuckle tactics behind the American Dream. (Library of Congress)

monopoly. Among the dazzling innovations of the entrepreneurs, it seemed, were a few ideas for minimizing competition. One of them was the *stock pool*, where two or three large producers of a given commodity would concentrate their ownership in the same hands and thereby coordinate their pricing. Another was the *holding company*, where one corporation would buy a controlling interest in its major competitors and bring about the same result. Then, in 1879, a lawyer named Samuel C. T. Dodd hit upon the most cunning device of all. A single authority could control the activities of any number of "competitors," he said, if they would commit their stock into the hands of a central *trust*. And just as a fiduciary trust might have final say in the affairs of a minor heir, Dodd's invention would similarly rule

with an iron hand. It was significant, perhaps, that his first client was John D. Rockefeller.

For the muckrakers, the word trust, used generically to denote any monopoly, became a term of extreme opprobrium. (It had the right ring to it and the right touch of irony.) And as muckrakers viewed turn-of-the-century America, they saw trusts in increasing profusion. There was a tobacco trust headed by the American Tobacco Company, a copper trust ruled by Amalgamated Copper, and a rubber trust under United States Rubber. The farm implement industry was a trust (International Harvester), as was the chemical industry (Du Pont), the steel industry (U.S. Steel), and the meat-packing industry (Armour). Garment making, sugar refining, cattle ranching, mining, milling, smelting, timbering—all were increasingly controlled by trusts. In 1900 there were some seventy-eight corporations that might fairly qualify as monopolies. And by 1909, a mere one percent of the nation's industrial firms were producing almost half of its total goods.

Some trusts were natural monopolies, like the railroads that passed through small towns on the prairie, for to compete with them by establishing duplicate facilities was virtually impossible. Other trusts grew out of inventions, such as Edison's electric light and Pullman's sleeping car. A few corporations, like Carnegie Steel, dominated the market simply by running their competitors out of business.

Standard Oil

There was one trust, however, that came especially to mind. Like many giant corporations in the Gilded Age, Standard Oil of Ohio shone forth as a symbol of American pride. Although its owner, John D.

Rockefeller, had not started out as a bobbin boy, he was nonetheless a figure out of Horatio Alger. Beginning as a produce merchant in Cleveland, Rockefeller invested in a local oil refinery during the Civil War, and by 1865 was engaged in the oil business full time. After the war, the industry expanded at a dizzying pace, and Rockefeller's company more than kept up. His orderly mind constantly searched for ways to perfect his organization, make better use of his resources, and improve his productive efficiency. For instance, by reducing the solder used in sealing an oil drum from forty drops to thirty-nine, Rockefeller saved thousands of dollars annually.

To such a mind, the bruising competition of the oil industry did not make very good sense. Why, asked Rockefeller, should competitors slash each other's throats when the expanding market afforded opportunities for everyone? Through the 1870s, Standard Oil quietly bought up its rivals or drove them out of business, and by 1879 it controlled 90 percent of the nation's oil-refining capacity. Soon Rockefeller was a millionaire eight hundred times over.

At that point, Standard Oil naturally caught the eye of the muckrakers. In 1879 Henry Demarest Lloyd began an investigation of the company and its practices, and the published result, titled *Wealth and Commonwealth,* made for lively reading. Equally lively was a series of articles in *McClure's* magazine by a young journalist named Ida Tarbell—or "Tar Barrel" as Rockefeller pronounced it—who had launched an investigation of her own. Both presented a shockingly different view of the American success story.

To begin with, Rockefeller paid informers to infiltrate the organizations of rival businesses and to track down their

Ida Tarbell: A downside of American success. (Library of Congress)

customers. He also, it seemed, paid judges to hand down favorable decisions, and lawmakers to vote for Standard Oil's interests. (He did everything to the Pennsylvania legislature, quipped Lloyd, but refine it.) And then there was the matter of shipping rebates. Wielding his clout heavy-handedly, Rockefeller forced railroads to refund a substantial portion of the freight rates he had paid for shipping his goods to market. He even forced them to pay "drawbacks" on the goods shipped by his competitors.

The oil magnate used another bag of tricks on the independents who dared to defy him. Drawing on the strength of his national organization, he could cut prices in a given locale until every single competitor had been driven to the wall. He could even supply his own dealers, most of them small grocery stores, with low-priced inventories of meat, flour, and sugar in order to drive *their* competitors to the wall. And, as for dealer loyalty, Rockefeller could, by threatening to withdraw his business, force the owner of any country store not to carry the products of his competitors.

Taken together, these tactics were overwhelming. They enabled Rockefeller to ruin his competitors piecemeal and then buy them out for a song. Once the competition was gone, Standard Oil could quickly recoup its losses by jacking up prices at will. And that was exactly what it did.

These revelations had a singular effect. Since almost everyone used petroleum products in some way, almost everyone tended to feel personally defrauded and victimized. Beyond that, there was a deeper sense of betrayal. The American people, as we have seen, had an enormous psychological and emotional investment in their system. Suddenly it appeared that the system had not only failed them, it had turned on them as well. Cartoonists portrayed Rockefeller as a serpent, a monster, a dragon poised to devour humankind; but their favorite image was of a huge octopus with its tentacles curling into every neighborhood. The captains of American industry, once universally admired, were now casually referred to as the tycoons, the magnates, or, most descriptively, the Robber Barons.

The Sins of the Trusts

Public apprehension was both reflected in and intensified by further investigations. If Standard Oil was capable of such shenanigans, people asked, what were the rest of the trusts up to? In a long catalogue of evils, the muckrakers began to respond. The following were numbered among their discoveries:

Private Power. Political power, we recall, was something the Founders had profoundly mistrusted and desperately sought to contain. Constitutions and bills of rights could limit the power of the politicians, but what about the power of the tycoons? No checks and balances constrained the authority of Standard Oil and presumably none could. What was more, the power of the trusts was purely private in character. There were no elections to legitimize it, no organizations to oppose it, and no court system to hold it in check. If a Rockefeller got some notion into his head, there was nothing short of personal integrity to stop him from pursuing it.

The use of private power was not hard to illustrate. Everywhere one looked, it seemed, the big corporations could be seen throwing their weight around. They arranged for legislation friendly to their interests, subverted judicial processes, and steamrolled political opposition. Virtually every large railroad had been built on public lands and financed by public loans, but as soon as the company was profitably in business, it typically turned its back on the public. In California the builders of the Southern Pacific, all of them multimillionaires, defaulted on $59 million worth of bonds, claiming that, after all, the railroad benefited everyone.

Time and again the contest between public and private power was shown to be an uneven one. Tariffs were repeatedly raised on manufactured goods (causing consumers to pay more for them) in the face of widespread opposition. Strikes were broken by hiring private gunmen to intimidate the strikers. Franchises were awarded,

A Victim of the Octopus

For the muckrakers, it was often only the pleasure of the kill that seemed to explain life in the business jungle. In his novel, *The Octopus*, Frank Norris portrayed a scene in which a small farmer named Dyke was ruined by the Pacific and South-Western Railroad. Based on the railroad's assurance of a two cent per pound freight rate on hops, Dyke borrowed heavily and put in a large crop. When it was time to ship, however, he came in for a nasty surprise:

> In the list that was printed below, Dyke saw that the rate for hops between Bonneville . . . and San Francisco was five cents.
>
> For a moment Dyke was confused. Then swiftly the matter became clear in his mind. The railroad had raised the freight on hops from two cents to five.
>
> All his calculations as to a profit on his little investment he had based on a freight rate of two cents a pound. He was under contract to deliver his crop. He could not draw back. The new rate ate up every cent of his gains. He stood there ruined. . . .
>
> "Good Lord," he murmured, "Good Lord! What will you people do next? Look here. What's your basis of applying freight rates, anyhow?" he suddenly vociferated with furious sarcasm. "What's your rule? What are you guided by?"
>
> But at the words, S. Behrman, who had kept silent during the heat of the discussion leaned abruptly forward. For the only time in his knowledge, Dyke saw his face inflamed with anger and with the enmity and contempt of all this farming element with whom he was contending.
>
> "Yes, what's your rule? What's your basis?" demanded Dyke, turning swiftly to him.
>
> S. Behrman emphasized each word of his reply with a tap of one forefinger on the counter before him: "All—the—traffic—will—bear."

For Norris, who researched his fiction with meticulous care, there would be no happy ending. Dyke, in a frenzy, stole a locomotive and took it on an open-throttle blast across the San Joaquin Valley. For this obvious act of madness he was sentenced by the railroad-controlled court to life imprisonment.

right of ways granted, and monopolies established by state and local governments too weak to resist. And even the federal government could be pushed around. In the face of pressure from timber, cattle, and mining interests, it gave away huge segments of the national domain for next to nothing.

Was private power something the United States could live with? The reformers doubted it. Power was power, they said, and too much of it in anyone's hands, public or private, boded ill for the Republic. In 1895, when U.S. gold reserves dipped dangerously low as the result of a recession, federal bankruptcy was staved off by a timely loan from J. P. Morgan. That a private financier should have such resources—and hence such power—struck many as intolerable.

Corruption. The power of the trusts was seldom used for worthy purposes, it was almost always used for corrupt ones. For men who were worth millions, it was nothing to bribe a local judge or pay off a few venal politicians. In the Erie War, Commodore Vanderbilt and Jay Gould vied with each other to buy votes in the New York legislature, but other states fell prey just as easily. It seemed that there were few state lawmakers with enough gumption to resist.

California's politics was particularly gruesome. By the 1880s the Southern Pacific Railroad, which monopolized every form of transportation in the state, had a stranglehold on the government in Sacramento. It handpicked the governor, appointed both senators, and maintained its own political machine in every metropolitan center. In San Francisco, for instance, the notorious "Little Pete" machine in Chinatown—specializing in opium, gambling, and slave prostitution—was directly linked to the railroad and flourished under its protection.

Nor was the federal government immune. When the builders of the Union Pacific found a way to make themselves rich by overcharging for construction supplies, they covered their tracks by selling stock at a discount to members of Congress. And when the restless Jay Gould attempted to corner the gold market in 1869, he took the precaution of setting up a gold account for Orville Babcock, the president's brother-in-law, who agreed to use his influence accordingly. A great many public scandals had the fingerprints of the Robber Barons all over them.

Corruption, we recall, was something the Founders had worried a great deal about, but even they had not foreseen this. Corruption on a scale that the Rockefellers and Vanderbilts could afford was something new in human history, and it was more than a little frightening. What did it mean for the future of republican government, asked the progressives, when corruption was big business and big business was corrupt?

Monopoly. For Adam Smith and the proponents of the market system, the idea of free competition was a given. In order for market mechanisms to operate as they should, it was necessary for competitors to struggle viscerally with one another, to knock down and drag out with abandon. Only the reality of competition, not just the idea or the threat of it, could keep self-interest within bounds.

By definition, of course, the trusts did not like competition and made haste to do away with it. Using fair means or foul, they either welded the leading producers of an industry into some sort of cartel monopoly or else one of them simply gobbled the others up. When teaching his Sunday School class in Cleveland, John D. Rockefeller occasionally lectured on the virtues of the American Beauty rose, which could be grown to an impressive size, as he demonstrated, by carefully pruning away all other buds on the stem. That more or less summarized his view of competition.

Once a trust had amassed size and power, it could throttle most of its competition handily. The small, independent producer, so vital to the operation of the market system, was particularly vulnerable, for, as the Standard Oil experience had shown, enormous leverage could be brought to bear on him. Indeed, destroying small competitors seemed to

Jacob Riis on Life in the Slums

Notwithstanding their general avoidance of the slums, middle-class Americans came to have a certain fascination with them. Artist George Bellows and others of the so-called Ashcan School found a strange sort of beauty in the tenements, capturing on canvas their forbidding darkness, their teeming humanity, their miasmic atmosphere of clotheslines. But it took a black-and-white camera to see the slums as they really were. That was the significance of police photographer Jacob Riis, whose assignments often called for picture taking. Some of Riis' photographs were of the human refuse that found its way to precinct headquarters; others were of the material conditions that spawned such lives. All of them were disturbing. Riis himself was moved to compose lengthy poetic captions for them:

Riis's photograph of children sleeping in the slums: How the other half lived. (Library of Congress)

> It was the death of little Giuseppe that brought me to his home, a dismal den in a rear tenement down a dark and forbidding alley. I have seldom seen a worse place. From this hole Giuseppe had come to the [Mott Street Industrial] school a mass of rags, but with that jovial gleam in his brown eyes that made him an instant favorite. Giuseppe was sent to an Elizabeth Street tenement for a little absentee. "This girl is very poor," he said, presenting her to the teacher, with a pitying look. [He] fished his only penny out of his pocket—his capital for the afternoon's trade [as a newsboy]. "I would like to give her that," he said. After that he brought her pennies regularly, and took many a thrashing for it. There came an evening when business had been so bad he thought a bed on the street healthier for him than the Crosby Street Alley. With three other lads in similar straights he crawled into the iron chute that ventilated the basements of the post office and snuggled down on the grating. They were all asleep, when fire broke out in the cellar. The three climbed out, but Giuseppe, whose feet were wrapped in a mail-bag, was too late.

Viewers were horrified by Riis' photographs, which seemed to come out of a netherworld totally alien to the Gilded Age. For the thoughtful, however, they marked the beginning of what Robert Hunter would call "the discovery of poverty" in the United States.

become, as the muckrakers viewed it, a kind of blood sport among the lords of industry—like hunting for the pleasure of the kill.

And when competition disappeared, other forms of hunting became possible. Customers, for example, made easy prey. In dealing with their shippers, railroads of the Gilded Age regularly discriminated in favor of the Rockefellers and Carnegies, with their vast daily cargos, and against the small and powerless. Thus, farmers in the Midwest, who could rarely choose among railroads as the large industrialists could, were forced to pay exorbitant rates for the use of railroad silos, loading ramps, and cattle pens. As for freight rates, it often cost more to ship from central Illinois to Chicago (on a route where there was no competition) than it did to ship from Chicago to New York.

Railroad monopolists, in fact, could become downright dictatorial. The Southern Pacific in California often demanded to see a shipper's books before deciding what rate to charge him, thereby securing every nickel he could afford to pay. It played fast and loose with its public land grants, too, selling them to unsuspecting buyers under extremely dubious circumstances. And when a group of farmers in the San Joaquin Valley strenuously objected to such high-handed treatment, the railroad hired gunmen to keep them in line. In 1880, at a place called Mussel Slough, there was an old-fashioned shootout in which seven people were killed. With this tragedy the muckrakers had a field day.

Progressives mourned the demise of competition with a special poignancy. As far as they were concerned, economic individualism, with its independent producers, its entrepreneurial inventiveness, and its restless kinetic energy, had lain at the very heart of the American success story. And just as the reformers feared for the Republic when too much power was held in too few hands, they began to fear similarly for the market system.

Exploitation. Muckrakers charged that the trusts shamelessly exploited labor, demanding long hours, paying low wages, and turning the workplace into a nightmare of lethal hazards. It was in the steel industry that the loudest complaints were heard. Big steel producers gained an advantage at the outset by massively recruiting their labor abroad. Once assured of a generous and virtually endless supply, the steel magnates could treat their workers pretty much as they saw fit.

Typically steelmen worked a twelve-hour day, six or seven days a week, with shifts rotating between day, night, and swing. That it was bone-crushing, spine-wrenching work was attested by the appalling number of accidents—old, retired steelworkers were something of a rarity. Wages were sufficient to lure young men away from their dirt farms in the Balkans, perhaps, but not sufficient to provide them with the sort of life promised in the recruiters' handbills. Most of them wound up in dark tenement ghettos, where rats infested the alleyways, where children played in the open sewers, and where two and three families huddled together in a single flat. When the muckrakers visited such places, they found plenty to write about.

But many other industries were as bad as steel. Their hours were equally long, their conditions equally poor, and their wages equally meager. Moreover, with technology moving at such a brisk pace,

Survival in the Jungle

Workers in a Chicago meatpacking plant: Perils and hazards everywhere. (Library of Congress)

much of their machinery was new and untried, and only through experience did the workers learn of the dangers. In the textile mills, for example, wheels were humming and belts flying at incredible speeds—before the electrical age, power had to be delivered to the looms mechanically—and it was all too easy to catch a hand, a dress, or (worst of all) long hair in the works. That these establishments were largely manned by young children did not add to their appeal.

Furthermore, according to legal doctrines of the day, factory and mill owners were not held responsible for industrial accidents. If a worker ended up in the hospital, he was expected to meet the expense through savings. Not infrequently, families found themselves quite literally in the poorhouse upon the death or dismemberment of a wage earner.

Of course, the surviving widow could take a job. (Often she had one already.) Yet life in the workplace was no better for her than it had been for her husband. For a few cents an hour, immigrant women were employed in the hundreds of "sweatshops" that dotted the Lower East Side. Here, in cold, grimy apartments and filthy, crowded cellars, babushka-clad women put

When his magnum opus, *The Jungle*, became a front-page American scandal, Upton Sinclair was not elated. "I aimed for America's heart," he said ruefully, "and by mistake I hit it in the stomach." And that was just what happened. Sinclair had not written the book to show the public what it was eating for breakfast; he had written it to show the unspeakable conditions of labor in the meat-packing industry. Had it not been for the gory details of embalmed beef and poisoned rats, the author almost certainly would have hit his mark.

For he was equally vivid in describing the horrors and hazards of the workplace. There were, for example, the hands of the boners and trimmers, cut so often that they became mere lumps of scar tissue; there were the fingers of the wool-pluckers, eaten away by their constant immersion in acid; there were the backs and shoulders of the hoisters, permanently humped by incessant ducking under rafter beams, "so that in a few years they would be walking like chimpanzees"; there were the lungs of the men in the cooking rooms, virtually all of them shot through with tuberculosis. "And as for the other men," Sinclair concluded,

> who worked in tank rooms full of steam, and in some of which there were open vats near the level of the floor, their peculiar trouble was that they fell into the vats; and when they were fished out, there was never enough of them left to be worth exhibiting—sometimes they would be overlooked for days, till all but the bones of them had gone out to the world as Durham's Pure Leaf Lard!

Such charges were not inconsequential, and a government commission hastened to look into them. Unhappily, the commission reported that Sinclair had told the truth about life in the packing houses, and in fact, that he had overlooked some things. At that, of course, the public outrage burst forth anew.

in ten- and twelve-hour days at a sewing machine, emerging at night to wend their way home through the slums. The sweatshops were vile establishments by anyone's reckoning, and were often against the law, to boot. But in the grip of necessity people had to work in them.

Was there any escape from such circumstances? Not for most people. Government had virtually nothing to do with working conditions—that was one of the things *laissez faire* ("leave alone") meant to leave alone—and the courts were similarly blind. Some workers took refuge in labor unions, but these were no match for most employers. If faced with a union challenge, virtually any mine or mill owner could resort to the use of strikebreakers, scabs, or armed mercenaries known as Pinkertons. And if the strike grew really vicious, as some did, the company could even call in the law.

But it was increasingly difficult to still the voice of the reformers. Some of the most effective muckraking of all time was addressed to the plight of American laborers, and middle-class readers could not help but sympathize. Indeed, in 1911 there occurred an event that brought the entire situation sharply into focus. It went down in history as the Triangle Fire.

Victims of the Triangle Fire: The way the system really worked. (Library of Congress)

The Triangle Shirtwaist Company occupied the upper three floors of the eight-story Asch Building in lower Manhattan, and fire safety had never been much on the minds of its owners. At 4:30 in the afternoon of March 25th, a flash fire broke out in one of the rag bins on the eighth floor. In the clutter of cotton scraps, the fire quickly passed out of control, forcing the five hundred employees to the exits. But there were no exits. The doors had been locked in the interest of keeping the young Italian and Jewish immigrant girls on the job. Only the elevators gave access to the room, and those were hopelessly inadequate for the clawing, shrieking mass of humanity.

One by one, each girl made her grim choice: the fire or the windows. Some chose the fire. They huddled on the stone ledges and burned to death in full view of the onlookers below. Others chose the windows, their clothes and hair trailing smoke as they plummeted earthward. "Thud—dead! Thud—dead! Thud—dead!" So began an eyewitness account of the Triangle tragedy by reporter William Gunn Shepherd. It was simply the worst thing he had ever seen.

No accounting was ever made for the 146 girls who died. Lawsuits were not deemed appropriate, and the trial of the Triangle owners for manslaughter ended in acquittal. Such an outcome spoke volumes about the American economic system and the way it worked.

Destruction of the Environment. Big business was in nowise unique in its disregard of the environment, for most Americans took nature quite for granted. It happened, though, that the pillagers John Muir ran into were big businessmen. Monopoly had become a way of life in turn-of-the-century California. What the Southern Pacific didn't control, the Comstock silver kings or the Sierra timber barons did. And all of them had a common interest in development. As a result, they were cutting down the redwoods by the square mile, filling in San Francisco Bay to create more real estate, and damming up the Sierra valley of Hetch Hetchy as a water resource.

It was at Hetch Hetchy that Muir drew the line. He was a religious man in his own way, and for him the glacier-cut valley with its towering granite walls was nothing less than God's own cathedral. He took Teddy Roosevelt on a climb of Half Dome in the Yosemite and made an environmentalist out of him. Then, organizing the Sierra Club, he went to work on everyone else.

As muckrakers, Muir and his followers were extremely good, and in time they got even better. Muir alone turned out more than sixty-five newspaper and magazine articles, most of them righteously angry about the ongoing despoilation. Of the Hetch Hetchy controversy he wrote: "These temple destroyers, devotees of ravaging commercialism, seem to have a perfect contempt for Nature, and instead of lifting their eyes to the God of the Mountains, lift them to the Almighty Dollar."

The Sierra Club lost its battle for Hetch Hetchy, which became the San Francisco municipal reservoir, and soon afterward a brokenhearted John Muir went to his grave. But in the course of the controversy many Americans came to believe that those who felled the forests and tore up the mountains were the same greedy capitalists who jacked up freight rates and foreclosed mortgages.

Bad Faith. Like environmentalism, consumerism got its start with the muckrakers, and with one of them in particular. Upton Sinclair was a prolific novelist, a radical, a socialist, and in 1904, an angry young man. That year he went to live in Chicago's Packingtown in order to see for himself how the meat-packing trust conducted its affairs. His sympathies were with the immigrant workers who lived dangerously in Packingtown's slaughterhouses and miserably in its clapboard slums. Once inside the plants, however, Sinclair couldn't help but notice something else— that consumers were being victimized by a gigantic (and poisonous) swindle.

Accordingly, as he scrawled out his soon-to-be-famous novel, *The Jungle,* Sinclair made sure that it contained graphic descriptions of what he had seen. He told of cattle covered with boils, which would "splash foul-smelling stuff into your face" when the knife was plunged in; of moldy sausage sent back from Europe, dosed with borax, and made over again for U.S. consumption; of meat that tumbled onto the floor, "where workers had tramped and spit uncounted billions of consumption germs." One passage was especially vivid:

There would be meat stored in great piles in rooms; and the water from leaky roofs would drip over it, and thousands of rats would race

A Gilded-age Strike

At first, Chicagoans thumbing through their morning papers could not believe it was really the Pullman Sleeping Car factory that was out on strike. For, all who had visited the company town of Pullman, Illinois, had come away favorably impressed. With its manicured lawns, its artificial lake, its posh hotel and shopping arcade, and most of all, its scrubbed and painted workers' cottages, Pullman seemed like an industrial vision of Utopia.

The workers themselves, however, knew another side. They knew, for example, that George Pullman was buying water from the city and retailing it to the townspeople at a 500 percent profit, that the gas selling in neighboring Hyde Park for seventy-five cents a thousand cubic feet was selling in Pullman for $2.25, and that the prices of everything else in the model town were similarly jacked up out of reason. And they knew that at fourteen dollars per month, rents for the picket-fence cottages were at least 25 percent higher than in Chicago. Still, Pullman *was* pretty, and so the workers had grudgingly gone along with the gouging.

Until George Pullman started cutting their pay. With the onset of depression in 1893, he reduced wages five separate times, until the average had fallen from fifty dollars a month to thirty-six dollars. Of course, prices in the town, including rents, remained exactly where they were. Soon children were going to the carpentry shop and begging for wood scraps to take home and burn. Picture-book Pullman was a scene of want and desolation.

The strike was touched off when a group of hungry Pullmanites sought out the railroad-car tycoon in his Chicago office and tried to reason with him. Not only did he refuse to budge on prices or wages, he fired the leaders of the delegation for good measure. By mid-May of 1894, Pullman's once bustling factory stood silent.

about on it. It was too dark in the storage places to see well, but a man could run his hand over the piles of meat and sweep off handfuls of the dried dung of rats. These rats were nuisances, and the packers would put poisoned bread out for them; they would die, and then rats, bread, and meat would go into the hoppers together.

The book touched off a terrific uproar, which didn't subside for months. And even after regaining their appetites, Americans long remained warily suspicious. After all, if trusted names like Armour and Swift could be guilty of such foul abuses, what were the lesser-known companies capable of? Readers began looking more skeptically at advertising copy. Was it really true,

they wondered, that Listerine Antiseptic prevented colds? Was it accurate to claim that with Old Gold Cigarettes there was "never a cough in a carload?" And what about the famous Carbolic Smoke Ball—did it truly cure cancer? Perhaps there were things besides meatpacking that needed government supervision.

Progressive Reform

In some ways the indictments of the muckrakers were unfair. Much of what they had supposedly unmasked as capitalistic evil was nothing more than market weakness,

The striking workers tried to keep things orderly. They remained calm, played baseball in the park, and kept a twenty-four-hour guard on the shut-down facilities in order to prevent damage. Only when it was clear that Pullman was not going to negotiate did they appeal for outside help. Writing to Eugene V. Debs, head of the American Railway Union, they laid out their grievances and asked the cooperation of the parent organization. Debs complied. He ordered that no trains be moved nationwide if they were carrying Pullman cars.

This broader strike tied Chicago railroading, with its twenty-four trunk lines, into a veritable knot. It also gave George Pullman the leverage he needed to break the strike, for now it could be argued that the union was preventing the movement of the mails. Attorney General Richard Olney obtained a federal injunction against the American Railway Union, and over the head of Gov. John Altgeld (who deeply sympathized with the strikers) federal troops were brought in.

It was then that all hell broke loose. Patient for months, the strikers took on the army toe to toe, overturning cars, throwing brickbats, burning and pillaging. And, for their part, the authorities fought back with mounting violence. By July 7, when a day-long pitched battle was fought at the Chicago rail yards, soldiers were simply firing pointblank into the crowds. "The ground over which the fight had occurred was like a battlefield," wrote a *Tribune* reporter, "The men shot by the troops and police lay about like dogs."

Before the Pullman Strike was over, the death toll reached thirty-four, with hundreds wounded and over seven hundred in jail. In dribs and drabs the sullen workers of Pullman returned to their former jobs (at their former wages), for there was no hope of beating the United States Army. And George Pullman took his place in the American industrial pantheon, beside Carnegie and Rockefeller.

as we saw in chapter twelve. The despoilation of the environment, for example, was really only an *externality*, the peculiar blindless of the market toward the interests of third parties, not a deliberate program of destruction. Indeed, if there was a real culprit behind corporate wrongdoing, it was probably change. U.S. economic and technological development were proceeding so rapidly that their effects simply spun out of control.

Nevertheless, the image of the evil capitalist began to loom large in the American imagination. Karl Marx had warned of the downfall awaiting capitalistic society, and much of what the muckrakers were bringing to light seemed a fulfillment of his prophecies. (Socialist candidates would poll over a million votes in the election of 1912.) Moreover, the sins of the trusts made Americans feel less special. Their faith had held that self-interest and virtue could exist side by side, just as in the pages of Horatio Alger, and that the American Way was living proof of it. Now, with rapacious men seemingly in control everywhere, the American Way seemed less extraordinary.

However explained, the progressives' sense of loss was both real and poignant. A happier, nobler time was slipping away, and they felt they must somehow call it

Advertisement for the water-cure: Perhaps other things needed supervision. (Library of Congress)

back. But what, exactly, could they do? There was little agreement. Some of the reformers embarked on crusades that could only be called romantic. For example, settlement-house workers like Jane Addams and Florence Kelly waded into the slums with the apparent thought of cleaning them up single-handedly. And, in the same spirit, political thinkers like Louis Brandeis proposed to "bust" the trusts—that is, legally break them up—and turn back the clock to better days. Other progressives were more forward looking. Placing their faith in science, they argued that a meticulous investigation of the problems would surely bring forth the right answers. From progressive learning centers, such as the University of Wisconsin, came a flood of proposals for resolving this or that difficulty. Some supposed that if science became sharp enough, even the trusts could be brought under control.

Intervention

With science in mind, many progressives gradually came to see big business in a different light. The chief spokesman of the new view was a political thinker named Herbert Croly. In a pathmaking book titled *The Promise of American Life*, Croly argued that the world of Thomas Jefferson was gone for good—swept away by the winds of change. Whether Americans liked it or not, he said, urbanization, industrialism, bureaucracy, and many other features of modern life were here to stay. And so was bigness. It would do no good to complain about big business, big labor, or big anything else in the century now dawning, for bigness was the wave of the future.

If there was no turning back the clock, then, what was there? Croly's answer was uncompromising. Meet the new era on its own terms, he admonished. Don't try to bust the trusts—*regulate* them. Accept the fact that they will and must exist and work on ways to improve their behavior. Croly apparently believed that the market economy was also a thing of the past. What remained, he argued, was for the United States to develop some sort of new economy, one in which big producers like Standard Oil and U.S. Steel would respond to signals not from the marketplace but from the government. Big government, so it seemed, was the most inevitable bigness of all.

What Croly was talking about, of course, was government intervention. Almost a century had passed since Americans deleted that term from their political vocabulary, but now, clearly, it was back. For, according to Croly's analysis, intervention was the necessary price of living in the modern world. When everything else became big and powerful and officious, government simply had to do the same. In order to control the trusts, in order to regulate the activities of a complex society, in order to monitor the interplay of capital and labor and consumption, much more public power was needed. The only way, said Croly, that an economic system could function adequately in the twentieth century was when government supervised everything.

It took time for some progressives to catch Croly's vision. Theodore Roosevelt, for example, began his presidential career by fulminating against the trusts and even by busting a few. It was at his insistence that the Justice Department, on the authority of the Sherman Antitrust Act, initiated suits against the Northern Securities Trust, the American Tobacco Company, and the granddaddy of them all, Standard Oil. But by 1912, when he again ran for the White House as the candidate of the Progressive party, Roosevelt had changed his tune. What was needed, he explained in the campaign, was not a lot of anachronistic trust busting; it was a government capable of supervising the trusts and making them behave. Big government, scientifically inspired and democratically controlled, could be thought of as a Hamiltonian means of producing a Jeffersonian end. Roosevelt called his program the New Nationalism.

The possibilities for such intervention were graphically demonstrated a few years later by World War I. Twentieth-century warfare, no longer the business of a few professionals, required the mobilization of every resource the nation could command.

In the interest of victory, the United States—under the leadership of another progressive, Woodrow Wilson—found itself undertaking precisely what Croly had outlined. Production was rationalized and carefully orchestrated. Resources were allocated and tightly controlled. Railroads, once the most individualistic of enterprises, were nationalized into a single administrative unit and placed under the command of a "czar." In an economy where planning had rarely been mentioned, there was now planning down to the smallest detail.

The Waning of Progressivism

In the main, however, the progressives were a good deal less advanced in their thinking. If they agreed with Croly that bigger government might be necessary in the future, they still looked back fondly on the past. Like Roosevelt himself, they were often of two minds about the modern world, and occasionally the two were in conflict. Apart from the war experience—which was highly unusual—progressives were rather timid in applying Croly's ideas.

They did take a few measured steps. For instance, they began to regulate the railroads. These were not totally private anyway, for most had been built with public funding; and in any case, they served a public purpose. Accordingly, beginning with the Interstate Commerce Act in 1887, reformers sought to curb railroad abuses by means of ever-tighter government regulation. By 1920, with the passage of the Railway Transportation Act, the railroads were supervised so closely by the Interstate Commerce Commission that many of them found it difficult to survive.

There were several other regulatory forays. Progressives sought to limit the hours of working women, to abolish child labor, and to require employers to provide "workman's compensation" for the victims of disabling accidents. With two new federal agencies, the Food and Drug Administration and the Federal Trade Commission, they struck at the meatpacking abuses detailed in Sinclair's novel, at the antics of patent-medicine vendors, and at some of the worst excesses of advertising. Finally, they reorganized the nation's banking system with the creation of the Federal Reserve, an institution that committed enormous economic power into the hands of a very few people.

Beyond this, though, there was little else. For the progressives' actual experience with intervention—as opposed to their warm advocacy of it—was not altogether happy. Intervention, it seemed, was a difficult and perplexing business, and one never knew what its outcome might be. The Sherman Act, whose purpose was to control the trusts, wound up controlling labor unions instead, and the Interstate Commerce Commission, which was designed to regulate railroads, originally approved nearly everything the railroads did.

After the World War, progressivism went into decline. To be sure, individual reformers were still active in public life and their concern for the future remained anxious. But with the Jazz Age and Prohibition and a roaring bull market on Wall Street, there were other things for people to think about. Besides, with Montgomery Ward selling at $138 a share, U.S. Steel at $262, and AT&T at $304, the trusts didn't seem quite so bad. Most Americans, still believing in progress, continued to hope that their political-economic system, conceived in liberty, would somehow right itself automatically.

The Legacy of the Progressives

Yet something of the old progressive crusade still remained: a deep and abiding mistrust of business in general and big business in particular. There would still be business heroes in America—Henry Ford preeminent among them—and stupendous business success stories. But the old naiveté about businessmen and their morals was gone. Whenever there were new revelations about the misdeeds of the trusts, people simply greeted them with a shrug. Horatio Alger went abruptly out of vogue.

The progressives left another legacy. The notion of government intervention in the economy, once universally abhorred, was now seen in a far more favorable light. Those who continued to fret about the country's economic problems—such as the devastating farm depression—did not discount the possibility of a major intervention later on. For, if something did go seriously wrong, what else but a large, powerful, Crolyan government would be in a position to deal with it?

The Great Depression and the New Deal

Objectives

The Great Depression
The New Deal
National Recovery Administration
Agricultural Adjustment
Administration
Welfare
Wagner Act
Keynesian Economics
Intervention and Consequences

Victims of the Great Depression (Culver Pictures)

Hard Times

Although Ben Isaacs had never been well-to-do, he lived a fulfilling, comfortable life. He was in business for himself, selling clothing door-to-door on credit. In a good week, he might take in four or five hundred dollars from his neighborhood customers, and nearly half of that was profit. He and his wife lived in a well-appointed Chicago apartment, dressed their children stylishly, had a modest passbook savings, a little property, and a tidy stash of gold bonds. Ben had thought about putting his money in the stock market—plenty of other people were doing that—but concluded that "the stock market goes up and down." Gold bonds, on the other hand, were "just like gold." As he approached his mid-forties, it was a point of special pride with him that never in his life had he had to accept charity.

In 1928, however, business began to fall off. Isaacs attributed the slackness to speculation, which seemed to be claiming his customers' extra income. By the following year things were bad, but they were soon to get worse. One day in October he was on his way to see a customer when he heard the newsboys blaring a strange headline: the stock market had crashed. "It came out just like lightning."

Very shortly Ben Isaacs' life began turning to ashes. From the five-hundred-dollar-a-week level, his business nose-dived to the two hundred, the one hundred, the fifty, the ten. Nobody would pay. Nobody *could* pay. His customers were losing their own jobs, and clothing was the first thing they could afford to cut. Sometimes, if their consciences bothered them, they might give him a dollar or two on the account, but more often they only managed a shrug.

By turns he lost everything. The bonds that were supposedly good as gold became worthless overnight. His investment property was sold for taxes. His car became useless to him, for he couldn't afford a license for it; he sold it for fifteen dollars to buy food. When the rent came due, he stalled frantically, hoping for some sort of reprieve. Soon he was unable to buy even cigarettes. He literally didn't have a nickel in his pocket.

He tried to find some other kind of work, but none was available. Day after day he pounded the pavement and night after night he came home empty-handed. He blamed himself, not the Depression: he must have done something wrong, made a mistake of some sort. How was it that he had gone through life and only qualified himself to sell clothing?

Then he noticed the taxis bumping along in the streets. Surely people would always need taxis, he reasoned. It was demeaning work, driving a taxi, but it beat starvation. After talking it over with his wife, he withdrew the last of his savings, two hundred dollars, for a down payment on a taxi. With the money tucked away in his pocket, he went downtown to the Checker Cab Company. But there was a hitch: the right kind of car wasn't available; he should check back in a week. Back on the street, he felt in his pocket for the money. It was gone. In his numbness, he had dropped it, mislaid it, or allowed it to be stolen from him. Now he was really broke.

Friends urged him to apply for relief. He had seen the bread lines downtown: men standing in the cold, shuffling miserably, staring at the pavement. No, he thought, he could not become a ward of charity. He walked the streets aimlessly, dazedly, hunger and worry gnawing at his stomach. Occasionally the thought of

The Great Depression affected masses of individuals
(UPI/Bettmann Newsphotos)

suicide flickered through his mind. Others were doing it—taking pills, jumping out of windows—and some of them were better off than he was. But the children kept appearing before his eyes. "Somebody has to take care of those kids. . . ."

At last he went to the relief office, tears streaming down his face, and began filling out the forms. "Shame? You tellin' me? I would stand on that relief line, I would look this way and that way and see if there's nobody around that knows me. I would bend my head low so nobody would recognize me." After a personal investigation and a great deal of red tape, the relief office granted him forty-five dollars a month. His rent was thirty dollars—and his family couldn't live on fifteen.

So, the family surrendered its comfortable apartment and found a cheap flat, "a dirty, filthy, dark place," heated only by the kitchen stove. Their meals were narrowed to two a day and their meat reduced to baloney. The children shivered with the cold. They began to get sick. Isaacs knew he had to find better for them, money or no money, so he buttoned up his threadbare coat and went out searching again.

He turned up a slightly better lodging for an appreciably higher rate, but supposedly it had steam heat. The cold found them here, too. After taking their rent, the landlord abandoned the building. Hot water became cold water and then, as the city shut off service, no water at all. Mrs. Isaacs had to borrow two pails full from a neighbor every morning and lug them up the stairs. They would make it last until bedtime, for cooking and washing alike, and then use what was left to flush the toilet.

Meanwhile Isaacs kept looking for work. Finally he decided to go back to selling, if not clothing, then razor blades and shoelaces. He would spend an entire day going door-to-door and come home in the evening with fifty cents. But it gave him someone to talk to. "That was the only way we could drown our sorrow," he later reminisced. "We'd come to each other's house and sit and talk and josh around and try to make a little cheerfulness."

It was 1944 before anything like prosperity returned. Isaacs and his wife worked throughout the war, he in a munitions factory, she as a waitress in a cheap restaurant, while their children grew up, got married, and moved away. When they had saved up four hundred dollars, he went back to the clothing store, took out a new consignment of merchandise, and headed back out on his old beat. Though he was now approaching sixty, and the younger salesmen gave him looks of pity, he made a go of it. But it was hard to resist the notion that a huge chunk had been taken out of his life.

In chapter twenty-one we saw that the re-publican government devised by the Founders harbored the seeds of its own near destruction, that in the decade of the 1850s these seeds sprouted into a full-scale crisis, and that in dealing with the crisis Americans were eventually obliged to modify their Constitution. In the early 1930s, virtually the same fate would befall the market system. For it, too, had its im-perfections, as we have seen, and it was only a matter of time before several of them combined to produce an historic disaster.

Again like the Civil War, the Great Depression became one of the central events in American history. We have suc-ceeded only partly in understanding its causes, and even less at penetrating the emotional and psychological aspects of its experience. The one thing that does seem clear is its results—which marked a major turning point in our national develop-ment. It is not too much to say that today, nearly half a century afterward, we are still living in the Great Depression's shadow.

The Great Depression

It began with the stock market crash in Oc-tober of 1929. Stocks on the New York ex-change, dizzily high only a few weeks before, now suddenly plummeted, and there seemed no end to their fall. U. S. Steel tumbled from 262 dollars a share to 22, American Telephone and Telegraph from 304 to 72, Montgomery Ward from 138 to 4. The stock of United Founders fell fur-thest of all: from 75 dollars to 75 cents. When the crash finally guttered out, three-quarters of the value of American invest-ment had vanished.

By that time the Depression was well under way. It commenced with the usual layoffs and plant closures as business after business retrenched. Many forecasters pre-dicted the imminent rebirth of pros-perity—always just around the corner—but gradually the hopeful talk faded. The fail-ures and layoffs continued their down-ward spiral, each round triggering the next. By 1932 automobile production had

Scene fom the Dust Bowl: On top of everything
else, the destruction of the land. (Library of
Congress)

The stock market crash of 1929 (UPI/Bettmann
Newsphotos)

The Bonus March

They came from all over the country—on freight trains, in old jalopies, sometimes even on foot—converging like homing pigeons on Washington, D.C. Eventually there were twenty thousand of them, all veterans of World War I, all victims of the Depression, all desperately in want. And, in their own minds at least, they were not coming to ask for handouts or favors, but for something that was legally and morally due them: their "bonus." It seemed that in 1924 Congress had allocated a special benefit for the vets, to compensate for their low pay as soldiers, but it was not payable until 1945. It only amounted to five hundred dollars, hardly a car payment in today's economy. To the hard-strapped "bonus marchers," however, it seemed like the difference between life and death.

They settled, willy-nilly, in a Potomac marshland known as Anacostia Flats. It was not the Ritz. "The men are sleeping," reported John Dos Passos, "in little lean-tos built out of old newspapers, cardboard boxes, packing crates, bits of tin or tarpaper roofing, every kind of cockeyed makeshift shelter from the rain scraped together out of the city dump." In such a situation mere survival posed a daily problem. But one local baker donated a hundred loaves of bread, and another a thousand pies, and the men themselves arranged boxing tournaments at nearby Griffith Stadium and raised a little cash. Somehow they survived.

Their purpose was to petition Congress for an early payment of the bonus. The House was willing to go along but the Senate steadfastly refused. As for President Hoover, to whom the veterans sought to make a special appeal, he sent word back that he was just too busy to see them. (That week he had to confer with a heavyweight wrestling champion, meet members of the Eta Epsilon Gamma sorority, and award prizes in a high school essay contest.) Understandably, the bonus marchers were miffed. Even so, Will Rogers could describe them as "the best behaved hungry men assembled anywhere in the world."

Inevitably, though, they had to be evicted. (Their very presence, it was said, was getting on the president's nerves.) On July 28, 1932, the D.C. police had a confrontation with them on Pennsylvania Avenue, and before it was over two marchers were dead. That afternoon Gen. Douglas MacArthur was ordered to get rid of them once and for all. He assembled six tanks, a squadron of machine guns, four troops of cavalry, and four companies of infantry, all of them ready for battle. When

slumped from its 1929 level of 4.5 million units to a scant 1.1 million. Ford had shut down completely.

Nor was Ford alone. One hundred eighty-five thousand businesses had failed, 25 percent of the work force was idled, and per capita income had been wrenched back a quarter of a century. What was worse, individual resources for coping with the catastrophe were jeopardized by bank failures. Some four thousand banks had already closed their doors, and with the

One of the Great Depression's many bread lines:
Not the Ritz. (National Archives)

they first saw the army coming, the veterans thought it was a military parade—in *their* honor. Only when the tear gas began flying did they put down their American flags and take cover.

The destruction of Anacostia Flats was not pleasant to watch. Old timers said it reminded them of a battle. And, indeed, it ended with a cavalry charge, led by hot-blooded George S. Patton, across the smoldering ruins of the Hooverville. In the melee, two more veterans were shot to death and two babies died from tear gas. Among the dozens of minor casualties was Joseph T. Angelino, who had won the Distinguished Service Cross for saving the life of a young officer—named George Patton—in the Argonne Forest.

collapse of each had gone the personal savings of thousands. In one failure alone, four hundred thousand depositors had been wiped out.

Farmers had never recovered from their own chronic depression, and now their plight was truly pitiable. Florida growers left mountains of oranges to putrefy. Iowans burned their corn for fuel. Minnesota dairymen emptied milk cans onto the road. "You don't pick three-cent cotton," said a gaunt Mississippi share-cropper, "you just leave it sit."

Christmas in a "Hooverville:" We shall never know how much the Depression really cost. (Library of Congress)

Most farm families did at least eat; the same could not be said for some city dwellers. Local charity quickly collapsed under the Depression's weight, and many people simply went hungry. In Alabama a family of four survived on neighborhood dogs and cats. In New York City bag ladies rummaged through garbage cans for food. And out in California's Salinas Valley, Dorthea Lange came upon an abandoned mother and her three small children, only a day or so from actual starvation.

Almost as hurtful was the damaged pride. People who had been climbing up the ladder of success all their lives now suddenly had to begin climbing down. Executives were demoted to shipping clerks, and shipping clerks to custodians. "You'll always have a job here," a railroad promised the head of its freight department, "even if it's only waving a lantern." Some, of course, lost even that. They stood on the streets and sold apples, still dressed in the suit and tie they had worn to the office.

Because of its pride, the middle class tried to hide its pain. People stayed indoors, not wanting friends and neighbors to learn that the furniture had been repossessed. They told—and lived—complex lies. Finally, when the house went up for sale and dissembling was no longer possible, they did desperate things. Every so often someone down the street put a gun to his head and pulled the trigger.

More often, though, the down-and-outer simply took flight. He went off, supposedly to look for work, and never returned. Sometimes he wound up in a skid row hotel somewhere, paying a dollar a week and fending off the rats. Sometimes he took to riding the rails, sleeping in boxcars or haystacks. Sometimes he came to rest in one of the Depression's many shantytowns (contemptuously called "Hoovervilles"), in a hovel made of tin and tarpaper. And once in a while he ended up on the pavement—stone cold in the dawn.

An entire generation was stunted by the ordeal. World War II medics were appalled by the incidence of flat feet, pigeon chests, curved spines, and rickets—consequences of a malnutritioned childhood. The spiritual damage was even worse. No one was ever quite the same afterward, and even today there are those who must hoard compulsively against the day of another famine. We shall never know how much the Depression really cost.

The Demand for Change

The poverty discovered by the old progressives had been profoundly unsettling. How, the reformers had asked, could freedom survive in the face of such deplorable conditions? By comparison, the poverty of the Great Depression far exceeded that found around the turn of the century, and it made the survival of freedom more doubtful than ever.

Still, in the face of their agony, the American people remained remarkably patient. Nothing better attested the strength of their public virtue—as well as

the soundness of their institutions—than the fact that their patience lasted as long as it did. In Germany, where the Depression was shorter in duration but greater in intensity, the people demanded sweeping change, even at the cost of losing their freedom. What they wound up with was Adolf Hitler.

Some sort of Hitler was possible for the United States as well. By 1936 there were a number of cures for the Depression in the air, and some of them bore familiar markings. In California a physician named Francis Townsend proposed to tax the rich massively and pay out the money in regular and sizable pensions to the aged. The pensioners would be required to spend their funds immediately, Townsend explained, and the force of the collective expenditure would get the economy rolling again.

Huey Long was an even greater menace. As governor of Louisiana, he had created a political machine which had all but snuffed out the state's democracy. Then, traveling to Washington as a U.S. senator, he began appealing to the American public. He too promised to soak the rich and, like Robin Hood, give the money to the poor. Long's "Share Our Wealth" program promised a house, a car, an education, and a decent income to every American family. The only problem was that the arithmetic behind it did not even begin to add up.

A media-minded cleric named Charles E. Coughlin was more demagogic still. In the beginning, his weekly radio broadcasts on social and political themes were harmless enough, but as the Depression deepened and festered, they took on an accusatory tone. Who was responsible? Coughlin asked his eager listeners, and every week he supplied a fresh answer.

It Can't Happen Here!

Watching the rise of Hitler in Germany, some Americans grew nervous about their own situation. For in the midst of the Great Depression, dictatorship had undoubted appeal. One American fascist by the name of William Dudley Pelley was almost a caricature of the German Fuehrer, from the jerky salutes, to the rabid Jew-baiting, to the brawling bodyguards known as Silver Shirts. And another one named Art J. Smith did a pretty good rendition of Mussolini. Striding about in a khaki shirt, riding breeches, and a gorgeous plumed headdress, he instructed his followers in the details of taking over Washington. But characters of this ilk were way out on the fringe. An American Hitler, if there was one, would probably not resemble the German one. He would probably look more like, say, Huey Long.

Huey Long: One man wore a crown. (Library of Congress)

Like many a presidential aspirant, Long was born in a log cabin and to a life of grinding poverty. He was not, however, destined to remain in the back bayous of Louisiana very long. A quick wit, a glib tongue, and a brilliant mind soon had him out hawking a new brand of shortening called Cottolene, and after making a tidy sum at that, he breezed through the three-year law course at Tulane University in a heart-stopping eight months. At the ripe old age of thirty-five he was governor of the state.

And what a governor he was. Laying stiff new taxes on business and industry, he proceeded to make good on campaign promises that to dirt poor Louisianans sounded like a pipe dream. There were new schools, free textbooks, state hospitals, and twenty-five hundred miles of paved roads. And in Baton Rouge there was a bold and vibrant new leadership proclaiming: "Every man a king, but no man wears a crown." Except, of course, Huey himself—*he* wore one. Not content with merely being governor, "the Kingfish," as they called him, wanted to be the entire government.

Using martial law, a subverted judicial system, a cynically bribed legislature, and secret-police terrorism, he turned Louisiana into an airtight dictatorship. On one occasion he rammed forty-four bills through the legislature in twenty-two minutes. But Louisiana was just a start; Huey had much bigger things in mind. In 1932 he had himself elected to the U.S. Senate, where he became a mover and shaker. Sauntering about in flamboyant lavender shirts and canary-yellow ties, waving his arms and beating his chest, telling off-color jokes and guffawing loudly, insulting his colleagues left and right, the Kingfish became a power unto himself. And as the Depression deepened and festered, he became a danger to the Republic.

His program was called "Share Our Wealth." It promised to tax away all fortunes in excess of $50 million and all incomes in excess of $1 million a year, and in return to provide each U.S. citizen with a radio, a washing machine, an automobile, a homestead, a college education, and a $5,000 income. And how to accomplish all this? Long confided to his biographer that he would have to outlaw the Democratic and Republican parties and become "the dictator of this country."

A good many voters thought it was wonderful. Share Our Wealth clubs sprang up across the South. There was a national newspaper, *American Progress*, and a theme song that promised:

> You can be a millionaire
> There's enough for all people to share.

Long estimated his following at around five million.

Of course, the number of people who wanted to kill him grew too. "I am not gifted with second sight," a political foe told Long in January of 1935, "But I can see blood on the polished floor of this Capitol." One of those out gunning for the Kingfish was a Louisiana physician named Carl Austin Weiss, three members of whose family had become victims of the Long regime. Pistol in hand, Weiss waited behind a pillar in the state capitol rotunda, and as Long approached with his entourage of bodyguards, he stepped out to fire a single fatal shot. Eerily, there *was* blood all over the polished marble floor.

The Kingfish was buried on the capitol grounds in Baton Rouge, amid a three-acre sea of flowers. The poor of Louisiana memorialize him to this day in a song that goes:

> Oh, they say he was a crook
> But he gave us free school book
> Tell me why is it that they kill Huey Long?

But after his death a number of politically savvy Americans breathed a good deal easier. Once again it was fashionable to say of totalitarian dictatorship: "It can't happen here."

Bankers, industrialists, and other dark conspirators came in for heaping portions of blame, and so, ominously, did the Jews. The Radio Priest's litany of hatred was enthusiastically received by his embittered audience. Sitting high in the Detroit tower which had been constructed as his studio, stroking his Great Dane and chain-smoking cigarettes, Coughlin wondered how best to capitalize on his mushrooming influence.

All of the demagogues had followings. Both Townsend and Long numbered their adherents in the millions, and Father Coughlin received more mail than the president of the United States. In a curious way, their popularity had been prepared for them by the old-time muckrakers. For, having grown up with the muckraking tradition, Americans generally believed the worst about business and were not slow to blame it for the Depression. They noted, for example, that the tax structure laid in place by tycoon Andrew Mellon (as Harding's secretary of the treasury) had favored the rich for more than a decade. They noted that an imbalance in foreign trade had been worsened by the demand of American bankers for repayment of the Allied war debt. They noted that Wall Street investors had moved quickly—and sometimes cynically—to protect themselves in the stock market crash. Never had businessmen been lower in the public esteem. For many Americans, the entire market system was washed up.

At the very least, a demand for fundamental changes in the U.S. political economy became sharp and insistent. It was not the demand of a single class or party; it welled up from rich and poor, from Republicans and Democrats, from liberals and conservatives, from white- and blue-collar workers, and, yes, even from business

itself. When the Seventy-third Congress convened in January of 1933, it was ready to give the newly elected president, Franklin D. Roosevelt, virtually a free hand.

The New Deal

Roosevelt, The Enigma

The president himself symbolized the new sense of things created by the Depression. The earliest American Roosevelt had helped Peter Stuyvesant govern New Amsterdam, and never since that time had the family known want. Indeed, the Roosevelt estate in the Hudson Valley reflected the graciousness and charm of a dozen generations of wealth. As a politician, Roosevelt had begun as a progressive. His distant cousin, Theodore, had been one of the great progressive presidents, and he himself had served in the Wilson administration as assistant secretary of the navy. Democratic progressives were generally more conservative than Republican ones about using government intervention to solve problems, and young Franklin was no exception. From childhood he had held the market system in deep respect.

But economic catastrophe effected a drastic change in him. Roosevelt was elected governor of New York in 1928, and it was in that capacity that he experienced the Depression's early devastation. New York's problems were especially grim, of course, owing to the poverty of so many city dwellers. In his earlier years, Roosevelt might have ignored their desperation—as did so many other politicians—but in 1921 he had suffered a disaster of his own, a paralyzing case of poliomyelitis, and had learned about misfortune firsthand. He became a pioneer in the use of governmental power to alleviate human suffering.

As president, Roosevelt was often viewed as an enigma. Trying to figure him out, said one pundit, was like trying to peel an onion: there was always another layer beneath. Yes, there was a streak of the opportunist in him. Yes, he wielded his power with great relish. Yes, he could be shortsighted and Machiavellian and sometimes plain wrongheaded. But at the onion's elusive inner core was a patriot of the stature of Washington and Lincoln. At bottom, Roosevelt was motivated by two essential concerns: he wanted to extend real help to the Depression's truly unfortunate, and he wanted to save the American system from total collapse. The means by which he sought to accomplish these ends became known as the New Deal.

Bold, Persistent Experimentation

Roosevelt knew little more about the Depression's possible causes or cures than anyone else, and he freely admitted it. Accordingly, he called not for a specific program but rather for "bold, persistent experimentation." Retaining the old progressive faith in science, he believed that somewhere in the United States there were men of sufficient intelligence and learning to come up with the right answers. And he was willing to try almost anything.

So it was that the New Deal came into being. It was confessedly a mishmash of ideas, some of them inspired by the old progressives, some turned out by the president's "brain trust" of academic advisors, and some even contributed by foreigners like John Maynard Keynes. As a result of this pluralism, the New Deal seemed to flow in every direction at once. There were

Poster for the NRA: But was public virtue enough? (National Archives)

programs to deal with the banking crisis, programs to forestall mortgage foreclosures, and programs to save floundering businesses. The farm situation was high on Roosevelt's priority list, but so was idled industry. Most pressing of all was the problem of poverty relief, which was so acute that it literally could not wait until morning: while the presidential trunks were still being bumped up the White House stairs, relief administrator Harry Hopkins ensconsed himself in a stairwell, set up a makeshift desk, and wrote out checks totaling $5 million.

Franklin Roosevelt and the American Character

Franklin Roosevelt surrounded by admirers: An
aristocrat with the common touch. (Library of
Congress)

Possibly the New Deal's greatest impact was on the American character. Before the Great Depression, Americans had customarily viewed life from the self-interested side of their nature. The cynical H.L. Mencken had spoken for many in the 1920s when he stated that doing good was in bad taste. But the bitter experience of the Depression changed much of that, and the New Deal changed even more. Raised anew were all of the Founders' old questions about the role of virtue in American life.

Those questions were aptly symbolized in the person of Franklin Roosevelt. He, too, had his self-interested side, the side of the crafty politician, the power broker, the worldly man of affairs. Yet there was another side of FDR, a deeper, more spiritual one, born of his tragic affliction with polio. Amid disruption and despair, Roosevelt remained a man of hope, of courage, and of an infectious and inspiring good cheer. The merry twinkle in his eye, the cigarette holder clamped rakishly in his teeth, the hearty laugh, the jaunty smile, the manner of easy confidence, rarely failed to win people over. To see the crowds of gaunt Americans grasp for his hands and touch his clothing put one in mind of Jesus.

What Roosevelt said to his countrymen, over and over, was that they had a responsibility to one another. Speaking to them in his famous "fireside chats"—while they huddled in silence around their radios—he echoed the tones of a wise and loving father. There were forgotten men and forgotten places in the United States, he said, and it was his duty as president to call them back to mind. People could not always go it alone in the modern world, for, as he pointed out, interdependency had quite outmoded rugged individualism. Americans—as Americans—had an obligation to be compassionate.

What infused the New Deal with such excitement, especially in the early years, was the sense of togetherness the president stirred. Americans, often angry and sullen, suddenly saw themselves as working together, pulling together, sacrificing together in ways they had not known since the Civil War. With the National Recovery Administration (NRA), they pledged to deal justly with one another in the marketplace. With the Civilian Conservation Corps (CCC), they sent young men into the mountains to stem erosion and plant trees. With the Agricultural Adjustment Administration (AAA), they dealt collectively for the first time with the problem of rampant individualism. In all of these programs, successful and unsuccessful, the amazing new spirit often prevailed. The willingness of Americans to devote themselves to a moral cause—which would justly win them fame in the war against Hitler—had its beginning here.

And Franklin D. Roosevelt, who knew how to appeal to that side of the American character, must be credited with beginning it. From a man taken by his enemies to be manipulative and cold, here was nothing less than a renaissance of virtue in the twentieth century. He truly did belong on Mount Rushmore.

Critics of the New Deal tirelessly pointed up its inconsistencies. There was no way, they said, that all these disparate programs could work together coherently. But coherence was one thing that Roosevelt never strove for. He was only experimenting, boldly and persistently, in the hope that some of the experiments might work.

The National Recovery Administration. Roosevelt's experimental approach to government is illustrated by the first New Deal program to win the president's full favor, the National Recovery Administration. Its aim was to cure the Depression by reversing the operation of certain economic laws. The laws of supply and demand, ordinarily a stabilizing influence, could wreak havoc in society if, as in the present situation, they once began spiraling downward. Retailers who could not move the goods on their shelves called the factories and canceled their orders. The factories then laid off their workers. The workers in turn purchased even fewer goods than before, and the whole thing spun around again.

Architects of the early New Deal thought that there might be a way to turn the tailspin around. If the consumers would only agree to keep buying, then the retailer could agree to keep ordering from the factory, the factory owner could agree not to lay off his workers, and the workers—who also happened to be the consumers—could honor their agreement to keep buying. That, in essence, was what the NRA attempted to do. Under its authority representatives from each industry met together and worked out a series of production quotas, prices, and wages. These "codes" would theoretically enable the industry in question to limit production, raise demand, stabilize prices, and still pay a decent wage.

This, of course, was precisely how cartel monopolies worked, and that was essentially what the NRA amounted to. Cartel monopolies, as we have seen, had certain basic difficulties, and every one of them soon surfaced in the NRA. For instance, when drawing up production quotas for a given industry, the large producers (who had the most political clout) always assigned themselves extremely generous allotments. That tempted the smaller producers to cheat on the cartel—to sell more than their designated share by cutting code prices. As a result, the traditional mechanisms of the market had to be replaced by appeals to virtue. One should support the NRA, it was urged, not out of self-interest but out of good old-fashioned patriotism.

But was patriotism enough? Franklin Roosevelt hoped so. He appointed Brig. Gen. Hugh "Old Iron Pants" Johnson to head the NRA and suggested he make use of high-powered salesmanship. Johnson did. He made the NRA seem like World War I all over again, with flags, banners, parades, songs, and speeches. Even Will Rogers, the popular wit, made public pitches, telling his radio audience that it was NRA or else—"or else there ain't goin' to be nothin' else." Supporters of the NRA could post a large blue eagle symbol in their store windows.

Yet all the hoopla was to little avail. Large producers continued to elbow out small ones in determining production quotas, and the small producers continued to cheat. In 1935 one of the cheaters, Schechter Poultry Co. of New York, was hauled into court for violating the NRA code for poultry—and for selling diseased products to boot. When the case reached the Supreme Court, the entire NRA was declared unconstitutional. As one wag put it, "The sick chicken made a dead duck out of the blue eagle." President Roosevelt grumbled a little but he eventually accepted the decision. He had realized for some time that the blue eagle was indeed a gone goose.

New Deal Expansion

The NRA experience might have reinforced a lesson learned by the old progressives: that government intervention into a market economy, however well intentioned, always carried a price. The public virtue preached by General Johnson was not achievable by ordinary Americans, and all the propaganda in the world could not make it otherwise. Without the competitive mechanism to hold self-interest in check, the players themselves made havoc of the game.

Still, the New Deal was committed to its course. If the NRA would not work, then something else must be tried in its place. Roosevelt's future experiments would include various programs of public works, the Tennessee Valley Authority (where the government would build and operate a series of large industries), Keynesian economics (in which the government's fiscal power would be used to counter recession), a drastic new farm program, the Social Security system, a vigorous new attack on the trusts, and the forging of a partnership between government and organized labor. Such a sprawl of new agencies would appear in Washington—typically designated by their initials—that the result would be a veritable alphabet soup. NRA, AAA, RFC, CCC, HOLC, FDIC, FCA, CWA, FERA, WPA, PWA, TVA, SEC,

Civilian Conservation Corp (CCC): Working together to solve a national problem. (Library of Congress)

and NLRB were only the more prominent of the new entities. Intervention had arrived in spades.

New Deal Invervention: Four Cases

Virtually all of the New Deal's programs affected the structure or operation of the U.S. political economy. Even minor activities of the Roosevelt administration—such as taking the United States off the gold standard—had far-reaching consequences. We can gain an idea of the New Deal's impact by examining only a few of its many programs. The four chosen here represent the wide range of its interests and give a sampling of its various techniques.

The Agricultural Adjustment Administration

The problems brought on by the Great Depression were nothing new for American farmers. Ever since the 1870s they had

Oklahoma family heading for California: In flight
from the Depression's brutal ravages. (Library of
Congress)

been struggling with overproduction, which created a downward spiral of its own. Surplus commodities on the market reduced prices and profits; profit reductions led the farmer to boost his production; and production increases further glutted the market. If ever there was a situation made for economic planning, this was it.

Roosevelt handed the farm problem to a soft-spoken Iowa Republican known for his radiant idealism and collectivist point of view. Henry A. Wallace, along with other New Deal planners, determined that the only solution was for farmers to decrease production, if not out of self interest, then in response to command. The idea was not immediately popular. Farmers who were barely surviving on their current production shuddered at the thought

of producing even less, and consumers thought it bizarre to destroy food in a time of hunger. But destroy it the government did. Under the AAA's direction, twelve thousand acres of peaches were pulled off the trees, a fifth of the tobacco crop was plowed under, and six million piglets were taken squealing from their mothers and slaughtered. Almost on every farm, it seemed, corn, wheat, or cotton were chopped to shreds with disk harrows, while gaunt farmers and their families looked on.

As the AAA matured, the business of reducing farm production became systematized. Each farmer was given an allotment for cultivation, usually some fraction of his total acreage. Then, in exchange for his willingness to cooperate, he would receive a cash payment from the Department of

Agriculture equal to what he might have gained by planting. The money came from a special processing tax levied against the commodity in question. It was a complicated system and a mountainous bureaucracy was needed to make it work. Moreover, it raised more constitutional questions. For instance, didn't the processing tax amount to an unconstitutional transfer of wealth from one individual to another?

As with all government intervention in the marketplace, the AAA did not always work out as intended. Farmers could fudge a little on their acreage allotments and still pick up their government checks. And there were lots of little loopholes. A man could exempt a field up on the north forty by claiming that its product was for home consumption, and if the product later wound up on the market, well, accidents happened. There ensued a game of hide-and-seek between such Pharisees and the Department of Agriculture, obliging the latter to add more and more agents to its staff, and obliging the agents to become nosier and fussier than ever. Still, the system did work. Beginning in the fall of 1933 commodity prices began to rise, and gradually they continued to do so. By 1935 farmers were speaking hopefully of the Depression's end.

Welfare

The problem of welfare was not only real but critical when Franklin Roosevelt came into office, for private charity had long since exhausted itself. Thus, in those first hectic months of the New Deal, few debated either the wisdom or morality of the government's massive welfare programs.

Extreme proponents of the market system suggested that hunger had its place in the world—as a spur to industriousness

and creativity—and therefore ought not be removed. President Roosevelt, by contrast, saw hunger solely in terms of compassion: what sense did it make, he asked, to preach rugged individualism to the vanquished spirits slumped beside the railroad tracks? Even so, the New Dealers, like most Americans, were wary of the dole. They reasoned that wherever possible welfare recipients ought to do a day's work for a day's pay. Accordingly, money that had simply been ladled out in the early days of the New Deal was administered far more carefully later on. A day's work for a day's pay was what the Works Progress Administration insisted on.

But that policy necessitated makework. Men were counted into gangs and set to cleaning the park, sweeping the streets, or painting the fence around the post office. Some literally dug holes and filled them up. A critic dubbed it "boondoggling"—after the current fad of weaving plastic yarn—and the term stuck. Editorial cartoonists pictured corps of WPA workers leaning listlessly on their shovels, while "WPA" came to stand for "We Poke Along."

The imaginative Harry Hopkins, President Roosevelt's principal relief administrator, began making adjustments. It was inappropriate for concert pianists to dig ditches, he reasoned, and so he put them to work giving concerts. By the same logic, artists were invited to paint murals in public buildings, playwrights were set to writing plays, and folklorists began collecting perishable Americana. (We are indebted to WPA interviewers for priceless oral histories of slavery and the Civil War.) Labor such as this invited far less shovel leaning—but now it could be charged that the New Deal was taking over private enterprise. Nervous critics, sensing a seismic shift in American institutions, fretted about dire consequences in the long run. "People don't eat in the long run," Hopkins snapped back, "they eat every day."

Yet the critics had their point. Hopkins and the others were indeed broadening their conception of welfare, and in the process were broadening their conception of government. In order to end hunger for good, they were beginning to reason, it was necessary to end the *causes* of hunger. The way markets dealt with that problem was by making everyone better off through economic growth. Impressive as growth had been in the United States, it did take time and it did work its injustices. There was, as we have seen, at least one other way to end poverty, and the New Deal planners began to think seriously about it. They could simply redistribute wealth from the haves to the have-nots.

Redistribution had some obvious advantages. The gains it brought to any given individual would not have to depend on intelligence, training, skill, or good fortune. The system would work just as well in bad times as good ones. It would serve the special needs of the aged, the incapacitated, and the unfit. And, not least, it would earn its sponsors an abiding store of political goodwill. It is easy to see how the New Deal fell in with it.

Social Security was the first step, taken in 1935. It was not originally conceived as a participatory program but rather as a simple transfer of wealth. (Anyone reaching retirement age, regardless of circumstances, would qualify for pension benefits.) This, however, would have left the program politically vulnerable, and so Roosevelt decided to make it participatory—everyone buying into it like life insurance. "No damn politician can ever scrap my social security program now," the president boasted, and so far he has been right. Social Security has become a part of the American consensus, accepted by virtually everyone.

The Wagner Act

In May of 1935 a dramatic shift occurred in President Roosevelt's attitude toward organized labor. Heretofore he had supposed that labor and management could sit down and work out their differences amicably, sharing equally in the benefits of recovery. But two years of continuing labor strife had disillusioned him. Not only had many employers refused to recognize the unions—as Section 7A of the National Industrial Recovery Act had required—they had worked out ingenious new methods for subverting them.

When the Supreme Court pronounced the NRA unconstitutional on May 27, the president decided on bold action. He threw his support behind a piece of legislation sponsored by Senator Robert F. Wagner of New York reenacting the pro-union provisions of Section 7A. Now, as a matter of law, it would be impossible for employers to bust unions or refuse to bargain with them in good faith. Organized labor was to be protected by the power of the government.

Roosevelt's reasoning for the move was quite clear. He believed that if businessmen could not restrain their selfishness voluntarily, as the NRA had tried to make them do, then the government must cultivate some countervailing power, such as organized labor, to restrain it for them. Market theory had never taken much account of labor unions, for ideally employers and employees were supposed to bargain with each other individually. But, theory aside, unions in America, in spite of their rough treatment, had significantly improved the lot of the workingman. Maybe they could help keep business in hand too.

This shift in policy had far-reaching effects. By committing itself to the protection and encouragement of organized labor, the New Deal was surrendering the traditional neutrality of government toward collective bargaining. It was also fomenting political revolution, for big business was bound to be all the more hostile to the Roosevelt administration and big labor all the more supportive. Finally, there were a host of new operational questions, some of them frankly troubling. Would employees now be *required* to join unions? Could employers refuse to knuckle under to union demands? And who was to decide what employment practices were in fact unfair to the unions?

But one thing was clear: federal officials would have a vastly expanded role in U.S. industrial relations. The National Labor Relations Board was set up to hear and decide complaints from union organizers, company officials, and even individual workers. In the workaday battles between labor and management, government was now officially the umpire.

Keynesian Economics

British economist John Maynard Keynes came up with a tantalizing idea for combatting recession, as we saw in chapter sixteen. Government, he said, could exercise a regulatory effect on the economy solely by means of its fiscal policy—its powers of taxing and spending. Imagine, for example, how a heavy dose of government spending in the midst of a severe recession might stimulate demand and get the economy rolling again. Suppose there was a little steel town on the Ohio River where virtually all economic activity had ceased. Suddenly, a government agent appears at the town's idled plant and places an order for a million tons of steel. What happens next? Laid-off workers are immediately called back to their jobs while their wives rush out to do months' worth of deferred shopping. Store owners, now seeing customers again, begin placing orders with their suppliers, and the suppliers call their own workers back. Furthermore, if the government man has done this same thing elsewhere in the country, our local steel mill might soon receive *other* orders. Recovery, in other words, no longer depends on the government!

In the meantime, it is true, the government would have a million tons of steel on its hands, and someone would have to pay for it. Keynes had an answer for that problem, too. As soon as the economy was back up to speed, he explained, the government could recoup its losses by raising taxes. The added revenue, moreover, would not only rebalance the budget, it would dampen the inflationary boom that might otherwise lead to another collapse. In place of the high peaks and deep troughs of the ordinary business cycle, Keynes' manipulations would keep the economy purring along evenly.

Taken for granted today, Keynesian economics struck Roosevelt's generation as something out of Arabian Nights. There was a bit more to it than calling genies out of lamps, however: the government had to massively spend money it did not have. Deficit spending was an unwholesome phrase to fiscal conservatives, who likened government budgets to those of a private business. But that, said Keynes, was merely Victorian stodginess. Governments could not go bankrupt.

Intoxicated with the possibilities, American Keynesians clamored for the ear of the president. Unhappily, however, the Hyde Park aristocrat proved to be one of those Victorian stodgies himself, unwilling to spend the government into the poorhouse. His New Deal was already heavily in the red just paying the bill for welfare. Indeed, the president had become so anxious about even that, that in 1937, when the economy seemed to be improving, he ordered the WPA budget drastically cut. The result, right out of Keynes' textbook, was a sharp recession.

Roosevelt and his advisors were amazed. Not only was Keynesian economics dramatically vindicated, but they themselves had apparently been making use of it. The WPA, with its gargantuan expenditures, had been supercharging the economy since the day Roosevelt took office. The president was suddenly a believer.

By 1938 the Keynes effect was not only visible but conspicuous in the U.S. economy. The rising threat of another world war had occasioned a desperate military buildup, and as the spending for tanks and planes increased exponentially, basic industries were fired up, small business began to thrive, and soon even the WPA could be dismantled. New Dealers were enormously impressed. If depression ever threatened America again, they told one another confidently, they would summon forth the Keynesian genie and banish it.

The Legacy of the New Deal

Friends and foes alike point to the legacy of the New Deal as an abiding feature of modern America—but there the agreement ends. What we must do now is sort through the debate between the two sides and pick out what seems to be of most value. The questions involved are extremely important—both as an assessment of the past and a guide to the future.

Did the New Deal Succeed?

One of the myths of the New Deal era holds that Roosevelt's programs did not succeed in the least, that they were a gigantic boondoggle from start to finish. We need to examine that contention first.

It is true that the New Deal did not cure the Great Depression. The causes of that misfortune were deep, complex, and elusive. We don't fully understand them today. It is quite pointless, then, for us to debate whether more New Deal, or less New Deal, or a different New Deal would have been better—except to note that when there was no New Deal (during the first three years of the Depression), the result was disastrous. What did cure the Depression in the end was the orgy of wartime spending.

On the other hand, virtually every New Deal program did succeed in what it attempted to do. The Agricultural Adjustment Administration significantly raised farm prices. The WPA kept millions of the unemployed from sinking into complete degradation. Social Security provided a safety net of old-age benefits for those who otherwise had none. The New Deal's labor policies measurably improved the situation of workers. And Keynesian economics exerted an inflationary influence on the economy. Only the NRA has to be put down as a washout—and it was the program most reliant on private enterprise!

But it is in other ways that we must judge the New Deal's greatest success. For example, its political impact was nothing short of revolutionary. Before Roosevelt, American politicians did not even talk of the poor and disadvantaged, much less act in their behalf. Now, of course, we take the politics of compassion quite for granted. If nothing else, the New Deal infused American democracy with a vibrant new spirit.

And the system—did the New Deal save it from ruin? The answer depends, in part, on what we mean by save. Obviously market economics was neither unscathed nor unaltered by the Great Depression, and no candidate capable of winning election in 1932 could have made the case otherwise. If capitalism was not doomed in America, *laissez-faire* capitalism certainly was.

Nevertheless, in the post-New Deal world much of the old system not only remained intact, it flourished as never before. Corporations were larger and more powerful than they had been in the 1920s; entrepreneurial activity was accelerated; and stocks on the New York exchange were soaring to new heights. American creativity, far from extinguished, was about to give the world jet aviation, telecommunications, mindboggling medical breakthroughs, the new science of computers, and a stunning space program. Even more importantly, the economic growth which

had touched the lives of so many Americans continued to expand its reach. Whether by the New Deal or otherwise, the system had indeed been saved.

Side Effects and Consequences

There remains, however, a completely different set of questions to answer. The old progressives learned that intervention in the market system, no matter how worthy the purpose or desirable the outcome, came at a price. There were always, it seemed, unanticipated side effects to deal with, and there were often some unwelcome long-range consequences. Mixing into a market economy was a little like mixing into nature.

Many of the New Deal's side effects were evident at the outset. Its programs vastly increased the size and complexity of government and endowed it with a host of new responsibilities. Before the New Deal it was unthinkable that government should worry about the employment of its citizens; afterward the employment question became a perennial ticking bomb. The dynamics of the entire system were altered.

The New Deal's long-term consequences were even more unsettling. Looking at each of our four programs above, for instance, we find difficulties, sometimes serious ones, that continue down to the present.

Agriculture. By saving the American farmer, the Agricultural Adjustment Administration saved the farm problem as well. After World War II, U.S. agriculture continued to improve its efficiency. Where in 1900 one farm worker had fed seven people, by 1965 he could feed more than thirty. No government program could handle increases on such a scale, but the notion was now entrenched that overproduction, like underemployment, was the government's problem. Storage programs, price supports, cutback incentives were tried and found wanting by Republican and Democratic administrations alike. Stored wheat grew into mountains. Stored butter filled warehouses. Stored cheese reached such proportions that a desperate Ronald Reagan finally gave it away. Meanwhile, the interests affected kept food prices high, farm politics volatile, and scandals simmering in the press.

Welfare. The New Deal's welfare programs also cast a long shadow. Half a century of unparalleled prosperity has not vanquished poverty in America—even though the struggle against it has steadily broadened. In the United States today there are agencies that supplement inadequate income, agencies that ameliorate poor housing, and agencies that improve mass transportation. The hungry poor are supplied with food stamps; the unhealthy poor are covered by Medicaid; and the elderly poor are attended with home-delivered meals. Poor households qualify for energy assistance, poor neighborhoods receive tax breaks, and poor enclaves of the foreign-born are taught English. Even poor criminals are defended in court free of charge. This welter of activity has confronted us with astronomical costs, mind-boggling rules, and a hydra-headed bureaucracy. It is the welfare state or the welfare mess, depending upon one's point of view.

Labor. Roosevelt's alliance with organized labor made unionism permanent and largely respectable in the United States. And, for their part, the unions have helped secure the good life for working Americans. But industrial relations have never been the same. Labor and management, traditionally at each other's throats, no longer seem to be hostile: they negotiate the next round of contracts—and price hikes—with absolute bonhomie. The resulting labor costs, which grow higher by the year, have the unfortunate effect of pricing American goods out of many markets. At the same time, union work rules, which have a tendency toward "featherbedding," rarely add much to productivity. (For example, diesel locomotives had to carry firemen for years, just because the old coal-burners did.) Finally, union domination has brought forth a raft of troublesome issues dealing with the right to work. The good life for workers has not been without its costs.

Keynesian Economics. For years it was accepted that Keynes had solved the riddle of recession once and for all. Thus, when business activity faltered in 1958, Dwight Eisenhower intensified federal spending and the economy quickly righted itself. And when hard times threatened again in 1961, John Kennedy applied a modified Keynesian approach—a large tax cut instead of increased spending—to the same good effect. But shortly thereafter forces began whirling the economy in new directions. In 1973 there was an embargo of Arab oil and then a fourfold increase in oil prices. The economy responded strangely, somehow inflating and stagnating at the same time. Soon the strange behavior had transformed into hyperinflation, pummeling prices into double-digit acceleration. Finally, in 1980 there commenced a recession that broke all the rules. As economists from the left to the right scratched their heads in puzzlement, only one thing seemed clear: Keynesian spending would not help. The 1984 budget ran $200 billion in the red just to make ends meet.

From such examples, we can see how profoundly the political economy of the United States has been altered. By establishing the precedent of massive government intervention in the market system, the New Deal has had as far-reaching an impact on American institutions as the Civil War. Yet, if that is one hard truth, there is also another. The New Deal in Germany was Adolph Hitler, and the New Deal in Italy was Benito Mussolini. Other countries adopted a rigid state socialism in response to economic chaos, and still others succumbed to anarchy and civil war. In the United States, the New Deal, fraught though it was with mistakes and excesses, was more than a creative compromise among the "isms" of the twentieth century—it was an honest, well-intentioned, and in the end, thoroughly American response to overwhelming catastrophe. We can look to it for much of the prosperity—and liberty—that we enjoy today.

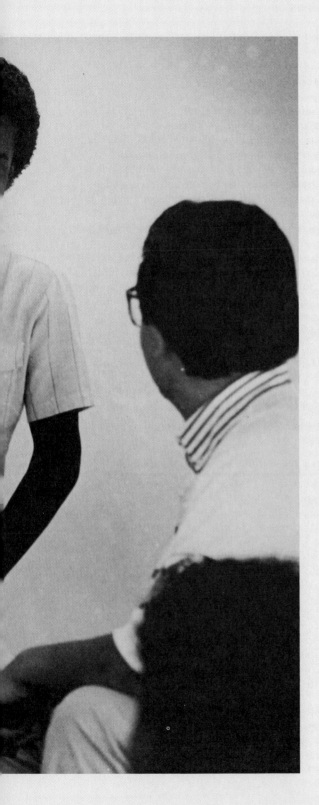

26
The New Society

Concepts

Traditional Society
Modern Society
The American Dilemma
The Civil Rights Revolution
Women's Movement
Melting Pot versus Salad Bowl
Pluralism

Dissolving artificial barriers (James L. Shaffer)

597

The Montgomery Bus Boycott

The Montgomery City Lines knew how to handle "uppity" Negroes. During 1955, five women and two children had been arrested and one man shot to death as a result of disobeying bus drivers' orders. So, when Mrs. Rosa Parks was arrested and booked on December 1 for refusing to honor a driver's request, she was not getting unusual treatment. But she was tired that day. She had put in a long shift in one of the downtown department stores, and her feet hurt. Besides, the thought of standing up—according to Alabama law—so that a white male could take her seat suddenly struck her as odious. She was a radiant, soft-spoken person, and she endured the obloquy of her arrest with calm forbearance. That was what seemed to irk Montgomery's blacks the very most.

Some of them wanted to dig out their baseball bats and "beat the hell out of a few bus drivers." But calmer heads prevailed. E. D. Nixon, a former state chairman of the NAACP, after putting up Mrs. Parks' bond, sat on the edge of his bed that night and said to his wife: "You know, I think every Negro in town should stay off the buses for one day in protest for Mrs. Parks' arrest. What do you think?"

"I think you ought to stop daydreaming," she replied. "Turn out the light and get some sleep."

Others, however, were having the same daydream. The following day, after a flurry of phone calls, Montgomery's black leaders held a meeting in the basement of the Dexter Avenue Baptist church and resolved to give the boycott a try. They stayed up all night to mimeograph seven thousand leaflets which read:

> Don't ride the bus to work, to town, to school, or any place Monday, December 5.
>
> Another Negro woman has been arrested and put in jail because she refused to give up her bus seat. . . .
>
> Come to a Mass Meeting, Monday at 7:00 p.m., at the Holt Street Baptist Church for further instructions.

"Martin! Martin! Come quickly!" It was 6:00 a.m. on the appointed morning, and Coretta Scott King was calling excitedly to her husband, the Reverend Martin Luther King, from the living room of the Highland Avenue Baptist parsonage. The first bus was lumbering by, and there were no blacks on it. King stared in blank amazement. Soon he was in his car driving about the city, and, sure enough, blacks were not riding the buses. Nothing like this had ever happened before.

Still a bit wonder-struck, the black leaders huddled again in the afternoon, organized the Montgomery Improvement Association, and drew up a pathetic list of demands. (One was that the color line in bus seating might be applied more flexibly.) They then chose a president. Rev. King was young, inexperienced, and a newcomer to boot, but old-timers like Ralph David Abernathy liked the cut of his jib. They elected him unanimously.

That evening King delivered the first of many memorable speeches to an overflow crowd in the Holt Street Baptist church. With but twenty minutes for preparation—less five minutes for fervent prayer—he pretty well had to speak impromptu. But the resonant baritone voice, the rolling cadences, the dramatically measured pauses were all in place and working. "There comes a time," he began, "when people get tired. We are here this evening to say to those who have mistreated us so long that we are tired—tired of being segregated and humiliated, tired of being kicked about by the brutal feet of oppression." Yet King was by no means spoiling for a fight. "Our actions," he continued, "must be guided by the deepest principles of our Christian faith. Love must be our regulating ideal. Once again we must hear the words of Jesus echoing across the centuries: 'Love your enemies, bless them that curse you, and pray for them that despitefully use you.'"

The future held abundant opportunities for turning the other cheek. The one-day boycott was so successful that the Montgomery Improvement Association voted to continue it indefinitely, until the bus company gave in. Blacks car pooled back and forth to work. They hitched rides with their white employers. They clambered aboard black-owned taxies, which charged them no more than the ten-cent bus fare. Mostly, however, they just walked, painfully, wearily, some of them as far as ten miles every day.

The city fathers addressed the problem soothingly (though without concessions) for the first few days. Then they took off the gloves. A whisper campaign charged that King, Abernathy, and the others were pocketing MIA funds. Newspapers published false stories of a settlement. Black drivers were arrested for speeding and black pedestrians for loitering and vagrancy. Obscene and threatening phone calls began. "Listen, nigger," snarled a voice in the night to King, "we've taken all we want from you. Before next week, you'll be sorry you ever came to Montgomery." The young minister felt stricken with desolation.

And then the bombing started. King's parsonage was first. Coretta was home at the time with their three-month-old daughter and several house guests. The bomb bounced onto the porch before detonating, shattering the front of the house. (Miraculously no one was injured.) In the ensuing weeks, dynamite was hurled at four Baptist churches, including King's, and three homes of MIA leaders. The temperature of the rhetoric mounted, too. A Citizens Council leaflet shrieked:

> In every stage of the bus boycott we have been oppressed and degraded because of black, slimy, juicy, unbearably stinking niggers. The conduct should not be dwelt upon because behind them they have an ancestral background of Pygmies, Head hunters and snot suckers.

King, however, somehow maintained control. Standing in the doorway of his smoldering house, flanked by pale and shaken city officials, he said: "We cannot solve this problem through retaliatory violence. . . . We must love our white brothers no matter what they do to us. We must make them know that we love them." The real struggle, as King knew, was between fear and courage.

Meanwhile, the boycott grew ever more effective. Beginning at around 80 percent, it increased with every new outrage until it became nearly total. Hundreds of blacks were fired from their jobs. Thousands were intimidated by police and the Klan. Ninety of the movement's leaders were arrested for violating an obscure antiboycott law. Yet they hung on. By the end of March the downtown stores had lost an estimated $1 million in business, and the Montgomery City Lines was eager to call it quits. But the city officials doggedly held out. To cave in now, they feared, would spell segregation's doom.

That remained the situation on November 13, nearly a year after Rosa Parks' arrest, when the U.S. Supreme Court finally cut through the knot. Segregation on Alabama's buses, it declared, was unconstitutional. As suddenly as it had begun, the bus boycott ended. However, for Martin Luther King, for Ralph David Abernathy, and for southern blacks as a whole, the battle for civil rights was far from over. It had only just begun.

In the 1960s and 1970s, the United States ran headlong into a new tangle of problems. These were not created by a single dramatic event like the stock market crash of 1929—unless it was the Supreme Court's decision in *Brown v. The Board of Education* in 1954—nor were they characterized by an all-encompassing term such as the Great Depression. Their symptoms were as diverse as images in a kaleidoscope: white violence in the South, black violence in the North, Native American takeovers of federal property, a boycott of grapes in California, an outbreak of virulent feminism, the sudden appearance of a counterculture. For those who feared that change might run out of control, it added up to a nightmare come true.

At the very least, it was the debut of a new social order—a new *kind* of social order. Thus, just as the march of history reshaped American politics and the market economy, it reshaped American society as well, and with dramatic consequences. It is toward an understanding of these consequences that this chapter is aimed.

From Traditional to Modern Society

In order to comprehend recent social developments, we must first learn something about the society our ancestors knew. For,

even though traditional society was swept away two centuries ago, in some ways it haunts us still.

Traditional Society

Traditional society stretched far back into the past. Although it was complex and sometimes difficult to fathom, we can gain a rough sense of it by examining a few of its principal assumptions. First, it was assumed that any organized group of people must be viewed as a single, coherent unit, just as, say, an organized group of leaves and branches must be viewed as a tree. Miscellaneous individuals might be thrown together by fate but they did not comprise a *society*. Second, it was assumed that society needed to be homogeneous in important ways. The various members of a group might have differing talents and personalities, but their values, their outlook, and their style of life needed to be broadly similar. And third, it was assumed that society existed for some transcendent—usually religious—purpose. If we asked someone in a medieval village why people lived together, he would probably reply that it was to bring about their common salvation.

All three assumptions could be illustrated by a widely invoked metaphor of the day. In the twelfth chapter of 1 Corinthians, the apostle Paul compared Christian society to a human body. "The body is not one member but many," he observed. "If the foot shall say, Because I am not the hand, I am not of the body; is it therefore not of the body?" The answer was obvious: the body needed all of its members, feet as well as hands, and all were equally pleasing to God.

These verses summarized traditional society's view of itself. The people of various European communities comprised what Paul termed the "Body of Christ." They were assembled organically, as hands and feet and ears and eyes, and addressed to a common pursuit of the Lord's purposes. The metaphor could be used to describe a family, a church congregation, or a civil community, for all worked basically the same way.

The Body of Christ metaphor had some important implications. The qualities that society needed most—such as stability and unity—could be achieved only at the expense of competition. Feet could not aspire to be hands, and hands could not aspire to be eyes. Fixed and permanent inequality was thus built into the system.

Consider the family, for example. No family could hope to be stable and unified if it lacked a clearly defined hierarchy of authority. If husbands and wives were considered equal, they would undoubtedly spend their time bickering about who was supposed to do what. The same was true for a civil community. If it was not settled in advance that some would be, say, the "brains" of the community, nothing but squabbles would ensue. That was why a prayer of the day intoned: "Bless the squire and his relations and keep us in our proper stations."

Even though traditional society seems alien to the modern mind, it was not without its rewards. In it there was a place for everyone, and one's place, whether at the top or the bottom, was regarded with respect. (After all, the body needed feet as well as hands.) There was no fear about losing one's place—one was probably stuck in it for life—and no spur to forsake it for something better. In modern society, by contrast, no one has a secure place, and no one's place is ever quite satisfactory. Vice presidents want to be presidents and presidents want to be chairmen of the board. In anxiety and neurosis, we pay a stiff price for our freewheeling competition.

Many of our own founding communities, such as Plymouth, were prime examples of traditional society. Their ministers often preached the twelfth chapter of I Corinthians and explained its implications in detail. In order to be "knitted together" as a single people, they pointed out, some would have to be the feet and like it. These communities stamped the American colonial experience with much of its unique character.

America and Social Change

In America, however, traditional society, which was already doomed in the modern world, quickly broke down. One reason why was the market system, which, as we have seen, encouraged each individual to pursue his or her personal vision of happiness. It may have made Christian sense to be meek and lowly but it never did much for self-interest. When the merchants of Boston were asked to charge a just price for their goods, they thought about it, and charged market prices instead.

Then, too, America became a land of diversity. Various communities, often with inconsistent or conflicting purposes, came to form the body politic of most colonies. In Pennsylvania, for example, there were, in addition to the original Quaker founders, literally dozens of other groups.

Moravians, Amish, Schwenkfelders, Dunkards, River Bretheren, and High Church Lutherans comprised only some of the communities of central Pennsylvania, while Scots, Irish, and Scots-Irish were found farther west. The only thing Pennsylvanians had in common was their residence in Pennsylvania.

Finally, the colonies experienced a rising tide of egalitarian feeling. Out on the frontier, where everyone could own land in abundance, it was difficult for anyone to regard himself as a "foot." The most humble of immigrants were soon buying farms, sending their children to school, and even running for the colonial assembly. No longer wishing to bless the squire and his relations, they had thoughts of becoming squires themselves.

Once the transformation began, it proceded rapidly. This was because modern society operated by a very different logic than its traditional cousin, and things that were taken for granted in the old order no longer made sense in the new. For example, in traditional society it seemed entirely logical to expel religious dissenters, for the only thing a dissenter could be to the Body of Christ was a thorn in the side. However, as soon as there were *a number* of dissenters, everything changed. Not only did it no longer seem logical to expel them, it no longer seemed logical to call them dissenters. Once there was no hope of regaining total Christian unity, complete tolerance was the only policy that made sense.

The New Social Logic

In similar fashion, almost everything about the old order came to seem absurd. A case in point was the notion of occupying a permanently low status. For, if there was no

real Body of Christ seeking the common salvation, there was surely no reward for being a foot. When people reached that conclusion, there was suddenly a scramble after every station in society. Competition became the rule.

The logic of modern society, then, was a logic of fair and open competition—much like the logic of democratic politics or the marketplace. It held that:

1. All people must be free from formal restraint so that they could compete on an even footing. Laws or legal actions that held anyone back were manifestly unfair.
2. Within reasonable limits, opportunities that were available to one person ought to be available to another. If some children should enjoy free public education, for example, then all children should.
3. All people must be given a voice in government. Quite beyond the consent required for the rule of law, people needed equal access to power if they were to compete successfully.

Taken together, these three requirements add up to what we meant in chapter four by the term legal equality. Legal equality did not make people equal by any means— there are gross inequalities in modern society—but it did make for an equal chance to compete.

By the new social logic, legal equality had to be accorded to everyone. Once the assumptions of traditional society were abandoned, there was no longer any logical justification for the stifling of competition. In fact, the reverse was true. The more competition there was, the more productivity there was all around. This truth was illustrated by the social cost of religious intolerance in the colonies. Those colonies which persisted in persecuting religious minorities faced political unrest at home and expanding complications abroad. Their foreign trade suffered, their economic development languished, and on occasion they even lost their charters.

Reality, of course, could not always deliver the conditions that pure logic might require. In actual fact, legal equality was often the exception rather than the rule. And it was here that the weakness of modern society became painfully evident. For in modern society—unlike the traditional—a person who, for one reason or another, was denied legal equality could not simply take his place as a foot of the social body. On the contrary, such people became outcasts and pariahs, who stood to be ignored, abused, exploited, ridiculed, or expelled. There was no "place" in modern society for those not allowed to compete.

The American Founders were beginning to sense the danger of this when they wrote the Constitution. The document they created was emphatically addressed to modern, not traditional, society. It proclaimed that as long as everyone abided by the law, everyone was free to compete. There was to be no favored class, no favored party, no favored interest, no favored religion, no favored anything.

Diversity and the American Dilemma

Diversity was the one fly in the ointment. Diversity had never been a problem in traditional society. If a square peg happened along, he was speedily shooed off, as we have seen. On the other hand, diversity would become a fundamental aspect of modern society, as any glance around us would demonstrate. Diversity of religion,

of thought, of values, of life style, of culture, of language, of race—all have come to characterize modern life.

As a matter of logic, once again, modern society had no trouble with diversity. Once the assumptions of traditional society were discarded, any sort of law-abiding diversity was logically acceptable. If a group of people wanted, say, to wear little beanies and converse in Pig Latin, well, that was their business.

The problem, rather, was human nature. It could only abide so much diversity. Historically speaking, human beings have tended to perceive marked departures from the norm as being inferior, contemptible, or threatening. Unfortunately, this has been particularly true of democratic societies. Witness, for example, the fits of blind conformity that have characterized much of our own national life. Even those spectacular nonconformists who moved into San Francisco's Haight Ashbury District in the 1960s felt obliged to conform to one another.

The question in America thus became: How much diversity—what degree of difference—would the people as a whole tolerate? The logic of modern society drew no lines whatever—*but human nature did.* The fact that lines would be drawn and that there would be no rational place to draw them became the essence of the American Dilemma.

Grappling with the American Dilemma

With the American Dilemma in mind, we can see our national history as a slow, grudging expansion of the types and degrees of difference we would tolerate. Americans in the year 1900 accepted far more diversity than had their ancestors a century earlier, and it seems clear that their descendants in the year 2000 will accept far more still.

What caused the pale of acceptability to expand? Several things. In the first place, modern logic, as we have seen, has never been on the side of bigotry, so Americans were inclined to be persuaded by liberal arguments. Then, too, as Americans gradually came to think of themselves as a nation of minorities, toleration became an article of faith. It was the one thing that stood to benefit everyone.

But the most important factor in improving American toleration was competition itself. If a group was not formally denied legal equality—that is, if its members were even more or less allowed to compete—then no matter how despised the group was, it could almost always force open the door of acceptance. Its people could get jobs, make money, send their children to school, and improve their situation in life. Not least, they could make the politicians sit up and take notice of them.

The Irish Experience

All of this was graphically illustrated by the Irish experience. In the days of Thomas Jefferson, the American idea of religious tolerance generally stopped short of Catholicism, whose theology and worship lay beyond the existing norm. At the time there were few Catholics to worry about, but that would soon change. With the onset of the great potato famine in 1841, the trickle of Irish immigrants into the United States suddenly swelled into a flood. Entire villages left the old country together, loaded like cattle into freighters and dumped without ceremony on American docksides. They wound up in ghettos such as the Fort Hill district of Boston, where life was far from idyllic. Barefoot, ragged, illiterate, often alcoholic, they had to make do with an animal existence.

For a number of reasons, then, the new immigrants were unacceptably different. Cartoonists portrayed them as bandylegged and barrel-chested, with stubble beards, apelike faces, and noses red from drink. Soon signs were going up in saloons that read: "No Dogs or Irishmen Allowed."

Real persecution followed. The Irish could find no employment save at the dirtiest and most thankless of tasks. Their children were denied entrance into schools. Their very presence was unwelcome outside of their steaming neighborhoods. And by 1850 a powerful new movement known as nativism was campaigning to eliminate the "Catholic menace" altogether. Nativists went so far as to burn an Ursaline convent to the ground.

Two things, however, worked to the newcomers' advantage. In the first place, they were not denied legal equality. No actions were formally taken against them and no laws singled them out for special restraint. As for their opportunities, while meager enough by present standards, they were not entirely foreclosed. The Irish could work as day laborers, draymen, and the like. When gold was discovered in California, some thirty thousand of them trooped off to the gold fields, and more than a few came back rich. Most importantly, they were not denied political power, which they learned to use effectively in their own behalf. Soon Paddy the fireman and Clancy the cop were familiar figures on the American street corner, as was the Irish political boss who secured them their jobs. By the 1870s Irishmen were sitting in the halls of Congress.

And secondly, except for their Catholicism, the Irish could become exactly like other Americans. Despite the cartoonists' fancies, there was no way to tell an Irishman by his looks, and when the second and third generations adopted a Yankee style of life, little else Irish remained.

The Irish, in a word, were rescued by the logic of modern society. Despised as they were, it made no sense to formally exclude them from competition. And so, except for the persecutions of the nativists, there was nothing to hold the Irish back permanently. Their eventual integration into the American mainstream helped expand the pale of acceptability.

The Mormon Experience

At the same time, however, another religious minority came to grief in America. To the Protestant mainstream, the Mormon religion—with its angels, visions, and practice of polygamy—was even further beyond the norm than Catholicism. Thus, in contrast to the Irish Catholics, Mormons were repeatedly denied legal equality. In western Missouri, where they congregated in 1830, and again in Nauvoo, Illinois, where they later built a thriving community, the laws never quite worked in their favor. Their leaders were arrested on trumped-up charges while their enemies were afforded legal protection. At one point, the governor of Missouri went so far as to issue an "extermination order" against them. And even after trekking westward to the Utah Territory, they saw polygamy outlawed, statehood denied, and an expeditionary force sent to harass them. For years hostility smoldered between Utah and the United States.

The Mormons came to know firsthand what happens to those in modern society who are not allowed to compete. They became, in effect, stepchildren in their own land. And that situation continued indefinitely. Before the Mormons could be accepted into the American mainstream, they had to materially alter the tenets of their religion.

Successive instances of the American Dilemma became increasingly difficult—more like the Mormon experience than the Irish-Catholic.

The "New Immigrants"

With the expansion of heavy industry after the Civil War, a new sort of immigrant began arriving in the United States, and in ever larger numbers. Heretofore most immigrants had come from northern and western Europe, and especially from the United Kingdom. By contrast, the New Immigrants, as they were called, came from southern and eastern Europe, from Italy to the Ukraine. They had all of the difficulties of the earlier Irish plus a few more. They wore strange clothing, ate exotic foods, and conversed in a babel of guttural tongues. Their religion was frequently non-Western—Greek or Russian Orthodox—and sometimes even non-Christian. A large number of them were Jewish.

What proved most damaging to them, however, was race. As Jews, Slavs, or Latins, they were recognizably different from the English, Irish, Germans, and Scandanavians who had come earlier. The pseudoscience of eugenics purported to claim that the racial characteristics of the newcomers were distinctly—and dangerously—inferior to those of Anglo-Saxons, and for the first time Americans became seriously concerned about compromising their racial purity. There was another worry, too: could the New Immigrants ever

An Anti-Mormon cartoon: Stepchildren in their
own land. (Library of Congress)

fit in? If, in addition to being racially distinctive, they continued to live in tightly
knit communities, wasn't it possible that
they would never blend into the general
populace?

With such fears lurking, nativism again
erupted in the United States. The newcomers were made the butt of jokes and the
subject of spiteful cartoons. Political rhetoric took a deadly turn against genetic pollution, and several Jews were actually
lynched. The brouhaha reached such proportions that, in 1924, the New Immigration was effectively cut off.

Even so, the story of the New Immigrants ended happily. Like Stevan Lazich—
who was one of them—they worked hard,
saved their money, sent their children and
grandchildren to ever better schools, and
took an active part in politics. When they
began flocking to the polls by the millions,
office seekers hastened to polish up their
ethnic stories and foreign phrases.

By the Second World War, the New
Immigrants were largely accepted. Despite
barriers of race, culture, and religion, they
proved themselves to be American in every
respect. Indeed, the third generation—

THEY ARE PRETTY SAFE THERE.

When Politicians do Agree, their Unanimity is Wonderful.

"GIVE IT TO HIM, HE'S GOT NO VOTE NOR NO FRIENDS!"

The lot of the unmeltable: A casualty of the American Dilemma. (Library of Congress)

those whose parents were born in the U.S.—were practically indistinguishable from their peers. It was an important success story, demonstrating that the logic of modern society could still expand toleration, and that toleration was still expandable. In reflection of the New Immigrants' experience, Americans began to speak proudly of the melting pot.

The Unmeltables

But there was no happy ending for several other groups. The horizons of American toleration may have been expanding, but for the fortunes of many they were not expanding fast enough. Each of the following came to know the costs of living in modern society and not being allowed to take part.

The Chinese. The West Coast Chinese had been rounded up in gangs and shipped to gold-rush California as laborers. They were model workers in every way, and if that was all that counted, they should have easily followed the path of the Irish. But because the Chinese were a distinctive racial type, everything worked differently for them. Their culture was depicted not only as strange, but as decadent and evil, an underworld of fan-tan parlors, opium dens, and slave bordellos. Stories were told of the secret tunnels beneath Chinatown, where lepers were supposedly stashed away and ritual murders carried out. It was soon clear that the Chinese would not win acceptance.

As a result, their right to compete freely in American society was summarily revoked. They were relegated to the activities that no one else wanted: cooking, cleaning, laundering. And persecution became a way of life for them. On the streets of San Francisco, young hoodlums spat in their faces and threw pepper in their eyes. One gang leader, a girl of fourteen, confessed to stringing Chinese up by their hair. And they were blamed for everything that went wrong. In 1877, after a severe recession, ruffians rampaged through Chinatown for a week, completely undeterred by the law.

The Japanese. With Japanese-Americans, the story of the Chinese essentially repeated itself. They, too, arrived as unskilled laborers and wound up providing more than enough competition. By 1920 Japanese farmers dominated the fruit and berry industries of California, for which they seemed to have a special genius. Nor could it be said of them—as it was of the Chinese—that they were rootless aliens: they bought property, built homes, and sent back to Japan for picture brides. They pursued the American Dream as eagerly as any Caucasian.

Nevertheless, they too were denied legal equality. Many doors of opportunity were slammed shut in their faces, and even in farming they suffered disabilities. In 1913, California, which had already tried segregating Japanese school children, passed an Alien Land Law that made it much more difficult for them to own property.

The lot of the pariah in modern society gained further illustration, if it needed any, at the outbreak of the Second World War. People of Japanese ancestry who had been American citizens for three generations were charged en masse as enemy aliens, stripped of their possessions, and bundled off to relocation camps. It was an outrage without parallel.

Native Americans. The story of the Native Americans was further complicated by the fact that they were here first. Lands occupied by the whites had once been their lands, and the whites' way of life had all but destroyed their own. Making matters still worse was the fact that Native Americans, for understandable reasons, did not really want to melt in.

In this situation, the choices were particularly painful. The reservation system, which gave Native Americans some protection and preserved some semblance of their traditional culture, made their integration into the mainstream virtually impossible. As a result, they would be left impoverished, ill-educated, often resentful, and, worst of all, wards of the government. On the other hand, Native Americans who sought to make a life outside the reservation found themselves in the situation of other despised minorities. Either way they seemed to lose.

Hispanics. Some Hispanics could also claim to have been here first. After all, Santa Fe had been a trading center long before the American westward movement, and the Spanish *Californios* went back far beyond the gold rush. Nevertheless, most Hispanics came into the United States afterward. From both Cuba and Mexico, which suffered political and economic turmoil, they filtered in to find work and sometimes peace. And from Puerto Rico, which became an American possession in 1898, they came to New York City as territorials.

For things Hispanic, it seemed, Americans reserved a special contempt. There were political animosities running all the way back to the Mexican War—visitors to the Alamo are still asked to remove their hats in respect to the patriots who died there—and beyond those were a host of cultural conflicts. Hispanic life was simple, rural, semifeudal, slow paced, and above all, Catholic, almost the reverse of the bustling Yankee style.

As a result, most Hispanics tried to make themselves invisible. They drifted silently from farm to farm in the growing season, getting by on the meagerest of incomes. In their *barrios*, such as East Los Angeles, life went on much as it had in the old Irish or Polish ghettos of the nineteenth century. But unlike the earlier cases, conditions never seemed to improve. For to be an American Hispanic was to remain very much on the outside of things.

Blacks. Black Americans were the worst off of all. They had had the misfortune of coming to America as slaves and the double misfortune of possessing a black skin. Black meant many things to Englishmen of the time, all of them bad. It suggested wickedness, heathenism, lustfulness, backwardness, and God's curse upon Ham. Some

Segregated beach: An incalculable price. (Library of Congress)

even explained it as crossbreeding between humans and apes!

Every horror that could befall an outcast in the modern world became a part of the black experience. They were enslaved, exploited, brutalized, degraded, ridiculed, and kept in ignorance. Nor did their life improve much after slavery. They were required to live in separate neighborhoods. Their children were taught in all-black schools. They were forbidden in white restaurants, theaters, and recreational facilities, and made to occupy segregated areas in public conveyance. In popular culture blacks were depicted as mindless, infantile, and comically credulous, all flashing teeth and rolling eyes. Black scientists were addressed as "boy." Black writers could not be read in the schools. And Marian Anderson, undoubtedly the finest contralto in the United States, was forbidden to perform at the Daughters of the American Revolution's Constitution Hall in Washington.

Nor was it, apparently, within anyone's power to change things. In 1896 the Supreme Court examined the so-called Jim Crow laws of the South and pronounced them constitutional. The armed forces of the United States remained rigidly segregated and the Civil Service was lily-white. In a land where to "smell a nigger in the woodpile" was a phrase of daily conversation, the great majority of blacks went through life as dishwashers, porters, and shoe-shine boys.

But all of the unmeltables suffered legal inequality. All of them faced laws or administrative actions that restricted their freedom, denied them opportunity, and left them bereft of political power. Casualties of the American Dilemma, they were not allowed to compete on any terms. For this, of course, there was no logical reason. The unmeltables were simply different—too different. And there was no way they could be otherwise.

Women

The situation of women was not precisely that of a despised minority, but it was often equally bad. Rather than being unacceptably different, women suffered from an anachronistic application of traditional social logic. In the interest of the family's stability and unity, they were confined to a "place." Men insisted that the place was not necessarily an inferior one—indeed sometimes it was up on a pedestal—but that was not the point. The point was that in modern society, the benefits of remaining in a place—*any* place—had all but disappeared.

The result, once again, was legal inequality. Women were denied equal opportunity in both education and employment. Innumerable laws discriminated against them. And they had absolutely no voice in government. Against these disabilities they struggled valiantly for almost a century, but generally in vain. After decades of strenuous agitation, they finally won the right to vote in 1919, yet they failed to use its power effectively. (Instead of voting for women's issues, they divided along the same lines as their male counterparts.) Although they went to court repeatedly to fight the discriminatory laws and restrictions, once again they did not

make much headway. In the enlightened 1980s, women still made only sixty-two cents for every dollar earned by males.

Growing Restiveness

Ironically for a world based on free competition, all of the groups listed above wound up living in a political, economic, and spiritual no man's land. Talented black athletes were made to play the role of clowns. Brilliant women were forced to be lackeys. The Japanese, who would one day give the world Sony, Seiko, Yamaha, and Mitsubishi, were forbidden to own land. That such a condition should exist continually bothered the thoughtful. The logic of modern society kept whispering that it was crazy.

The Second World War did much to dramatize the situation. American blacks went to war in their segregated units and distinguished themselves in battle. The famous 442 Infantry Battalion, composed entirely of Japanese-Americans, became the most decorated outfit of the war—while their people back home were being kept behind barbed wire. And women went into the factories and proved they could weld and rivet as well as any man. The war also made Americans reexamine their ideals. On close inspection, the evils they were fighting abroad looked suspiciously like the defects in their own society. How much difference was there, people asked themselves, between America's treatment of the blacks and Hitler's treatment of the Jews?

The Civil Rights Revolution

By the war's end, the situation was ripe for revolution. The Supreme Court's decision in *Brown v. The Board of Education*, requiring

The great Civil Rights March of 1963: No more
riding in the back of the bus. (Library of Congress)

the desegregation of all U.S. school systems, proved to be a match in the tinder
box. The Court had caught the mood of the
country and courageously given voice to
it. There was no turning back.

Blacks Lead the Way

The galvanizing effect of the *Brown* decision was soon evidenced by a new spirit
among blacks. The following year, in
Montgomery, Alabama, a foot-weary black
woman on her way home from work decided, on the spur of the moment, not to
give up her bus seat to a white passenger,
as required by law. Her arrest sparked a
calm, orderly, but deadly efficient boycott
of the city's transit system. Blacks walked
for miles to and from work while empty
buses rattled by them on the streets. Eventually the city surrendered uncondition-
ally.

In a dozen other southern cities, blacks
sat down at white lunch counters for the
first time in a century and asked for service. For their pains, they were reviled, spit
on, beaten up, arrested, and jailed. On several occasions police attacked them with

The Films of Sidney Poitier

For decades, popular culture helped nourish and strengthen racism in the United States. Popular songs, ethnic jokes, magazine stories, even advertising reinforced the image of blacks as so many Sambos. Possibly the worst offender was Hollywood, which got a great deal of mileage out of its "Amos 'n Andy" conception of black character. Only fittingly, then, the American film industry, at the outset of the Civil Rights Revolution, began doing what it could to repair the damage it had caused earlier.

The herald of the new Hollywood black was Sidney Poitier. Handsome, well-spoken, and every inch the gentleman, Poitier was precisely the opposite of the scatterbrained, eye-rolling "darkies" of old. In literally dozens of films made between 1950 and the present, Poitier convincingly demonstrated to the American public that its ideas about race were simply wrong. Consider, as examples, three films released in 1967, at the height of the Civil Rights Revolution.

In *To Sir With Love*, Poitier played the part of a skilled engineer who, for want of more suitable employment, winds up teaching high school on London's East Side. The tough, greasy, and ill-behaved students reject his civilized ways in favor of a "rocker's" life. But he goes to work on them. Treating them as grownups, speaking to them with respect, guiding them into the world of high culture, he slowly begins to win them over, a fact symbolized by their use of "Sir" as a form of address. "It is your duty to change the world, if you can," he tells them, "not by violence—peacefully, individually—not as a mob." By the end of the film, Sir has clearly captured their hearts. At the end-of-the-term dance they make an emotional speech of appreciation, hand him a beautifully wrapped gift, and present a card with all of their signatures: "To Sir, With Love."

The genius of *To Sir With Love* was that it made absolutely no difference that the hero was black. By contrast, in the murder mystery titled *In the Heat of the Night*, it made all the difference in the world. The small, Faulkneresque town of Sparta, Mississippi, finds itself with an extremely embarrassing murder on its hands and no apparent way of solving it. (Bill Gillespie, the town's redneck cop, can barely handle his malfunctioning air conditioner.) It happens, though, that suave and sophisticated Virgil Tibbs, played by Poitier, is on leave from the Philadelphia Police Department where he is a crack detective, and in town visiting his mother. In order for Tibbs to solve the murder, Gillespie and the townspeople have to swallow their southern pride and do a lot of growing up. At one point, when Tibbs explodes wrathfully at white stupidity, Gillespie, with a look of wonder on his face, exclaims: "My God, you're as bad as we are!"

The tensions that were merely implicit in the first two films became fully explicit in the third one, *Guess Who's Coming To Dinner*. For the bottom line of the American racial conundrum has always been the question of intermarriage. Joey Drayton, the daughter of a liberal San Francisco journalist, meets and falls in love with dashing John Wade Prentice, played by Poitier. At which point Joey's father has all sorts of second thoughts about the values he has so carefully instilled in her. "It's so interesting," says a family friend, "to see a broken-down old phony liberal come face to face with his principles." But eventually the father does accept the situation. "The only thing that matters," he says at the end, "is what they feel, and how much they feel, for each other."

That was a long way from Amos 'n' Andy.

dogs, and on several more they were knocked off their feet with high-pressure fire hoses. But eventually they were served.

Even bloodier trials awaited them. In 1961 a group of blacks joined forces with white liberals for a bus tour through the South. News of the "freedom riders" spread before their Greyhound like a prairie fire, and at each stop ever uglier crowds awaited them. Finally, in Birmingham, the bus was waylaid by chain-wielding Klansmen, who proceeded to wreak vengeance upon the passengers. James Zwerg, a white student from Fisk University, was seized by several of the assailants and beaten until his face was a bloody pulp. Yet months later, in a voice still quavering with emotion, Zwerg insisted that he would go through it all over again. If nothing else, the Civil Rights Revolution sparked virtue.

Because reason and justice were on their side, blacks, under the leadership of the Reverend Martin Luther King, Jr., were able to keep the revolution nonviolent. And for precisely the same reason, the federal government was obliged to come to their aid. At Little Rock, Arkansas, in 1957, Dwight Eisenhower called in the U.S. Army to supervise school desegregation. Later on, the Kennedy brothers, after initially hesitating, threw their own support behind the cause. But the real champion of civil rights was Lyndon Johnson. A Democrat, a southerner, and a Texan's Texan, Johnson might have been anything but sympathetic to black Americans, but he rose heroically above background and circumstance. If the power of government could be used to combat the Great Depression, vowed Johnson, who had gained his political tutelage under Franklin Roosevelt, it could be used to secure racial justice as well.

The turning point was reached in the mid-1960s. The Civil Rights Act of 1964 abolished the Jim Crow laws of the South: no more would blacks have to ride in the back of the bus. Even more important was the Voting Rights Act passed a year later. By destroying the various subterfuges by which blacks had been disenfranchised over the years, this law presented the specter of ten million new black voters. The effect was almost magic. Politicians who only months earlier were fanning the flames of racial hatred suddenly began speaking of peace, harmony, and cooperation.

Revolutionary Spin-Offs

Other groups were encouraged by the success of the blacks. Native Americans began speaking hopefully of "red power." In order to dramatize the message, they occupied the town of Wounded Knee, South Dakota—the site of a tragic massacre of their people in 1890—and Alcatraz Island in San Francisco Bay. Hispanics also came into a revolutionary self-awareness. In the early 1960s they rechristened themselves *Chicanos* and began speaking proudly of La Raza. Cesar Chavez's successful grape boycott in California demonstrated that Chicanos could flex their muscles as well as anyone. Life in Chinatown changed at the same time. The relative peace enjoyed by the Chinese had been purchased at the price of opportunity, and many were growing unhappy with the trade. Even groups like the handicapped, whose situation in life often paralleled that of the outcast minorities, caught the new spirit. If competition was the name of the game in the United States, they wanted to compete too.

If the Men Were All Transported
Far Beyond the Northern Sea

Emily Wilding Davison was one of the patron saints of the international women's movement. As one of Mrs. Pankhurst's English suffragettes, Davison dropped acid into mailboxes, slashed paintings in art galleries, and once, in the Holloway Prison, jumped down a stairwell in an effort to kill herself. If these tactics seemed questionably related to the problem of securing the vote for women, Davison had a ready explanation. Only her death, she said, could make the women's cause be taken seriously. That was why, in 1913, she ran out onto the track at Epsom Racecourse and threw herself in front of the king's horse as it sped toward the finish line.

Davison's life—and death—illustrated the psychological difficulty of all disadvantaged minorities. In focusing exclusively on their own plight, they tend to turn inward, lose perspective, and in the end court self-defeat. This is not to suggest that their plight is not real. American women of the 1980s still meet discrimination at every turn: they are needlessly foreclosed from many activities, hobbled by archaic laws, and woefully victimized in the workplace. For every dollar earned by males, women make sixty-two cents.

But virtually wherever and whenever women have striven to rectify their condition politically, they have come up against the Davison syndrome: what begins as a legitimate crusade against a painfully real evil often ends slipping off the rails. It happened to the suffragettes of Carrie Chapman Catt's day, and it happened to their granddaughters in the 1960s and 1970s. In Betty Friedan's book, *The Feminine Mystique* (1963), the woman's problem in modern society was compellingly set forth. The subsequent literature of the movement, however, moved inexorably toward radicalism. Together, Kate Millett's *Sexual Politics* (1970) and Germaine Greer's *The Female Eunuch* (1971) approached the realm of a Davisonean narcissism.

Soon the women's movement was becoming known, not for the legitimacy of its complaints, but for its media-hype zaniness. Essential to feminism, it seemed, was the ritual bra burning, the advocacy of unisex clothing and generic restrooms, and the renunciation of cleanliness, grooming, and civility. In the minds of middle-of-the-road Americans, whose support was essential to any reform, the typical feminist was no longer the single mother of three who faced sexual harassment and job discrimination, but rather a cigar-chomping female wrestler.

By 1969 a group calling itself FEMINISTS had taken the movement to what they saw as its logical conclusion. "We must destroy love," they proclaimed. "Love promotes [a woman's] vulnerability, dependence, possessiveness, susceptibility to pain,

Feminists on the march: In the shadow of Emily
Wilding Davison.

and prevents the full development of her human potential." Nor was that all. "We
must destroy the institution of heterosexual sex, which is a manifestation of the male-
female role." In its place, Ti-Grace Atkinson suggested "nonexploitive physical
relations" which "would not necessarily involve genital emphasis."

Marriage, of course, had to be scrapped first of all. "Marriage exists for, and is a
condition of, rape, enslavement and imprisonment." With that general philosophy in
mind, a group calling itself WITCH descended upon the New York Bridal Fair in
February to "Confront the Whoremakers." They performed guerrilla theater, waved
placards that read "Always a Bride, Never a Person," and set loose 150 mice among the
trousseau fashion show. As the police dragged them off to the paddy wagon they
screamed: "I *won't* get married, no, no, I *won't*."

None of this was unique to feminism. It was part and parcel of the battle of any
outside group for its place in the sun. Extremists in the Civil Rights Movement were
led toward black power and race war, while their counterparts in the Latino
renaissance applauded leftist terrorism abroad. Something about the visceral struggle
for acceptance and equality—and the relentless concentration upon self that it
entailed—seemed to drive its participants toward social madness.

The Liberated Society

Where, exactly, is pluralism taking us? The city of San Francisco may offer a pretty good glimpse of the future, for it presents the liberated society in all its fullness.

As far back as the gold rush, San Francisco was known for its toleration. Irish immigrants came to the city as forty-niners and immediately found acceptance. New Immigrants created a thriving Little Italy in the North Beach District, complete with wine making, pasta shops, and Fisherman's Wharf. The San Francisco Chinese once had a rough time of it, to be sure, but the abrasions of the nineteenth century were eventually forgotten. (Chic apparel shops now display their fashions on Oriental manikins.) Chicanos made peace with San Francisco, too, and the Mission District came to throb with a latinesque vitality. And in the Fillmore District, blacks began renovating Victorian houses with a palette of vibrant colors.

So cosmopolitan did San Francisco become that the poet Allen Ginsberg found it the perfect setting for his Beat Generation. Slouching in their wrought-iron furniture, drinking cheap wine, and reading poetry until dawn, "beatniks" were different, all right, but San Francisco could handle that. Indeed, the beats became something of a tourist attraction.

But there were even better tourist attractions in North Beach. The nightclubs were already becoming a bit risqué there, and with the arrival of the beatniks they grew even more so. Bimbo's 365 Club offered "the girl in the fishbowl," a titillating bit of optical illusion, but that was soon eclipsed by Carol Doda's act at the Condor Club. One night in 1964 she unhooked her bra in the midst of a go-go dance and went "topless." Soon topless and bottomless became San Francisco's gift to the world.

The beats also got into the use of mind-altering drugs such as LSD. This marked yet another new twist, but San Francisco was up to that. In fact, among the "hippies,"

The Women's Movement

The most important spin-off was the women's movement. As with other groups, what most of the feminists wanted was only a chance to compete fairly. In their case, however, the demand was received differently. In order to understand why, we must compare traditional and modern society once again. Where in traditional society legal equality was given up for stability and unity, modern society strove for legal equality and let stability and unity blow to the winds. As a result, many of the institutions of traditional society had suffered mightily. Both the church and the community had lost much of their influence and the family was disastrously weakened. In traditional society, all positions in the family were kept subordinate to the male parent (or grandparent) in order to bind the family together. With the advent of legal equality nothing could bind the family together but goodwill.

as beatniks were becoming known, being different became a kind of quest. Greasy hair grew to the shoulders and was tied into a ponytail. Denims became faded and patched. Shirts were opened to the waist or replaced by mod leather vests. Shoes were discarded entirely. And the hippies evolved a lifestyle to match their clothing, including open-air concerts, alley-cat sex lives, and communal living in the California hills. At this point further innovation was almost impossible, but one hippie commune did manage a new wrinkle. Charles Manson and his "family" began dabbling in recreational murder.

By 1970 the barriers that had constrained the Pilgrims of old had been swept away in the new Babylon. Where Plymouth had allowed only one religion, San Francisco welcomed hundreds of them. Zen monks squatted on the sidewalks. Cosmic nuns wandered Haight-Ashbury. And the First Church of Satan zealously worshipped the devil. Only Jim Jones found the city's religious atmosphere confining, and moved his People's Temple to Guyana.

Where Plymouth had accepted but a single concept of chastity, San Francisco floated free: Couples "lived in" on a regular basis, swinger's directories advertised odd forms of sex, and women strolled the streets effectively naked. Even the conformism of Plymouth had been turned on its head. The only sort of conformity imposed by San Francisco was that of *non*conformity.

Here for the world to see were all the strengths of the new society—its color, its variety, its dynamism. Fortunes were made and broken like clockwork. New ideas succeeded or failed resoundingly. Useful experiments were constantly brewing and bubbling. But here, too, equally conspicuous, were the new society's critical weaknesses. Where every sort of diversity was encouraged, nothing seemed to possess integrity. Where change was fast paced and kaleidoscopic, nothing appeared worth hanging on to. Where every value seemed to apply, there was often a sense of no values whatever.

This fact made the women's situation doubly difficult. For, if women were now to be accorded perfect legal equality—as contemplated in the proposed Equal Rights Amendment—it would likely weaken the family even further. On the other hand, many women in the modern world had no family involvement whatsoever; what sense did it make to hobble *them*? These dilemmas were exceptionally difficult for contemporary Americans. They had learned to answer all such questions in the light of modern social logic—but in this case no answer seemed forthcoming.

Pluralism

We cannot overstate how important and far-reaching the Civil Rights Revolution was. Just as the Civil War revolutionized the U.S. constitutional system and the Great Depression revolutionized the market economy, the Civil Rights Revolution completely changed American society. Historically that society had searched for some kind of unity, some essence of Americanism that bound everyone together. The idea of the melting pot was precisely such an essence.

After the Civil Rights Revolution, the search for an American essence began to fade. Americans seemed to accept the fact that they were not one people, one style, or one set of values, but many. Blacks, for example, were noticeably prouder of being black and being different. Indeed, the apostles of black power gave up on integration and spoke instead of a return to things African.

Other groups, such as Native Americans and Hispanics, sounded the same way. Although they still demanded free competition, they no longer seemed to want to melt in. Indeed, some groups which had *already* melted in began to reassert their identity. There were frantic attempts to keep Old World cultures and languages alive—or in some cases to resurrect them.

Nothing was more symptomatic of the new wave than the so-called counterculture. This, after all, consisted of people deliberately separating themselves from the mainstream. Children from American middle-class homes—many of whose parents had struggled to provide a lifestyle in keeping with the norm—donned tie-dyed grubbies, let their hair grow long, and set out for a hippie commune. Being different became an end in itself.

The acceptance and encouragement of diversity—such a departure from man's historic need for homogeneity—is called pluralism. That everyone should be equally accepted and free to do his or her own thing is the essence of the pluralistic ideal. We can think of its capital as San Francisco, where a dizzying array of cultures and lifestyles coexist, and we can think of its anthem as "Anything Goes." Pluralism, needless to add, is the logical end point for the development of modern society. In our own time the United States has become a fully pluralistic society.

Has that been good or bad? Probably a little of both. In a pluralistic society, everyone is unrestrained, everyone has opportunity, and everyone has access to political power. Society is conceived as an open competition—within the law—among all peoples, all ideas, and all values. Thus, pluralism in America has had important implications for both freedom and democracy, and has more or less laid the American Dilemma to rest.

On the other hand, where does pluralism logically end? Should there be a total acceptance of everything the modern world can come up with? Should homosexuals be considered only another deserving minority? Should drug users be regarded as only another interest group? What about prostitutes, pornographers, subversives bent on destroying freedom? What about religious cults that practice torture and mind control? What about terrorists, neo-Nazis and the Ku Klux Klan? And what about cold-blooded criminals? Shouldn't there indeed be limits to toleration?

Another set of questions concerns public virtue. With all its faults, traditional society had its respect for the common well-being woven right into the social fabric. In modern society, by contrast, no similar respect exists, and we seem at a loss to reproduce it artificially. When society is reduced to a slugfest among contending groups, there is apparently little in the way of virtue felt by any of them.

Such questions had no easy answers, of course, nor were Americans close to achieving a consensus on them. (Consensus is hard to come by in a pluralistic society.) However, the election and reelection of Ronald Reagan seemed to indicate a chill in the enthusiasm of Americans for social experimentation. Perhaps the New Society they had been developing for the past two hundred years was not all they had hoped it would be.

27
Among the Nations

Bad ending to a divisive war (UPI/Bettmann Newsphotos)

The Fall of Saigon

It was, in all, a bad ending to a bad war. When the advancing North Vietnamese began shelling Tan Son Nhut Airport, late in the evening of April 28, 1975, word was passed among Americans in Saigon that the evacuation would have to be made by helicopter instead. When they heard Bing Crosby's "White Christmas" played on the Armed Forces FM station, American personnel were to quietly disengage themselves and make their way to one of the previously arranged staging areas. They were to be careful not to tell the Vietnamese they were leaving, as a panic might set in. Julie Forsythe, an American working for a Quaker organization, heard all this from her Vietnamese neighbors.

On the morning of the 29th there was a charge in the air. The sky was filled with helicopters, their rotors thumping a pulsing tattoo through the muggy tropic air. Some headed for the roof of the Pittman Apartments, where Americans stood ready to climb aboard. Others headed for the American embassy. The Vietnamese were not blind. By noon the roads were thronged with bicycles and motorscooters hauling people with bags and suitcases. Many of *them* were heading for the embassy, too. Everyone expected a blood bath when the North Vietnamese entered the city. Anyone who had worked for the Americans, or served in the government of Nguyen Van Thieu, was well advised to get out.

Flickers of panic began to appear in the early afternoon. A bus rounding up the Americans got lost down at the waterfront, and as it tried to leave, Vietnamese desperately jumped aboard. A mother with an infant under her arm leaped for the running board but in the process lost her grip on the child, which tumbled beneath the wheels. The unnerved driver roared off through the dust.

By midafternoon a sea of humanity surged about the gates of the embassy, waving papers and documents, imploring the Marines to let them through. Two towering guards, 6'3" and 6'5" respectively, wearing flak jackets and carrying M-16s, waded among the Vietnamese to usher Americans through. Americans first. No one had said it in so many words, but the policy was all too clear. Thousands of Vietnamese had received promises of safety from their Yankee employers, but now, when the chips were down, they knew in their hearts they were going to be left behind. Chun Wan Lin, a child in each arm, stood in the crowd, fighting back her tears. "I felt more hurt than angry," she recalled. "I felt that I had been abandoned by my best friend."

This, in a sense, was how the whole war had gone. Coming to help, the Americans, in the eyes of many Vietnamese, had only hindered. With them had come their rock music, their hard drugs, their licentiousness, and worst of all, their promises. Pacification. Stabilization. Vietnamization. The story of the war could be told in the euphemisms that were used to make the nightmare acceptable. The generals had come and the politicians had come and, yes, even the president had come, and all had gone back to the United States to proclaim "We can win." And they had lost.

Helicopter sorties from the deck of the *Midway* continued through the night. Sloshing with coffee or drugged with No-Dōz, the pilots, many of them awake for the past seventy-two hours, flew lights-out through the inky blackness, watching the flames of the city below them. Lines of tracers climbed up through the night, and an occasional rocket swooshed by. The Viet Cong, who had commandeered Air America Hueys, were also beating around over the city. Here and there the silhouette of one would suddenly loom ahead.

"Throw away your suitcases," State Department official Joe McBride told the Vietnamese inside the embassy compound. "You can't take anything with you." The Vietnamese instantly obeyed. They were the lucky ones, the ones inside the gates, and they would do nothing to foul up their chances of going now. Slowly the line of them climbed the stairwell and onto the roof, where the choppers swung out of the oblivion and threw open their cargo hatches. As McBride climbed aboard one of the last ones, he was struck by the Dantean illumination of the red cabin lights, and by the high-pitched whine of the turbines. Then suddenly the engines roared and they were off into the night.

At 5:00 in the morning there were still 420 Vietnamese inside the embassy compound. Six more helicopters were supposedly on their way. Suddenly Maj. James Keane, the senior Marine, walked up to Col. John Madison and announced, "Sir, the evacuation is over. It's Americans only." The order had come directly from Washington. Capt. Stuart Harrington had the hapless job of covering everyone else's retreat. He stood in the courtyard, radio in hand, confidently talking to helicopters that weren't there. "Are the helicopters coming?" asked a pretty Vietnamese girl, her dark eyes wide with alarm. "Yes, there's a big one on its way," he answered. A few minutes later he excused himself to urinate behind a bush—and made a mad dash for the embassy door.

As the last chopper lifted from the roof, BBC reporters, watching it from a nearby hotel, sprinted over to the embassy to cover their last Vietnam dateline. The grounds were littered with desks and chairs. Wooden drawers were upended. Papers, classified and unclassified, were scudding along in the morning breeze. A group of Vietnamese were stuffing explosives into a steel safe in the consulate, calling merrily to one another. When the safe blew, there were thousands of dollars to pass around.

Meanwhile, the first North Vietnamese tanks rolled up to the Bin Hoa Bridge. Minutes earlier a frantic South Vietnamese colonel, his lips flecked with foam, had confiscated a large, pink Cadillac and pulled it crossways onto the bridge. The tanks rolled over the top of it without ceremony, smashing it flat, and swung down the city's main thoroughfare. One of the BBC men, in a moment of bravado, hitched a ride on the lead tank. He was still bumping along behind the gun turret when the tank burst through the gates of the presidential palace.

But at the American embassy no one seemed to notice. Hundreds of Vietnamese were still sitting patiently on their suitcases, waiting for the helicopters to come and take them away.

Shortly after the United States felt the birth pangs of the New Society, it found itself mired down in a disastrous foreign war. The experience was a conundrum of irony and paradox. The war itself was undeclared and extralegal—yet fifty thousand servicemen were killed in it. The official enemy was North Vietnam—yet most of the hostile combatants came from the "friendly" South. American troops employed the world's most sophisticated military technology—yet could not overcome men armed with zip guns. The conflict was a civil one, in a small, unimportant country—yet it constantly threatened to embroil the superpowers. The U.S. became involved in it at the height of its own power and influence—and got its first bitter taste of defeat.

In order to understand how the United States could find itself in such a situation—one that symbolized its increasingly troublesome relations with the world—we must begin at the beginning, when the newly minted American Republic first took its place among the nations.

The Main Themes of U.S. Foreign Relations

It was a beginning marked by reluctance and trepidation. After all, the American Republic was not only a new government, it was a new *form* of government, and its very existence posed a challenge to the monarchical powers. Then, too, both its friends and its enemies had only recently recovered from the War of the American Revolution, and they were still glowering darkly at one another. America's closest friend, France, was soon to become revolutionary France—a loose cannon on the deck of Old World politics. And next to France, oddly enough, America's closest ties were to its recent enemy, England. The whole situation was fraught with difficulty and danger.

Besides, on its own side of the world, the United States had pressing problems to attend to. Unfriendly powers, such as the Spanish in the lower Mississippi and the English in Canada, were perilously near. Various Indian tribes contested American claims beyond the Appalachians, and they were easily stirred into action. And then there was a continent to settle and the problems of nationhood to work out. Little wonder that when American statesmen looked at their position in the world, they concluded that *isolationism* might well be the best policy.

Isolationism

Isolationism did not mean ignoring the world or severing all ties to it; it meant holding *political* relations with it to a minimum. In the world of eighteenth-century diplomacy, alliances between nations were often made and broken according to the coldest calculation of self-interest, and any alliance had the capacity to haul its signatories into war. It was like an ongoing chess match among masters of the game, and certain would-be participants were better off never to play.

The Farewell Address. George Washington, upon retiring from the presidency in 1797, determined that the United States clearly fell into that category. As president, he had tried to steer among the rocks and shoals of the French problem and the sailing had never been smooth. The best thing to do, he concluded, was stand aloof from both revolutionary France and its British nemesis. In his Farewell Address, he accordingly advised his countrymen to pursue a course of national independence, minimize foreign political relations, and avoid permanent alliances. The Farewell Address became one of the founding documents of American isolationism.

The Monroe Doctrine. The other founding document was drawn up a quarter century later, in 1823. In the interim, the United States had learned the hazards of the diplomatic game firsthand, having twice been drawn into European conflicts. U.S. statesmen were especially concerned about the possibility of European powers entering the Western Hemisphere to rebuild their crumbling empires. Accordingly, a doctrine enunciated by President Monroe in his annual message to Congress stated that it would be the policy of the United

States to oppose any new incursions into the Americas. Europe for the Europeans, the Monroe Doctrine declared, and America for the Americans.

America and the Great Passions

Like the foreign policies of most nations, the American policy of isolationism was a reflection of political self-interest. Virtue may have had its place *within* national borders, but few held it to apply outside. As a result, the powers often dealt with one another in extremely cynical ways. Indeed, in nineteenth-century Europe, foreign affairs were marked by great tides of passion that swept national self-interest to new heights. Among these passions were the following:

Nationalism. The nations of Europe seemed to grow increasingly conscious of their distinctiveness. Far from seeing themselves as fellow Europeans with common interests and values, they saw themselves ever more clearly as Englishmen, Frenchmen, or Germans, and emphasized the differences that set them apart. It was difficult to discuss nationality at all without falling into a blustering quarrel about who was better than whom. Even the intellectuals got into it. In coldly dispassionate treatises or stirringly romantic prose, they sang the virtues of this people or that—as against all others. "My country, right or wrong," said the nationalists, and they meant it.

Imperialism. The war of words soon grew into a scramble for empire. In reality, the contest dated back to Columbus, who had claimed the lands he discovered for the king and queen of Spain. It was not until the nineteenth century, however, that the colonial rivalry really hit its stride. In the belief that colonies were needed to supply raw materials and ready-made markets for European industries, the entire globe was rapidly carved up. In China, for example, England moved into the Yangtze valley and warned the other powers to keep away. Germany took possession of the Shantung Peninsula in the same spirit. Russia began a railroad across Manchuria in the north of China, and Japan laid plans for a competing line. The French, who arrived late on the scene, had to establish their own holdings southward—in what the natives called Vietnam. Whatever possessions the powers held, it seemed, they were never quite enough.

Militarism. No empire could be kept secure without a powerful and mobile military force. Armies came in handy for this purpose but navies came in still handier. Steam-powered ships could sail into any colonial situation and train their guns on the beach, and if need be they could square off against rival colonial powers. In light of this fact, there was a sudden premium on bigger, faster, and ever more heavily armed seacraft, and it was not long before Europe was engaged in a frantic naval arms race. Ships of the line called dreadnoughts (after HMS *Dreadnought*) proved to be the last word in naval perfection, for they could knife through the seas at twenty-one knots and pack twelve-inch guns. Submarines were useful too, for they could scuttle a dreadnought with a single torpedo. England built dreadnoughts in ever greater numbers, but Germany more than matched it with U-boats. The more ships each side got, of course, the more each seemed to need.

As the United States became wealthier and more populous, it began to think of itself as a great power too. Isolationism had

The Frankenstein of Modern War

At the dawning of the nineteenth century, most peoples of the Western world equated science and technology with progress. New inventions, they believed, were bound to make the world ever better. By 1818, however, when Mary Wollstonecraft Shelley wrote *Frankenstein*, doubts were beginning to gather in a number of minds. It was just possible that science and technology, so beneficent when applied to the peaceful arts, might, when applied to the military ones, become Frankenstein's monster.

And that was essentially what happened. The monster was created, oddly enough, not by imperial Germany or czarist Russia, but by the Western democracies: France, Great Britain, and the United States. The latter especially, renowned for its brilliant technology, moved steadily into the forefront of the new military hardware, which came to include the following:

Heavy Cannon. Variously called howitzers and Big Berthas, the new guns were veritable monsters. The Germans created one with a barrel as long as a crane boom that could throw a projectile seventy-six miles, while the French developed another, fired from a giant railroad car, with a sixteen-inch bore and a two thousand-pound shell. Even so, the Modéle 1916, as it was called, was only half the size of the German mortars that pounded the Belgian fortress of Liége into rubble.

Machine Guns. Invented by an American in 1884, the Maxim gun revolutionized modern warfare. By utilizing recoil energy to operate the loading, firing, and ejecting mechanisms, the Maxim could get off as many as 780 rounds of ammunition in a minute. It was too bulky (160 lbs.) for effective offensive use, but placed at the edge of a trench and encircled with concertina wire, it was all but invincible. In the Second Battle of the Somme, 1916, machine guns mowed down the attacking forces like wheat, and in the end claimed more than a *million* casualties.

Tanks. As early as 1899, a Maxim gun was mounted on a motor car in the United States. To complete the evolution of the tank, only a track was needed, and this was supplied by British engineers in the fall of 1915. Seeing the first "Big Willie" slogging across the mud in no man's land did not convince the Germans of its usefulness, and they declined to duplicate the weapon; but on November 20, 1917, 474 British tanks achieved a spectacular breakthrough at Cambrai. Ground fighting in the next war would clearly belong to the Rommels and the Pattons.

Dreadnoughts. Of all the ships developed in the nineteenth century, nothing so captured the imagination of naval strategists as the "dreadnought." The first of these, HMS *Dreadnought*, commissioned in 1906, was the direct result of Dewey's victory over the Spanish at Manila Bay, which proved that heavy guns alone were useful in a face-off of armored ships. Accordingly, *Dreadnought* was armed with a battery of ten twelve-inchers. Not to be outdone, the U.S. began building dreadnoughts of its own, the Texas class, with guns a full two inches larger. And not to be outdone by that, the British responded with the Queen Elizabeth class, packing fifteen-inch guns. Which meant that the Americans had to come back with the Colorado class, upping the bore size to sixteen inches. And so on.

Submarines. Ever since the shootout between the *Monitor* and the *Merrimac* in the American Civil War, the advantages of a small, hard-to-sight, hard-to-hit ironclad were apparent. With a bit more tinkering, the *Monitor*, whose decks were almost awash

The United States' Great White Fleet: Whose ships
were bigger than whose? (Library of Congress)

anyway, became a submersible, able to duck under the waves for up to two hours.
Something else to come out of the Civil War were torpedoes. Confederate sappers used
stationary ones (actually mines) against Union vessels, and a few years later a Scottish
engineer named Robert Whitehead learned how to make them self-propelled. The
horror of the submarine did not become evident until World War I, when a German U-
boat torpedoed and sank the British liner *Lusitania* with appalling loss of life.

Aircraft. Balloons were used in the Civil War, too, for reconnaissance and artillery
spotting. Inspired by that, Germany built huge, steel-framed dirigibles, five hundred
feet long, and loaded them with high explosives to drop on London. In all there were
fifty-one Zeppelin raids in the world war and thousands of casualties. There was even
an attack planned against New York.

As for the airplane, the Wright brothers hoped that it would somehow outmode
war by making troop movements fully observable. Instead it became an instrument of
war itself. Seven years after the first flight at Kitty Hawk, Glenn Curtis, an American
aviator, was dropping dummy bombs on a shiplike target, while others were trying to
figure out how to mount a machine gun so that it would not shoot off the plane's own
propeller. The first aircraft to achieve this, Germany's Fokker Eindecker, swept the
skies over the western front—and then began strafing the trenches.

As early as 1910, airplanes were even taking off from, and landing back onto, the
decks of the new turbine-driven scout cruisers, and once again Americans were
leading the way. One group of Yankee engineers even worked up a plane that would
fly by remote control, a sort of pilotless bomb, as they conceived it. Now, if there were
just some really big explosive they could mount in it. Coincidentally, another group of
Americans were puzzling over Einstein's relativity equations and wondering if some
really big explosive couldn't be produced from atomic fission.

Frankenstein's monster had blinked open its eyes.

never meant the absence of economic, social, or cultural ties with the rest of the world, and as contact with Europeans increased, Americans began to be swept along by the currents of the age.

American Nationalism. American citizens felt little sense of nationalism in the beginning, for each state thought of itself as a separate nation. That situation was changed by the War of 1812. The war itself was a stalemate and nowhere was the fighting distinguished, but in the rosy glow of memory it became a grand patriotic adventure. Americans especially savored the Battle of New Orleans, where a motley band of frontiersmen under a border captain named Andrew Jackson routed a force of disciplined British regulars. With rising Yankee pride, a song of the day depicted the British retreat:

Well, they ran through the briars an' they ran
    through the brambles,
An' they ran through places where a rabbit
    couldn't go.
They ran so fast that the hounds couldn't catch
    'em,
On down the Mississippi to the Gulf of Mexico.

In "Old Hickory," as Jackson was dubbed, the young Republic found a true national hero and got its first taste of military grandeur. Why, if a bunch of Yankees could fight like that, people speculated, they could probably do almost anything. American folklore began spinning out its Paul Bunyans, Tony Beavers, and Pecos Bills, and Americans' self-reputed brains, pluck, humor, know-how, virtue, and folksy wisdom became embodied in a new symbol of the United States—Uncle Sam.

Though it was harmless enough in the beginning, American nationalism soon took on a note of belligerence. One of the things Yankees boasted they could do was whip ten Mexicans apiece if it came to a fight. And in 1846 it did. Spread-eagle nationalism was not the sole cause of the Mexican War, but it was certainly a contributing factor. For what might have been a negotiable difficulty between the two countries (the U.S. acquisition of breakaway Texas) was amplified tenfold by braggadocio and fighting talk. The war turned out to be a long and difficult one for both sides, and there was little gratification to be found in it. Yet, for many Americans, nationalism bathed it in an aura of romance.

American Imperialism. How the United States reacted to the rush for empire was not simple. On the one hand, Americans had once been part of an empire themselves, and the memory was not a happy one. On the other hand, they became increasingly concerned about competing against the colonial powers. Some began to think of pursuing empire themselves.

There were several reasons for the growing interest. Americans had always looked toward the Pacific, and they ventured into its waters with increasing confidence. Gray whales patrolled the California coast and blue whales were found out near Hawaii. Protestant missionaries headed for the same islands, and by mid-century they had taken the gospel there in force. American clippers crossed the Pacific too, born westward by the trade winds to Canton and Shanghai. That was the most tantalizing fact of all.

Indeed, American merchants fairly dreamed of the China trade. Why, to put a single shirt on the back of every Chinese, they calculated, would drive the U.S. textile industry at full throttle for a year. This, of course, was the familiar rationale for imperialism, and it was by no mere chance

General George Patton: the personnification of
American nationalism and militarism (UPI/
Bettmann Newsphotos)

that other powers were moving in on
China at the same time. Unawares, the
United States began drifting into the im-
perialistic struggle.

In order to compete successfully in
the China trade, it would be necessary
for the United States to expand and mod-
ernize its navy, build a canal across the
Isthmus of Panama, and secure strategic
bases in the western Pacific. These points
were brought to the attention of expan-
sion-minded Americans by a leading
theorist of empire, Capt. Alfred Thayer
Mahan, USN. Spreading his maps before
him, Mahan argued that all power in the
modern world came down to naval power

in the end, and that the United States was
capable of developing an extraordinary
degree of it. Of course, it would have to
have those islands: Hawaii, Samoa, Guam
perhaps, maybe even the Philippines. And
they all happened to belong to someone
else.

American Militarism. Americans watched
the buildup of European armaments with
a morbid fascination. They were a peace-
loving people, they told themselves, and
yet war was clearly a part of their experience. At one time they themselves had led
the way in developing military hardware,
but the ironclad ships of the Civil War were

old hat now and Yankee inventors had turned to other things. By 1888 the once-proud U.S. Navy was ranked twelfth in the world (out of perhaps thirteen) while the army was practically nonexistent.

Some Americans did not like this state of affairs. Capt. Mahan, for example, became an evangelist for American naval power, tirelessly preaching its gospel to politicians, diplomats, and military planners. In time, his audience included some influential people, not the least of them a rising New York police commissioner named Theodore Roosevelt. But it was James G. Blaine who first acted. As President Benjamin Harrison's secretary of state, Blaine persuaded the Republican party, which he largely controlled, that the United States deserved a navy second to none.

During the 1890s the Great White Fleet came into being. Although it was no match for the earth-girdling British Fleet, it was modern, well equipped, and impressive on the high seas. In 1908 Theodore Roosevelt, now president, was so moved by the sight of it that he sent the fleet on a cruise around the world. Like the heads of other great powers, Roosevelt was using the specter of naval might to awe would-be enemies. It was one of imperialism's oldest tricks.

Mission

Some Americans could not countenance a foreign policy that was so aggressive and self-serving. To cast eyes at neighboring possessions, to build a fleet of menacing dreadnoughts, to pick quarrels with Old World powers, seemed entirely against the spirit of republicanism. What, after all, was the meaning of America, they asked, if not to advance the cause of humanity?

These dissenters gradually articulated an alternative concept of U.S. foreign policy. Borrowing a term from Jefferson, they argued that the United States had a Mission to perform for humankind. The Mission was not to beat the other powers at the game of diplomacy. It was not to out-bluster the jingoists or outgun the militarists, and it was certainly not to outconquer the makers of empire. Rather, they urged, the Mission of America was to set a moral example before the nations, to show forth republican virtue in the conduct of its foreign affairs. America, in a word, ought to be a beacon of light to the world.

Contradictions and Ambiguities

By the end of the century, it was clear that the United States was soon to become a world power in its own right. Yet it would not, at first, really know how to play that role. Unlike the traditional powers of Europe, whose experience stretched back into the centuries, America, only recently out of the cocoon of isolationism, would decidedly be new at the game. Before the U.S. could develop a consistent and meaningful relationship with the nations, several troubling ambiguities would have to be resolved.

First of all, with threads of both self-interest and public virtue wound into its thinking, how would the U.S. put its power to use? Would it muscle its way around, as suggested by the Roosevelts and Mahans, or would it light a beacon, as suggested by the advocates of Mission?

Second, given their history of isolationism, could the American people sustain long-term international commitments? By anyone's reckoning, the geopolitical game required patience and perseverance, and no player could hope to win every round. Americans, by contrast, were a go-ahead, can-do people, impatient with long-term difficulties. They would be tempted to try quick solutions in their foreign policy—and if those solutions failed, they would be tempted to cut and run.

Third, would Americans similarly be tempted by the arms race? There was reason to think so. The United States in 1890 was the mightiest industrial power on earth. Its factories were capable of astronomical production, and its technology was moving ahead at full gallop. If, as some feared, the future was to be determined by the possession of military hardware, who but the Americans would be better able to compete?

Finally, given the monumental success of their own institutions, how would Americans react to foreign ones? Would a market-oriented U.S. be able to deal with socialistic rivals in the world? Would a democratic U.S. be able to deal with monarchy, anarchy, and totalitarian dictatorship? There was a distinct possibility that the American Mission to the world might become that of converting the world to Americanism.

Stepping Onto the World Stage: The Spanish-American War

The incident that vaulted the United States onto the stage of world politics began obscurely. In 1898, Cuba, for centuries a colony of Spain, had long been the scene of a smoldering brushfire-revolt. It was a bloody affair, and the Spanish had taken desperate measures to end it. American newspapers, hoping to boost their readership, had printed lurid details of Spanish atrocities—sometimes entirely fabricated—and before long a burning sense of outrage had been kindled. Who were these Spanish anyway, it was asked, with their evil decadence and their rapacious blood lust?

When the USS *Maine*, stationed in Havana Harbor to protect American interests, was blown to eternity on a quiet tropical night in February, war between the United States and Spain became virtually unavoidable. (Ironically, there was no real reason to believe the Spanish were responsible for the explosion, and several reasons to believe they were not.) The war itself was short. Chaos and bungling marked the U.S. effort to land an army in Cuba, but the Great White Fleet fulfilled its every promise. One squadron under Adm. William T. Sampson bottled up a Spanish force in Santiago and destroyed it piecemeal. Another under Adm. George Dewey steamed into Manila Bay in the Philippines—a place hardly relevant to Cuba—and also commenced hostilities. Making pass after pass in the morning hours of May 1, Dewey's dreadnoughts raked the Spanish fleet with their thirteen-inch guns and utterly demolished it.

After the war Americans looked around to find they had acquired much of the Spanish empire. Cuba became an American protectorate, and the islands of Guam in the Pacific and Puerto Rico in the Caribbean became outright possessions. Most surprising of all was the U.S. acquisition of the Philippines.

What had happened? The intervention into Cuba had originally been inspired largely by the virtuous side of American thinking—by the sense of Mission—but as the fighting progressed, self-interest had come charging to the fore. Those who had

Teddy Roosevelt charging up San Juan Hill: The war created heroes. (Library of Congress)

thought about joining the game of world politics suddenly saw their chance and seized it. It was a truly startling development.

Still, the experience gave Americans much to ponder. It was now they, not the Spanish, who were seen as the oppressor in the Philippines, and soon a revolt against *their* rule was under way. Then, too, ownership of the Philippines sucked the U.S. into the Pacific power struggle—and into an extremely vulnerable position, at that. Even with Cuba, the United States acquired new difficulties. An unstable government in the vicinity of the Panama Canal promised endless political headaches, and on more than one occasion U.S. marines had to be landed. Thoughtful Americans began to wonder if the sally into imperialism hadn't been a mistake.

World War I

The United States thus backed away from empire building virtually at the moment of its success. And none too soon. The passions of Old World diplomacy were at that moment leading toward a disaster that would change the course of history. In August of 1914 the field guns which had been perfected over the past twenty years began firing across the Franco-German border. The world was suddenly at war.

American isolationists, still a potent influence, were horrified at the thought of possible U.S. involvement. They watched newsreels from the front and stared aghast at the scale of the slaughter. Modern weapons had revolutionized warfare, it seemed, and both the weapons and the warfare were now taking their toll. How lucky it was, Americans told one another, that the United States was not a part of it.

But it *was* a part of it. America's throbbing factories were capable of supplying any of the belligerents with the wherewithal of victory, and in recognition of that fact the war moved out of the trenches and onto the high seas, where the Allies' transatlantic lifeline lay exposed. In 1917, the German High Command, increasingly desperate, decided to go for broke and use its submarines to attack U.S. shipping. Against its will, the United States was drawn into the war.

The American Expeditionary Force, led by Gen. John J. Pershing, reached the trenches of the western front in the spring of 1918, just in time to meet Germany's final offensive. The Germans pushed the battle-weary Allies back to the Marne, only fifty miles from Paris, before the weight of the new forces was felt. American troops stalled a ferocious assault at Chateau-Thierry in May and broke through the

Trench warfare on the western front: A whole new
way of fighting. (Library of Congress)

German line at Belleau Wood in June. In
the center of the line, between Reims and
Soissons, eighty-five thousand Americans
participated in the seesaw battles that
ended in an Allied victory in August. As
the Kaiser's army reeled back toward the
Rhine, the fighting steadily intensified. It
transpired in an inferno of shell craters,
shattered trees, and cordite smoke, with the
scream of artillery everywhere. No
doughboy who lived through it was ever
quite the same.

The Question of the League

When the smoke cleared it became obvious
that American forces, while they had not
borne the brunt of the fighting, had indeed
made a critical difference, and in that sense
they had won the war. When President

Wilson traveled to Europe for the peace
negotiations, he was regarded as a savior;
surging crowds roared their approval of
him and girls strewed flowers in his path.
It was a role he was ready to play.

The son of a Presbyterian minister and
a man of searching conscience, Woodrow
Wilson had deeply pondered the causes of
the Great War and arrived at some important conclusions. The problem, as he saw
it, was that diplomacy was an inherently
selfish business, and the passions of the
nineteenth century had made it ever more
so. Self-interest, in a word, had run amok.

Although America had not been free
of selfishness in its own foreign affairs, it
had come to balance self-interest with a
measure of political virtue. (It had promised the Philippines, for example, that

The Failure of Moral Leadership:
Hitler's Reply to Roosevelt

In April of 1939, as the world braced itself for the final showdown with Nazi Germany, President Roosevelt, in a desperate attempt to avoid war, sent a telegram to the German Fuehrer. In it he reaffirmed his faith in negotiation and asked specific assurances that Hitler would not attack any of thirty-one countries listed. The telegram was America's last exercise in moral leadership.

On April 28 Hitler gave his reply in the German Reichstag. William Shirer, who was there, remembered how the deputies rocked with laughter at the Fuehrer's masterly irony and sarcasm. Was it true, as Roosevelt affirmed, that "all international problems can be solved at the council table?" Hitler's answer:

> I would be very happy if these problems could really find their solution at the council table. My skepticism, however, is based on the fact that it was America herself who gave sharpest expression to her mistrust in the effectiveness of conferences. For the greatest conference of all time was the League of Nations . . . representing all the peoples of the world, created in accordance with the will of an American President. The first State, however,

President Woodrow Wilson: A belief in American Mission. (Library of Congress)

when politically mature they would be set free.) Moreover, the U.S. had had other experience at controlling self-interest, in the operation of its market economy and in the workings of its government. It seemed to Wilson that what the world community needed was something similar. There needed to be a sort of parliament of the nations in which structural devices would help keep human passions under control.

The institution that developed from these ideas was called the League of Nations. It was much like the present-day United Nations except that, in theory, it had sharper teeth. Article X of the League Covenant made decisions of the world organization binding on member nations, and could be construed as a limitation of

that shrank from this endeavor was the United States. . . . It was not until after years of purposeless participation that I resolved to follow the example of America.

The freedom of North America was not achieved at the conference table any more than the conflict between the North and the South was decided there. I will say nothing about the innumerable struggles which finally led to the subjugation of the North American continent as a whole.

I mention all this only in order to show that your view, Mr. Roosevelt, although undoubtedly deserving of all honor, finds no confirmation in the history of your own country or of the rest of the world.

Hitler climaxed his peroration by reading out, one at a time, the names of the countries on Roosevelt's list. With each of them he paused, and in mock solemnity forswore any aggressive intention, while the roars of gleeful laughter grew ever louder. He even pointed out that two of the countries on the list, Ireland and Syria, had told him that they felt more worried about Great Britain than the German Reich. It was a wonderful performance.

And it was not until much later that William Shirer stopped to think that Hitler had slyly left Poland off the list of his replies. That, undoubtedly, was because three weeks earlier he had issued final orders for the destruction of Poland by September 1.

their sovereignty. Thus, in the event that England got into a squabble with, say, Russia and the League took the Russian side, it was conceivable that the United States would be obliged to apply sanctions against a friend. Isolationists were not pleased. The League of Nations seemed to be everything George Washington had warned against in the Farewell Address.

Other Americans, however, saw the League in terms of Mission. Woodrow Wilson believed that the United States must lead the way toward Camelot, for it alone possessed unchallengeable moral authority. Campaigning strenuously for the League, the president seemed to be on the verge of convincing the American public when he suddenly collapsed and suffered a paralyzing stroke. In the end, the Senate refused to ratify American membership in the League of Nations.

Moral Leadership

Americans on both sides of the League question agreed on certain fundamentals, however. They were ready to wash their hands of all bullying and bluster in their own foreign policy. To the extent that they would shape world affairs in the future, they agreed that it must be by *moral* means, not political or military. Moral leadership was probably the best thing they could have given the League anyway, they told themselves, and that sort of leadership could be supplied in other ways. Indeed, within two years the United States had hosted a disarmament conference in Washington and had offered to take the lead in dismantling naval weaponry.

Thus, by 1920, the United States had begun to fashion a new role for itself among the nations. It would not conduct diplomacy the way the world did. It would never again steal possessions from a weak neighbor or attempt to gain objectives by force. Self-interest would remain present in its diplomacy, to be sure, but self-interest would be balanced and tempered by virtue. Above all, it would provide the world with impeccable moral leadership. Mission had become its guiding principle.

World War II

Owing to the continuing influence of the isolationists, American moral leadership remained passive throughout most of the 1920s. The United States held itself aloof from world politics (as well as from the League of Nations) and concentrated instead on the making of grand gestures. For example, in 1928 the U.S. jointly sponsored a multinational treaty to "outlaw" war. The Kellogg-Briand Pact, as it was called, perfectly exemplified the moralistic approach to diplomacy.

The Gathering Storm

Teaching the world by moral example was not without its hazards, however, and naked aggression happened to be one of them. Conquerers throughout history have seldom been deterred by grand gestures. Adolph Hitler, for one, had a program of aggrandizement in mind from the day he came to power, and no amount of U.S. moralizing dissuaded him from a jot of it.

In that sense, the United States was partly responsible for the holocaust that followed. Had it played a more conventional role in world affairs, it is conceivable that Hitler and Mussolini might have been stopped before they got started. The League of Nations tried to take a stand against both dictators as they reached out for conquest, but without the cooperation of the United States, the effort proved futile.

Stopping Japan would have been another matter. The Japanese believed that geography and history had endowed them with a "special"—that is, imperialistic—relationship to China, and they openly resented Yankee intermeddling. But the intermeddling continued. Americans themselves wanted to trade with China, which they regarded as being ripe for Western-style democracy and a Christian way of life. So, when Japan attacked Manchuria (northern China) in 1931, the United States, though it took no action, entered bitter complaints. By 1937 the war had spread to southern China, and Japanese bombers were wreaking havoc on the coastal cities. With supreme reluctance, Americans began beating their plowshares back into swords.

On September 1, 1939, the Second World War broke out in Europe. Hitler's piecemeal conquests of his neighbors—Austria, Czechoslovakia, and now Poland—had finally forced England and France to act. For a while it appeared that general hostilities might still be avoided, but in the spring of 1940 Hitler struck westward with stunning ferocity. Mighty France, which had withstood German assaults for four long years during World War I, crumpled like a wad of paper before Guderian's tanks, and by midsummer England was fighting for its life.

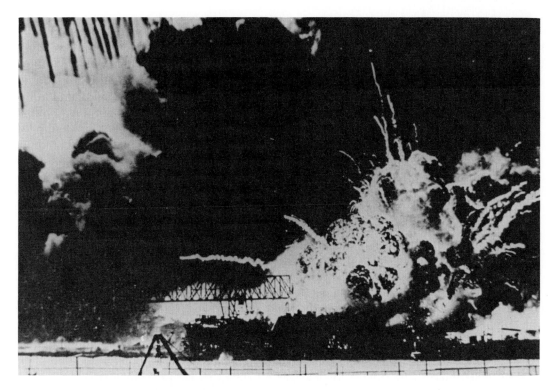

The Japanese attack on Pearl Harbor, December 7, 1941: Settled with dramatic simplicity. (Library of Congress)

Only then did it become evident—with a shock—that the American policy of moral leadership had failed. Grand gestures had not deterred the march of aggression nor had they preserved the peace. U.S. trade with China, the well-being of friendly powers, and the maintenance of world stability had all been weakened by American uncertainty—and yet the uncertainty dragged on. So horrified had Americans been of World War I, and so disillusioned by the treaty that ended it, that for more than two years the United States still kept clear of the conflict. Then, on a Sunday morning in December of 1941, the Japanese settled everything with dramatic simplicity. They attacked the American fleet at Pearl Harbor and bombed most of it into oblivion.

Leader of the Free World

As though aroused from a sound slumber, Americans quickly brought doubt and vacillation to an end. They cleanly repudiated isolationism and gave up on the idea of moral leadership. For better or worse, the United States was in the world at last.

Indeed, for the first time in the twentieth century, the U.S. had found a winning role for itself on the world stage. It had played the aggressor in its dealings with Spain, and it had played the cat's-paw (or thought it had) in World War I. But here was a situation made to order. In fighting for a stable world, a rational world, and a world reasonably accessible to American enterprise, the U.S. was clearly fighting for its own interests. Yet in fighting to destroy

American Virtue and the Second World War

The Founders had often wondered what, if anything, would keep American virtue alive. One answer, sadly enough, was war. In the Civil War, as we have seen, there was a tremendous outpouring of public spiritedness, on both sides of the Mason-Dixon line. There was an equally impressive one during World War II.

The virtue was manifest first of all in America's war aims, which could scarcely have been more selfless. It is true that U.S. interests were threatened by the Axis powers, but it is equally true that Americans fought simply for the Four Freedoms. This was made clear by their treatment of conquered enemies. Germany and Japan were both helped to their feet after the war. Their peoples were fed and clothed, and their economies brilliantly reconstructed. And as soon as democratic elements were able to assert control in each country, constitutions were drafted, elections held, and the occupation forces speedily withdrawn. In Japan, which expected a Carthaginian peace and even the loss of the emperor, the rule of Douglas MacArthur was so beneficent and evenhanded that he remains a national hero to this day.

Virtue of a more personal sort was required to sustain the daily war effort. Civilians on the home front cheerfully put up with rationing, shortages, restrictions, and blackouts. Consumer goods were in short supply, gasoline and rubber (hence travel) were stringently rationed, and even some food items, such as meat and sugar, were limited. Beyond that, consumers were expected to salvage scrap metal, to save fat and grease, to donate blood, and to plow their earnings into war bonds. At their jobs they worked hard, kept absenteeism low, put in long hours, and generally forswore the privilege of striking. In heavily congested regions like the San Francisco Bay area, some workers slept in "hot beds" in six-hour shifts, while others commuted up to five hours a day. But the dedication paid off. Henry Kaiser's Richmond, California, shipyard was soon building Liberty Ships in five days flat.

Women in the labor force were a special wonder. Rosie the Riveter, as she was called, handily learned to weld, solder, and operate a gantry crane. In Henry Ford's mile-long assembly line at Willow Run, where thousands of Rosies were employed, giant B-24 Liberators roared to life at the rate of one an hour and flew off (with female pilots at the controls) for the battlefront. The world had never seen anything like it.

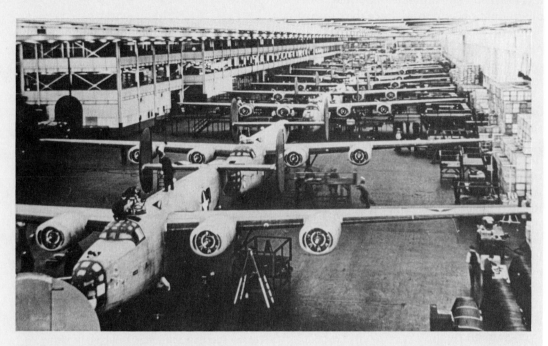

B24 Liberators rolling off the assembly line at
Willow Run: The world had never seen anything
like it. (Library of Congress)

In war, of course, the ultimate sacrifice was death on the battlefield. Hitler was
quite certain that Americans were not up to much of that, especially where their own
soil was not threatened, but again he was wrong. The bloody carnage at Iwo Jima,
Monte Cassino, and Utah Beach amply attested to U.S. fighting morale. In a war that
offered neither gain nor glory, the American G.I., so aptly symbolized by Bill
Mauldin's "Willie and Joe" cartoons, was quietly dedicated to getting a nasty job over
with—and to making the world safe for democracy.

dictatorship, to promote national self-determination, and to advance the cause of human freedom, the U.S. was equally in pursuit of Mission. Both sides of the American mind, self-interest and virtue, could finally work together.

Meanwhile, the United States was suddenly a leader in a world at war. Although the conflict itself is beyond our scope here, a couple of general points are worth remembering. First, America neither fought nor won the war single-handedly: for every American killed in combat twenty-five Russians lost their lives. Second, however, American industrial production again made the difference between winning and losing, not just for the United States but for everyone. Despite the fact that German U-boats were sinking half a million tons of Allied shipping a month, American factories managed to keep up with the losses and even gain on them.

A third point to bear in mind is that not only production but technology played a role in the war, and here again the United States held the winning cards. Were aircraft carriers the key to the Pacific? U.S. shipyards turned out ever bigger and better ones, and constantly improved the planes that landed on their decks. Was strategic bombing a critical factor? The United States produced ever faster and heavier bombers, and armed them with ever deadlier weaponry. Did explosive devices prove decisive? The United States perfected the most powerful explosive device known to man, and ended the war by dropping it on Japan.

Even so, the fighting progressed slowly. Hitler entrenched his armies across the length and breadth of Europe and then launched a massive attack on the Soviet Union. Battles on the Russian front were so immense as to dwarf the imagination, counting their casualties in the millions.

Advertisement promoting the American war effort: For the first time self-interest and public virtue worked together.

Through a number of such engagements, Russia held the Germans at the gates of Moscow and slowly began driving them back. Meanwhile, the United States and Great Britain landed in North Africa in 1942 and swept Rommel's panzers from the desert. They then blasted their way across Sicily and on into Italy, where a disheartened Mussolini was knocked out of the war.

By the summer of 1944 the Allies were prepared to assault Hitler's "Fortress Europe." A gigantic invasion crossed the English Channel in the morning hours of June 6 and hit the beaches at Normandy. After six weeks of heavy fighting, General Patton's tanks broke out at Saint-Lo and swept eastward across France. There would remain a few dying gasps from Hitler's once-victorious army (the most audible

Churchill, Roosevelt and Stalin at the Yalta
Conference: A few wrinkles to iron out later on.
(U.S. Army)

being the Battle of the Bulge in December)
but the writing was clearly on the wall. The
only question remaining was how to build
from the Allied victory a lasting world
peace.

The Cold War

As the war drew to a close in the spring of
1945, some predicted the dawning of an
American Century. After all, the United
States was now virtually alone on the world
stage. Russia was broken and bleeding.
France had been conquered. Britain only
barely survived the conflict and its once-
mighty empire was ready for the scrap
heap. China had been badly mauled by
Japan—and Japan lay smoldering in ruins.
Presumably the U.S. could have negotiated any sort of peace it wanted.

Yet, incredibly, within five years the
United States would be back at war—a
hopeless, winless war—and the peace that
followed would be the most vexatious,
troublesome, and threatening in history.
Why did the *Pax Americana* become the
Cold War? Generally speaking, because the
world, after centuries of comparative stability, had suddenly undergone a fundamental change. With the abrupt exit of the
traditional powers, an unstable political
vacuum had opened from Europe to the Far
East. To make matters worse, the U.S. and
the Soviet Union, the only real powers left,
happened to be ideological adversaries,
each with its own deeply held "ism." And
finally, nuclear weapons had now made it
possible for either side to utterly destroy
the other—along with the rest of mankind. It was an ironic twist. The United

The Berlin Airlift

Just how far the United States was willing to go in countering Soviet aggression was revealed in the summer of 1948, when the Russians, in a deliberate provocation, suddenly closed the overland access routes to West Berlin. Their city still in ruins from the Allied bombing, Berliners now found themselves pawns in the most ruthless power play of the Cold War—for Stalin had determined to starve them into communism.

He hadn't figured, however, on the inventive mind and steel-trap will of the U.S. military governor, Gen. Lucius D. Clay. A soft-spoken, courtly mannered Georgian, Clay began shaping an American response to the Soviet outrage on the spot. Indeed, within hours of the blockade's announcement, a battered C-47, loaded with foodstuff, rolled off the runway at Frankfurt's Rhein-Main Airbase and headed northeast for the beleaguered city.

What? Supply two and a half million people by air? Keep food on their tables and clothing on their backs and coal in their fireplaces? Keep their factories running and their jobs intact—with airplanes? The notion was too preposterous to think about. Joseph Stalin hadn't, either.

But while the world looked on in blank astonishment, Clay set about to do just that. In cooperation with the British, American air transports filled the skies over Berlin with the angry throb of their engines. Every three minutes, day and night, week in and week out, summer and winter, a cargo ship taxied to a stop at Tempelhof Aerodrome and was immediately engulfed by stevedores. Its food, clothing, and 110-pound sacks of coal were loaded into waiting trucks while the pilot grabbed a Coke in the orange and white control tower. Then it was back into the air and westward toward Frankfurt.

It was the can-do sort of challenge that Americans liked best, and in accepting it they were clearly in their element. One had only to listen to the radio voices emanating from the Tempelhof tower:

Give me an ETA on EC 84. . . . That's flour coming in on EC 72. . . . Roger. . . . Ease her down. . . . Where the hell has 85 gone? Oh yeah, overhead. . . . Wind is now north northwest. . . . The next stupid Charlie 47 has nothing on his manifest. . . . Are you in charge of putting de-icer fluid in aircraft? Well, who the hell is?

The costs, of course, were astronomical. A fifteen dollar bag of coal cost $175 to tote over the air bridge, as the Germans called it. At four thousand tons of supplies a day, the tab exceeded $500,000. Then, too, the old C-47s, already clunkers, were worn to exhaustion in a few short months. The landing gear collapsed on one. Another flew

American air transports filled the skies over Berlin
(UPI/Bettmann Newsphotos)

without a door. A third came in streaking flames. In the first four months alone, there were two fiery crashes and a half-dozen fatalities. Still the echo of aircraft engines droned on.

The Soviets were dumbfounded. Here was an issue of their own choosing, and they were losing badly on it. Yak fighter planes occasionally buzzed the transports testily, but, short of starting World War III, there was little else they could do. The United States, by contrast, reaped a harvest of goodwill. German children, taught from birth to despise the "Amis," gazed skyward in awe as each new installment of Operation Vittles lumbered past. Occasionally, they even found candy floating down to them in little parachutes.

And thirteen months later, when the Soviets figured they had taken enough of a beating, they lifted the blockade.

States, having come to terms with the Old World at last, suddenly found itself grappling with a new one.

The two sides immediately got off on the wrong foot. President Roosevelt had made a number of wartime agreements with the Soviet leadership—agreements that were critically necessary while the bombs were still falling—and all of them were now subject to misunderstanding. Who had promised to do what in exchange for what? Different parties remembered things differently. And Roosevelt, who at the Yalta Conference in January of 1945 had only a few weeks to live, had made some of the agreements rather lightly, confident that he could iron out the wrinkles later on.

The critical misunderstanding came over Poland. It was there that the war had begun in the first place, and Polish-Americans were eager to restore its lost freedom. Joseph Stalin took a different view. He saw Poland as a corridor for the tanks that had ripped into his homeland in 1941, and was determined that it would never be so used again. His promise to hold free elections in Poland was a promise he never meant to keep.

Soon charges of bad faith were hurling back and forth. Harry Truman, still dazed by his elevation to the presidency after Roosevelt's sudden death on April 12, made a bad situation worse with his quarterdeck bluntness. For his part, Stalin took Truman's bluster seriously and used it to justify further advances. By 1947 an "iron curtain" had fallen across the European continent.

But if American diplomats made beginner's mistakes, they also scored some critical bull's-eyes. With the so-called Marshall Plan, for example, the United States moved surefootedly to stabilize and rejuvenate the teetering European economy. And when Russian machinations threatened to topple the governments of Greece and Turkey, a veteran Kremlinologist by the name of George Kennan came up with a method for countering them. The U.S. could economically rehabilitate the imperiled governments, Kennan suggested, and thus contain the Soviet threat.

Indeed, containment, in various guises, became the centerpiece of American foreign policy for the next twenty years. It was another twist of irony. The once-aloof United States now found itself the fireman of the world, rushing here and there to quench the latest conflagration. The Soviets were adept at lighting new fires, too, endlessly testing their adversary's resolve.

Meanwhile the world was becoming ever more dangerous. Nuclear weapons grew increasingly more sophisticated and their delivery systems increasingly impervious to enemy defenses. Soon the only defense for either side was its ability to annihilate the other. It was fervently hoped that this mutual deterrence would continue to protect life on earth while the two superpowers went on jousting at one another in Berlin, in the Middle East, in the Caribbean, in the Horn of Africa, and in Southeast Asia.

Korea and Vietnam

The mounting pressures of the Cold War sent Americans into a deep psychological turmoil. Indeed, the soul-searching virtually recapitulated their diplomatic history. Were they being too self-interested? they asked. Was their opposition to the Soviets really only "Yankee imperialism" in

Vietnam precipitated a spiritual crisis among the American people (UPI/Bettmann Newsphotos)

backed one party and the United States backed the other. In June of 1950 the conflict became military when Kim decided to reunite Korea by force.

It was a bleak, messy, unhappy war, only slightly less absurd than it was portrayed on episodes of "M.A.S.H.," and neither side came close to winning it. Before it was over the United States had to fight not only the Soviet-armed North Koreans, but Communist China as well. As the Chinese rushed wave upon wave at American positions in the dismal winter of 1951, it occurred to some policy makers that containment had gone awry.

George Kennan himself was one of them. It was not possible to contain Soviet expansionism *militarily*, Kennan pointed out, only *economically*. If it came to a shooting war, and especially a conventional shooting war, then the Communist nations with their superior numbers would have the advantage. Having learned that lesson painfully, the United States extricated itself from the Korean "police action."

Vietnam

And yet within a decade, the Korean debacle was repeating itself, like a serial nightmare, in Vietnam. The two Vietnams, North and South, had once been part of French Indochina. In the 1930s a communist-inspired liberation movement led by Ho Chi Minh began to make life difficult for the French, and after World War II it steadily gained momentum. The French continued to ride the tiger until 1954, when Vietnam was partitioned by the United Nations, divided between Ho's followers and a pro-Western regime, and left to its fate.

disguise? Was it wise for them to be committed all around the world—wasn't some sort of isolationism really a better idea? Were they trying to accomplish too much with military hardware and too little with negotiation? Were their methods—especially their covert methods—a betrayal of their own ideals? And was their unflagging defense of capitalism well advised—when so many capitalistic regimes happened to be so unadmirable?

Korea

U.S. involvement in two extralegal, undeclared wars brought the soul-searching to a head. The Korean War began as a family quarrel between the fanatic Kim II Sung in the northern half of the Korean Peninsula and a newly minted democracy (of sorts) in the southern. The Soviet Union

Ho's insurgency sputtered on, of course, now virtually unopposed, and that fact posed a now familiar dilemma. Had the United States any business intervening in an Asian civil war in order to stop the spread of communism? Presidents Eisenhower and Kennedy both thought so, if the scale of the intrusion could be kept small. They sent a handful of military advisors.

What followed seemed to be straight out of an isolationist's textbook. The government of South Vietnam proved to be corrupt and incompetent, despised by its own citizens. The war itself proved to be a quagmire, pulling the United States in deeper and deeper with its every move. And the enemy proved to be absolutely indomitable. "You will kill ten of us for every one we kill of you," prophesied North Vietnam's General Giap, "and it is you who will tire of it."

Young Americans tired of it quickly. It was they who had to bear the brunt of the fighting, and they found the issues of the war beyond fathoming. Some dodged the draft in artful ways. Others fled abroad. And still others formed themselves into a peace movement that shook the foundations of the republic. Chanting "Hell no, we won't go," they rampaged through the streets, burning their draft cards and firebombing recruitment centers. They muscled the ROTC off dozens of college campuses and then began shutting down the colleges themselves.

The morale of U.S. troops was often not much higher. Many soldiers had been drafted out of the ranks of the peace movement, and they took along their drugs and their radicalism. Relations between themselves and the Vietnamese went from bad to worse. Viet Cong (guerrilla) suspects were sometimes pitched out of helicopters as a part of their "interrogation," while whole villages were obliterated in fire fights. At the village of My Lai 4, an American patrol threw men, women, and children into a ditch and machine-gunned them all.

By 1966 the American presence in Vietnam had escalated to half a million men. The decision to raise the ante had been made by Lyndon Johnson, who had become president upon the assassination of John F. Kennedy in 1963. Johnson came into office with the hope of establishing a "Great Society" in the United States, and of perfecting the promise of American life. But everywhere he turned he saw Vietnam—and soon his Great Society was in tatters. So controversial did the war become that in 1968 Johnson threw in the towel.

The Turning Point

It was a year of decision for others as well, for Vietnam had precipitated a spiritual crisis among the American people. Just where *did t*hey stand, Americans asked themselves, in regard to their role among the nations? A century ago they had looked upon world politics—with its nationalism, imperialism, and militarism—with supreme disdain. Now voices whispered that it was they who were the spread-eagle nationalists, they who were the neo-imperialists, they whose generals were out of control. America had not only joined the world, it was said, it had surpassed it.

But other voices spoke contrarily. Vietnam was not self-interest run amok, they said; Vietnam was in the highest tradition of republican virtue. After all, hadn't the United States gone halfway around the world, and at no small expense, to succor a struggling democracy? What better example of American Mission could be found?

It was a question over which Americans would remain bitterly divided. Both sides agreed, however, that the United States could not go on as it had. It lacked the resources—military, economic, and moral—to continue being the all-purpose fireman. The calls for a peace with honor in Vietnam grew ever more hollow, until it was clear that the U.S. would accept peace on any terms.

The American Role

In 1974, when the last shots were fired, the United States had been standing on the world stage for three quarters of a century. It had ushered in no *Pax Americana*, nor had it solved the diplomatic problems of the ages. On the contrary, American influence had often made situations even more complex and morally ambiguous than they already were. The problem, it was suggested, was that American thinking about the world had always been double-minded. On the one hand, Americans were a self-interested people, and they had thought of the world as their oyster. On the other hand, they had thought of themselves as being above the fray of geopolitics, and had searched for some sort of higher Mission. With one side of their being pulling toward self-interest and the other pulling toward virtue, the result had been contradiction.

Undoubtedly, there was some truth to the observation. At times the United States had indeed acted in its narrow self-interest, and in the mid-1980s it continued to do so. If diplomacy beyond Vietnam showed anything, it was that America could play the international game pretty much as others did. It committed its resources to the areas of its own interests—Central America, the Middle East—and was not too fussy about the morals of its allies or the methods of its agents. If Chile's Allende posed a problem, plot his downfall. If Salvadoran death squads murdered people, kindly ask them not to. If Nicaragua proved unfriendly, bankroll a guerrilla war against it.

Yet American foreign policy also continued to reflect the nation's better self. By and large, it was a foreign policy that worked, as it always had, to expand human freedom. Beyond the ambiguities of application, whenever the United States had come down squarely on a moral issue, however unpopular the position, however difficult the action, and however unfortunate the outcome, it had usually been for the purpose of defending someone's liberty. With all its faults, it was the foreign policy of a free—and freedom-loving—people.

28

The America Question

Concepts

The America Question
Watergate
Structural Fallacy
Judicial Activism

We are also "The People" (Jon Jacobson)

Watergate

The final goodby was pitiful. The president, worn, haggard, his eyes red-rimmed, stood before the members of his administration and rambled extemporaneously for nineteen minutes about his mother, his father, and his hero, Teddy Roosevelt, who had also known some setbacks. The world needed good people, he noted irrelevantly, good farmers, good businessmen, good carpenters. There was an uneasy stir in the room when he mentioned good plumbers, but he seemed not to notice. He finished the speech abruptly and exited to polite applause. With his family, he walked through the East Room and out onto the south lawn, where a red carpet incongruously rolled down to a waiting olive drab helicopter. Then, shaking the hand of Gerald Ford, his appointed successor, Richard Nixon embarked on his last flight as president of the United States.

The road into exile was a long one. It had begun more than two years earlier, in January of 1972, when G. Gordon Liddy, a self-styled soldier of fortune and member of the secret White House Plumbers (whose job it was to "stop leaks"), had spelled out to Attorney General John Mitchell, Presidential Counsel John Dean III, and Acting Director of the Committee to Re-elect the President (CREEP) Jeb Stuart Magruder, a comprehensive intelligence-gathering plan that would include electronic surveillance, abduction of radical leaders, and the use of call girls to pry information out of leading Democrats. But the world first knew of the affair the following June, when an alert security guard at the Watergate Hotel noticed that a door lock had been taped open. Upon the arrival of the D.C. police, five men were arrested in the offices of the Democratic National Committee.

Although everyone in the Nixon administration denied knowledge of "this very bizarre incident," Press Secretary Ron Ziegler noted prophetically that "certain elements may try to stretch this beyond what it is." Indeed they did. Throughout the election summer Democrats referred back to it repeatedly. But, then, they were losing badly; what else could they do?

The burglary was also taken seriously by two reporters from the *Washington Post*. Carl Bernstein and Robert Woodward were anything but journalistic superstars. Being young, hitherto undistinguished, and not conspicuously talented, they had been assigned to the police-court beat, and they were sitting in the courtroom the day the burglars were arraigned. Something about it all smelled fishy to them. For one thing, names in the burglars' address books connected them to both E. Howard Hunt, a one-time CIA agent, and G. Gordon Liddy, formerly with CREEP. And for another, they had in their possession thirty-two crisp, sequentially-numbered hundred-dollar bills, obviously freshly laundered.

Like a pair of eager bloodhounds, the reporters set about to track down the money. They were aided by a tip from an inside source—known to this day only as Deep Throat—who told them that the trail was indeed worth following. But the tracking proved to be hard work. Dozens of doors were slammed in their faces. Scores of leads petered out. Almost everyone connected with the White House, with CREEP, or with the burglars themselves was either afraid or unwilling to talk. And there were only so many news stories that could be written on the basis of speculation and hearsay. The day soon arrived when *Post* editor Ben Bradlee, himself out in deep water, told the reporters to fish or cut bait. Finally, though, they got a bite. Almost fortuitously they learned that the burglars' money could definitely be traced to a slush fund at CREEP.

With this revelation, U.S. District Court Judge John J. Sirica was certain that he was not trying an ordinary case of burglary, and he hounded the Watergate defendants mercilessly to tell what they knew. Faced with the prospect of forty years in jail (Sirica's provisional sentence), the burglars' stone wall of silence began to crack. By March 23, chief burglar Frank McCord was willing to admit that perjury had been committed at the trial and that higher-ups had been involved in the break-in.

Meanwhile, the Senate had voted 77-0 to establish a select committee under North Carolina's Sam Ervin to probe into the Watergate affair. Plain-spoken, down-to-earth, and quintessentially Southern, Ervin respected the law and the Bible about equally, and pursued Watergate culprits with a wrathful vengeance. Under the committee's relentless questioning, the real story of the break-in began to unfold. Acting FBI Director L. Patrick Gray disclosed that John Dean, who had supposedly investigated the affair and given the White House a clean bill of health, had received FBI reports to the contrary. Jeb Stuart Magruder confessed to perjuring himself at the burglary trial, and went on to implicate Dean and Mitchell. Dean, in turn, implicated H.R. Haldeman and John Ehrlichman, the two men closest to the president, and stated categorically that Nixon himself had taken part in the coverup. And there had been plenty to cover up. The burglary at the DNC had merely been the tip of an iceberg that included blackmail, extortion, intimidation, influence peddling, bribery, campaign-law violations, illegal wiretaps, political sabotage, and coldly systematic obstruction of justice.

By now the sharks were swimming in ever tighter circles about Richard Nixon. "What did the president know and when did he know it?" asked Republican Howard Baker again and again of the Ervin Committee witnesses. Could the testimony of John Dean, a self-confessed liar, really be accepted? It was the job of Harvard Law Professor Archibald Cox to find out. Named special prosecutor on May 18, he began to sift through the mounting evidence and formulate specific indictments. The White House, meanwhile, began visibly falling apart. Officials who only weeks before were smiling about "a third-rate burglary attempt" were now accusing one another of felony. Dean, Mitchell, Magruder, Chapin, Krogh, and Strachan were all offered up for sacrifice. On April 30 Nixon asked for the resignations of Ehrlichman and Haldeman, proclaiming his own innocence yet again.

Then came the bombshell. On July 16 a former White House aide testified that a secret recording system had been installed in the Oval Office, and that most of the incriminating conversations existed on tape! Both Cox and Ervin subpoenaed the tapes immediately, of course, but Nixon, stoutly claiming "executive privilege," refused to give them up. While the case of *U.S. v. Nixon* made its way through federal appeals, Watergate took another unseemly turn. On a lively Saturday evening in October, Nixon suddenly fired the special prosecutor, presumably on account of his excessive zeal, and before the dismissal could be carried out, he had to accept the resignations of two attorneys general as well. After this "Saturday Night Massacre," the House Judiciary Committee began looking into the possibility of impeachment.

When the Supreme Court finally decided, 8-0, that the president must indeed surrender the tapes, more pulling and hauling ensued. Two of the tapes mysteriously disappeared. A third fell victim to an eighteen-minute buzz, the result of at least five separate erasures. But even among what remained the evidence was damning. Richard Nixon, in a conversation laced with crude expletives, could be heard talking to Haldeman on June 23, six days after the break-in, and matter-of-factly arranging for the CIA to thwart the FBI's investigation. Senator Baker learned at last what the president knew and when he knew it.

On July 24, 1974, the House Judiciary Committee began voting affirmatively on articles of impeachment. A week later, under pressure from Presidential Counsel James St. Clair, whose own hearing of the June 23 tape had left him stunned, Nixon publicly admitted his role in the coverup. It was the last and heaviest of the Watergate bombshells, and, although Nixon seemed not to realize it at the time, it made his resignation of the presidency absolutely mandatory.

In the course of U.S. history, seasons of difficulty have always thrust the America Question back to the fore. The Civil War, the Great Depression, the Civil Rights Revolution, the Korean and Vietnam Wars each caused Americans to examine themselves all over again. But nothing brought the America Question into sharper focus than Watergate. "What went wrong?" Americans asked themselves with perplexity. Had their materialism finally caught up with them? Were their institutions slipping from their moorings? Had the corruption feared by the Founders finally eaten away their sense of virtue? Had history overtaken them?

Much, of course, *had* changed. Since the American Republic had come into the world, its territory had more than doubled in size, its population had grown seventy-five-fold, its prosperity had eclipsed all precedent, its technology had revolutionized the world, its society had grown enormously complex, and its foreign relations had vastly proliferated. But had the *basic* things changed? Was human nature still capable of producing political virtue and still controllable by a constitutional structure? Was the rule of law still a working reality? Had or had not the American

system, so appropriate to the eighteenth century, been outmoded by the passage of time? In the light of Watergate, these were questions worth thinking about.

The Market System

To begin with, how was the market system faring in the era of Watergate? There was no simple answer. The self-interest that made the market system operate was still in evidence, of course, and the system still seemed capable of controlling it. But the system itself was much altered. The Great Depression and the New Deal—whose influence was still very much alive—had given *laissez-faire* capitalism a thorough going over. In the workplace there were now maximum hours and minimum wages. Social insurance in the form of Social Security, Medicare, and Medicaid was firmly entrenched. Regulatory agencies oversaw almost every aspect of business life, and a variety of tariffs, quotas, and price supports were now a part of the American scene. Richard Nixon, a conservative Republican, had recently reacted to brushfire inflation by clamping down wage and price controls.

For all that, the system still seemed sound. Real income stood twenty times higher than in Jefferson's day, and continued economic growth was virtually taken for granted. Poverty was still a problem, to be sure, and probably always would be. But, to keep the problem in perspective, it was well to remember that the official poverty level in the United States was above the per capita income of Brazil.

What did the future hold for the market system? No one, of course, could say. But the easy public confidence it had enjoyed before the Great Depression had not yet returned and quite possibly never would. Americans had become sophisticated about economics, and their sophistication had taught them to be skeptical. Where they once saw nothing but sunny skies overhead, they now scanned the horizon for clouds. Among the clouds they watched most closely were the following:

Population. The U.S. population continued its upward climb, not solely through the birth rate, which had begun to fall off, but through immigration. For economic growth to continue, of course, GNP had to expand faster than population. This promised to be especially difficult for countries like Mexico, whose population explosion had begun to drive hundreds of thousands across the American border. And U.S. labor had begun to fret about the threatened loss of jobs.

Declining Resources. It seemed equally clear that the day of cheap U.S. resources was near an end. Diminishing rapidly were the virgin continent's endless forests, its huge mineral deposits, its accessible supplies of energy. Indeed, during the Watergate embroglio, an Arab oil boycott brought this situation home with a shock.

Motorists waited in line for hours to buy gasoline, and when supplies resumed the price had quadrupled. A memorable cover of *Newsweek* showed Uncle Sam standing in the snow on a dark winter's night, peering into an empty cornucopia.

Environmentalism. Concern for the environment in the era of Watergate was both real and well founded. Industrial pollution, which had already turned Lake Erie into a cesspool, had come to threaten a vast number of American waterways. The Los Angeles smog alert, once only occasional, seemed to ring incessantly, while in the East, acid rain was melting bronze statues like bars of soap. Garbage ringed American cities, landfills oozed toxic chemicals, pesticides turned up in the bone marrow of children. Americans suddenly awoke to the fact that they might be destroying the earth.

Yet what was the alternative? The industry that created the pollution also created the wealth. Zero pollution, the goal that many environmentalists seemed to espouse, quite simply meant zero jobs, and on that basis compromise was hard to reach. And so, without market mechanisms to guide them, Americans continued to debate extreme alternatives—no pollution on the one hand, no growth on the other—and to hope that somehow the problem might go away.

Inflation, Recession, and Economic Justice. The U.S. economy continued to experience inflation and recession. Inflation simmered steadily at 6 to 7 percent and occasionally threatened to boil into double digits. Recession visited the American scene every three to five years and wrought its customary havoc. The enormous expenditures of the Vietnam War had kept it at bay for almost a decade, but as soon as the fighting decelerated it began to creep back. Before the decade's end, the economy would witness "stagflation," where, to confound conventional wisdom, inflation and stagnation would somehow appear at the same time.

The question of economic justice also continued to dog the system's heels. This was partly due to the new social pluralism, which generated more and more groups contesting for slices of the economic pie. It seemed that no group ever got as much of the pie as it wanted, needed, or believed it had a right to. (Even the white middle class felt cheated.) To this problem there could never be a solution, for justice, like beauty, was in the eye of the beholder. Nevertheless, the perception that the market system could not deliver justice continued to work against it.

Intervention. Government intervention in the economy had always come at its price, as even the happiest of New Dealers would admit, but by the eve of Watergate the price had begun to seem onerous. Whether it was the Vietnam War and its accompanying anarchy, or the disastrous failure of Johnson's Great Society—big government at its biggest—something clearly had gone sour. Americans across the political spectrum suddenly seemed to turn away from the ethic of intervention and back toward that of the marketplace. However, whether they would actually dismantle what they had built and return to *laissez faire* seemed unlikely.

Market Virtues. Finally, what about the old market virtues: hard work, imagination, willingness to take risks? Some Americans fretted that such qualities were disappearing fast. In an oft-cited comparison, they pointed out that Japanese workers worked harder and longer for less compensation, and saved more of their income for investment. And Japanese businessmen clung to their companies with samurailike loyalty, used recreation time to brainstorm with colleagues, and returned to the office after supper. Were Americans, they asked themselves, still up to that?

For these and other reasons, the changes that had overtaken the market system seemed irreversible. Smokestack industries, once the pride of America, were dying by the score. Agribusiness still seemed to require massive subsidies. High interest rates, worsening trade imbalances, and worrisome government deficits always seemed to be throwing something out of kilter. And even flush times failed to bring the easy growth of the 1950s and 1960s. That Americans felt differently about the future was all too evident: polls revealed that for the first time in a century U.S. children did not expect to do as well as their parents had.

Where there was change, however, there was also opportunity, and Americans would prove that they could still seize it. With the development of the microprocessor, the world of computers opened before them, and they strode into it with confidence. Indeed, it was almost like the days of Henry Ford, with backyard tinkerers leading the way. One such hacker, Steven Wozniak, a boy still in school, put together a computer whose compactness, performance, and affordability reminded old-timers of the Model T. The fabulous success of Apple Computers was a much needed addendum to the American Dream.

Other tales of economic heroism were still in the making. An inventor named Robert Jarvik was tinkering with mechanical hearts; within the decade he would implant one in a human patient. Young George Lucas, operating in the film industry, was at work on a trilogy of science-fiction fantasies that would become the top-grossing movies of all time. And in the heart of the Rustbelt, a cashiered auto executive named Lee Iacocca would lay hold of the moribund Chrysler Corporation and produce in one year more profit than it had totaled in the previous sixty. The future of the market system was not without hope.

The Political System: Republican Virtue

What about the political system? The Founders, we recall, had based its operation on simple human virtue, especially *public* virtue, with what they called *auxiliary precautions* as a kind of backup system. How well had their plans been borne out by history? The question seemed especially relevant as the horrors of Watergate unfolded.

Republican Virtue and Historical Change

As some of the Founders had feared, history had not been particularly kind to American political virtue. The winds of change that gusted through the nineteenth century had blown much of the old thinking away. And the institutions that had anchored virtue had themselves been altered. Take the family, for instance. In early republican America, fathers were expected to teach their children patriotism in the ordinary course of things. As time passed, however, the family itself grew

troubled, and fathers were less and less able to teach anything. The inculcation of values fell to other institutions.

But those institutions also faltered. The church, for example, faltered badly. For the children and grandchildren of the Puritans, public virtue had been fostered by the tenets of a General Religion. With the passage of time, the General Religion began to fade, and individual churches seemed less and less effective at instilling moral precepts. Mainstream Christianity became formal and decorous once again, and the fires that had driven the Puritans in search of freedom seemed to burn ever lower.

The decline of religion was accompanied by the luxuriant growth of materialism. As grubby tenements gave way to tidy apartments and then suburban ramblers, the middle class had ever less concern for public responsibilities and ever more for creature comforts. Soon automobiles, boats, and campers were added to the list of American distractions, along with televisions, stereos, and home computers. Gadgets and gismos flooded the marketplace, promising to answer the phone, balance the checkbook, teach the kids arithmetic, and protect the house from burglars. One Abercrombie & Fitch item for "the man who has everything": a seventy-five dollar pistol that shot rubber bands.

Popular culture made its own contribution. Advertisements hammered away at the theme of me, me, me: *my* house, *my* car—*my* personal happiness. And for many Americans, such obsessive egoism needed little encouragement. After all, every night on prime-time television one could watch people presumably like oneself getting what they wanted any way they could. With a kind of nightmarish twistedness, programs like "Dallas," "Dynasty," and "Falcon Crest" came to represent what

Espionage: A Commentary on American Public Virtue?

Not since the Rosenberg case of the 1950s had a story of espionage so stunned the United States. Arrested and charged with spying were John Walker, his brother Arthur, his son Michael, and an associate, Jerry Whitworth. All of the accused were Navy men, and their careers situated them perfectly for espionage. Together they may have seriously compromised the United States in submarine warfare, amphibious operations and weaponry, communications coding systems, naval intelligence, and carrier tactics.

People, of course, asked why. After all, Arthur Walker and his wife were pillars of their community, described by neighbors as an all American family. Michael was something of a party-goer and beach bum, voted best-looking male graduate of his high-school class. And John, the ringleader, kept a photo of Ronald Reagan on his desk and "talked like a real patriot." None of them, obviously, had acted out of ideological considerations. Indeed, the apparent motive was much simpler: greed. John Walker, for one, was used to life in the fast lane. He owned a houseboat, an airplane, a prosperous suburban dwelling, and kept expensive female company. While attempting to recruit his daughter into the family spy ring, he said: "Why don't you let me help you make a lot of money."

Nor was this the first such case. Since 1975, thirty-eight people have been charged with espionage in the United States, and 21 have been convicted. Here are a few of their stories:

After leaving the CIA in 1970, David Barnett returned to Surabaja, Indonesia, and tried his hand at several businesses. After six years and serious losses, he typed out a note offering his services to the KGB for $70,000 and delivered it to the Soviet cultural attaché in Jakarta. They took him up on it.

William Holden Bell, an engineer with Hughes Aircraft in California, fell into financial difficulty in spite of his $50,000-a year income. A sympathetic Polish neighbor offered to bail him out in exchange for a few pictures of unclassified material. Once the hook was in, Bell couldn't stop, and soon he was photographing the plans for top secret weapons systems. He made $110,000.

American life was supposed to be about. Indeed, to many viewers, Watergate seemed like just another soap opera.

Ominous Straws In the Wind

Yet there were times when virtue seemed to stir back to life. There was an outpouring of public spirit in the early days of Kennedy's New Frontier, when everyone seemed to be volunteering for VISTA and the Peace Corps. However, there were other moments in the 1960s when virtuous behavior seemed utterly to have vanished. Among them were the following:

The Milgram Experiment. In one of the most unsettling experiments of modern times, residents of New Haven, Connecticut, were invited to participate in a Yale-sponsored study on learning. The study

In Silicon Valley, James D. Harper, Jr., found a bonanza of his own. By handing over details of a project for protecting Minuteman missiles from nuclear destruction, he was given an envelope stuffed with a thousand hundred-dollar bills. Harper's motivations were described by his lawyer as a desire for money and adventure.

And in Los Angeles, Richard Miller, overweight, slovenly, debt ridden, and reprimanded by his FBI bosses for poor performance, decided that selling Amway products from his government car was the hard way to get rich. In 1984 he was accused of offering FBI secrets to Russian emigres for $65,000. Two years later he was found guilty.

With these and other instances in mind, former CIA Director Richard Helms made a neat summary. "People are not particularly patriotic anymore," he said. "When they are faced with the opportunity [to spy], they say, 'Screw it. If I can make some money, why not?'" It is a logic that David Hume would have understood all too well.

John Marshall with a U.S. marshall: A logic David Hume would have well understood (UPI/Bettmann Newsphotos)

was actually psychological, and the community volunteers were its real subjects. They were taken, one at a time, into a room in which another human being was strapped to a chair and fitted with electrodes. The volunteer was then handed an adjustable rheostat and told that he controlled the amount of current to be passed through the human guinea pig. As the experiment proceeded, the guinea pig was supposedly given a learning exercise—matching pairs of words—in which every mistake was to be punished by higher and higher doses of electric shock. To the amazement of the researchers, the community volunteers quite willingly watched fellow human beings writhing in an agony (faked of course) that they themselves were causing. It was easy to see how the My Lai massacre had come about in Vietnam.

The Kitty Genovese Murder. On the night of March 13, 1964, Kitty Genovese, twenty-eight, manager of a bar in Queens, New York, was returning home to her apartment when an assailant stepped from the shadows, drew a knife, and sprang at her. She screamed: "Oh my God, he stabbed me! Please help me! Please help me!" But no one helped. Residents of the middle-class neighborhood threw open their windows and peered out into the darkness. One man shouted, "Let that girl alone." The rest went back to bed. The assailant, meanwhile, drove around in his car and returned. He calmly searched out the wounded girl, who had crawled into an alley for safety, and finished his night's work. Of the thirty-eight witnesses to the murder, only one, belatedly, called the police. Even more chilling were the excuses they offered when a reporter asked them why. "I didn't want my husband to get involved," explained a housewife through her half-opened door. "I was tired," said another. "I don't know," replied a third.

The New York Blackout. On the evening of July 17, 1972—one month after the Watergate break-in—the lights of Brooklyn, New York, suddenly blinked out, the result of an improbable electrical gridlock. For the most part, calm prevailed—indoors at least. Out in the streets it was a different situation. Lit eerily by the headlights of automobiles, people could be seen running through the blackness. They hurled rocks through store windows and jammed crowbars through the door locks, helping themselves to the merchandise inside. Before the power came back on, they had carted off literally millions of dollars worth of televisions, stereos, and assorted appliances, trundling the loot through the streets like so many deliverymen. They were white as well as black. They were middle-class as well as poor. And, most distressingly, they were of the law-abiding, as well as criminal, element. For five surreal hours, the restraint that controls all free societies simply vanished.

As straws in the wind, these incidents were ominous indeed. Moreover, they explained many of the actions of Watergate. For there, too, virtue seemed utterly to have collapsed. Minor functionaries, blameless themselves, refused to aid the investigation out of some skewed notion of loyalty. Accountants falsified documents, attorneys perjured themselves, and the head of the FBI burned evidence along with the Christmas trash. From the hirelings of CREEP to the president himself, everyone acted solely out of self-interest.

Public Virtue and Watergate

Or so it first appeared. Gradually, however, a broader view emerged. After all, Eliot Richardson and William Ruckelshaus had behaved well enough, both of them sacrificing their cabinet posts in the Saturday-Night Massacre. And John Sirica, the U.S. District Court judge who consistently ruled against Nixon, had displayed his own high courage. Republican members of the Ervin committee, such as Lowell Weicker and Howard Baker, had put their necks on the block to press the Watergate investigation, and their counterparts on the House Judiciary Committee had voted to impeach the head of their own party.

This, however, was the virtue of officeholders; what about the critically important virtue of the public? Reporters Bernstein and Woodward tenaciously stuck to their investigation of the Watergate break-in, even though dozens of doors were slammed in their faces. Their positions on the *Washington Post* became steadily more precarious as the investigation continued. Others on the *Post* had even more to lose. The editor, Ben Bradlee, stood to become a laughingstock among colleagues in the publishing world, who repeatedly advised him to forget about Watergate. And the owner, Kathryn Graham, had the possibility of legal action to think about. John Mitchell had confidently warned her not to "get caught in the ringer."

Now and then there were other players in the Watergate drama who might well have acted out of public virtue. Of Deep Throat's motives—as well as his identity—we shall probably never know. John Dean, though his own motives may have been mixed, came forward, despite darkly whispered threats, and told his story to the congressional investigators. Hugh Sloan wrathfully resigned from CREEP when the slush fund got out of hand. And one of the perpetrators, Dwight Chapin, became a born-again evangelist while serving time for his Watergate crimes.

Finally, there were a number of extremely courageous little people in the Watergate drama: bookkeepers, secretaries, clerks. They had little or nothing to gain by telling what they knew—and a great deal to lose. They lived by a code which held loyalty to the boss as the highest of virtues and indiscretion as the worst of sins. Nevertheless, here and there one of them was willing to come forward. Cowering like a frightened kitten and twisting her handkerchief into a tight spiral, an unnamed bookkeeper for CREEP told Carl Bernstein of the secret slush fund at committee headquarters from which the burglars received their pay. Why did she talk? Possibly she herself didn't know. But possibly, too, she heard the whispering of conscience.

There was another dimension to public virtue: the actions of the public at large. As angry letters and phone calls began to rain down upon the elected officials, it became clear that a small revolution was in progress. In the past, Americans had put up with a good deal of public misbehavior, but no more. There was a new wall of distrust between the people and the government—precisely as public virtue presupposed. On the other hand, the people also remained remarkably patient. If their faith was shaken in the government of the moment, it was not shaken in the system itself. As the system creaked along in pursuit of the malefactors, Americans calmly awaited the outcome.

Still, Watergate badly frightened them. For the first time, they faced the possibility that republican virtue could indeed fail. In 1976 Jimmy Carter campaigned for the Presidency on the theme of returning to American values. The theme was repeated again and again in the campaigns that followed. In calling for a recommitment to home, family, and community, winners and losers alike were attempting to articulate something they felt stirring within the American psyche. There was a part of the Constitution that was not written on paper, and without it constitutional government could not survive.

The Political System: Auxiliary Precautions

If Watergate proved a disappointment for those who believed in virtue, it proved a soaring triumph for those who favored auxiliary precautions. For, the shabbier

Evidence for the proposition that public virtue still lives may be found in the modern-day phenomenon of the "whistle-blower." Viewed solely in terms of self-interest, there are not many reasons to come forward and expose an employer's waste, mismanagement, or violation of public trust, and there are some excellent reasons against it. Whistle-blowers are often isolated, ostracized, and punished in subtle ways; more often still they are simply fired. Some typical examples:

Bertrand Berube, an official with the General Services Administration, uncovered wasteful GSA spending to the tune of $1.5 billion. His reward was to be demoted three times in succession, presumably as an inducement to resign.

James B. Nagel, a hospital administrator in Washington, D.C., discovered that staff members were misspending federal funds. When he complained publicly, he was reassigned as supervisor of maintenance. Nor was that all. "All of my working files and . . . my address book disappeared. All the knobs on my air-conditioning unit were removed and hidden. I was placed under constant surveillance."

A. Ernest Fitzgerald, a civilian cost analyst with the Air Force, disclosed a $2 billion cost overrun on the development of the C-5A military transport. Suddenly it was discovered that his civil service tenure had been granted in error, the result of a wildly improbable computer glitch. While reeling from that shock, he was informed that his job had been eliminated as part of a cost-saving retrenchment program. He spent years in the courts and hundreds of thousands of dollars before getting his job back.

Two engineers at B. F. Goodrich, after repeatedly trying to convince superiors that the braking system being developed by their company was in no way capable of stopping an A7D fighter on the runway, finally went to the FBI. Both of them were fired.

And in the most famous case of them all, Karen Silkwood, a Kerr McGee employee in Cimarron, Oklahoma, was on her way to talk to reporters about radiation hazards in the company's production of plutonium when, amid unexplained circumstances, her car was run off the road and she was killed.

If these are the costs, what are the benefits? The only conceivable one is the knowledge of making a contribution to the well being of society. For most whistle-blowers that, apparently, is enough.

virtue looked, the more impressive seemed the achievement of the system. Among the structural controls that operated precisely as the Founders had intended were the following:

Separation of Powers. It proved to be extremely fortunate, in the first place, that powers in the American government had been made separate. For the executive branch, as Watergate plainly demonstrated, was honeycombed with corruption. Both president and vice president (Spiro Agnew) were tainted. The attorney general wound up in jail. The CIA was neutralized in the early days of the coverup and the FBI soon followed it. As for the White House staff, the corruption had spread from the presidential assistants at the top to scores of functionaries throughout.

Congress, by contrast, was free of implication and hence free to act. Of course, members of the White House staff tried to halt its investigations. They used whatever tricks they still had in their bag to block the insistent question asking, but most of the tricks were found wanting. Ehrlichman and Haldeman could threaten and cajole those who had to answer to the president, but they could never intimidate Congress.

The independence of the courts also proved to be crucial. Nothing in the Watergate story was more significant than the fact that every pivotal question—including the custody of the White House tapes—was settled by a U.S. District Court. Judge John Sirica was not on anyone's list of prestigious federal officeholders. But because the Constitution had given him ample judicial power, and, more importantly, because it had given him total independence, he was able to order a sitting president to hand over necessary evidence. History offers very few parallels to that.

Checks and Balances. Several checks and balances were called into service by Watergate, but two of them were especially important. The first was the congressional power of investigation. It was a power that had sometimes been abused in the course of American history, but here it was used as the Founders had intended. We must remember that the Watergate burglars had already been put on trial, and that the judicial system had failed to pry the truth out of them. Before the Select Committee on Watergate, however, they began to spill everything. Simple perjury was one thing, it seemed; contempt of Congress was something else.

The second was the power of impeachment. We overlook its use because President Nixon was not in fact impeached. The more important fact, however, was that Nixon, like so many of his aides, stonewalled all action until the threat of impeachment became imminent. The press, the Congress, the people themselves had been clamoring for his resignation for some time, and his only reaction had been to go on television and swear "I am not a crook." It was only when the House Judiciary Committee voted affirmatively on three articles of impeachment that he finally decided to relinquish the presidency.

The Free Press. It was the press, of course, that broke Watergate open in the first place. Jefferson would have been pleased. Still, it was fortunate that the *Washington Post* enjoyed the protection of the First Amendment. The president's men, as would soon become clear, had stopped at almost nothing in dealing with their enemies.

"Dirty tricks" had been played on political opponents. Reputations had been smeared and careers ruined. Extortion and blackmail had been freely employed, illegal wiretaps installed, and the office of Daniel Ellsberg's* psychiatrist brazenly burglarized. Without the First Amendment as a shield, there is little doubt that Bernstein and Woodward would have been stopped in their tracks.

The Two-Party System. The party system itself lent a hand. When Watergate began to unravel, it was seen as a political godsend to the Democrats, who, after all, had taken quite a beating in the election. Time and again votes for decisive action divided neatly along party lines. In time, however, Republicans began to support the investigation too. Why let the Democrats become the party of integrity? they asked themselves. The effect of Watergate was to make veracity the primary political virtue.

The Structural Fallacy

Some Americans derived a different sort of lesson from the Watergate experience. If the Constitution's structural controls worked this effectively, they reasoned, then perhaps such controls were all that was really needed. The Founders had supposed that *virtue* was the foundation of a free society, and that the *auxiliary precautions* were merely a backup. For Americans living in the era of Watergate, it seemed possible that the Founders had had it backwards. It was the Constitution, not some vague notion of virtue, that seemed to be the keystone of liberty.

*Daniel Ellsberg was the one who filched the famous Pentagon Papers during the Vietnam War and published them.

Clearly this must be fallacious. For, how well would the Constitution's structure have worked without republican virtue? Could the Ervin committee really have dug out the truth if all of its witnesses, every single one of them, had been committed to stonewalling? No matter how well the Constitution's auxiliary precautions have served us, they have not served us *that* well. Political virtue is as necessary today as it was when the Constitution was first promulgated.

The Rule of Law

Equally problematic—and equally important—in the Watergate era was the question of whether, and to what extent, the United States had succeeded in maintaining the rule of law. And change was evident here as well. The rule of law, as the Founders had learned for themselves, was an exceptionally delicate flower. Quite apart from qualities of public virtue or the workings of a constitution, it often became a casualty in the modern world.

Modern Threats to the Rule of Law

Fear of Subversion. One theme of modern life that continually threatened the rule of law was fear of enemy subversion. In the days of isolationism, when there were few enemies to worry about, Americans found little reason to abridge the rule of law. In the twentieth century, however, all of that changed. When the United States entered World War I, it suddenly saw enemies everywhere: German-Americans were persecuted, opponents of the war villified, and political oddballs brutally silenced. Rose

Pastor Stokes, the wife of a prominent socialist, was sentenced to ten years in prison for saying: "I am for the people and the government is for the profiteers."

And in World War II it happened again. Despite the lessons of 1917, Japanese-Americans, some of them citizens for three generations, were ignominiously rounded up and shipped off to "relocation centers." In the age of total war, it seemed, constitutional freedoms were simply too risky.

Things grew even worse during the Cold War. After it was established that Soviet spies had stolen U.S. atomic secrets in 1949, a climate of suspicion and fear became almost palpable. A Wisconsin senator by the name of Joseph McCarthy took advantage of the paranoia to advance his own political ambitions. Declaring that there were hundreds—the exact number varied considerably—of "known communists" in the U.S. State Department, he embarked upon a sensational odyssey of witch hunting. Reputations were ruined, jobs were lost, careers were dashed, and hundreds of innocent people were persecuted before sanity returned.

Significantly, it was fear of subversion that was offered as a justification of Watergate. Radical groups were operating inside and outside the antiwar movement, and classified information was draining through a score of government leaks. In order to plug the leaks, the White House Plumbers were set up and placed in the charge of one G. Gordon Liddy. And while they were at it, they decided to check up on the Democrats.

Judicial Activism. At least one modern constitutional development also took its toll. Commencing with the liberal activists appointed to the Supreme Court by Franklin Roosevelt, federal judges began to subtly extend the reach of their authority. Capitalizing on the Constitution's occasional loose phrases and implied ideas, they created a world of possibilities for judicial intervention, as we saw in chapter nine. And, if these jurists stretched the limits of constitutional interpretation far enough, they found they could effectively write their own legislation.

The prime example—though there were other noteworthy ones—was abortion. Nowhere, of course, did the Constitution mention abortion, much less endow it with legal protection. By the doctrine of implied rights, however, it was possible to discern a right of privacy in the document, and that, in turn, could be applied to abortion. In the landmark case of *Roe v. Wade* in 1972, the Court argued that such a right indeed existed, and that neither state nor federal governments could abridge it.

Just how Americans felt about judge-made law reflected how they felt about specific issues. Liberals hailed *Roe v. Wade* while conservatives excoriated it. But this was precisely the point. To many Americans, pro and con, abortion was a matter for the democratic process to resolve, not the courts. For, once the courts stepped into the realm of the legislature, what was to stop them from creating an entire agenda of their own? To some Americans it seemed particularly chilling that *Roe v. Wade* was a product of the Watergate summer.

Big Government. The growth of powerful, interventionist government seemed to threaten the rule of law in a different way. When the Founders sketched out the American government on paper, it had a certain size in their minds, as well as a certain shape and organization. The growth of big government in the twentieth century vastly altered those proportions. And the growth did not occur in the areas described in the Constitution; it occurred in the bureaucracy further down. The Department of Agriculture, for example, had just twenty thousand employees in 1924, when farmers were still a sizable segment of the population; in 1980 it had 129,139.

Proliferating bureaucracy posed a new sort of difficulty. No matter how honest, how efficient, or how well-intentioned a government agency happened to be, it existed in a world essentially free from auxiliary precautions. Presidents had to answer to Congress, and vice versa, when it came to determining the broad contours of public policy, but in the lower echelons of the Post Office, the Customs Bureau, or the Internal Revenue Service, the operatives answered to no one. They wielded enormous power over the lives of citizens, and there was very little to hold them in check.

Then, too, government agencies tended to operate by their own logic. They were set up to solve a specific problem—but if the problem was really solved, simply and finally, they would be out of business. Accordingly, the problem tended never to be solved. Indeed, the problem often proliferated, making necessary the expansion of the agency in question. Meanwhile, a certain drift might set in. An office set up to forecast the weather might begin to forecast the climate, and then to forecast earthquakes. In time it might forget about the weather entirely.

This, too, was exemplified by Watergate. In the beginning, the White House Office was a small, secretarial affair, given custody of the president's paperwork. But as more and more people needed to see the president about more and more things, the WHO staff steadily expanded. Soon it was a sprawling organization with its own rules, its own behaviors—and its own ethics. By the eve of Watergate it had become a power unto itself. In one tiny office, far removed from the president's eye, sat Dwight Chapin, whose job it was to dream up "dirty tricks."

Beyond changes in the way the system itself operated, the rule of law may have lost ground in the hearts of the people. For, just as the nature of republican virtue seemed to change through time, so too did respect for the law. John Adams could boast that in America "the law is king." History has rendered that proposition rather doubtful.

For example, massive evasion of the Volstead Act during Prohibition, regardless of what one personally thought of drinking, did not speak well for the rule of law. Nor, for that matter, does equally massive evasion of the drug laws today. And in both cases what began as public disrespect for the law soon played into the hands of hardened criminals. Indeed, the merest glance at American history suggests that where unpopular (or controversial) laws exist, it is but a short step to general lawlessness.

This attitude is reflected in American popular culture, whose fascination with crime and violence has become legendary. To be sure, in our numberless Hollywood shoot-'em-ups, the good guys usually win. But do the good guys really represent law and order? Dirty Harry, gun in hand, grins at his quarry and says: "Go ahead! Make my day!" It is not, of course, abstract justice that will make the day in question—it is the animal pleasure of licensed murder. Such fare offers a dubious commentary on our respect for the rule of law.

San Jacinto County, Texas, is out in what used to be called the badlands. The population is a meager 11,500. Eighty percent of the land is federally owned. So it was a little surprising to some people that in San Jacinto County, with a law-enforcement establishment of one sheriff and five deputies, there were as many drug-related arrests as there were in sprawling Houston.

But, then, those people didn't know Sheriff J. C. Parker. "Humpy" Parker, as they called him, was a character right out of *Smokey and the Bandit*, drawling, paunchy, and supremely arrogant. Early in life, he was known for his ability to imitate a hound dog. More recently, he was known for law and order.

Here is how the system worked. Parker's men would station themselves along the highway at night, using their high beam headlights to scan the passing cars. If they saw a hippie, say, or a beat-up old car with no hubcaps, or a bumper sticker advertising Houston's leftward leaning K-101 rock station, they would pull it over.

Maybe the mufflers were too loud, the deputies would allege, or maybe the license plate was not well enough illuminated. (That was easy to charge: while one deputy spoke to the driver, another walked around behind and put out the light with his gun-butt.) Whatever the accusation, it was sure to be followed by a full-scale search.

And full-scale meant *full*-scale. The car's occupants stood with their hands on their heads, often at gunpoint, while Parker's men did their work. Sometimes they were stripped naked, men and women alike. Sometimes they got even worse.

Confiscated wholesale were any drugs the car might contain, along with anything else that happened to catch the deputies' eyes: one victim lost $2,500 worth of stereo equipment, plus a hundred records and tapes. The booty was resold—$300,000 worth of it in 1981 alone—and the funds stashed in San Jacinto's coffers. Twenty-one percent of the county's budget came from Parker's "customs service."

There was more to the San Jacinto reign of terror, much more. There were tow trucks hovering in the darkness like vultures, hauling forty-five or fifty cars a night back to town for a fat fee. There were bail-bondsmen moving in on the hapless victims, charging one hundred dollars for the necessary thousand-dollar bail. There were assorted fines and court costs totaling well into six figures. And there was even outright torture. If an arrestee complained too loudly about the abuse of his constitutional rights, it was amazing how his mind could be changed by handcuffing him to a chair, wrapping a towel around his head, and dripping water into it until he began to suffocate. Said one deputy: "The sheriff had a feeling he could get away with anything."

Long accustomed to the protections of the Constitution, many Americans say "it could never happen here." But it did.

A Feeling of Powerlessness

On a sandy landfill at the edge of New York Harbor, in the shadow of the World Trade Center, there stands a giant orange megaphone. It is so large that one has to climb ten feet to get to the mouthpiece. Its official name is the Freedom of Expression National Monument.

Its use? Shouting at the establishment. Arrayed before it are the towers of steel and glass that house the powers of America. You can shout at Wall Street if you so desire, or, by turning the megaphone a few degrees, you can shout at virtually any corporate headquarters in the country. Even city government:

"Hey, Koch, try some long-term thinking! Try the next hundred years!"

The shouter is a young man in his twenties. His German shepherd sits by patiently while the message is delivered. Then the two of them depart.

The megaphone was the brainchild of performance artists John Malpie and Erica Rothenberg and architect Laurie Hawkinson. It was funded by *Creative Times'* Art on the Beach Project. The idea was to provide the means for yelling at authority. People use it all day long. A girl, for instance, in a long dress and layered sweaters:

"Look up at that blue sky! Those white clouds! Enjoy it! Don't look at the steel, the concrete, the dog poop! Look up at the sky!"

She is more philosophical than most. Most, in fact, have a specific gripe: taxes, pollution, apartheid. They don't feel they can actually do anything about the problem in question, as citizens in a republic are supposed to, so they go out to the megaphone and simply shout about it. Indeed, the bronze plaque at its base reads:

This megaphone was designed to combat the sense of powerlessness felt by ordinary citizens in an age of omnipotent electronic media. You are cordially invited to step up and speak up.

Watergate took place amid just such an atmosphere. In the minds of the perpetrators, legal process had become totally eclipsed by the elemental passions. If someone was opposing them, no matter how legally, he had to be dealt with, no matter how *illegally*. Moreover, they assumed that everyone else was playing by their own alley-fight rules. Previous administrations had broken the law, they said. Their adversaries were breaking the law. Why couldn't they break the law too? One of the chief exponents of this logic, chillingly enough, was the attorney general himself.

We the People

So the America Question still remains unanswered. The Founders would probably not be surprised, for they did not regard the American Republic as complete for all time. In their minds, the Republic was like the uncapped pyramid still visible on the dollar bill: a good piece of work but unfinished.

Why? Because the Founders understood that the real constitution of a people was something more than words committed to parchment. The total constitution included the people's beliefs and values, their collective wisdom and intelligence, their sense of tradition, their particular way of doing things, and, not least, their accumulated historical experience. It was an unspoken agreement—a consensus—covering the multitude of things they held in common. It could never be complete, for it, too, changed with history.

In an autocracy, the constitution of the people did not count for much, because what happened in the end was determined by a privileged few at the top. In a republic, however, the constitution of the people counted for everything—and it remained literally in the people's own custody. Witness how the Founders themselves patiently molded and shaped it. They spent ten years of their lives arguing about how things ought to be in the British Empire. They then invested more years in fighting the Revolutionary War and struggling with the Articles of Confederation. Finally they recommenced their constitution making at Philadelphia.

The document written at Philadelphia worked so well that, to many Americans, it signaled the end of constitution making. Roughly the same thing happened with the market system. There was a season of lively debate about how economic society should be organized. At length the market system emerged and was itself incorporated into the national consensus.

By the eve of the U.S. Centennial in 1876, the consensus had become so strong and stable that Americans widely spoke of their institutions as having been inspired by God. Although this sense of givenness has in many ways served us well, it has also created the impression that the American Republic, despite what the Founders believed, is indeed finished for all time. This view, of course, conveniently minimizes our own involvement and responsibility. There is no sense in fretting about a pyramid that is already completed to perfection.

Yet, if Watergate taught us anything, it must be that what can be built by the hand of man can be destroyed the same way. One could argue, in fact, that in American history, construction and destruction have more or less run nip and tuck. Quite clearly, the Constitution of 1787, good as it was, was not perfect: we had to fight a Civil War to straighten out some wrinkles. Nor was the market system perfect: had it been so we would have escaped the Great Depression. And there have been other wrenching lessons. The battles we have fought over civil rights, the foreign wars into which we have been drawn, the changing nature of our society all have reworked the constitution of the people.

It is for this reason that the faith of the Founders must also be our faith. They believed that men could understand problems and find solutions to them. And they believed that in a republic it was the first responsibility of the citizen—every citizen—to do just that. They may not have envisioned a Philadelphia convention every few years, but they certainly did envision a continuing process of building, altering, refining and reforming. They might not have been surprised by Watergate—it was just the sort of thing they expected—but they most certainly would have been saddened by our inability to learn from it.

Near the close of the twentieth century we stand very much where the Founders stood before us. We look ahead and see only uncertainty. We look back and find history already far behind. Between the imperfectly perceived future and the imperfectly understood past, we have only ourselves, our humanity, and hopefully, our spark of divinity. How we will be viewed by those who come after us depends absolutely on what we choose to do with our own moment of time. We, too, are the people.

Aggregate. Refers to the whole economy (ex. aggregate demand, aggregate supply, etc.).

Aggregate demand. The total demand for goods and services in the economy as a whole.

Agricultural Adjustment Administration. A program aimed at controlling farm output through quotas and subsidies to farmers.

American Dilemma. Feeling uncomfortable with ethnic and cultural heterogeneity, with political diversity and with absolute equality of opportunity, people seek to "draw lines." Yet in a pluralistic/modern society, there is no logical place where such lines may be drawn.

American Dream. The idea that in America, a person with nothing but ambition, courage and character, can rise from rags to riches.

America Question. The United States is a nation quite unlike any other, seeming to operate successfully on a set of principles different from any other nations. The America Question is, then, What was it that made for those successes?

Amoral. Not making moral distinctions or judgments. Not caring about right or wrong.

Anarchy. Literally, "rule of no one." Mob rule. Chaotic lawlessness due to the absence of governmental control.

Antitrust policy. Laws passed by the national government to inhibit monopolies and promote competition.

Aristocracy. Rule by a small clique of society's "best" citizens, the selection of which may be based on birth, wealth, ability, social standing or ecclesiastical position.

Auxiliary precautions. The term used by the Founding Fathers to describe structural controls. Consequently, structural controls are auxiliary (or, a back up system) to public virtue.

Balance of payments. A summary of financial transactions involving trade and investment between the United States and foreign countries.

Bicameral legislature. Two-house legislature, each endowed with a different character to check the other and maintain the balance within.

Bill of rights. The first ten amendments to the Constitution, emphasizing the protection of individual liberties.

Boundaries. Divisions for consideration of economic equity. e.g. city, state, nation, world

Bureaucracy. Systems of organizing and processing information. Have become so massive and complex that they cannot respond to human needs.

Business cycle. The "boom and bust" pattern of general economic activity, especially in a market economic system.

Capital. The equipment, plants, buildings, and inventories that are available to society for production of other goods and services.

Capital gain. The increase in value above the price originally paid for an asset.

Capitalism. An economic system where resources are privately owned, prices and profits allocate resources, and decentralized decisions are based on economic incentives.

Capital-labor ratio. The amount of capital per worker. An increase in this ratio increases output per worker.

Cartels. A industry group acting together as a monopolist to regulate price and increase profits.

Caucus. A meeting of state party leaders in which the delegates to the national party convention are selected.

Checks and balances. The sharing of the same kind of power between the three branches of government, in order to maintain separation of powers, avoid deadlock, and promote cooperation. Creates atmosphere in which major policy decisions involve at least two separate branches.

Civil rights. Government acts designed to protect persons against arbitrary or discriminatory treatment by government or individuals.

Coalition blackmail. Occurs while forming ruling coalitions in a proportional representation system. If a tiny splinter party controls the important "swing" votes, it may blackmail the major coalitions before joining them, thereby exerting disproportionate influence.

Coalition politics. The American political system is based on compromise within the parties. In order to capture a majority, several different interest groups must coalesce and moderate their views.

Command economic system. An economic system which is characterized by government ownership of most businesses, land, and capital. Resource allocation is determined by economic planners making centralized decisions.

Commerce. Trading of goods, especially on a large scale.

Commercial republic. Highly differentiated economy depends upon a large market area—proliferating economic interests and variety or kinds of property—which produces the moderate conflict upon which the constitutional system depends.

Commodities. Usually refers to agricultural goods or precious metals.

Common law. The cumulative body of judge-made law, as expressed through court decisions. These decisions are shaped according to prevailing custom, rather than actual written law.

Communism. A system in which all economic and social activity is controlled by the government.

Confederal government. A league of independent, sovereign states. A central, or administrative government handles those matters of common concern (usually defense) delegated to it by the member states.

Conservative. One who opposes major changes in the political, economic, or social principles and/or institutions of a society. Although the term has no consistent meaning throughout the history of American politics, conservatives generally oppose government regulation of the economy and favor a more modest role for government.

Consumer durables. Consumption goods that last longer periods of time such as houses and automobiles.

Consumerism. A modern movement for the protection of the consumer against useless, inferior, or dangerous products, misleading advertising, unfair pricing, etc.

Consumer sovereignty. Consumers in a market economy are economically sovereign, meaning that the market responds to consumer demand in order to determine the quantity and quality of goods and services produced.

Consumption. Purchases by households of goods or services to increase happiness or satisfaction.

Containment. The policy of restricting, or "containing," the territorial expansion or ideological influence of a hostile nation.

Counterculture. The culture of those people, especially young people, who reject the traditional institutions, values and behavior of the existing society.

Counterpoise. The term used by the Founders to describe the underlying philosophy of structural controls—the setting of ambition against ambition.

Covert. Secret, hidden, or disguised.

Deficit spending. Government spending above the level of revenues collected. Spending financed by borrowing.

Deflation. Generally falling prices.

Demand deposits. Any funds deposited in a savings institution that can be withdrawn at any time with no penalty. Usually checking accounts.

Democracy. Governmental system in which ultimate political authority lies with the people, through direct participation.

Depreciate. To lose value or purchasing power.

Depression. A severe recession, usually with higher than 10 percent unemployment.

Desegregation. The elimination of all laws, customs, or actions that promote racial discrimination, by restricting different races or groups to specific schools, neighborhoods, or other public facilities.

Deterrence. Discouragement or restraint from acting or proceeding, by means of fear or doubt. In the area of modern foreign policy, deterrence (or nuclear deterrence) is the policy of keeping the peace by threatening would-be enemies with massive retaliation in the event of a first strike.

Dictatorship. Rule by a tyrant or leader who governs with absolute power.

Discrimination. To act on the basis of prejudice. To treat an individual or group differently because of an irrelevant characteristic.

Disposable income. Total income minus income paid as taxes. (More or less, take-home pay)

Distribution of income. Distribution of income among households, families or groups. Usually expressed as the percentage of total income going to each group. For example the poorest 20 percent of all households received 5 percent of total income.

Distribution of wealth. Distribution of wealth among households, etc. Measured in the same way as income.

Due Process of Law. Protection against arbitrary state deprivation of life, liberty, or property. More particularly, substantive due process of law emphasizes protection from legislative or executive acts that are arbitrary or lacking in reasonableness, covering subject matter beyond the legitimate reach of government.

Duty. A tax levied on imported or exported goods.

Economic competition. Because of the large number of buyers and sellers, the participants in the exchange process assume the price or terms of the exchange is beyond their control.

Economic equity. Characterized by a fair distribution of economic rewards; may or may not imply equality.

Economic growth. A general increase in the standard of living; usually measured by the growth in real GNP per capita.

Economic injustice. A situation where the distribution of economic rewards is unfair. What actually is "unfair" is a subjective decision.

Economic mobility. Movement of individuals, families, or other groups up and down the economic ladder.

Economies of scale. As a firm increases in size, its long-run average costs decrease.

Efficiency. An economy is efficient when society's resources are allocated such that it is impossible to make someone better off (by reallocating resources) without hurting someone else.

Egalitarian. Asserting a belief in the equality of all men.

Elastic currency. The idea that the Federal Reserve would increase or decrease the money supply to meet the needs of the economy.

Electoral college. An assembly elected by the voters to formally elect the president and vice-president. Electors of each state, equal in number to its members in Congress, are expected to cast their votes for the candidates selected by the popular votes in their state. Political parties that nominate pledged electors have distorted the original intention that electors be chosen based on their own merit, to exercise complete discretion in the selection of the president (indirect election).

Embargo. A government order prohibiting trade in a certain commodity or with a certain country.

Eminent domain. Inherent power of government to take over private property, if taken for a public purpose and just compensation is given.

Employed. Includes all full-time and part-time employees.

Enlightenment. A period in intellectual history opening towards the end of the seventeenth century. A basic premise of the Enlightenment was that it was possible for man, through reason and with an appreciation that there are laws governing human nature, to set up a governmental system that could avoid the Human Predicament.

Entrepreneurship. Innovation, organization, and risk-taking in business.

Enumerated powers. Powers of the national government that are specifically written into the Constitution.

Equality. Everybody has the exact same value, quantity, or measure as another. For example, an equal distribution of income means that all incomes are exactly the same.

Equality of Opportunity. Each participant in the economy has an equal chance of economic success or failure; outcomes depend on individual performance.

Equality of Result. Each participant in the economy receives the same economic rewards.

Equilibrium Price. In a free market, the price at which the quantity that individuals want to purchase equals the quantity that firms want to supply.

Equity. The fair distribution of the resources of an economy.

Executive privilege. The power of the executive to refuse to appear before a legislative committee or a court, or to withhold information from them. This is claimed as an inherent executive right under the constitutional separation of powers.

Export. Goods that are produced in a given country and then sold in another country.

External benefit. Occurs whenever a third party not directly involved in an exchange benefits from a trade without payment.

External Cost. Occurs when a third party is damaged by an exchange between two individuals or firms without compensation.

Externalities. The beneficial or damaging effects of an exchange on a third party not directly involved in the exchange.

Extralegal. Outside or beyond the normal application of law.

Faction. A group of citizens who are united and actuated by some common passion or interest, adverse to the rights of other citizens or the interests of the community as a whole.

Factional behavior. Factions tend to bring out the worst in human nature, encouraging extreme, irrational, and/or hysterical behavior.

Fallacy of Composition. The assumption that what is true for one is true for the group. (ex.: If one person stands up at a football game, he can see better. If everybody stands up, nobody can see better).

Federal deficit. The difference between government revenue (taxes) and government expenditures for a given year is that year's deficit.

Federalism. The division of power between the national and state government. Both act directly upon the people, are supreme within their proper spheres of authority, and must consent to constitutional change.

Federal Reserve System. A centralized banking system given authority to regulate banking and the money supply in the United States.

Federal structure. The exercise of popular sovereignty was divided in two. Powers delegated to the national government were carefully enumerated. All other powers not designated national, nor prohibited to the states, were reserved to the states respectively, or to the people.

Filtered consent. In defending popular government from pure democracy, the Founders attempted to process consent through a set of filters to purify the popular will. These filters include representatives, indirect election, staggered elections and overlapping terms of office.

Fiscal policy. Policy determining the level and kinds of government expenditures and taxes.

Freedmen. Those who have been freed from slavery.

Freedom. Beyond merely the absence of tyranny and anarchy, freedom is a noble instinct, characterized by a desire for truth, respect for justice, sense of mercy, and the will to be free. Implies more responsibility than simply doing anything one wishes. In politics, the highest form of freedom is held to be democratic self-government. In an economic context, it is the freedom to make trades or exchanges, to use property as desired, or to form business enterprises.

Freedom of Religion. Freedom of worship and religious practice addressed in the Bill of Rights. Government cannot establish a national church (separation of church and state), nor can it prohibit the free exercise thereof.

Freedom of Speech. Right to expression without prior restraint. Subject to penalties for the abuse of the right.

Free-rider problem. Exists when people enjoy the benefits of a good or service without paying the cost. Applies especially to public goods and externalities.

Freeze factor. In the two-party system, because both parties are scrambling for predominantly the same voters, they often can wind up so evenly matched that any debate on substantive issues is essentially frozen, while the parties attempt to immobilize each other, debating only secondary issues.

Gains from trade. The difference between our own cost of production and the cost we pay for the good through exchange.

General Religion. The generalized Christianity consisting of those aspects of the gospel which were common to all churches. Central to the General Religion were Christian ethics (going the extra mile, turning the other cheek, etc.), as well as the Puritan notion that society as a whole, not just the individual, must be pleasing to the Lord.

GNP. Gross National Product—The dollar value of all final goods and services produced in one year by an economy.

Government intervention. Direct government action to alter the operation of a market. It usually involves regulation of prices or other components of exchange.

Government spending. Government purchases of goods and services.

Graft. The acquisition of riches or gain by dishonest or unfair means, especially through abuse of one's position in government.

Great Depression. Beginning with the stock market crash in October 1929, and lasting through most of the 1930's, it was the longest and most severe recession in American history.

Households. The generic term used in economics to represent a single consuming unit. A household could be a single individual, a family, or a group living together.

Human nature. The qualities of the individual's heart and soul. Also, the psychological and social qualities that characterize mankind.

Human Predicament. The historically cyclical movement of tyranny, revolution, anarchy, factions and tyranny again. Freedom lies elusively within the circle, difficult to obtain, let alone maintain.

Hyperinflation. Very rapid inflation, usually greater than 100 percent per month.

Ideological. Committed to an ideology or cause. Doctrine and principle are more important than winning elections. An ideological politician would "rather be right than president."

Impeachment. Formal accusation, or indictment, rendered by the House, that commits an accused civil officer for trial in the Senate. Impeachment is the first step in a two-stage process.

Imperfect information. Faulty information that causes exchanges to take place that are not mutually beneficial.

Imperialism. The policy of extending the rule or authority of a nation by acquiring and holding colonies and dependencies.

Implied rights. Rights not specifically mentioned in the Constitution, which have been inferred from stated rights.

Import. Goods that are produced in another country and then purchased in a given country.

Incidence. Who actually bears the burden. For example, the incidence of a tax refers to who actually has to pay the tax.

Income. The amount an individual earns or receives in a given time period.

Indexation. Connecting a price or payment to an index for inflation so that the price will move with the inflation rate, and reflect a constant value level.

Indirect election. The people elect representatives who then elect representatives of their own.

Inflation. Generally rising prices; inflation is thought to be largely caused by excessive growth of the money supply.

Interdependence. Being mutually dependent upon other individuals or nations for economic well-being, due to specialization and exchange.

Interest rate. The reward for saving or the price for borrowing

Intermediaries. "Middlemen" who provide information to buyers or sellers in order to facilitate exchange.

Internal Cost. Costs borne directly by the parties involved in an exchange.

Interstate Commerce Clause. Article I, Section 8 of the Constitution is the clause upon which most government intervention in the economy is based. Gives Congress the authority to regulate commerce between the states.

Investment. Addition to the capital stock.

Isolationism. A policy of noninvolvement in the political affairs of other nations.

Judicial activism. Also known as "judicial intervention," an approach to judicial decision-making that maintains that a judge should use his or her position and policy making ability to promote desireable social ends, rather than deferring to the legislative and executive branches, who are more directly accountable to the people.

Judicial legislation. When the court clearly crosses over the fine line between interpreting the law and making law, in favor of making law (judge-made law).

Judicial reinterpretation. Judges reshaping the Constitution through interpretation according to time, place and circumstance.

Judicial review. Power of the court to declare laws or acts of the legislative or executive branches unconstitutional. The Constitution is supreme law, acts contrary to it are unconstitutional, and thus null and void.

Keynesian economics. The belief that fiscal policy could be used to control the business cycle.

Labor. The physical and mental effort that people apply to production.

Laissez Faire. Roughly translated, to "let alone." In a market economy, it is the term used to express the idea of completely free and competitive exchange.

Land. Similar to natural resources. Anything from nature, including minerals, forests, land, and water.

Law of comparative advantage. Every individual, group, or nation can produce at least one good or service at lower opportunity cost than others. To maximize their standard of living, they should specialize in the production of such goods or services.

Law of demand. As the price of a good or service increases, individuals will buy less of that good or service.

Law of supply. As the price of a good or service increases, firms will want to supply more of that good or service.

Legislative tyranny. According to republican theory, people naturally allocate predominant authority to the body most responsive to them—the legislature, leaving the rule enforcer weak. Unfortunately, tyranny is often the result.

Libel. Publication of knowingly false or malicious statements that damage someone's reputation.

Liberal. One who seeks political, economic, or social change in an attempt to aid in the development of the individual. There is no consistent definition of liberal throughout American political history, but modern liberals generally view government as a means to eliminate problems and expand individual freedoms, rather than as a threat to freedoms, as traditional liberals saw government.

Libertarian. Those who desire liberation from all but the most necessary governmental authority.

Licentiousness. Used by the Founding Fathers to mean lack of discipline and self-restraint, excessive freedom, constituting an abuse of liberty. We normally use the term license today.

Low-cost producer. The low-cost producer of a good or service is the one with the lowest opportunity cost of production.

Macroeconomics. The study of the economy as a whole, rather than dealing with individual markets or individual consumers and producers.

Majority. More than half of all votes cast.

Market economic system. A system characterized by unrestricted free exchange, where competition determines prices and profits, which in turn allocate resources.

Market weaknesses. Areas where a market does not provide efficient prices and quantities of goods and services.

Martial law. Law that is enacted upon a society by the military when civil authority has broken down. Can be accompanied by a suspension of the writ of habeas corpus. May be invoked by the President when necessary for the security of the nation.

Mass culture. A popular culture, embraced by the common people, because high culture was seen to be "lapsing into incomprehensibility."

Median. The middle of a distribution. For example, if all households were ranked from richest to poorest, the median income would be the income where 50 percent of the households were richer, and 50 percent were poorer.

Medium of exchange. Any objects accepted in exchange for goods and services. See Money.

Mercantilism. A philosophy of the eighteenth century that emphasized exports and the hoarding of gold and silver. Mercantilist policies sacrificed the interests of a colony to the interests of the mother country.

Militarism. The glorification and buildup of military power and technology. Military strength is seen as the ideal of the state.

Miracle of exchange. That both parties are made better off by trade even though no additional goods have been produced.

Mission. American foreign policy asserting that the only proper role of the US in world relations is as a beacon or light to other nations. Emphasizes US moral authority and leadership.

Mobility. Movement of individuals, families, or other groups up and down the economic ladder. Also, the ability to travel great distances with increasing ease.

Modern society. Follows a logic of fair and open competition (legal equality), without favored class, party, interest, religion, etc. Emphasizes human reason.

Monarchy. Rule by one, usually a king or queen.

Monetary policy. Policy regarding the money supply and interest rates.

Money. Anything that is widely accepted in exchange for goods and services, paying debts or taxes is money. The medium of exchange for an economy.

Money supply. Usually defined as currency and demand deposits; under the control of the government (The Federal Reserve in the United States).

Monopoly power. A situation where a firm can affect the price of a good by controlling the quantity produced.

Muckraking. A style of investigative journalism from the early 1900's. Usually aimed at exposing commercial or political corruption.

National debt. The total amount of money the government still owes on money borrowed from lending institutions.

Nationalism. Prevailing spirit in individuals or populations of devotion to country and promotion and defence of its interests. Tends to emphasize separateness and differences between groups.

Nationalistic (interpretation). Broad constitutional interpretation to maximize national authority and jurisdiction.

National Recovery Administration. A series of production quotas, prices, and wages meant to stop the downward spiral of the economy. The basic idea was to use cartel monopoly to raise prices.

Natural law. Human relations are governed by an immutable set of higher laws or self-evident truths, similar to the physical laws of the universe, and discernible through human reason. Constitutes the foundation for natural rights philosophy.

Natural monopoly. A firm that is protected from competition by its ownership or control of nonreproduceable resources, making it a monopolist.

Natural resource. The base materials, taken from the earth, that labor and capital use to produce goods.

Natural rights. Individuals are endowed by their creator with certain unalienable rights that may not be abridged by government.

New Deal. A series of programs implemented during Franklin Roosevelt's term in office aimed at curing the depression.

Nostalgia. A wistful longing for the past, whose themes identify those highly idealized qualities that Americans believe have been left behind in the tides of change.

Not in labor force. Includes everyone over sixteen years of age who is not in school and is not employed or actively seeking employment.

Obscenity. A legal term to describe forms of expression that are offensive to modesty or decency (pornography).

Oligarchy. Government in which a small elite group has the ruling power—usually those with wealth, military power, or social position.

Oligopoly. A type of market where a few mutually interdependent sellers have some influence over the price of their good or service.

Open market operations. The buying and selling of U.S. government bonds in order to control the money supply.

Opportunity cost. The cost of any choice is measured by the value of the best foregone alternative.

Original consent. Consent of the people to create, alter, or abolish a form of government, i.e. ratification of new constitution, amendment provisions, etc.

Paternalism. Government's feeling of obligation to prevent damage from occurring to individual citizens because of their own mistakes.

Patronage. A system whereby one person in society is dependent upon some higher person—his patron—for many of the opportunities of life. Operates on the basis of favors and informal understandings.

Periodic consent. Once a form of government is chosen, regular consent of the people is obtained to select its officers, and to give guidance as to the policies they should pursue.

Personal exemptions. A reduction in taxable income based on number of dependents or family members.

Planned economic system. A system which is characterized by government ownership of most businesses, land, and capital. Resource allocation is determined by economic planners making centralized decisions.

Pluralism. The willingness of a society to tolerate and even encourage social, cultural, intellectual, and racial diversity among its people.

Plurality. The largest block of all votes cast.

Political-Economic System. The organization of ownership and allocation of resources, and decision-making arrangements for a society to coordinate the economic interests of groups or individuals. The two dominant political-economic systems are market and command or planning.

Popular government. Natural rights concept stating that ultimate power rests with the people, who can create, alter, or abolish government. In practice, popular government avoids direct contact with the people, opting rather for representative institutions, as filters between.

Popular sovereignty. The doctrine asserting that the people are sovereign. Just before the Civil War, a term used to indicate that the people living in the territories should be free from government interference in determining a policy on slavery.

Practical. Emphasizes political results. It is acceptable to bend principles a little in order solve political problems. A practical politician would "rather be president than right."

Precedent. A court ruling that has bearing on future court decisions in similar cases.

Price ceiling. A maximum price above which prices cannot legally rise. (ex.. rent controls)

Price floor. A minimum price below which prices cannot legally fall. (ex.. minimum wage)

Price indexes. Measures a particular year's cost of a given market basket as a percentage of the cost of the same market basket in some base year.

Productivity growth. Growth in the productivity of capital. Increases in the output per laborer.

Profits. The difference between total revenue from sales and total costs for a firm.

Progressive tax. Tax rate increases as income increases.

Progressivism. A movement in response to the economic and political abuses of the unregulated industrialization and urban expansion in the late nineteenth century, advocating, among other things, popular government, direct elections and women's suffrage.

Property rights. The right of an owner to use or exchange property.

Proportional representation. An electoral system that allocates seats in the legislative body to each party based approximately on its percentage of the popular vote. This provides democratic representation to minority parties, but tends to result in unstable coalition governments.

Proportional tax. Everyone pays the same percentage of income in taxes.

Public goods. A good that can be consumed by one individual without diminishing the amount available for others to consume.

Public virtue (classical). The classical ideal of public virtue was characterized by an independent, male landowner of extreme discipline, self-denial and militarism. Political participation is his self-realization. Difficult to subdue.

Public virtue (new). In the American experience, public virtue becomes less extreme than the classical public virtue, yet as powerful and more stable in the long run. While individual political participation is still necessary, there is a healthy merging of public virtue and self-interest as individuals are involved in their own "pursuit of happiness."

Pure market system. A system that is characterized by competitive free exchange. All exchanges are allowed to take place, and no single individual or firm has control over the terms of exchange.

Quota. Limits on the amount of foreign goods that can come into the country.

Radical. One who favors substantial political, economic, or social change. More extreme than liberals.

Reactionary. One who favors substantial political, economic, or social changes, advocating a return to principles and institutions of earlier times. More extreme than conservatives.

Real. A measure of economic performance that has been adjusted for inflation in order to look at its value in constant dollar values.

Real GNP. The value of GNP adjusted for the effects of inflation (rising prices) so that constant dollar value comparisons of GNP can by made.

Real GNP per capita. Real GNP divided by the population of a country gives the value of output per person in an economy.

Recession. An economy is in a recession when output falls significantly below the output possible when resources are fully employed.

Referendum. A vote of approval or rejection by the people on a measure either passed or proposed by the legislature.

Regressive tax. Tax rate falls as income increases.

Representation. A system where selected leaders represent a larger group of citizens.

Resource. Composed of land, labor, and capital, resources are the basis of production.

Resource market. The market for the resources of production.

Revenue powers. Article I, Sections 7 and 8 of the Constitution identify the powers and limits the national government has in raising revenue.

Right to Fairness. Implied right that the treatment of all persons charged with crimes ought to be impartially measured against a general standard (procedural due process).

Right to Privacy. An implied right to determine ones personal affairs and the information concerning oneself, free of governmental interference and control.

Role of profits. Firms and resources will be attracted to industries with high profits and will leave areas with low profits.

Rule of Law. In the private sphere of human activities, the government may not act except in the enforcement of a known, general rule. Impartial law rules, rather than capriciousness. For the rule of law to exist, five elements must be present: Generality, Prospectivity, Publicity, Consent, and Due Process.

Scale. The institutions of society—business, labor and government—enormously expand their size and power relative to the individual.

Scarcity. Unlimited wants in the face of limited resources means that there will not be enough goods and services to satisfy all wants.

Scientific tyranny. Science, instead of as a means to understand and control human behavior, could be used to change human nature. Tyrants could use this new scientific knowledge to go beyond mere control of people's actions, to change the human mind itself, according to the tyrant's will.

Secede. To formally withdraw from an alliance or federation, as in the withdrawal from the Union of 11 southern states in the period 1860-1861, an act which precipitated the Civil War.

Sedition. Actions or criticisms that incite rebellion or discontent against duly established government.

Self-interest. Those personal tastes or ends (material, moral or religious) that apply solely to the individual and determine an individual's motives and actions.

Separation of powers. Traditionally seen as the placing of rule making and rule enforcing powers in separate hands. Contemporary separation of powers includes a division of the rule enforcer, consequently the power is now distributed among three branches of government. The officials of each branch are selected by different procedures, have different terms of office, and are independent of one another. Designed to prevent tyranny.

Socialism. A system which adheres to the belief of collective ownership and government control of resource allocation. Socialism is one type of command economic system.

Sovereign. Supreme in decision-making power.

Sovereignty. The power of making final decisions, free from external interference.

Specialization. Limiting production to the narrow range of goods or services in which a firm or an individual has a comparative advantage.

Stagflation. An incident of simultaneous serious inflation and high unemployment.

State of nature. Assumes that people had rights in a "state of nature" and created government to protect these rights.

States' rights. Term used to imply opposition to the increasing power of the national government, at the expense of the states. Calls for limited national government with its assumed implied powers, and expanded interpretation to reserved powers of states.

Structure. An overall organizational system composed of structural controls, using the predominance of self-interest to channel human nature towards a desirable outcome.

Structural controls. A carefully designed system using the predominance of the self-interested aspect of human nature to produce a beneficial outcome. Structural controls will operate basically without moral consideration. The basic idea with structural controls is to set ambition against ambition—also called counterpoise.

Structural fallacy. The incorrect assumption that asserts that if structural controls work so well in manipulating self-interest, then they are perhaps all that is needed.

Subsidy. Monetary aid from the government to individuals or firms. Usually used by government to stimulate the economy, correct a market weakness or redistribute income.

Subversion. The act of overthrowing or undermining the establishment.

Suffrage. The right to vote in a political election.

Tariff. A tax on foreign goods coming into the country.

Tax Brackets. The range of incomes that a particular tax rate applies to.

Tax rate. The percentage of income to be paid as taxes.

Technological change. The discovery of more advanced equipment and efficient production methods, thereby allowing more output from the same amount of resource.

Traditional society. A group of people organized as a single, homogeneous, static, coherent unit, that exists for some transcendant—usually religious—purpose.

Transaction Costs. Costs associated with the process of exchange or trade.

Transfers. Government transfer of taxes collected from one group to another group where the recipients did not provide any goods or services in exchange.

Treason. A violation by a citizen of his allegiance to the sovereign state. In the United States this consists of either waging war against the US, or aiding its enemies.

Two-party system. Dividing of voter loyalties between two major political parties, resulting in the virtual exclusion of minor parties from seriously competing for political power.

Tyranny. Rule by a person (or group) who uses the power of government to further his (or their) own ends. Rule of will.

Unemployed. Includes all individuals over sixteen years of age who are not in school and are actively seeking work.

Unemployment rate. The number of unemployed (those looking for but unable to find work) divided by the number in the labor force.

Unitary government. A centralized government in which local, or sub-divisional governments use only those powers given to them by the central government, basically acting as administrative units.

Urbanization. The tendency of the population to become more and more concentrated in the cities. Gradually, the values and the lifestyle of the country are replaced by those of the city.

Virtual representation. A system in which leaders represent generalized points of view, rather than geographical districts or specific groups of voters. The representatives rarely had to live with the consequences of their own decisions.

Wage-price spiral. Unions negotiate higher wages, causing management to raise prices, causing unions to negotiate higher wages.

Wagner Act. Enactment that guarantees the right of unions to organize and bargain collectively through representatives. Government has power to disband businesses that participate in unfair labor practices.

Wants. Those things which we desire to own or consume, but do not need for basic survival.

Wealth. The value of one's total assets (real estate, cash, stocks, bonds, etc.) minus the value of one's liabilities (debts).

Welfare. Make-work and transfer programs intended to provide for the physical well-being of the people.

Winner-take-all. An all-or-nothing elective system in which minor parties are usually unable to win any share of political power. In a presidential election, for example, the winning party in each state gets all the electoral votes. Tends to create two-party politics. A corollary to winner-take-all could be "loser-take-nothing."

We the People of the United States, in Order to form a more perfect Union, establish Justice, insure domestic Tranquility, provide for the common defence, promote the general Welfare, and secure the Blessings of Liberty to ourselves and our Posterity, do ordain and establish this Constitution for the United States of America.

The Constitution of the United States

Article I

Section 1. All legislative Powers herein granted shall be vested in a Congress of the United States, which shall consist of a Senate and House of Representatives.

Section 2. The House of Representatives shall be composed of Members chosen every second Year by the People of the several States, and the Electors in each State shall have the Qualifications requisite for Electors of the most numerous Branch of the State Legislature.

No Person shall be a Representative who shall not have attained to the Age of twenty five Years, and been seven Years a Citizen of the United States, and who shall not, when elected, be an Inhabitant of the State in which he shall be chosen.

Representatives and direct Taxes shall be apportioned among the several States which may be included within the Union, according to their respective Numbers, which shall be determined by adding to the whole Number of free Persons, including those bound to Service for a Term of Years, and excluding Indians not taxed, three fifths of all other Persons. The actual Enumeration shall be made within three Years after the first Meeting of the Congress of the United States, and within every subsequent Term of ten Years, in such Manner as they shall by Law direct. The Number of Representatives shall not exceed one for every thirty Thousand, but each State shall have at Least one Representative; and until such enumeration shall be made, the State of New Hampshire shall be entitled to chuse three, Massachusetts eight, Rhode-Island and Providence Plantations one, Connecticut five, New York six, New Jersey four, Pennsylvania eight, Delaware one, Maryland six, Virginia ten, North Carolina five, South Carolina five, and Georgia three.

When vacancies happen in the Representation from any State, the Executive Authority thereof shall issue Writs of Election to fill such Vacancies.

The House of Representatives shall chuse their speaker and other Officers; and shall have the sole Power of Impeachment.

Section 3. The Senate of the United States shall be composed of two Senators from each State, chosen by the Legislature thereof, for six Years; and each Senator shall have one Vote.

Immediately after they shall be assembled in Consequence of the first Election, they shall be divided as equally as may be into three Classes. The Seats of the Senators of the first Class shall be vacated at the Expiration of the second Year, of the second Class at the Expiration of the fourth Year, and of the third Class at the Expiration of the sixth Year, so that one third may be chosen every second year; and if Vacancies happen by Resignation, or otherwise, during the Recess of the Legislature of any State, the Executive thereof may make temporary Appointments until the next Meeting of the Legislature, which shall then fill such Vacancies.

No Person shall be a Senator who shall not have attained to the Age of thirty years, and been nine Years a Citizen of the United States, and who shall not, when elected, be an Inhabitant of that State for which he shall be chosen.

The Vice President of the United States shall be President of the Senate, but shall have no Vote, unless they be equally divided.

The Senate shall chuse their other Officers, and also a President pro tempore, in the Absence of the Vice President, or when he shall exercise the Office of President of the United States.

The Senate shall have the sole Power to try all Impeachments. When sitting for that Purpose, they shall be on Oath or Affirmation. When the President of the United States is tried, the Chief Justice shall preside: And no Person shall be convicted without the Concurrence of two thirds of the Members present.

Judgment in Cases of Impeachment shall not extend further than to removal from Office, and disqualification to hold and enjoy any Office of honor, Trust or Profit under the United States: but the Party convicted shall nevertheless be liable and subject to Indictment, Trial, Judgment and Punishment, according to law.

Section 4. The Times, Places and Manner of holding Elections for Senators and Representatives shall be prescribed in each state by the Legislature thereof; but the Congress may at any time by law make or alter such Regulations, except as to the Places of chusing Senators.

The Congress shall assemble at least once in every Year, and such Meeting shall be on the first Monday in December, unless they shall by Law appoint a different Day.

Section 5. Each House shall be the Judge of the Elections, Returns and Qualifications of its own Members, and a Majority of each shall constitute a Quorum to do Business; but a smaller Number may adjourn from day to day, and may be authorized to compel the Attendance of absent Members, in such Manner, and under such Penalties as each House may provide.

Each House may determine the Rules of its Proceedings, punish its Members of disorderly Behaviour, and with the concurrence of two thirds, expel a Member.

Each House shall keep a Journal of its Proceedings, and from time to time publish the same, excepting such Parts as may in their Judgment require Secrecy; and the Yeas and Nays of the Members of either House on any question shall, at the Desire of one fifth of those Present, be entered on the Journal.

Neither House, during the Session of Congress, shall, without the Consent of the other, adjourn for more than three days, nor to any other Place than that in which the two Houses shall be sitting.

Section 6. The Senators and Representatives shall receive a Compensation for their Services, to be ascertained by Law, and paid out of the Treasury of the United States. They shall in all cases, except treason, felony and breach of the peace, be privileged from Arrest during their Attendance at the Session of their respective Houses, and in going to and returning from the same; and for any Speech or Debate in either House, they shall not be questioned in any other Place.

No Senator or Representative shall, during the Time for which he was elected, be appointed to any civil Office under the Authority of the United States, which shall have been created, or the Emoluments whereof shall have been encreased during such time; and no Person holding any Office under the United States, shall be a Member of either House during his Continuance in Office.

Section 7. All Bills for raising Revenue shall originate in the House of Representatives; but the Senate may propose or concur with Amendments as on other Bills.

Every Bill which shall have passed the House of Representatives and the Senate, shall, before it become a Law, be presented to the President of the United States; If he approve he shall sign it, but if not he shall return it, with his Objections to that House in which it shall have originated, who shall enter the Objections at large on their Journal, and proceed to reconsider it. If after such Reconsideration two thirds of that House shall agree to pass the Bill, it shall be sent, together with the Objections, to the other House, by which it shall likewise be reconsidered, and if approved by two thirds of that House, it shall become a Law. But in all such Cases the Votes of both Houses shall be determined by Yeas and Nays, and the Names of the Persons voting for and against the Bill shall be entered on the Journal of each House respectively. If any Bill shall not be returned by the President within ten Days (Sundays excepted) after it shall have been presented to him, the Same shall be a Law, in like Manner as if he had signed it, unless the Congress by their Adjournment prevent its Return, in which Case it shall not be a Law.

Every Order, Resolution, or Vote to which the Concurrence of the Senate and House of Representatives may be necessary (except on a question of Adjournment) shall be presented to the President of the United States; and before the Same shall take Effect, shall be approved by him, or being disapproved by him, shall be repassed by two thirds of the Senate and House of Representatives, according to the Rules and Limitations prescribed in the Case of a Bill.

Section 8. The Congress shall have Power to lay and collect Taxes, Duties, Imposts and Excises, to pay the Debts and provide for the common Defence and general Welfare of the United States; but all Duties, Imposts and Excises shall be uniform throughout the United States;

To Borrow Money on the Credit of the United States;

To regulate Commerce with foreign Nations, and among the several States, and with the Indian Tribes;

To establish an uniform Rule of Naturalization, and uniform Laws on the subject of Bankruptcies throughout the United States;

To coin Money, regulate the Value thereof, and of foreign Coin, and fix the Standard of Weights and Measures;

To provide for the Punishment of counterfeiting the Securities and current Coin of the United States;

To establish Post Offices and post Roads;

To promote the Progress of Science and useful Arts, by securing for limited Times to Authors and Inventors the exclusive Right to their respective Writings and Discoveries;

To constitute Tribunals inferior to the supreme Court;

To define and punish Piracies and Felonies committed on the high Seas, and offences against the Law of Nations;

To declare War, grant Letters of Marque and Reprisal, and make Rules concerning Captures on Land and Water;

To raise and support Armies, but no Appropriation of Money to that Use shall be for a longer Term than two Years;

To provide and maintain a Navy;

To make Rules for the Government and Regulation of the land and naval Forces;

To provide for calling forth the Militia to execute the Laws of the Union, suppress Insurrections and repel Invasions;

To provide for organizing, arming, and disciplining, the Militia, and for governing such Part of them as may be employed in the Service of the United States, reserving to the States respectively, the Appointment of the Officers, and the Authority of training the Militia according to the discipline prescribed by Congress;

To exercise exclusive Legislation in all Cases whatsoever, over such District (not exceeding ten Miles square) as may, by Cession of particular States, and the Acceptance of Congress, become the Seat of the Government of the United States, and to exercise like Authority over all Places purchased by the Consent of the Legislature of the State in which the Same shall be for the Erection of Forts, Magazines, Arsenals, dock-Yards, and other needful Buildings;—And

To make all Laws which shall be necessary and proper for carrying into Execution the foregoing Powers, and all other Powers vested by this Constitution in the Government of the United States, or in any Department or Officer thereof.

Section 9. The Migration or Importation of such Persons as any of the States now existing shall think proper to admit, shall not be prohibited by the Congress prior to the Year one thousand eight hundred and eight, but a Tax or duty may be imposed on such Importation, not exceeding ten dollars for each Person.

The Privilege of the Writ of Habeas Corpus shall not be suspended, unless when in Cases of Rebellion or invasion the public Safety may require it.

No Bill of Attainder or ex post facto Law shall be passed.

No Capitation, or other direct, Tax shall be laid, unless in Proportion to the Census or Enumeration herein before directed to be taken.

No Tax or Duty shall be laid on Articles exported from any State.

No Preference shall be given by any Regulation of Commerce or Revenue to the Ports of one State over those of another; nor shall Vessels bound to, or from, one State, be obliged to enter, clear, or pay Duties in another.

No Money shall be drawn from Treasury, but in Consequence of Appropriations made by Law; and a regular Statement and Account of the Receipts and Expenditures of all public Money shall be published from time to time.

No title of Nobility shall be granted by the United States; And no Person holding any Office of Profit or Trust under them, shall, without the Consent of the Congress, accept of any present, Emolument, Office or Title, of any kind whatever, from any King, Prince, or foreign State.

Section 10. No State shall enter into any Treaty, Alliance, or Confederation; grant Letters of Marque and Reprisal; coin Money; emit Bills of Credit; make any Thing but gold and silver Coin a Tender in Payment of Debts; pass any Bill of Attainder, ex post facto Law, or Law impairing the Obligation of Contracts, or grant any Title of Nobility.

No State shall, without the Consent of the Congress, lay any Imposts or Duties on Imports or Exports, except what may be absolutely necessary for executing it's inspection Laws; and the net Produce of all Duties and Imposts, laid by any State on Imports or Exports, shall be for the Use of the Treasury of the United States; and all such Laws shall be subject to the Revision and Control of the Congress.

No state shall, without the Consent of Congress, lay any duty of Tonnage, Keep Troops, or Ships of War in time of Peace, enter into any Agreement or Compact with another State, or with a foreign Power, or engage in War, unless actually invaded, or in such imminent Danger as will not admit of delay.

Article II

Section 1. The executive Power shall be vested in a President of the United States of America. He shall hold his Office during the Term of four Years, and together with the Vice President, chosen for the same term, be elected, as follows

Each State shall appoint, in such Manner as the Legislature thereof may direct, a Number of Electors, equal to the whole Number of Senators and Representatives to which the State may be entitled in the Congress: But no Senator or Representative or Person holding an Office of Trust or Profit under the United States, shall be appointed an Elector.

The Electors shall meet in their respective States, and vote by Ballot for two Persons, of whom one at least shall not be an Inhabitant of the same State with themselves. And they shall make a List of all the Persons voted for, and of the Number of Votes for each; which List they shall sign and certify, and transmit sealed to the Seat of the Government of the United States, directed to the President of the Senate. The President of the Senate shall, in the Presence of the Senate and House of Representatives, open all the Certificates, and the Votes shall then be counted. The person having the greatest Number of Votes shall be the President, if such Number be a Majority of the whole Number of Electors appointed; and if there be more than one who have such Majority, and have an equal Number of Votes, then the House of Representatives shall immediately chuse by Ballot one of them for President; and if no

Person have a Majority, then from the five highest on the List the said House shall in like Manner chuse the President. But in chusing the President, the Votes shall be taken by States, the Representation from each State having one Vote; A quorum for this Purpose shall consist of a Member or Members from two thirds of the States, and a Majority of all the States shall be necessary to a Choice. In every Case, after the Choice of the President, the Person having the greatest Number of Votes of the Electors shall be the Vice President. But if there should remain two or more who have equal Votes, the Senate shall chuse from them by Ballot the Vice President.

The Congress may determine the Time of chusing the Electors, and the Day on which they shall give their Votes; which Day shall be the same throughout the United States.

No Person except a natural born Citizen of the United States, at the time of the Adoption of this Constitution, shall be eligible to the Office of President; neither shall any Person be eligible to the Office who shall not have attained to the Age of thirty five Years, and been fourteen years a Resident within the United States.

In Case of the Removal of the President from Office, or of his Death, Resignation, or Inability to discharge the Powers and Duties of the said Office, the Same shall devolve on the Vice President, and the Congress may by Law provide for the Case of Removal, Death, Resignation or Inability, both of the President and Vice President declaring what Officer shall then act as President and such Officer shall act accordingly, until the Disability be removed, or a President shall be elected.

The President shall, at stated Times, receive for his Services, a Compensation, which shall neither be increased nor diminished during the Period for which he shall have been elected, and he shall not receive within that Period any other Emolument from the United States, or any of them.

Before he enter on the Execution of his Office, he shall take the following Oath or Affirmation:—"I do solemnly swear (or affirm) that I will faithfully execute the Office of President of the United States, and will to the best of my Ability, preserve, protect and defend the Constitution of the United States."

Section 2. The President shall be Commander in Chief of the Army and Navy of the United States, and of the Militia of the several States, when called into the actual Service of the United States; he may require the Opinion, in writing, of the principal Officer in each of the executive Departments, upon any Subject relating to the Duties of their respective Officers, and he shall have Power to grant Reprieves and Pardons for Offences against the United States, except in Cases of Impeachment.

He shall have Power, by and with the Advice and Consent of the Senate, to make Treaties, provided two thirds of the Senators present concur; and he shall nominate, and by and with the Advice and Consent of the Senate, shall appoint Ambassadors, other public Ministers and Consuls, Judges of the supreme Court, and all other Officers of the United States, whose Appointments are not herein otherwise provided for, and which shall be established by Law; but the Congress may by Law vest the Appointment of such inferior Officers, as they think proper, in the President alone, in the Courts of Law, or in the Heads of Departments.

The President shall have the Power to fill up all Vacancies that may happen during the Recess of the Senate, by granting Commissions which shall expire at the End of their next Session.

Section 3. He shall from time to time give to the Congress Information of the State of the Union, and recommend to their Consideration such Measures as he shall judge necessary and expedient; he may, on extraordinary Occasions, convene both Houses, or either of them, and in Case of Disagreement between them, with Respect to the Time of Adjournment, he may adjourn them to such Time as he shall think proper; he shall receive Ambassadors and other public Ministers; he shall take Care that the Laws be faithfully executed, and shall Commission all the Officers of the United States.

Section 4. The President, Vice President and all civil Officers of the United States, shall be removed from Office on Impeachment for, and Conviction of, Treason, Bribery, or other High Crimes and Misdemeanors.

Article III

Section 1. The judicial Power of the United States, shall be vested in one supreme Court, and in such inferior Courts as the Congress may from time to time ordain and establish. The Judges, both of the supreme and inferior Courts, shall hold their Offices during good Behaviour, and shall, at stated Times, receive for their Services, a Compensation, which shall not be diminished during their Continuance in Office.

Section 2. The judicial Power shall extend to all Cases, in Law and Equity, arising under this Constitution, the laws of the United States, and Treaties made, or which shall be made, under their Authority;—to all Cases affecting Ambassadors, other public Ministers and Consuls;—to all Cases of admiralty and maritime Jurisdiction;—to Controversies to which the United States shall be a Party;—to Controversies between two or more States; between a State and Citizens of another State;—between Citizens of different States;—between Citizens of the same State claiming Lands under Grants of different States, and between a State, or the Citizens thereof, and foreign States, Citizens or Subjects.

In all Cases affecting Ambassadors, other public Ministers and Consuls, and those in which a State shall be Party, the supreme Court shall have original Jurisdiction. In all the other Cases before mentioned, the supreme Court shall have appellate Jurisdiction, both as to Law and Fact, with such Exceptions, and under such Regulations as the Congress shall make.

The Trial of all Crimes, except in Cases of Impeachment, shall be by Jury; and such Trial shall be held in the State where the said Crimes shall have been committed; but when not committed within any State, the Trial shall be at such Place or Places as the Congress may by Law have directed.

Section 3. Treason against the United States, shall consist only in levying War against them, or in adhering to their Enemies, giving them Aid and Comfort. No Person shall be convicted of Treason unless on the Testimony of two Witnesses to the same overt Act, or on Confession in open Court.

The Congress shall have Power to declare the Punishment of Treason, but no Attainder of Treason shall work Corruption of Blood, or Forfeiture except during the Life of the Person attained.

Article IV

Section 1. Full Faith and Credit shall be given in each State to the public Acts, Records, and judicial Proceedings of every other State. And the Congress may by general Laws prescribe the Manner in which such Acts, Records and Proceedings shall be proved, and the Effect thereof.

Section 2. The Citizens of each State shall be entitled to all Privileges and Immunities of Citizens in the several States.

A Person charged in any State with Treason, Felony, or other Crime, who shall flee from Justice, and be found in another State, shall on Demand of the executive Authority of the State from which he fled, be delivered up, to be removed to the State having Jurisdiction of the Crime.

No Person held to Service or Labour in one State, under the Laws thereof, escaping into another, shall, in Consequence of any Law or Regulation therein, be discharged from such Service or Labour, but shall be delivered up on Claim of the Party to whom such Service or Labour may be due.

Section 3. New States may be admitted by the Congress into this Union; but no new State shall be formed or erected within the Jurisdiction of any other State; nor any State be formed by the Junction of two or more States, or Parts of States, without the Consent of the Legislatures of the States concerned as well as of the Congress.

The Congress shall have Power to dispose of and make all needful Rules and Regulations respecting the Territory or other Property belonging to the United States; and nothing in this Constitution shall be so construed as to Prejudice any Claims of the United States, or of any particular State.

Section 4. The United States shall guarantee to every State in this Union a Republican Form of Government, and shall protect each of them against Invasion; and on Application of the Legislature, or of the Executive (when the Legislature cannot be convened) against domestic Violence.

Article V

The Congress, whenever two thirds of both Houses shall deem it necessary, shall propose Amendments to this Constitution, or, on the Application of the Legislatures of two thirds of the several States, shall call a Convention for proposing Amendments, which, in either Case, shall be valid to all Intents and Purposes, as Part of this Constitution, when ratified by the Legislatures of three fourths of the several States, or by Conventions in three fourths thereof, as the one or the other Mode of Ratification may be proposed by the Congress; Provided that no Amendment which may be made prior to the Year One thousand eight hundred and eight shall in any Manner affect the first and fourth Clauses in the Ninth Section of the first Article; and that no State, without its Consent, shall be deprived of its equal Suffrage in the Senate.

Article VI

All Debts contracted and Engagements entered into, before the Adoption of this Constitution, shall be as valid against the United States under this Constitution, as under the Confederation.

This Constitution, and the Laws of the United States which shall be made in Pursuance thereof; and all Treaties made, or which shall be made, under the Authority of the United States, shall be the supreme Law of the Land; and the Judges in every State shall be bound thereby, any Thing in the Constitution or Laws of any State to the Contrary notwithstanding.

The Senators and Representatives before mentioned, and the Members of the several State Legislatures, and all executive and judicial Officers, both of the United States and of the several States, shall be bound by Oath or Affirmation, to support this Constitution; but no religious Test shall ever be required as a Qualification to any Office or public Trust under the United States.

Article VII

The Ratification of the Conventions of nine States, shall be sufficient for the Establishment of this Constitution between the States so ratifying the Same.

DONE in Convention by the Unanimous Consent of the States present the Seventeenth Day of September in the Year of our Lord one thousand seven hundred and Eighty seven and of the Independence of the United States of America the Twelfth IN WITNESS whereof We have hereunto subscribed our Names,

G.º WASHINGTON—Presidᵗ
and deputy from Virginia

New Hampshire	John Langdon
	Nicholas Gilman
Massachusetts	Nathaniel Gorham
	Rufus King
Connecticut	Wm. Saml. Johnson
	Roger Sherman
New York	Alexander Hamilton
New Jersey	Wil: Livingston
	David Brearley
	Wm. Paterson
	Jona: Dayton
Pennsylvania	B Franklin
	Thomas Mifflin
	Robt Morris
	Geo. Clymer
	Thos FitzSimons
	Jared Ingersoll
	James Wilson
	Gouv Morris

Delaware	Geo: Read
	Gunning Bedford Jun.
	John Dickinson
	Richard Bassett
	Jaco: Broom
Maryland	James McHenry
	Dan of St Thos Jenifer
	Danl Carroll
Virginia	John Blair—
	James Madison Jr.
North Carolina	Wm. Blount
	Richd. Dobbs Spaight
	Hu Williamson
South Carolina	J. Rutledge
	Charles Cotesworth Pinckney
	Charles Pinckney
	Pierce Butler
Georgia	William Few
	Abr. Baldwin

Amendments

[The first 10 Amendments were ratified December 15, 1791, and form what is known as the "Bill of Rights."]

Amendment 1

Congress shall make no law respecting an establishment of religion, or prohibiting the free exercise thereof; or abridging the freedom of speech, or of the press; or the right of the people peaceably to assemble, and to petition the Government for a redress of grievances.

Amendment 2

A well regulated Militia, being necessary to the security of a free State, the right of the people to keep and bear Arms, shall not be infringed.

Amendment 3

No Soldier shall, in time of peace be quartered in any house, without the consent of the Owner, nor in time of war, but in a manner to be prescribed by law.

Amendment 4

The right of the people to be secure in their persons, houses, papers, and effects, against unreasonable searches and seizures, shall not be violated, and no Warrants shall issue, but upon probable cause, supported by Oath or affirmation, and particularly describing the place to be searched, and the persons or things to be seized.

Amendment 5

No person shall be held to answer for a capital, or otherwise infamous crime, unless on a presentment or indictment of a Grand Jury, except in cases arising in the land or naval forces, or in the Militia, when in actual service in time of War or public danger; nor shall any person be subject for the same offence to be twice put in jeopardy of life or limb; nor shall be compelled in any criminal case to be a witness against himself, nor be deprived of life, liberty, or property, without due process of law; nor shall private property be taken for public use, without just compensation.

Amendment 6

In all criminal prosecutions, the accused shall enjoy the right to a speedy and public trial, by an impartial jury of the State and district wherein the crime shall have been committed, which district shall have been previously ascertained by law, and to be informed of the nature and cause of the accusation; to be confronted with the witnesses against him; to have compulsory process for obtaining witnesses in his favor, and to have the Assistance of Counsel for his defence.

Amendment 7

In Suits at common law, where the value in controversy shall exceed twenty dollars, the right of trial by jury shall be preserved, and no fact tried by a jury, shall be otherwise re-examined in any Court of the United States, than according to the rules of the common law.

Amendment 8

Excessive bail shall not be required, nor excessive fines imposed, nor cruel and unusual punishments inflicted.

Amendment 9

The enumeration in the Constitution, of certain rights, shall not be construed to deny or disparage others retained by the people.

Amendment 10

The powers not delegated to the United States by the Constitution, nor prohibited by it to the States, are reserved to the States respectively, or to the people.

Amendment 11
(Ratified February 7, 1795)

The Judical power of the United States shall not be construed to extend to any suit in law or equity, commenced or prosecuted against one of the United States by Citizens of another State, or by Citizens or Subjects of any Foreign State.

Amendment 12
(Ratified July 27, 1804)

The Electors shall meet in their respective states and vote by ballot for President and Vice-President, one of whom, at least, shall not be an inhabitant of the same state with themselves; they shall name in their ballots the person voted for as President, and in distinct ballots the person voted for as Vice-President, and they shall make distinct lists of all persons voted for as President, and of all persons voted for as Vice-President, and of the number of votes for each, which lists they shall sign and certify, and transmit sealed to the seat of the government of the United States, directed to the President of the Senate;—The President of the Senate shall, in the presence of the Senate and House of Representatives, open all the certificates and the votes shall then be counted;—The person having the greatest number of votes for President shall be the President, if such number be a majority of the whole number of Electors appointed; and if no person have such majority, then from the persons having the highest numbers not exceeding three on the list of those voted for as President, the House of Representatives shall choose immediately, by ballot, the President. But in choosing the President, the votes shall be taken by states, the representation from each state having one vote; a quorum for this purpose shall consist of a member or members from two-thirds of the states, and a majority of all the states shall be necessary to a choice. And if the House of Representatives shall not choose a President whenever the right of choice shall devolve upon them, before the fourth day of March next following, then the Vice-President shall act as President, as in the case of the death or other constitutional disability of the President—The person having the greatest number of votes as Vice-President, shall be the Vice-President, if such number be a majority of the whole number of Electors appointed, and if no person have a majority, then from the two highest numbers on the list, the Senate shall choose the Vice-President; a quorum for the purpose shall consist of two-thirds of the whole number of Senators, and a majority of the whole number shall be necessary to a choice. But no person

constitutionally ineligible to the office of President shall be eligible to that of Vice-President of the United States.

Amendment 13
(Ratified December 6, 1865)

Section 1. Neither slavery nor involuntary servitude, except as a punishment for crime whereof the party shall have been duly convicted, shall exist within the United States, or any place subject to their jurisdiction.

Section 2. Congress shall have power to enforce this article by appropriate legislation.

Amendment 14
(Ratified July 9, 1868)

Section 1. All persons born or naturalized in the United States, and subject to the jurisdiction thereof, are citizens of the United States and of the State wherein they reside. No State shall make or enforce any law which shall abridge the privileges or immunities of citizens of the United States; nor shall any State deprive any person of life, liberty, or property, without due process of law; nor deny to any person within its jurisdiction the equal protection of the laws.

Section 2. Representatives shall be apportioned among the several States according to their respective numbers, counting the whole number of persons in each State, excluding Indians not taxed. But when the right to vote at any election for the choice of electors for President and Vice President of the United States, Representatives in Congress, the Executive and Judicial officers of a State, or the members of the Legislature thereof, is denied to any of the male inhabitants of such State, being twenty-one years of age, and citizens of the United States, or in any way abridged, except for participation in rebellion, or other crime, the basis of representation therein shall be reduced in the proportion which the number of such male citizens shall bear to the whole number of male citizens twenty-one years of age in such State.

Section 3. No person shall be a Senator or Representative in Congress, or elector of President and Vice President, or hold any office, civil or military, under the United States, or under any State, who, having previously taken an oath, as a member of Congress, or as an officer of the United States, or as a member of any State legislature, or as an executive or judicial officer of any State, to support the Constitution of the United States, shall have engaged in insurrection or rebellion against the same, or given aid or comfort to the enemies thereof. But Congress may by a vote of two-thirds of each house, remove such disability.

Section 4. The validity of the public debt of the United States, authorized by law, including debts incurred for payment of pensions and bounties for services in suppressing insurrection or rebellion, shall not be questioned. But neither the United States nor any State shall assume or pay any debt or obligation incurred in aid of insurrection or rebellion against the United States, or any claim for the loss or emancipation of any slave; but all such debts, obligations and claims shall be held illegal and void.

Section 5. The Congress shall have power to enforce, by appropriate legislation, the provisions of this article.

Amendment 15
(Ratified February 3, 1870)

Section 1. The right of citizens of the United States to vote shall not be denied or abridged by the United States or by any State on account of race, color, or previous condition or servitude.

Section 2. The Congress shall have power to enforce this article by appropriate legislation.

Amendment 16
(Ratified February 3, 1913)

The Congress shall have power to lay and collect taxes on incomes, from whatever source derived, without apportionment among the several States, and without regard to any census or enumeration.

Amendment 17
(Ratified April 8, 1913)

The Senate of the United States shall be composed of two Senators from each State, elected by the people thereof for six years; and each Senator shall have one vote. The electors in each State shall have the qualifications requisite for electors of the most numerous branch of the State legislatures.

When vacancies happen in the representation of any State in the Senate, the executive authority of such State shall issue writs of election to fill such vacancies: Provided, That the legislature of any State many empower the executive thereof to make temporary appointments until the people fill the vacancies by election as the legislature may direct.

This amendment shall not be so construed as to affect the election or term of any Senator chosen before it becomes valid as part of the Constitution.

Amendment 18
(Ratified January 16, 1919)

Section 1. After one year from the ratification of this article the manufacture, sale, or transportation of intoxicating liquors within, the importation thereof into, or the exportation thereof from the United

States and all territory subject to the jurisdiction thereof for beverage purposes is hereby prohibited.

Section 2. The Congress and the Several States shall have concurrent power to enforce this article by appropriate legislation.

Section 3. This article shall be inoperative unless it shall have been ratified as an amendment to the Constitution by the legislatures of the several States, as provided in the Constitution, within seven years from the date of the submission hereof to the States by the Congress.

Amendment 19
(Ratified August 18, 1920)

The right of citizens of the United States to vote shall not be denied or abridged by the United States or by any State on account of sex.

Congress shall have power to enforce this article by appropriate legislation.

Amendment 20
(Ratified January 23, 1933)

Section 1. The terms of the President and Vice President shall end at noon on the 20th day of January, and the terms of Senators and Representatives at noon on the 3d day of January, of the years in which such terms would have ended if this article had not been ratified; and the terms of their successors shall then begin.

Section 2. The Congress shall assemble at least once in every year, and such meeting shall begin at noon on the 3d day of January, unless they shall by law appoint a different day.

Section 3. If, at the time fixed for the beginning of the term of the President, the President elect shall have died, the Vice President elect shall become President. If a President shall not have been chosen before the time fixed for the beginning of his term, or if the President elect shall have failed to qualify, then the Vice President elect shall act as President until a President shall have qualified; and the Congress may by law provide for the case wherein neither a President elect nor a Vice President elect shall have qualified, declaring who shall then act as President, or the manner in which one who is to act shall be selected, and such person shall act accordingly until a President or Vice President shall have qualified.

Section 4. The Congress may by law provide for the case of the death of any of the persons from whom the House of Representatives may choose a President whenever the right of choice shall have devolved upon them, and for the case of the death of any of the persons from whom the Senate may choose a Vice President whenever the right of choice shall have devolved upon them.

Section 5. Sections 1 and 2 shall take effect on the 15th day of October following the ratification of the article.

Section 6. This article shall be inoperative unless it shall have been ratified as an amendment to the Constitution by the legislatures of three-fourths of the several States within seven years from the date of its submission.

Amendment 21
(Ratified December 5, 1933)

Section 1. The eighteenth article of amendment to the Constitution of the United States is hereby repealed.

Section 2. The transportation or importation into any State, Territory, or possession of the United States for delivery or use therein of intoxicating liquors, in violation of the laws thereof, is hereby prohibited.

Section 3. This article shall be inoperative unless it shall have been ratified as an amendment to the Constitution by conventions in the several States, as provided in the Constitution, within seven years from the date of the submission hereof to the States by the Congress.

Amendment 22
(Ratified February 27, 1951)

Section 1. No person shall be elected to the office of the President more than twice, and no person who has held the office of President, or acted as President, for more than two years of a term to which some other person was elected President shall be elected to the office of the President more than once. But this Article shall not apply to any person holding the office of President when this Article was proposed by the Congress, and shall not prevent any person who may be holding the office of President, or acting as President, during the term within which this Article becomes operative from holding the office of President or acting as President during the remainder of such term.

Section 2. This article shall be inoperative unless it shall have been ratified as an amendment to the Constitution by the legislatures of three-fourths of the several States within seven years from the date of its submission to the States by the Congress.

Amendment 23
(Ratified March 29, 1961)

Section 1. The District constituting the seat of Government of the United States shall appoint in such manner as the Congress may direct:

A number of electors of President and Vice President equal to the whole number of Senators and Representatives in Congress to which the District would be entitled if it were a State, but in no event more than the least populous State; they shall be in addition to those appointed by the States, but they shall be considered, for the purpose of the election of President and Vice President, to be electors appointed by a State; and they shall meet in the District and perform such duties as provided by the twelfth article of amendment.

Section 2. The Congress shall have power to enforce this article by appropriate legislation.

Amendment 24
(Ratified January 23, 1964)

Section 1. The right of citizens of the United States to vote in any primary or other election for President or Vice President, for electors for President or Vice President, or for Senator or Representative in Congress, shall not be denied or abridged by the United States or any State by reason of failure to pay any poll tax or other tax.

Section 2. The Congress shall have power to enforce this article by appropriate legislation.

Amendment 25
(Ratified February 10, 1967)

Section 1. In case of the removal of the President from office or of his death or resignation, the Vice President shall become President.

Section 2. Whenever there is a vacancy in the office of the Vice President, the President shall nominate a Vice President who shall take office upon confirmation by a majority vote of both Houses of Congress.

Section 3. Whenever the President transmits to the President pro tempore of the Senate and the Speaker of the House of Representatives his written declaration that he is unable to discharge the powers and duties of his office, and until he transmits a written declaration to the contrary, such powers and duties shall be discharged by the Vice President as Acting President.

Section 4. Whenever the Vice President and a majority of the principal officers of the executive departments, or such other body as Congress may by law provide, transmit to the President pro tempore of the Senate and the Speaker of the House of Representatives their written declaration that the President is unable to discharge the powers and duties of his office, the Vice President shall immediately assume the powers and duties of the office of Acting President.

Thereafter, when the President transmits to the President pro tempore of the Senate and the Speaker of the House of Representatives his written declaration that no inability exists, he shall resume the powers and duties of this office unless the Vice President and a majority of the principal officers of the executive department or such other body as Congress may by law provide, transmit within four days to the President pro tempore of the Senate and the Speaker of the House of Representatives their written declaration that the President is unable to discharge the powers and duties of his office. Thereupon upon Congress shall decide the issue, assembling within forty-eight hours for that purpose if not in session. If the Congress, within twenty-one days after receipt of the latter written declaration or, if Congress is not in session, within twenty-one days after Congress is required to assemble, determines by two-thirds vote of the House that the President is unable to discharge the powers and duties of the office, the Vice President shall continue to discharge the same as Acting President; otherwise, the President shall resume the powers and duties of his office.

Amendment 26
(Ratified July 1, 1971)

Section 1. The right of citizens of the United States, who are eighteen years of age or older, to vote shall not be denied or abridged by the United States or by any State on account of age.

Section 2. The congress shall have power to enforce this article by appropriate legislation.[1]

---

[1]Six amendments have been proposed but not ratified. The first and second were proposed on September 24, 1789, along with ten others which became the Bill of Rights. The first of these dealt with the apportionment of members of the House of Representatives. It was ratified by ten states, eleven being the necessary three-fourths. The second provided that "no law, varying the compensation for the services of the Senators and Representatives, shall take effect, until an election of Representatives shall have intervened." It was ratified by six states, eleven being necessary. A third was proposed on May 1, 1810, which would have abrogated the citizenship of any persons accepting foreign titles or honors. It was ratified by twelve states, fourteen being necessary. A fourth was proposed on March 4, 1861, which prohibited the adoption of any amendment "to abolish or interfere, within any state, with the domestic institutions thereof, including that of persons held to labor or service by the laws of that state." This was approved by three states. The fifth, the proposed child-labor amendment was proposed on June 2, 1924. It contains the following provisions:

Section 1. The Congress shall have power to limit, regulate, and prohibit the labor of persons under eighteen years of age.

Section 2. The power of the several States is unimpaired by this article except that the operation of State laws shall be suspended to the extent necessary to give effect to legislation enacted by Congress.

This has been ratified by twenty-eight states and rejected in eleven. The approval of thirty-eight states is necessary.

The sixth, providing equal rights for women, was proposed on March 22, 1972. It states:

Section 1. Equality of rights under the law shall not be denied or abridged by the United States or by any State on account of sex.

Section 2. The Congress shall have the power to enforce, by appropriate legislation, the provisions of this article.

Section 3. The amendment shall take effect two years after the date of ratification.

Index